Resistance to Christianity

RESISTANCE TO CHRISTIANITY

*A Chronological Encyclopaedia of
Heresy from the Beginning to
the Eighteenth Century*

Raoul Vaneigem

Translated by Bill Brown

ERIS

ERIS

86–90 Paul Street   265 Riverside Dr. #4G
London EC2A 4NE   New York, NY 10025

All rights reserved.

Copyright © 2023 by ERIS
English translation © 2023 by Bill Brown
La Résistance au christianisme: Les hérésies des origines au XVIIIe siècle by Raoul Vaneigem
© 1993 Librairie Arthème Fayard

Cover image: detail from Hieronymus Bosch, *The Garden of Earthly Delights*, oil on oak panels, Museo del Prado, Madrid

Printed and bound by Maple Press
Distributed by Columbia University Press,
New York, NY, and London, England

Edited by Angus Ledingham
Designed by Alex Stavrakas

ISBN 978-1912475-60-5 (paperback)
       978-1916809-92-5 (hardback)
       978-1912475-45-2 (ebook)

No part of this publication may be reproduced, stored in a retrieval system, or transmitted in any form or by any means, electronic, mechanical, photocopying, recording or otherwise, without prior permission in writing from the Publisher.

eris.press

Contents

Translator's Introduction 11

Author's Foreword 19

1 A Nation Sacrificed to History 31

2 Diaspora and Anti-Semitism 49

3 The Judean Sects 59

4 The Men of the Community, or the Essenes 75

5 The Baptist Movement of the Samaritan Messiah Dusis/Dositheos 95

6 Simon of Samaria and Gnostic Radicalism 103

7 The Phallic and Symbiotic Cults 117

8 Three Esseno-Christian Christs 147

9 The Messianic Sects of Joshua/Jesus 171

10 Quarrels about Prophets and Apostles 177

11 Marcion and the Hellenization of Christianity 209

12 The Inventors of a Christian Theology 219

13 Marcus and the Hellenization of Jewish Hermeticism 243

14 Carpocrates, Epiphanius, and the Tradition of Simon of Samaria 251

15	The New Prophecy and the Development of Popular Christianity 257
16	Tatian and the Fabrication of the New Testament 277
17	Three Local Christianities 291
18	Novatian, the Apostate Clergy, and the Anti-Montanist Reaction 301
19	Arianism and the Church of Rome 307
20	Donatus and the Circumcellions 315
21	The Spirituals, Also Called Messalians or Euchites 321
22	Monophysites and Dyophysites 327
23	Pelagius and Augustine 335
24	Priscillian of Ávila 341
25	Paulicians and Bogomils 347
26	Christs and Reformers 359
27	The Communalist Prophets 369
28	Philosophy Against the Church 377
29	The Cathars 385
30	The Waldensians and the Adepts of Voluntary Poverty 399
31	The Movement of the Free Spirit 409
32	Beghards and Beguines 425
33	The Millenarians 437

34	The Flagellants	453
35	The Fraticelles	461
36	The Eastern Reformers	471
37	The Men of Intelligence and the Picards of Bohemia	477
38	The Victory of the Reformers and the Birth of the Protestant Churches	483
39	The Dissidents from Lutheranism and Calvinism	495
40	The *Alumbrados* of Spain	509
41	The Spiritual Libertines	515
42	The Anabaptists	529
43	The Individualist Messiahs	547
44	Ironists and Skeptics	561
45	Levelers, Diggers, and Ranters	569
46	The Jansenists	583
47	Pietists, Visionaries, and Quietists	593
48	The End of the Divine Right	609
	Afterword to the English Edition	619
	Notes	627
	Bibliography	701
	Name Index	735
	Authors' bios	744

Resistance to Christianity

Translator's Introduction

Born on 21 March 1934 in Lessines, Belgium, Raoul Vaneigem is the author of nearly fifty books and more than twenty prefaces, postfaces, and articles, only a handful of which have been translated into English. He is perhaps best known for his membership in the Situationist International (the 'SI'), which he joined in 1961 and stayed with until his resignation in 1970. A small but incredibly fertile and highly influential grouping of radical European artists, filmmakers, and writers, the SI was founded in 1957 and dissolved in 1972. During those fifteen years, the group developed a new critique of modern capitalism, reinvented the theory of proletarian revolution, and propagated these ideas through a journal called *Internationale situationniste*, several books (including Vaneigem's *Traité de savoir-vivre a l'usage des jeunes générations*, first published in 1967 and translated into English as *The Revolution of Everyday Life*), and a number of scandalous provocations. The SI was deeply involved in the protests, riots, and occupations that nearly toppled the French government in May–June 1968.

Vaneigem's post-SI work has covered a wide variety of subjects, including Surrealism, the poetry of Louis Scutenaire, contemporary revolutionary movements in Chiapas, Oaxaca, Greece, and Chile, and, of course, the situationists. In recent years he has also written passionately about *Charlie Hebdo*, the Yellow Vests, and COVID-19. But there is a subject to which he has returned several times and with great intensity: religion, particularly the Christian religion and the so-called heresies against which it fought in order to establish its own unquestionable authority, even when the content of those allegedly heretical beliefs was clearly social and political rather than religious.

Vaneigem has in fact written nearly half a dozen books on these closely related subjects. In chronological order of their publication, they are *Le Mouvement du libre-esprit*, published in 1986 by Ramsay[1] and translated into English in 1994 as *The Movement of the Free Spirit*[2]; *Les Controverses du christianisme*, published under the pseudonym Tristan Hannaniel in 1992 by Bordas and not yet translated into English; *La Résistance au christianisme: Les Hérésies des origines au XVIIIe siècle*, published in 1993 by Fayard (the first edition is still in print) and translated into English here for the first time; *Les Hérésies*, published in 1994 by PUF (collection "Que sais-je?") and not yet translated into English; and *De l'inhumanité de la religion*, published in 2000 by Denoël and also not yet translated into English.

But Vaneigem is not an expert in these matters. "I am not an expert in anything", he told the Belgian newspaper *Le Soir* in November 2020[3]. His "subjective investigations", as he calls them in his Introduction to *The Movement of the Free Spirit*, "do no more than satisfy a personal curiosity". These are "cursory" projects, he says, and "the sheer number of texts that had to be uncovered and translated added to the cursory character of this project"[4].

But this doesn't mean that he's written these books for his personal pleasure alone. In the aforementioned introduction, he says,

> I want to challenge the view of those who dehumanize history, seeing it as fated and fatal: hence my wish to pay homage to those who refused to give in to the idea that history moves toward some inevitable outcome. I want also to seek out signs of life, behind the edifices of religious and ideological obscurantism, and in so doing I hope to dispense once and for all with the cherished but no less dubious notion of a Christian Middle Ages.[5]

This idea is echoed by his 1993 Preface to the American Edition of *The*

TRANSLATOR'S INTRODUCTION

Movement of the Free Spirit: "The Middle Ages were no more Christian than the late Eastern bloc was communist"[6].

In other words, something that called itself Christianity was present and quite powerful in the Middle Ages, but it was an impostor, and it wasn't embraced or accepted by the vast majority of the people who lived during that era. In fact, Christianity was constantly challenged and sometimes even completely ignored. Its history is not the history of its ineluctable global triumph, but the history of the implacable resistance that it encountered. Unfortunately for us, Vaneigem notes in his Introduction to *The Movement of the Free Spirit*, "historians for the most part have ignored or misapprehended the struggle waged through the ages against religion's impregnation of consciousness and behavior". But Vaneigem is not a historian and he doesn't imagine his readers to be students of history. "Readers who take pleasure in paying history the same undivided attention they pay the struggles of their own passions", he writes, "will discover a naive but valuable confirmation in this book: lies serve their own purposes, their own ends; while the love of pleasure has none"[7].

If we substitute 'Western civilization as a whole' for 'the Middle Ages', we will get an idea of what Vaneigem is up to in *Resistance to Christianity*, which both continues and expands upon the ground already covered in *The Movement of the Free Spirit*. In fact, the present volume offers nothing less than a complete historical account of the development of Christianity as a whole.

* * *

In this incredibly ambitious undertaking, Vaneigem both relies heavily upon and disagrees with a number of traditional historians, but especially Norman Cohn, the author of *The Pursuit of the Millennium: Revolutionary Messianism in Medieval and Reformation Europe and its Bearing on Modern Totalitarian Movements*. Originally published in 1957, and revised and reprinted in 1961, this pioneering and exceptionally influential work claims that,

[a]lthough it would be a gross over-simplification to identify the [medieval] world of chiliastic exaltation with the world of social unrest, there were many times when needy and discontented masses were captured by some millennial prophet. And when that happened movements were apt to arise which, though relatively small and short-lived, can be seen in retrospect to bear a startling resemblance to the great totalitarian movements of our own day. [...] The time seems ripe for an examination of those remote foreshadowings of present commotions. If such an enquiry can throw no appreciable light on the workings of established totalitarian states, it might, and I think does, throw considerable light on the sociology and psychology of totalitarian movements in their revolutionary heyday.[8]

As Greil Marcus notes in *Lipstick Traces: A Secret History of the Twentieth Century,* "the situationists would carefully plunder"[9] Cohn's book, which was published in France in 1962 under the title *Fanatiques de l'apocalypse.*

Significantly, in 1970, when a third edition of *The Pursuit of the Millennium* was published, it bore a different subtitle: *Revolutionary Millenarians and Mystical Anarchists of the Middle Ages*[10]. This change did not reflect revisions to the book itself, but changes in the world in which its author (and everyone else) lived. In addition to totalitarianism and the Nazi movement of the 1930s and 1940s, "one may also", Cohn writes in his new Conclusion, "reflect on the left-wing revolutions and revolutionary movements of this century". "Those who are fascinated by [...] emotionally charged phantasies of a final, apocalyptic struggle or an egalitarian Millennium" now include "the populations of certain technologically backward societies" and "certain politically charged marginal elements in technologically advanced societies—chiefly young or unemployed workers and a small minority of intellectuals and students". In other words, people just like Raoul Vaneigem and the other members of the Situationist International, who were living proof that, in Cohn's words, "revolutionary millenarianism and mystical anarchism are with us still"[11]. He is clearly unhappy with this state of affairs: "For the ideal of a total emancipation of the individual from society, even from external reality itself—the ideal, if you will, of self-divinization—which some nowadays try to realize with the help of psychedelic drugs, can be recognized already in that deviant form of medieval mysticism"[12].

Perhaps predictably, the situationists tended to see the validity of Cohn's hypothesis only when it was inverted. In *La Société du spectacle* (first published in 1967 and since then translated into English as *The Society of the Spectacle*), Guy Debord, a co-founder of the SI, points out that:

> The great European peasant revolts were [...] a *response to history*—a history that was wresting the peasantry from the patriarchal slumber hitherto guaranteed by the feudal order. This was the moment when a millenarian utopianism aspiring to *build heaven on earth* brought back to the forefront an idea that had been at the origin of semi-historical religion, when the early Christian communities, like the Judaic messianism from which they sprang, responded to the troubles and misfortunes of their time by announcing the imminent realization of God's Kingdom, and so added an element of disquiet and subversion to ancient society. [...] So, contrary to what Norman Cohn believes he has demonstrated in *The Pursuit of the Millennium*, modern revolutionary hopes are not an irrational sequel to the religious passion of millenarianism. The exact opposite is true: millenarianism, the expression of a revolutionary class struggle speaking the language of religion for the last time, was already a modern revolutionary tendency, lacking only the consciousness of being *historical and nothing more*. The millenarians were doomed to defeat because they could not recognize revolution as their own handiwork. The fact that they made their action conditional upon an external sign of God's will was a translation onto the level of thought of the tendency of insurgent peasants to follow outside leaders.[13]

Though he generally accredits this analysis, Vaneigem's position in *Resistance to Christianity* is somewhat more nuanced. As he states in Chapter 33, "The great revolutionary movements later gave to millenarianism a more ideological than religious form. Nevertheless, it would be a mistake to underestimate the role of irrational and Joachimite faith in Nazi millenarianism—that is to say, in that which was the very antithesis of projects for a classless society or an ecological paradise, both of which were brought to the fore by the successive waves of the burgeoning economy". Unlike Debord, who once half-jokingly proclaimed that "The Cathars Were Right"[14], Vaneigem does not see a general consistency or uniformity in millenarianism[15]. In his Preface to the American edition of *The Movement of the Free Spirit*, he says: "the partisans of the Free Spirit were divided on one fundamental issue".

> Driven by their will to follow nature, some identified with God and the ordinariness of his tyranny, using force, violence, constraint and seduction to secure the right to gratify their whims and passions. Others refused to countenance such a union between a despotic God and a denatured nature, a union whose exploitation found perfect expression in the myth of a divinity at once pitiful and pitiless. Instead they saw the refinement of their desires and the quest for a ubiquitous and sovereign amorous pleasure as a way of replacing the spiritualized animal and its labor of adaptation with an authentic human species capable of creating the conditions favorable to its own harmonious development.[16]

All through *Resistance to Christianity*, Vaneigem will highlight this fundamental difference between the so-called heretics. It is in fact the central theme of the book. He says 'no' to the likes of the Cathars, the Flagellants, and Thomas Müntzer, who, "far from giving up Judeo-Christian comportment", engaged in "its most odious practices: self-sacrifice, cults of the martyr, guilt, making people feel guilty, hatred of amorous desire, scorn for the body, fascination with the Spirit, quests for salvational suffering, fanaticism, and obedience to a master, a cause"; and he says 'yes' to the likes of Simon of Samaria, Eloi Pruystinck, and Marguerite Porete, "who resisted obscurantism, who were dead set against oppression, who extolled the emancipation of men and women, who anticipated by their insolent modernity the behaviors of the radicalism that is emerging today"[17].

"It is time to say it again, with force", Vaneigem writes in his 2005 Preface to a reprint of the French edition of *The Movement of the Free Spirit*. "Nothing prevents someone from practicing a religion, following a belief, defending an ideology, but no one should impose it upon others or—a still more unacceptable thing—indoctrinate children. All convictions can freely express themselves, even the most aberrant, the stupidest, the most odious, the most ignoble, on the express condition that, dwelling in the state of singular opinions, they can not oblige anyone else to receive them against their will"[18].

* * *

I have changed the book's subtitle from "Heresies from the Beginning to the Eighteenth Century" to "A Chronological Encyclopedia of Heresy from the Beginning to the Eighteenth Century" because I think that the latter is a better description of what the book actually offers its readers.

The original French volume includes both footnotes and endnotes by the author: the former, which are generally reserved for commentary (there are a few exceptions), are marked by asterisks; the latter, which are always reserved for the attribution of source materials and quotations, are marked by Arabic numerals. In this volume, the author's commentary has been integrated into the text, placed between parentheses, and prefaced with the word 'Note'. Attributions of source materials and quotations appear in this volume as endnotes, and every effort has been made to flesh them out with all available bibliographical information. The same goes for the book's bibliography.

As the reader will see, I have also taken the liberty of offering my own endnotes. I have done so in order to translate words or phrases that were not in French in the original text; to elucidate references that might be obscure to Vaneigem's readers in the English-speaking world; and to draw the reader's attention to connections that she might find interesting.

When necessary, I have supplied within brackets [thus] words that make the text easier to understand. When I have relished a certain play on words or have chosen a non-literal rendering of a word or phrase, I have supplied the original French in italics and within brackets [*ainsi*]. When the author's sentences have contained a great many sub-clauses, I have occasionally used parentheses (like this) for the sake of clarity and to avoid confusion. And when square brackets appear in extended quotations taken from the works of other writers [like this], they have been supplied either by Vaneigem or myself, or, when indicated, by the secondary source being quoted. (Material enclosed within round or angled brackets originates in the source being quoted, unless otherwise indicated.)

In instances in which Vaneigem offers a French translation of a work that was originally written in English, I have used the original instead of translating the French back into English. And in the vast majority of those instances in which he offers a French translation of a work that was originally written in German, Italian, Latin, or Greek, I have endeavored to locate an already existing, direct translation from the original language into English and to use that instead of offering what would amount to a double translation (e.g. from Latin to French and then from French into English). In those instances in which an English-language version was not available, I have appended an endnote that indicates that I have translated the passage from Vaneigem's French.

* * *

I would like to thank all the people who, having seen my first efforts at translating this book (they were uploaded to the internet), sent me emails conveying their appreciation, encouragement, and/or suggested corrections. My special thanks go to Greil Marcus, whose writings introduced me to the Situationist International back in 1983 and who has been a strong supporter of my efforts since then to keep the situationist flame alive; to Raoul Vaneigem, for patiently answering my questions and for volunteering to write an Afterword for this edition, despite the fact that he was busy with other projects; and especially to Angus Ledingham, whose commitment to this project has been unshakeable right from the start and whose hard work copyediting the manuscript has been crucial to bringing it up to the high level of quality that it currently enjoys.

Bill Brown
New York City
—June 2023

Author's Foreword

The rising tide of the commodity has not left standing a single traditional value of the past on the shore on which the two thousand years of the Christian era have been brought to an end. Did not this tide, by drowning the mass ideologies that had themselves hastily brought the religious edifice crashing down (at the moment in history at which the State was taking over from God in the conduct of terrestrial affairs), also inevitably push towards annihilation the last remnants of a Church whose mysteries had already been domesticated by the Second Vatican Council[1]?

The indifference into which those beliefs that are governed by rituals performed by the Party or by the ecclesiastical bureaucracy have sunk has awakened a new interest in the history of those beliefs. This interest is not motivated by any sort of obsolete desire—be it to make apologies or to denigrate. It is a curiosity that is quite simply preoccupied with its own pleasure and that takes pride in its ability to play the game of discovering that which the official truths tried so zealously to bury beneath the *ultima ratio*[2] of their dogmatic canon.

Could one even imagine that Christianity, once it had been cleansed of its sacred apparatus by the powerful waters of commercialism, would have been able to escape from the crusher that, in less than a half-century, has smashed the sacrificial rocks—known under the names of nationalism, liberalism, socialism, fascism, and communism—that generations of people have adored with a mixture of fascination and terror?

Now that nothing remains of yesterday's shipwrecks but a sea that is relatively calm and only weakly agitated by ripples of derision, this curiosity supplies that form of archaeology that is best suited to examining objects that have long been coated with holiness. Inspiring respect or profanation, these objects have until now only called for . . . I wouldn't say impartiality, but the naïve indiscretion of truth-seekers who are without either prejudices or guile.

In the same way as it is now possible to examine the birth, development, and decline of Bolshevism without exposing oneself to accusations of materialism, spiritualism, Marxism, revisionism, Stalinism, or Trotskyism (which today give rise to smiles and yet once were paid for in blood), attention can now be focused on the Christian religion without reference to the repudiations and praises dispensed by theology and philosophy, or to that archaic *trompe-l'oeil* confrontation in which the God of some and the non-God of the others meet up at the same vanishing point in the celestial realm of ideas—that is to say, at the same level of abstraction from corporeal and terrestrial reality.

Today, along with a feeling for the preeminence of the living, there is, at least for those who remain naïve, an astonishment that wants to understand why and by which channels the world of ideas has so often required a pound of flesh slashed from the heart in exchange for a glimpse at its own chimerical horizons.

The current crisis of transformation, which is today forcing the economy either to destroy itself or to reconstruct itself (one way or the other, it will take the world along with it), has the merit of opening minds to the origins of inhumanity and to the available means of remedying it. The politics of sterilization, which has rendered the entire planet (as well as whole societies, mindsets, and bodies) gangrenous, has also highlighted, thanks to the extremity of the situation to which it has given rise, the ways in which mankind—subjecting nature and human beings to market exploitation—produces, at the expense of the living, an economy that subjugates it to a power that was initially mythical in nature and that subsequently became ideological.

Driven by a system of exchange that they themselves created and that, even as it tore them from themselves, shaped them without ever completely mechanizing their bodies, their consciousnesses, or their subconscious minds, individuals have, over the course of the millennia, been insignificant compared to the formidable power that has fed upon their blood. How could their miserable condition not have induced them to place the halo of an absolute authority, as perfect as the celestial vault, on the transcendence of a Father whose decrees—administering fortune and misfortune alike—proclaimed his eternal and capricious authority over endless generations?

Invested with an extra-terrestrial sovereignty, the mythical meaning of which only the priests had the ability to decipher, the economy nevertheless revealed its fundamental materiality through the interests that, in a free-for-all that was secularized and could therefore no longer be profaned, brought forth temporal masters and business leaders.

Religion—that is to say, 'that which binds' [*ce qui relie*]—placed in the hands of a fantastic deity the central link of a chain that, interlocking tyranny and slavery from one end to the other, also anchored to the earth the celestial power that people's own scorn for themselves had consecrated as sovereign, unchanging, and intangible.

Thus God drew from the cyclical and archaic world, which was enclosed within the moats and ramparts of the agrarian economy, a permanence that, during great tumults concerning the 'end of time', was ceaselessly contradicted by the innovative politics of commerce and free-exchange—a politics that unclasped the links of mythic time, corroded the sacred with acerbic spittle, and introduced into the citadels of conservatism the Trojan Horse of progress.

Nevertheless, despite the state of conflict that repeatedly opposed the conquest of new markets to the ownership of land, the antagonistic emanations of these competing economic models—these emanations being temporal and spiritual kings, on the one hand, and priests, philosophy, and theology, on the other—continued to constitute the two halves of God (that is, for as long as the agrarian structure and its mentality remained dominant).

By decapitating Louis XVI, the last monarch of the Divine Right, the

French Revolution slew the two-headed hydra of temporal and spiritual power, which not long before (in the last of a lengthy series of crimes) had sent the young Knight de la Barre[3] to the scaffold for allegedly committing the crime of impiety[4].

If the Roman Church, now deprived of the secular arms that had once enforced the truth of its dogma, slowly descended to the rank of a spiritual scarecrow, this was because the era of the lords and priests and its dominant economy had come to an end, thereby depriving Rome of the penal ferocity that had previously underwritten the Church's arrogance.

The *Ancien Régime*, having been definitively crushed beneath the inexorable weight of market freedom and of the 'democracy' of that which is profitable, was dismantled at the same time as its ramparts, palaces, siege mentalities, and old mythic ways of thinking were being demolished.

At that moment, God succumbed to the hatchet blow dealt by a State that was thenceforth able to rule without the guarantees provided by its former celestial accomplice. Christianity then entered the spectacular history of the commodity. Come the dawn of the twenty-first century[5], Christianity will emerge from that history crushed, just as other herd-mentality ideologies have been.

The fact that a kind of religious spirit and the sinister colors of fanaticism continue to subsist at the heart of the systems of ideas that have supplanted Christian mythology—including opinions that are furiously hostile to Christian allegiances—is demonstrated well enough by the exaltation of militants and the hysteria of crowds that we see during the great Masses that are solemnly presided over by the tribunes and tub-thumpers of nationalism, liberalism, socialism, fascism, and communism.

The hysterical uprooting that pulls a man out of his body in order to identify him with a collective and abstract body (a nation, a State, a party, a cause) is indistinguishable from a spiritual adherence—I might even say a spiritual adhesion—to a God whose gaze, imbued with both solicitude and scorn, symbolically expresses the relations between the mechanical abstraction of profit and the living matter that is subjected to ruthless exploitation.

There have been more upheavals in the last three decades than in the previous ten millennia. By selling off ideologies from the shelves of indifference, the *self-services*[6] of consumption-at-any-price have, *volens nolens*[7], stripped the individual of the character armor[8] that conceals him from himself, and have thereby condemned him to constrained desires (and this without offering him any other way of letting off steam than engaging in the dead passion for destroying and being destroyed)[9]. Thus, little by little, one sees the gradual awakening of a will to live that has never ceased to appeal to the conjoined creation and enjoyment of oneself and the world. Isn't the situation now a matter of each person attaining amorous possession of the universe for him- or herself?

The individual, which only yesterday was an object manipulated by a Spirit and nourished by its very substance, today becomes—by discovering on the earth and in his or her own flesh the place of his or her living reality—the subject of a destiny that will be constructed by means of a renewed alliance with nature. Bored and wearied by artificial desires that ascribed to him a profit-minded ability to reason and that, over the centuries, led him to a place where he had nothing to do, the individual today contemplates with an amused curiosity the objects that once objectified him or her and that now litter the shores of his or her past—fragments of a death that is, today, refused.

The feeble enthusiasm now shown for herd-like gatherings is indicative of a steady decline of religious and ideological faith within the industrialized countries. Nonetheless, the hacks employed by the newspapers—who can only galvanize a desperately lethargic, everyday spectacle by fits and starts—haven't failed, when faced with a few outbursts of archaic and barbaric behavior, to cry out for the return of religion and nationalism. But, as Diderot asks, which ass will pass this shit?[10] Which economic imperative could provide a buttress for the ramparts of a bygone age—hastily rebuilt by desperation and resentment—or indeed prevent them from collapsing under the weight of an economic shortfall?

There is no doubt that the end of religious institutions does *not* mean the end of religiosity. Driven out of the mainstream by the debacle of the great ideologies, and imperfectly satisfied by the sects that are increasingly poorly housed within the Catholic and Protestant Churches—which are filled with the intolerable, lingering odors of the latest totalitarianism—the Christian sentiment now searches for new trickle beds [*lits d'ecoulement*].

Will it find them in a landscape that ecological transformation is preparing to remodel? Some people suspect as much in the wake of the advent of an ecological capitalism that seeks to obtain from environmental remediation a profitability that the desertification of soils, sub-soils, and hopes for survival can no longer guarantee. When celestial abilities are attributed to terrestrial divinities (Gaia, Magna Mater, sylphs, dryads, or other elementary forces), it makes little difference to me who is doing the attribution. As long as it does not require self-sacrifice, no belief is repugnant to that which is truly human.

On the other hand, I am delighted by people learning about the autonomy that, due the collapse of the supporters of and supports for the past, engenders the necessity of going it alone. I am delighted by the end of crowds, by the emergence of individuals' awareness of the fight for life, by their resolution to vanquish the fear of the self (from which all the other fears are derived), and by the emergence of a creativity that is substituting itself for the necessity of working for a living—a necessity that does not allow new generations to move toward a true humanity. Even if its advent is not inevitable, for the first time in history this creativity is in the hands of men, women, and, most especially, children who are educated in the enjoyment of life rather than in its morbid refusal.

Such is the perspective according to which I wish to examine the resistance with which the inclination to natural liberty has, for nearly twenty centuries, responded to the *antiphysis*[11] of Christian oppression.

Regardless of the domain (historical, scientific, philosophical, social, economic, or artistic), I cannot conceive of an analysis that could claim to work outside of the individual life history in which are inscribed the everyday gestures of the person who has resolved to undertake that analysis. Although circumstances have spared me from contact with religion, I have always experienced a singular revulsion for the deadly empire that is emblazoned with a cross and that has been driven into the hearts of all those who have been born into life. I therefore understand the indignation of Karlheinz Deschner when, in his *Kriminalgeschichte des Christentums*[12], he excoriates the murders, impostures, and falsifications committed by the Catholic Church, but I do not know that his polemic, which penetrates far into the adversary's terrain, has gained for him the recognition and interest that he had every reason to expect. And one might ask, in any case: why revive the embers of the millennium pyre with angry breaths, when the winds of a new era have condemned them to extinguished?

Besides, shouldn't there be something that dissuades us from the use of a condemnatory tone [such as Deschner's] in the simple, obvious fact that atheists, freethinkers, anti-clericals, and other militants of the "Good God in Shit"[13]—far from abandoning the Judeo-Christian comportment—have most often adopted its most odious practices: sacrifice, cults of martyrdom, guilt, making people feel guilty, hatred of amorous desire, scorn for the body, fascination with the Spirit, quests for salvational suffering, fanaticism, and obedience to a master, to a cause, to a party? What better tribute to orthodoxy is there than heresy, than a nonconformism that infatuates itself with contesting the axis around which it in fact gravitates?

Little interested in arbitrating the dubious combat between victims and executioners, I prefer to liberate from the past—in which the forgotten, scorned, misunderstood, prejudged, and calumnied have been buried and stratified by the famous objectivity of the historians—the healing that human tissue, irrigated by the freedoms of nature, untiringly performs upon itself in order to reconstitute and strengthen itself by weaving the social network (and this in spite of the deleterious effects of fear, dereliction, suffering, faith in the beyond, and the consolations of death).

The act of taking hold of the life that is trapped underneath death, which has seized hold of life through a subtle mix of violence and persuasion, in fact revives beings and things that are no longer identified according to the traditional perspective in which God, the State, and the Economy collect the tears of terrestrial valleys in exchange for a happiness that is endlessly deferred; these beings and things now quiver in response to the beating of the wings of the living, which is more perceptible today because it is no longer stifled by the weight of ancient oppression.

Therefore, the reasons for being amazed by a life that is so obstinate that it flowers again by breaking through the asphalt of an inhuman history also raise, in counterpoint, several doubts about the honesty and quality of the scholars and specialists who are accustomed to regarding this history as if it were conquered terrain.

I accept the facts that a theologian—who bases his career on painting glossy pictures of his God in order to expound upon His radiance to those who are too blind to perceive its obviousness in day-to-day life—orders things according to his personal beliefs; that he gives his jargon the appearance of reasonable language, calling desire 'temptation', pleasure 'sin', and the embrace of lovers 'fornication'; that he venerates with the title of 'saint' the forerunners of the Heroes of the People who were honored by Lenin[14]; and that he uses the Gospels in much the same way as Joseph Stalin attributed truthfulness to the *Great Soviet Encyclopedia*[15]. This is what results, not from lies, but from proselytism. Encountering the same attitude in a historian who isn't inspired by such vast designs is enough, it will surely be agreed, to leave one perplexed.

What is one to think of those university scholars who are trained in the science of discrediting the authenticity of manuscripts that have been handed down from copyist to copyist and stuffed full of interpolations along the way, but who nevertheless comment upon certain works as if they were original texts, and who set the date of the composition of the Epistles at the very beginning of the Christian era, when they were in fact rewritten, if not actually written, by Marcion, reorganized by Tatian, and submitted to corrections up until the fourth century, and yet are nonetheless attributed to a certain Saul, known as Paul of Tarsus, a Roman citizen who allegedly lived around 60 CE, when in point of fact Tarsus was only Romanized in 150 CE?

No one is unaware that the manuscripts of the canonical Gospels and of the Acts of the Apostles appeared in the fourth century (at the earliest) and constituted—under the aegis of Constantine—the library of propaganda that Eusebius of Caesarea and his scribes revised and distributed to all the Churches, which were thereby united upon the same dogmatic base. Apparently these facts aren't of the type to trouble the good consciences of those researchers who, with a beautiful unanimity, take them for reports by living beings who were near contemporaries of the witnesses or apostles of an Adonai, *Kyrios*, or Lord whose name (Joshua/Jesus) didn't actually impose itself in its symbolic meaning of 'God saved, saves, will save' until the end of the first century. The only sources of dissonance in this ecstatic concert are the atheists Dupuy, Alfaric, Couchoud, Kryvelev, and Dubourg; the Catholics Loisy and Guillemin; and the Protestant Bultmann.

In their attempts to define polytheism and the various cults as 'strangers to the faith', few scholars have had qualms about using the terms 'pagans' and 'paganism', by which the Church expressed its scorn for the beliefs of the *pagani*—the peasants, yokels, and bumpkins who proved impermeable to the civilization of the towns. What about the angels of the Jewish pantheon, the semi-legendary Paul and Peter, the anti-Gnostic Irenaeus, the philosopher Augustine of Hippo, the anti-Semite Jerome, the spiritual master of the Inquisition, Dominic de Guzmán, and the murderer of the Fraticelles, John of Capistrano? Many of them were given the title 'saint', with which the Church compensated its real and mythical servants. There are likewise several biographies of Stalin in which he is referred to without irony as 'Little Father of the People'.

It has been left up to atheism to furnish with the weapons of critique one of the Church's most preemptory claims—namely, the historical existence of this Joshua/Jesus, on which the legitimacy of the Church's temporal power is based. Sufficiently enraged to deny the divinity of Christ, an allegedly freethinking militancy nevertheless falls into the trap set by this Jesus, who is said to be a friend of the poor and a kind of Socrates preaching the truths of a Gospel-based socialism before dying on the cross due to his pacifistic insolence. Back in the second half of the second century, Tertullian and the Christian movement of the New Prophecy could not have dreamed of a better future for their hero, whom the atheists have purged of his Jewishness and disguised as Zorro[16] for the edification and salvation of the working class.

Once we have granted the existence of this agitator who founded the Church and who was crucified under the orders of Pontius Pilate—and this without any contemporary corroborating testimony, and notwithstanding the fact that, at the time, the name 'Jesus' still had the meaning of the Biblical 'Joshua'—why should we be surprised to learn that erudite people have also accepted the following: the fraudulent listing of popes and bishops that was drafted by Eusebius of Caesarea; the back-dating of canonical texts; the interpolation of citations that actually date from the controversies of the fourth and fifth centuries into writings allegedly drafted in the second century; and the accusations of 'heresy' that were made against the Dosithian, Nazarene, Sethian, Naassene, Ebionite, Melchizedekian, Elchasaite, Carpocratian, Basilidian, Marcionite, anti-Marcionite, Montanist, Valentinian, Marcusian, Bardesanian, and Novatian doctrines that, hundreds of years before the establishment of Christian orthodoxy, mixed together ideas of many origins and that the Constantinian Church—by crushing, remodeling, and readjusting them—would subsequently use to build the unstable foundations of its dogma?

In the manner of Stalin recuperating Bolshevism while shooting Lenin's companions, the Catholic 'fathers' *a posteriori* condemned as heterodoxy not only non-Christian religious choices (*hairesis* in Greek), but also the diverse Christianities upon which the throne of Constantine had been raised. And the historians have followed suit by managing to discern around Peter—'the first Pope of Rome'—the existence and praiseworthy efforts of a Catholic Church that was struggling against heretical perversions that threatened to corrupt the integrity of its canonical teachings.

Although it does not seem to me useless to highlight such impostures even at a time when it is difficult to imagine the pontifical authority and the clerical bureaucrats surviving the collapse of the last totalitarian citadels, I have found less charm in trying to rectify the opinion that nothing other than some kind of inertia of thought can explain the ambition to uncover from beneath the leathery history of the past the nervous excitations of the living, which are often weak and yet nonetheless manage to generate a force that is incomparably more effective than intellectual critique in the attempt to crush the tombstones of oppression.

What is it that is discovered under the label of heresy, under the labels by which the Church subjected to its control (by naming them) various human and inhuman behaviors, the condemnation of which reinforced the predominance of orthodoxy? Episcopalian rivalries and internecine struggles, such as Arianism, monophysism, and English Lollardism. Or one discovers the movements of the body as it limps from constraint to license, from asceticism to debauchery, from repression to release, all of which were exploited with remarkable skill by the markets in penitence and death. Or even a more secretive attitude, one that was an object of perplexity to the religious police: the individual will to create—in opposition to the social forms of *antiphysis*—a destiny that is better suited to the promises of a nature that has, until now, been relegated by its exploitation to the 'beyond' of the human. One will easily divine the types of 'heresies' or irreligious afterglows to which my curiosity is the most strongly attached.

For the sake of readers who are familiar with the *Traité de savoir-vivre*, the *Livre des plaisirs* and the *Adresse aux vivants*[17], I wish to make it clear that my apostil in *Mouvement du libre-esprit* is also applicable here: "The genius of a book is nothing other than what can be drawn from it that allows one the pleasure of living better. It is thus understood, from the start, that the study of the Free Spirit is not intended to do that for me personally"[18].

On the other hand, a single merit must be granted to this work: it hopefully ignores the solicitations of the pleasures of knowing and the pleasures of the gay science[19] as infrequently as possible. As a summary that, over the course of time, gradually reveals itself to be a clearing out of dead wood from an uncertain history, this book will, I feel, at least succeed in avoiding the risk of competing for the greatest number of errors, ignorant remarks, and fraudulent hypotheses with the majority of the volumes, monographs, and scholarly works that have, in our era, been piled on top of the heads of Jesus, the apostles, and their universal legatees.

If it is, finally, necessary to furnish an excuse for a style of writing in which one can hardly be said to find the care that I try to give to books whose subjects are not too far removed from my own way of my life, I would like simply to say that each subject has been given the treatment that it merits.

—January 1992

CHAPTER ONE

A Nation Sacrificed to History

There is no more singular and paradoxical destiny than that of the Jewish people. The Books or *Biblia* that, under the name 'Bible', founded the Hebraic mythology raised the Jews to the elective glory[1] of a unique God who aspired to reign over all of humanity. Invested with an eternal and universal truth, the Jews only entered the design that they attributed to YHWH at the cost of their effacement from time and space, of which no nation offers such an unhappy example.

The arrogance of the God of the holy wars was born from a statist centralism that unified the nomads and that soon became sedentary on newly conquered territories. By a cruel irony, this arrogance continued to be puffed up by the winds of prediction even as the temporal power of the Hebrews—far from seizing the world in order to propagate obedience to YHWH—ended up succumbing to the blows of the Assyrians, Persians, Greeks, and Romans, and thereby found itself extirpated from the very places in which it had been established over the course of nearly two millennia.

That a nation unanimously placed its fate in the hands of a God and experienced hostility, hate, and scorn everywhere and for so long—its strange specificity doesn't lie in this. But what surprises us is the fact that this nation kept faith and confidence in, and accredited, a deity that proved so detrimental to its interests.

Situating themselves within a mythical history—the temporal aspect of which was a mere shadow of the divine will—the Jews submitted (as to a malediction to which they subscribed in advance) to a historical exclusion from which they only returned in the twentieth century by replacing religious preoccupations with social ones. Few believers will today deny that the army and the cooperative system offer to Israel better guarantees than those of YHWH.

It's about time. Vilified, oppressed, massacred, and imprisoned in ghettos, they continued to interpret their nightmare exegetically. The malediction confirmed their status as the Chosen People; it conferred upon them—through water, fire, the blood of sacrifice and redemption, ordeal and salvation, expiation and redemption—an existence that was, so to speak, metaphysical, *sub specie aeternitatis*[2].

Expelled from Palestine in 135 CE, after the collapse of their last insurrection, the Jews would subsequently be stripped of their religion by a Christianity that issued from Judaism, the political career of which would emerge in the West in the fourth century under a Catholicism that conducted pogroms.

There is insufficient space here to clarify the detours by which a conquering will was transformed into resignation—dereliction, even—but it is nonetheless worth emphasizing what one can call the opening out of Hebrew expansionist ambitions.

While a succession of reversals—which were saluted by prophetic agitators as just (and divine) punishments—swelled with anger and blood the unmerciful myth of the God of Israel, a more pacific conquest also became apparent. This took the form of a Diaspora that extended to the four corners of the world colonies of Jews who—notwithstanding the intransigence with which they treated the question of the one God—did not find it repugnant to compromise with their new neighbors when this proved necessary to the safeguarding of their right to asylum and their financial interests. It was here, in the opening of the spirit that imposed the laws of commerce, that cruel YHWH gave way to a more compassionate God, while Mosaic rigor accommodated itself to a relaxation of its own rituals. It was here that the 'treason' of Judaism fomented itself—i.e. that Essenean Judeo-Christianity was established so as to Hellenize itself.

Egyptian, Babylonian, Persian, Greek, and Roman imperialism included in their respective expansionist politics the recognition of the Gods honored by the vanquished nations. After Babylon, however, the Greeks and Romans destroyed the Temple of Jerusalem and proscribed the cult of YHWH, who allowed no other God than Himself.

Once it had accomplished the conquest of the territories of Canaan, the young and precarious Hebrew state remained on the defensive. It took root in an agrarian structure. Reassembling the nomads, it cemented the nation in a monotheistic bloc in which God, in solidarity with his people, created the earth so that they could cultivate it and impose his law everywhere.

YHWH was still a God in formation when the Babylonian invasion of the seventh century BCE brought a serious blow down upon the unitary myth, which had already been dented by the schism between Judea and Samaria. YHWH had scarcely begun to distinguish himself from the Canaanite God El—a God of women and children whose plural form, Elohim, was not unrelated to the future dualism of Samaritan Jewish Gnosticism.

The local trading posts of the Diaspora did not constitute bridgeheads—that is, billets of troops who would have been quick to open up paths for the merchants. But there were Jewish slave communities where the synagogue represented the Temple of Jerusalem. Although they were proselytes, these slaves isolated themselves in a defensive posture, as if the immobility of the sacerdotal caste that ruled over Judea, Samaria, and Galilee was weighing them down.

The dynamism of the industrious Jewish classes got entangled in the nets of the Sadducean bureaucracy, which was the aristocratic caste of the functionaries of the Temple. Its conservatism concretized the God of conquest who had afflicted His powerless believers and who held onto the gift that they made to him (in the form of salutary expiation) every day of their existence.

The development of the modernist party, Phariseeism, arrived too late, when the Jewish nation was a mere colony that successive empires indirectly inherited. The Pharisees also clashed with revolts of the extremist type that limited their ambitions to massacring the *goyim* (nonbelievers) and adoring YHWH. When Essenism broke with the Yahwehism of the Temple, it undertook to promote an ascetic rigor that would nourish the fanatical guerrillas of the Zealots who fought against the Roman occupation and Pharisee collaboration.

Lacking a bite on history, the Jewish people—having been rendered toothless by the all-powerful God who had chosen them—ended up condemned to various holocausts.

Many times rewritten and revised, the original kernels of the first Biblical texts date from the tenth and eleventh centuries before the Christian era BCE, shortly after the establishment of the Hebrews in the land of Canaan.

They lived there as semi-nomads and in a mosaic of city-states of the tribes of the Semitic race. Nomads themselves, the Hebrews—whose tribes had visited Mesopotamia and Egypt and had gleaned from them religious beliefs and techniques of organization—seized hold of a part of the land of Canaan under the leadership of a person to whom their mythology gave the name Moses.

The formation of the Jewish nation took place around the priest/warrior, who presented himself as the instrument of a patriarchal and creative divinity.

The military victories against the raids led by the 'peoples of the sea' (the Philistines of the Bible) reinforced the political unity of the Hebraic tribes and outlined—with the grand stature of El (who would become YHWH)—the triumphant symbol of the Hebraic power that was annihilating the Semitic nations and their archaic Gods: Dagan (the Dagon of the Bible), Ashtoreth or Astarte, and Baal-Zebub, popularized much later by way of the diabolical traits of Beelzebub.

Around 1000 BCE, perhaps, King David inaugurated monotheistic syncretism, because statist centralism needed a transcendent power to impose its cohesion on the tribes, which had traditionally been independent. Arrogating to himself the functions of the high priest, this temporal monarch canonized his power to guide the people chosen by El—the Father, creator of the universe and mankind, conceived in order to be obeyed.

The legend attributes to Solomon, son of David, the construction of the first Temple of Jerusalem: the symbol of the faith and supremacy of the Jews, a monument to the monotheism that had hastened to destroy the invaders, and an edifice that would one day be replaced by the Basilica of Rome.

Nevertheless, the tyranny of Solomon provoked the secession of the northern tribes. Upon his death, they refused obedience to his son and, strong with the consent of Egypt, founded in 900 BCE an independent kingdom in which the cult of El-YHWH, imperfectly implanted, clashed with the partisans of the ancient Gods.

From then on, Palestine was split between two rival regions: in the South, the Kingdom of Judea, with Jerusalem as its capital; in the North, the Kingdom of Israel, including Samaria and Galilee (today the West Bank).

Over the centuries, hate and scorn pitted Judea against Samaria—the former taking shelter in the jealous cult of YHWH and the latter, more tolerant, opening itself to new ideas and Greek influences.

Because the Samaritans weren't part of the Judean tribe, the Judeans considered them to be not Jews but *goyim*—that is, non-believers, who were generally associated with the anathema, "May their bones rot [while they are still alive]".

The opposition between Judeans and Samaritans explains an important part of the Hellenization of Jewish Gnosticism, which was omnipresent in the first Christianities. It especially explains the anti-Judaism that animated the 'Men of the Community', the Essenes, and the fact that Greco-Roman racism would disguise itself as anti-Semitism.

Priding themselves on being the true children of Israel, the Samaritans rejected rabbinical Judaism and retained as sacred texts only the books of the Pentateuch: Genesis, Exodus, Leviticus, Numbers, and Deuteronomy.

On the mountains of Ebal and Gerizim, places of worship were built that the Samaritans believed were more powerful than the Temple at Jerusalem. For them, YHWH, God of war and conquest, had not abolished El, the Father, from whom He issued, nor had He abolished the tetrad that He originally formed with his wife Asterath (Ashtoreth, Astarte), and their sons and daughter.

For the Samaritans, two feminine divinities attenuated the pitiless patriarchy that the Judeans claimed for themselves. So it was not by chance that women occupied a preponderant place in the philosophy of the physician and philosopher Simon, to whom all the varieties of Christianity—and Catholicism in its turn—would impute the origin of a thought that was radically hostile to the religious spirit.

In 722 BCE, Samaria succumbed to Assyrian invaders. The population, reduced to servitude, took the road of exile. Thenceforth, foreigners reigned over the territories that the legendary Moses had decreed 'the Promised Land' and into which Joshua had led his people.

In 586 BCE, Nebuchadnezzar seized the Kingdom of Judea, razed the Temple, and destroyed Jerusalem. Among those who survived, the notables and rich people were led away as slaves and "there only remained very few people [...]. The historians designate the form taken by the religion of the Jewish people after the destruction of the First Temple and the captivity in Babylon as Judaism"[3].

This defeat—the first in a long series—brought forth an apology as desperate as it was frenzied for the all-powerful God, as well as an exacerbated feeling of collective guilt. Upon each reversal, the litany of wandering prophets exalted the grandeur of YHWH, brooding in psalm-like fashion over the calling of the Jewish people to dominate the world and to prove in its heart the righteous expiation of its lack of faith.

Thus Biblical mythology resounds with hymns to expansionist boastfulness at the same time that it charts (in counterpoint) the harsh harmonies of a ceaselessly repeated guilt. The beating of guilt gives rhythm to the Bible and the flight of broken wings punctuates Hebraic power.

Polytheism could, without too much difficulty, revoke one or the other of the divinities who proved incapable of granting the prayers that were addressed to them. Does the supplicant not dare to threaten persecutory measures against the god who does his job maladroitly? But what about when it is a question of a unique God, the father of a national family whose children must fear, tremble, venerate, and love Him? YHWH was, after all, supposed to multiply the Chosen People until they were as numerous as the grains of sand by the sea and to guarantee them an unequaled prosperity; all peoples were supposed to give in before the grandeur of Israel and serve it without a murmur. That history continued to defy the promise of such brilliant glory—this is not what troubled the believer, who was little disposed to accuse the just and terrible YHWH of perjury, powerlessness, and perversity.

No, it was obvious to the ancient Jews that the guilty ones were the Jews themselves, unworthy men who—due to the split between the kingdoms of the North and the South—had profaned the heritage of David and the weakness of whose zeal had drawn down upon them the just wrath of the Lord. The cruelest of enemies—the Babylonians, Persians, Greeks, and Romans—wove for them between the hands of the Eternal a net of unhappiness and redemption. But if the children of Israel amended themselves, resigned themselves, welcomed misfortune with a morbid joy—and proclaimed their unshakable confidence in the fire of the ordeal—then divine mercy would bring down upon them its perpetual grace. Such is the essential message of the Biblical prophets and the canonized texts; men are invited to cover themselves with imprecations in order to redeem the incongruous conduct of a God who, having chosen to overwhelm an emerging empire with opprobrium, would be no less hesitant about annihilating the whole of the universe that He had created.

No doubt this is a unique phenomenon in history: a state—possessed by an invincible God and yet dispossessed of any victory—in which germinated the projects of a universal theocracy, a millennium sanctifying the earth, and a holy war in which the combatants had no weapons with which to confront the enemy other than their own teardrops.

Once more, it was in Samaria that, against Yahwist intransigence, there emerged a dualism that opposed a good God, unknowable, ungraspable and not of this world, to the God of war, the Demiurge, creator of a bad world; this was an idea later adopted by Christianity of the Nazarene type, as well as by the hedonistic Gnostics of the Carpocratian school.

Where the political and military development of Judea ends, there begins the myth of religious imperialism.

A veritably imprecatory saga, remodeled from older texts, was inscribed on the steps of the Temple that was sacked by the Babylonians.

For its past heroes it had the 'Judges', priests and warriors who were charged with leading holy war in the name of YHWH. They were helped—and here there was the heritage and recuperation of the pre-Yahwist cults—by women, prophetesses, such as Deborah, who commanded the tribes of the North. The *nazirs* [non-believers], ascetics and combatants devoted to God (Samson, for example), composed the shock troops.

The traditional rivalry between the temporal prince and the priest shows through in the fate reserved for the kings: honored in the narrative books of the Bible, they were shamed in the prophetic books and the Psalms. For the fanatics of holy war, God was king and had no need of leading His people to the type of victory won by a head of state. Nevertheless, it happened that a particularly pious king took on the traits of a saint and was called 'Messiah', 'anointed by the Lord', which the Greeks translated as *Christos*.

Eli and Elise propagated the cult of YHWH in the towns and countrysides against the sectarians of Baal and the ancient Gods. Jeremiah, agent of the Assyrian party against Egypt, preached the uselessness of the struggle against Nebuchadnezzar. He placed the stubborn defense of religion above political preoccupations, as if the unquestionable supremacy of God implied the infallible grandeur of a people among whom growing misery was merely the secret sign of a triumph that was all the more assured by its delays in manifesting itself on the derisory level of human temporality.

Under the Roman occupation, the Pharisee party would not act otherwise, collaborating with the enemy for the greater glory of the God who thereby tested it. Situating itself under the eternal gaze of the divinity, the spirit of Judaism wanted to appear to be ahistorical. Prophets and heroes changed names and eras but ultimately remaining the same. Adam, Moses, Joshua, and Isaiah never stopped being present at every moment.

Around 550 BCE, the Babylonian empire could not resist the assault of the Persians. In 536 BCE, Cyrus allowed the Jews to return to their homeland and reconstruct the Temple. Only the poorest returned to Palestine. Many exiles enriched themselves in Assyria and Babylon as merchants, entrepreneurs, and bankers—in Nippur, the Murashu bank offered a perfect example of the successful Jew. These Jews felt themselves to be among their co-religionists, now regrouped in little communities.

Thus began the pacific phenomenon of expansion—a mix of forcible exile and voluntary emigration—that the Greeks would give the name *diaspora*.

The particularity of the Diaspora resided in its founding Jewish trading posts that constituted so many enclaves of monotheistic Judaism in *goyische* territory. The closed theology of the agrarian myth was coupled with a spiritual opening that implied commercial practices and the circulation of commodities.

Established within a polytheistic environment, the synagogue represented the Temple of Jerusalem but was disentangled from the sacerdotal despotism of the Sadducees and was consequently more receptive to religious innovations. It was the site of the confrontation between the Pharisee party and the diverse Esseno-Christian tendencies in the first century.

The end of exile did not involve the reestablishment of a monarchy. Under the control of the Persians, the Jewish State was transformed into a theocracy. The high priest of Jerusalem directed a sacerdotal bureaucracy that led a dissolute existence while also employing itself in collating and revising the ancient texts—the corpus of which would sanctify the unity of the nation under the shepherd's crook of the supreme God, the only one who was called upon to reign over the world that He had created. The outcome of the power rivalries in the leadership caste would, much later, produce the Sadducean party, the conserver of orthodoxy in the Kingdom of Judea that claimed a monopoly over Judaism.

Those who were subjected to despotism sometimes responded to the people of the Temple—whose rapacity was matched by a ritualism that they substituted for faith—with indifference and passivity, and at other times with bouts of religious vehemence and appeals for purification, mortification, and asceticism. These latter were propagated by prophets who were quick to enflame the latent insubordination of artisans, small merchants, and the plebeians. Through revelation or 'apocalypses' (as the Greeks called them), the illuminati announced in great cries the imminence of the end of time and easily gained the adhesion of crowds in which shoemakers, carpenters, woodworkers, and bakers did not disdain playing the Rabbi or lending to their claims the rags of religious speculation. Such would be the ferment of future sects.

Even before 450 BCE, the old Samaritan schism engendered dissent from Yahwehism. The *Letters from Elephantine* (Assouan), which were rewritten on the occasion of a frontier skirmish between Israeli mercenaries in the service of the king of the Persians and the Egyptians, demonstrate the importance in the fifth century of religions that were distinct from Judean monotheism[4]. The author of these *Letters* honored the God Iao, who was derived from El but was seemingly distinct from YHWH. Sometimes confused with the Demiurge Ialdabaoth, Iao would be invoked much later by many Gnostic sects, including the Sethians. His name would frequently be mentioned in magical conjurations, charm rituals, execration slabs, and talismanic stones called *abraxas*. Also celebrated in the *Letters* was the goddess Anath-Bethel, from whom the mysterious Barbelo of the non-Christian Gnostics may have issued. Assim Bethel, child of Iao and Anath, had already passed for the Son of God.

In 400 BCE, the Persian Empire crumbled in the face of the power of the economic, political, and cultural imperialism of Greece. In 331 BCE, the victory of Alexander marked the end of Persian domination.

Upon the death of Alexander in 323 BCE, the Hellenic empire exploded, Egypt passed into the hands of Ptolemy, and Syria and Palestine became part of the Seleucid Empire.

It was at this time that the often-backdated books of the Bible were drafted in order to halo them with the prestige of ancient times. The Catholic Church would likewise move back the dates of its canonical Gospels, and for identical reasons.

Deuteronomy, falsely dated back to 622 BCE and inspired by the return from Babylon, would be redefined within the more ancient framework of the exodus in order to accentuate—to update, as it were—the role of Moses, around whom was restructured the unitary myth that created a synthesis of three great currents of thought (royal, sacerdotal, and prophetic).[5] The Book of Ezekiel, which had been projected back to between 586 and 536 BCE, presented its heroes as if they were prophets and priests, even though the sacerdotal function did not exist at that time. The priests described were identical to the 'Sons of Sadoq', a sect founded around 300 BCE. The last part of Ezekiel proposed a religious and nationalist eschatology: a great river flowed underneath the Temple in order to irrigate the holy earth while the final struggle against Gog— the enemy of Israel, whom Torrey identifies with Alexander[6]—took place.

In its first nine chapters the Book of Proverbs betrays a Hellenic influence; several aspects recall a book of Egyptian wisdom called *The Wisdom of Amenemope*. It is significant that the counsels of politeness and everyday civility gradually dressed themselves up in religious ritualism.

Favored by Hellenization, books of wisdom founded a tradition that would play an important role in the second-century redaction of the *logia*—that is, the remarks attributed to Joshua/Jesus.

Through perpetual rewriting, the corpus of the sacred books—with the Greek plural noun *biblia* ending up in the singular noun 'Bible' as if to suggest the idea of a single book dictated by the one God—claimed to be a celestial monument dedicated to the absolute power of YHWH, sculpted with bitterness, hatred, dereliction, and megalomania, and secreting a mentality resigned to supporting the foreign yoke and drawing from suffering its reason to exist. And this book, which only ever reflected the ignominy imposed on its scribes, was proposed for generations as a model to more than half the world.

The Sadducees would credit the epic hero Moses with having prescribed, in all their details, the rites, costumes, habits, and objects of the cult around which the priests moved (and therefore with instilling the omnipresence of God in the prevailing routine of gestures and comportments). The most ancient texts, which were legendarily attributed to the same 'Father', would be periodically reviewed—nay, corrected— by prophets such as Dositheus, who, in a manner that was not uncommon, characterized himself as the 'new Moses'.

Also backdated, the text known under the name of Isaiah contains a part titled "The Songs of YHWH's Servant" (chapters 50–3), the theme of which inaugurated the legend of the suffering Messiah. The Servant, a man resolved to sacrifice himself and die for the salvation of the nations, was scorned and misunderstood: "He was despised and rejected by men, a man of sorrows and acquainted and with grief [...]. | Surely he has borne our griefs and carried our sorrows [...]. | But he was pierced for our transgressions; he was crushed for our iniquities; | upon him was the chastisement that brought us peace, | and with his wounds we were healed" (53: 3–5)[7]. Here there appeared for the first time the literary prototype of the envoy of God who dies for the salvation of all. The Essenes applied this model to their Master of Justice—who was put to death around 60 BCE—before the Nazarenes and their enemies in the Pauline School applied it to the Messiah that they called Joshua and the Greeks called Jesus.

Encouraging Samaria's refusal of obedience to Judea, the Greek occupation allowed the Samaritans to erect in the region near Ebal and Gerizim a temple distinct from the one in Jerusalem. Samaria thus encountered in the North the welcome that Judea had refused to give. From the conjunction of Judaism and Greek philosophy was thus born in Samaria a thought that was oriented around knowledge of self and the world (i.e. Gnostic thought) and that sometimes took root in religious speculation and at other times in a feeling for life that revoked all forms of religion in favor of a magic Hermeticism—nay, a somatic analysis—such as that of Simon of Samaria.

Such a modern spirit would easily propagate itself in the communities of the Diaspora—in the Jewish colonies of Mesopotamia, Egypt, Syria, Asia Minor, Rome, and the Gauls.

From the Samaritan schism derived the sects that put forth different conceptions of Judaism: the Sadducees, the Pharisees, and the Esseno-Baptists who, through the Nazarene and Ebionite groups, would form the original Christianity.

The Samaritans recognized as sacred texts only the Pentateuch and the book by Joshua (who, under the name of Jesus, had a certain future). These texts and the manuscripts discovered at Qumran present similarities that accredit the close relations between the Samaritans and the Essenes; they differ from the Masoretic texts, which were exegetical enterprises on the sacred books written by Masoretes or Jewish theologians.

From 300 to around 165 BCE, the Hellenization of Palestine impregnated religious literature with a thought that was radically foreign to the Jewish mentality. Two civilizations clashed: one that was closed in upon its agrarian economy and that situated its commercial activities beyond its own frontiers (in trading posts and communities withdrawn into intransigent monotheism); and another, essentially mercantile, that propagated its logic and rationality in every location that was penetrated by its system of exchange.

Nothing is more antagonistic than the relationship between the mythic, analogical, and ahistorical spirit of the Jews and the Greek *Logos*—the latter comprising the linear time of the historians, the usage of syllogism, analysis, and synthesis, and a reality in which the Gods derived their splendor from the capricious facets of destiny.

The Indo-European structure of the Greek language very imperfectly rendered Hebraic idioms, with their atemporal verbs, word play, magical sounds, phonetic equivalences, and numerical values attributed to letters—elements that lent to the pre-Gospel *midrashim* significations that developed Kabalistic speculations but that proved to be dead ends for the Greeks and resulted in mistranslations. ("*Midrash*: Jewish (or Samaritan) exegesis. Term derived from the Hebrew *DRS*, 'to seek, to search'. Among all the rabbinical *midrashim* and the commentaries on the Torah and then on the Bible in its entirety, it is fitting to cite the *Midrash Rabbah*, the Great Midrash, a Hebraic compilation of which certain portions date back to an epoch long before the first century"[8].)

Although it attests to the universal curiosity of the Greeks, the translation of the Biblical texts by the 'Seventy' (so-called because it was legendarily attributed to seventy translators) appeared to the Masoretes and Jewish theologians as a sacrilege and a betrayal of the Biblical message. It is worth noting that it is here that 'Joshua' was first translated as *Iesous*, Jesus.

From the Alexandrian epoch came two literary genres which were diametrically opposed and yet which both fed into the fabrication of the 'novels' about Jesus: the 'wisdom' that bore the stamp of Hellenic morality, and the 'apocalypses' or 'revelations', which were prophecies that were hostile to the Greek and then to the Roman occupiers, and which were rooted in the Hebraic myth of an all-powerful God for whom punishments were the wages of love and redemption.

Issuing principally from Egypt, 'wisdom' became Hellenized in Palestine through two texts that were destined to be highly influential. The first was *The Wisdom of Ben Sira* or, more precisely, *Wise Instruction and Conscientious Proverbs by Simeon, Son of Jesus, Son of Eleazar, Son of Sira*. Although the Pharisees excluded it from their canon, the Talmud cites it close to eighty times. It became one of the Catholics' preferred books under the title that was imposed on it around 250 CE by Cyprian, the Bishop of Carthage: the *Ecclesiasticus liber*, also known as the Ecclesiasticus. (Not to be confused with the *Qohelet*, 'He who speaks in the assemblies', which the Catholics called Ecclesiastes—in Greek, 'assembly' is *ekklēsia*, the Church—and which is a text from the fourth century BCE that communicated what were then unusable banalities about the bitter destiny of man and the ignominy of woman.) The epistle falsely attributed to Jacob borrows from it a great number of expressions, as do the *logia* (attributed to Jesus), in which Simeon, who became called Simon-Peter, appears.

An early Hebrew manuscript version dating from the eighth century CE was exhumed in 1896 from the *gennizah* (a reserve in which sacred books that were no longer used were stored) in a synagogue at Cairo. The authenticity of the text was confirmed by the discovery, in 1964, at Masada—the high place of the Zealot resistance to the Romans—of a scroll that contained important fragments in the original Hebraic versions. (Yadim dates the redaction of the text to the pre-Herod period—around 40 BCE, between Chapter 1 of Isaiah and the *Manual of Discipline*[9].) The *Wisdom* was attributed to Rabbi Sira (around 190 BCE). His grandson Joshua/Jesus had it translated into Greek around 117 BCE.

In the era of Rabbi Sira, the Seleucids—the masters of Syria and Palestine—attempted to break the monotheistic rigor of the Jews by way of forced Hellenization. In 165 BCE the revolt led by Mattathias Maccabee and his son Judah demonstrated once again that state tyranny never puts an end to religious tyranny but rather reinvigorates it with the same authoritarian principles that eventually destroy it. The insurrection would offer a model of heroic and desperate holiness to the struggle that the Zealots—on the initiative of Judah of Gamala and his two sons, Jacob and Simeon—would later conduct against the Romans.

By prohibiting the practice of worship in the Temple, the Seleucid King Antiochus IV Epiphanes (215–163 BCE) succeeded in convincing the Jews of the vanity of terrestrial empires and of the much greater interest of a celestial kingdom, the imminence of which had been proclaimed by prophetic agitation.

The author of the *Wisdom* did not reject Hellenism but strove to assimilate it into Judaism, as Philo of Alexandria did later on. Rabbi Sira's faith in the final victory of the Chosen People did not reject the luminaries of Greek thought.

The true son of Israel was a sage. Wisdom [*sagesse*] would save him, because "he who is practiced in the Law will come to Wisdom"[10]. Crowning messianic hope, *Sophia* (Wisdom) plays the role of a great mediator between God and man: "Motherlike she will meet him, like a young bride she will embrace him, | Nourish him with the bread of learning, and give him the water of understanding to drink"[11].

The Greek word *sophia*, which translates the Hebrew *Hochma* and the Aramaic *Achamoth*—two feminine terms that also designate the Spirit—assumed a considerable importance in the Esseno-Christian Gnosticisms and the hedonistic currents in which figured, under a great variety of names and forms, that which brings salvation to men. Wife, mother, and virgin, Sophia was at the origin of Miriam-Mary (the virgin mother) and her companion Mary of Magdalene (as presented in the Gospel attributed to Thomas), but also of the Holy Spirit that descended upon the Messiah.

The second of the two texts through which 'wisdom' became Hellenized in Palestine was the *Wisdom of Solomon*—drafted around 50 BCE—which allied with Judeo-Greek thought a magical conception that would appear in the Hermetic current and would become very popular, in particular, in Alexandria. In *Antiquities of the Jews*, Flavius Josephus recalls that "God also enabled him [Solomon] to learn that skill which expels demons, which is a science useful and sanative to men. He composed such incantations also by which distempers are alleviated. And he left behind him the manner of using exorcisms, by which they drive away demons, so that they never return"[12].

An extract from the *Wisdom* attributes to Solomon knowledge of "the violences of winds and the thoughts of men, | The diversities of plants and the virtues of roots"[13].

Researchers have wanted to detect here the ideas of an Essene community on the Lake Mareotis—which Philo names Therapeutes—and it is true that Judeo-Greek magic is not absent from the texts found at Qumran[14]. Christian Gnosticism of the first and second centuries included thaumaturgical groups from which diverse evangelic novels concerning Jesus took inspiration in order to disguise their heroes as exorcists, healers, and miracle workers.

Rejected by the Pharisee synod of 80–90, the *Wisdom of Solomon* would later enter the Catholic canon. The Platonism into which Biblical mythology seemed to merge allows us to glimpse the surpassing of Judaism, for which the Hellenized Christianities were working from the second half of the second century.

On the other hand, the hostility of Judaism towards Hellenization was exacerbated through an original mode of original expression: 'revelation', which was better known under its Greek form 'apocalypse'—a term that much later assumed the meaning of 'universal catastrophe'.

A cyclical thought that loops around in a dazzling shortcut of birth and death, the origin and the end of time, the alpha and omega of a world created in order to annihilate itself in its terrestrial form and be reborn in a cosmic beyond, apocalypse drains away in a sudden rage the multiple reasons for putting an end to an existence that is condemned to tragedy. Its suicidal resolution has avenging accents, because no power can escape the egalitarian leveling of the death that it (the apocalypse) announces. Over the centuries the oppressed human creature discovered in apocalypse a panacea for the maledictions of injustice—the end of the centuries that founds the hope for the Great Night and the days after it that sing. It is the song of an immobile history, fixed in its glaciation, which can only set off a total explosion. Born from archaic Judaism's rupture with history, it reappears on every occasion that dreadful oppression [*l'oppression désespérante*] explodes beneath the blows of a desperate revolution [*une revolution désespérée*].

Judaic and Christian literature contains fifty apocalypses. Two of them burn with a particularly intense glare in the speculative torrent that would furrow the historical landscape in which Christs and Messiahs proliferated.

Attributed to the legendary patriarch Enoch, the *Parables* contain an apocalypse whose influence marked the myth of Jesus that circulated among the Christians. At the end of an ascension that leads him to the kingdom of the heavens, Enoch sees the Son of Man—that is to say, Adam—and discovers his true nature: the Son of Man collaborated in the creation of the world as an integral part of YHWH; he then sits at His right hand and, at the end of time (which is imminent), he returns to earth to deliver mankind from its pitiful condition.

The Apocalypse attributed to Daniel reflects the struggle of religious Jews against the political Hellenization of Antiochus IV Epiphanes. Through an artifice that reveals less a deliberate lie than a cyclical vision of history, this work claimed to be from an earlier epoch and thus to have foreseen the future. The author backdated the prediction of events that he in fact witnessed—around 165 BCE, during the revolt of the Maccabee family and their partisans, the defenders of the faith.

Obeying a mythic logic—and also conforming to the structure of Hebrew, which hardly accords with the rationality of the Greek language (which fails to render it)—this narrative transposed the political situation to the divine plane. Michael, the chief of the angels and the protector of Israel, uses his power to save his people. The visionary prophesied the ruin of four great oppressive empires: the Babylonian, the Assyrian, the Persian, and the Greek. The effective disappearance of the first three in 165 BCE of course augured the ruin of the fourth and revived the ardor of the combatants by demonstrating that God would never surrender his people to an impious domination. The fact that the crushing of the Jewish insurgents (once again) threw a bitter shadow on the antiphony "the time is near for His power and His justice to restore Israel to its glory"[15] did not exhaust the source of a type of inspiration that was stimulated rather than discouraged by failure.

The last Jewish apocalypse would also—in its zealously Christianized form—be the only one that was retained by the Catholic canon, despite those that flourished up to the sixth century. *The Original Jew* (now lost) no doubt stigmatized the Roman politics of Tiberius, who, from the year 19 CE, encouraged the pogroms in Rome and prohibited the Jewish religion in Italy.

The Greek version (attributed to John) adopted the schema of all the other revelations: evil has disturbed the divine order; order must be restored so that the kingdom of the heavens and the saints can be propagated on earth. The unleashing of calamities sounds the announced hour of the Days of the Savior, the extermination of the wicked, and the glory of Jerusalem. The era of prosperity, peace, and heavenly happiness will coincide with the triumph of the 'communities'—the Essene Churches.

By claiming that only blind faith in God would vanquish the enemy, the Apocalypse attributed to Daniel clothed in divine emanations the manifesto of the Assideans—the fanatical observers of Mosaic law and the shock troops of the Maccabean insurrection. Along the same lines, the apocalypse later attributed to John resounds with echoes of the Zealot program; perhaps the rage to destroy Rome was not unrelated to the fire of 64 CE, which has been so unreasonably imputed to Nero.

The Maccabean wars also date the Psalms—songs of praise addressed to God by the devout—whose rhythms and repetitions were carefully adhered to in order to permeate people's minds and comfort their faith.

CHAPTER TWO

Diaspora and Anti-Semitism

While the Hebrew word *galout* (exile) was used in a theological context and implied an eschatology of uprooting and return, the Greek term *diaspora* referred to an historical phenomenon: the dispersal of the Jews across the world.

In the beginning, the Jews of Judea and Samaria were chased from Palestine by a conspiracy of violence and political constraints. In 722 BCE Israel, the Kingdom of the North, fell to the power of Babylon; in 586 BCE the Kingdom of Judea succumbed in its turn.

Part of the population submitted to deportation, drawing from its unhappiness the hope of a return under the leadership of a hero chosen by God in order to help his people (now sanctified by their ordeals).

The realities of the situation, however, took the upper hand over the tortuous designs of providence. Many exiled Jews—little concerned with regaining their homeland because they held comfortable places, despite their transplantation—created communities, practiced their worship, and instaurated a politics of mutual assistance amongst themselves, with the affluent supporting the poorest.

The first Diaspora thus began as a movement of voluntary dispersal. It escalated after Alexander's conquest, when Palestine—now inserted into the Greek world—participated in that world's intense commercial activity. The Jews thus propagated themselves in regions that were subjugated to Ptolemy and the Seleucids, of whom they were now the subjects.

To the longstanding communities in Egypt and Babylon were added those of Syria, Asia Minor, and, soon after, the entire Greco-Roman Empire.

A second Diaspora extended from the second century before the Christian era to the beginning of 135 CE, when Hadrian's crushing of the revolt by Bar Kokhba marked the beginning of a third, dramatic exodus. The flame of persecution, revived by the return [*relaps*] of Judaism in the Greco-Roman Christianity of the second century and in the Catholicism of the fourth century, would consume the Jews all the way up to the twentieth century.

In the course of the second century before the Christian era, the Asmonean dynasty built diplomatic relations with Rome, where Jewish communities were multiplying.

"One cannot easily find", wrote Strabo, who lived from 58(?) to 25(?) BCE, "a spot on the inhabited world that hasn't given asylum to this people and that isn't mastered by them"[1]. And Agrippa, in a letter to Caligula, wrote: "Jerusalem is the metropolis not only of the country of Judea, but of many others due to the colonies that it has sent out, according to the occasion, in neighboring countries, including Egypt, Phoenicia, many parts of Asia, as far away as Bithynia, equally in Europe, Thessaly, Boeotia and Macedonia"[2].

As in the majority of the great towns of South Gaul, there were Jews in Lyon, where, along with Christians of the New Prophecy, they were the victims of the pogroms of 177.

The statuettes in baked earth that caricatured Jews with circumcised phalluses—which attest to the presence in Trèves, around 275, of a quite ancient community—were intended to stir up anti-Semitism.

The Jewish settlements in the towns explain the urban character of Judeo-Christianity and of the Hellenized and de-Judaicized Christianities that succeeded it. The insulting qualification *goyim*, which designated non-Jews (non-believers), would in fact appear among the anti-Semitic Christians of the second century (because of the towns' scorn for the conservatism of the countryside) in their use of such terms as *pagani*, 'peasants', 'hicks', 'bumpkins', and, in French, 'pagans'. (Historians have adopted without scruple the scorn that monotheism nourished with respect to polytheism, by speaking of 'pagans' and 'paganism'.)

Among the population of the Roman Empire, Jews constituted seven to ten percent of the total—that is, around six million people. This number exceeded the number of inhabitants in Judea.

In the first century of the Christian era, the Jewish colony in Rome numbered between 40,000 and 50,000 people. It possessed fifteen synagogues, in which rival sects often sprung up: Sadducees, Pharisees, Essenes, Nazarenes, Ebionites, Naassenes, Sethians, and converts to Judaism from all nationalities—a diversity into which the Zealot movement and its terroristic struggle against the Romans would introduce trouble.

For six centuries, the propagation of Judaism appeared to be a form of conquest. Unlike in future epochs—during which numbers would decline—a very active proselytism multiplied the numbers of adepts among the dominant classes as well as in the disadvantaged milieus. Excited by monotheistic intransigence and incessant nationalistic and extremist revolts, the hostility of the state was accentuated under Tiberius and culminated in the sacking of Jerusalem in 70 and the annihilation of the Jewish nation in 135.

Nevertheless, four centuries later, the political principle of monotheism—'One God, One State, One Nation'—would seduce Roman power at the end of a long evolution that would see the Jews robbed of their sacred texts by the Greco-Roman Christianities, which were themselves for the most part excluded from the Roman and Byzantine Churches, whose reign began in Nicaea in 325.

Jewish Proselytism and Anti-Semitism

The Bible of the Seventy, the Greek version of the sacred texts, formed the iron lance of Jewish proselytism in the Greco-Roman Empire. It responded to a will to open up to the world of the *goyim*; the Pharisees expressed it first, before pitting themselves against the modernism of certain Judeo-Christian sects that—not content with rejecting the sacrifices and priests of the Temple (as Essenism did)—put into question the meticulous rituals of Mosaic law, especially circumcision, which was a major obstacle to obtaining conversions.

Jewish orthodoxy wasn't deceived; it held the Greek translation to be a betrayal of the spirit and the letter of the law.

With the Bible of the Seventy, a civilization that was dominated by commercial capitalism seized hold of an agrarian civilization, which was walled up in its immobility and its mythic thought. Here began the plundering of the Jewish nation's sacred writings. Did not the apologist Justin affirm around 160 that these texts had ceased to belong to the Jews because they no longer understood them? For the first time, Adonai became *Kyrios*, the Savior; Joshua was transformed into Jesus; and 'Messiah' became *Christos*, Christ.

Whereas Hellenized Judaism distanced itself from the Judean tradition—a tendency for which anti-Judean Essenism clearly paved the way—the Pharisees, the only orthodox Jewish sect that survived the disaster of 70, fell back on the traditional Biblical corpus, the Talmud. Attacked from all sides, the Pharisee community took refuge in a defensive attitude; it surrounded itself with dogmatic ramparts, but not without opening the great window of Kabbalah onto the cosmic visions of Gnosticism.

Hellenized Judaism easily took root in Samaria, where the old refusal of YHWH still smoldered. From the Kingdom of the North radiated the Baptist Dunstan/Dositheos, Nazarenism, Essenism, and the philosophy of Simon (the 'father of all heresies').

Alexandria, the incubator of scholars and curious spirits, possessed an important Jewish colony. Greek anti-Semitism occasionally released upon it ferocious pogroms. It was a crucible in which the most diverse opinions mixed and clashed. There gushed from Alexandria—alongside a powerful Hermetic current that cultivated the mysteries of Egypt—apologetic texts such as the *Letter of Atisteas*, the *Fourth Book of the Maccabees*, Flavius Josephus's *Against Apion*, and the works of Philo (who lived around 20 BCE to 50 CE), in which Judaic faith absorbed Greek wisdom and was absorbed by it in turn.

Even if Philo kept to the heart of Jerusalem, a metropolis and spiritual homeland, his conception and language were Greek. A philosopher of the Diaspora, he scattered the seeds of Judaism on foreign soils where the stones of anti-Semitism abounded and where anti-Judean Essenism had already been confused with Judeo-Christianity.

From the beginning of the first century, the idea of a renewed Judaism that renewed Mosaic law coincided with the dynamism of a market in full expansion, where the commercialism of the Diaspora assisted and by turns competed with the places of Greek and Roman business.

"For a merchant", Josy Eisenberg writes, "to be or become Jewish was an assurance of easily establishing business-relations in a number of countries, of benefiting from a warm welcome and great hospitality. For the poor, belonging to Judaism could represent the guarantee of assistance and regular aid [...]. In Alexandria, there were shipowners and bankers who possessed great Jewish fortunes. But, to consider the entirety of the Empire, the majority of the Jewish population were people of small means. There were slaves among them. In Rome, neither the Trastevere neighborhood, nor those of the Porte Capere or Suburra, could pass for distinguished. What one most often reproached the Jews for was not being sewn from gold, but, rather, for being dressed in tatters and sordid"[3].

Around the beginning of the third century, the historian Dio Cassius (155–235) asked himself about the phenomenon of Jewish expansion. "I do not know how this title [the word 'Jews'] came to be given them, but it applies also to all the rest of mankind, although of alien race, who affect their customs. This class exists even among the Romans, and though often repressed has increased to a very great extent and has won its way to the right of freedom in its observances" (xxxviii. 17).[4] For Dio Cassius—and this is 200 years after the supposed birth of Christianity—there was no notable difference between the Pharisees and the Marcionite Christians, the Christians of the New Prophecy, the Valentinian Christians, the Naassenes, the Sethians, and Gnostics of all types.

The discredit that affected many of the ancient and modern forms of worship that were practiced in the Empire; the honors that were rendered to a God and to despots who made a spectacle of their own degeneration and who embellished with bloodthirsty caprices their characteristic incapacity to impose a coherent politics on the State; a sharp derision of protestations of austerity and patriotic grandeur—all of this prompted nostalgia for a unity in which religious faith buttressed the fervor of the citizenry, matched calculating reason with the charm of mystery, ordered a new marriage of the heavens and the earth, and united audacious and mercantile modernity with the prudent virtues of agrarian conservatism.

Jewish monotheism exactly proposed the principle of a unity founded on a community practice dominated by solidarity. The businessmen as well as the poor classes of the towns discovered a communal interest. After having favored emigration from Palestine, the high birthrate—justified by the fact that not having children "diminishes the image of God"[5]—worked in favor of the rapid demographic growth of the Jewish colonies, whose social and economic power grew.

"The multitude of mankind itself", Flavius Josephus noted in the first century, "have had a great inclination of a long time to follow our religious observances; for there is not any city of the Grecians, nor any of the barbarians, nor any nation whatsoever, whither our custom of resting on the seventh day hath not come, and by which our fasts and lighting up lamps, and many of our prohibitions as to our food, are not observed"[6].

Nevertheless, it was on the reef of complex rituals that the proselytism of the Jews would run aground. Their intransigence proceeded from a conservatism that proved to be irreconcilable with the Greco-Roman mentality. The history of Judeo-Christian and early Christian sects unfolded along the lines of an incessant revision of Jewish monotheism and messianism—as dictated by a nostalgia for a nationalized God who was made strong by the obedience of the nations.

Although its unitary doctrine made it attractive, the Jewish religion's intolerance and fanaticism also made it irritating. The destruction of the monuments of other cults in the name of YHWH's disapproval of idolatry caused scandal and kindled the racial hatred of the pogroms.

From the first century onwards, incidents and conflicts eventually (and sooner rather than later) exploded wherever Jewish communities settled.

In 19, Tiberius, who reigned from 14 to 38, took as his pretext the troubles in Rome caused by "three extravagant devoted Jews and a great woman converted to Judaism" to prohibit the Judaic cult in Rome and in the entirety of Italy. According to Mommsen, "those who did not consent to publicly repudiate their faith and throw their sacred vessels into the fire were chased from Italy, or at least those who were not judged suitable for military service—these latter Jews were incorporated into the disciplined companies, but their religious scruples led to a great number of them to being brought before the war counsels"[7].

Rome, which had up to 19 observed with respect to Judaism the tolerance that it applied to other religions, suddenly used anti-Semitism as a distraction from the real or imaginary menace that the frequency of rebellions in Palestine represented in the Latium [Central Italy]. The repression inaugurated by Tiberius was no doubt not unrelated to the decision of the evangelic novelists to situate the historical existence of Jesus under his reign.

When Gaius, Tiberius's successor, stirred up the great pogrom in Alexandria in 38, Philo did not hesitate, in his *In Flaccum*, to castigate the passivity of Flaccus and the Roman power that had supported the Greek party, which was superior in numbers to the Jews.

In a letter dated 41, Emperor Claudius threatened the Jews of Alexandria with punishment if they did not renounce their subversive schemes. He accused them of being "fomenters of what is a general plague infecting the whole world"[8].

In 49, this same Claudius chased the Jews from Rome because they had provoked trouble there. In 64, taking the burning of Rome as a pretext, Nero organized a pogrom that official Catholic history would later present as the first persecution of the Christians.

Hatred for the Jews grew even more after the insurrection in Palestine, which, between 66 and 70, ended in the long guerrilla war of the Zealots. "In the neighboring Greek towns—Damascus, Caesarea, Ashkelon, Scythopolis, Nipos, and Gadara—the Greeks massacred the Jews. In Damascus alone, between 10,500 and 18,000 Jews were put to death"[9].

Other pogroms took place in Alexandria, Antioch, and Pella. All of the persecutions of the first century—which the Catholics recorded in their martyrology with a view to substantiating their own long history—were in fact pogroms. The refusal to make 'sacrifices to idols', so frequently recalled in hagiographical legends, properly belonged to Jewish religious obstinacy. In 38, Philo of Alexandria interceded with the Emperor in favor of the Jews who refused to render homage to his statue.

Up to the end of the third century, the catacombs served as a sepulcher and refuge for Jews and several (probably Naasean) Gnostics, whom the imperial power hunted down without making any distinctions.

The reproaches addressed to the Jews by Roman moralists most frequently emphasized their impiety—which was alleged because of the absence of priests from their communities—and their immorality, which was an accusation traditionally leveled against mystical communities that were poorly understood or that had evaded the control of the state. Celsus left no doubt in his *True Doctrine*. In the words of Origen: "They cannot tolerate temples, altars, or images. In this they are like the Scythians, the nomadic tribes of Libya, the Seres who worship no god, and some other of the most barbarous and impious nations in the world"[10]. Celsus also referred to the 'orgiastics'—persecuted in 42 BCE by the Empire—who constituted secret groups and revived the traditions of the Dionysian cults. The same argument would later serve the Church many times in its condemnations of heretics.[11]

Furthermore, the Zealots' guerrilla war contributed to the popularization of the image of 'the Jew with a knife between his teeth', which the anti-Semitism of the twentieth century would regurgitate without being aware that it originated with the Pharisee Jew Flavius Josephus, a friend of the Romans for whom the Zealots were *lestoi*—bandits, hired killers or 'knife-wielding killers'[12].

The stupidity of Greco-Roman anti-Semitism did not pale in comparison with the ignominy of its modern resurgence (and this should come as no surprise). The poet Horace (65–8) was irritated to see his friend Fuscus convert to Judaism, observe the Sabbath, and refuse to "affront the circumcised Jews"[13].

Petronius (10–66) ridiculed the Jews by assuring his readers that they adored a Pig-God and gave thanks to the head of an ass[14]. If the idea of a Pig-God ironically mocks the prohibition on eating pork, the reference to a God with the head of an ass is not without interest: such a representation appeared on a number of Sethian magical amulets and confirms the presence in Rome—in the Jewish milieu of the 50s—of a group for which the Messiah was Seth, Son of Man; that is to say, the Son of Adam[15].

For Pliny the Elder (28–79), the Jews were "a nation remarkable for the contempt which they manifest of the divinities"[16], and, according to Lysimachus of Alexandria, Moses "charged them to have no kind regards for any man"[17]. Martial (c. 40–c. 104) had recourse to the leitmotif of fantastical frustration, which provided racism with a violent form of release. "Nor do you shun the lecheries of circumcised Jews", he said to Caelia indignantly, conscious of the peril hanging over Roman virility[18].

Around 120, Tacitus denounced what he saw as the decline of the Empire and the corruption of ancestral virtues in the frequent conversions to Judaism of members of the Roman aristocracy and even the familiars of the imperial court. He indicated that the Jews "are obstinately loyal to each other, and always ready to show compassion, whereas they feel nothing but hatred and enmity for the rest of the world"[19]. He speaks of them being "sunk in superstition"[20] and believes them "less guilty of having burned Rome than of hating humanity"[21].

After the crushing of Bar Kokhba by Hadrian and the end of the Jewish nation, the anti-Judaism of the Judeo-Christians transformed into anti-Semitism among the Hellenized Christians, as much under the influence of Marcion—the inventor of Saul/Paul—as under that of anti-Marcionites such as Justin, who would attempt to get closer to Rome by alleging his hostility to all forms of Judaism.

"Judaism", writes David Rokeah, "produced a replacement that came forth to conquer the pagan world. From the middle of the second century CE, the activity of the Christian 'mission' was intensified"[22].

When Philostratus affirmed around 230 that "the Jews have long been in revolt not only against the Romans, but against humanity; and a race that has made its own life apart and irreconcilable, that cannot share with the rest of mankind in the pleasures of the table nor join in their libations or prayers or sacrifices, are separated from ourselves by a greater gulf than divides us from Susa or Bactra"[23], his remarks could have been countersigned by those who would later accuse the Jews of deicide—namely, the fathers of ecclesiastic anti-Semitism: John Chrysostom, Jerome, Athanasius, and Augustine of Hippo[24].

Judaism maintained such a morbid propensity to hold itself responsible for the ordeals inflicted by a 'just God' that it attracted—in the manner of the masochist soliciting the sadist—the donkey's kick that, after the definitive loss of 135, it would receive from a movement [i.e. Christianity] that was born from the very heart of Judaism and that would, over the centuries, martyr the Jews in the name of the love of Christ and in that of a good God. A double abuse of authority presided over the birth of Christianity: the plundering of the Jews' sacred texts and the legend of a crucified Messiah whose blood would fall upon them. The bloody irony of what Deschner calls the "criminal history of Christianity" is that Catholicism simply ratified the incessant rewriting of Jewish texts by the prophets, the Essenes, the Christian Jews and their *midrashim*, and the hatred of the Esseno-Baptists for Jerusalem, whose priests had executed their Master of Justice.

CHAPTER THREE

The Judean Sects

The term 'sect' did not originally carry pejorative connotations. It designated certain political and religious factions that involved a part of the population.

One can confirm the existence of a Samaritan sect—which derived from the separation between the Kingdoms of the North and the South— starting from the era of Alexander and Greek domination. Hellenization encouraged this sect by allowing it to build a temple distinct from the one in Jerusalem. Its members knew and recognized only the Pentateuch (the first five books of the Bible) and the Book of Joshua/Jesus, whose influence on the mythic genesis of the messianic Savior was revealed in a sermon by Origen, written in the first half of the third century. The Samaritan Bible differed from the (subsequently established) Masoretic text and is close to the manuscripts discovered at Qumran.

The Sadducees

It is believed that the sect of the Sadducees appeared about 300 years before the Christian era and was inscribed in the political line of Yahwehist centralism. Backdated to the exile (586–536 BCE) but actually drafted in the fourth century BCE, the Book of Ezekiel describes priests who are consistent with the idea that one has of the Sadducees, 'the Sons of Sadoq' (or Tsadoq). Combining the role of prophet and the function of the priest, Ezekiel unified in the same ministry two religious attitudes that had often been opposed: the popular agitator and the temple functionary.

A priest who claimed to have ordained Solomon (Kings 1: 38), Sadoq evokes the idea of justice in accordance with the Semitic practice of wordplay known as *themoura*—"a Kabalistic practice by which, on the basis of a logical table of permutations, one replaces one Hebrew letter with another. When applied to Biblical texts, these replacements permit one to multiply their hidden meanings (or what are held to be such)"[1].

Here the key word is *tsedeq*, 'justice', which would be used by the Judeo-Christian sect of Melchizedek. One also finds it in the Essene cult of the Master of Justice, in the name they conferred upon themselves, 'Sons of Sadoq', and even in the quality of 'Justness', ascribed to Jacob, who was later held to be an apostle by the Christian and Catholic evangelic legends.

The Sadducees believed in the unitary doctrine of the state and monotheism. A sacerdotal ruling class, the Sadducees made the Temple of Jerusalem the axis of its temporal power and the privileged place in which God manifested his will to guide his people. High functionaries of the divine judgment, the Sadducees especially devoted themselves to quarrels concerning precedence and to rivalries for power.

Tasked with accomplishing the sacrifices of the Temple and with watching over the observance of the rites with which YHWH punctuated everyday existence, the Sadducees' mindset differed little from that of the Prince-Bishops of the Middle Ages and the Renaissance who, living in opulence and debauchery, only professed their faith in order to better secure for themselves the prerogatives of the Church and its sacred authority.

Good conservatives, the Sadducees absorbed revolt into change and apostasy into prophetic proclamations. Quite attached to their privileges, which they claimed came from an all-powerful God, they didn't hesitate to collaborate with invaders or to ferociously repress those Jews who did not accommodate themselves to them.

The Pharisees treated the Sadducees as if they were Epicureans, which the Pharisees thought to be an insulting term. The Christians accused the Sadducees of not believing in anything, a reproach that—following a malign turn of events—Celsus and his contemporaries addressed to the Christians, with whom (as late as the second century) they still confused the Orthodox Jews who had disappeared after 70 CE. The Sadducees, it is true, rejected the three great Pharisee teachings that were later reprised by the Christians: the expectation of a Messiah; the immortality of the soul; and—evoked for the first time in the Book of Daniel in 165 BCE—the resurrection of the body.

The Sadducees' support for Antiochus IV Epiphanes's politics of Hellenization provoked the Maccabean insurrection. In 169 BCE the pillaging of the Temple and the massacre of the factions hostile to the Greek party, which was followed two years later by the instauration in Jerusalem of the cult of the Olympian Jupiter, triggered a popular nationalist and religious upheaval that was led by a certain Mattathias. The movement participated in great prophetic agitations that demanded strict and universal obedience to Mosaic law.

Killed in 166 BCE, Mattathias was succeeded by his son, Judah, surnamed Maccabee. Under his leadership the rebellion grew and, in 164 BCE, forced Antiochus IV Epiphanes to abrogate the measures he had taken against the religion. Despite the amnesty and the reestablishment of the cult, Judah pursued the fight against the occupiers. Because his campaign also struck the partisans of Hellenism, his fanaticism alienated a faction of the Jews who were open to the freedoms of Greek thought and the merits of rational critique. The death of Judah in 160 BCE during the course of combat brought down a pitiless repression.

The ascension to power of John Hyrcanus I (134–104 BCE) marked the beginning of the Asmonean dynasty. Hyrcanus made himself odious to the Samaritans by seizing their country. He destroyed the Temple on Mount Gerizim; he annexed Idum to the south of Judea and Judaicized cosmopolitan Galilee. His son Aristobulus succeeded him but died a year later, in 103 BCE. His widow married Alexander Jonathan (103–76 BCE), who arrogated the title of king for himself.

According to Flavius Josephus, a new party intervened in the quarrel between pontifical and monarchial power—that old quarrel between the temporal and the spiritual. The Pharisees confronted the Sadducees, who, thanks to an alliance with the despots of the day, had maintained their privileges.

The Pharisees came out against the attribution of the royal title to Alexander Jonathan. He soon thereafter crucified 800 Pharisees; the throats of their women and children were cut before their eyes.

From the same tormented matrix would come a third sect—that of the Sons of Sadoq, or the Men of the Community, whom the Greeks called the 'Essenes'. Hostile to both the Sadducees and the Pharisees, they were also violently opposed to Jerusalem, the Temple, and the practice of sacrifices.

Collaborators with all the occupiers of Palestine, the Sadducees did not survive the war of the Zealots, which ended with the sacking of Jerusalem and the destruction of the Temple in 70 CE. At the end of the first century, the Pharisees possessed a monopoly on Jewish orthodoxy.[2]

The Pharisees

The Hebrew word *peroushim* means 'separated, placed apart' and alludes to the schism that led to a nationalist and holy war against the Greek occupation by Mattathias and his son, Judah Maccabee, in 163 BCE. Better known by their Hellenized name 'Pharisees', these sectarians extolled the strict observance of Mosaic laws and opposed the Sadducees' hypocrisy with popular fervor.

Vituperators of the dissolute morals of the sacerdotal caste, the Pharisees—precursors of the reform movements that castigated the morals of the Roman Church—celebrated the virtues of ascetic morality, emphasized the importance of solidarity, encouraged piety, and rallied a crowd of oppressed people whose feelings of frustration, disorder, and envy they channeled.

In their struggle against the Sadducees' domination, the Pharisees used two institutional weapons that demonstrated their organizational power: the Rabbinate and the assemblies of the faithful, or synagogues, which were the model for the Churches of the future.

Whatever his trade, the *rabbi* ('my master'), a secular pedagogue, dispensed religious instruction among the working classes. After the defeat of 70 CE and the disappearance of the Sadducees, there were rabbis who imposed modernity on the Jewish religion, fixed the canon of sacred texts, defended orthodoxy, and condemned the heresies of the *minim* (dualists or Gnostics) and the *noisrim* or Nazarenes.

The synagogues (the source is the Greek word *synagoge*, which means 'meeting') were the houses for priests, studies, and meetings. The Essenes would imitate them by calling theirs 'communities' (from the Greek word *ekklēsia*: 'church' designates the place and 'Church' the assembly that meets therein).

When bloody repression by Alexander Jonathan, allied with the Sadducees, fell upon them in 100 BCE, the Pharisees in large part left Judea and went to Galilee. There they were rivals with the Nazarenes in the second half of the first century before the Christian era. In the cities of the Diaspora, their influence continued to grow until the great anti-Semitic waves of 70 and 135.

When Pompey seized Jerusalem in 63 BCE, thereby inaugurating a Roman domination that would last until 324 CE, the Pharisees, in their turn, chose to collaborate with the occupiers.

In the same period, under the pontificate of John Hyrcanus II, a dissident rabbi (the head of an Essene community who was known by the name Master of Justice) was put to death with the consent, if not on the instigation, of the Pharisees. The Essenes declared a hatred of the Pharisees that was equal to that which they felt for the Sadducees and for Judaism in general. Not only would the execution of the Christ or the Essene Messiah lend its dramatic aura to the crucifixion of Jesus (as reported by the evangelic legends), but it would also accredit the notion of a death clamored for by the Pharisees.

Although little taken with the kings chosen by the Romans (such as Herod the Great), the Pharisees estimated that sovereigns govern by reason of a divine will and supported the principle that it was necessary "to render unto Caesar what belongs to Caesar".

The Pharisees took the side of Rome in its struggle against the Zealots, whom one of their most celebrated sectarians, the historian Flavius Josephus, called *lestoi*—'bandits' and 'terrorists'. Wasn't it with the consent of the Roman authorities that, a little before the destruction of Jerusalem, the great rabbi Johanan Ben Zaccai and the Pharisees left the town? That exodus, voluntarily undertaken in order to avoid a confrontation of which the Pharisees disapproved, would, in a falsified version, enter into the apologetic novel known as Acts of the Apostles (end of the second century). In this text the Pharisees have become Christians and are therefore accredited with nurturing no hostility towards Rome (from the second half of the second century on, the politics of the diverse Christianities strove to obtain a certificate of good citizenship from Roman imperial power). They took refuge at Pella, in Macedonia. Like the Sadducees, the Pharisees made a pact with the powers-that-be so as better to situate their religion beyond terrestrial contingencies. The Catholic Church took the same approach all the way through the nineteenth and twentieth centuries. On the other hand, the Pharisees drew upon themselves the hatred and scorn of the Zealots and of the Essene factions that were favorable to them.

The Pharisees popularized the practice of the *midrash* or biblical commentary. The so-called sacred texts were recopied, revised without scruple as a function of ongoing polemics, read in public, explained, glossed, corrected by the evolution of mindsets, and brought up to date—nay, even suppressed, as was the case with the Book of Tobias. A whole literature—*targum, midrash, mishna, Talmud*—was thus forged in the fires of the assemblies and from the necessity of extracting from these texts a moral rule applicable to the community or to the entirety of the believers.

The Pauline current, which Marcion would impose around 140 CE in order to counter the Judeo-Christian communities that claimed Peter and James for themselves, took a large part of its doctrine from the Pharisees' teachings: notably, the beyond in which the dead would be individually resurrected after a Last Judgment that would divide them up into the blessed (who would be elected to a celestial Eden) and the damned (who would be hurled down into Gehenna); the existence of angels (agents and intercessors of Divine Grace); the end of the world, in which a Messiah sent by God annihilates the terrestrial kingdoms in order to substitute for them the kingdom of God; and the imminence of the times in which the power of the Savior will be revealed.

Like the Essenes, the Pharisees practiced the Holy Communion or

Eucharistic banquet, but they defended a more personal religion—one that was less austere and that better accorded with human weaknesses. Although they were attached to sacrifices and to the meticulous rigors of the observances, they were otherwise much more accommodating, which elicited the reproach of laxity from the Essenes, who themselves refused the sacrifices of the Temple in order to substitute for them the sacrifice of existence and the maceration of the body.

The Pharisees were ardent proselytizers, but, unlike the Essenes, the Nazarenes, and the Elchasaite Christians (who were mentioned in a letter from Pliny the Younger to Emperor Trajan), they were rather inclined to discourage neophytes. Another paradox: like the Christian Jews in the Epistle attributed to Barnabas (90? 100? 110?), they did not remove the obstacles of circumcision, the Sabbath, the rites of purification, or prohibited foods.

Placing their emphasis on active solidarity, the Pharisees made the synagogues places of mutual assistance and encounter. In them they developed a kind of social security system that provided assistance to the poor, the elderly, widows, and the sick. The Churches (first the Judeo-Christian ones, then the de-Judaicized ones) claimed for themselves the charitable politics of the Pharisees, investing in them in order to establish themselves more easily in the working-class milieus.

The Zealot Movement

The Zealots constituted a national guerrilla front that brought together (in a shared hatred for the Roman occupation) diverse religious tendencies in Palestine and across the Diaspora. They were not a religious sect, properly speaking.

Herod, who was king from 37 to 4 BCE, did not fail to rebuild the Temple, appease religious scruples, and assure himself of the favor of the Sadducees and Pharisees. Nevertheless, an agitation that no doubt issued from the Essene and Baptist milieus (Dositheans and Nazarenes) ravaged the State that was under his control.

Speaking about the revolt led by Judah of Gamala, Flavius Josephus mentions a bandit by the name of Ezekias: "There was also Judas, the son of that Ezekias who had been head of the robbers; which Ezekias was a very strong man, and had with great difficulty been caught by Herod"³.

Judah [or Judas] of Gamala (or Galilee) seems to have been the leader of the revolt that took place in the year 6. The crucifixion of his father, Ezekias, took place around 30 BCE.

The endemic state of the revolt worsened after Herod's death in 4 BCE. "At this time there were great disturbances in the country [...]. Simon, one of the servants to the king, relying upon the handsome appearance, and tallness of his body, put a diadem upon his own head also; he also went about with a company of robbers that he had gotten together, and burnt down the royal palace that was at Jericho, and many other costly edifices besides"⁴. A shepherd, Athronges, also put on a diadem and traveled the country, killing Romans and the King's people. In response, the Roman General Varus was sent in with two legions and four regiments of cavalrymen.

In 6, the census organized by Quirinus, the legate of Syria, gave the signal for a general insurrection that was conducted for religious reasons — because "only God can number his people" (which is how the census taken by David is described in 2 Samuel 24: 1, as a numbering)⁵ — but was above all caused by the miserable lot of the disadvantaged classes. The insurrection was led by Judah of Gamala, to whom Flavius returns several times.

> A certain Galilean, whose name was Judas, prevailed with his countrymen to revolt; and said they were cowards if they would endure to pay a tax to the Romans, and would, after God, submit to mortal men as their lords.⁶

> There was also Judas, the son of that Ezekias who had been head of the robbers; which Ezekias was a very strong man, and had with great difficulty been caught by Herod. This Judas, having gotten together a multitude of men of a profligate character about Sepphoris in Galilee, made an assault upon the palace [there], and seized upon all the weapons that were laid up in it, and with them armed every one of those that were with him, and carried away what money was left there; and he became terrible to all men, by tearing and rending those that came near him; and all this in order to raise

himself, and out of an ambitious desire of the royal dignity; and he hoped to obtain that as the reward, not of his virtuous skill in war, but of his extravagance in doing injuries.[7]

Yet was there one Judas, a Gaulonite, of a city whose name was Gamala, who, taking with him Sadduc, a Pharisee, became zealous to draw them to a revolt, who both said that this taxation was no better than an introduction to slavery, and exhorted the nation to assert their liberty; as if they could procure them happiness and security for what they possessed, and an assured enjoyment of a still greater good, which was that of the honour and glory they wou[l]d thereby acquire for magnanimity. They also said that God would not otherwise be assisting to them, than upon their joining with one another in such counsels as might be successful, and for their own advantage […].[8]

Whence arose seditions, and from them murders of men, which sometimes fell on those of their own people (by the madness of these men towards one another, while their desire was that none of the adverse party might be left), and sometimes on their enemies; a famine also coming upon us, reduced us to the last degree of despair, as did also the taking and demolishing of cities; nay, the sedition at last increased so high, that the very temple of God was burnt down by their enemy's fire. Such were the consequences of this, that the customs of our fathers were altered, and such a change was made, as added a mighty weight toward bringing all to destruction, which these men occasioned by thus conspiring together; for Judas and Sadduc, who excited a fourth philosophic sect among us, and had a great many followers therein, filled our civil government with tumults at present, and laid the foundations of our future miseries, by this system of philosophy, which we were before unacquainted withal; concerning which I shall discourse a little, and this the rather, because the infection which spread thence among the younger sort, who were zealous for it, brought the public to destruction.[9]

But of the fourth sect of Jewish philosophy, Judas the Galilean was the author. These men agree in all other things with the Pharisaic notions; but they have an inviolable attachment to liberty; and say that God is to be their only Ruler and Lord. They also do not value dying any kinds of death, nor indeed do they heed the deaths of their relations and friends, nor can any such fear make them call any man Lord; and since this immoveable resolution of theirs is well known to a great many, I shall speak no further about that matter; nor am I afraid that any thing I have said of them should be disbelieved, but rather fear, that what I have said is beneath the resolution they show when they undergo pain; and it was in Gessius Florus's time that the nation began to grow mad with this distemper, who was our procurator, and who occasioned the Jews to go wild with it by the abuse of his authority, and to make them revolt from the Romans; and these are the sects of Jewish philosophy.[10]

Flavius Josephus's text calls for several remarks. The movement of the Zealots or those who are "zealous for the law"[11] was not born under the government of Gessius Florus—that is to say, in 65. It emerged instead from the failure of Judah of Gamala, who was called the Galilean—as was the Messiah Jesus (of whose existence Flavius Josephus is unaware)—and who also wanted to become king of the Jews.

The name of the Pharisee, Sadoq, whom Flavius Josephus (himself a Pharisee) held in only middling esteem, evokes the idea of justice, as does the Essenes' Master of Justice and the Judeo-Christians' Jacob/James. Finally, the grouping together of diverse religious tendencies that the historian calls the "fourth sect"—does it not suggest the idea of a religious syncretism in which each combatant, recognizing no other authority than that of God, is the brother of and witness for Adonai, *Kyrios*, the Savior?

In 45, Cuspius Fadus—named the governor of Judea by Emperor Claudius—had to face an insurrection led by the Messiah Theudas (aka Judah or Thomas), who was followed by a great many poor people. In the manner of Elijah and Elisha in Hebrew mythology, he promised his troops that they would take Jerusalem and cross the River Jordan without getting their feet wet. By promising to lead his flock into the holy land, he repeated the gesture of Joshua. Fadus suppressed the revolt. Theudas was decapitated, his partisans massacred.

Between 46 and 48, Tiberius Alexander, who succeeded Fadus,

ordained the crucifixion of the two sons of Judah of Gamala: Simeon (Simon) and his brother Jacob (James).

Under Agrippa III, around 49, new clashes broke out between Jews and Zealots. Battles were fought beside the Temple. In 66, Caesarea was the theater of battle between Jews and Greeks. Two years later, another incident brought fire to the powder. Eleazar, son of the great priest Anania and leader of the Temple's guards, killed the third son or the grandson of Judah of Gamala—Menachem, one of the leaders of the Zealot movement (his name means 'paraclete' [in Greek] and 'comforter' [in Latin]). The general war against Rome and the independence of Israel were proclaimed in a great confusion, because Jews from rival factions were killing each other in Jerusalem. This would last up until 70 CE.

Flavius Josephus, who had been the governor of Galilee, said the following with full knowledge of the causes of the Vespasian campaign[12]:

> Now all those Galileans who, after the taking of Jotapata, had revolted from the Romans, did, upon the conquest of Taricheæ, deliver themselves up to them again. And the Romans received all the fortresses and the cities, excepting Gischala and those that had seized upon mount Tabor; Gamala also, which is a city over against Taricheæ, but on the other side of the lake, conspired with them. This city lay upon the borders of Agrippa's kingdom, as also did Sogana and Seleucia. And these were both parts of Gaulanitis; for Sogana was a part of that called the Upper Gaulanitis, as was Gamala of the Lower; while Seleucia was situated at the lake Semechonitis, which lake is thirty furlongs in breadth, and sixty in length; its marshes reach as far as the place Daphne, which in other respects, is a delicious place, and hath such fountains as supply water to what is called Little Jordan, under the temple of the golden calf [13], where it is sent into Great Jordan. Now Agrippa had united Sogana and Seleucia by leagues to himself, at the very beginning of the revolt from the Romans; yet did not Gamala accede to them, but relied upon the difficulty of the place, which was greater than that of Jotapata, for it was situated upon a rough ridge of a high mountain, with a kind of neck in the middle: where it begins to ascend, it lengthens itself, and declines as much downward before as behind, insomuch that it is like a camel in figure, from whence it is so named, although the people of the country do not

pronounce it accurately. Both on the side and the face there are abrupt parts divided from the rest, and ending in vast deep valleys; yet are the parts behind, where they are joined to the mountain, somewhat easier of ascent than the other; but then the people belonging to the place have cut an oblique ditch there, and made that hard to be ascended also. On its acclivity, which is straight, houses are built, and those very thick and close to one another. The city also hangs so strangely, that it looks as if it would fall down upon itself, so sharp is it at the top. It is exposed to the south; and its southern mount, which reaches to an immense height, was in the nature of a citadel to the city; and above that was a precipice, not walled about, but extending itself to an immense depth. There was also a spring of water within the wall, at the utmost limits of the city.

As this city was naturally hard to be taken, so had Josephus, by building a wall about it, made it still stronger, as also by ditches and mines under ground.[14]

Situated to the east of Lake Tiberias (Genesareth), Gamala—despite its privileged situation—fell into the hands of Titus, son of Vespasian, after tough fighting.

In August 70, the Roman Decima Legio seized Jerusalem, sacked it, and ruined the Temple. The Zealots' desperate resistance was sustained until the fall of Masada, their last fortress, in 73.

In the first half of the second century, revolt broke out again under the leadership of the Messiah Bar Kokhba. Hadrian crushed it in 135, reducing the Jewish nation and state to nonexistence for the next nineteen centuries.

If Flavius Josephus spoke of the Zealots as if they were a sect, this was because the insurrection had been experienced like a veritable national and religious epic, a saga whose scattered fragments nourished *midrashim* of anger, despair, and eschatology before being revised and faultily translated into Greek and implanted in propaganda narratives (first Christian, then Catholic) that falsified their meaning.

Jews of all beliefs numbered among the Zealots. Flavius Josephus—a Hellenized aristocrat and a functionary of the Roman Empire—reproached them for their violence and fanaticism. (Nothing excludes the possibility that the fire that ravaged Rome in 64 CE, to which Nero's pogroms responded, was the work of a hardcore faction of the Zealots who were active in Rome's Jewish community. In 49, troubles attributed to the Jews had exploded in Rome. Assuming that it isn't an interpolation, the formula "impulsatore Christo", which Suetonius employs around 130 in his *The Twelve Caesars*—"with the prompting of a Messiah", with *Chrestos* or *Christos* simply translating the Hebrew 'Messiah'—refers to those troubles.) But, with xenophobia and nationalist messianism serving as catalysts, these religious tendencies amalgamated themselves into an apparent unity, from which Judeo-Christianity would draw a kind of specificity after the defeat [of 70 CE].

The Pharisees promulgated the hope for salvation, the imminent end of the world, the approach of the Last Judgment, and resurrection.

Despite the pacifism with which they are generally credited, the Essenes did participate in the Zealot movement. The Decima Legio would raze the site of Qumran. Among the texts discovered at Masada—in addition to *The Wisdom of Ben Sira*—was a specifically Essenean ritual, namely the Sabbath prayer chanted in union with the angels of heaven.[15]

What about a Judeo-Christian presence of the Ebionite or Nazarene type among the Zealots? The works of Flavius Josephus mention many names that also appear in the exegetical and propagandistic literature; they pop up in the Hebrew or Aramaic *midrashim* of the first century, and in the Catholic texts of the fourth, fifth, and sixth centuries. It therefore seems that—due to the ahistorical spirit of Judaism—the two Zealot leaders, Jacob/James and Simon, son of Judah of Gamala, respectively 'became' Jacob of Kepher Schanya, the leader of the Nazarene community who was executed between 41 and 42 on the orders of Herod Agrippa, and Simon the Essene, the enemy of Jochanaan (John the Baptist). The first of the two would later become James the Just and the second Simon/Peter, a descendant of Simon Cephas (Simon the Rock, Simon the Stone, Simon the Bald, Simon the Cruel, Simon the Unshakable?).

The agitator Theudas contains the *doublon*[16] Jude/Judas and Thomas. The evangelic legends call him 'Athlete' (according to the Essene expression 'athlete of virtue') and 'father of the Savior'. These four names later would be included in the communion of the apostles who were selected as the patrons of diverse communities. Around the end of the second century, the assembly of the apostles would constitute the team members of the only hero of whom no trace exists outside of Hebrew mythology: Joshua/Jesus.

Brandon's thesis, according to which Jesus was a Zealot put to death alongside fellow brigands or *lestoi*, is not without interest in this context. Saul/Paul, an adversary of the communities or Churches that claimed James and Simon/Peter for themselves, erected Jesus as the exemplary value in his (Saul/Paul's) soteriological and penitential system. In order to please Rome, he substituted for the terrorist a saint put to death not by the Romans but by the Jews, who did not pardon him, his pacifism, or the ecumenism of his God of Kindness. These are fictions that—well into the twentieth century—took up the reins from the canonical Gospels in order to firm up the notion of an historical Jesus by according an increasing amount of credit to the Zealot hypothesis, which supposes that Jesus was the brother of James and Simon, and therefore the son of Judah of Gamala. (One would be remiss not to cite one of the two remarks that do *not* conform with the kindness of the Messiah and that have survived the composite redaction of the Gospels: "'But as for these enemies of mine, who did not want me to reign over them, bring them here and slaughter them before me'. And when he had said these things, he went on ahead, going up to Jerusalem" (Gospel attributed to Luke, 19: 27–8).)

Although Bernard Dubourg's thesis of a Biblical Joshua (incarnated in many prophets) confirms the nonexistence of the notion of a historical Jesus as late as the second half of the second century (in 150, a work recognized by all the Churches of the epoch under the title *The Pastor of Hermas* does not mention him), it does not exclude the possibility of an intervention—in the long struggle of dissident Jews against Rome—by a 'new Joshua' with whom Theudas/Thomas (much later called the 'twin brother of Jesus') might have identified himself.

After 70, Rome imposed upon Palestine the peace of the cemetery. The Sadducee aristocracy disappeared; the last Zealot party desperately resisted at Masada. The Samaritans and the Essenes entered the war on the side of the Judeans, were decimated, and took refuge in the cities of the Diaspora. Only the Pharisees—friends of Rome and defenders of the peace—escaped the violence of the conquerors, only to fall victim to the animosity of the vanquished; that is to say, the Esseno-Christians, who themselves broke up into a multitude of sects that repudiated the bloody God of Israel, contested Mosaic law, and rediscovered the pacifism that they had briefly forsaken.

CHAPTER FOUR

The Men of the Community, or the Essenes

Only Flavius Josephus and Philo of Alexandria use the words *essenoi* or *essaoi* (from the Hebrew *esah'*, meaning 'council' or 'party'), which Dupont-Sommer[1] translates as "congregation" [*congrégation*] or "men of the community" [*hommes de la communauté*], to refer to the Jewish dissidence that was hostile to the two sects that dominated Judea and the Diaspora: the Sadducees and the Pharisees.

Hadot does not rule out the influence of the Aramaic word *ossio* ('doctor') in the origin of the appellation *Therapeutes* (or the 'doctors of the soul'), which Philo gives to an Essene sect located not far from Alexandria.

If it is possible to judge from the manuscripts discovered at Qumran, they called themselves the 'Men of the Community', 'Council of God', 'Council of the Community', 'Sons of Sadoq' (or Tsadoq), 'Sons of the Just', or 'Sons of Justice'. In a general way, they called themselves the 'Loyal' or the 'Pious'. In Hebrew, the word is *châssé*; in Syrian, it is *hasaya*, which means 'pious' or 'holy', and is phonetically similar to 'Essenean'. "The eastern door of Jerusalem, which overlooked the country of the Essenes, kept the name *Bab Essahioun*, which seems to recall the name of this mysterious community".[2]

According to Qumranian texts from a later date, the Essenes formed a sect of the 'New Alliance', a formula that Marcion—in all probability inspired by the Christian Jew Saul—would translate as 'New Testament' in order to oppose it to the Old one (with a measure of success that cannot be denied).

In its two centuries of existence, Essenism—the expansion of which followed the tracks of the Diaspora—did not fail to borrow from diverse streams and embrace many doctrines. Philo speaks of the 'Therapeutes' of Lake Mareotis. In certain texts, the Men of the Community are identified with the *ebyonim*, the 'poor', who had every reason to approach the Judeo-Christian sect of the Ebionists, who were close to or rivals of the Nazarenes and to whom the *rebym*, the 'many' (a term used by Saul/Paul to designate his disciples), seem to have been opposed.

History of the Sect

Rejecting the early hypothesis that traces the origin of Essene dissidence to the Asmoneans Jonathan and Simon, Dupont-Sommer traces it instead to Alexander Jannaeus (103–76 BCE).

Opposition to the monarchal pretentions of the great priest Alexander Jonathan incited the leader of the Essenes to withdraw into the desert with his partisans, just as Moses did.

> We know through Flavius Josephus that Aristobulus the First, successor to the great priest John Hyrcanus, his father, would add the title of king to that of great priest. A year later, in 103 BCE, his brother Alexander Jannaeus succeeded him and did not disavow this bold initiative: he took the title of king in his turn. Of the three great Jewish parties, only the Essenean party was strongly opposed to this innovation.[3]

The resolution to leave Jerusalem and enter the desert is evoked in *War of the Sons of the Light Against the Sons of Darkness*[4].

Where was the community located? The historian Dio Chrysostom (around 42 to 125) speaks of Essenes living near Sodom. For Saulcy, Qumran would be Gomorrah[5]. Doresse contents himself with stating that "Sodom and Gomorrah count among the places in which their colonies were established"[6].

In *The Damascus Document*, the first master of the sect carried the title of priest. He issued from the sacerdotal family of Gemul and his dissidence derived, at least at its origin, from a power struggle within the Sadducee caste, which was mythically attached to Sadoq, the great priest under Solomon.

His title referred to the sacred notion of justice, to those just or holy people whom God designated as his chosen; in Christianity, Jacob/James would be an example of such a person. This was also the destiny of Melchizedek, a secondary biblical personage who, among certain Essenes, was elevated to the dignity of Messiah by the symbolic consonance of his name (*tsedek*, 'justice'). Fragments that came from *midrashim*, reprised in the notes attributed to Saul/Paul, again attest to the veneration shown with respect to an *alter ego* of the Master of Justice.

Around 100 BCE there developed in Qumran a Jewish sect that broke away from the Sadducees and that was hostile to the Pharisees who were persecuted by Alexander Jannaeus. Upon the death of the monarch and great priest, his widow, Alexandra (76–7), occupied the throne and set up her son Hyrcanus II as the sovereign pontiff.

Upon the death of Alexandra, a war broke out between Hyrcanus II (67–63) and his brother, Aristobulus II. The Pharisees took the side of the former, while the Sadducees chose the latter.

Around 65 BCE, persecution by Hyrcanus II fell upon the Essenes who had taken refuge in Damascus, the holy city of which the Hebrew name (*DMS*) means 'sanctuary'.[7] Its mythical foundation was attributed to Seth, the Son of Man (that is to say, the Son of Adam), whose importance—emphasized in the Qumran manuscripts, as well as in the texts discovered at Nag Hammadi—demonstrates the existence of sects that believed Seth was the Messiah. *The Damascus Document* situates the persecution a little before the arrival of Pompey in Judea in 63 BCE.

Between 65 and 63 BCE a drama exploded, the eschatological consequences of which surpass the history of the Essenes: the putting to death of the Master of Justice, who was, according to the "Commentary on Habakkuk", "the Priest [in whose heart] God set [understanding] that he might interpret all the words of His servants the prophets"[8]. Was this Onias the Just, put to death in the camp of Hyrcanus II, as suggested by Dupont-Sommer? (According to J. M. Rosenstiehl[9], the ancient kernel of the *Apocalypse of Elijah* dates from the epoch of Hyrcanus II. An unanointed king persecutes the virgin Tabitha, who personifies the Community of Qumran, but the Anointed One, the Messiah, comes to deliver her and lead her to terrestrial paradise. The return of Enoch evokes that of the Master of Justice.)

Whatever the case, the Qumran texts thenceforth combined veneration of the victim—the 'Last Priest' or the 'Messiah of the Spirit'—with execration of the despot or the 'Impious Priest'. Philonenko sees in the martyrdom of Isaiah a transposition of the history of the sect and the sacrificial execution of its Messiah[10].

When Pompey seized Jerusalem and razed the Temple in 63 BCE, the Essenes propagated the rumor of a just punishment inflicted by God on the Judeans, who were guilty of the death of the Messiah. This scenario, which colored anti-Judaism with anti-Semitism, would, in the second century, enter the fictional elaboration of the death of Jesus.

Little by little, the Men of the Community regained the region of the Dead Sea, and not without leaving important colonies in the cities of the Diaspora and in Damascus, the sanctuary city in which the legendary biography of Saul/Paul situated the prophet's illumination and his revelation of the Messiah.

An invasion by the Parthian Empire, which ravaged the Qumran region between 40 and 38 BCE, and an earthquake combined to ruin a secular community whose numerical strength was attested to by the architectural development of its buildings, the extensiveness of its agriculture, its irrigation system, and even its cemetery, in which both men and women reposed.

The tolerant attitude of Herod (37 BCE–4 CE) favored the Essenes' freedom of movement. They traveled the roads that, from Jerusalem to the Dead Sea, followed the banks of the River Jordan. There an important Baptist movement was born. Can one see an evolved Essenism, stripped of its elitism, or the perpetuation of the teachings of the Messiah called Dunstan/Dositheos (who was crucified) in the Nazarenism that was established in Judea, Galilee, and Samaria well before the Christian era?

From 4 BCE onwards, the guerrilla war against Rome provoked a new flow of people into Qumran. It is more than probable that a faction within Essenism supplied doctrinal weapons to the Zealot movement. There were Essenes at Masada for whom *The War of the Sons of the Light Against the Sons of Darkness* brought together eschatological combat and nationalist warfare.

In 68 CE, Qumran was devastated by the Decima Legio Fretensis, the elite military horde sent by the Romans to crush the Jewish insurrection. But the development of Essenism was not broken; in fact, it had only just begun.

With the divine punishment that fell upon Jerusalem and the Temple, which they never ceased to execrate, the Men of the Community showed themselves—in the broad daylight of the Diaspora—to be what they had always been: messianic Jews expecting the imminent return of their *Kyrios*, their Savior; enlightened ones whom the Greeks at the beginning of the second century called *chrestianoi* or *christianoi*—that is to say, quite simply messianics and not, as the historians have falsely suggested, disciples of a unique Christ.

Contrary to what Renan affirms, Christianity is not an Essenism that succeeded; it is nothing other than the entirety of the Essene sects, encompassed by the general term Judeo-Christianity, and set in opposition to the Pharisees.

Spared from Roman repression, the Pharisees tightened their ranks and fell back upon a rigorous canonicity that was concretized by the Talmud and its commentaries. They fought two heresies: the *nosrim* or Nazarenes, who were preoccupied with the reform of Mosaic law, and the *minim* or Gnostics, 'those who know', which included the dualists, who opposed the Good God and YHWH with the Simonian doctrine of individual salvation through self-creation.

Monachism and Ecclesial Organization

Essenism evolved a great deal over the course of two centuries. If its archaic form, which was of the monastic type, had not disappeared (due to the persecution pursued by Decius) from the hermitages and Coptic monasteries founded by Pachomius and Macarius around 251, then its doctrines would have taken on the more modern colorations that were expressed by Ebionism, Nazarenism, the Epistle attributed to Barnabas, the teachings of Saul/Paul—nay, the Elchesaitism of the *Homilies of Peter* attributed to Clement[11]—not to mention the Enochians, Melchizedekians, and Sethians.

The excavations at Qumran have uncovered a square building flanked by a tower that was perhaps intended to watch for the return of the Messiah, who was put to death around 63 BCE.

A system of canals that began at a mountain stream fed seven pools equipped with a stairway and several round basins, which were reserved for the baptism of neophytes and purifying ablutions.

The monastery was dedicated to worship and meetings and did not shelter the members of the community, who were lodged nearby. A meeting hall served as a space for the reading and exegesis of biblical texts, which were rewritten and revised without scruple by sectarians who were convinced that they were the only ones who held the truth. Did they not praise their Christ for having revealed to them the meaning of the Scriptures and for thereby elevating them to the status of God's chosen ones, saints, 'perfect ones'?

There in the monastery were celebrated the sacred banquets or 'Holy Communions', ritual meals of bread and wine (or water) by which the faithful communed with the presence of God (the Catholic Eucharist was inspired by it and added the symbolism of the Flesh and the Blood, which was borrowed from the Phrygian cult of Attis).

According to estimates, the average population of Qumran was around 200 people. Its autocratic system was founded on agriculture, which was given over to the care of neophytes, while the Perfect Ones devoted themselves to praising the Savior, singing hymns, and the exegesis of sacred texts. Flavius Josephus estimated the number of Essenes in Alexandria (where Philo knew them by the name 'Therapeutes'), Damascus, Greece, Asia Minor, and Italy to be 4,000.

The cemeteries have yielded the skeletons of men and women—probably the wives of the converts assigned to labor activities—who were accorded the right to marry with the goal of procreating. The Essenes interred their dead with their heads facing north. They differed in this regard from other Jews, whom they considered to be non-believers: they judged themselves to be the only representatives of the true Israel. They included in this execration the Sadducees and the Pharisees, who were deemed guilty of spilling the blood of the Messiah. Refusing the sacrifices made under the aegis of the Great Priest, they called for divine vengeance upon the Temple, the object of infamy that had been rebuilt by Herod.

As for Jerusalem, they nurtured the ambition to deliver it from the Jews who had profaned the holiness of the place with their impious doctrines. Among several attempts effectuated in this regard, there was the tumult stirred up by Theudas/Thomas and his 4,000 'poor people' (*ebyonim*), who partook of the Essene spirit.

Their apportionment of time also distinguished the Essenes from their co-religionists. The only true observers of Mosaic laws, they claimed that their calendar derived from divine revelation. Unlike the Judean calendar, theirs was solar, not lunar.

Following Ezekiel's directions, the year was divided into four trimesters and into months of thirty or thirty-one days, with the result that festivals fell on fixed dates. Easter echoed Wednesday 14 Nizan, two days before the Easter celebrated in Jerusalem.[12]

This was the calendar to which the evangelic novel of Joshua/Jesus referred and which was later adopted by Catholic orthodoxy when—appropriating the control of time in its turn—it arbitrarily anchored at zero the beginning of the Christian era.

The Essenes replaced sacrifices at the Temple with the sacrifice of the body: mortification extinguished the fire of desire and stoked the ardor of the spirit, to which their miserable existence reduced itself. Their fanatical asceticism nourished the misogyny that is characteristic of patriarchal peoples and intensified it to a state of neurosis. The Qumran manuscripts include a poem against women—the source of all the evils and troubles that afflicted men.[13]

The *Rule of War* proscribes sexual relations and excludes women, young men, and the impure (understood to be those who ejaculate) from the ranks of the Enlightened Ones[14].

A subsequent text, issued from Damascus, tolerates marriage as a last resort, but with the sole objective of perpetuating the sect through procreation.

Scorn for women runs in counterpoint through all the divisions of

Christianity. Saul/Paul (an Essenean or Nazarene) tolerated their presence in the ecclesiastical assemblies only on the condition that they kept quiet; the Marcionites, Elchesaites, Montanists, and Catholics all treated them as if they were impure beasts. To affirm that this was all quite commonplace, given the prejudices of the times, would be to ignore the fact that, at the same time, the schools—nay, even the sects—recognized in women and love the priceless privileges of creating life and saving humanity. This was the case with Simon of Samaria, certain Naassenes, and the Barbelites.

No doubt Pliny the Elder was right to paint an unlikable portrait of the Essenes: "they have no women among them; to sexual desire they are strangers; money they have none; the palm-trees are their only companions"[15]. Love was travestied by their adoration of God and their clannish solidarity. As for the absence of money, which was the result either of an autocratic economy or (as was the case among the Ebionites) of voluntary poverty, this was something that would later haunt the collective and millenarian dreams that, taking root in crises brought on by economic and social transformation, would demand a return to an egalitarian, fraternal, and disinterested Christianity—the cathartic prelude, in other words, to the reign of the holy.

Essenism Was the Real Original Christianity
In the eighteenth century, the scholar Bernard de Montfaucon stirred up a polemic on the subject of the Therapeutes described by Philo of Alexandria. To Montfaucon they were a Christian sect, an assertion that he backed up with serious argumentation[16]. His critics retorted that other Jewish milieus presented the same singularities. Both were right: the Therapeutes were both Jewish and Christian. Until the beginning of the second century, the only existing form of Christianity was inscribed in the framework of a reformed and anti-Judean Judaism—that is, before Marcion rejected it in the name of a Greek Christianity.

Essenism brought together all the traits of primitive Christianity: it was baptist, believed in a Messiah, founded Churches, and was marked by a duality of paths, Light and Darkness—nay, by the duality of the Demiurge and the Good God.

The Sadducees and the Pharisees used baptism as a ritual of purification, but among the Essenes it did not take on the value of a spiritual engagement and a communitarian rite of initiation. Thus a hymn proclaims:

> It is by the humility of the soul with respect to all the precepts of
> God that the flesh will be purified
> when one sprinkles it with purifying [*lustrale*] water
> and sanctifies it in running water.[17]

Symbolically, water cleanses the body of its natural impurity, washing from it its sensual passions, exonerating it from its material gravity and elevating it towards God in the ascendant movement of the spirit. Baptism remains without effect if it is not accompanied by a conversion of the heart. The doctrine of Saul/Paul gives baptism the same spiritual meaning, inverting the baptismal conception honored by certain Alexandrian Gnostic sects, for which water meant a return to the maternal matrix and re-birth in the heart of the host community.

The current state of research does not permit us to conjecture as to whether Dositheosian or Nazarenean baptismal practices influenced Essenism, but certain Essene traits undoubtedly proceeded from the Samaritans' freedom with respect to Judaic orthodoxy.

The Messiah

The doctrinal system of the Men of the Community and the Book of Enoch 1 had the same lineaments as the Gnosticism and messianism that would dominate first the Jewish and then the Hellenic Christianities up to and beyond the second century.

In this system the angels, the Princes of Light, confronted the fallen angels, the Princes of Darkness; the 'couples' or syzygies opposed Michael and Raphael to Belial and Satan.

The theory of the Son of Man (Adam) is expounded in the section devoted to the ascension of Enoch. When Enoch asks the angel who accompanies him about the Son of Man—"who he was, and whence he was"—the angel responds: "This is the Son of Man who hath righteousness.

With whom dwelleth righteousness, and who reveals all the treasures of that which is hidden. Because the Lord of Spirits hath chosen him"[18].

The angel specifies that he is also "engendered by Justice"[19], which is a reference applicable to the Essene Master and to Melchizedek, his consort or *alter ego*.

As the Son of Man was incarnated in the Master of Justice, he will return in the features of a new Messiah, whom Enoch's parable names the Chosen One, according to the tradition inaugurated by the stanzas on the 'Servant of YHWH' in the Book of Isaiah (42: 1).

Thus, as Philonenko[20] emphasizes, there exists a veritable Christology in the Qumran texts. It reaches such a degree of precision that people have supposed that in certain writings—such as the Testaments of the Twelve Patriarchs (the parting remarks of the twelve sons of Jacob to their children: Ruben, Simeon, Levi, Judah, Issachar, Zabulon, Dan, Naphtali, Gad, Asher, Joseph, and Benjamin)—there must be interpolations by various Greek Christianities, or even by Catholicism. Comparing the manuscripts found at Qumran with the revised versions, Philonenko reveals a small number of interpolations, most of them limited to the addition of the word *Christos*. Here was a Messiah ready to assume the emblematic name Joshua/Jesus.

Essene Christology evolved from a primitive conception to a modern vision of the Christ. The most ancient texts evoked two Messiahs: one, sacerdotal, who indicates to the faithful the road to sanctification; the other, royal, who leads Israel to victory over the *goyim*. Forty years later a single Messiah was expected: the Master of Justice, the Chosen One, the *Kyrios* chosen by God to reveal the 'New Alliance' (the *Novum testamentum* of which Marcion would later speak).

The wait had begun many years before the Christian era. While the *Rule Annex* (1 Q. Sa 2/11–2) speaks of a time when "God will have engendered the Messiah"[21], the part devoted to Benjamin in the *Testaments of the Twelve Patriarchs* clearly evokes the coming of a unique Messiah, the reincarnation of the Master of Justice[22].

> Then shall we also rise, each one over our tribe, worshipping the King of heaven, [who appeared upon earth in the form of a man in humility. And as

many as believe on Him on the earth shall rejoice with Him]. Then also all men shall rise, some unto glory and some unto shame. And the Lord shall judge Israel first, for their unrighteousness; [for when He appeared as God in the flesh to deliver them they believed Him not].[23]

Let's recall that this is a question of a text unearthed at Qumran that does not include any subsequent interpolations. It is difficult not to discern in it the source of the mythical person called Jesus and the essentials of the doctrine attributed to Saul/Paul. Amplified by *midrashim*, completed by particular communitarian practices and by modern polemics, and adapted to the Greco-Roman mindset, the speculations arising around the Essene Messiah who was tortured around 63 BCE would sketch out the scenario of a syncretic Messiah derived from Joshua, whose drama would be transposed so that it took place during the Zealots' war under Tiberius. As for James and Peter, the heroic witnesses and disciples of the *Kyrios* who had guided their acts, they died while being crucified.

The secret name of such a Messiah formed the stakes in a long struggle in the places that had been penetrated by Jewish eschatology. Each Essene community or Church produced its own proofs and testimonies with a view towards winning approval for its Christ.

Grotto 4 at Qumran yielded an Aramaic text, the terms of which entered into the composition of the future Joshua/Jesus.

> He will be great on the earth [O King, and he will make] peace and each will serve him. He will be called the Son of the Great God and by this name he will be called. He will be saluted as the Son of God and we will call him the Son of the Most High and his kingdom will be an eternal kingdom.[24]

He will be the heavenly figure of the Son of Man announced by the Book of Enoch: "the Lord of Spirits hath chosen him"[25]. "The light of the Gentiles"[26], he will possess the spirit of wisdom, science, and strength, the three qualities that would appear in the *logia* or in the remarks attributed (in the second century) to Jesus.

A number of traits that are arranged anecdotally in Jesus's evangelic novels abound in the Qumran writings. The apocalypse included in the

Testament of Joseph nourished the legend of a virginal birth: "And I saw in the midst of the horns a virgin [wearing a many-coloured garment, and from her] went forth a lamb"[27].

The manuscript labeled 1 Q H 6, 12 imputes to this Christ-Lamb a calling that is no longer nationalist but universal, following an overture that the Church characteristically attributed to the school of Saul/Paul: "All nations recognize your truth and all people glory you"[28].

Moreover, the Master of Justice appears, in the manner of the future Joshua/Jesus, as a suffering Messiah and as the founder of Churches: "God had wanted it that, in his sorrows, the Master of Justice built his glorious Church, and, although the Hymns of the Master of Justice do not explicitly present his sufferings as capable of expiating the sins of the others, this was a fundamental doctrine of the sect, and one finds in the 'Songs of the Savior' (which figure in the Book of Isaiah and inspired Qumranian hymns) that the Savior 'was pierced for our transgressions; he was crushed for our iniquities [...]. | Yet he bore the sin of many, and makes intercession for the transgressors' (Isaiah, 53: 5, 12)"[29].

Another function of the Master of Justice was attributed to Joshua/Jesus and to Saul/Paul: announcing the Good News, which in Greek is the *Evangelion*, the Gospels.

The Qumranian hymns stipulate that God gave him the mission to be, "according to His truth, the one who announces the Good News [in the time] of His Goodness, evangelizing the humble ones according to the abundance of His mercy, [watering them] at the source of holiness, and consoling those who are contrite of spirit and afflicted" (XVIII. 14–5)[30].

This hymn inspired the 'Songs of the Savior' in Isaiah.[31]

The Spirit of the Lord God is upon me,
because the Lord has anointed me
to bring good news to the poor,
he has sent me to bind up the brokenhearted [...].

Nothing is missing from the ensemble of the fundamental materials that, through rewriting and revision, ended up in the texts of the various

Hellenic Christianities and of Catholicism, and even in the text of 'New Testament' that Marcion would brandish like a weapon against the 'Old' one.

Dupont-Sommer does not fail to reveal it[32]. Essenism (or at least an Essene party that was perhaps Saul's, one that was opposed to the partisans of Jacob, Peter, and Thomas) claimed to be *the* sect of the New Alliance, otherwise known as the New Testament (Hymn V, 23; *The Damascus Document*).

R. H. Charles, after studying the Books of Enoch, which were a part of the Essene canon, remarks that the Testaments of the Twelve Patriarchs is "a product of the school that prepared the road to the New Testament". He goes further, emphasizing that the famous Sermon on the Mount attributed to Jesus "in several passages reflects and goes as far as reproducing the same phrases from our text"[33]. Charles adds that Paul seems to have used it like a *vade-mecum*. Dupont-Sommer reveals the following, among other examples, in the *Manual of Discipline* (also known as *The Community Rule*): "I will pay to no man the reward of evil"[34]. There are even recommendations of the apostolic type: "They shall practise truth and humility in common, and justice and uprightness and charity and modesty in all their ways"[35].

Regarding Saul/Paul, Teicher has collated a great many analogies between the fragments of his letters and several Qumran manuscripts (according to Teicher's thesis, the manuscripts are of a late date and express the opinions of Judeo-Christianity and, in particular, those of the Ebionites)[36].

Nevertheless, although the divergences between rival groups were inscribed on a common foundation, the cleavage seems to have been of a political—not to say, strategic—nature. The Essenean Churches of the Ebionite or Nazarene type that laid claim to James, Peter, and Thomas—even those laying claim to the John the Essene mentioned by Flavius Josephus—conserved a relatively firm, elitist, and perhaps esoteric structure, whereas the schools propagated by Saul appealed to the *rebbim*, to the 'many', and thus affirmed themselves to be exoteric and populist.

The Essene Churches

The Church of the Master of Justice claimed to be present in the whole world, to be universal, which is a term that translates the Greek word *catholicon*. This Church was built to "serve as an impregnable refuge for the Chosen Ones during the war that, at the end of time, the forces of evil would conduct against them"[37].

Hymn XI reveals the origin of the *Kephas*, the 'rock', the 'stone/Peter' [*pierre*] that—combined with Simon the Zealot and Essene—would end up in the wordplay that would found the Church of Rome ("and on this rock I will build my church"[38]). Sure enough, one can read in that Hymn the following:

> the way of my steps is over stout rock
> which nothing shall shake;
> for the rock of my steps is the truth of God
> and His might is the support of my right hand.[39]

The Church is the community, the Assembly:

> My eyes have gazed [...]
> on a fountain of righteousness
> and on a storehouse of power [...].
> God has given them to His chosen ones
> as an everlasting possession,
> and has caused them to inherit
> the lot of the Holy Ones.
> He has joined their assembly
> to the Sons of Heaven
> to be a Council of the Community [...].[40]

The Essenean Churches organized themselves in relations of hostility to and competition with the Pharisee synagogues of the Diaspora. While the synagogal assemblies drew their unity from a Phariseeism that was endowed with a spiritual center (the holy city of Jerusalem, whose orthodoxy was guaranteed by the Temple), the Essenean communities—which were devoted to the unceasing revision of the sacred texts—decreed the end of time, speculated on the imminence, nature, and name of the Messiah, and constituted rival Churches that were fecund with new doctrines. It would take three centuries for ecclesial monarchism to end up with the supremacy of the Bishop of Rome—which was contested up until the seventh century—and the imposition of the universality (the *catholicon*) desired by the Master of Justice, the 'Just Messiah'.

The *Manual of Discipline* makes clear the mode of organization: "Whenever there are ten men of the Council of the Community there shall not lack a Priest among them. And they shall all sit before him according to their rank and shall be asked their counsel in all things in that order"[41].

As among the Pharisees, the first places were reserved for the old ones, *prebyteroi*—that is to say, long-sighted people [*presbytes*], priests. One of them, someone who was known as 'the inspector of the many' (the *rebbim* or 'many' refers to the faithful, who are distinguished from the 'perfect ones'), became the leader, archon, the *episcopos* (Greek for 'bishop'). He was invited to carry himself like a shepherd, like a pastor, which is a title that around 140–50 would inspire the writing of a Judeo-Christian novel attributed to Hermas in which the author deplores the discord among the diverse Churches of Rome.

Towards the end of the second century, some Churches obeyed a collegiate leadership structure (with a council of archons), while others adopted the monarchal form privileged by the politics of unification.

When Marcion provoked a rupture with Jewish Christianity, he attempted to found unified Churches that he wanted to have under the control of Rome: federations of Churches that were favorable to Saul's school and that rejected the communities that had chosen to place their legitimacy under the patronage of Zealot heroes, Ebionites, Nazarenes, James, Peter, Thomas, and Clement, whose partisans treated 'Paul' like a false prophet. It was still the Testaments of the Twelve Patriarchs that justified the number of companions of a Messiah whose name—unknown to Hermas in 140—would now begin to impose its revelation: Joshua/Jesus, the one who 'saved, saves, will save'. This was a minor skirmish within the multitude of sects that bordered and confronted each other in Alexandria, Antioch, Corinth, Colossae, Edessa, Rome . . .

A Dualist Tendency

The Jewish, Sadducee, and Pharisee orthodoxies abominated all dualisms that, suspiciously revoking the uniqueness of YHWH, threatened the State and the national mystique. The Samaritans, by contrast, were often reticent with respect to the imported Judean God and never made a mystery of their attachment to the plural God El-Elohim—nay, to the dualism of the Divine Father/Divine Mother.

Essenism did not totally extirpate the Samaritan influence from its heart. The Jewish Gnosticism attested to by the Books of Enoch (which in fact combated other Gnostic tendencies) continued to exist within the diverse primitive Christianities—which were Jewish in the case of the Elchesaites' *Homilies of Peter* (c. 110), Judaicized in the case of *The Shepherd of Hermas* (c. 140), and Hellenized and anti-Semitic in the case of Marcionism—as late as the second half of the second century, which ended with the popular development of the New Prophecy or 'Montanism'.

Dualist thought manifested itself in Essenism in diverse ways. No manuscript from Qumran implicitly expounds the idea that two Gods can exist. Nevertheless, certain currents accredited the syzygy of the Good God and the Demiurge, which was present in the doctrines of Cerinthus, Marcion, the Naassenes, the Sethians, the Barbelites, and many other sects (Christian or otherwise).

The Arab historian Al-Shahrastani (c. seventh century) affirms that, in the fourth century, Arius borrowed the doctrine according to which the Messiah was the first angel of God from the Magharians[42], "who lived four hundred years before Arius and were known for the simplicity of their way of life and for their serene abstinence"[43].

Who were the Magharians, whose existence dates back to the first century before the Christian era? Their Arab name leaves little doubt; it means 'people of the cavern or the cave', because—as Shahrastani makes clear—they hid their sacred texts in caverns.

There is nothing surprising in the fact that the doctrine of the Angel-Messiah (the *Angelos-Christos*) was originally Essenean, since it was shared by the various Christianities and prevailed until the second half of the second century, when the campaign to make Jesus a historical figure began.

In addition, this Arab historian explains that the refusal of an anthropomorphic YHWH induced the Magharians to impute the creation of the material universe to a Demiurge.[44] It is therefore not impossible that the dualist conception of a good and inaccessible God and a God who created the bad world (whom Marcion in his hatred of Judaism identified with YHWH the Bloody) existed in certain Essenean Churches and was defended by Marcion.

Without crediting Essenism in general with a position that was regarded as scandalous by the Pharisees (and much later by the monarchal current—for which there was only one God and one Bishop—to which the leaders of the Christian communities would attach themselves in reaction to Marcionism), dualism was unambiguously expressed in the doctrine of the two roads and even in the 'couples' or syzygies that were still attested to by the *Homilies of Peter*. The struggle between the Sons of Light and the Sons of Darkness dominated the thought of the Men of the Community. To them, God "disposed for man two spirits [...] the spirit of truth and the spirit of perversion" (*Rule of War*)[45].

In each generation, the Sons of the Prince of the Light and the Sons of the Angel of Darkness confront each other in a war from which the saints—the pure ones, who renounce the flesh and possess knowledge (*gnosis*)—will emerge victorious.

Due to the privileges that they accorded knowledge, the Essenes belonged to Jewish Gnosticism, which would be perpetuated in Kabalistic investigations.

"You have given me the intelligence of your faith and the knowledge of your admirable secrets", declares Hymn VII (25)[46]. *Gnosis* is nothing other than secret knowledge. But from its essential root grew a great diversity of options, of choices (which translates the Greek word *hairesis*, heresy): dualism; the refusal or the surpassing of religion; monotheism; salvation by the individual himself, by a community, or by a Christ; and rational, mystical or magical approaches to the *Logos*. *Gnosis* implies the primacy of knowledge over *pistis*, faith, and over the secret (the *apocryphon*, an apocryphal text that the Church—as part of its seizure of language and meaning—would identify with the 'false, falsification').

In the cities of the Diaspora, more so than in Judea, the esotericism of the Essenean groups became an exotericism that was better suited to compete with the Pharisees' proselytism. Such, no doubt, was the tendency of the school of Saul/Paul. Esotericism itself borrowed from different sources. The secret Gospels (the *Apocrypha*) and the Hermetic remarks of Jesus (the *logia*) could only have come from the same Churches that—according to a manuscript from Grotto 4 at Qumran studied by J. T. Milik[47]—inferred from the morphology of individuals born under certain zodiacal signs their belonging to the cohort of the 'spirits of Light' or to the horde of the 'spirits of Darkness'. (Such speculations could be found in the Christian astrology of Bardaisan, and also in divinatory magic, in the spirit of the quarrels over predestination, and in the art of recognizing sorcerers and sorceresses in the sixteenth and seventeenth centuries.)

Towards a Judeo-Christian Syncretism

The thesis, accredited by the majority of historians, of a prophet named Jesus who founded a Church upon dogmatic truths that in fact only emerged after a long and painful period of labor in the fourth, fifth, and sixth centuries underestimates the marginal character of those religious speculations by concealing from view the profusion of Messiahs, sects, schools and communities in the particular milieus that they touch upon.

Dositheos, the crucified Samaritan Messiah; the Master of Justice, put to death by the Judeans; Melchizedek the Just; Enoch, who was guided by the Son of Man; Barbelo, who collected sperm in order to save the world; Naas, the *Ophis-Christos* or Serpent-Redeemer; Three-Times-Great Hermes; Seth, the Son of Man with the head of a horse or donkey; Abrasax, with ophidian legs and a cockscomb, the saver of souls threatened by the Archons—these were all so many Christs, among whom Joshua/Jesus (whose name secretly means 'God saved, saves, will save') would later carve out a place for himself in the form of an angel sent by God.

And, among the four or five thousand Essenes of whom Flavius Josephus speaks, what a confusion! Partisans of James the Just, Simon-Peter, John the Essene, Jochanaan (also known as John the Baptist), Theudas/Thomas, Saul known as 'Paul' (in accordance with Marcion), Cerinthus,

Zacchaeus/Clement and so many others who commented upon and adapted the biblical texts by taking extracts from the *midrashim* (sometimes translated into Greek)—the majority of which had disappeared, but about which it is possible to get an idea through a text that was not accepted by the Church but that illustrates the passage from Judeo-Christianity or Essenism to a Hellenized Christianity that was ready to ride roughshod over its Judaic roots: the *Didachē*.

In the current of the first century, there circulated among the non-Pharisee Judaicized milieus (Essene or Samaritan) a moralizing pamphlet titled *Doctrine of the Two Roads*, the title of which indicates its origin.

Recopied, revised, developed, and Hellenized, it ended up in a version that its last redactor (circa 140–50) gave the title *Didachē kyriou dia tōn dōdeka apostolōn tois ethnesin* (*The Lord's Teaching Through the Twelve Apostles to the Nation*).

An analysis of the various states of this text and the strata of its rewriting has permitted us to extract the oldest kernel of the *Didachē*, which was inspired by the *Manual of Discipline* and makes clear "the disciplinary order that is imposed on the community"[48]. In it, the higher-ups are called *episkopoi kai diakonai*, bishops and deacons. Moral comportments are ordered according to the 'two roads'. Also covered are baptism, fasting, prayer, and the sharing of bread (much later called the Eucharist).

The second great revision dates from 140–50 and is therefore contemporaneous with the hostility adopted with respect to the original Judeo-Christianity. The text, known under the title *Didachē* or *Doctrina apostolorum*, was honored in the Greco-Roman Churches that, in the Diaspora, had separated themselves from the Jewish and Christian Churches that had issued from Essenism. It is contemporaneous with the *Shepherd* attributed to Hermas of Rome (still Judeo-Christian), the *Homilies of Peter* attributed to Clement of Rome (based upon an Elchasaite text contemporaneous with Trajan), and the Epistle of Barnabas (around 117–30, according to Erbetta)[49].

A Trinitarian doxology would be added in the fourth century, due to polemics against Arius.

For a long time held as canonical, the *Didachē* would finally be excluded from the Catholic Scriptures. A modern version of Judeo-Christianity, it refused the Judaic sacrifices and rituals, especially circumcision, which it spiritualized and interpreted symbolically. The name 'Jesus' does appear, but in association with features that were particularly embarrassing to the future Catholic orthodoxy: in the manner of the Master of Justice, he carried the title of Servant of God, and, in addition, he is perceived as an Angel-Messiah—an *Angelos-Christos*—in accordance with the traditions of the time and notably in agreement with the Epistle of Barnabas, in which Jesus is simply the biblical Joshua.

CHAPTER FIVE

The Baptist Movement of the Samaritan Messiah Dusis/Dositheos

If Samaria constituted an object of scandal for Judea, its neighbor to the south, this was because of the ancient cults that continued to exist there and which engaged in a religious and nationalist resistance that was resolved to impede the invasion-politics of Yahwehism and its terrible, avenging, and bellicose God.

The Samaritans only tolerated an archaic form of YHWH, one that was still close to El, the Father, and to the angelic plurality contained in his Elohim form. Holding that the sanctuary at Sichem on Mount Gerizim was the only true Temple, Samaritanism recognized as sacred texts only the Torah or Pentateuch (the first five books of the Bible) and the Book of Joshua, which Hellenization, soon established in Samaria, propagated under the name *Book of Jesus* (which is how Origen would refer to it around 250).

The hatred between the Judeans and the Samaritans was exacerbated by the destruction of Sichem during the reign of John Hyrcanus, an Asmonean prince and the Great Priest of Jerusalem (135–105 BCE).

Nevertheless, Hellenization received a warmer welcome in Samaria than it did in Judea. It is true that the (quite hardy) Canaanite and Philistine substrata were not strangers to Achaean settlement during the migrations of the second millennium before the Christian era. The persistence of cultural forms that issued from the Magna Mater, allied with the audacious critiques of Greek philosophy, introduced into the closed universe of the Gods a quite corrosive mixture, of which the teachings of Simon and Barbelite practices offer singular examples—that is, after one excavates them from beneath the silence and the calumnies that were layered over them by the eradications performed by the Church and its complacent historians.

This light from Samaria doesn't accord well with the shining and virtuous road chosen by Essenism. Nevertheless, it illuminates the birth of certain dissident sects, including the still poorly known Sethians, whose Messiah-Son of Man one frequently encounters in the Qumranian manuscripts.

Located between Judea and Galilee, Samaria extended up to the banks of the Dead Sea, where the original kernel of Essenism was established. These places were propitious for the implicit constitution of a front hostile to the Temple, to Jerusalem, and to Judean beliefs—nay, even to the law of Moses.[1]

Did not Essenean dualism have its origin in the Samaritan distinction between YHWH and his angelic component, Elohim? In any case, the heresy of the 'two celestial powers' (a veritable crime against the unique God in the eyes of Jewish orthodoxy), although condemned by the Books of Enoch, was surreptitiously slipped into them in the form of the confrontation between the Good Angels and the Bad Angels.

Such a doctrine even impregnated the thought of the quite Phariseean Philo of Alexandria, when he opposed the beneficial power of *Theos*, the Good God, to the punitive function with which the *Kyrios*, the Savior (the Greek translation of *Adonai*, the equivalent of the Tetragrammaton YHWH), was tasked. Marcion limited himself to specifying the difference between the God of the Jews—the creator of a bad world—and the Good God that de-Judaicized Christianity substituted for YHWH as the creator of a world in which the good would be realized through the intervention of the Messiah-Redeemer.

But both Essenism and Samaritanism, despite the diverse views that they nourished, discovered in Dusis/Dositheos a messianic figure, the importance of which few researchers have emphasized until now.

The Messiah Dusis/Dunstan/Dositheos

In the fourteenth century, the Samaritan chronicler Abu'l Fath spoke of a certain Dusis or Dunstan around whom, at the time of the crisis engendered in 135 BCE by the destruction of the Temple at Gerizim by Hyrcanus II, was united a messianic and baptist group that he called the Dunstanites.

Was a second expansion of Dunstanism manifested by a new eschatological prophet named Dositheos, as Isser suggests?[2] He would have had a prophet named Aulianah as his successor.

But the name Dositheos, *Dosi-theos*, which refers to Dusis and means 'Gift of God', recalls Dusis's status as an Angel-Messiah. No doubt he establishes a connection with another Messiah who came from Galilee: Hanina Ben Dosa (that is to say, son of Dusis).[3]

Dositheosism seems to have presented in a Hellenized form the old Dunstanite movement, which was a baptist and messianic movement that resulted from a schism within Samaritanism.[4]

As in Essenean dissidence, Dusis's schism was accompanied by a reworking of the calendar: the adepts counted thirty days in each month. A century later, the Elchasaites—anecdotally expressing in the *Homilies* the scorn they felt for Saul (identified with Dositheos and Simon)—reported that Dositheos founded a sect comprising thirty men and a woman named the Moon, the latter of whom had been a prostitute in a brothel at Tyre and the mistress of the prophet before she threw herself into the arms of Simon.

In the sixth century, Bishop Euloge encountered in Alexandria Samaritan groups that still reproached Dositheos for having altered a great many sacred texts. Abu'l Fath shared that same indignation.

In truth, if the Dunstanite prophet rewrote the sacred messages—as the Essenes, Nazarenes, Marcionites, anti-Marcionites, and Catholics also did—this was because Moses supposedly spoke through his voice and thus titled him to revise the law and adapt it to his divine truth.

Did Dusis's disciples push the critique of Judean and Mosaic doctrines even further? This is the hypothesis advanced by Fossum[5]. Dositheos— the Hellenized version of Dusis—rejected the prophets accepted by the Jewish canon, called for the reform of Mosaic law, and even advocated the abolition of religious duties.

At that time, all of the milieus that were preoccupied with Judaism debated the observance of and the challenges to the rituals that had allegedly been decreed by Moses. After 140, the Hellenization of Judeo-Christianity did not take place on any other terrain. The rejection of the prophets foreshadowed Marcion.

As for the irreligious attitude, it tallied with the philosophy of Simon of Samaria, whom the heresiologues communally characterized as a disciple of Dositheos and as the father of all heresies. But the confusion of Dositheos with Simon appears to have derived from the same polemical vein as the identification of Saul with Simon, which was made by the partisans of the Churches of James and Simon-Peter.

The Dositheosians participated in the general reform movement that—by way of Essenism, Ebionism, Nazarenism, and Paulinism—would end up in the Hellenized Christianity of the Marcionites and anti-Marcionites of the second century.

According to Abu'l Fath, the Dositheosians were called "the children of the Apostle"—the apostle being Moses.[6]

At the cusp of this era, which was subsequently officially decreed to be Christian, the apostles and their children were quite numerous. To efface their memory, it proved necessary to have a conspiracy [*conjuration*] of ecclesiastical interests impose the symbolic power of Joshua leading the nations toward the mythical beyond of the River Jordan—a power that was furthermore imposed under the redemptive name 'God has saved, saves, will save'. This conspiracy would later be obliterated in its turn by the fabrication of a historical Jesus.

In the figure of Dositheos, Christian historicism wanted to incarnate a disciple of Jesus named Nathaniel, whose name in Hebrew matches Dositheos: Gift of God.[7]

The novels devoted to Jesus abound in effects of this type, in which reality, travestied and put on stage, works to the glory of the protagonist. The mythical hero thereby subjugates beings and symbols from which his legend in fact derives.

Dusis preceded, foreshadowed, and prepared the effervescence—quite limited until the Zealot movement gave it a large audience—in which Messiahs, apostles, prophets, illuminati, and charlatans carved out popular reputations for themselves by advocating the reform, rebirth, or abolition of Judean conservatism.

Like Essenism, Dositheosism or Dunstanism was a baptist, messianic, and reformist movement. Baptism occupied a primary place in it. Prayers were offered up in symbolically fertile waters such as bathing pools or the River Jordan.

The erudite blinders worn by researchers exploring (with the Church's prejudices) an epoch upon which the Church fraudulently established its foundations have seldom permitted them to disentangle what united and what distinguished the baptist and Samaritan currents of Dunstan/ Dositheos (born around 135 BCE), Essenism (around 100 BCE), Nazarenism (around 50 BCE), and the Johanism of Jochanaan/John the Baptist—all of which adhered to a great ascetic rigor and a scorn for the body, for the world, for women, and for life.

Even more troubling is that Dusis was also a crucified and resurrected Messiah.

The *Kitab al-Tarikh* of Abu'l Fath mentions a group called the *saduqay*, which "erred in saying that the world would endure: for did (not) Dūsīs die his disgraceful death? Was not Levi stoned to death? Dūsīs did indeed die, and (in him) all the innocent of the world died as well"[8].

Reserved for slaves and common criminals, the 'shameful death' meant execution on the cross. The idea that Dusis, raised up to heaven, had not been struck down by a real death prevails, when applied to Jesus, in all the Christianities of the first three centuries—nay, even beyond, and up to what Catholicism condemned under the name of 'Docetism'.

Incarnated as the Spirit of God and the reincarnation of Moses in a terrestrial existence marked by redemptive suffering, Dusis does not fail to evoke the syncretic Messiah of the Judeo-Christian Elchasaites, who expressed themselves around 110 in the *Homilies of Peter*: "There is only one true prophet: the one who, since Adam, has been incarnated in the patriarchs Enoch, Noah, Abraham, Isaac, Jacob, and Moses, and who, in the end, finds his rest by incarnating himself in Jesus"[9].

Like the Master of Justice, Dusis—a suffering and glorious Messiah—assured his faithful an eternal survival and a resurrection according to the spirit. Do not Dusis, the Master of Justice, Dositheos, Jochanaan,

James, and Simon-Peter all trace out both the line of the successive syncretisms that were hostile to Yahwehist syncretism and an ecumenicalism of diverse tendencies that would—after the 'apocalypse' of 70—be united according to the myth of Joshua the Unifier?

It is worth noting that Levy, a disciple of Dusis who was put to death by stoning, is found in the novels of Jesus in the figure of Levy the Publican (alias Matthew), to whom is attributed a secret Gospel and a Gospel that was consecrated by the Catholic canon.

Close to the Johanite, Ebionite, and Nazarenean sects, the Dositheosians were opposed to the Naassenes. The *saduqay* mentioned by Abu'l Fath in fact taught that "the Serpent would govern the life of creatures until the day of the resurrection"[10]. They identified the Serpent with the Cosmocrator, the Demiurge, the Bad God who ruled the world, unlike the Naassenes, for whom *NHS*, the Serpent, revealed the road to salvation. The Naassenes, nevertheless, sometimes shied away from asceticism and chastity, which were uniformly preached by Esseno-Christianity.

Did not the hostility to Yahwehism engender in Dositheosism the identification of YHWH with the Demiurge that would prevail in Marcionism? In a *midrash* from the third or fourth century, the Samaritan Marqua evoked an ancient tradition in which YHWH revealed himself to be the supreme destroyer. He also reported an action of which one finds traces in the evangelic legends: "At midnight, YHWH destroyed all the first-born of Egypt"[11].

The exegetes of the New Testament betrayed a certain embarrassment when they were faced with the lie that attributed to Herod the mass extermination known as the 'massacre of the innocents'. The imputation of a heinous crime that Marcionism would count as one of a number of wrathful manifestations of the God of Israel to an absolutely bloody Jewish king is an indication of the willingness of the fabricators of the Gospels to give to symbols and abstractions an anecdotal and historical character.

Finally, in the eschatological tumult of the times, Dositheosism carried a resonance that was not foreign to the leanings attributed to the mysterious Saul, so fabulously known under the name Paul of Tarsus.

According to Fossum[12], a Dositheosian prophet named Aulianah (should we identify him with Hanina Ben Dosa?) proclaimed that divine forgiveness was on the verge of being accomplished. His disciples, sectarians of the Messiah Dusis, believed "that they already live in the period of divine grace".

According to Fossum, they affirmed that "salvation and the period of divine grace are not future events: paradise and the resurrection are to be found here and now". Does not Saul/Paul express this notion in another fashion, by supporting the idea that the Messiah had already come, redeemed men of their sins, and saved all those who (imitating his example) had sacrificed their flesh to the spirit?

CHAPTER SIX

Simon of Samaria and Gnostic Radicalism

Stripped of the lies and calumnies in which the Judeo-Christian and Catholic traditions have clothed him, as if in a laughable frock coat, Simon of Samaria evokes those thinkers who, as much as Heraclitus or Lucretius, have irresistibly inscribed themselves in the modernity of each epoch.

A Hellenized Samaritan who according to the heresiologues was born in the outskirts of Getta, in the last years of the first century before the Christian era, Simon was no doubt a philosopher and doctor in the manner of Paracelsus, whom he resembled in the care with which he simultaneously approached the microcosm and the macrocosm, the body of man and the totality of the world.

The few surviving fragments of his lost oeuvre suffice to suggest a radical will in the precise sense of the term: that which attaches itself to the root of beings and things. Growing out of Greek rationality, his analysis undertook to return to the *materia prima* of the body (from which the mythical visions of the Pentateuch derived) that the Hebraic religion had snatched from the luxuriance of desires in order to transpose it—through a cathartic and castrating function—into the domain of the spirit.

The majority of the Church censors were afflicted by a very particular malediction. Fascinated by the works that they execrated and overwhelmed by their own denatured and destructive rage, they succumbed to a compulsion to cite extracts from works whose existence they endlessly deplored.

Around 230–50, the first version of a collection titled *Philosophoumena e kata pason aireseon elenchos* (*Philosophoumena or Refutation of All Heresies*), abbreviated as *Elenchos*, began to circulate[1]. Successively attributed to Origen and to Hippolytus, the Bishop of Rome, the *Elenchos* probably emanated from the Christianity of the New Prophecy. It actually ranked among the heretics another Roman bishop, Callixtus, who was accused of permitting the remarriage of widows and of pardoning Christians who abjured their faith in the face of torture—both of which were seen as crimes by followers of the New Prophecy.

A chapter in this work devoted to Simon quotes extracts from his work *Apophasis megale* in order to refute them, which is does with great awkwardness. (A kind of objective irony has contrived things such that the most serious study to date of Simon of Samaria comes from a Jesuit named Salles-Dabadie. Not content with publishing the Greek text with a critical apparatus, he went as far as establishing a typographical distinction between the text of the author, the remarks of Simon, and the interpolations. The entirety of the text illustrates quite clearly the treatment applied by Christian or Catholic panegyrists to the manuscripts that they transcribed. To the extracts—which were interpreted in accordance with the polemics of the time—were added canonical citations, which were most often multiplied by later copyists. It became a question of proving first of all that the alleged heretic was familiar with these citations and secondly that he had deformed them or interpreted them falsely. The canonical traditions were thereby backdated.)

According to Salles-Dabadie, the *Apophasis megale* "is the testimony of an archaic gnosis and not a later one"[2].

Fragment 1 *incipit* offers the original title (stripped of additions): *Apophasis tes megales dynameos* (*Revelation of the Great Power*). The work would much later be cited under the title *Megale apophasis* (*Great Revelation*) at the instigation of Christians or religious sects that wanted to dress the philosopher up as a prophet and to call him *ó hestôs uios*, the Son of 'He who holds himself upright'. (The Judeo-Christians of the *Homilies of Peter* would make him into an impostor, a rival of Joshua/

Jesus, but, by attacking the anecdotal Simon, they were actually aiming at the 'false prophet' Saul/Paul).

The meaning of the text, Simon makes clear, "will be sealed, (and) kept secret, (and) hid, (and) will repose in the habitation, at the foundation of which lies the root of all things"[3]. According to Hippolytus, Simon "asserts that this man who is born of blood is (the aforesaid) habitation, and that in him resides an indefinite power, which he affirms to be the root of the universe"[4].

The Great Power is nothing other than a fire whose nature is both hidden and apparent. Hippolytus writes:

> And the manifest portion of the fire comprises all things in itself, whatsoever any one might discern, or even whatever objects of the visible creation he may happen to overlook. But the entire secret (portion of the fire) which one may discern is cognised by intellect, and evades the power of the senses; or one fails to observe it, from want of a capacity for that particular sort of perception.[5]

Conscious and unconscious, Fire is the energy of life.

An eternal fire also engendered the cosmos. An unbegotten energy conferred six roots upon it: *Nous* and *Epinoia* (spirit and thought), *Phone* and *Onome* (voice and name), and *Logismos* and *Enthymesis* (reason and reflection). The Great Power is enclosed in the six roots, but only in a state of potentiality.

Does it therefore remain asleep? It doesn't accede to the unity of its perfection. It "vanishes, he [Simon] says, and is destroyed in such a way as the grammatical or geometrical capacity in man's soul. For when the capacity takes unto itself an art, a light of existent things is produced; but when (the capacity) does not take unto itself (an art), unskillfulness and ignorance are the results; and just as when (the power) was non-existent, it perishes along with the expiring man"[6].

The six roots of being participate inseparably in the individual body and the cosmos. *Nous* and *Epinoia* are male and female, the heavens and the earth, where the fruits of the macroscopic tree settle in order to reproduce themselves. *Phone* and *Onome* are the sun and the moon, and

Logismos and *Enthymesis* are air and water.

With its equals, each element composes a unity in which the Great Power that is enclosed within the elements is recreated. By gathering together the elements into which it was scattered—just like Barbelo, the Judeo-Greek form of the *Magna Mater*, who collected within herself the sperm of all the scattered beings in order to impregnate herself with a new universe—the Great Power revealed itself as the 'seventh power'. (The seventh power would become the Hebdomad in the Valentinian systems.) At the same time, it manifests the presence in the macrocosm and the microcosm of the *Hestôs*: the one who has stood up, stands up, will stand up. (Salles-Dabadie is surprised by the bizarreness of this formula, but all it is doing is translating into Greek [*estôsa, stanta, stèsomenon*] the timeless character of the Hebrew words. The principle of a man assuming his potential divinity, standing at the center of himself and of the world, is, of course, the opposite of the principle that the name Joshua/Jesus expresses: God saved, saves, will save.)

The unbegotten fire/energy thereby engendered man and placed him at the heart of corporeal and cosmic matter. Simon undertook to interpret the books of the Pentateuch—the only books recognized by the Yahwehist Samaritans—as the expression of the corporeal and terrestrial reality from which he judged them to have emerged.

What does the Book of Genesis mean? Paradise is the womb, Eden is the placenta, and "a river flowed out of Eden to water the garden" (Genesis 2: 10) is the umbilical cord.[7]

> This navel, he [Simon] says, is separated into four principles; for on either side of the navel are situated two arteries, channels of spirit, and two veins channels of blood.[8] But when, he says, the umbilical vessels proceed forth from Edem, that is, the caul in which the fœtus is enveloped grows into the (fœtus) that is being formed in the vicinity of the epigastrium—(now) all in common denominate this a navel—these two veins through which the blood flows, and is conveyed from Edem, the afterbirth, to what are styled the gates of the liver; (these veins, I say), nourish the fœtus. But the arteries which we have spoken of as being channels of spirit, embrace the bladder on both sides, around the pelvis, and connect it with the great artery, called the

aorta, in the vicinity of the dorsal ridge. And in this way the spirit, making its way through the ventricles to the heart, produces a movement of the fœtus. For the infant that was formed in Paradise neither receives nourishment through the mouth, nor breathes through the nostrils: for as it lay in the midst of moisture, at its feet was death, if it attempted to breathe; for it would (thus) have been drawn away from moisture, and perished (accordingly). But (one may go further than this); for the entire (fœtus) is bound tightly round by a covering styled the caul, and is nourished by a navel, and it receives through the (aorta), in the vicinity of the dorsal ridge, as I have stated, the substance of the spirit.[9]

(Note that, for Simon, *pneuma* [the spirit] meant 'breath of life'. The Barbelites would identify *pneuma* with *sperma*. For the Judeo-Christians it was the Spirit, before ending up, among the Catholics, as the Holy Spirit.)

The four branches or vessels into which 'the river that leaves Eden' was divided correspond to the four senses of the fetus: sight, smell, taste, and sound. Touch only appears after the birth of the infant.

The river is what Moses called the Law, and each Book of the Law addresses one of these senses.

Genesis illustrates sight, the look gaze that encompasses the cosmos. Crossing the Red Sea, Exodus is the road of blood that leads, through ordeals and bitterness, to the knowledge of life. There begins taste, beginning with the 'bitter water' (blood) that knowledge and the *Logos* change into sweet water, the source of life.

Explaining the transmutation of blood into sperm, Simon cites the flower of life offered by Hermes in the *Odyssey* (10.339–41): "Its root is black and its flower white as milk | and the gods call it moly. Dangerous for a mortal man | to pluck from the soil but not for the deathless gods"[10].

Smell and breathing are linked to the third book, Leviticus; sound to the fourth, Numbers, the rhythm of which refers to speech. Finally, Deuteronomy refers to the sense of touch in the newborn, who discovers the world by appropriating it. As Deuteronomy recapitulates the preceding books, touch summarizes and contains the other senses.

This is the most important part of Simon's doctrine: the man who, in the formation and perfection of his senses, becomes aware of the presence in himself of the Great Power, and so acquires the ability to restore and recreate it in his future.

> All things, therefore, he says, when unbegotten, are in us potentially, not actually, as the grammatical or geometrical (art). If, then, one receives proper instruction and teaching, and (where consequently) what is bitter will be altered into what is sweet—that is, the spears into pruning hooks, and the swords into ploughshares[11]—there will not be chaff and wood begotten for fire, but mature fruit, fully formed, as I said, equal and similar to the unbegotten and indefinite power. If, however, a tree continues alone, not producing fruit fully formed, it is utterly destroyed. For somewhere near, he says, is the axe (which is laid) at the roots of the tree. Every tree, he says, which does not produce good fruit, is hewn down and cast into fire.[12]

There is an indissoluble relation between the microcosm of the individual body and the macrocosm. If man does not realize his nature of Fire, his original and immanent energy, "he will perish with the cosmos". (Note that the First Epistle to the Corinthians (11: 32) attributed to Saul/Paul borrows an expression from Simon). This borrowed passage is not the only residual trace of Gnosticism in the writings of this enemy of James and Peter. In fact, the Epistle gives a singular credit to the *Homilies*, in which Simon stands in for Paul.)

What is the nature of the Great Power from the moment it materializes itself in an engendered being? According to Simon, fire or the eternal energetic flux is identified with the reproductive [*génésique*] principle, sexual force.

> Of all things, (i.e.) of whatsoever there is a generation, the beginning of the desire of the generation is from fire. Wherefore the desire after mutable generation is denominated 'to be inflamed'. For when the fire is one, it admits of two conversions. For, he says, blood in the man being both warm and yellow, is converted as a figured flame into seed; but in the woman this same blood is converted into milk. And the conversion of the male becomes generation, but the conversion of the female nourishment for the foetus.[13]

For Simon, there is a somatization of the Great Power: it manifests itself in the power to engender beings through desire, but also in the power of desire to engender in its turn—or, more exactly, to recreate in the unity of its scattered fragments—the *Dynamis* of which all life is simultaneously the effect, the immanence, and the future.

Becoming aware of the permanent flux of life involves seeing in libidinal energy the source of a will capable of realizing in each person the Great Power in action, which is none other than the government of destiny. This is what the religious spirit means by the expression 'to become God'. Assuredly, no other man in antiquity, with the exception of Lucretius, dared to affirm so strongly the primacy of the earth over the heavens and the man of desire over the spiritualized brute.

Completing his demythologizing of Genesis, Simon explains that the fire/desire energy is the "flaming sword that turned every way to guard the way to the tree of life" (Genesis 3: 24).

> For the blood is converted into seed and milk, and this power becomes mother and father—father of those things that are in process of generation, and the augmentation of those things that are being nourished; (and this power is) without further want, (and) self-sufficient. And, he says, the tree of life is guarded, as we have stated, by the brandished flaming sword. And it is the seventh power, that which (is produced) from itself, (and) which contains all (powers, and) which reposes in the six powers. For if the flaming sword be not brandished, that good tree will be destroyed, and perish. If, however, these be converted into seed and milk, the principle that resides in these potentially, and is in possession of a proper position, in which is evolved a principle of souls, (such a principle,) beginning, as it were, from a very small spark, will be altogether magnified, and will increase and become a power indefinite (and) unalterable, (equal and similar) to an unalterable age, which no longer passes into the indefinite age.[14]

The amorous conjunction of man and woman therefore realizes, through the act of creation, the incarnation of the Great Power. From its conception, the infant receives, with the *Logos*, the spark of the *Megale Dynamis*. It will be up to him or her to increase the ardor of this spark as fire and *Logos*—otherwise known as desire and consciousness of the creative act—in order to realize in him- or herself the eternal presence of the energy that creates and recreates itself without beginning or end, and which is a flux of life.

As long as he or she develops through desire and its consciousness (fire and its thought) the *Megale Dynamis* of which he or she has received the spark, each person is in a position to pass from the state of energy-receiver to the ability to act on him- or herself and on the cosmos. Surpassing the monstrous couple formed by humanity and its Gods, the human being of the Great Power invents a universe that belongs to him or her completely.

Simon is a Gnostic only because of the importance that he attaches to consciousness of the energy by which each person is assured of the privilege of becoming the totality of the life that he or she carries inside.

How could he not reject the men who had created Gods by debasing themselves in the idea that the Gods had created them? And how could he not be subjected to the hatred of the people for whom the spirit religiously exalts itself through its scorn for the earth, the body, and desire?

The first slander against Simon involved saddling him with the reputation of being a God-Man. Justin the Apologist incorrectly affirms that a statue was erected in Rome to the glory of this philosopher. (He specifies in chapter 26 of his *Apology* that Simon was as adored as Zeus was. He speaks of a woman called "the first idea generated by [Simon]"[15]. She was Epinoia, in whom was incarnated the *Nous* that Athena symbolized in Greek philosophy. Anecdotally translated by Justin, the allegorical Epinoia became Helene, mistress of Simon, prostituted in a brothel in Tyre.) Judeo-Christian stagecraft erected Simon as a rival of another God-Man named Jesus, whose project was to destroy and diminish the energy that Simon invoked in order to edify and increase it.

When all is said and done, perhaps we must impute to the disciples of Simon the deification of him spoken about by the Christian communities that claimed James the Just and Simon-Peter for themselves. Perhaps these communities' insistence on calling Saul/Paul by the name 'Simon the Magician' implies a criticism of Saul/Paul's apparent self-deification, in which the presumed author of the Epistles identifies the Great Power with the suffering and glorious Messiah who is incarnated in each person. (Didn't Paul identify himself with the *Hestôs*, with the God living in his heart, whom he called Joshua/Jesus and whose champion he set himself up as?)

In "The Name of God"[16], Fossum explains that, for the Samaritans, the Great Power, the *Megale Dynamis*, designated the divine name as well as the human force assumed by the divine manifestation. Although Simon removed its religious meanings in order to identify the Great Power with a flux of creative life whose spark—rekindled by love—offers to the individual the ability to create him- or herself, the dominant mindset obeyed the religious conditioning that impregnated the sects that were both close to and radically at odds with Simon's teachings, such as the Naassenes and the Barbelites, for whom sexual fusion was still governed by obedience to a divinity.

Simon's other singularity concerns the primacy that he accorded to the individual person and to his or her body, which was in solidarity with the cosmos. His project resided in the realization and the mastery of destiny, not in the notion of salvation that Christianity would impose for nearly two thousand years.

Simon appeared at a point of fracture. The unitary Jewish myth declined in the face of the desacralizing critique offered by Greek rationality, which was a *market* rationality. And in the same way that the European Renaissance saw liberty concretized in the radicalism of Paracelsus and La Boétie, the beginning of the first century manifested a human presence—in creators such as Simon of Samaria and Apollonius of Tyana—whose memory the regression into Christian myth would suffocate until both myth and the sacred disappeared in their turn.

The teachings of Simon would not escape the regression that imposed a return to religious forms, a return whose triumph a Hellenized and rationalized Judaism—now purged of its orientalism—would consecrate by crowning with its spider's web the bureaucratic empire that Rome had propagated in the world.

Simon's influence surfaced among the Naassenes and the Barbelites. It touched Saul/Paul and Marcion, and expressed itself in certain manuscripts at Nag Hammadi. It even penetrated the anti-Gnostic Christianity of the New Prophecy, in which Priscilla affirmed that the Christ "visited" her and slept near her in Pepuza (the New Jerusalem): he took the form of fire and "put his Wisdom in her".

But it is especially in the Hermetic current—which was very important in Alexandria—that the connection with Simon is evident, although it is not easy to determine which one came first.

"It was indeed a new conception of the world", Annequin writes, "that theurgists such as Alexander of Abonoteichus and Apollonius of Tyana proposed"[17].

According to a remark attributed to Apollonius of Tyana, the earth, water, air, and vegetal fire compose an alchemy of a microcosmic and macrocosmic fulfillment that Simon would not have disavowed: "The doors of the earth are open; the doors of the heavens are open; the road of the flowers is open. My spirit has been understood by the spirit of the heavens, by the spirit of the earth, by the spirit of the sea, and by the spirit of the flowers"[18].

Wasn't it against such a teaching that the Talmudists warned? "Whosoever prieth into the four things in the matter of the chariot in Ezekiel's vision—what is above, what is beneath, what is before, or what is behind—it were better for him if he had never been born"[19].

The *gnosis* of Hermes Trismegistus presents a spiritualized version of Simonian doctrine ("If you are made of Life and Light, and if you *know* it, you will one day return to Life and Light"[20]). On the other hand, the tradition that is expressed in the *Apocalypse of Asclepius* (the eighth scripture in Codex 6 of Nag Hammadi) belongs to the Simonian theory of the *Megale Dynamis*:

> And if you wish to see the reality of this mystery, then you should see the wonderful representation of the intercourse that takes place between the male and the female. For when the semen reaches the climax, it leaps forth. In that moment the female receives the strength of the male; the male for his part receives the strength of the female, while the semen does this.[21]

A countercurrent to the morbidity that would be propagated by generations of Judeo-Christians, Gnostics, Marcionites, anti-Marcionites, and

Catholics, the *Apocalypse of Asclepius* denounced those who scorned the world and "preferred death to life"[22].

Inversely, an abstract and speculative tendency was illustrated by the *Poimandres*, which would go on to inspire several Gnostic cosmogonies. After the separation of the light from the darkness, a struggle between two antagonistic principles ensued. The divine entity, seduced by the image that it projected in matter, desired to unite with it. The father creator, in androgynous form, thus engendered a composite creature: half-*Logos* and half-*Anthropos*, or primordial man (Adam, according to Jewish mythology).

From his superior part, man radiates a luminous particle, ejaculated by the divinity and imprisoned in him. In the beginning, the spermatic emission of the divine power spurted. However, this panspermia is both spiritualized—the *pneuma* or breath of life transcends the *sperma*—and identified with a fall, a cascading slide from the light into the terrestrial matrix, into obscurity, chaos, and matter.

In fact, what fundamentally distinguished Simon's teachings from those of the religious or Hermetic Gnostics is the nature of the amorous relation, which is a truly fundamental one: it is exalted as a creative force in the case of the former, and it is burdened with guilt, tied together with the idea of decline, and mortified through renunciation, abstinence, and asceticism, in the case of the latter.

Running counter to Simonian radicalism is the line that leads from brutal repression of the Esseno-Christian type to the hierogamiac rituals of the Naassenes and Barbelites, for whom ejaculated sperm nourished the divine *pneuma*. (Attacking the Cainites, Irenaeus wrote: "they call this Hystera [uterus] the creator of heaven and earth"[23]: "Hysteram autem fabricatorum coeli et terrae vocant". Likewise, at the end of the second century, the Gospel attributed to Philip called the *Pleroma* [the Totality] the *koinon*, the "nuptial chamber" or the "place of union"[24].) This line even leads to magical practices. (Delatte speaks of a magic stone called the "key to the matrix", no doubt tied to a rite of participation in the inseminating and sexual vitality that is the privilege of the Gods, a vitality that the magus hopes to appropriate like a particle of eternity[25]. Here there is a magic inherent in fetal creation: the womb forms the athanor; the transmutation of the sperm and the ovum refers to the notions of *surrectio* and *resurrectio*. The idea risked incurring the condemnation of the rabbis, according to a fragment collated by Köller: "God reserves three keys that he has not wanted to entrust to any intermediary: those to the womb, the rain, and the resurrection"[26].)

The So-Called Disciples of Simon

Because of our ignorance about the life and work of Menander, we must believe the claim of Justin the Apologist (which is hardly easy) that he was among the disciples of Simon. A Gnostic Samaritan, he taught at Antioch, where the Nazarenes enjoyed a certain influence. Irenaeus accused him of magical practices intended to vanquish bad angels and to resurrect the dead, which was a program that was, to say the least, vague, and one that did not exclude the Esseno-Christian viewpoint.

The same is true of Satornilus. Irenaeus attributed to him a dualism of the Samaritan type, one which distinguished between El the Father—here become the YHWH of the Judeans—and Elohim, his angelic cohort, around whom rebel elements had created the bad world[27]. A Savior-Messiah would only come at the end of a universe that had yielded to the forces of evil. And here Satornilus, close to Essenism but not to Simon, advocated a strict asceticism. It seems that Satornilus conferred upon his Messiah-Savior the emblematic name Joshua/Jesus, and that he was among the first to do so.[28]

As for Cerinthus, he was one of the Judeo-Christian philosophers preoccupied with the name and nature of the *Angelos-Christos*. Indications from Epiphanius of Salamis, who in the fourth century treated him as a false apostle, and from Irenaeus, who engaged in a polemic with the Apostle John, throw *a contrario* a certain light upon the fundamental text much later revised as the canonical Gospel attributed to John. We know that this text at first carried traces of Naassenism and belonged to Christian Gnosticism. It isn't impossible—but these are only hypotheses—that Cerinthus was the author of a *midrash* that was revised many times before being placed under the name of John, and that the meaning of this *midrash* obeyed the syncretic will to match Naassenism with Nazarenism, the Serpent-Redeemer or *NHS* thereby assuming the name of the Messiah Joshua/Jesus, who was himself identified with the crucified Serpent.

On the other hand, the shadow of Simon stands out more clearly upon the group founded by Carpocrates and his son Epiphanius, and upon the Gnostic Justin (not to be confused with the apologist decapitated in 165), the presumed author of the *Book of Baruch*, in which Genesis is analyzed in light of the self-creation of man (the *autogenous*). God planted the Garden of Eden by mating two unbegotten principles, Elohim and Edem, from which would be born a third principle—the most elevated, Priapus—in whom Good and Life were concentrated.

The names of the Great Power multiplied with the number of sects. Michel Tardieu studied the concept of *Bronte*, the Thunder, in the *Untitled Writing* (2d of Codex VI in the Nag Hammadi Library) and showed that it is identified with the *Megale Dynamis* and with the Great Power that the *Apocryphon of John* called Ennoia, the Valentinians called Sophia, the Barbelites called Barbelo, and the Naassenes called Brimo-Demeter.[29]

The collection at Nag Hammadi includes a hymn, *Ego eimi* (NHL II, 8, 34–5), which celebrates with a singular force the will of the individual to become his or her own creator in the fusion of universal forces:

> I am part of my Mother and I am the mother, I am woman, I am the virgin, I am the consoler of sadness, my spouse is he who engendered me and I am his mother and he is my father and my lord; he is my strength; what he wants, he says; in any case, I become, but I have engendered a lordly man.[30]

CHAPTER SEVEN

The Phallic and Symbiotic Cults

The conquest of the lands of Canaan by the Hebrew invaders began by Judaicizing the agrarian cults that were honored by the vanquished and then by prohibiting and defaming their persistent observance. The same went for the rites adoring the Serpent, whose symbolism involved both phallic power and mysteries of fecundation.

Despite the danger presented by certain species, serpents evoked by the grace of their movements the dance of love, to which the bodies of the lovers surrender themselves. Doesn't the allegorical representation of health—the caduceus in which two serpents intertwine—conserve the memory of the force of life inherent in pleasure and its slow crawling? More than any other mythology, the Bible changed the serpent into an object of abjection, terror, and evil.

I would like to conjecture that the religious spirit that substitutes itself for an analogical and totemic approach to the serpent—an approach that in a certain sense removes from the serpent the perils of venom and strangulation—has emphasized to the point of hyperbole the danger of death that in fact results from the anathema hurled against the part of life and pleasure that is so hostile to the power of the Spirit and its priests.

The Hebrews annexed the cult of the serpent to their gestating monotheistic syncretism, hence the *seraphim* (the 'seraphs', much later changed into angels).

In Deuteronomy (8: 15), *nahash seraph* designates the burning serpents[1] that murder people in the desert. Numbers (21: 6) speaks of *nahashim seraphim*[2]. If the word 'seraph' is applied to serpents, this is because of an idea about a 'burning bite'—the root of the word in Semitic languages is the verb 'to burn' and, more precisely (as in Jeremiah 7: 31[3]), the act of burning infants on the altar of Baal.[4]

Fecundation and the expiating sacrifice of the newborn infant or animal inscribe themselves in the essence of the religions: the production of lives reduced to their power to work implies the destruction or repression of non-productive libidinal energy.

The serpent (*nahash*, NHS) plays a predominantly sexual role in Genesis. It is a condemned sexuality, as is well illustrated by a Talmudic tradition (*Avodah Zarah*, 22 b): "At the time when the snake came upon Eve, at the time of the sin of her eating from the Tree of Knowledge, it infected her with moral contamination, and this contamination lingers in all human beings"[5]. And Genesis is no less explicit in Adam's resolution (3: 20) to call his wife Hawwah (Eve), playing on both the Hebrew word *hayah*—which expresses the idea of life—and the Aramaic *hivyah*, 'serpent'. Much later, Clement of Alexandria would remark that, "if one thickens a little the pronunciation of the name of the first woman, one evokes in Jewish ears the word for the female of the serpent species"[6].

Sexual initiation, with its wantonness or its art of caressing, originally increased the benefits of having the woman. The patriarch, whom the violation of the earth by agricultural plowing had elevated to absolute power, behaved towards women in the same spirit of exploitation. The lascivious and feminine undulation of exuberant life fell under a prohibition, while the phallic 'plowshare'—symbolized by the bronze serpents that Moses held aloft in the desert, carriers of a deadly life—was erected as a sign of power. The venom of those serpents impregnated women and nature, and both were condemned to produce until they were exhausted.

This serpent, the triumph and terror of virile politics, would be transformed in Hebrew mythology into Satan. Alan Rowe has shown the importance of the cult of the serpent at Beth-Shan, where he led a campaign of excavations. Beth-Shan was the House of the Serpent-God, and Shahan the divine serpent. Rowe remarks that *shahan* read backwards is *nahash*—the root *NHS* expressing in its diverse permutations the idea of the serpent in all the Semitic languages[7].

It was to the archaic cult of the serpent—simultaneously proscribed and recuperated by Judaism—that the sects attached themselves at the time of their encounter with the various Judeo-Christianities and the Hellenized Christianities; they strove to integrate it into their myths of salvation and influenced certain of its tendencies before it was condemned by the New Prophecy and Catholicism.

The Naassenes or Ophites

Late and rudimentary study has left us in ignorance concerning the history of the sect that—between Judaic antiquity and the sect's appearance in Egypt, and particularly in Alexandria—speculated about the redemptive nature of the Serpent or *NHS* (*nahash*).

The Naassenism of Alexandria may have constituted a syncretism that brought together Jewish, Phoenician, Egyptian, and Greek elements. The Phoenicians gave to the serpent the name *Agathodaimon*, 'beneficent being' (the apotropaic meaning is not obvious). The Egyptians translated *Agathodaimon* as *kneph*, which one finds in the *knouphis* (coiled serpents) depicted in amulets (*abraxas*). The contributions made by the old Ophidian cult of the Greeks would lend to Naassenism the belated name 'Ophitism'.[8]

When Nazarenism became increasingly important towards the end of the first century, the Naassenes, in their desire for ecumenical unity, did not reject the integration of the name Joshua/Jesus into their diverse list of names for their *Ophis-Christos*, their Serpent-Messiah: *Kneph, Agathodaimon, NHS*, and *Abrasax*.

Around 230–50, the competition between Jesus and the *Ophis-Christos* still worried Origen and made him indignant. Objecting to the teachings of a Naassene prophet named Euphrates, he considered it worth stating the problem in precise terms: "These are not the words of Christians, but of those who are altogether alienated from salvation, and who neither acknowledge Jesus as Savior, nor God, nor Teacher, nor Son of God"[9].

As Fossum remarks, moreover, the confusion between Christians and Naassenes proceeded from a belated evolution: "The serpent became a redeemer, while the God of the Old Testament found himself degraded into a harmful Demiurge, devoid of wisdom, named *Ialdabaoth*, who doesn't know that there is a God above him"[10].

Whatever the case, in the first century Naassenism entered the quarrel of Messiahs that agitated religious milieus on all sides. Despite all the revisions and rewritings, both the canonical Gospel attributed to John and the apocryphal Gospel attributed to Thomas retain traces of an underlying text that belonged to the Naassene current in which the *Ophis-Christos* was substituted for the *Iesous-Christos*: "And as Moses lifted up the serpent in the wilderness, so must the Son of Man be lifted up, that whoever believes in him may have eternal life" (canonical Gospel attributed to John 3: 14–5)[11].

Due to the necessity of falsifying history in order to prove its own antiquity, the Church advanced the ideas that the Naassenes were inspired by Jesus and that *NHS* was a suffering and redeeming Messiah. Even though Naassenism came well before Christianity, the Church, unconstrained, managed to detect the influence of that belief system (Christianity) on the martyrdom of the Master of Justice and Dusis. The primary nature of the seraphim that are the closest to God is that of the serpent, as the Book of Enoch recalls (20: 7, 61: 10, and 71: 7). The serpent wanted to reveal to Adam and Eve the pleasure and knowledge that are contained in the union in which divine immortality dwells. This is why the jealous God punished the serpent, nailing it to the ground or—according to certain texts attributed to Moses—to the Tree of Life on which its skin hung, crucified.

The *Gospel of Truth*, discovered at Nag Hammadi, still tells the story of the Garden of Eden from a Naassene point of view: the serpent, being the principle of divine wisdom—the equal of Sophia, the Angel-Messiah, or the *pneuma*—proposed to offer knowledge to Adam and Eve. God, possessive and jealous, prohibited them access to *gnosis* and, expelling them from Paradise, condemned them to a mortal destiny.

NHS—the serpent of knowledge and pleasure in the manner of the *Kundalini*, which awakens the body to its potential richness—introduced into male and female human beings alike the vital breath, which later became the *pneuma* or the Spirit in the cults.

From the fact that their Serpent-God penetrated into Eve and into Adam, breathing immortality into them, some people have inferred that the Naassenes practiced coupling with a lack of sexual differentiation that symbolically recreated the original androgyny. Perhaps it was to them that the remark, sometimes attributed to Simon of Samaria, was applied: "All earth is earth, and it does not matter where one sows seeds".

No doubt there existed a diversity of sects in Naassenism, since certain tendencies advocated asceticism (and thereby approached Esseno-Christianity), while others practiced sexual liberty in the name of the fusion of man, woman and world, all intertwined in *NHS*.

The invocation of a primordial erotic entity is expressed in a representation that was frequently engraved on talismanic stones or amulets in the form of a cameo, to which one gave the name *abraxas* through a deformation of the name of the depicted power, Abrasax.

This was a tutelary God with the head of a rooster and legs in the form of serpents. Armed with a shield and a whip, he repelled hostile forces and erected himself in a phallic manner in the interior of an oval that symbolized the female sex organs. Celestial [*solaire*] because of his head and terrestrial because of the ophimorphic legs that formed the supports of his sexual power, he was a God of fusion, the invocation of whom was modeled on the "song of the seven vowels"[12] that corresponded to the seven spheres that the initiate—elevated by amorous ecstasy— had to cross in order to attain the Great Power.

It is possible that there developed among the Naassenes an idea of health-through-sexual-enthusiasm that approximated Tantrism and dressed up the thought of Simon in religious garb.

The idea that the *Logos* had—in the manner of a serpent coiling up in the form of a circle and thereby forming the *ouroboros* or the serpent that bites its own tail, which often figured on the *abraxas*—descended into matter and then returned to God (from which it had issued) suggested to the Naassenes an interpretation of Genesis that imitated Simon's:

The Ocean that flows in circles from high to low and low to high, and the Jordan that descends and resumes its course, are images of a single and same Logos that moves and constitutes the most intimate essence of the living world. Another symbol of this process is that of the serpent, *naas*, or *ophis*, in the form of the serpent that bites its tail and thereby figures the cycle of becoming, *Hen* to *Pan*[13]. The serpent is not the only object of their cult. "And these affirm that the serpent is a moist substance, just as Thales also, the Milesian, (spoke of water as an originating principle,) and that nothing of existing things, immortal or mortal, animate or inanimate, could consist at all without him. And that all things are subject unto him, and that he is good, and that he has all things in himself, as in the horn of the one-horned bull[14]; so as that he imparts beauty and bloom to all things that exist according to their own nature and peculiarity, as if passing through all, just as the river 'flowed out of Eden to water the garden, and there it divided and became four rivers'"[15]. Eden[16], whence flows the river, is the brain of man; the celestial spheres are the membranes that envelop the brain. The paradise that crosses the river is the head of man. The four branches into which it is divided—the Pison, the Gihon, the Tigris and the Euphrates—are sight, sound, breathing and mouth. From the mouth comes prayer, the Logos as word; into the mouth comes nourishment, the spiritual nourishment obtained by prayer: "(The mouth) makes glad, and nurtures and fashions the Spiritual Perfect Man".[17]

Likewise, according (as always) to the *Elenchos*—which seems to be referring to a Christianized Naassenism, since what it describes differs radically from the philosophy of Simon—the Naassenes divided man into three parts. "For, say they, of this man one part is rational, another psychical, another earthly. And they suppose that the knowledge of him is the originating principle of the capacity for a knowledge of God, expressing themselves thus: 'The originating principle of perfection is the knowledge of man, while the knowledge of God is absolute perfection'"[18]. And, the author of the *Elenchos* adds, accrediting a connection between some Naassenes and the Nazarenes: "These are the heads of very numerous discourses which (the Naassene) asserts James the brother of the Lord handed down to Mariamne"[19].

Who was Mariamne? Not the Jewish queen—the wife of Herod who was put to death at the age of ninety (she lived from 60 BCE to 29 CE)—but another name for the Jewish Achamoth, the Greek Sophia, who would later become Miriam-Mary, the Virgin and Mother of the Savior in the evangelic novels about Jesus.

It was Mariamne, issued from the ancient *Magma Mater*, whom the Naassenes placed above Chaos. She engendered the Son of Man (Adam), of whom *NHS* was one of the incarnations (so as to save the men of the bad world who are held prisoner there by the Demiurge), at least according to the Ophites whose doctrines are reported by the *Elenchos*. (Celsus speaks of Christians drawing their origin from Mariamne. Cf. Origen, *Contra Celsum*, book 5, chapter 6.)

The work of the Demiurge produced corruption and death. Hence the intervention of the *Ophis-Christos*, born to the Virgin Mariamne:

> "No one, then, he says[20], can be saved or return [into heaven] without the Son, and the Son is the Serpent. For as he brought down from above the paternal marks, so again he carries up from thence those marks roused from a dormant condition and rendered paternal characteristics". One might say that the entire cycle is conceived as a natural cycle—almost physical. The higher Logos once again attracts to itself the spiritual element of matter: "as the naphtha drawing the fire in every direction towards itself; nay rather, as the magnet [attracting] the iron and not anything else, or just as the backbone of the sea falcon, the gold and nothing else, or as chaff is led by the amber. In this manner, he says, is the portrayed, perfect, and consubstantial genus drawn again from the world by the Serpent; nor does he [attract] anything else, as it has been sent down by him" (*Elenchos*, book 5, chapter 12).[21]

Perates, Cainites, Nicolaites, Koukeens

The proliferation of sects didn't just affect Esseno-Baptism; it also characterized the great religious currents derived from other Judean and Samaritan sources. Naassenism was divided into rival groups, communities, or Churches. In the doctrinal confusion of the first two centuries of the Christian era, the fundamental agreement among them proceeded less from the name and nature that they attributed to the

Messiah—*NHS*, Seth, Joshua, Dusis, Adam, Sophia, Barbelo, etc.—than from behavior marked by asceticism and renunciation or given over either to the pleasures of love or to the release of constrained desires.

An aggressive remark in the *Elenchos* in fact provides an observation: "The priests, then, and champions of the system, have been first those who have been called Naasseni, being so denominated from the Hebrew language, for the serpent is called *naas* (in Hebrew). Subsequently, however, they have styled themselves Gnostics, alleging that they alone have sounded the depths of knowledge. Now, from the system of these (speculators), many, detaching parts, have constructed a heresy which, though with several subdivisions, is essentially one, and they explain precisely the same (tenets); though conveyed under the guise of different opinions, as the following discussion, according to its progresses, will prove" (*Elenchos*, book 5, chapter 1)[22].

Koukeens, Phibionites, Stratiotics, Levitics, Perates, Cainites, Nicolaites—so many mysterious names: either local designations of groups anchored (despite their particularities) in a shared faith or the fantastical inventions of the heresiologues, who were always anxious to exhibit the chaos of the heterodoxies in order to emphasize the unity of the 'true' belief in the 'true' Messiah.

The preeminence of a saving Mother Goddess and a symbiotic cult of the phallic serpent brought a kind of unity to Naassenism, which was otherwise prey to behavioral variations that ranged from Essenean abstinence to the creative love advocated by Simon of Samaria.

According to the *Liber scholiorum*, written by the Syrian heresiologue Theodore Bar Koni[23], the poetic cosmogony of the Koukeens was as follows:

> God was born from the sea situated on the Earth of Light, which they call the Bright Sea. The Sea of Light and the Earth are more ancient than God.
>
> When God was born from the Bright Sea, he sat on the waters, looked at them, and in them saw his own image. He extended his hand, took [this image], took it as a companion, made love with it and engendered with it a crowd of Gods and goddesses.

The idea of a God in love with his reflection, with his Spirit, with his Wisdom or Sophia, was not foreign to Judeo-Christian speculations on the nature of the *Angelos-Christos*.

The position of the Nicolaites appears to have been closer to Essenism:

> The Darkness [the abyss and the waters], rejected by the unbegotten Spirit, rose up, furious, to attack it; this struggle produced a kind of womb that, for the Spirit, engendered four Eons, which engendered fourteen others; after which 'right' and 'left', light and darkness, were formed. One of the higher powers that emanated from the Spirit, Barbelo, the Celestial Sea, engendered the bad entity [Ialdabaôth or Sabaôth], creator of the lower world; but, repenting, she used her beauty to develop the health of the lower cosmos.[24]

A rumor has it that the Nicolaites—a name that comes from a certain Bishop Nicolas, who was the governor of their community—were made the object of polemics, to which the Greek text of the Apocalypse attributed to John bears witness. If one remembers that the same name, John, was used to sign a Gospel originally derived from a Naassene *midrash*, it is not improbable that, at the end of the first century—while Judeo-Christian philosophers such as Cerinthus, Satornilus, and the partisans of Saul/Paul were confronting each other in Ephesus, Antioch, Pergamon, Alexandria, and Corinth—a program of Esseno-Christian reunification that excluded the old forms of Naassenism was added to the original Jewish version of the Apocalypse. The text of the Apocalypse (2, 6, and 15–16) especially attacks the Nicolaites who were influential in Ephesus and Pergamon, where they seem to have striven to reconcile Naassenism and Essenism.

In all probability, the Perates constituted a later branch of the Naassenes. In his study of *WAW*, the Hebrew letter that symbolizes the Messiah, Dupont-Sommers traces their name to the Greek word *parátaxis*—the 'crossers', those who cross the waters of corruption[25]. Perhaps they were confused with the Cainites, who, according to the *Elenchos*, believed that the serpent was "the mark that was set upon Cain, that any one who findeth him might not kill him" (book 5, chapter 11)[26].

In North Africa, Naassenes of the Cainite type rallied many adepts around a prophetess named Quintilla. These adepts professed the existence of two divinities. As with Marcion much later, their Demiurge was identified with YHWH. Cain, like the Serpent, is YHWH's expiatory victory: "The serpent is Cain whose offering the God of this world did not accept, whereas he did accept the bloody sacrifice of Abel, because the master of this world wallows in blood"[27].

It is possible that the Cainites of North Africa, who were absorbed by the Christianity of the New Prophecy (which was particularly influential in Carthage around 160–70), convinced it to give to its redeemer the generic name of the God who saves: Joshua/Jesus.

The sect of the Perates, which was perhaps contemporary with the *Elenchos* (the text lingers over it at great length), testifies to the existence of a late and Hellenized version of Naassenism.

The author of the *Elenchos* rejects in particular two prophets, bishops or founders of communities: Euphrates the Perate and Kelbes the Karystian.

> They denominate themselves, however, Peratæ, imagining that none of those things existing by generation can escape the determined lot for those things that derive their existence from generation. For if, says (the Peratic), anything be altogether begotten, it also perishes [...]. But we alone, he says, who are conversant with the necessity of generation, and the paths through which man has entered into the world, and who have been accurately instructed (in these matters), we alone are competent to proceed through and pass beyond destruction [...]. This death, (the Peratic) says, seizes the Egyptians in the Red Sea, along with their chariots. All, however, who are ignorant (of this fact), he says, are Egyptians. And this, they assert, is the departure from Egypt, (that is,) from the body. For they suppose little Egypt to be body, and that it crosses the Red Sea— that is, the water of corruption, which is Cronus—and that it reaches a place beyond the Red Sea, that is, generation; and that it comes into the wilderness, that is, that it attains a condition independent of generation, where there exist promiscuously all the gods of destruction and the God of salvation.

Now, he says, the stars are the gods of destruction, which impose upon existent things the necessity of alterable generation. (*Elenchos*, book 5, chapter 11)[28]

The interpretations that Simon of Samaria applied to the texts of the Bible are found here, but they are made in the context of that scorn for the body that is common to all the religions.

The Redeeming and Perfect Serpent is opposed to the serpents that inject death. According to the *Elenchos*, speaking of the Peratic:[29]

Now, he says, the stars are the gods of destruction, which impose upon existent things the necessity of alterable generation. These, he says, Moses denominated serpents of the wilderness, which gnaw and utterly ruin those who imagined that they had crossed the Red Sea. To those, then, he says, who of the children of Israel were bitten in the wilderness, Moses exhibited the real and perfect serpent; and they who believed on this serpent were not bitten in the wilderness, that is, (were not assailed) by (evil) powers. No one therefore, he says, is there who is able to save and deliver those that come forth from Egypt, that is, from the body and from this world, unless alone the serpent that is perfect and replete with fullness. Upon this (serpent), he says, he who fixes his hope is not destroyed by the snakes of the wilderness, that is, by the gods of generation. (This statement) is written, he says, in a book of Moses. This serpent, he says, is the power that attended Moses, the rod[30] that was turned into a serpent.

(Note that the serpent as the principle of pleasure—defined as perdition by the Perates—was vanquished by the phallic symbolism of the staff of commandment.)

The serpents, however, of the magicians—(that is,) the gods of destruction—withstood the power of Moses in Egypt, but the rod of Moses reduced them all to subjection and slew them. This universal serpent is, he [the Peratic] says, the wise discourse of Eve. This, he says, is the mystery of Edem, this the river of Edem; this is the mark that was set upon Cain, that any one who findeth him might not kill him. This, he says, is Cain, whose sacrifice the god of this world did not accept. The gory sacrifice, however, of Abel he approved of; for the ruler of this world rejoices in (offerings of) blood. This, he says, is he who appeared in the last days, in form of a man, in the times of Herod[.]

(Note that the Serpent incarnated in human form was evoked in the Semitic substrata of the Gospel attributed to John before being given—like Melchizedek, Seth, and the Master of Justice—the name Joshua/Jesus. The image of the crucified Serpent would be perpetuated in alchemical representations.) For the Peratic, the serpent appeared:

> in the likeness of Joseph, who was sold by the hand of his brethren, to whom alone belonged the coat of many colors. This, he says, is he who is according to the likeness of Esau, whose garment—he not being himself present—was blessed; who did not receive, he says, the benediction uttered by him of enfeebled vision. He acquired, however, wealth from a source independent of this, receiving nothing from him whose eyes were dim; and Jacob saw his countenance, as a man beholds the face of God[31]. In regard of this, he says, it has been written that he was "like Nimrod a mighty hunter before the LORD"[32]. And there are, he says, many who closely imitate this (Nimrod): as numerous are they as the gnawing (serpents) which were seen in the wilderness by the children of Israel, from which that perfect serpent which Moses set up delivered those that were bitten [...]. According to the likeness of this was made in the desert the brazen serpent which Moses set up.

(Cf. the text of the Gospel attributed to John: "And as Moses lifted up the serpent in the wilderness, so must the Son of Man be lifted up, that whoever believes in him may have eternal life" (3: 14–5).)

> Of this alone, he says, the image is in heaven, always conspicuous in light.
> This, he says, is the great beginning respecting which Scripture has spoken. Concerning this, he says it has been declared: "In the beginning was the Word, and the Word was with God, and the Word was God. He was in the beginning with God. All things were made through him, and without him was not any thing made that was made. In him was life [...]".[33]

(The *Apocryphon of John* also belonged to this Naassenean or Peratean literature.)

> And in Him, he says, has been formed Eve; (now) Eve is life. This, however, he says, is Eve, the mother of all living,—a common nature, that is, of gods, angels, immortals, mortals, irrational creatures (and) rational ones.

(One final note: Eve as the principle of life and universal mother also appears in the doctrines of the Barbelites.)

Opposite the *Logos*, which is similar to the serpent, matter rises up and curls in upon itself; it appears under the symbol of water, which one also encounters among the Naassenes.

> But water, he says, is destruction; nor did the world, he says, perish by any other thing quicker than by water. Water, however, is that which rolls around among the PROASTIOI, (and) they assert (it to be) Cronus. For such a power, he says, is of the color of water; and this power, he says—that is, Cronus—none of those things existent by generation can escape. For Cronus is a cause to every generation, in regard of succumbing under destruction, and there could not exist (an instance) of generation in which Cronus does not interfere. This, he says, is what the poets also affirm, and what even appalls the gods:—
>
>> Earth be my witness now, the vaulting Sky above
>> and the dark cascading waters of the Styx—I swear
>> by the greatest, grimmest oath that binds the happy gods.[34]

The *Elenchos* (book 5, chapter 9) quotes a fragment of a Peratean hymn:

> I am a voice of arousal from the slumber in the age of night. Henceforward I commence to strip the power which is from chaos. The power is that of the lowest depth of mud, which uprears the slime of the incorruptible (and) humid expanse of space. And it is the entire power of convulsion, which, ever in motion, and presenting the color of water, whirls things on that are stationary, restrains things tremulous, sets things free as they proceed,

lightens things as they abide, removes things on the increase, a faithful steward of the track of the breezes, enjoying the things disgorged from the twelve eyes of the law, (and) manifesting a seal to the power which along with itself distributes the downborne invisible waters, and has been called Thalassa. This power ignorance has been accustomed to denominate Cronus, guarded with chains because he tightly bound the fold of the dense and misty and obscure and murky Tartarus.[35]

The syncretism of the Perates was not content with harmonizing the Greek and Hebrew mythologies; it furthermore incorporated into its doctrine of salvation an astrological speculation that was also present in Essenism and in the Christianities of Bardaisan and Priscillian.

The universe and the individual knew an existence subjected to astral influences that the Perates identified with the power of the Archons—agents of the Demiurge. The art of the Serpent-*Logos* consisted in escaping from them.

In the same way that the stars tend towards the center of the world in order to move away from it again, the entire Creation moves away from its center—the Divinity—in order to return to it. The fall is designated by the left side of circular movement; ascension is on the right side. The heavens themselves offer a great fresco of the combat between the Logos (the Good and Perfect Serpent) and the master of this world (the Bad Serpent). The Logos is figured by the constellation of the Dragon; it has on the right and left sides of its head the Crown and the Lyre. Before the Dragon is kneeling the 'pitiful' man, the constellation of Hercules, who touches the end of the right foot of the Dragon. Behind him, the Bad Master of the world—the constellation of the Serpent—approaches in order to abduct the Crown, but Ophiuchus surrounds Him and prevents Him from touching the Crown.[36]

Note that the theme of the two serpents is evoked in the Book of Isaiah (27: 1)[37].

Still later, Epiphanius of Salamis attributed to those whom he called 'Ophites' a Eucharist held in honor of the Serpent-Redeemer. (Certain sects practice this Eucharist today.)

They have a real snake and keep it in a basket of some sort. When it is time for their mysteries they bring it out of the den, spread loaves around on a table, and call the snake to come; and when the den is opened it comes out. And then the snake—which comes up of its own accord and by its villainy—already knowing their foolishness, crawls onto the table and coils up on the loaves. And this they call a perfect sacrifice.

And so, as I have heard from someone, not only do they break the loaves the snake has coiled on and distribute them to the communicants, but each one kisses the snake on the mouth besides—whether the snake has been charmed into tameness by some sort of sorcery, or coaxed by some other act of the devil for their deception. But they worship an animal of that sort and call what has been consecrated by its coiling around it the eucharistic element. And they offer a hymn to the Father on high—again, as they say, through the snake—and so conclude their mysteries. (Epiphanius, *Panarion*, iii. 37. 5, 6–7).[38]

From the serpent of the lewd temptation to the *Ophis-Christos*, passing through the phallic and magical rod of Hermes Trismegistus, the ancient totemism of the animal that coils, intertwines, wriggles, penetrates, unites, and ejaculates venom or life was spiritualized and incorporated into religious stereotypes without losing its ambiguous nature.

Uprooted from its original androgyny—which was celebrated by certain Naassenean groups hostile to Puritanism—the *ophis* was made a Redeemer Messiah and a Destroyer Messiah, a virgin of iron and terror who reigned over nature, beasts, and women in order to impose on the world the order of pure renunciation (incarnated in Jesus) and the order of pure release (incarnated in Satan, the *alter ego* of the Messiah).

Perhaps it was also by means of the *Ophis-Christos* that the cult of Hermes-*Logos*—which the Greeks called *agathephoros*, carrier of the good (as the *agathodaimon*), and which offered the erect phallus to popular veneration—succumbed to a kind of castration.

Whatever the case, Essenean asceticism invaded the Greco-Roman world and, by way of the antagonistic tendencies of Marcionism and Montanism, propagated within that world fanatical tastes for continence, mortification, and the martyred body.

But while the rod of Moses was substituted for the 'golden staff of Hermes', the rites of sexual fusion acquired a vivacity that was not always as clandestine as one might suppose, since Epiphanius of Salamis was able to learn about the existence of the Barbelites, who called themselves 'Christians' (thereby restoring to the word the sense of 'messianic'). Their Messiah was not named Jesus, but Barbelo.

At the end of the fourth century, Priscillian of Avila considered it worth making clear that "neither Armaziel nor Mariame nor Ioel nor Balsamus nor Barbilon are God, but Jesus Christ" (*Corpus eccles. latin.*, xviii. 29)[39]. Mariamne was the Mother-Spirit-Sophia-Virgin and Mother of the Naassenes. Barbilon was Barbelo, the sperm-eating and redeeming divinity of the Barbelites.

Justin the Gnostic and the Book of Baruch

In the mid-second century, Justin the Gnostic—a Greek who was familiar with the Jewish texts and who became the master of an esoteric school in which instruction was dispensed under the seal of the secret—drafted the *Book of Baruch*, of which the *Elenchos* conserved extracts. (It's not impossible that Justin frequented milieus of Kabalistic Jews who, under the cover of Phariseean obedience, perpetuated and amplified the *gnosis* of the Hermetic groups of Egypt and Asia Minor.)

The *Book of Baruch* offers a Judeo-Greek syncretism quite different from that of Justin's contemporary, Marcion, which was elaborated on the basis of the authority of Saul/Paul.

Justin refers to a myth, reported by Herodotus, according to which Hercules made love with a being who was half-young woman and half-serpent, and who gave him three children. From this myth Justin drew a Trinitarian theology. In the words of the *Elenchos*[40]:

> This (heresiarch) makes the following statement. There are three unbegotten principles of the universe, two male (and) one female. Of the male [principles], however, a certain one, is denominated good, and it alone is called after this manner, and possesses a power of prescience concerning the universe. But the other is father of all begotten things, devoid of prescience, and invisible. And the female (principle) is devoid of prescience,

passionate, two-minded, two-bodied, in every respect answering (the description of) the girl in the legend of Herodotus, as far as the groin a virgin, and (in) the parts below (resembling) a snake, as Justin says. But this girl is styled Edem and Israel. And these principles of the universe are, he says, roots and fountains from which existing things have been produced, but that there was not anything else. The Father, then, who is devoid of prescience, beholding that half-woman Edem, passed into a concupiscent desire for her. But this Father, he says, is called Elohim. Not less did Edem also long for Elohim, and the mutual passion brought them together into the one nuptial couch of love. And from such an intercourse the Father generates out of Edem unto himself twelve angels. And the names of the angels begotten by the Father are these: Michaël, Amen, Baruch, Gabriel, Esaddæus...[41] . And of the maternal angels which Edem brought forth, the names in like manner have been subjoined, and they are as follows: Babel, Achamoth, Naas, Bel, Belias, Satan, Saël, Adonæus, Leviathan[42], Pharao, Carcamenos, (and) Lathen.

Of these twenty-four angels the paternal ones are associated with the Father, and do all things according to His will; and the maternal (angels are associated with) Edem the Mother. And the multitude of all these angels together is Paradise, he says, concerning which Moses speaks: "And the LORD God planted a garden in Eden, in the east"[43], that is, towards the face of Edem, that Edem might behold the garden—that is, the angels—continually. Allegorically the angels are styled trees of this garden, and the tree of life is the third of the paternal angels—Baruch. And the tree of the knowledge of good and evil is the third of the maternal angels—Naas. For so, says (Justinus), one ought to interpret the words of Moses, observing, "Moses said these things disguisedly, from the fact that all do not attain the truth". And, he says, Paradise being formed from the conjugal joy of Elohim and Edem, the angels of Elohim receiving from the most beauteous earth, that is, not from the portion of Edem resembling a monster, but from the parts above the groin of human shape, and gentle,—in aspect—make man out of the earth. But out of the parts resembling a monster are produced wild beasts, and the rest of the animal creation. They made man, therefore, as a symbol of the unity and love (subsisting) between them; and they depute their own powers unto him, Edem the soul, but Elohim the spirit. And the man Adam is produced as some actual seal and memento of love, and as an everlasting emblem of the marriage of Edem and Elohim. And in like manner also Eve was produced, he says, as Moses has described, an image and emblem (as well as) a seal, to be preserved for ever, of Edem. And in like manner also a soul was deposited in Eve,—an image—from Edem, but a spirit[44] from Elohim. And there were given to them commandments, "Be fruitful and multiply and fill the earth"[45], that is, Edem; for so he wishes that it had been written. For the entire of the power belonging unto herself, Edem conferred upon Elohim as a sort of nuptial dowry. Whence, he says, from imitation of that primary marriage up to this day, women bring a dowry to their husbands, complying with a certain divine and paternal law that came into existence on the part of Edem towards Elohim.

And when all things were created as has been described by Moses—both heaven and earth, and the things therein—the twelve angels of the Mother were divided into four principles, and each fourth part of them is called a river—Pison, and Gihon, and Tigris, and Euphrates, as, he says, Moses states. These twelve angels, being mutually connected, go about into four parts, and manage the world, holding from Edem a sort of viceregal authority over the world. But they do not always continue in the same places, but move around as if in a circular dance, changing place after place, and at set times and intervals retiring to the localities subject to themselves. And when Pison holds sway over places, famine, distress, and affliction prevail in that part of the earth, for the battalion of these angels is niggardly. In like manner also there belong to each part of the four, according to the power and nature of each, evil times and hosts of diseases. And continually, according to the dominion of each fourth part, this stream of evil, just (like a current) of rivers, careers, according to the will of Edem, uninterruptedly around the world. And from some cause of this description has arisen the necessity of evil.

When Elohim had prepared and created the world as a result from joint pleasure, He wished to ascend up to the elevated parts of heaven, and to see that not anything of what pertained to the creation laboured under deficiency. And He took His Own angels with Him, for His nature was to mount aloft, leaving Edem below: for inasmuch as she was earth, she was not disposed to follow upward her spouse. Elohim, then, coming to the highest part of heaven above, and beholding a light superior to that which He Himself had created, exclaimed, "Open me the gates, that entering in I may acknowledge the Lord; for I considered Myself to be Lord"[46]. A voice was returned to Him from the light, saying, "This is the gate of the LORD; the righteous shall enter through it"[47]. And immediately the gate was opened, and the Father, without the angels, entered, (advancing) towards the Good One, and beheld "what eye hath not seen, and ear hath not heard, and what hath not entered into the heart of man to (conceive)". Then the Good One says to him, "Sit at my right hand"[48]. And the Father says to the Good One, "Permit me, Lord, to overturn the world which I have made, for my spirit is bound to men. And I wish to receive it back (from them)"[49]. Then the Good One replies to him, "No evil canst thou do while thou art with me, for both thou and Edem made the world as a result of conjugal joy. Permit Edem, then, to hold possession of the world as long as she wishes; but do you remain with me". Then Edem, knowing that she had been deserted by Elohim, was seized with grief, and placed beside herself her own angels. And she adorned herself after a comely fashion, if by any means Elohim, passing into concupiscent desire, might descend (from heaven) to her.

When, however, Elohim, overpowered by the Good One, no longer descended to Edem, Edem commanded Babel, which is Venus[50], to cause adulteries and dissolutions of marriages among men. (And she adopted this expedient) in order that, as she had been divorced from Elohim, so also the spirit of Elohim, which is in men, being wrong with sorrow, might be punished by such separations, and might undergo precisely the sufferings which (were being endured by) the deserted Edem. And Edem gives great power to her third angel, Naas, that by every species of punishment she might chasten the spirit of Elohim which is in men, in order that Elohim, through the spirit, might be punished for having deserted his spouse, in violation of the agreements entered into between them. Elohim the father, seeing these things, sends forth Baruch, the third angel among his own, to succour the spirit that is in all men. Baruch then coming, stood in the midst of the angels of Edem, that is, in the midst of paradise—for paradise is the angels, in the midst of whom he stood,—and issued to the man the following injunction: "You may surely eat of every tree of the garden, but of the tree of the knowledge of good and evil you shall not eat"[51], which is

Naas. Now the meaning is, that he should obey the rest of the eleven angels of Edem, for the eleven possess passions, but are not guilty of transgression. Naas, however, has committed sin, for he went in unto Eve, deceiving her, and debauched her; and (such an act as) this is a violation of law. He, however, likewise went in unto Adam, and had unnatural intercourse with him; and this is itself also a piece of turpitude, whence have arisen adultery and sodomy.

Henceforward vice and virtue were prevalent among men, arising from a single source—that of the Father. For the Father having ascended to the Good One, points out from time to time the way to those desirous of ascending (to him likewise). After having, however, departed from Edem, he caused an originating principle of evil for the spirit of the Father that is in men. Baruch therefore was despatched to Moses, and through him spoke to the children of Israel, that they might be converted unto the Good One. But the third angel (Naas), by the soul which came from Edem upon Moses, as also upon all men, obscured the precepts of Baruch, and caused his own peculiar injunctions to be hearkened unto. For this reason the soul is arrayed against the spirit, and the spirit against the soul. For the soul is Edem, but the spirit Elohim, and each of these exists in all men, both females and males. Again, after these (occurrences), Baruch was sent to the Prophets, that through the Prophets the spirit that dwells in men might hear (words of warning), and might avoid Edem and the wicked fiction, just as the Father had fled from Elohim. In like manner also—by the prophets—Naas, by a similar device, through the soul that dwells in man, along with the spirit of the Father, enticed away the prophets, and all (of them) were allured after him, and did not follow the words of Baruch, which Elohim enjoined.

Ultimately Elohim selected Hercules, an uncircumcised prophet, and sent him to quell the twelve angels of Edem, and release the Father from the twelve angels, those wicked ones of the creation. These are the twelve conflicts of Hercules which Hercules underwent, in order, from first to last, viz., Lion, and Hydra, and Boar, and the others successively. For they say that these are the names (of them) among the Gentiles, and they have been derived with altered denominations from the energy of the maternal angels. When he seemed to have vanquished his antagonists, Omphalos—now she is Babel or Venus—clings to him and entices away Hercules, and divests him of his power, viz., the commands of Baruch which Elohim issued. And in place (of this power, Babel) envelopes him in her own peculiar robe, that is, in the power of Edem, who is the power below; and in this way the prophecy of Hercules remained unfulfilled, and his works.

Finally, however, in the days of Herod the king, Baruch is despatched, being sent down once more by Elohim[.]

The following offers a typical example of interpolation. It dates, at the earliest, from the fourth century, since Nazareth didn't exist before then.

Coming to Nazareth, he found Jesus, son of Joseph and Mary, a child of twelve years, feeding sheep. And he announces to him all things from the beginning, whatsoever had been done by Edem and Elohim, and whatsoever would be likely to take place hereafter, and spoke the following words: "All the prophets anterior to you have been enticed. Put forth an effort, therefore, Jesus, Son of man, not to be allured, but preach this word unto men, and carry back tidings to them of things pertaining to the Father, and things pertaining to the Good One, and ascend to the Good One, and sit there with Elohim, Father of us all". And Jesus was obedient unto the angel, saying that, "I shall do all things, Lord", and proceeded to preach. Naas therefore wished to entice this one also. (Jesus, however, was not disposed to listen to his overtures), for he remained faithful to Baruch. Therefore Naas, being inflamed with anger because he was not able to seduce him, caused him to be crucified. He, however, leaving the body of Edem on the [accursed] tree, ascended to the Good One; saying, however, to Edem, "Woman, thou retainest thy son"[52], that is, the natural and the earthly man. But (Jesus) himself commending his spirit into the hands of the Father, ascended to the Good One.[53]

Leisegang pertinently detects in Justin and his mythology the echoes of an amorous torment, here hypostasized as a cosmic drama. I leave the floor to the exegete. His sympathy for that vindictive man and his antipathy towards the woman—who here is given the same sentimental interest that Leisegang has in Justin elsewhere—shows quite clearly the sensual origin of all *hairesis*, of all choices that are supposedly religious or ideological.

Amorous desire and its satisfaction: such is the key to the origin of the world. The disillusions of love and the vengeance that follows them—such is the secret of all the evil and egotism that exists on the earth. The entire history of the world and humanity becomes a love story. We seek, we find, we separate, we torture ourselves, and then, finally, faced with a more acute pain, we renounce: that is the eternal mystery of love, the intrinsic paradox of which makes us desire to be delivered from women and from the feminine. All this marks a fine intelligence concerning the essential differences that separate men from women. The tragedy of the destiny of the universe begins with the amorous impulse that leads its Creator to leave the domain of the Good. By descending toward Edem[54], who watches out for him, Elohim finds himself charged with the first fault, which involved both a free decision and a natural instinct. When one considers that he left his wife, that he did not descend from the heavens to return to her, and that he repented of the consequences of his love and wanted to destroy all that issued from him, it is clear that his guilt is enormous. Though his conduct might well appear, from the angle of the earth, to be a frightful infidelity, it was much less blameworthy than the conduct and the vengeance of Edem[55], for which she found a partial justification. One thinks of a remark by Nietzsche: "Man fears the woman who loves: she will not recoil before any sacrifice, and all the rest will appear to her as without value. Man fears the woman who hates: because man in the depths of his heart is malicious, but the woman is bad" (*Ainsi parlait Zarathoustra*, trans. G. Bianquis (Paris: Aubier, 1946), 153[56]). Edem[57] was malicious: she did everything she could to thwart the ceaselessly renewed efforts by Elohim to efface the evil that had issued from him; efforts that would end successfully after millennia of perseverance. Sympathy was also shared between Edem[58] and Elohim. The sadness of God before the fatal consequences of his love and the distress of the disappointed woman were both intended to awaken the sympathy and emotions of the man who, in the course of his poor little existence, allows himself to be caught in this tragedy of love and experiences it. That Elohim finally reached salvation at the cost of laborious efforts, and that Edem[59]—

bent on saying no and on impeding the work of the Good—found her tragic end in an eternal abandonment and ended up as a de-spiritualized cadaver: this responds to the sentiment of justice, which demands the most severe punishment for irreconcilable hatred.[60]

The Adepts of Barbelo

Around 335, the young Epiphanius of Salamis, a future master-thinker of the Church and the author of a denunciatory list of heresies titled *Panarion kata haireseôn* (*Medicine Chest Against All the Heresies*), adhered to a sect that still called itself 'Christian' in the Greek sense of 'messianic'.

Its Christ or Messiah was named Barbelo. She was a modern emanation of the ancient Goddess-Mother and revealed herself in the features of a *Sophia* who would be the exaltation, not of the *pneuma* in its spiritual sense, but of the breath of life, the sensual power of the body.

Tormented by guilt, and later on converted to the frenzies of asceticism, Epiphanius overwhelmed his first co-religionists with the same indignant rage as that with which Augustine of Hippo repudiated the Manichaeism of which he had once been a zealous partisan.

Among the books that propagated the Barbelite doctrine, Epiphanius cites the *Books of Ialdabaoth*, the *Apocalypse of Adam*, the *Gospel of Eve*, the *Books of Seth*, the *Book of Noria*, the *Prophecies of Barkabbas* (cited by Basilides), the *Ascension of Elijah*, the *Nativity of Mary*, the *Gospel of the Apostles*, the *Great and Small Interrogations of Mary*, the *Gospel of Philip*, and the *Gospel of Perfection*.

Several hypotheses have been advanced concerning the name of the Goddess. For Leisegang it derived from the Hebrew *Barbhe Eloha* ('in four is God'), which was an allusion to the divine tetrad—not, that is, to the *tetragrammaton* YHWH, but to the ancient Semitic heavenly group: El the Father, the Mother (His wife), and their sons and daughter. These later became Father, feminine *pneuma*, Son, and Messiah or Christ. Others see in it a deformation of Baal (Belo) or the cult of the divinity named Bel—which derived from the rites of fecundity and light that persisted in Samaria despite the Yahwehist implantation—or even an emanation from Anath. In the *Book of Baruch* by Justin the Gnostic, the entity Babbel is identified with Aphrodite.

According to the report made by Epiphanius: "For some of them glorify a Barbelo who they claim is on high in an eighth heaven, and say she has been emitted by the Father. For some of them say she is the mother of Ialdabaoth, others, of Sabaoth. But her son has ruled the seventh heaven with a sort of insolence, and tyrannically. To the one below him he says[61], 'I am the first and I am the last; besides me there is no god'" (*Panarion*, ii. 25. 2,2)[62].

The tyrannical Eternal is none other than YHWH, the God of the Judeans, who was identified by anti-Judean Jewish *gnosis* and then by Hellenic *gnosis* with the Demiurge—the bloody God who was popularized under the name Ialdabaoth or Sabaoth. The Demiurge presides over the destiny of an irremediably bad world. That YHWH-Ialdabaoth was the son of the Goddess-Mother here recalls the eviction of the cults of the Woman and Mother by the patriarchy that rose to power alongside Neolithic agriculture.

Hearing these words, Barbelite mythology says, the mother of the divine despot decided to save humanity from the miserable lot to which God had reduced it. How did she resolve to restore the power that her odious son had stripped away? By ruse and seduction. She presented herself to the Archons—the servants of the Savior—in the voluptuous majesty of her femininity and, having excited their desires, received their sperm: "And she keeps appearing in some beautiful form to the archons and stealing the seed which is generated by their climax and ejaculation—supposedly to recover her power which has been sown in various of them" (*Panarion*, ii. 25. 2,2)[63].

The faithful to Barbelo thus imitated the saving gesture of the Goddess and, with all the good conscience that comes with making an offering, abandoned themselves to the pleasure of making flow—in place of the blood shed by so many religions—the sperm and the cyprine [vaginal lubrication] whose emission revives the energy of the *Natura Magma*.

In a passage that would much later inspire the inquisitors who accused Catharist and Waldensian ascetics of debauchery, Epiphanius reports the use of a sign of recognition (attested to by the Messalians, Beghards and Beguines) that—predating the twentieth century's hedonistic fashion for sexual liberties—was long perpetuated among young people, who indicated, by a caress in the palm of the hand, the imperious character of their desire:

> And if a guest who is of their persuasion arrives, they have a sign that men give women and women give men, a tickling of the palm as they clasp hands in supposed greeting, to show that the visitor is of their religion.
> And once they recognize each other from this they start feasting right away—and they set the table with lavish provisions for eating meat and drinking wine even if they are poor. But then, after a drinking bout and, let us say, stuffing their overstuffed veins, they get hot for each other next. And the husband will move away from his wife and tell her—speaking to his own wife!—"Get up, perform the Agape[64] with the brother". (*Panarion*, ii. 26. 4,1–3)[65]

Note that the Christian Churches that claimed Thomas for themselves allowed for the existence of an amorous relation between Jesus and Salome: "Salome said: 'Who are you, man, that you . . . have come up on my couch and eaten from my table?'" (*logion* 65 of the *Secret Sayings of Jesus*, popularly known under the title *Gospel of Thomas*)[66]. In the same order of ideas, the First Epistle attributed to John (3: 9–10) declares: "No one born of God makes a practice of sinning, for God's seed abides in him; and he cannot keep on sinning, because he has been born of God. By this it is evident who are the children of God, and who are the children of the devil".

The man and the woman take care to receive the sperm between their hands, and they pledge it to the Goddess-Mother so that she can fortify life in the world and also in them.

The sect frequented by Epiphanius offers an example of an archaic belief of the orgiastic type that was degraded by successive syncretisms. Even the Christianity erected at Nicaea as the religion of the State was impregnated by the currents in which it was at first formulated (before it settled down as a political and theological doctrine). Many tendencies fundamentally hostile to Christianity would survive by adapting themselves with varying degrees of flexibility to the norms imposed by Rome (the recuperation of the Celtic or Slavic mythologies, which were incorporated into the cult of the saints, is exemplary in this regard, as Robert Graves has shown[67].)

In the case of the Barbelites, who were belatedly denounced by Epiphanius, communion of the Christian type may have replaced the tribute that was formerly rendered to the 'breath of life' and that strongly expressed amorous pleasure. As Leisegang recalls, "the word *pneuma* is immediately tied to the evocation of a spermatic, reproductive matter. At the beginning, the *pneuma* had absolutely nothing to do with spirit; it was the 'wind', it was a 'hot air'. The conception according to which it is a *pneuma*-wind, and not a *pneuma*-spirit, that engenders human life, is encountered in the Greek tradition"[68].

The idea of a *sperma* that generates life, of a substance that creates man and the world, is not absent from the Greek translation of 'Spirit' by the word *pneuma* as it appears in the Old and New Testaments. Little by little, however, this translation obliterated the element that was least acceptable to a society dominated by religion: the act of self-creation, of the creation of the world and, randomly, of the child who contains in his or her substance the amorous union of man and woman. This submerged reality ironically reemerged among a few playful stoics and the voluntarily castrated Origen by way of the traits of the *logos spermatikos* that became, in Saint-Sulpicean imagery, the language of fire of the Pentecost.

For the Barbelites, man and woman possessed the *pneuma*, the breath of God, in their own seeds. And the individual came closer to the divine essence as he or she radiated his or her spermatic power and dispensed it in a symbiotic [*fusionnel*] orgasm.

"To unite with God", Leisegang specifies, "one must mix and merge together one's semen with the generating substance of the All. Salvation consists in removing one's semen from its terrestrial destination and leading it back to the celestial source of all semen"[69].

Here is what Epiphanius of Salamis reports about the group in which he had been an adept.

> The woman and man receive the man's emission on their own hands [...] and offer that stuff on their hands to the true Father of all, and say, "We

offer thee this gift, the body of the Christ". And then they eat it partaking of their own dirt, and say, "This is the body of Christ; and this is the Pascha, because of which our bodies suffer and are compelled to acknowledge the passion of Christ".

And so with the woman's emission when she happens to be having her period—they likewise take the unclean menstrual blood they gather from her, and eat it in common. And "This", they say, "is the blood of Christ". And so, when they read, "I saw a tree bearing twelve manner of fruits every year, and he said unto me, 'This is the tree of life[']", in apocryphal writings, they interpret this allegorically of the menstrual flux. (*Panarion*, ii. 26. 4,5–5,1)[70]

Epiphanius did not understand, or didn't want to understand, that the Christ, the Messiah of the Barbelites, was not Joshua/Jesus but Barbelo, whom Priscillian would call Barbilon. Epiphanius goes on to say:

But although they have sex with each other they renounce procreation. It is for enjoyment, not procreation, that they eagerly pursue seduction [...]. They come to climax but absorb the seeds of their dirt, not by implanting them for procreation, but by eating the dirty stuff themselves. (*Panarion*, ii. 26. 5,2–3)[71]

When Barbelo gave birth to the odious breed of the Eternal—YHWH-Ialdabaoth-Sabaoth (also called Kalakau)—she revoked her status as mother in order to be celebrated as the woman impregnated by the pleasure and love that she dispensed. The Barbelites also had recourse to a voluntary form of interrupted pregnancy, which is not without interest.

But even though one of them should accidentally implant the seed of his natural emission prematurely and the woman becomes pregnant, listen to a more dreadful thing that such people venture to do. They extract the fetus at the stage which is appropriate for their enterprise, take this aborted infant, and cut it up in a trough with a pestle. And they mix honey, pepper, and certain other perfumes and spices with it to keep from getting sick, and then all the revelers in this <herd> of swine and dogs assemble, and each eats a piece of the child with his fingers. And now, after this cannibalism, they pray to God and say, "We were not mocked by the archon of lust, but have gathered the brother's blunder up!" And this, if you please, is their idea of the "perfect Passover".

[...] Again, whenever they feel excitement within them they soil their own hands with their own ejaculated dirt, get up, and pray stark naked with their hands defiled. The idea is that they [can] obtain freedom of access to God by a practice of this kind.

Man and woman, they pamper their bodies night and day, anointing themselves, bathing, feasting, spending their time in whoring and drunkenness. And they curse anyone who fasts and say, "Fasting is wrong; fasting belongs to this archon who made the world. We must take nourishment to make our bodies strong, and able to render their fruit in its season". (*Panarion*, ii. 26. 5,4–8)[72]

Here 'the archon' refers to the God who created the world (the Eon)[73]. The expression 'archon' is frequently found in the letters allegedly written by Paul, but translators have unfailingly made it their duty to render it as 'world', 'century', or 'epoch' so that the Gnostic connotation is avoided.

Note that the *Gospel of the Egyptians* also justified the refusal to engender children: "When Salome asked the Lord: 'How long shall death hold sway?' he answered: 'As long as you women bear children'. [...] On this account he says: 'When Salome asked when she would know the answer to her questions, the Lord said, When you trample on the robe of shame, and when the two shall be one, and the male with the female, and there is neither male nor female'. [...] For when she [Salome] says, 'I would have done better had I never given birth to a child', suggesting that she might not have been right in giving birth to a child, the Lord replies to her saying, 'Eat of every plant, but eat not of that which has bitterness in it'" (quoted by Clement of Alexandria, *Stromata*, book 3, chapter 9:66[74], and by the *Second Epistle to the Corinthians* attributed to Clement).

In its most radical elements, the Barbelite doctrine was similar to the teachings of Simon of Samaria: the body is the earth, whose creative power merits the exclusive attention of men and people. The goal is the fusion of the me and the world, but whereas Simon identified the consciousness of pleasure with the consciousness of self-creation, the Barbelites, obeying the dictates of religion, ended in a mystical vision of pleasure that was, in the last instance, a tribute of the *soma* to the Spirit and the divine.

Like Tantrism, Barbelo, the orgiastic Goddess and sucker of the universal sperm, turns the pleasures of life into a heavenly duty, and sensual pleasure into a ritual obligation. What's therefore disgusting is *not* sensually communing in sperm and abnormal excitation, but rather travestying amorous exaltation as an ejaculation of the sacred.

The Barbelite religion fomented a theology that long predated that which Catholicism would impose after Nicaea.

Two forces were opposed: the Good God, of whom Barbelo was the emanation, and the God who had created the bad world. By way of the road of orgasm, Barbelo led man back to the kingdom of light, from which the Demiurge was exiled in order to enslave it to its own odious authority.

> Certain others of them make up some new names, and say that there were Darkness, Depth and Water, and that the Spirit in between them formed their boundary. But Darkness was angry and enraged at Spirit, and this Darkness sprang up, embraced it, they say, and sired something called "Womb". After Womb was born it conceived by Spirit itself. A certain four aeons were emitted from Womb, but fourteen others from the four, and this was the origin of "right" and "left", darkness and light. But later, after all these, a certain ignoble aeon was emitted. It had intercourse with the Womb we mentioned above, and by this ignoble aeon and Womb gods, angels, demons and seven spirits were produced. (*Panarion*, ii. 25. 5,1–3)[75]

The *Book of Noria*—Noria is not the daughter of Adam, as she was among the Ophites, but the wife of Noah—recounts that Noria did not enter the Ark, because she wanted to kill the Creator of this world along with the rest of humanity: because she did not serve this Creator but the superior powers and Barbelo, the enemy of the Archon. Noria set fire to the Ark three times, from which one must conclude that "what has been stolen from the Mother on high by the archon who made the world, and by the other gods, demons and angels with him, must be gathered from the power in bodies, through the male and female emissions" (*Panarion*, ii. 26. 1,9)[76].

It is in the *Gospel of Eve*[77] (the Hebrew word *Hawwah* means 'life') that the symbiotic [*fusionelle*] aspiration of the Barbelites—the identity of the 'I' and the world that offers the radiant presence of love in the flash of pleasure—appears with an astonishing poetry.

> "I stood upon a lofty mountain, and saw a man who was tall, and another, little of stature.[78] And I heard as it were the sound of thunder and drew nigh to hear, and he spake with me and said, I am thou and thou art I, and wheresoever thou art, there am I; and I am sown in all things. And from wheresoever thou wilt thou gatherest me, but in gathering me, thou gatherest thyself". (*Panarion*, ii. 26. 3,1)[79]

CHAPTER EIGHT

Three Esseno-Christian Christs: Seth, Melchizedek, and Joshua/Jesus

The diverse sects of the movement that was given the general name 'Essenism' placed at the front rank of their preoccupations—on which the Zealot movement conferred a dramatic reality—the question of the Messiah, the envoy to whom God would assign the task of leading the people towards a promised new earth.

Due to their collaboration with the Roman occupiers, the Pharisees condemned messianic speculations, particularly those that—hoping for the reincarnation of Adam or of one of his sons—claimed that the first man was a partner of God and that he took part in the creation of the world. For the Pharisees, no Messiah infatuated with any kind of power could arrogate to himself any of the rights or functions that were reserved exclusively for Adonai, the Savior, the Creator. Adam had chosen evil, and the Pharisees stigmatized as *minim* (Gnostics) those who affirmed that Adam had repented, chosen God, and been saved, which is what the *Epistula apostolorum* claims. (Note that "there were Jewish traditions concerning Adam that represented him as the Vice-Regent of God, as being established like a king in a sphere above the world from which he imposed his domination on the entirety of creation. Several rabbis perceived the danger of being contradicted and attempted to check the most perilous of these positions"[1]. There was soon a struggle between the rabbis, on the one hand, and, on the other hand, the groups that claimed to valorize Adam as the essence of the Messiah—nay, even as the Father of the Messiah who was called the Son of Man.)

Many Essene factions supported the thesis of Adam being seated at God's right hand—of his being simultaneously the redeemer of humanity and the Co-Regent of God. This proposition was inadmissible in the context of Yahwehist monotheism, but it nonetheless shows through in certain of the letters that were attributed to Saul/Paul.

The Letter to the Colossians (1: 15–8) makes the Christ a pre-existing agent of God in the creation. "The Messiah is called 'Image of God' and 'The Head of the Body', the latter of which originally signified the entire universe (the 'Church' is almost certainly an addition designed to destroy the parallelism between the hymn and the cosmic vision presented)"[2]. (Note that this is one of many examples of the falsifications introduced into the letters of Saul/Paul by his copyists and translators. They were intended to make the reader forget that Saul had belonged to Jewish Gnosticism.)

Nevertheless, the name of the Messiah varied according to the sect, meaning that the name was precisely what conferred power upon the community or Church. A fragment from an apocryphal *Book of Daniel* discovered at Qumran insists on the expectation of a savior delegated by God and carrying the Name: "He will be called the Son of the Great God and by his Name he will be named. He will be greeted as the Son of God; one will call him the Son of the Most-High"[3].

The quarrel was about the secret name of the Son of God: was it Adam reincarnated or the son of Adam, the Son of Man? The *Testament of Abraham*, a text of Jewish origin from the first century before the Christian era, describes an Adam crowned in the heavens. Such was also the vision of Saul/Paul in the second Letter to the Corinthians (22–3), which evoked the presence of Adam in Paradise or the third heaven.

The *Apocalypse of Adam*—another text of Judaic origin from the first century, discovered at Nag Hammadi (Nag Hammadi Library V)—contains the revelation of the future destiny of the Adamites, which is offered by Adam to his son Seth.

For Fossum, "Adam was the first manifestation of the True Prophet"[4]. Adam possessed the spirit of God, which brought knowledge (*gnosis*) of all things, past and future (*Homilies of Peter*, 3.17). The cycle of legends concerning Adam constituted the axis of Jewish speculations that centered on the nature of the Messiah. It originally explained the theme of the descent and ascension of the savior.[5]

According to the *Poimandres*, the heavenly Adam was made in the form and the image of God, a formulation that Saul/Paul took up when he assured his followers that Jesus was a form of God.[6]

The Messiah Seth

The new Adam and Son of Man that the Ebionites and Nazarenes would christen Joshua, was, for some Essenes, the third son of Adam, Seth. The important Sethian literature discovered at Nag Hammadi proves that the vogue for religious syncretism didn't hesitate to absorb the doctrines of other sects, including those of the Naassenes (some Sethians estimated that the savior had deceived the creator by assuming the form of a serpent), the Cainites (for whom Seth was Adam's brother), and the sectarians attached to Joshua (the *Gospel of the Egyptians* postulates an equivalence between Seth and Joshua/Jesus). (The collection at Nag Hammadi includes a great number of Sethian works, some of which—thanks to the successive syncretic waves of works by Naassenes, Barbelites and Joshua/Jesus-Christians—are barely distinguishable from one another: the *Three Pillars of Seth*, the *Epistle of Eugnostos* (which became *The Sophia of Jesus Christ*), and the *Paraphrase of Shem* (Seth), in which the mediating Spirit intervenes in the primordial struggle between Light and Darkness.[7])

Seth was born to Adam and the Virgin Eve. Their descendants were the 'spiritual', 'pneumatic', or 'perfect' Sons of the Light, who extolled asceticism and the stimulation of the spirit at the expense of the body.

According to Sethian mythology—insofar at least as it is discernible it in the writings at Nag Hammadi—Ialdabaoth (the God of Genesis) created a bad world. Nevertheless, in the man that he produced was perpetuated a heavenly spark that—aspiring to return to the superior places from which it had come—indicated the road to salvation. Like Sophia, Barbelo, and Naas, Seth was the Messiah of the Good God and was superior to Ialdabaoth.

The Sethians divided history into four periods: the age of Adam, the age of Seth, the age of the first Sethians, and the present, in which the Sethians prepared for the return of their Messiah. After the end of time, the faithful, the Sons of the Light, would enter a *pleroma* [a fullness] superior to the places created by the Demiurge. Because "their kingdom isn't of this world". Arrived from elsewhere—'non-natives', as they would say—they would return to the side of the Father in a universe illuminated by four entities: Harmozel, Oroiael, Daveithai, and Eleleth (in the same way that the Judeo-Christians selected four angels—Michael, Raphael, Gabriel, and Oriel—and that the Catholics would place the four canonical Gospels under four symbols that doubled the names Mark, Matthew, Luke, and John: the eagle, the lion, the bull, and the man).

The Messiah Seth announced the return to the 'other world'. The race of Seth, Puech says of Seth's sons and their descendents, is 'another' race, a foreign or strange race in the strong senses of these terms.[8] (Stroumsa thinks that the famous Elisha ben Abuyah—who was condemned by Jewish orthodoxy at the beginning of the second century because he rejected the Talmud and therefore became *aher*, 'other', a 'stranger/foreigner', 'non-native'—was a member of the Sethians[9]. *Sperma eteron* translates *zera aher*.) This idea was shared by other Christian sects, including those devoted to Joshua/Jesus, whose adepts, to the great scandal of the Greeks and Romans—for whom all of the religions assumed their meaning within the citizen-cult of the State—displayed the greatest scorn for death and punishment because they were assured of rejoining the true kingdom of light. (Such was still the profession of faith of Justin the Apologist, condemned to death around 165).

The *Elenchos* quotes extracts from a Sethian cosmogony in which (as among the Naassenes) one can perceive a religious recuperation of Simon of Samaria's attempt to return the mythological inspiration of the Pentateuch to the human body. Here the cosmos was in the image of the belly of a pregnant woman.[10]

> In the earth, from the infinite seals are produced infinite crowds of various animals. But into all this infinity of the different animals under heaven is diffused and distributed, along with the light, the fragrance of the Spirit

from above. From the water, therefore, has been produced a first-begotten originating principle, viz., wind, (which is) violent and boisterous, and a cause of all generation. For producing a sort of ferment in the waters, (the wind) uplifts waves out of the waters; and the motion of the waves, just as when some impulsive power of pregnancy is the origin of the production of a man or mind, is caused when (the ocean), excited by the impulsive power of spirit, is propelled forward.

Note that, in a process that is the inverse of that of Simon and his cosmo-somatism, the *sperma* (sperm) becomes *pneuma* (spirit); the coupling of man and woman that creates the world gives way to religious allegory, to spiritualization. The Sethians called themselves *Pneumatics* in opposition to the Hylics (the sons of Cain) and the Psychics (the sons of Abel).

When, however, this wave that has been raised out of the water by the wind, and rendered pregnant in its nature, has within itself obtained the power, possessed by the female, of generation, it holds together the light scattered from above along with the fragrance of the spirit—that is, mind moulded in the different species. And this (light) is a Perfect God, who from the unbegotten radiance above, and from the spirit, is borne down into human nature as into a temple, by the impulsive power of Nature, and by the motion of wind. And it is produced from water being commingled and blended with bodies as if it were a salt of existent things, and a light of darkness. And it struggles to be released from bodies, and is not able to find liberation and an egress for itself. For a very diminutive spark, a severed splinter from above like the ray of a star, has been mingled in the much compounded waters of many (existences), as says he, (David) remarks in a psalm[11]. Every thought, then, and solicitude actuating the supernal light is as to how and in what manner mind may be liberated, by the death of the depraved and dark body, from the Father that is below, which is the wind that with noise and tumult uplifted the waves, and who generated a perfect mind his own Son; not, however, being his peculiar (offspring) substantially. For he was a ray (sent down) from above, from that perfect light, (and) was overpowered in the dark, and formidable, and bitter, and defiled water; and he is a luminous spirit borne down over the water. When, therefore, the waves that

> have been upreared from the waters have received within themselves the power of generation possessed by females, they contain, as a certain womb, in different species, the infused radiance, so as that it is visible in the case of all animals. But the wind, at the same time fierce and formidable, whirling along, is, in respect of its hissing sound, like a serpent.

Note that the winged serpents are the *seraphim* (seraphs). As among certain Naassenes of the ascetic tendency, the Redeeming Serpent was opposed to the Serpent of Lust. Here the womb was impure, which was the inverse of the Simonian conception.

> First, then, from the wind—that is, from the serpent—has resulted the originating principle of generation in the manner declared, all things having simultaneously received the principle of generation. After, then, the light and the spirit had been received, he says, into the polluted and baneful [and] disordered womb, the serpent—the wind of darkness, the first-begotten of the waters—enters within and produces man, and the impure womb neither loves nor recognizes any other form. The perfect Word of supernal light being therefore assimilated (in form) to the beast, (that is,) the serpent, entered into the defiled womb, having deceived (the womb) through the similitude of the beast itself, in order that (the Word) may loose the chains that encircle the perfect mind which has been begotten amidst impurity of womb by the primal offspring of water, (namely,) serpent, wind, (and) beast. This, he says, is the form of the servant, and this the necessity of the Word of God coming down into the womb of a virgin. But he says that it is not sufficient that the Perfect Man, the Word, has entered into the womb of a virgin, and loosed the pangs which were in that darkness. Nay, more than this was requisite; for after his entrance into the foul mysteries of the womb, he was washed, and drank of the cup of life-giving bubbling water. And it was altogether needful that he should drink who was about to strip off the servile form, and assume celestial raiment.

It would suffice for the sects devoted to Joshua/Jesus to translate this myth into a legend of virginal birth, now embellished as a familial saga. Likewise, the triad Light, Pneuma, and Darkness—*alias* the Father, the Mother (or the feminine Spirit, the *Sophia*/Wisdom), and the Son— would engender future Arian and Catholic speculations on the Trinity.

The library of Nag Hammadi contains a Sethian text titled the *Epistle of Eugnostos*. It clearly expresses ideas that the Joshua/Jesus sects of the second and third centuries had no scruples about exploiting and recuperating in the name of their mythic hero.

> The First who appeared before the universe in infinity is Self-grown, Self-constructed Father, and is full of shining, ineffable light. In the beginning, he decided to have his likeness become a great power. Immediately, the principle [or beginning] of that Light appeared as Immortal Androgynous Man. His male name is 'Begotten, Perfect Mind'. And his female name is 'All-wise Begrettress Sophia'. It is also said that she resembles her brother and her consort. She is uncontested truth; for here below, error, which exists with truth, contests it.
>
> Through Immortal Man appeared the first designation, namely, divinity and kingdom, for the Father, who is called 'Self-Father Man' revealed this. He created a great aeon for his own majesty. He gave him great authority, and he ruled over all creations. He created gods and archangels and angels, myriads without number for retinue.
>
> Now through that Man originated divinity and kingdom. Therefore he was called 'God of gods', 'King of kings'.
>
> First Man is 'Faith' ['pistis'] for those who will come afterward. He has, within, a unique mind and thought [...]. Afterward another principle came from Immortal Man, who is called 'Self-perfected Begetter'. When he received the consent of his consort, Great Sophia, he revealed that first-begotten androgyne, who is called, 'First-begotten Son of God'. His female aspect is 'First-begotten Sophia, Mother of the Universe', whom some call 'Love'. Now, First-begotten, since he has his authority from his father, created angels, myriads without number, for retinue. The whole multitude of those angels are called 'Assembly of the Holy Ones, the Shadowless Lights'. Now when these greet each other, their embraces become like angels like themselves.
>
> First Begetter Father is called 'Adam of the Light'. And the kingdom of Son of Man is full of ineffable joy and unchanging jubilation, ever rejoicing

in ineffable joy over their imperishable glory, which has never been heard nor has it been revealed to all the aeons that came to be and their worlds.

Then Son of Man consented with Sophia, his consort, and revealed a great androgynous Light. His masculine name is designated 'Savior, Begetter of All things'. His feminine name is designated 'Sophia, All-Begettress'. Some call her 'Pistis' [faith].[12]

To affirm that the messianic sects deformed the dogmatic message of Jesus and his apostles is to suppose that this orthodoxy existed in the first century, when in fact it was still in its infancy in the fourth and fifth Centuries. With a strange complacency with respect to ecclesial falsifications, many historians have preferred to ignore the stratification of successive syncretisms that—drawing upon the doctrines of the Sethians, Naassenes, Barbelites, Elchasaites, Nazarenes and others—ended up, under the name of Joshua, offering to the federated powers of the bishops a powerful shield and a universality that was required by their political projects of conquest and Empire.

The *Epistle of Eugnostos* was thus cut out, recomposed on the model of a dialogue between Jesus and his disciples, and given the title *Sophia of Jesus*.[13] (The prologue to the Canonical Gospel attributed to John was also inspired by Sethian texts.)

The Messiah Melchizedek

The Epistle to the Hebrews—attributed to Saul/Paul by the Catholics, to Barnabas by Tertullian, and to Apollos by Luther—linked the priesthood of the Messiah Joshua-Jesus to the priesthood of Melchizedek. According to Fitzmyer, this epistle was addressed to the Essenes[14].

Who was Melchizedek? For biblical mythology and for orthodox Jews he was a person of no little importance: a priest-king of Salem (Jerusalem). Essenean texts therefore treated him with veneration and credited him—as well as Adam and Seth (with whom he was sometimes confused)—with the vocation of Messiah.

Cave 11 at Qumran revealed a *midrash* in which Melchizedek was held to be the announcer of the Good News (otherwise known as the Gospels) and none other than the Messiah through whom salvation would come.[15] Hero of the battle of the Sons of Light against the Sons of Darkness, he vanquished Belial, the master of evil ("He who announces the Good News is the Messiah"[16]).

Melchizedek furthermore came to be associated with Michael, the head of the angels. Other characteristics that completed the sketch of the figure of Archangel Michael would be of great consequence for Christo-angelology. One gave to Melchizedek the name 'Michael' and it was to him that one connected Psalm 110: 1 and 4. He was invested with a cosmogonic function: he was the maintainer of the universe. According to Enoch 69: 14 sq: "This angel requested Michael to show him the hidden name, that he might enunciate it in the oath [...] and he placed this oath Akae in the hand of Michael. These are the secrets of this oath and they are strong through his oath: The heaven was suspended before the world was created, and for ever. And through it the earth was founded upon the water and from the secret recesses of the mountains come beautiful waters from the creation of the world and unto eternity"[17].

The *Zohar* makes this precise, moreover: "Everywhere you find mentioned Michael, who was the first of the angels, the Shekhina is suggested"[18]. The Shekhina (or Achamoth) is therefore none other than the Spirit, which is feminine in Hebrew and is figured under the traits of Sophia, Mariamne, Miriam, and Mary.

The Book of Enoch, which was dear to the Essenes, called Melchizedek the Son of Man, in accordance with the Book of Daniel, which was adopted by the sects devoted to Joshua/Jesus to describe their Messiah.[19]

Spanning from the second century before the Christian era to the first century that inaugurated it, the text of Enoch existed in three manuscript versions in the eleventh and twelfth Centuries: Greek, Ethiopian and Slavic. One can distinguish an orthodox Jewish redaction in which YHWH mercilessly punishes the two hundred watchers or *Egregores*, and an Esseno-Christian redaction in which God, having judged their fault to be pardonable, reconciles himself with them, a softening that—like the salvation accorded to Adam and the Serpent by the Sethians and Naassenes—suggests the appearance of a God of kindness who opposes his mercy to the intransigence of the God of Israel.

The miraculous birth of Melchizedek in Enoch foreshadowed that of

Joshua-Jesus: without the intervention of a carnal father, he was engendered by a woman (the Spirit, the Shekhina/Achamoth/Sophia, Mariamne/Miriam and, much later, the Virgin Mary). Following the Epistle to the Hebrews (7: 16), the Messiah endowed with the name Jesus "was not made according to the law of carnal order"[20].

Finally, Melchizedek, whose name, as we have seen, contained an allusion to justice (*tsedeq*), participated in the Essene thematic of the Master of Justice. The *Testament of Levi* says: "Then shall the Lord raise up a New Priest. | And to him all the words of the Lord shall be revealed; | And he shall execute a righteous judgement upon the earth for a multitude of days"[21].

One manuscript from Nag Hammadi pushes this identification much further: it evokes heavenly messengers who assign to Melchizedek his future role as great-priest and predict for him the destiny of a Messiah who is condemned to undergo torments so as to triumph over death.

At the end of the second century, the devotees of Melchizedek would disapprove of Theodote the Banker (*trapezetes* in Greek), with whom they nevertheless shared the belief in an Angel-Messiah, an *Angelos-Christos*. They estimated that it was Melchizedek and not Joshua-Jesus who was the superior angel. The quarrel would reappear in the fourth century with Arius, who, far from being an innovator, remained loyal to the old angel-Christology, which was permitted by the ensemble of the Christian sects until the second half of the second century.

Werner has demonstrated that Arius interpreted the Epistle to the Hebrews as proof of angel-Christology (Jesus as angel of the Savior) and that he was inspired by the argumentation of the followers of Melchizedek who, drawing from the same Epistle, reached the conclusion that the Christ, in terms of his essence and rank, was not above but below the heavenly angel Melchizedek[22].

Joshua/Jesus, Unknown Prophet and Syncretic Messiah

The creature whose crucified body and spirit of sacrifice have dominated two thousand years of an inhuman civilization pursued abstinence and abnegation to such an extent that he left no traces of his own passage through history.

Neither historians, philosophers, authors, nor polygraphs[23]—no one in the first century ever heard the hero of the evangelic novels speak. Pliny the Elder (who was nonetheless aware of the existence of the Nazarenes), Justus of Tiberias, Juvenal, Martial, Dio Chrysostom, Philo of Alexandria, Petronius—none of them knew anything about him.

Flavius Josephus, an attentive observer of a war of the Jews in which he collaborated with the Romans, mentioned Theudas, James, and Simon (the son of Judah of Gamala). But the least echo of the exemplary sacrificial gesture of a New Joshua—named 'Jesus' by the Greeks—never reached him, except through the intervention of a copyist who added, to a Slavic version of Josephus's text from the twelfth century, information about Jesus, the absence of which struck him as inadmissible to contemporary historians. The patriarch of Constantinople, Photios, showed more honesty, if not naivety, in this regard. Commenting on a copy of the *Chronicles of the Kings of the Jews*, which has been credited to Justus of Tiberias (Photios possessed the manuscript, which has since disappeared), Photios—in his *Myriobyblion* (108), a collection of analyses of 279 different texts that he had read—was indignant about the silence concerning Jesus on the part of an author who had only lived a few kilometers from Capernaum, a city famous in the sacred geography of the Church.[24]

The Qumran manuscripts spoke of Seth, Melchizedek, the Master of Justice. They said nothing about Jesus; we have only a kind of Messiah archetype and a text plagiarized by the Sermon on the Mount.

In the Epistle attributed to Barnabas—a Judeo-Christian text from end of the first century or the beginning of the second century that advocated the abandonment of Mosaic law, not only in its spirit but in its letter (circumcision of the heart must replace circumcision of the sexual organ)—Jesus was none other than Joshua, the son of Nun. Around 230–50, Origen, in his sermon on Joshua/Jesus, celebrated the timeless and exemplary glory of the biblical Joshua, whom he called Jesus.

In 135 (and not between 80 and 90), the Phariseean convention condemned the heresy of the *noisrim* or Nazarenes but knew nothing of a community leader named Jesus.

One must wait until the beginning of the second century to find an allusion to the *chrestianoi*, otherwise known as the followers of the

Messiah (*Chrestos* or *Christos* translates the Hebrew word 'Messiah'). Around 111, a letter from Pliny to Trajan asked the Emperor about the fate reserved for the *chrestianoi*—in all probability, the Elchasaites—who "had been coming to a meeting on a given day before dawn, and singing responsively a hymn to Christ as to God" (*Christo quasi Deo*)[25].

In the same epoch, Tacitus's *Annals* and, a little later, Suetonius speak not of Jesus but of *Chrestos*, the cause of agitation under Nero. But there did exist at the same time a quite historical *Chrestos* who preoccupied Emperor Hadrian and aroused the disapproval of Greco-Roman public opinion: the nationalist Messiah Bar Kokhba, the hero of the last insurrection of the Jewish people. Tacitus and Suetonius were not unaware that the Rome of Claudius and Nero had repressed many agitations of Jewish messianism that had been precipitated by the Zealot movement. The Elchasaite behavior described by Pliny in his letter to Trajan, regarding which Pliny was inclined to be lenient, did not justify the revulsion felt by Tacitus and Suetonius: their insulting commentaries were inspired much more by the insults that were being directed at the Jewish religion more generally at the time and by the contemporaneous rise of anti-Semitism.

Around 160, the Christ or Messiah of a Christian such as Justin the Apologist was not a historical individual. He was a God incarnated in the form of a man, martyred on earth, and returned to the divine essence of which he was the emanation (this was the doctrine of the *Angelos-Christos* that Catholicism would condemn much later under the name Docetism). The irony was that the conjecture about a prophet born from a man and a woman originally emanated from a Jew. Justin reported in his *Dialogue with Trypho the Jew*:

> Those who affirm that the Christ was a man, and that he was anointed and became the Christ by election, seem to me much closer to the truth than your doctrine. Because we Jews expect the Christ as a man born from a man, and that Elijah will come to anoint him when he has come. But if the one of whom you speak claimed to be the Christ, one must conclude that he was a man born from a man. Yet, since Elijah did not come to anoint him, I do not believe that he was the Christ.[26]

(Note that Marthe de Chambrun Ruspoli, who quotes Justin, adds: "It is perhaps in response to this argument that we read in the Gospels that Elijah returned in the person of John the Baptist"[27].)

And Trypho also objected: "And you, having accepted a groundless report, invent a Christ for yourselves, and for his sake are inconsiderably perishing"[28].

How can the historians be so little attached to the testimony of attested facts that they have accredited the Catholic and Roman fable of a historical Jesus, when for Justin (a Saint and martyr, according to the Church) he was still an *Angelos-Christos*, and when Jesus possesses neither family nor history in the letters of Saul/Paul, whom Marcion was in turn the first person to mention?

In a challenge to the forgeries of Eusebius of Caesarea and 'the Church Fathers', the Emperor Julian—who in 350 or so wrote his *Against the Galileans* (as a precaution it was later destroyed, except for several quotations)—found himself justified in stating: "But if you can show me that one of these men is mentioned by the well-known writers of that time,—these events happened in the reign of Tiberias or Claudius,—then you may consider that I speak falsely about all matters"[29]. Julian obviously did not speak falsely.

On the other hand, in the fourth century, Jerome—a saint according to the Church—worked towards the truth by disseminating the letters that Seneca exchanged with Paul, proving that the author of the epistles (like the adventures imagined by the Acts of the Apostles) had an historical and dogmatic existence well before Marcion's discovery of it. (The question of the Gospels that, canonical or apocryphal, were only *Kultlegende*[30] to Soden[31] will be examined later in this book.)

Today it seems as though the historians, finally perceiving the enormity of the official lie, are now devoted to evoking a plausible, historical Jesus, notwithstanding the first two centuries in which he played the role of Angel-Messiah: a spark imprisoned in a body that freed itself from death and returned to God. Not ignoring the character of the 'pious fables' (cf. Loisy, Bultmann, Guillermin, and Schweitzer) that exoterically translated the elements of the myth, these historians draw from the New Testament—the texts of which were revised as late as the fourth century—information that is then coupled with events from the very first decade of the first century. Brandon thus advances the idea that Jesus was a Zealot crucified between two *lestoi* or brigands, which was the term Flavius Josephus used to describe the anti-Roman guerrillas[32]. In order to win the good graces of Rome, the Pauline school made a pacifist of the martyr who was crucified by the Jews (rather than by the Romans). As for Robert Amberlain—who bases his argument on the crucifixions of James and Simon (the sons of Judah of Gamala)—he infers that Jesus was their father and also a Zealot[33].

Elements of a Forgery

The seventy-odd canonical and apocryphal scriptures that were elaborated for the greater glory of the Messiah Jesus illustrate in an exemplary manner a remark by Robert Graves: "Almost all were explanations of ritual or religious theory, overlaid with history: a body of instruction corresponding with the Hebrew Scriptures and having many elements in common with them"[34].

Such a large number of elements entered into the fabrication of the historical Jesus that accounting for all of them would require several volumes and a quantity of energy that I would personally prefer to invest in more passionate matters. I will therefore content myself with recalling only the most obvious.

The only Jesuses known in the first century were the biblical Joshua, son of Nun, and Jesus ben Sirach, whose name appears in a book of wisdom.

The myth of Joshua carried a double eschatology: a national salvation recalled by the River Jordan—beyond which the successor of Moses led his people—and a universal salvation (because the crossing of that heavenly river, or the baptismal immersion in its waters, was accomplished without encountering any resistance from the kingdom of the Father). The syncretism born from the Zealot opposition to the Roman occupiers founded the preoccupations of the Zealots, Essenes, and Nazarenes in a universal eschatology. The reincarnation of the *Tsedeq*, the Just One martyred around 63 BCE, was revived in the crucifixion of James and Simon of Gamala—brothers or witnesses of God according to a midrashic expression that was reprised by the Apocalypse attributed to John.

In *Revolution in Judea*[35], Maccoby supposes that Barabbas and Jesus were actually one person: the first of the two, put to death as a 'bandit', was a political symbol of the second. I myself am inclined to examine the meanings of the two names: Bar Abbas, Son of the Father, and Joshua/Jesus, 'God saved, saves, will save'. Especially since a Naassene sect clearly evoked the trinity of Kalakau, or Adam, the man from on high; Salasau, the mortal man from below; and Zesar, the River Jordan that flows towards the high and that Adam deposed through the terrestrial suffering that was overcome in order to return to the Father.

It was still Joshua, the Jordan, and the soul imprisoned in matter that was described by a Naassene hymn transcribed in the *Elenchos* (book 5, chapter 5):

But Jesus said, Father, behold,
A strife of ills across the earth
Wanders from thy breath (of wrath);
But bitter Chaos (man) seeks to shun,
And knows not how to pass it through.[36]

At the instigation of Cyprian, the Bishop of Carthage, who died in 258, the Catholics referred to the *Sophia Iesou uiou Seirach* (the *Wisdom of Jesus, Son of Sira*)[37]—the last book of wisdom to figure in the Bible of the Seventy—as the *Ecclesiasticus liber* (or Ecclesiasticus). Written on the eve of the Maccabees' uprising, this work enjoyed a great reputation among the Zealots.

In the words of this book of wisdom, "he who is practiced in the Law will come to Wisdom". As for Wisdom herself: "Motherlike she will meet him, like a young bride she will embrace him, | Nourish him with the bread of learning, and give him the water of understanding to drink"[38]. As in all the Gnostic and Christian developments, this *Sophia*, who was simultaneously mother, wife, and virgin, ruled at the side of God and communicated her knowledge (her *gnosis*) to the Sons of Israel so that they could be saved. But her remarks encompassed more than just the Hebrew people. She meant to found an alliance in which God would encounter Israel in order to promote the order that would permit all of humanity to accede to salvation.

Thus the Essenean sects referred to a New Alliance (*Novum testamentum* in Latin), the universal message of which the Master of Justice would express through his return.

In his study of Lilith, Jacques Brill pertinently remarks with respect to the *Sophia Iesou uiou Sirach*: "The author is represented in it as a child whose marvelous deeds and gestures illustrate wisdom, in the same manner in which the deeds and gestures of Jesus are treated in the *Gospels of Childhood*"[39].

The Virgin wife and mother, the child nourished by divine wisdom—did they not offer to prophetic imaginations and to commentators on community rules elements sufficient for an anecdotal staging that would facilitate access to simple souls? The clumsy and confused didacts of the Hebrew and Aramaic *midrashim* easily found among Greek authors a novelistic form that pleased the people. The *Homilies of Peter*, the *Pastor of Hermas*, the Acts, and the apocryphal and canonical Gospels were all literary fictions with apologetic pretensions.

Before the creation of the staging and imagery that were used to illustrate certain allegories and symbols, there seems to have existed other compilations of wisdom that continued the saga of Jesus ben Sirach. This was the case with a work discovered at Nag Hammadi: *The Secret Sayings of Jesus*, which the Catholics later called the *Gospel of Thomas*[40].

The idea of Jesus developed from a tradition of wisdom that had opportunely given the Angel-Messiah a doubled human and divine nature. Here was sketched out the figure of the insurgent, the audacious thinker, and the philosopher proffering the truths of biblical morality, with which Jewish orthodoxy, ensconced in its sacerdotal rituals, did so little. The *Sophia* that was dispensed under his name served as a guide for the leaders of the Nazarene and Ebionite communities; it also bestowed upon them the authority of the master, which accrued to his disciples, witnesses, and brothers in spirit.

Other compilations of wise remarks made by Jesus ben Sirach had been disseminated ever since the second century, when Basilides stated that he'd received from Matthew the secret doctrines of the Savior—

the name Jesus being confounded therein with the saving role of the *Sophia*-Spirit. There existed under the name Matthew, *alias* Levi, both an apocryphal Gospel and a Gospel revised according to the Catholic canon.

The hypothetical conjunction of a sage born from the book of Jesus ben Sirach and the *Angelos-Christos* named Joshua is confirmed when one finds out that, around 100–10, the Christian Gnostic Satornilus of Antioch, who was the first to found his doctrine on the name of Jesus, established a distinction between a just and wise man named *Iesou*, on the one hand, and the Messiah or *Christos*—the intelligence of the transcendent God that united with him when he became an adult—on the other.

To the warrior Joshua, who prophesied the reconquest of Palestine, was added Joshua the Sage, who summoned men to the incarnation of the *Sophia*-Spirit that would conduct them to salvation. And to that amalgam was added the Adamic Joshua, the double of Melchizedek/Michael.

"From the start, the entire trajectory of Joshua/Jesus rests upon the Christianity of resurrection and salvation", Dubourg writes[41].

The *Gospel of the Ebionites* spoke of the final union of the Holy Spirit (the *Sophia*) with Jesus, the last of the prophets. And, according to the *Gospel of the Hebrews*: "the Holy Spirit [...] said to him: My son, in all the prophets was I waiting for thee that thou shouldest come and I might rest in thee"[42]. At the end of the first century, the Ebionites, Cerinthians, and Nazarenes managed to impose a syncretic and prestigious name of such a nature as to put an end to the quarrels over Messiahs into which had been mixed *NHS* the Serpent, Barbelo the Essential Woman, Sophia, Seth, and Melchizedek the Master of Justice (sometimes symbolized by another sign of messianic rallying, the sixth letter of the Hebrew alphabet *WAW*).[43] (Hermetic thought and magical practices were manifested in a number of sects in which abounded talismans and *abraxas* stones engraved with signs of power: *IAW, WAW, WW*, with the sign *W* transcribing the omega and the litany of the seven vowels. Jung was able to identify Jesus with *lapis*, 'stone', in latter-day alchemical texts.)

After the collapse of Palestine in 70, the warrior Joshua ceded place to his divine transcendence, to his spiritual *alter ego*. Having lost the war, he propagated in people's hearts a message of hope that was less contingent, more generously universal, and prudently timeless: 'God saved, saves, will save'. The meaning of the Name left no doubt.

Ptolemy writes "Him they also speak of under the name of Saviour, and Christ, and patronymically, Logos, and Everything, because He was formed from the contributions of all"[44].

Even the canonical Gospel placed under the name of Matthew did not dream of concealing it: "She will bear a son, and you shall call his name Jesus, for he will save his people from their sins" (Gospel attributed to Matthew, 1: 21).

Up to the end of the second century and even beyond, this Joshua/Jesus was none other than the Spirit-*Sophia* of God incarnated in the suffering of terrestrial existence, overwhelmed by death, resurrected, and then returned to the place of his divine origin.

For Justin the Apologist, the Christ was identified with the *Sophia* or the *Logos* described by Philo of Alexandria: "God engendered from himself a form of power and a rational beginning—preceding all of his works—whom he also called the Holy Spirit, the glory of the Savior, and, at other times, the Son, or sometimes Wisdom or the Angel of God or the Savior or Logos. He sometimes calls himself 'commander in chief' when he appears in the human form of Joshua, the Son of Noun"[45].

In the second century, the Christian Jew Aristo of Pella erected the Messiah with the divine name as the co-creator of the universe. His *Dialogue of Jason and Papiscos*, cited by Origen (*Contra Celsum*, book 4, chapter 52), stated that the first verse of Genesis had to be read "In filio Deus facit coelum et terram" ("God made the heavens and the earth in the person of his Son"[46]).

Even the canonical Gospel attributed to Matthew, despite being purged more than once of its Judeo-Christian and Gnostic residues, conserved the idea of a Son of Man who co-created the world with God: "When the Son of Man comes in his glory, and all the angels with him, then he will sit on his glorious throne. Before him will be gathered all the nations" (Gospel attributed to Matthew, 25: 31–2). We still cite the Jewish liturgical fragments of the *Constitution of the Apostles*, in which the Savior was simultaneously the Son, *Sophia*, *Logos*, Great Priest and Angel of the Great Council.

Henri Corbin writes:[47]

> It is the anthology of *christos-angelos* that requires reproduction here. In general, the question is so rarely present in the minds of our contemporaries that we ourselves must select a few references concerning the broad traits. There is the Christology of the Judeo-Christians and the Ebionites, for whom the *Christos* that descended upon Jesus at the moment of his baptism in the Jordan was one of the Archangels, who had power over the [other] angels and the creation in general, and who was the lord of the future *Aion*, as Satan was the lord of the current *Aion*. There were the Elchesaites (descended from the preceding sects), for whom the *Christos* appeared as an angel of immense stature and masculine sex, and revealed the Book to the founder of the sect, and who was accompanied by a feminine angel, his sister, who was the holy Angel-Spirit (*ruah* is feminine in the Semitic languages). Among the Valentinians, the *Christos* was an angel from the pleroma. In the Gnostic book of the *Pistis Sophia* and in the 'Books of Jeu', there was a *Christos-Gabriel*. And there was the *Pastor of Hermas*, which belonged to Judeo-Christian literature and in which the figure of the Archangel—or, rather, the figure of the *Christos-Michael*—was the dominant figure. In a very old treatise titled *Of the Triple Fruit of the Christian Life*, the *Christos* was one of the seven archangels created from the fire of the seven evangelic princes (*ex igne principum septem*). In the Book of the Ascension of Isaiah, there was the *Angelos-Christos* and the holy Angel Spirit.

A multiform Joshua, a son of the Virgin *Sophia*, a *Logos*, an *Angelos-Christos*, an author of wise remarks, an Adam who was the co-creator of the world—the Messiah was all of these things, but he was not the son of Joseph and Mary who was born in Bethlehem, preached the Good News, healed the lame, aided the widows and orphans, and succumbed to the wickedness of the Jews because he preferred humankind to Israel.

Nevertheless, the Catholic Church would describe as a "heretical perversion" the Christian vision that served as the basis for the instauration of its temporal and spiritual Church.

It is true that there existed an ecclesial Christology that inspired the mysterious Saul/Paul and his school to ordain the political project of their Churches. There was a crucified person—the victim not of the Jews but of the Judeans, and already quite dead in 63 BCE. But time means nothing to history when it comes to mythical matters. This crucified person contrasted sharply with the disorder of the wandering prophets and their partisans. Was it not assured (*Hymn* XVIII, 14–5) that God gave him the mission of being, "according to his truth, the one who announces the Good News [in the time] of his Goodness, evangelizing the humble ones according to the abundance of His mercy, [watering them] at the source of holiness, and consoling those who are contrite of spirit and afflicted"[48]?

Whereas the "Songs of the Savior" from Isaiah declared:

> The Spirit of the Lord GOD is upon me,
> because the LORD has anointed me
> to bring good news to the poor,
> he has sent me to bind up the brokenhearted[.][49]

And again, in the same text, there was this foreshadowing of the Annunciation of the Virgin Mary:

> The LORD called me from the womb,
> from the body of my mother he named my name.[50]

And his betrayal by some of his own disciples:

> And the men of my Council being in revolt
> And murmuring nearby
> And the mystery that You have concealed in me,
> They calumny among the sons of the unhappy.[51]

This Messiah was tailor-made for the men of power who were resolved to impose their authority on other communities—to federate the Churches, even—by nourishing the dream of one day offering Rome a State religion.

The true founders of the monarchal Churches would be Marcion and the 'Paul' whose letters he exhibited. But Marcion discredited himself through a tactical blunder. Blinded by his anti-Semitism, he rejected the Old Testament as a whole. He went even further: he undermined the very foundations of the temporal Church by imputing the creation of the world to a deranged and bloodthirsty God, to a Demiurge whose work reached such levels of perversity that there was nothing more urgent than renouncing it by rejoicing in the beyond presided over by a Good and Unknowable God.

The bishops of Smyrna, Carthage, Rome, Lyon, Antioch, and Alexandria suspected that they would not increase their control over the popular and aristocratic mindsets of the world if they professed a total disdain for terrestrial and corporeal matter. They invented a carnal Jesus who had both his feet on the ground: while he undoubtedly assumed divine grace and was invested with a salvific role, he nonetheless carried himself like any other human creature. He would be a God who shared the common existence—the temptations and weaknesses—of the humble people. The popular Christianity of the New Prophecy greatly contributed to the painting of this portrait of the Savior.

A proletarian on account of his father being a (slightly silly) carpenter, he could claim an incontestably divine ancestry by way of his mother, Mary the Virgin (who was *Sophia*, Mariamne), while his divine consort [*parèdre*], Prunicos the prostitute, became Mary Magdalene.

Mary herself is not a recent invention. In *Le Retour du phénix*, Marthe de Chambrun Ruspoli notes that, according to the old Egyptian religion, "TUM, in his capacity as Creator, sent across the abyss the soul of his Son, the Word, whom he engendered by himself from his own substance. And he pronounced these words: 'Is made flesh' (text from the Merenre Pyramid, line 97, discovered by Gaston Maspero). And the Spirit (Thoth), crossing the abyss to the earth, stopped before the sycamore at the feet of which stood NOUT, the Virgin. He made the divine germ penetrate her womb"[52].

Alexandria and Upper Egypt was an old crucible for speculations concerning the female Spirit, who was much later made virile by an angel procreating the New Joshua.

Why was Jesus supposedly born in Bethlehem? Because the biblical text Micah (5: 2) declared:

> But you, O Bethlehem Ephrathah,
> who are too little to be among the clans of Judah,
> from you shall come forth for me
> one who is to be ruler in Israel[.]

The cave and the date 25 December—borrowed from the mythology of Mithra—both accorded with the policy of recuperating the competing cults, whose references were Christianized.

And so it is with the symbolism of the bread and the wine, which was borrowed in the second century from the rituals of Attis and thereafter replaced the Essenean Eucharistic banquet, in which sharing bread and water simply reinforced the commensality that united the members of the same community.

The Passion (from *patiri*, 'to suffer') drew its inspiration from the torments of the Servant of the Savior that were reported in the Book of Isaiah and brought up to date in the epic of the Master of Justice, a suffering and glorious Messiah.

Nazareth, a market town that did not exist before the fourth century, was anecdotally substituted for the term 'Nazarene', which designated the sect that had invented the syncretic doctrine of the Joshua-Savior. The mention of Nazareth in a text, be that text apocryphal or canonical, clearly indicates that the revision dates from the era of Nicaea [325 CE] at the earliest.

The Messiah was killed on the Mount of Olives because Zacharias cited it as the place where the great miracle would be accomplished.[53]

The couple or syzygy of Mary and Mary Magdalene reproduced the doubling of the Virgin *Sophia* and the prostitute Prunicos, the latter being the former's form after she had fallen and been imprisoned in matter. The miracles popularly attributed to Apollonius of Tyana enriched the imagery of the therapeutic Messiah, whose life achieved its end at thirty-three years, in perfect accord with the number that signified purification among the Jews.

The third century began to invent for Jesus a childhood in which his mother, *Sophia*-Mary, was endowed with a morganatic husband. The idea of the cross came from a symbol in the works of Justin. In his *Apology* (chapter 60) he noted that in "the physiological discussion concerning the Son of God in the *Timæus* of Plato, where he says, 'He placed him crosswise in the universe', he [Plato] borrowed [...] from Moses [...]. Which things Plato read[,] [without] accurately understanding, and [without] apprehending that it was the figure of the cross"[54].

The instauration of a State religion in Nicaea in 325 *ad majoram Dei gloriam*[55] endowed the Truth with a dogma and an army finally determined to impose it on all of humanity. The Church, securing to its advantage the fluctuating power of the emperors, extended itself into those territories where the *pax romana* had buried the local civilizations under the rockslide of its authority.

Orthodoxy invented a past for itself and, having selected its doctrines from the purified and rewritten works of such thinkers as Paul, Justin, Clement, and Irenaeus, it condemned as heretical perversions the varieties of Christianity that had preceded it and from which it had extracted the rudiments of its theology. The predecessors of Jesus, of his apostles and his faithful, were thus condemned to the contempt and silence of the Jewish, Catholic, Protestant, and atheist historians, all of whom fell to their knees before the testimony of the New Testament—the effervescence of three centuries, the pleasant state of which Bernard Dubourg has summarized thus:

> All of the Gnostics, who squabbled and gutted each other on occasion, were Jews or Samaritans, as were the primitive Christians. Like the evangelists and the (pseudo-?) Paul who invented/discovered 'Jesus/Joshua', they all sculpted heaps of narrative, visionary, allegorical and eschatological (but especially not historical!) monuments; and all of them, by way of *midrash*, chiseled these monuments upon the unique basis of the same and unique Hebrew Bible. This meant that they recognized it and knew it (as sacred): because long and hard would be the battle between (and among) the Gnostics, orthodox Samaritans, Phariseean Jews, Sadducees, Essenes, Zealots and primitive Christians over the sacredness of the respective books of the

Bible. There would be brawls over Ezekiel, Enoch, the Canticle of Canticles, etc.—brawls over the beginning of the book of Genesis. And so many texts were discarded, excommunicated and buried in the *genizoth* (see the Dead Sea manuscripts).[56]

CHAPTER NINE

The Messianic Sects of Joshua/Jesus: Nazarenes, Ebionites, Elchasaites

At the confluence of Essenism, Samaritanism, and the baptist movement of Dunstan/Dositheos were formed sects in which a certain communality of doctrine and practice did not exclude rivalries and struggles for power. Their conjunction, no doubt precipitated by the Zealot insurrection, ended in the consecration of a syncretic Messiah invested with the secret name 'God saves', in whom was incarnated the long line of prophets 'anointed by Adonai' and persecuted for their untimely revelations.

All distinguished themselves by a rigorous asceticism; scorn for material goods, the body, women, and pleasure; recourse to the purifying and initiating rite of baptism; the foundation of communities or *Ecclesiai* (Churches); the propagation of the doctrine of two roads—one of Light and the other of Darkness—which was sometimes extended to a cosmic opposition between a Good God and a God who created a bad world; and the expectation of a Messiah or, more exactly, his return, because (having been sent by the Good God) he had been pitilessly put to death by the priests of the Temple of Jerusalem or their henchmen. The redemption promised by this Angel-Messiah would spread his grace to all of humanity, compensating the just and punishing the wicked.

Hostile to both the Sadducees and the Pharisees, these sects accommodated themselves to the philosophical speculations of Philo of Alexandria. His Judaic monotheism actually provided *gnosis* with a kind of safe-conduct, of which the supposed Fathers of the Church did not fail to take advantage. On the other hand, they execrated with perfect unanimity the Great Power of life that the works of Simon of Samaria had illustrated.

Nazarenes and Ebionites

Pliny the Elder, recopying reports drafted on the orders of Emperor Augustus by one of his generals, Marcus Agrippa, indicates in book 5 of his *Natural History* that not far from Apamea, in Syria, Nazarenes lived in a city called Bambyx, Hierapolis, or Mabog.

Marcus Agrippa having died in 12 BCE, Dubourg situates his historical investigations into the Nazarenes between 30 and 20. Accounting for the lapse of time required for the establishment in Syria of a sect born in Palestine, Dubourg judges plausible the presence of a Nazarene current around 50 BCE[1].

Initially a priest-warrior who consecrated to YHWH a life of piety and austerity, the nazir thereafter designated a man devoted to God by a vow of nazireat. This word suggested a connection with 'Nazoreans' or 'Nazarenes': 'the observers, the conservers'.

Aligned with the rigorous faction of Judaism and hostile to both the Sadducees and the Pharisees, the Nazarenes placed themselves in the general line of Essenism, of which they may have formed a community or Church. The Greek authors of the Acts of the Apostles, who compiled and rewrote ancient *midrashim* in order to reconcile the schools of Simon/Paul and Simon Cephas, staged a Jewish orthodoxy that vituperated the *hairesis ton nazoraion*—that is, the heresy of the Nazarenes.

The Phariseean rabbis knew them under the name *noisrim* and declared them to be heretics (*aher*, 'others'), not in 90 as is often claimed but in 135, when—after the revolt of the Messiah Bar Kokhba, which they refused to join—the legend of a Joshua/Jesus who was a pacifist and respectful of the Romans was born.

Bar Kokhba stigmatized the Nazarenes in his letters under the name 'Galileans'. In the second century, Hegesippus referred to one of the Jewish sects of his time in this way, but for Emperor Julian (331–63), cited by Cyril of Alexandria, 'Galilean' was still a synonym for 'Christian'. Moreover, several texts designated the Messiah Jesus by the word 'Galilean'.

Like the other anti-Judean Jewish sects, the Nazarenes did not escape the Zealot wildfire. Only their refusal to rally themselves to the troops of Bar Kokhba around 133–5 exonerated them from the reproach of violence and haloed them with the same pacifism by which the Greco-Roman Christian communities distinguished themselves from 'Semitic fury'.

Derived from Jewish extremism, Nazarenism paradoxically opened the door to an incessant revision of the Mosaic message and law. Their *midrashim*, which were disseminated in the assemblies of believers, laid the groundwork for the coming of the Messiah that Israel had invoked in the thick of the troubles of the war, corrected the prophecies of the past (adapting them to the modernity of the circumstances), and thereby formed the streams of the foreseeable torrent that would swell the Good News announced by the Hymns of the Master of Justice.

One would be deceiving oneself if one gave to Nazarenism a unity that contradicted the echoes of the quarrels between their leaders, whose names have been preserved: Theudas/Thomas the Egyptian, Jacob/James, Simon Cephas, John the Essene, Zacchaeus/Clement, Barnabas, Saul also known as Paul, and Jochanaan also known as John the Baptist.

A sect of the Ebionites, still active in the fourth century, was certainly derived from the *ebyonim* ('poor people') who had laid the foundations among the Essenes for voluntary poverty—the perilous virtues of which the Messalians, Waldensians, Beghards, Fraticelles, and Apostolics would later rediscover.

The Nazarenes, or at least the tendency for which Jochanaan represented the only prophetic authority, perpetuate themselves to this very day in Mandaeism, which is still alive between the Tigris and Euphrates. Their name means 'those who know'—the 'Gnostics'. They were also known as the 'Christians of Saint John', meaning Jochanaan/John the Baptist. Their doctrines, which arrived late in the day and have been clarified by an abundant literature (*Ginza* or *Treasure*, subdivided into a 'Right Ginza' and a 'Left Ginza'), formed a syncretism in which were mixed Judeo-Christian, Iranian, and Babylonian elements.

The Mandaeans claimed for themselves Hibil (Abel), Shitil (Seth), Anosh (Enoch), and John the Baptist, and formed one of the branches of Nazarenism, which, in search of a unique Messiah, rejected the accord established by the partisans of James, Simon/Peter and Saul/Paul under the name Joshua/Jesus, because, according to them, Anosh had shown that Jesus was a false prophet.

Elchasaites
In the third year of Trajan's reign, around 100–1, Nazarenism seemed to give way to a new generation of Christians: the Elchasaites. (Note that the diversity of the names need not confuse us. The 'Sampseans', whom Hegesippus called the 'Nasbotheans', only offer variants of the expression *seô ayya*, which means 'the Baptized'.) A sacred book was delivered to the prophet Elchasai, the head of a Christian community, by two angels, one male (the Son of God), the other female (the Holy Spirit)—which no doubt justified the investigation conduced by Pliny the Younger, the papal legate of Bithynia. The *Homilies of Peter* counted among their writings, at least in its original versions. The Elchasaites also constituted a Christianity that was different from the opinions that the Catholics of the fourth century tried to impose. This is why Epiphanius of Salamis—who was being ironic in his *Panarion* when he said of the Elchasaites, "Not being Christians, Jews, or pagans, but something of an intermediary; at base they are nothing"[2]—showed *a contrario* that they were in fact simultaneously Jews, Christians and pioneers of a Greco-Roman Christianity. (The Church, however, would attribute that pioneering role to the enemy of the Elchasaites, Saul/Paul, after it had snatched him from the hands of his discoverer, Marcion).

Did not Elchasaitism, with its real or mythical prophet—'Elchasai' is related to the Aramaic word *Ieksaï*, which means 'Hidden Savior'—foreshadow the great current of popular Christianity that, under the name New Prophecy, obeyed the Christ reincarnated in the prophet Montanus? It is difficult to come to a clear view on this question on the basis of the comings-and-goings of the various sects, prophets and apostles who clashed with the mainstream fanaticism of the accepted truths. The ancestors of the Mandaeans rejected Joshua/Jesus, while the respective partisans of James and Peter—who were hostile to Jochanaan, also known as John the Baptist—somehow managed to denounce the imposture of Saul/Paul, whose disciples in turn held Peter to be a traitor and renegade. Those who were faithful to Jude/Thomas triumphed at Edessa, but they did so without attracting a unanimous veneration for their master, because certain people saddled him with the role of Judas. Add to this the fact that Elchasaitism, which was hostile to Marcion and active in Rome with Alcibiades of Apamea, witnessed the birth of Mani, the future founder of a religion and the clear inspiration for the dogmas of Marcion.[3]

(Note that Mani, who was raised in an Elchasaite community, reprised the Samaritan titles 'Unique Envoy' and 'True Prophet'. The 'Unique Envoy' was an old Judeo-Samaritan name for the principal agent of God ("The Spirit of the Lord GOD is upon me, | because the LORD has anointed me | to bring good news to the poor": Isaiah 61: 1). This was also the status of the Master of Justice and Joshua/Jesus, which could have been claimed by all of the inspired prophets—by Elchasai as much as Montanus. One understands why Catholicism accorded exclusivity to Jesus, the only 'True Messiah', and why it prohibited any competition on pain of death.)

CHAPTER TEN

Quarrels about Prophets and Apostles: Jochanaan, Theudas/Jude/Thomas, Jacob/James, Simon-Peter, Barnabas, and Saul/Paul

If history did not preserve the least trace of someone named Jesus, his inventors and worshippers—disguised over the course of time as his brothers, companions, witnesses, disciples, or apostles—can easily be revealed by random testimonials from the first century. So it goes with John the Baptist, Thomas, James the Just, Simon Cephas, and Barnabas.

Paradoxically, regarding Paul—the best known, and the one upon whom biographers have expounded with the greatest gullibility—there remains almost nothing of the epistles that, being in reality only brief notes, served as the doctrinal holdall for both the Marcionites and anti-Marcionites before they were cleansed, purified, and resharpened several times according to the rectified line of the fourth century.

Jochanaan, Also Called John the Baptist
In *Antiquities of the Jews*, drafted around 95, Flavius Josephus spoke of a preacher named John:

> [He] was a good man, and commanded the Jews to exercise virtue, both as to righteousness towards one another, and piety towards God, and so to come to baptism; for that the washing [with water] would be acceptable to him, if they made use of it, not in order to the putting away [or the remission] of some sins [only], but for the purification of the body [...].[1]

(Note here the connection with the Master of Justice, James the Just, Tsadoq, and Melchizedek.)

> [Many] others came in crowds about him, for they were very greatly moved [or pleased] by hearing his words [...].[2]

The Greek version of Josephus's *War of the Jews* (written around 90) doesn't mention Jochanaan. Two Slavic versions, written much later and unreliable, return to this person. One reads in the first version[3]:

> At this time there lived among the Jews a man of strange costume; he applied the hides of animals to every part of his body that wasn't covered by his own hair. In his face, he was similar to a savage.
> He went to the Jews and summoned them to freedom, saying: "God sent me so that I can show you the Path of the Law, by which you can deliver yourselves from many powerful people. And over you will reign not a mortal, but the Very High who sent me".
> And when the people heard this, they rejoiced. And he was followed all over Judea, the region in the vicinity of Jerusalem. And he did nothing more than plunge them into the waves of the Jordan and then send them away, saying to them that they should renounce their bad works and that they would be given a king who would emancipate them and subjugate anyone who rebelled against them, but that he [John] himself would not be submitted to anyone.
> Some blasphemed, others believed him. And when he had been led before [Herod] Archelaus, and when the doctors of the Law had been assembled, they asked him who he was and where he had been until then. He responded: "I am a man, the Spirit of God has led me, and I feed upon reeds, roots and carob".
> They threw themselves upon him to torture him if he did not renounce his words and acts, but he said: "It is for you to renounce your abominable works and become devoted to the Lord your God".
> And Simon, originally an Essenean scribe, arose in anger and said: "We read the divine books every day. But you, who come from the forest like a beast, you dare to instruct us and seduce the crowd with inflammatory

discourse". He hurried to punish him physically. But he punished them by saying: "I will not reveal to you the mystery that lives in you, since you haven't wanted it. Through this will come on you an inexpressible unhappiness, and it will be your fault".

After having spoken thus, he went to the other bank of the Jordan and, [since the others] no longer dared to molest him, he continued to act as before.

In the second Slavic version, Herod intervenes[4]:

> This man whom one called a savage came alone before him [Herod] in anger and said to him: "Why have you taken the woman of your brother, infamous one? Because your brother died a pitiless death, you too will be cut down by the celestial scythe. The decree of God will not be lifted, but you will perish miserably in a strange country. Because you do not keep the name of brother alive; instead, you satisfy your carnal passion [instead of procreating], because he already had four children [and wanted no more]".
>
> As soon as Herod heard this, he became angry and ordered him to be beaten and chased away. But he did not cease to accuse Herod everywhere that he found himself, until Herod had him seized and ordered that he be killed.
>
> His character was strange and his life wasn't human. He lived like a spirit without flesh. His lips never knew bread. Even at Easter he didn't eat unleavened bread, saying that it had been given in memory of God, who had delivered his people from servitude and had provided consolation because the road had been sorrowful. As for wine and intoxicating drinks, he didn't even let them near him. And he had a horror of all animals. He disapproved of all infractions, and he made use of carob.

An anti-nature fanatic, an ascetic moralist, and a hysterical and extreme imprecator, Jochanaan inscribed himself in a current that continues even today to oppose against the freedom of life a system of corporeal and spiritual occlusion that propagates morbidity and death. Depending on the circumstances, such dispositions can prove compatible with the resentment of the disinherited—in this case that of entire an people who had been subjected to Roman colonization and who erected their God as a timeless machine of war against the imperialist violence of the West.

According to the Slavic manuscripts, Jochanaan's rage at the people of the Temple did not spare the masters of the country. Jochanaan was presented to Archelaus, who was the Ethnarch of Judea, Samaria and Edom from 4 BCE to 5 CE and who decided to banish him. According to the evangelic legends, Jochanaan later succumbed to the blows of Herod Antipas, who was the Tetrarch of Galilee from 4 BCE to 38 CE.

The news raged along the Jordan that Joshua—a conqueror, a thaumaturge, a maker of miracles (he stopped the sun) and a leader of the Jewish people—had crossed over, had surpassed a limit that was inseparably terrestrial and celestial.

As in Essenism, his baptism symbolically liberated the soul from the 'stain of the body' and consecrated a penitential choice: the renunciation of the goods of the earth and the mortification of the flesh. The least pleasures horrified this holy man and he execrated the animals, whose sexual liberty offended his aggressive chastity. If he covered himself with animal skins, it was in order to resemble a certain Esau, who is mentioned in Genesis (25: 25–6).

The hostility of the Sadducees and Pharisees did not prompt any of the Essene factions to rally around him, because a Man of the Community named Simon (so famous that Josephus cited him) violently took him aside and vented the animosity that reigned between the saints or perfect ones—who were devoted to prayer and study—and the preachers of voluntary poverty or *ebyôn*, the Ebionites. Here it was a question of rival currents of Essenism, because Simon would never have associated himself with the sacerdotal aristocracy of the Temple, which was in fact made up of his worst enemies.

A deep hostility towards John the Baptist therefore persisted among the Nazarenes-Elchasaites from whom the *Homilies* emanated. For the Elchasaites, who were adepts of James the Just and Simon-Peter, John the Baptist incarnated the Messiah's adversary. A syzygy was situated within the antagonism between the Light and the Darkness: a syzygy between Jesus, the Son of Man and the good path, and Jochanaan, the Son of Woman and the path of evil.

Opposed to the Essenism of the communities—the subsistence of which was assured by agriculture in the form of various meats and wine, which enabled the neophytes to marry and to satisfy themselves with a sexuality reduced to occasional coitus and geared towards procreation— the wandering prophets extolled absolute dispossession and complete sexual continence: they stigmatized the 'laxity' of their co-religionists.

Another sect derived from Essenism, Mandaeism (from *manda*, 'gnosis'), held John the Baptist to be its founding apostle and, having rejected the false Messiah named Jesus, professed an equal scorn for both the Jews and the sectarians of the impostor 'denounced by Anosh' (that is to say, by Enoch).

In the very heart of Nazarenism, contradictory *midrashim* retraced the complexities of the quarrels of the prophets. The echoes of these Hebrew and Aramaic texts (today disappeared) resounded clearly even in the latter-day canonical Gospels, which translated into Greek writings whose allegorical and Semitic meanings escaped their redactors.

In the Gospel attributed to Luke, John the Baptist was not the mere herald of Jesus but the announcer of the end of time and the imminent kingdom of God. The works placed under the names of Mark and Matthew present John the Baptist as being equal in importance to Jesus, whom he baptized. Jesus recruits his partisans from among the Jochanaanites and only advances to the front of the mythological stage once his master has been decapitated. Herod, moreover, sees in Jesus the reincarnation of John the Baptist.

The Gospel attributed to John, on the other hand, greatly reduced John the Baptist's role. He was neither prophet nor Elijah, but only "the voice of one crying out in the wilderness"[5]; not the Light, but a witness to the Light.

Whence comes the question: the John who was proposed to be the author of a Gospel that was initially Gnostic (Naassene or Sethian)— wasn't he based on John the Essene whom Flavius Josephus mentions? As for the Apocalypse, which was a Jewish text transcribed in Greek and which was also attributed to a certain John under the title 'Revelations', it cited neither Jesus nor Jochanaan but evoked two "witnesses of God"[6] struggling against the Beast—that is to say, against Rome. Put to death, they remain three days without burial and are then resurrected up to the heavens. According to Josephus, there were two Jewish and anti-Judean leaders who were victims of the Roman occupation. They were Jacob/James and Simon, the sons of Judah of Gamala, who were the mythic witnesses to the Angel-Messiah who was summoned to lead the just to final victory (despite the terrestrial failure of 70) and to conquer the world in the name of a God who was more powerful than the bloody and boastful God YHWH.

Theudas/Jude/Thomas
In 45, in *Antiquities of the Jews* (book 20, 97–8)[7], Flavius Josephus cited the tumult caused by the "magician" Theudas ('magician' was a qualifier frequently synonymous with 'Egyptian' due to the great vogue for Hermeticism in Upper Egypt). (Note that there is, on the other hand, no trace—other than in the composite novel titled Acts of the Apostles[8]—of an agitator who went by the name of Stephen, who speculated on the Torah, invented *midrashim*, rose up against the people of the Temple, and claimed to be a just man who had been cruelly persecuted and who would return to the earth. This 'imaginary Stephen' fits a portrait that could have included the majority of the Essenean preachers, all of whom modeled themselves on the Master of Justice in the midst of a "messianic agitation that soon began and didn't end until Bar Kokhba"[9].)

In the words of Flavius Josephus,

> Now it came to pass, while Fadus was procurator of Judea, that a certain magician, whose name was Theudas, persuaded a great part of the people to take their effects with them, and follow him to the river Jordan; for he told them he was a prophet, and that he would, by his own command, divide the river, and afford them an easy passage over it; and many were deluded by his words. However, Fadus did not permit them to make any advantage of his wild attempt, but sent a troop of horsemen out against them; who, falling upon them unexpectedly, slew many of them and took many of them alive. They also took Theudas alive, and cut off his head, and carried it to Jerusalem.[10]

The Talmud identifies the Theudas mentioned by Josephus with Ben Stada, who promised his partisans that he would destroy the walls of Jerusalem as Joshua had destroyed those of Jericho[11].

Theudas also enjoyed the posthumous privilege of having furnished the names for at least two recruits to the evangelic legends of the apostles. Theudas (or Thaddeus) corresponded to Judah (or Judas), who was in fact none other than Thomas. There's no mystery as to why the Acts and Gospels mistakenly called Thomas 'the twin brother of Jesus': Thaddeus, Jude, and Thomas all mean 'twin', from which came the unfortunate expression employed by the Greek translators, who were unaware of the original meaning of the name and thus mistakenly surnamed Thomas 'Didymus' (*didumos*, 'twin').

While the Nazarene disciples of James and Simon-Peter established themselves in Antioch, those loyal to Theudas/Thomas spread in Edessa, where their communities founded a specific kind of Christianity before entering the syncretic wave of the years 90–100. At the beginning, each sect expressed the truth of its quest for a unique Messiah by placing itself under the patronage of an elder—a witness or a 'brother' of the Savior. The unification of the various Judeo-Christian currents engendered the legend of a group of apostles who were initially united (complete with differences, doubts and betrayals) around the Lord, the Adonai, who had descended to the earth.

By guaranteeing the separation of the waters of the River Jordan for the crowd of his partisans, Theudas/Jude/Thomas identified himself with Joshua. His crossing transmuted the waters of death into the waters of life. In the mythic and messianic spirit of the age, Joshua and Thomas were mentioned at the same time in the *Acts of Thomas* (the manuscript dates from the sixth century and no doubt transcribed a much older text): "And the Lord said to him: I am not Judas, who is also Thomas; I am his brother. And the Lord sat down on the bed"[12].

Thomas/Theudas was/were probably referred to by the *Gospel of the Egyptians*, in which the will to asceticism common to all Esseno-Baptism expressed itself violently: Jesus came to abolish the works of women and procreation, and thus to abolish the death that affects everything brought into the world. (Note that, outside of the Christian milieu, this idea also existed in several Hermetic groups in Alexandria. According to the *Poimandres* (18), "desire is the cause of death"[13]. Asclepius supported the contrary thesis.)

The same spirit was encountered in a text discovered at Nag Hammadi and popularized under the arbitrary name the *Gospel of Thomas*[14].

This work had points in common with the *Gospel of the Egyptians*, the *Acts of Peter*, the *Acts of Philip*, the canonical Gospels, the doctrines of the Naassenes, the Sethians, and the Enochians (*logion* 11), Essenism (*monachos* does not mean 'monk', as one might expect, but the 'perfect man', as in the texts from Qumran), Marcion (*logion* 32), Theodotus and Heracleon (*logion* 144), and the *Recognitiones*, which was a Latin (and later) version of the *Homilies*, 1.84 (*logion* 39).[15]

The text of the *Gospel of Thomas* included 118 *logia* or remarks attributed to Joshua/Jesus, dramatized in the form of brief dialogues between James, Thomas and Simon-Peter. Marked by a number of Semitisms, the text seems to have been a collection of rewritten, translated and sequenced *midrashim*. It manifestly inspired the authors of the canonical Gospels, who purged it of doctrinal archaisms and strengthened its ascetic rigor.

In a reversal of the real that typifies the inhuman essence of religion, the condemnation of desire and pleasure ends in the identification of the Holy Spirit with an abstract Mother—a Mother who gives life—even as actual women who bring children into the world are said to engender death. (Note that this is the sense—that is to say, the sense of being contrary to nature—in which Jesus was called "the living Jesus" in the work attributed to Thomas[16].) The Adamism of a return to paradise implied a total defleshing of sexuality. In paradise, man was neither male nor female but identical to a putatively asexual child. As soon as it ate the forbidden fruit of sensual pleasure its primitive unity was lost, and the result was a man different from the woman. Only a spiritual androgyny—the pure spirit of a body without desire or impulses—would return to this human being the disincarnated unity in which it had originated. This same speculation was illustrated in the *Gospel of the Egyptians*. Catholicism would condemn as heretical the frenzied asceticism that was practiced until the third century by adepts of the communities devoted to Jude/Thomas (this is perhaps the reason why the evangelic novels recognized by the Church execrate the double of the good Thomas: the informer named Judas).[17]

Jacob/James

In his *Church History* (book 2, chapter 1: 3–4), Eusebius of Caesarea cites an extract from the *Hypotyposes* of Titus Flavius Clemens, also known as Clement of Alexandria, who was born around 150 and died around 210. Clement was a Christian philosopher classified among the orthodox by the Catholics, but one whom the patriarch and theologian Photios I (820–55) judged to be impious and heretical in many of his opinions.

A commentator on biblical texts, Clement belonged to anti-Marcionite Christian Gnosticism, as did the Christians of the New Prophecy and its disciple Origen. Clement drew his references from the Epistle of Jude, the Epistle of Barnabas, and the Apocalypse of Peter (all of which were later condemned as apocryphal) because he was unaware of the canons that didn't come into existence until after his death. Of course, his future copyists were careful to compensate for his legitimate ignorance by inserting backdated citations.

For Clement, *gnosis* allowed one to discover the topography of the celestial dwellings, which were inhabited by cohorts of hierarchically arranged angels. *Gnosis* revealed to him the superimposed or successive worlds through which the soul elevated itself in order to attain its supreme repose. And none other than Joshua/Jesus was the informed guide in this spiritual adventure.

According to the extracts produced by Eusebius, Clement declared: "The Lord after his resurrection imparted knowledge to James the Just and to John and Peter, and they imparted it to the rest of the apostles, and the rest of the apostles to the seventy, of whom Barnabas was one"[18]. (Note that this was enough for Eusebius to consecrate James as the "bishop of the church of Jerusalem"[19].)

In another work, the *Stromata*, in which he attempted to reconcile Greek philosophy and Jewish prophecy, Clement called the true *gnosis* 'Christian', unlike Irenaeus who, vituperating the Christian Gnostics Marcion and Valentinus, judged *gnosis* and the teachings attributed to Jesus to be irreconcilable. Clement referred to "the tradition of the blessed doctrine derived directly from the holy apostles, Peter, James, John, and Paul, the sons receiving it from the father"[20], thereby composing a list of ancient masters in which (out of a desire for unity) were brought together two antagonistic currents: that of Saul/Paul and that of James and Peter.

James, in whom the Master of Justice was reincarnated, played a role of the highest rank in a work discovered at Nag Hammadi: *The Secret Sayings of Jesus*, which proclaimed:

> The disciples said to Jesus: "We know that you will depart from us. Who is to be our leader?"
> Jesus said to them, "Wherever you are, go to James the righteous, for whose sake heaven and earth came into being".[21]

The phrase "for whose sake heaven and earth came into being" made James nothing less than the co-creator of the universe, at the same level as Adam and Jesus, who furthermore was his 'brother'. This remark, borrowed from a *midrash* that claimed for itself the authority of James, illustrates quite clearly how the self-legitimating acts of the Church— which, as it happened, established the terrestrial ruler as the auxiliary and right arm of God—were collected, collated, and harmonized to the extent that the initially disunited Nazarene Churches became federated and formed accords among themselves. There would thus appear—having been engendered by a community inspired by one Levi/Matthew—a work titled *The Secret Words That the Savior Said to Judas Thomas and That I, Matthew, Wrote Down While I Heard Them Speak to Each Other*, sometimes called the Gospel according to Matthew[22]. (Note that Saul/Paul also spoke of a vision in the course of which "he heard things that cannot be told, which man may not utter"[23].) The pious lies by virtue of which the local Churches invented witnesses or brothers of the Messiah would be seen as instances of inadmissible naivety in the eyes of the redactors of the New Testament, who took the precaution of adding the color of historical probability to these falsifications (or, more precisely, these myths) and thereby effaced the original documents, which were accused of being crude aberrations. (Note that, with respect to the invention of witnesses and brothers, the abbeys of the Middle Ages proceeded in the same fashion when they invented patron saints and exhibited their relics so as to attract the faithful, crowds, and alms.)

Incidentally, the figure of James wasn't exclusively connected to Judeo-Christianity, since the Naassenes—according to the *Elenchos* (book 5, chapter 1)—kept in their teachings "the heads of very numerous discourses which (the Naassene) asserts James the brother of the Lord handed down to Mariamne"[24]. Here the Lord was *NHS*, the Redeemer Serpent, and Mariamne corresponded to Miriam/Mary. It was also under the name of James that, after the second century, the *Gospel of James*—a recitation of the childhood of the Christ Jesus and the story of Mary and Joseph the carpenter—would be disseminated.

The original specificity of a Jamesian Christianity, with its own Church, was perpetuated in Nestorianism, which was condemned as a heresy and still exists to this day in Jacobite Churches.

James, prophet and Messiah, assumed the roles of witness, brother, and apostle of Joshua/Jesus to the extent that the diverse currents of Esseno-Christianity—even the Sethian, Naassenean, and Barbelite forms of messianism—slowly came together and grouped their respective patrons or founders together within the apostolic cohort of the Lord.

A fragment from the Judeo-Christian writer Hegesippus (end of the second century), transcribed by Eusebius of Caesarea, described James the Just as an ascetic "holy from his mother's womb"[25]—a trait that was also attributed to Jesus. This accounts for the mythical slide of James (the Messiah of an Essene community) into Jesus (the syncretic Messiah of the first Churches, which may have been federated by Elchasai).

Like Dunstan, Jochanaan, the Servant celebrated by Isaiah, and the other spawn of the Master of Justice, Jacob/James did not eat meat and never shaved, combed his hair, or washed. He dedicated all of his time to prayer. Hegesippus called him "Bulwark of the people", because "many [who] believed did so on account of James"[26].

Among the Elchasaites, James passed for the true founder of their community. The primitive text of the *Homilies* presented itself as a letter from Clement, *alias* Zacchaeus, to James.

History has preserved traces of two people named Jacob who were tied to messianic agitation; the ahistorical spirit of the *midrashim* easily united them in an identification that was made plausible by the common front of Zealotism and Essenism. According to Flavius Josephus (*Antiquities of the Jews*, book 20, chapter 5.2)[27], Jacob of Gamala, son of Judah and brother of Simon, was crucified around 45 under the reign of Tiberius Alexander, who had succeeded Caspius Fadus (responsible for the execution several months earlier of Theudas/Thomas) as procurator of Judea.

The first Jacob, a Zealot, was doubled by another, who was either a Nazarene or an Ebionite. The Talmud and a *midrash* set themselves against a Christian Jew named Jacob of Kepher Schanya (or Maya Simai), who was accused of contesting the orthodox rituals prescribed by Deuteronomy. Interrogating Rabbi Eliezer on a point of doctrine, Jacob was invited to give his opinion about it and to advance an interpretation drawn from Micah (2: 7) that emphasized God's solicitude regarding interests of men. Eliezer ended up supporting Jacob's explication and thereby drew upon himself the reproach of complacency with respect to Nazarenism.

Simon-Peter

Named governor of Bithynia in 111, Pliny the Younger solicited directives from Emperor Trajan regarding the conduct he ought to adopt with respect to the *chrestianoi*, whose behavior had aroused unfavorable reactions from the locals (*Letters* 10.96–7). Oscar Cullmann has shown that the incriminated Christian sect was that of the Elchasaites, whose doctrine synthesized the teachings of Nazarenism and Ebionism, if not of other messianistic sects[28]. Their ideas were expressed in an ensemble of texts that were revised many times and that were for a long time held to be orthodox by virtue of their being organized under Clement's name. Indeed, Clement (the 'Gentle')—a translation of Zacchaeus from the Bible—was the third Pope of Rome in the official histories of Catholicism. Rejected much later by the Church, these writings would be rebaptized *Pseudo-Clementines* by historians who (it should be noted) were in no rush to contradict absurd speculations concerning the era in which a Roman pontificate might have lived.

Under the name of Clement (the Pope of Rome and successor to Peter)—'Clement' was in fact a fictive person invented by Irenaeus and consecrated by Eusebius[29]—a body of work was disseminated that analysis reveals to have had three stages. First, the *Homilies* or the *Epistle of Peter to James* was a Greek revision of an old *midrash* placed under the name of Zacchaeus. Second, a Greek development, called the *Anagnosos*, was translated and revised under the title *Recognitiones* (*Recognitions*) by Tyrannius Rufinus, a notorious forger and censor of the works of Origen. Third and last, the *Sinai Epitome* represented the Catholic version, amputated from the text of the *Homilies of Peter*, which would reappear much later under the title *Acts of Peter by Clement*.

The Hebrew source has disappeared, but the primitive kernel, extracted by Cullmann, explicitly revealed the central theme of the speculations advanced by the author: "The true prophet and the intelligence of the law according to the teachings of the Mosaic tradition". Cullmann summarized it thus:

> The world with its sins and errors is compared to a house that is filled with smoke. The men who find themselves inside search in vain for the truth, which doesn't enter. Only the true prophet, by opening the door, can give it to them. This prophet is the Christ, who first entered the world in the person of Adam, anointed by the oil of the Tree of Life. For all beings, God made a prototype: for the angels, an angel; for the spirits, a spirit; for men, a *man* who is Adam-Jesus. Adam was without sin, notwithstanding certain mendacious passages in the Scriptures. Adam, the true prophet, announced the world to come. By contrast, Eve, who was inferior to him as the moon is inferior to the sun, was appointed to the present world as the prototype of the prophets born from women (whereas Adam was the 'Son of Man'). The feminine principle led the men of the first generation away from the path of truth. Their depravity manifested itself especially in the practice of *sacrifices*. But since the beginning of the world, the true prophet hasn't ceased to travel through the centuries, changing name and form. He was incarnated in Enoch, Noah, Abraham, Isaac, Jacob and Moses. Moses renewed the eternal law that Adam had already promulgated, but, at the same time, by authorizing sacrifices through a law, Moses made a concession to

the hardening of the Jews that also placed a curb upon their most serious excesses: sacrifices had to be offered to God only, and only in a particular place. But this permission was only provisional. Moses foreshadowed a future prophet who would abolish sacrifices. The true prophet finally reached his perfect repose in the Christ. He put an end to sacrifices and replaced them with *baptism*. Also, during the Jewish War, only the baptized were saved. Before dying, the true prophet chose twelve apostles, and, in the manner of Moses, tasked seventy-two doctors of the law with transmitting the truth. By abolishing sacrifices, the Christ did not abolish the law, but that which was not part of primitive law. He announced that, until the heavens and the earth had passed, not an iota or a trait of the Law would fall.[30]

The author (or authors) of the *Homilies* belonged to the reformist current that became increasingly critical of the biblical texts and Mosaic law. They eliminated not only the prophets who represented feminine principles, but also certain important parts of the Pentateuch. Of course, the Elchasaites, in conformity with the Essenean matrix, rejected the sacrifices of the Temple. "after a little the written law had added to it certain falsehoods contrary to the law of God" (homily 17, chapter 38)[31]. This argument recalled those of the Dunstanites or Dositheosians, whose prophet, James, mystically presided over the authority of a Church to which Peter himself was obliged to render account.

As for the defense of the unique God, it was inscribed in the polemic of the two Gods and their respective natures. Was it necessary—in the manner of Marcion circa 140, and perhaps also in the manner of Saul, the enemy of the Elchasaites—to postulate the existence of a Good and Christian God radically different from YHWH, the creator-God of a bad world, a bloody God who betrayed his people, a Demiurge who was master of a deplorable universe? Or was it necessary to rally to the Elchasaite thesis, from which would in fact be born the God of Irenaeus, Tertullian, and then of the Catholics and the Protestants ("He kills through the left hand, that is, through the evil one, who has been so composed as to rejoice in afflicting the impious. And he saves and benefits through the right hand, that is, through the good one, who has been made to rejoice in the good deeds and salvation of the righteous"[32])?

Finally, the Elchasaites, having entered the general quarrel concerning the 'true Messiah', were perhaps the first ones to produce—with Saul/Paul and Satornilus—the ecumenical name of Joshua/Jesus.

In the manner of the various Christianities of the first two centuries, the Elchasaites' conception of the Messiah was that of the *Angelos-Christos*. He had been created as one of the archangels—in the same way that Michael was also Melchizedek. "For all beings, God created a prototype: for angels, an angel; for the spirits, a spirit; for men, a *man* who was Adam-Jesus. Adam was without sin, notwithstanding certain mendacious passages in the Scriptures"[33].

Elchasaite Christianity believed in the successive reincarnations of the Messiah, who had, "changed his forms and his names from the beginning of the world, and so reappeared again and again in the world" (homily 3, chapter 10)[34].

No doubt the Messiah was manifested by the voice of Elchasai, just as he prophesied a half-century later through the mouth of Montanus in the popular Christianity of the New Prophecy, which was born in Phrygia, in the immediate neighborhood of the Bithynia of Pliny and the Elchasaites.

But what could be the means of preventing other visionaries from obeying the revelation of the Messiah? The two great enemies of Elchasaitism—like those of Montanism and Tertullian, but later on—had also heard Christ's message, after all.

Cullmann failed to detect in the primitive text of the *Homilies* what was in fact there, namely, a charge made against Marcion, which was refuted by a subsequent copyist who revised the text. And yet, as Ferdinand Christian Baur has demonstrated, the hostility manifested with respect to Simon 'the Magician' was in fact aimed at Saul/Paul, who was held to be a false prophet.

Nevertheless, the authors of the *Homilies* did not know any of the letters by Paul, nor the texts of the New Testament invented by Marcion. They simply preached the good news, the gospel, and rejected that of Saul, the founder of competing Churches.

According to the *Homilies* (homily 2, chapter 17): "as the true Prophet has told us, a false prophet must come first from some deceiver; and then, in like manner, after the removal of the holy place, the true Gospel must be secretly sent abroad for the rectification of the heresies that shall be"[35].

Which holy place? Jerusalem and the Temple? But Essenism didn't cease to demand the annihilation of the town consecrated to the 'impious priest'. Wasn't this instead a reference to Qumran or Damascus—that is to say, to *DMS*, the sanctuary, towards which (according to legend) Paul was travelling when he received the revelation of the Messiah? (Unless the allusion is to the era after 135.)

If Saul/Paul was treated as a false witness to the Lord, his own notes stigmatized his adversaries as "false brothers"[36]. Harmony certainly did not reign between the different communities invested with the divine message.

Towards the end of the second century, and more surely in the fourth century, the monarchal Churches—aiming to win the good graces of imperial power—effaced from their histories the divergences between the partisans of James and Peter and the disciples of Saul/Paul. Simon-Peter and Paul, finally reconciled, reigned as the patron saints of Rome, in which neither of them had ever set foot.

Nevertheless, hatred for the 'impostor' never completely disappeared from the restoration of the Christian edifice by Catholicism. A manuscript discovered by Shlomo Pines that conveys the opinions of a Jewish community from Syria in the fifth century[37] accuses Paul of Tarsus of having falsified the teachings of the Messiah. This false prophet rejected the Torah with the intention of attracting to himself the favors of Rome and of acquiring personal power and influence. Having flattered the anti-Semitism of the Romans, he was the one truly responsible for the destruction of the Temple in 70. And this text, caught up as it was in the polemical whirlpools of the fifth century—during which the Church invented the legend of 'Paul, apostle to the gentiles', who won the Empire over to Christian convictions—objects that "His Christianity was nothing more than pure Romanism; rather than converting the Romans into Christians, he converted the Christians into Romans"[38].

This manuscript furthermore denounces the impostures and contradictions of the canonical Gospels and accords credit only to the original

Gospel—the one drafted in Hebrew. This community, which made exclusive claims to the authority of James and Peter, existed until the tenth century, according to the Jewish philosopher Saadia Gaon.

Perhaps it was from the same milieu that emerged a kind of 'novel about Paul' that attacked the official novel known as the Acts of the Apostles. Epiphanius of Salamis (438–96) echoed it in his discussion of the Ebionites' beliefs about Paul in *Panarion* (ii. 30. 16,9):

> They then claim that he was Greek and the son of a Greek mother and Greek father, but that he had gone up to Jerusalem, stayed there for a while, desired to marry a daughter of the high priest, and had therefore become a proselyte and been circumcised. But since he still could not marry that sort of girl he became angry and wrote against circumcision, and against the Sabbath and the legislation.[39]

The (no doubt quite limited) vogue for Elchasaitism survived the Jewish revolt of 133–5 that ended in the defeat of Bar Kokhba and the end of the Palestinian nation. The future of Christianity henceforth belonged to the Pauline tendency, which the shipowner and founder of Churches, Marcion, exploited before he himself was rejected by the popular development of a Hellenized Christianity, whose birth in Phrygia clearly demonstrates its relation to the Christianity of the prophet Elchasai, which was established in Bithynia.

As for Simon-Peter, the disciple or younger brother of James, his name derives from the Hebrew *Symeon* and from the Aramaic sobriquet *Kepha*, 'rock'. Hence Simon the Rock, Simon the Pitiless, or Simon the Bald.

His only historical traces lead back to Simon, son of Judah of Gamala and brother of Jacob, who was put to death as a Zealot. Was he confused with Simon the Essene, whose violent hostility to John the Baptist was indicated by Flavius? The *Homilies* do indeed execrate Jochanaan. Another trace of Essenism, the *Testamentum Domini* (a discourse addressed to the Sons of Light), was inserted into the *Homilies*.

The *Recognitions*, a development and revision of the *Homilies*, preserved a list of couples or syzygies: the Antichrist was opposed to the

Christ as Cain was opposed to Abel, Ishmael to Isaac, Isaiah to Jacob, Aaron to Moses, John the Baptist to the Son of Man, and Paul to Peter. (It is worth recalling that the first description of the Antichrist—as well the Messiah's horoscope—were discovered among the manuscripts at Qumran.)

The authority of Simon-Peter eclipsed that of James around the end of the second century. He triumphed over Saul at Antioch, where he acted as James's delegate. It was in Simon-Peter's company that Clement was instructed in Caesarea, and Clement learned from his mouth the doctrine of the 'true prophet'. The legend of his death, invented by Tertullian and reprised in the *Acts of Peter*, entered the dogma of the Church in the fourth and fifth Centuries by virtue of the efforts that were undertaken to offer to Rome, the Emperor, and the citizenry (none of whom were particularly eager to embrace Catholicism) the venerable patronage of two pillars of faith: Peter and Paul, united despite themselves for the greater glory of God. (Note that the *Acts of Peter*, still part of the canon in the fourth century, were rejected as 'apocryphal' upon the triumph of the belief that Peter had founded the Roman Church. In the twentieth century certain archeologists—who, like the historians, were motivated by a sense of Christian duty—strove to discover his tomb. The Light of Faith only illuminated their absurdity.)

Barnabas

No historical certitude gives plausible contours to the person named Barnabas. In his study of the apocryphal books of the New Testament, Erbetta made him a Levite from Cyprus, a Jewish member of the minor clergy involved with the services at the synagogue[40]. He was supposedly the companion of a certain Mark, the author of a secret Gnostic Gospel in the line of Essenean teachings. A *Letter to Theodore* by Clement of Alexandria (end of the second century) affirmed that this Mark "composed a more spiritual Gospel for the use of those who were being perfected. Nevertheless, he yet did not divulge the things not to be uttered"[41].

All the evidence suggests that the apocryphal text attributed to Mark, whose name would later crown a canonical Gospel substituted for the Gnostic one, was similar in its contents to the epistle placed under the name of Barnabas, which is a text of great interest for an understanding of Judeo-Christianity at the end of the first century and the beginning of the second. In Erbetta's opinion, this epistle was composed in Alexandria, Syria, or Asia Minor, and in its Greek form dated from the years 117 to 130. Transcribed again for the fourth-century Sinaiticus manuscript, it was held as canonical until Pope Gelasius's decree set it aside.

Originally written in Hebrew or Aramaic, the text defined in its entirety the program of revising Judaism undertaken by Essenism, and, more particularly, by the diasporic sects that adapted anti-Judean Christianity to Greco-Roman ways of thinking.

The reproach addressed to Phariseean orthodoxy much later nourished the anti-Judaic polemic. It was less a question of globally rejecting Yahwehism—as Marcion desired—than of expelling the Jews from biblical exegesis, of which they had 'shown themselves to be unworthy'. Hadn't they chosen to interpret the writings of the Bible literally rather than in a spiritual sense? The Epistle of Barnabas thus recommended the practice of circumcision of the heart and not that of the flesh ("Circumcise therefore the foreskin of your heart, and be no longer stubborn"[42]). (The abandonment of circumcision as a component of the rites of conversion undoubtedly aided the cause of proselytism and the recruitment of non-Jewish believers.)

In the same way, the prohibition of certain foods had to be understood symbolically, as a refusal to associate with people shaped by immorality. The Temple of Jerusalem had to give way to a true temple that lived in the heart of the believer. So as to break more clearly with Jewish practice, the Sabbath was shifted from the sixth to the seventh day, which was consecrated *dies Domini*, Sunday.

The second part of the Epistle corresponded almost entirely to the Hebrew manual that was revised, corrected, and disseminated by Jewish Christians under the name *Didachē*. One notably finds in it the doctrine of the two paths (Barnabas 18–20), which conforms with the Essenean combat between the Light and the Darkness.

But, in the Epistle of Barnabas, the two most significant elements of Judeo-Christianity that were undergoing a process of Hellenization demonstrate the obvious influence of Naassenism and of a strictly biblical conception of Jesus. For the Christians who were contemporaries with the famous letter of Pliny, Jesus—insofar as he was the Christ—was none other than the successor to Moses: Joshua, the holder of the New Alliance or *Novum testamentum.*

As for Naassenism: "For the Lord caused all manner of serpents to bite them, and they died (forasmuch as the transgression was wrought in Eve through the serpent), that He might convince them that by reason of their transgression they should be delivered over to the affliction of death. Yea and further though Moses gave the commandment, *Ye shall not have a molten or a carved image for your God*, yet he himself made one that he might shew them a type of Jesus. So Moses maketh a brazen serpent, and setteth it up conspicuously, and summoneth the people by proclamation. When therefore they were assembled together they entreated Moses that he should offer up intercession for them that they might be healed. And Moses said to them; Whensoever, said he, one of you shall be bitten, let him come to the serpent which is placed on the tree, and let him believe and hope that the serpent being himself dead can make alive; and forthwith he shall be saved" (Epistle of Barnabas 12: 5–7)[43].

As for Jesus, his person presents no historical trace at all. There is not the least allusion to the anecdotes complacently reported by the canonical and Catholic texts. He was simply Joshua, son of Nun or Nahum, an angel of God, co-creator of the world, the alpha and omega, an immanent being without any connection to the events that unexpectedly took place in the era of Tiberius and Procurator Pontius Pilate.

> What again saith Moses unto Jesus (Joshua) the son of Nun, when he giveth him his name, as being a prophet, that all the people might give ear to him alone, because the Father revealeth all things concerning His Son Jesus? Moses therefore saith to Jesus the son of Nun, giving him this name, when he sent him as a spy on the land; *Take a book in thy hands, and write what the Lord saith, how the Son of God shall cut up by the roots all the house of Amalek in the last days.* Behold again it is Jesus, not a son of man, but the Son of God, and He was revealed in the flesh in a figure. Since then men will say that Christ is the son of David, David himself prophesieth being afraid and understanding the error of sinners [...]. (Epistle of Barnabas, 12: 8–10)[44]

It is fitting to compare the Epistle of Barnabas to a letter attributed (not without some difficulty) to Saul/Paul by the Catholics: the Epistle to the Hebrews.

In his *De pudicitia* (20), Tertullian attributed this epistle to Barnabas. Luther placed it under the name of Apollos, one of the opponents supposedly encountered by Paul.

For Prosper Alfaric, the text was of Alexandrian origin and took up a *midrash* from the 60s that was revised and Hellenized around 135:

> Christ, the first-born Son of God, enthroned Sovereign-Sacrifice-Performer, shed his blood "once for all"[45] so as to remove sorrow and death from the lives of men. Divine promoter of a New Alliance, he had—upon the order of his Father [...]—to descend "for a little while lower than the angels"[46], to take human form and submit to a Passion. His death and resurrection rendered the immolations of the Temple null and void, and rendered useless the sacrifice-performers [*les sacrificateurs*] of the race of Aaron; because his divine nature, perfected by suffering, made him the Perfect Victim. Passing through 'the door' to the heavens in which the Just would rejoin him [...], he immolated himself in his celestial sanctuary, not in a temple constructed 'by the hand of man'; he worked the purification of sin by his blood, but he did not take their sins upon himself and did not become a 'scourge'.[47]

The drama of the timeless Christ excluded all terrestrial historical existence. Moreover, he did not live on the earth: he "appeared" in flesh (9: 26) so as to identity himself with the humans whom he was charged with saving. The prototype that is suggested here is Melchizedek, who was, like Jesus, "without father or mother, without genealogy, having neither a beginning to his days nor an end to his life". Those who denied Christ would be trampled by him (10: 13); Gehenna awaited the impious.

Many of the features exhibited in the primitive kernel of the Epistle to the Hebrews were found again in the notes that were, perhaps, drafted by Saul/Paul.

Saul, Called Paul of Tarsus
Catholics, Byzantines, Protestants, and Christians of all kinds have

erected Paul and his Christian theology as a pillar of the Church. His biography offers fewer lacunae than that of Hölderlin. Bernard Dubourg notes with an ironic tone that "Everywhere one speaks of the psychology of Paul, the voyages of Paul, the doctrinal efforts of Paul, the difficulties of Paul, etc.—as one speaks, elsewhere and in no particular order, of the mood-swings of Caligula, the peregrinations of [the Count of] Lapérouse, the hypotheses and theories of Kepler, and the tribulations of Socrates. That's right: in learned opinion, Paul is the Socrates of the Church [...]. Even better, he is a Socrates who writes"[48].

On what has such striking certitude been based? On a composite novel whose late-second-century redactors compiled it from apologues and from Jewish *midrashim*, the meaning of which escaped them and which they translated and explicated anecdotally, thereby historicizing the Hebrew myths. And on fourteen letters recorded in manuscripts that were contemporaneous with the instauration of Catholicism and State orthodoxy.

Picking out the incoherencies and improbabilities of the first document, Dubourg emphasized the *midrashic* elements that were revealed by a retroversion of the text into Hebrew.

According to the Acts of the Apostles, Paul was a Jew who became a Roman citizen and was originally from Tarsus, in Cilicia. He then changed his Jewish name, Saul, to Paul. His writings do indeed bear the mark of many Semitisms that are perceptible in the Greek redaction.

It is impossible to be a Jew and a Roman at the same time, Smallwood declares. Adhesion to Roman citizenship "involved the duty to participate in both pagan social rites and religious observances that were incompatible with Jewish orthodoxy"[49].

The fact that the authors of the Acts of the Apostles attribute to Paul Roman citizenry in Tarsus provides a good indication of the epoch in which they forged this biographical fantasy. Tarsus was not made Roman until the second half of the second century. Voltaire did not fail to perceive the following in his *Philosophical Dictionary*: "Was Paul a Roman citizen, as he boasts? If he was from Tarsus in Cilicia, Tarsus wasn't a Roman colony until 100 years later; all the antiquarians agree".

Paul's pilgrim's journey evokes that of Aeneas. After a journey to

Malta, Paul borrowed an Alexandrian vessel "with the twin gods as a figurehead" (Acts of the Apostles 28: 11) in order to return to Rome. An attempt to harmonize the Hebrew myths with Greek philosophy, in which the symbolism of the Dioscuri or twins [Castor and Pollux] assumed no small importance, this apparently journalistic detail awoke echoes of the voyages of initiates, such as that of the Argonauts. Particularly since Paul's inventor—the Christian dualist and anti-Semite Marcion—used his profession as a shipowner and a businessman to found his own Churches everywhere.

Due to a curious amnesia, the historians and biographers of Paul generally forget to mention that he was indeed a product of Marcion—the *bête noire* of Irenaeus, Tertullian, Justin, various Phariseean or Christian Jews, and, much later, Catholic apologists.

But it was Marcion and Marcion alone who, around 140 or 150, revealed the existence of ten epistles written by somebody named Paul, the founder of Churches in the East.

Nevertheless, these letters existed prior to Marcion, and they attest to quarrels between diverse communities or Esseno-Christian Churches. The hostility between these groups, some sworn to James, Peter or Thomas, the others sworn to Saul/Paul, led the historian Bauer to conjecture that the person of Simon caricatured in the *Homilies* was in fact a stand-in for Saul, who—unlike the 'true witnesses', James and Simon Cephas—claimed to have received the revelation of the Messiah.

Who was the original author of Paul's epistles, which were recopied in the fourth century in an atmosphere of dogmatic fabrication and revised on the basis of a Roman past that the Church of Constantine and Theodore falsified without scruple? Loisy doubts their integrity and authenticity. Meaks holds seven of Paul's letters to be authentic, and attributes Thessalonians I and II, Timothy I and II, Philemon, Hebrews, and Titus to the Pauline schools of the second century[50].

For Ory, "the interpolations in the letters of Saint Paul are certain and obvious; they distort the appearance of Paulinism in an extravagant manner"[51]. According to Deschner, opinion today agrees to recognize the existence in the first century of several short notes: echoes of pastorals, polemics, and *midrashic* speculations on the Messiah (whom Saul/Paul did not, in any case, present as a historical person)[52]. The word 'Christ' comes from the Bible, specifically from Isaiah; on the other hand, it is not impossible that 'Jesus' was an addition made at the beginning of the second century.

To whom were the letters addressed? The historians obedient to Catholicism and Protestantism have designated them as being addressed to the *goyim*, the non-Jews, whom Catholicism called the *gentiles* (kind people) or *pagani* (peasants).

In Medieval Hebrew, *goyim* had the connotation of impiety, which was emphasized by the anathema: "May their bones rot [while they are still alive]". Dubourg remarks: "But in the Hebrew of the Bible or Qumran, 'GWY, GWYM', mean 'nation, nations'. The epistles of Saul/Paul were not addressed to the Romans, Ephesians, Galatians or Corinthians, but to the Jews or the Judaicized people of the Diaspora. They were addressed to the Jews of all nations. They carried traces of the *midrashim* of rival groups before they were revised by Marcion, who cut them loose from their purely Jewish foundations"[53]. The letters transmitted the revisionist and anti-Judean theses common to Essenism, Nazarenism, Ebionism and Elchasaitism.

If Marcion used the authority of Saul/Paul to give an apostolic character to the Churches he founded everywhere in opposition to Jewish Christianity, this was because he had discovered in them many arguments against orthodox Judaism, and even against YHWH.

Saul's *midrashim* and polemical fragments thus fell into the hands of Marcion, who opposed the Nazarene/Elchasaite current. Marcion recopied them, but not without distorting their meaning in order to fit the polemical orientations of his times. He intended to federate his Christian Churches by imposing upon them the central reference point of Rome, thereby foreshadowing the politics instaurated by Catholicism two centuries later. Nevertheless, his authoritarianism and his arrogance as a businessman (legend has it that he attempted to buy the Judeo-Christian communities established in Rome, whose myths, legends and polemics were collated by the *Pastor of Hermas*) set against him the Judeo-Christians and the Hellenized Christians who—while also hostile to Christian Jews—refused Marcion and his doctrine, having judged his dualism and his global condemnation of Hebrew mythology (the Old Testament) to be unacceptable.

Paul's letters were revised by Marcion and then subjected to corrections that the anti-Marcionites—Justin, Polycarp, Tertullian, and Irenaeus—judged to be useful. In addition, Tatian—the presumed author of the first version of the three 'synoptic' Gospels—enhanced their aesthetic qualities by polishing them and harmonizing them with the Greek version.[54] Tatian, who was later condemned for the extreme asceticism that he shared with those faithful to the New Prophecy, delivered the Pauline epistles to which orthodoxy would require several adjustments to be made. So many revisions, interpolations, and harmonizations followed each other, stacked up, stratified—all to produce the historical authenticity of manuscripts from the fourth century! And yet hundreds of scholars have founded their studies and staked their reputations on the supposed authenticity of these letters, now arbitrarily backdated to the first century.

The two Letters to Timothy—known as 'pastorals'—are marked by anti-Marcionite developments. (Although the voyages evoked therein might well be those of Marcion. The names Titus, Mark, and Luke also figure in those letters.) They emanated from the enemies of the ship-owner. The author, who had no scruples about signing these texts 'Paul, apostle of the Christ', was—according to Deschner[55]—a bishop named Polycarp (second half of the second century), who was close to the Christian current of the New Prophecy.

The two Letters to the Thessalonians disavowed an older letter by Paul.[56]

The Letter to the Galatians retained something of the quarrels between the Jews of the Diaspora. The first Letter to the Corinthians extolled asceticism and advanced the Phariseean idea of the resurrection of the body. The second evoked differences with Apollos.

In the Letter to the Colossians, the word 'Church' took on a Catholic meaning that it did not have in the other texts. The letter must therefore have been written at a later date.

Priscillian still held the Letter to the Laodiceans to be an authentic text from Paul, when in fact it was a Marcionite text from the years 160–90.[57]

Must we recall that all of the so-called Catholic letters, which were placed under the names of Peter (I and II), John (I, II, and III), James and Jude, were forgeries? Origen mentioned them for the first time in the middle of the third century and judged them to be subject to controversy.

The correspondence between Seneca and Paul—no doubt inspired by Jerome, 'Father of the Church'—offered the slightly too clairvoyant merit of presenting Paul as the contemporary of Nero and as a perfect Roman citizen. These letters met the fate of the letters exchanged between Jesus of Nazareth and King Agbar. Disparaging a few outrageous fakes makes it easier to attribute authenticity to the apostle's epistolary dabbling.

What remains of Saul/Paul after he's been screened by the critique that we can legitimately bring to bear on every dubious historical personage?

He was assuredly a Jew—perhaps Hellenized, but certainly not a Roman citizen. Perhaps he adhered to the doctrines of the Pharisees, as his legends suggest. In any case, his syncretism retained the Phariseean idea of the resurrection of the body and an ecclesial organization for which the synagogue offered an efficacious model. "But this I confess to you, that according to the Way, which they [Paul's accusers] call a sect, I worship the God of our fathers, believing everything laid down by the Law and written in the Prophets, having a hope in God, which these men themselves accept, that there will be a resurrection of both the just and the unjust"[58]. (Note: *odos*, the 'Way' [*la voie*], and not *hairesis*, the 'choice'[59].)

There is no shortage of traces of Essenism in the Pauline corpus. Murphy O'Connor has detected their presence.

As Dubourg has noted, the symbolism of the conversion of Paul on the road to Damascus—not to the city, but to *DMS*, the sanctuary—would be added to the doctrine of the two paths (Light and Darkness), to anti-Judaism, and to the refusal of the sacrifice of animals in the name of penitential sacrifice. Saul rejected anti-Essenean Phariseeism and encountered the revelation of the expected Messiah. He affirmed the return of the Master of Justice, of the Just Person of whom Jacob/James affirmed himself to be the brother. He saw him in the light of Essenism.

And he founded Churches and thereby aroused the animosity of the established communities, which treated him as a false prophet.

If Paul extolled the universal Church, he did so in strict obedience to the Master of Justice, for whom the Church "wants to be universal, present in the entire world, eternal; it feels itself to be in communion with Eden and even with Sheol"[60].

There may be some confusion in the novel called Acts of the Apostles between Paul and the Egyptian—that is to say, Theudas/Thomas. Did Saul not momentarily rally the groups loyal to the 'twin brother of the Lord' before erecting himself as a privileged witness?

Just as Moses heard the voice of God in a flaming bush, Saul perceived the Messiah and heard his voice in an illumination. He proclaimed that he had "been individually selected as an apostle by the Christ himself, in a face-to-face meeting to which he was the only witness"[61].

Here we find the only holder of the truth, privileged by his own authority among the apostles, about whom the Qumranian manuscript *The Damascus Document* says this: "Those 'called by name' are those who hold themselves upright until the end of time"[62]. Simon of Samaria used this same expression, but in a completely different sense: the *Hestôs*, The-One-Who-Holds-Himself-Upright, was the man who created his destiny by being aware of the Great Power (the *Megale Dynamis*) present within him. Although the doctrine of Saul/Paul was situated in a perspective that was radically opposed to that of Simon, his adversaries stigmatized him by identifying him with Simon, 'who wanted to be God'. (Note that, in the biblical texts, there is a Saul who was a son of Simon, who may have been the malicious inspiration for this polemic.)

There's no shortage of traces of quarrels. A legendary tradition reported by Eusebius has it that Paul assassinated James the Just. The *Homilies* contained a direct attack on Saul, as Cullmann emphasizes: "Truth doesn't need to be sought in an ecstatic way; it imposes itself on whoever believes in the true prophet. By this natural path, the truth was revealed to Peter when he made his confession: You are the son of the Living God. Simon (that is to say, Paul), on the other hand, rested his supposed knowledge of Jesus on a vision that had no value and that did not confer upon him the right to the apostolate"[63].

For their part, the Paulinians did not spare Peter. An evangelic fable accused him of having denied Christ—of behaving, in sum, like another traitor, like Judas/Thomas. Thus did the apologetic novels translate the quarrels concerning ascendancy that took place between the diverse Esseno-Christian communities of the first century.

The Letter to the Galatians (2: 11–4) rejects Simon-Peter in particular: "But when Cephas came to Antioch, I opposed him to his face, because he stood condemned. For before certain men came from James, he was eating with the Gentiles; but when they came he drew back and separated himself, fearing the circumcision party. And the rest of the Jews acted hypocritically along with him, so that even Barnabas was led astray by their hypocrisy".

The allusion to circumcision—inconceivable for Saul, a Jew—sounds like an intervention by the anti-Semite Marcion. (Horace gave the practice an insulting connotation and spoke of "offending the circumcised"[64].)

In the second Letter to the Corinthians (12: 11), Saul balked: "For I was not at all inferior to these super-apostles, even though I am nothing".

This response makes the nature of the reproach clear. Another interesting passage appeared in the Letter to Timothy, a text falsely attributed to Paul that implored its addressee to remain in Ephesus so as to combat those who "devote themselves to myths and endless genealogies"[65]. Don't we have grounds for supposing that certain Churches undertook to confer a historical existence upon Jesus, who was, from that point on, very different from the Messiah of whom Saul/Paul spoke?

Because the only Messiah that Paul recognized was the *Angelos-Christos*, the envoy of Adonai. And on this point he agreed with the Judeo-Christians, the Marcionites, and anti-Marcionites such as Justin the Apologist. Renan was perceptive when he wrote: "For Paul, Jesus is not a man who lived and taught, but a completely divine being".

Irony has so contrived things that the Catholic Church's favorite prophet was undeniably vulnerable to accusations of heresy, accusations that would have been dictated to Catholicism by its interest in fabricating the historical existence of Jesus. The heresy in question at the time [circa 325] was Docetism: the belief in an Angel-Messiah who assumed human form for the brief duration of a voluntary terrestrial descent.

The incarnate, dead, and resurrected Savior had nothing in common with a rabbi who agitated the people, nor with the slightly Brahmanic sage who dispensed his secret wisdom in the *logia* that were piously and falsely compiled by Matthew and Thomas.

For the Christians who followed Paul, for the Nazarenes, the Ebionites, the Elchasaites, the Marcionites, and the anti-Marcionites (at least up to Justin), Joshua/Jesus had neither childhood, parents, nor any adventures other than his descent into the darkness of matter and his ascension towards the Light. He appeared suddenly, without anyone knowing whence he came. He was a heavenly Adam and a *Logos*. Even the canonical Gospel placed under the name of Mark knew nothing of the baby Jesus and was content with the anecdotal staging of his wise remarks (*logia*) and his penitential message.

Like all Christians up to the 150s or 160s, Paul was a Gnostic. "In Pauline Christianity", Maccoby writes, "the *gnosis* which the saviour brings is nothing but the knowledge of the saving power of his own death. He functions as a sacrifice, but only if the initiate is aware of his sacrificial power and shares, by 'faith', in the saviour's sacrificial experience"[66].

The Greek text of the letters presents numerous expressions that were used in Gnostic writings; the Latin and other translations took care to efface them. Speaking of the assault of the forces of evil against the Messiah, the Greek version literally said, "None of the rulers of this age [*archonton tou ainos toutou*][67] understood this [his glory], for if they had [known] [*gnosis*], they would not have crucified the Lord of glory" (1 Corinthians 2: 8)[68]. The Christ is a *pneuma*: "Now the Lord is the Spirit" (2 Corinthians 3: 17).

"It is no longer I who live, but Christ who lives in me", Paul wrote in the Epistle to the Galatians (2: 20), but since Christ was a *pneuma*, Paul was a *pneumaticos*, a 'Perfect One' possessed by the spirit that expressed itself in him. (Note that Paul's conception of a pneumatic baptism was opposed to the baptism by water of the Elchasaites and Nazarenes.) And Leisegang remarks: "It is no longer he who lives but the Christ who lives in him, speaking through his mouth, becoming him. Such is the sense in which Simon [of Samaria] was aware of being the Great Power God"[69].

Paul's dualism was expressed by the incompatibility he saw between the path of Light and the path of Darkness, the internal man and the external man, and the struggle between the Christ and Belial, the leader of the ages. Nevertheless, no allusion to the two Gods put Jewish monotheism into question.

At Corinth, moreover, Paul struggled against other Gnostics—Nicolaites or Barbelites—who estimated that the ecstasy through which the pneuma or Holy Spirit revealed itself gave one the freedom to act according to one's desires (1 Corinthians, 6, 12, 15, 16). Once more, the choice between a daily practice governed by asceticism or one governed by hedonism determined the demarcation among the various Gnosticisms.

The Letter to the Colossians evokes the Pauline current's opposition to a Hermeticist group that practiced the astral magic possessed by amulets or *abraxas*. This epistle explicitly rejects the doctrine of the *stoicheia* [first principles]. One had to renounce this doctrine in order to follow Christ, "for in him the whole fullness of deity dwells bodily"[70], and "in the same way we also, when we were children, were enslaved to the elementary principles of the world" (*upo ta stoicheia tou cosmou*)[71]. (Note that the theory of the *stoicheia* attributed to magical rites and incantations such as the 'song of the seven planetary vowels' the power to act upon the stars and the destinies of men.)

The Letter to the Colossians, on the other hand, alluded to a secret doctrine—secret in the sense in which the Gospels revealed *apocrypha* or hidden things. "I know a man in Christ who fourteen years ago was caught up to the third heaven—whether in the body or out of the body I do not know, God knows. And I know that this man was caught up into paradise [...] and he heard things that cannot be told, which man may not utter" (2 Corinthians 12: 2–4)[72]. Did not Valentinus—who around 140 left Egypt for Rome, where he knew and fought against Marcion—claim that "he himself learned Paul's secret teachings from Theudas, one of Paul's own disciples"[73]? Theudas was none other than Thomas, under whose name appeared the *Logia of Jesus* discovered at Nag Hammadi. Note that the canonical Gospel attributed to John was related to the Gnostic Gospels by way of its vocabulary and ideas. The Christ existed *en arche* (at the beginning of the world); he was the *Logos* of God, the

Zoe (the Life) and the *Phos* (the Light) that spread the *pneuma* (the Spirit) of life. This does not preclude a refusal of Samaritan *gnosis*, which is evoked in the interview between Jesus and a Samaritan woman to whom he explains that the salvation of the Samaritans will in fact come from Judea.

The Good News (the Gospel) of Paul was the only Gospel to which Christians of all kinds referred until the third century. The Epistle attributed to Clement, which emanated from a Judeo-Christian milieu at the beginning of the second century, let it be understood that the Messiah whose return had so often been promised had still not appeared.

The Good News of Paul—but should we not say the Good News of Marcion?—was that the Redeemer had in fact been manifested in a suffering Messiah. Not only did the Jews not recognize him, but they also put him to death.

CHAPTER ELEVEN

Marcion and the Hellenization of Christianity

Despite the passage of two centuries and the accusations of heresy that separated him from the State religion, Marcion (born in Rome in the fourth century) deserves to be considered the true father of the Catholic Church—a clumsy father who abandoned to the world a runt that only his enemies would bring to maturity.

Missionary zeal; the determination to found communities; the hope for supreme authority (the investiture with which he would receive in Rome); the monarchal organization of the *Ekklēsia*; virulent anti-Semitism; the conception of a Christian philosophy purified of its Judaism; a theology inspired by Greek thought: these qualities of Marcion's proved to be a great many of the fundamental traits of the future Catholic Church.

With Marcion, Christianity—contemptuous of the historical truth—arrogated for itself a Hellenic genesis by way of the myth of Paul, 'apostle to the Gentiles'. Even today, many historians shamelessly ratify this supposed birth of Christianity from Greek origins.

Marcion's talents were those of a businessman. Due to the events of his time, he understood that Christianity would be renouncing any possible future if it didn't break all ties with Judaism, which was disapproved of throughout the Greco-Roman world because of the endemic state of insurrection in Palestine and in the cities of the Diaspora.

In 115, the Jews destroyed the temple of Zeus in Cyrene. An agitator named Lukuas or Andrew (a name annexed by the apostolic legends) took power and was acclaimed King of the Jews. Andrew called for the destruction of all the monuments of idolatry before the arrival of the Day of the Lord. A rumor was propagated that the insurgents ate their enemies and anointed themselves with their blood. The massacre of non-Jews struck good Greek and Roman consciences with horror; there is a letter—sent by the mother of a general who was sent to put down the rioters—in which she prayed that her son would not be "roasted by the Jews". It is well known how the falsehoods common to tumults of this type—which have occurred repeatedly over the course of almost two thousand years of religious criminality—have nourished the grievances of Catholic, Protestant, Byzantine, and atheistic mobs that have unleashed pogroms against peaceful ghettos.

That same year, the insurrection of the Jews of Alexandria spread to the Delta and the Thebaid and gained ground in Palestine, Syria, Mesopotamia, and Cyprus. In their holy war against the *goyim*, the Jews destroyed Salamis. Around 117, Trajan moved to end the revolts. Ten thousand Jews were executed.[1]

Nevertheless, Simon Bar Kokhba took up arms in 132 and fought against Rome. In 135, he was beaten and killed in his fortress at Betar. The Jewish nation was banned by Greco-Roman 'civilization', in which elevated thought accommodated itself easily enough to circus games.

Well before the new insurrection, the Judeo-Christians—unlike the Essenes of the first century—had distanced themselves from the holy war. They had refused to give their support to the Messiah Bar Kokhba: one of their letters had condemned the attitude of the 'Galileans'. Thereafter, the Christians accentuated what separated them from the Jews: the profession of a pacifist faith; non-violence; the virtues of sacrifice; and the rejection of circumcision and the Jewish ritual observances (the impetus for the latter was particularly great, because Hadrian, taking his stand on the Roman law that prohibited corporeal mutilations, formally prohibited circumcision).

After 135, the Jewish communities were persecuted mercilessly. Rabbi Joshua ben Hananiah was burned alive; Rabbi Akiba was skinned alive. In his *Contra Celsum*, Origen recalled the great massacres of the 'circumcised'. Even if this Christian refused the worship of idols and abstained from offering sacrifices to the Emperor, he demanded his Greek or Roman citizenship and proclaimed his absolute difference from the Jews.

Marcion's anti-Judaic reforms survived the disorder caused by the political wildfire at the heart of Judeo-Christian churches that had fallen prey to internecine struggles for influence. Those reforms advocated an ecclesial politics that would be centered upon Rome and strengthened by its rupture with 'Jewry'. The few biographical elements available to us confirm this.

Marcion would have been born in the last years of the first century in Sinope, on the Pont (around 95 or 100, according to Harnack[2]).

Marcion soon came into conflict with the Judeo-Christian communities. His father, the overseer of an *Ekklēsia*, chased him away for having expressed opinions hostile to the faith that were doubtless inspired by Saul and his disciples. Marcion went to Asia Minor, where he clashed with the local Christian churches, which would in all probability have been Elchasaite.

A wealthy ship-owner, Marcion had the practical intelligence of a businessman. His rationality, seduced by Greek philosophy, was repulsed by the analogical spirit of the *midrashim* and by the Hebrew wordplay that Greek translations reduced to absurdities. The bloody and inhuman character of the biblical texts furnished him with an argument that was opportunely confirmed by the violence of the Jewish revolts. In place of the latent dualism of the Esseno-Christians, Marcion explicitly substituted the two irreconcilable characters of YHWH—God-creator of a world of war and misery—and a Good God to whom the schools of James, Simon-Cephas, Thomas, Clement, and Saul/Paul implicitly referred.

Marcion placed his bets on anti-Judaism and hostility towards the people of the Temple, Jerusalem, the Pharisees, and the murderers of the Master of Justice. He supported his doctrine with compelling arguments and with promises of a beautiful future in the Church, but, before that future came to pass, he contented himself with insulting the voluntary poverty of the communities: he offered 200,000 sesterces to the Roman Churches in an attempt to subject them to his authority (with an eye to an international federation).

Marcion was the first to understand that Rome, constituting as it did the center of a civilization that was being proposed as an example for the whole world, was the axis of gravitation from which Christianity, purified of its barbarity, might hope to radiate a 'universal' glory. (The word *catholicon* came into play towards the end of the second century and was popularized in the fifth.) Tertullian avowed: "For he [Marcion] has filled the whole world with the lying pretence of his own divinity"[3].

Around 140, in a Rome in which the Churches—still Judeo-Christian—were being torn apart by rivalries for power (according to the contemporary novel by Hermas, *The Pastor*), Marcion met Cerdo, a disciple of Satornilus of Antioch. Marcion composed two works, which were lost or destroyed by the Church.

The *Apostolicon* was a compilation of letters attributed to Saul, Romanized as Paul. The *Evangelion* expounded the Good News, the unique Gospel, the Gospel of Paul, to which both the Marcionites and the anti-Marcionites referred. Taking his stand on the letters that he had recopied and rewritten (stripping them of their Semitisms in the process), Marcion thereby drafted Paul's evangelic message.

Raschke believed the canonical Gospel attributed to Mark to be the work of Marcion, subsequently corrected by the anti-Marcionites[4]. He noted that Jesus's childhood was not mentioned in the text, that Jesus's opposition to the Torah wasn't at all ambiguous, and that the staging of the remarks or *logia* didn't break with the conception (common to Judeo-Christianity, Saul/Paul and Marcion) of an *Angelos-Christos* incarnated in a being of wisdom—that is, in an emanation of the Sophia.

In the course of the reaction against Marcion, anti-Marcionite prologues were added to the Gospels attributed to Mark, Luke, and Matthew. Conceived in order to combat the notion of an Angel-Messiah, they added the traits of a historical Roman personage to the allegorical material. The Montanist propagandistic narratives about Pilate, Paul, and Peter (the Gospel of Nicodemus, the Acts of Paul and Thecla, the Apocalypse of Peter, etc.) contributed to the eventful staging of this drama.

Marcion died around 165, after an adventurous life in which the backdated journeys of Paul figured prominently. Did he not derive his apostolic legitimacy, everywhere that he presented himself, from the simple assertion that Paul had been present several generations previously?

His disciple Apelles continued his work in Rome and Alexandria. He demonstrated the absurdity of the biblical texts in his *Syllogisms* (now lost). He seems, however, to have broken with the Marcionite doctrine of the two Gods. He admitted only one: a good one, the creator of the angelic world, from which escaped a perverse angel—the Demiurge—who inclined all things towards evil. Apelles came close to the Christianity of the New Prophecy: he gave to Jesus not a mere human *appearance* but a real body, and the mission of correcting the unfortunate work of the Demiurge. His *Revelations* (now lost, unless it was in fact the apocalypse of Paul or Peter) retranscribed the visions of a prophetess called Philomene. A polemic opposed her to Rhodon, a disciple of Tatian.

Marcion invented a Western Christianity, one without a Jewish [i.e. Eastern] past. He rejected the *midrashim* of the Nazarene and Elchasaite Churches, elements of which later entered the Greek Gospels attributed to Matthew, Thomas, James, Andrew, and Philip. According to Joseph Turmel[5], Marcion—using the short notes written by Saul—gave to his Churches, which were 'Catholic' before the advent of Catholicism, a Roman master, a citizen of the town of Tarsus (which was Romanized in 140 or 150).

Marcion's ascetic renunciation did not contravene the morality of Christianity in its entirety (except for the sects in which Naassene or Barbelite syncretism dominated). The New Prophecy, hostile though it was to Marcionism, abounded in the same ascetic practices, albeit with different meanings attached. Marcion refused sexuality, pleasure, and even marriage, which he judged propitious for the work of the Demiurge. The New Prophecy limited itself to encouraging detachment from the body to the profit of the spirit.

In its violent rejection of Judaism, Marcion's dualism did not yet take on the scandalous character that State Catholic monotheism would subsequently imprint upon it. Is an example of this needed? In his *Dialogue with Trypho the Jew*, Justin the Apologist—a determined anti-Marcionite—hears a remark made by his interlocutor that evokes the trouble caused by belief in a Good God:

> We have heard what you think of these matters. Resume the discourse where you left off, and bring it to an end. For some of it appears to me to be paradoxical, and wholly incapable of proof. For when you say that this Christ existed as God before the ages, then that He submitted to be born and become man, yet that He is not man of man, this [...] appears to me to be not merely paradoxical, but also foolish.[6] Tell me first how you could prove that there is another God alongside the one who is the Creator of all things, and then show me how this God also deigned to be born from a virgin.[7]

Marcion's missionary activity and his determination to establish non-Jewish and unified Churches everywhere did not, in themselves, offer any grounds for official condemnation because, thanks to a trick proper to the Catholic Church and to all power, the glory that the Church took away from Marcion accrued to the person of Paul, the sacred 'apostle to the Gentiles'.

Marcion's activity was so effective that, in 400, there were still Marcionite Churches in Rome, in all of Italy, in Egypt, Palestine, Arabia, Syria, Armenia, Cyprus, and even Persia, where Manichaeism developed. He propagated everywhere the unique Gospel inspired by Paul and the appellation adopted by Catholicism, the 'Old Testament', to which he opposed the New Testament, translating in this fashion the expression 'New Alliance', which according to the manuscripts of Qumran defined the Church of the Master of Justice.

Leisegang summarizes Marcion's conceptions as follows:[8]

> The Gospel of the Christ teaches merciful love, while the Old Testament teaches a malevolent punitive justice. The Christ is the Son of a God of love, and faith in this God is the essence of Christianity. The history of the world from Adam to Christ described in the Old Testament forms an immoral and repulsive drama, one staged by the God who created this world—which is as bad as possible—and who, departing, could not be any better than his

lamentable creation. It is therefore impossible that the Christ is the Son of the creator revealed in the Old Testament. This creator is just and cruel, whereas Jesus is love and kindness personified. Jesus is, by his own words, the Son of God. He could therefore only be the Son of a God completely different from that of the Old Testament. He is the Son of a Good God, one who has until now remained unknown to man and a stranger to this universe, because he has absolutely nothing in common with it. This God is the Unknown God that Saint Paul announced at the agora of Athens. This God is the father of the Christ.

The Old Testament lost its status as the Holy Scripture of Christianity. It did not know the True God and knew nothing about Jesus. The words of the prophets and the psalms, until then considered to be prophecies referring to the Christ, had to be submitted to a literal reinterpretation, after which they no longer applied to Jesus. The Law and the prophets ended with John the Baptist. John was the last Jewish prophet; like his predecessors, he preached a Demiurge of cruel justice and knew nothing of the Good God, who remained foreign to all the Jews. That this was the case, Jesus himself confirmed. He [Jesus] did not cease, in his language as well as in his conduct, to violate the Law of the Old Testament, or to disobey the God who instituted it. He declared an open war on the doctors of the Law, the scribes and the Pharisees. Jesus welcomed sinners while turning away from those who passed for just in the sense of the Old Testament. Jesus showed that the last prophet of the Old Testament, John the Baptist, was an ignoramus and the subject of scandal. John himself had said that the Son was the only one to know the Father and that all of those who had come before him had known nothing of him, and had preached another God [...].

When Jesus spoke of the bad tree that could only bear bad fruit and of the good tree and its good fruit, he understood the bad tree to be the God of the Old Testament, who had only created and could only create what is bad. The good tree, on the other hand, is the Father of the Christ, who can only produce good things. And, by denouncing the stitching of a new piece into an old frock and the putting new wine into old bottles, Jesus expressly prohibited the establishment of any kind of connection between his Gospel and the religion of the Old Testament with its [bad] God.

And when Marcion wrote, "O marvel of marvels, rapture and subject of amazement, one absolutely cannot say or think what surpasses the Gospel; there is nothing to which one can compare it"[9], he provided the tone for generations of historians for whom Christianity was the product of Greek civilization and had nothing to do with the Jews.

Nevertheless, Marcion stirred up lively disapproval in his own lifetime. Is it necessary to point out his authoritarianism, his extreme rigor, the envy of the other Church leaders, or the hatred felt for him by the Judeo-Christians whose anti-Judaism did not imply a rejection of the Bible?

The response to this question resides in the reactions and polemics that were engendered by his theses. Gospels and Acts were drafted against them that reported that Jesus was a Jewish agitator who, though undoubtedly put to death by the Jews, was nonetheless nourished by the milk of biblical wisdom. The Gospel placed under the name of Luke detailed the childhood of the Christ, a man born from a woman, even if the *sperma* was called *pneuma*, 'Spirit'.

Paul, the Marcionite apostle, penetrated the anti-Marcionite texts that attested to his 'veritable existence'. Thus the Acts of the Apostles—a novel that presents itself as a historical chronicle—reconciles the apostles Simon-Peter and Paul.[10]

Other letters by Paul were written: the so-called 'pastorals'. Joseph Turmel has established that the letters of Ignatius of Antioch—the same ones that tradition cites as featuring the first appearance of the word 'Catholic'—reveal the existence of a Marcionite version of the pastorals (135, at the earliest) that was revised around 190–210 by another bishop of Antioch, Theophilus, who, despite his hostility to Marcion, complacently relied upon the inspiration of the *Novum testamentum*[11]. This Theophilus did not hesitate to speak of the letters of Paul as the "holy and divine Word"[12], but not without preliminarily ridding them of their Marcionite expressions. He also borrowed from Theodotus the notion of the trinity and, as Deschner remarks, undertook the "harmonization of the Gospels, which appeared to him almost devoid of harmony"[13].

In seeking to demolish Marcion, Theophilus was joined by Denis of Corinth, Philip of Gortyn, Hippolytus of Rome, Clement of Alexandria,

Irenaeus of Lyon, Justin the Apologist, Bardaisan of Edessa, Tertullian, Rhodon, and Modestus. These were mostly men who enjoyed a certain amount of power as leaders of Christian communities.

But the worst enemy of Marcion was Marcion himself. How could a founder of Churches, engaged in politics and in temporal and spiritual affairs, hope to build the power of God upon the foundation of a world that he condemned because it was the work of a Demiurge—a bloody and pernicious God? How could he succeed in establishing a Universal Church in an odious society, a society that simple faith invited one to renounce right away? And to which authority could a bishop go in order to durably legitimate a Jesus who had not lived the life of the humble people whom he ruled?

By breaking with Jewish mythology, did Marcion not completely undermine his faith in a Christianity that was borrowed in its entirety from biblical exegeses? Justin understood this very well when he condemned Marcion and explained to Trypho that—the Jews having lost the key to its interpretation—the Bible thenceforth belonged to the Christians, who were the only ones in a position to confer upon it its true meaning.

Irenaeus, the Bishop of Lyon, had no sympathy for the inventor of Paul; his *Epideixis* explained Christian doctrine on the basis of biblical prophecies. Neither did Tertullian, though he was in other ways close to the one who called marriage trash and an obscenity. Because if Marcion, despite his dualism, was not a Gnostic—for him faith (*pistis*) took precedence over *gnosis*, and adhesion to Christ was not founded upon knowledge (*gnosis*)—he nevertheless stripped the martyrdom of Jesus of its penitential meaning when he separated it from the tradition of Isaiah and the other biblical prophets. Deprived, then, of the sacrificial model of the man dead upon the cross, the Church lost its meaning and utility.

CHAPTER TWELVE

The Inventors of a Christian Theology: Basilides, Valentinus, Ptolemy

In the crucible of Alexandria, the expectation of a Savior who would untangle the obscure paths of the destiny of humanity produced disparate developments on the basis of ancient Egyptian wisdom, Greek thought, Eastern magic, and the Hebrew myths.

From opposite directions, Philo of Alexandria and Simon of Samaria cast the shadow of an absent person. This absence was highlighted both by Judeo-Christian asceticism and by the aspiration of man to save himself.

Against Nazarenism and Elchasaitism, which were forms of Essenism that had been offered up to Greek modernity, there arose the will to emancipate oneself from the Gods, which was celebrated by men such as Lucretius of Rome, Simon of Samaria, Carpocrates of Alexandria, and his son, Epiphanius. Between these two extremes, various schools, sects, secret or Hermetic societies, and inner circles of magicians or sorcerers intermingled and produced—for their own use and according to the rules of existence that they advocated—an astonishing wealth of concepts, visions, and representations in which a multiplicity of internal and external worlds brought together (beyond or below the best and the worst of those worlds) the most extravagant imaginings.

In Alexandria there was born—amid the daily interpenetrations of infernal and paradisiacal universes, interpenetrations that were punctuated by riots, pogroms and social struggles—a theology that successive prunings, rational readjustments, and polemical motivations transformed into a dogmatic edifice that was shakily built upon nebulous foundations, foundations which the Church did not cease to shore up through the combined action of bribed thinkers and State terrorism.

When modern historians have refused to follow Eusebius of Caesarea, for whom the Catholic Church had illuminated the world from the beginning of the Christian era and had thereby aroused the envy of Satan and his henchmen—

> As the churches throughout the world were now shining like the most brilliant stars, and faith in our Saviour and Lord Jesus Christ was flourishing among the whole human race, the demon who hates everything that is good, and is always hostile to the truth, and most bitterly opposed to the salvation of man, turned all his arts against the Church. [...] Instigated by him, impostors and deceivers, assuming the name of our religion, brought to the depths of ruin such of the believers as they could win over[1]

—perhaps these historians have been attempting to make it possible for themselves to extricate the ideas and opinions from which the dogmatic writings of the New Testament and the theses of Nicaea were born from the various philosophical and moral systems that were hastily assembled under the heading of 'gnosis'.

Basilides of Alexandria
To this day, all that we know of Basilides comes from Eusebius's diatribes, which mention an ancient refutation of Basilides' ideas made by a certain Agrippa Castor; from Irenaeus, who was so hostile to Valentinus that he placed all of the Gnostics on his list of adversaries; and from the *Elenchos*, whose author was determined to demonstrate that *gnosis* came from Greek philosophy.

What can one divine of Basilides' existence? A contemporary of Carpocrates, he led a Pythagorean school in Alexandria—he conserved Pythagoras's theory of metempsychosis—that was adapted to the tastes of the times. Basilides' renown peaked around 125 or 135. His son Isidore continued his teachings.

Perhaps due to Philo's influence, Basilides' syncretism encompassed the Judaic elements of Elchasaitism and Naassenism.

Basilides referred to Barkabbas and Barcoph, the presumed sons of Noah and brothers of the Noria who were attested to in Naassenean, Sethian, and Barbelite writings. Clement of Alexandria (who lived between 150 and 215) took Basilides to be the master of a certain Glaucias, a 'disciple of Peter'—that is to say, an Elchasaite or Nazarenean Christian. Many of his moral reflections later appeared in the remarks that the Gospels attributed to Luke and Matthew would attribute to Jesus.

Basilides' morality attempted to trace, through a just moderation, a median route between the extreme asceticism of the Judeo-Christians and the sexual liberty of Carpocrates and the Barbelites. Although he did evoke Pelagius's thesis, there is insufficient evidence for us to determine whether Augustine's adversary actually knew the Alexandrian philosopher.

Basilides supposed that man had a will to perfection that was apt to assure his salvation as a spiritual being. According to the relation of each person to his sexual impulses, Basilides distinguished three categories of individuals: those who had no attraction to women; eunuchs; and men of desire whose merit was vanquishing their passions, thereby permitting the triumph of the spirit over the body:

> Some men, from their birth, have a natural sense of repulsion from a woman; and those who are naturally so constituted do well not to marry. Those who are eunuchs of necessity are those theatrical ascetics who only control themselves because they have a passion for the limelight. [...] Those, then, who are eunuchs of necessity have no sound reason for their abstinence from marriage. But those who for the sake of the eternal kingdom have made themselves eunuchs derive this idea, they say, from a wish to avoid the distractions involved in marriage, because they are afraid of having to waste time in providing for the necessities of life.[2]

To that third category, Basilides—the enemy of obsessive abstinence and the ferocity that it involves—extolled the virtues of intermittent relief and assuagement, which nonetheless remained subject to the regulations of the will and the spirit. Speaking of Basilides' disciples, Clement writes:

> And they say that by the words "it is better to marry than to burn" the apostle means this: "Do not cast your soul into the fire, so that you have to endure night and day and go in fear lest you should fall from continence. For a soul which has to concentrate upon endurance has lost hope". In his *Ethics*, Isidore says in these very words: "Abstain, then, from a quarrelsome woman lest you are distracted from the grace of God. But when you have rejected the fire of the seed, then pray with an undisturbed conscience. And when your prayer of thanksgiving", he says, "descends to a prayer of request, and your request is not that in future you may do right, but that you may do no wrong, then marry".[3]

(Note that this remark would later be reprised, no doubt in an anti-Marcionite sense, in the first Letter to the Corinthians 7: 9, attributed to Saul/Paul: "it is better to marry than to burn with passion".)

> But perhaps a man is too young or poor or suffers from weak health, and has not the will to marry as the apostle's saying suggests. Such a man should not separate himself from his brother Christian. He should say, I have come into the sanctuary, I can suffer nothing. And if he has a presentiment that he may fall, he may say, Brother, lay your hand on me lest I sin, and he will receive help both spiritually and physically. Let him only wish to accomplish what is right and he will achieve his object.
>
> "Sometimes, however, we say with our mouth 'I wish not to sin' while our mind is really inclined towards sin. Such a man does not do what he wishes for fear lest any punishment should be in store for him. Human nature has some wants which are necessary and natural, and others which are only natural. To be clothed is necessary and natural; sexual intercourse is natural but not necessary".[4]

The responsibility of the individual for choosing a virtuous morality extended to suffering or experiencing misfortune; these were punishments for faults. Basilides' sense of guilt and nature as the sources of defilement and impurity proceeded from a Judaic vision that Christianity inherited. Even a child was potentially guilty. Clement of Alexandria writes that:

Basilides, in the twenty-third book of the *Exegetics*, respecting those that are punished by martyrdom, expresses himself in the following language: "For I say this, Whosoever fall under the afflictions mentioned, in consequence of unconsciously transgressing in other matters, are brought to this good end by the kindness of Him who brings them, but accused on other grounds; so that they may not suffer as condemned for what are owned to be iniquities, nor reproached as the adulterer or the murderer, but because they are Christians; which will console them, so that they do not appear to suffer. And if one who has not sinned at all incur suffering—a rare case—yet even he will not suffer aught through the machinations of power, but will suffer as the child which seems not to have sinned would suffer". Then further on he adds: "As, then, the child which has not sinned before, or committed actual sin in itself, but has that which committed sin, when subjected to suffering, gets good, reaping the advantage of many difficulties; so also, although a perfect man may not have sinned in act, while he endures afflictions, he suffers similarly with the child. Having within him the sinful principle, but not embracing the opportunity of committing sin, he does not sin; so that he is not to be reckoned as not having sinned. For as he who wishes to commit adultery is an adulterer, although he does not succeed in committing adultery; and he that wishes to commit murder is a murderer, although he is unable to kill; so also, if I see the man without sin, whom I specify, suffering, though he have done nothing bad, I should call him bad, on account of his wishing to sin. For I will affirm anything rather than call Providence evil". Then, in continuation, he says expressly concerning the Lord, as concerning man: "If then, passing from all these observations, you were to proceed to put me to shame by saying, perchance impersonating certain parties, This man has then sinned; for this man has suffered;—if you permit, I will say, He has not sinned; but was like a child suffering. If you were to insist more urgently, I would say, That the man you name is man, but that God is righteous: 'For no one is pure', as one said, 'from pollution'".[5]

(Note that the reference in the last line is to the Book of Job, 14: 4[6]. Such ideas nourished the letters attributed to Saul/Paul.)

A fragment attributed to Isidore, the son of Basilides, expounded a theory about free will that would later be adopted by Catholicism. According to Clement of Alexandria:

Isidorus, in his book, *About the Soul Attached to Us*, while agreeing in the dogma, as if condemning himself, writes in these words: "For if I persuade any one that the soul is undivided, and that the passions of the wicked are occasioned by the violence of the appendages, the worthless among men will have no slight pretence for saying, 'I was compelled, I was carried away, I did it against my will, I acted unwillingly'; though he himself led the desire of evil things, and did not fight against the assaults of the appendages. But we must, by acquiring superiority in the rational part, show ourselves masters of the inferior creation in us".[7]

In order to provide a cosmic foundation for his morality of the 'perfect', the 'pneumatic', or the 'man who lives according to the spirit', Basilides appealed to a cosmogony, many elements of which made their way into future theological quarrels. Leisegang rightly points to a connection between Basilides' idea of a superior God and the conception attributed to Dionysius the Areopagite[8].

The *Elenchos* says the following about Basilides:

(Time) was, says (Basilides), when there was nothing. Not even, however, did that nothing constitute anything of existent things; but, to express myself undisguisedly and candidly, and without any quibbling, it is altogether nothing.[9]

In his remarks on "the pre-eminent Cause of every object of intelligible perception", Pseudo-Dionysius writes,

On the other hand, ascending, we say, that It is neither soul, nor mind, nor has imagination, or opinion, or reason, or conception; neither is [the abstraction] expressed, nor conceived; neither is number, nor order, nor greatness, nor littleness; nor equality, nor inequality; nor similarity, nor dissimilarity; neither is standing, nor moving; nor at rest; neither has power, nor is power, nor light; neither lives, nor is life; neither is essence nor eternity, nor time; neither is Its touch intelligible, neither is It science, nor truth; nor kingdom, nor wisdom; neither one, nor oneness; neither Deity, nor Goodness; nor is It Spirit according to our understanding; nor Sonship, nor Paternity; nor any other thing of those known to us, or to any other existing being; neither is It any of non-existing nor of existing things, nor do things existing know It, as It is; nor does It know existing things, *qua* existing; neither is there expression of It, nor name, nor knowledge; neither is It darkness, nor light; nor error, nor truth; neither is there any definition at all of It, nor any abstraction. But when making the predications and abstractions of things after It, we neither predicate, nor abstract from It; since the all-perfect and uniform Cause of all is both above every definition and the pre-eminence of Him, Who is absolutely freed from all, and beyond the whole, is also above every abstraction.[10]

Therefore, from this God—who was all-being and all non-being, and who was *Sige*, pure Silence (the disciples of Basilides were apparently required to be silent for five years)—there ejaculated a seed from which three entities were born. The first was the Son of God, *consubstantial* with his Father; the term used by Basilides was the famous *homoousios* [consubstantiality] around which the quarrel of Arianism and the break with Byzantium took place. The Son was thus of the same nature as his Father. The second birth was that of the *pneuma*, the Spirit, the spark of God that plunged into matter and that aspired to return to its celestial kingdom. And the third, the veritable scrapings of the divine sperm, was none other than the earth, the body, and matter, fortunately clarified by the *pneumatic*, spiritual spark.

The *pneuma* frolicked between two spaces: the lower cosmos, which is our universe, and a hyper-cosmos. Thus the *pneuma*, by raising itself up and believing that it had attained the highest place, made itself the Lord (the archon) and created a son who appeared so beautiful to it that it had him sit on its right. It then conceived the Ogdoad, or the eighth heaven, in which it reigned over the celestial creatures.

When the ethereal beings—still issued from the *Logos Spermaticos* that produced the divine nothingness—were ordered to rise, a second archon was summoned to rule over the seven other heavens, or Hebdomad. The archon of Hebdomad was the one who spoke to Moses and identified himself with the Demiurge. His creation multiplied the material and spiritual traps that the *pneumatics* had to overcome in order to regain the *pneuma*, which was co-regent with the Lord of the Ogdoad.

In the same way that sin entered the world because the first archon claimed to have a power that, due to his nature, wasn't his, all the sins of man resided in the will to power that incited him to surpass the limits of his nature.

Both extreme asceticism and license came from sin, because they set themselves aside from the happy medium prescribed by Epicurean morality.

Irenaeus later presented a version of Basilides' theology to which the scraps of the legend of Jesus would be joined:

> He [Basilides] sets forth that Nous was first born of the unborn father, that from him, again, was born Logos, from Logos Phronesis, from Phronesis Sophia and Dynamis, and from Dynamis and Sophia the powers, and principalities, and angels, whom he also calls the *first*; and that by them the first heaven was made. Then other powers, being formed by emanation from these, created another heaven similar to the first; and in like manner, when others, again, had been formed by emanation from them, corresponding exactly to those above them, these, too, framed another third heaven; and then from this third, in downward order, there was a fourth succession of descendants; and so on, after the same fashion, they declare that more and more principalities and angels were formed, and three hundred and sixty-five heavens. Wherefore the year contains the same number of days in conformity with the number of the heavens.
>
> Those angels who occupy the lowest heaven, that, namely, which is visible to us, formed all the things which are in the world, and made allotments among themselves of the earth and of those nations which are upon it. The chief of them is he who is thought to be the God of the Jews; and inasmuch as he desired to render the other nations subject to his own people, that is, the Jews, all the other princes resisted and opposed him. Wherefore all other nations were at enmity with his nation. But the father without birth and without name, perceiving that they would be destroyed, sent his own first-begotten Nous (he it is who is called Christ) to bestow deliverance on them that believe in him, from the power of those who made the world. He appeared, then, on earth as a man, to the nations of these powers, and

wrought miracles. Wherefore he did not himself suffer death, but Simon, a certain man of Cyrene, being compelled, bore the cross in his stead; so that this latter being transfigured by him, that he might be thought to be Jesus, was crucified, through ignorance and error, while Jesus himself received the form of Simon, and, standing by, laughed at them. For since he was an incorporeal power, and the Nous (mind) of the unborn father, he transfigured himself as he pleased, and thus ascended to him who had sent him, deriding them, inasmuch as he could not be laid hold of, and was invisible to all. Those, then, who know these things have been freed from the principalities who formed the world; so that it is not incumbent on us to confess him who was crucified, but him who came in the form of a man, and was thought to be crucified, and was called Jesus, and was sent by the father, that by this dispensation he might destroy the works of the makers of the world. If any one, therefore, he declares, confesses the crucified, that man is still a slave, and under the power of those who formed our bodies; but he who denies him has been freed from these beings, and is acquainted with the dispensation of the unborn father.

Salvation belongs to the soul alone, for the body is by nature subject to corruption. He declares, too, that the prophecies were derived from those powers who were the makers of the world, but the law was specially given by their chief, who led the people out of the land of Egypt. He attaches no importance to [the question regarding] meats offered in sacrifice to idols, thinks them of no consequence, and makes use of them without any hesitation; he holds also the use of other things, and the practice of every kind of lust, a matter of perfect indifference. These men, moreover, practise magic, and use images, incantations, invocations, and every other kind of curious art. Coining also certain names as if they were those of the angels, they proclaim some of these as belonging to the first, and others to the second heaven; and then they strive to set forth the names, principles, angels, and powers of the three hundred and sixty-five imagined heavens. They also affirm that the barbarous name in which the Saviour ascended and descended, is Caulacau.

He, then, who has learned [these things], and known all the angels and their causes, is rendered invisible and incomprehensible to the angels and all the powers, even as Caulacau also was. And as the son was unknown to all, so must they also be known by no one; but while they know all, and pass through all, they themselves remain invisible and unknown to all; for, "Do you", they say, "known all, but let nobody know thee". For this reason, persons of such a persuasion are also ready to recant [their opinions], yea, rather, it is impossible that they should suffer on account of a mere name, since they are like to all. The multitude, however, cannot understand these matters, but only one out of a thousand, or two out of ten thousand. They declare that they are no longer Jews, and that they are not yet Christians; and that it is not at all fitting to speak openly of their mysteries, but right to keep them secret by preserving silence.

They make out the local position of the three hundred and sixty-five heavens in the same way as do mathematicians. For, accepting the theorems of these latter, they have transferred them to their own type of doctrine. They hold that their chief is *Abraxas*; and, on this account, that word contains in itself the numbers amounting to three hundred and sixty-five.[11]

(Note that those who were "not yet Christians" nevertheless constituted a branch of the Esseno-Christian tree: they were a Hellenized branch distinct from Marcionism, although the absence of women from their cosmogony confirmed their tendency towards asceticism.)

Disentangled from the Christianity of the 180s, in which Irenaeus located them, the Basilideans' syncretism suggests a connection—because of the importance given to Abrasax and to magic carvings [in stones] called *abraxas*—to the cult of Mithras, from which the sects devoted to Joshua/Jesus borrowed the specific image of a solar divinity. It is probable that Basilides facilitated the exchange between Mithraism and Christianity.

The importance of magic, on the other hand, appears unquestionable. Bonner has studied talismans that bear representations of Abrasax, the Anguiped divinity with the head of a rooster who united the sun and the earth, light and darkness, male and female[12].

Based on the reports concerning Abrasax and Mithras:

Jerome, *In Amos* III (P.L., XXV, col. 1018 D), notes that Basilides designated his all-powerful God with the magic name Abraxas; by adding up the respective numerical values of each Greek letter in this name, one obtained the number of circles that the 'Sun' describes in the course of a year; this is the same god as Mithras, [because] that name, although formed with different letters, totals the same numerical value:

$$A\text{-}B\text{-}P\text{-}A\text{-}\Xi\text{-}A\text{-}\Sigma$$
$$1+2+100+1+60+1+200 = 365$$

$$M\text{-}E\text{-}I\text{-}\Theta\text{-}P\text{-}A\text{-}\Sigma$$
$$40+5+10+9+100+1+200 = 365$$

From then on, the meaning of the 365 heavens is clear. Just as the circuit of the seven planets distinguishes seven heavens, each circle described by the sun forms a heaven—that is to say, a spherical envelope traced out by this circle. Each day, then, the sun traverses a circle that is slightly different from that of the preceding day, and it is thus that—following Egyptian computations, which count months of thirty days each—there are 360 circles or heavens. The five other circles echo the planets—apart from the sun and the moon, which are assigned particular roles—and the annual interstitial week of five days, which comes to the same thing because the days of the week carry the names of the planets. The sun is Helios, and Mithras-Abraxas is the Archon who embraces the totality of the solar circle as a unity. Mithras and Helios are in a father-son relationship. Mithras is the Great God; Helios is his *Logos*, thanks to whom he developed and thus created the world; Helios plays the role of mediator between man and God. He had the same function as the *Christos-Logos*; see the 'liturgy of Mithras' and the speech of Emperor Julian about King Helios.[13]

According to Basilides, the Great Archon had a son, the Christ of the Ogdoad. The Hebdomad then had his Archon and he, in his turn, had a son, also Christ, the solar Christ, the simultaneously divine and human twin of the superior Christ of the Ogdoad.

Thus Abrasax became the prototype of the *Christos-Helios* and of the epoch that he governed.

Abraxas, like Mithras, signifies the God who unites in himself the power of the seven planets, because his name is composed of seven letters. Because these seven letters have a total value of 365, it follows that he contains within him 365 partial or subaltern Gods. As temporal grandeur, he contains a whole year or every year that the world lives; he is the Eon, the Eternity. Each partial god presides over one day. An echo of this belief subsisted in the calendar of the Catholic Church, in which each day carries the name of a saint, the king of that day. The Christian Gods simply took the place of the pagan Gods.[14]

Valentinus and the Valentinians

In a letter to the consul Servianus, Emperor Hadrian (117–38) gave an idea of the confusion of the messianic sects that were then called 'Christian':

> I am now become fully acquainted with that Egypt which you extol so highly. I have found the people vain, fickle, and shifting with every breath of opinion. Those who worship Serapis are in fact Christians; and they who call themselves Christian bishops are actually worshippers of Serapis. There is no chief of a Jewish synagogue, no Samaritan, no Christian bishop, who is not an astrologer, a fortune teller and a conjuror. The patriarch himself, when he comes to Egypt, is compelled by one party to worship Serapis, by the other, Christ. [...] They have but one God [...]—him Christians, Jews, and Gentiles worship all alike.[15]

It was from the microcosm of Alexandria that Valentinus came; along with Philo and Basilides, he was the father of speculative theology. Fleeing the troubles and repressions of the last war of the Jews, he went to Rome, where he stayed from 136 to 140. While he was there he crossed paths with the Judeo-Christians (whose dissensions the *Pastor of Hermas* deplored), with Marcion and his Pauline Churches, with the disciples of Carpocrates (for whom hedonism traced out the path to salvation), and with the mob of bishops and leaders of Christian sects who had uncertain doctrines and appetites for unbridled domination.

A brilliant rhetorician, a poet, and the author of letters and essays, Valentinus shared with Christianity only a certain propensity for asceticism and references to a redeemer: the Christ-*Logos*, or a spiritual entity tasked with guiding souls towards the kingdom of the ineffable and good God. He was the author of the treatise *The Three Natures* (now lost) and the *Gospel of Truth*, which was discovered at Nag Hammadi.

Did Valentinus prophesy in the manner of Elchasai or, twenty years later, of Montanus, Priscilla, and Maximilla, the initiators of the New Prophecy? Nothing permits one to be sure of this, but note the importance that he allegedly accorded to ecstasy, as described in a later report made by Epiphanius of Salamis:

> "Greeting from <unnameable>, indestructible Mind to the indestructible among the discerning, the soulish, the fleshly, the worldly, and in the presence of the Majesty!
>
> "I make mention before you of mysteries unnameable, ineffable, and supercelestial, not to be comprehended by principalities, authorities, subordinates or all commingled, but manifest to the Ennoia of the Changeless alone". (*Panarion*, ii. 31. 5, 1–2)[16]

The Valentinian theological system developed Basilides's cosmo-genesis with a complexity reminiscent of the tortuous discourse of scholasticism. According to the *Gospel of Truth*, the divine world or Pleroma (which expresses well the modern term 'totality') was founded on a duality: the Ineffable, the male principle, and Silence, the female principle. From their coupling was born a second duality, and from that came a quaternary principle, with the whole forming the Ogdoad ($2 + 2 + 4 = 8$). Eleven couples of Eons (entities, powers, forces) proceeded from it; men and women sketched out this amorous adventure of creation, which was as foreign to Judaism as it was to Catholicism. The total was $8 + 22$—that is, 30 Eons—of which the last one, the youngest, was none other than Sophia. Relegated to the place furthest away from the primordial duality, Sophia was pregnant with desire and revolt, and engendered the Demiurge, the God of Genesis and the world.

By striving to separate her desire from the obscurity that reigned beyond the Pleroma, Sophia abandoned into flesh a fragment of spirit and soul. So as to save the spirit thus imprisoned in matter, the celestial

Messiah sent the Christ Jesus to teach men the nature and destiny of their souls, with the result that, having crossed the threshold of death, they were able to return to their place of origin.

Platonism, which was inherent in the idea of a world that imperfectly reflected the primordial Eon, explains the manner in which Valentinus's theology not only prefigured the simplifications and desexualizations wrought by Catholic dogma, but also foreshadowed the legalisms of the theologians, from Arianism to Jansenism.

As for Jesus, if he was no longer Joshua—because Valentinus's Christianity wanted to be purely Greek—then he remained the descendant of *Sophia*, the *pneuma* or Spirit, here designated by the term *Logos*.

In a poem, Valentinus illustrated the following remark, which was ascribed to him by the *Elenchos*: "Valentinus [...] alleges that he had seen an infant child lately born; and questioning (this child), he proceeded to inquire who it might be. And (the child) replied, saying that he himself is the Logos"[17]. This manner of proceeding on the part of the author of the *Elenchos* is a good illustration of that text's reduction of philosophical discourse to the level of anecdote. Here is the poem, as transcribed in an earlier passage in the *Elenchos*: "I behold all things suspended in air by spirit, and I perceive all things wafted by spirit; the flesh (I see) suspended from soul, but the soul shining out from air, and air depending from aether, and fruits produced from Bythus, and the foetus borne from the womb"[18].

It was in reaction against such conceptions that the Gospels recounted the childhood of Jesus, his escapades, and his family. They derived principally from a popular Christianity, a Christianity that rejected the abstractions and elitism of the Valentinians because it needed exemplary legends to help support its martyrs and faith (the *pistis*). The New Prophecy, carrying even further the simplicity of Elchasaitism, condemned speculations about the Savior, the *Sophia*, the Good God, and the bad world, all of which were incomprehensible to the humble people. Clement of Alexandria wasn't wrong when he wrote, in his *Stromata*: "the followers of Valentinus assign faith to us, the simple, but will have it that knowledge springs up in their own selves (who are saved by nature) through the advantage of a germ of superior excellence, saying that it is as far removed from faith as the spiritual is from the animal"[19].

Clement was also a philosopher, but, in the manner of Irenaeus, the Bishop of Lyon, he adhered, if not directly to the New Prophecy, then at least to the fervent movement that it inspired and that would only later alienate his excessive taste for martyrdom and aggressive puritanism. Irenaeus took up the pen against "so-called gnosis" while Clement identified *gnosis* with the Christian faith, but both of them chose—instead of the Hellenization of Christianity that was gradually assimilating it [Christianity] into a renewal of Greek philosophy—the social and non-violent ferment that united in the Churches and under the authority of the bishops all those (rich and poor alike) whose mythical and ecumenical spirit described (for the first time) a Jesus who was stripped of his angelic nature and portrayed as an agitator: a Jesus who chased the merchants from the Temple, healed the unfortunate, incurred the betrayal of his friends, submitted to an infamous death, and was resurrected in glory in the kingdom of the heavens, according to the hopes of the Montanist martyrs. In fact, on the question 'Who is the Rich Man That Shall Be Saved?', Clement wrote a homily in which he extolled the collaboration of the classes in their shared detachment from the benefits of this world. (An echo of this sentiment would be retained in the composition of the Gospel attributed to Matthew towards the end of the second century.)

Nevertheless, the future theological corpus of the Church came from Valentinus. The *Tripartite Tractate* discovered at Nag Hammadi revealed a trinitarian conception of God, one composed of the Father, the Son and the *Ekklēsia* (in the sense of the 'mystical communities of the faithful' illustrated by Hermas). According to Tertullian, the same conception was found in the works of Heracleon, a disciple of Valentinus. Theodotus, also a Valentinian, spoke of the Father, the Son, and the *Pneuma*-Spirit more than a century and a half before Nicaea.

The *Treatise on the Resurrection* (Nag Hammadi), which was of Valentinian origin, supported a doctrine according to which "the resurrection of the believer has already happened" and exhorted Christians to live as if they had already been resurrected[20]. The New Prophecy fought against a similar assertion, and two letters placed with impunity under the name of Paul—the Letters to Timothy—attempted to combat this Valentinian argument.

The *pneumatics* or Perfect Ones attempted to accede to the state of pure spirit. Their conception of Jesus responded to their aspirations: he was the son of a carpenter and a friend of the poor. Such was the populism of Montanus.

According to Clement[21], the Valentinians believed that Jesus "ate and drank in a manner peculiar to himself, and the food did not pass out of his body. Such was the power of his continence that food was not corrupted within him; for he himself was not subject to the process of corruption". Perhaps the Barbelites and the Carpocratics were not wrong to make fun of such a concordance between spiritual asceticism and constipation.

The incorruptible *Logos* became the principle of eternity. In the words of a homily written by Valentinian: "Ye are originally immortal, and children of eternal life, and ye would have death distributed to you, that ye may spend and lavish it, and that death may die in you and by you; for when we dissolve the world, and are not yourselves dissolved, ye have dominion over creation and all corruption"[22]. These would be admirable remarks if they did not involve a perspective that was radically hostile to life, because they implied a spiritualization in which the body and its desires were reduced to precisely nothing.

Especially as it was developed by Mark, Valentinianism did not exclude a relationship with Hermeticism. According to the *Elenchos*, a certain Monoime—in all probability a symbolic name, like Allogenes or Autogenes—took his stand on the first letter of the word *Iesou* and was inspired by Plato and Pythagoras when he argued: "For cubes, and octahedrons, and pyramids, and all figures similar to these, out of which consist fire, air, water, (and) earth, have arisen from numbers which are comprehended in that simple tittle of the iota. And this (tittle) constitutes a perfect son of a perfect man"[23]. Such doctrines flourished among the doctors of Kabbalah, as well as among Renaissance scholars such as Marsilio Ficino. Accommodating themselves poorly to the political will of the bishops and their flocks to push Jesus toward the steps of the Imperial Palace, they encountered only condemnation and scorn.

Ptolemy

Ptolemy occupied a distinctive position in the Valentinian school. He was known through an *Epistle to Flora* that Epiphanius recopied—albeit not without garnishing it with quotations from the canonical Gospels with all the care of a Catholic who wanted to confirm the antiquity of a dogma that was in fact a distortion of the thought of the perverse and heretical Ptolemy—in his *Panarion.*

Confronted with the variety of the doctrines that composed Christianity in the second half of the second century, Flora had lost the light of the Spirit. Marcionism and anti-Marcionism were at that point agitating the Christian, Jewish, and Greco-Roman milieus.

Ptolemy estimated himself so well prepared to suggest a philosophical supersession of the two positions [i.e. Marcionism and anti-Marcionism] that he confessed his past adherence to Marcionism: "I, who have benefited from the knowledge of the two Gods"[24].

More than two centuries after the birth of Essenism, the problem of Mosaic law continued to nourish speculations in those milieus that preoccupied themselves with the choice of a religious path. In the words of Ptolemy's *Epistle to Flora*[25]:

> The law established by Moses, my dear sister Flora, has in the past been misunderstood by many people, for they were not closely acquainted with the one who established it or with its commandments. I think you will see this at once if you study their discordant opinions on this topic. [...] For some say that this law has been ordained by god the father; while others, following the opposite course, stoutly contend that it has been established by the adversary, the pernicious devil; and so the latter school attributes the craftsmanship of the world to the devil, saying that he is "the father and maker of all this universe"[26]. <But> they are <utterly> in error, they disagree with one another, and each of the schools utterly misses the truth of the matter.

Ptolemy distinguished three stages in Mosaic Law: a Law of God, a Law of the Jews, and a revision according to the Spirit (the *pneuma*) that founded Christianity[27].

The first, the law of god that is pure and not interwoven with the inferior, is the decalogue or Ten Commandments inscribed on two stone tablets; they divide into the prohibition of things that must be avoided and the commanding of things that must be done. Although they contain pure legislation they do not have perfection, and so they were in need of fulfillment by the savior. [...]

The second, which is interwoven with injustice, is that which applies to retaliation and repayment of those who have already committed a wrong, commanding us to pluck out an eye for an eye and a tooth for a tooth and to retaliate for murder with murder. This part is interwoven with injustice, for the one who is second to act unjustly still acts unjustly, differing only in the relative order in which he acts, and committing the very same act. But otherwise, this commandment both was and is just, having been established as a deviation from the pure law because of the weakness of those to whom it was ordained; yet it is incongruous with the nature and goodness of the father of the entirety. Now perhaps this was apt; but even more, it was a result of necessity. For when one who does not wish even a single murder to occur—by saying, "You shall not murder"[28]—when, I say, he ordains a second law and commands the murderer to be murdered, acting as judge between two murders, he who forbade even a single murder has without realizing it been cheated by necessity.

For this reason, then, the son who was sent from him abolished this part of the law, though he admits that it too belonged to god: this part is reckoned as belonging to the old school of thought, both where he says, "For god commanded, 'Whoever reviles father or mother must surely die'"[29] and elsewhere. [...]

And the third subdivision of god's law is the symbolic part, which is after the image of the superior, spiritual realm: I mean, what is ordained about offerings, circumcision, the Sabbath, fasting, Passover, the Feast of Unleavened Bread, and the like.

Now, once the truth [i.e. the savior and his teachings[30]] had been manifested, the referent of all these ordinances was changed, inasmuch as they are images and allegories. As to their meaning in the visible realm and their physical accomplishment they were abolished; but as to their spiritual meaning they were elevated, with the words remaining the same but the subject matter being altered. For the savior commanded us to offer offerings, but not dumb beasts or incense: rather, spiritual praises and glorifications and prayers of thanksgiving, and offerings in the form of sharing and good deeds.

And he wishes us to perform circumcision, but not circumcision of the bodily foreskin, rather of the spiritual heart; and to keep the Sabbath, for he wants us to be inactive in wicked acts; and to fast, though he does not wish us to perform physical fasts, rather spiritual ones, which consist of abstinence from all bad deeds. [...]

Nevertheless, fasting as to the visible realm is observed by our adherents, since fasting, if practiced with reason, can contribute something to the soul, so long as it does not take place in imitation of other people or by habit or because fasting has been prescribed <for> a particular day. Likewise, it is observed in memory of true fasting, so that those who are not yet able to observe true fasting might have a remembrance of it from fasting according to the visible realm. Likewise, the apostle Paul makes it clear that Passover and the Feast of Unleavened Bread were images, for he says that "Christ, our Passover lamb, has been sacrificed" and, he says, be without leaven, having no share in leaven—now, by "leaven" he means evil—but rather "be a new lump"[31]. [...]

And so it can be granted that the actual law of god is subdivided into three parts. The first subdivision is the part that was fulfilled by the savior: for "you shall not murder", "you shall not commit adultery", "you shall not bear false witness"[32] are subsumed under not being angry, not looking lustfully at another, and not swearing at all. [...]

The second subdivision is the part that was completely abolished. For the commandment of "eye for eye, tooth for tooth"[33], which is interwoven with injustice and itself involves an act of injustice, was abolished by the savior with injunctions to the contrary, and of two contraries one must "abolish" the other: "But I say to you, Do not resist the one who is evil. But if anyone slaps you [singular] on the right cheek, turn to him the other also"[34]. [...]

And the third subdivision is the part whose referent was changed and which was altered from the physical to the spiritual—the allegorical part, which is ordained after the image of the superior realm. Now, the images and allegories are indicative of other matters, and they were well and good while truth was not present. But now that truth is present, one must do the works of truth and not those of its imagery. [...]

His disciples made these teachings known, and so did the apostle Paul: he makes known to us the part consisting of images, through the passage on the paschal lamb and the unleavened bread, which we have already spoken of. The part consisting of a law interwoven with injustice, he made known by speaking of "abolishing the law of commandments expressed in ordinances"[35]; and the part not interwoven with the inferior, when he says, "So the law is holy, and the commandment is holy and righteous and good"[36].

If these quotations from Paul pertained as much to Judeo-Christian revisionism as to Marcionism, the end of the letter by Ptolemy sketched out a return to monotheism. Thanks to the impetus of Augustine of Hippo and his thesis of the weakness of man, Catholicism developed the Ptolemaic explication of the evil introduced into the world.

> Thus I think I have shown you, as well as possible in a brief treatment, both that there is human legislation which has been slipped into the law and that the law of god himself divides into three subdivisions. [...]
>
> Now it remains for us to say what sort of being this god is, who established the law. But this too I believe I have demonstrated to you (sing.) in what I have already said, providing you have followed carefully. [...]
>
> For since this division of the law (that is, god's own law) was established neither by the perfect god, as we have taught, nor surely by the devil—which it would be wrong to say—then the establisher of this division of the law is distinct from them.
>
> And he is the craftsman and maker of the universe or world and of the things within it. Since he is different from the essences of the other two <and> (rather) is in a state intermediate between them, he would rightfully be described by the term intermediateness. [...]
>
> And if the perfect god is good according to his nature—as indeed he is, for our savior showed that "there is only one who is good"[37], namely his father whom he manifested—and if furthermore the law belonging to the nature of the adversary is both evil and wicked and is stamped in the mold of injustice, then a being that is in a state intermediate between these and is neither good, nor evil or unjust, might well be properly called just, being a judge of the justice that is his. [...]

And on the one hand this god must be inferior to the perfect god and less than his righteousness precisely because he is engendered and not unengendered—for "there is one God, the Father, from whom are all things"[38], or more exactly, from whom all things depend; and on the other hand, he must have come into being as better and more authoritative than the adversary; and must be born of an essence and nature distinct from the essences of the other two. For the essence of the adversary is both corruption and darkness, for the adversary is material and divided into many parts; while the essence of the unengendered father of the entirety is both incorruptibility and self-existent light, being simple and unique. And the essence of this intermediate produced a twofold capacity, for he is an image of the better god.

And now, given that the good by nature engenders and produces the things that are similar to itself and of the same essence, do not be bewildered as to how these natures—that of corruption and <that> of intermediateness—which have come to be different in essence, arose from a single first principle of the entirety, a principle that exists and is confessed and believed in by us, and which is unengendered and incorruptible and good.[39]

Ptolemy then announced in his letter-preamble to a Christian rite of initiation that Flora had to elevate herself to a superior degree of instruction. His status as the leader of a community or as a bishop, which was legitimized by a claim to apostolic descent, authorized him to confer such instruction:

> For, god permitting, you will next learn about both the first principle and the generation of these two other gods, if you are deemed worthy of the apostolic tradition, which even we have received by succession; and along with this you will learn how to test all the propositions by means of our savior's teaching. [...]
>
> I have not failed, my sister Flora, to state these matters to you briefly. And what I have just written is a concise account, though I have treated the subject adequately. In the future these teachings will be of the greatest help to you—at least if, like good rich soil that has received fertile seeds, you bear fruit.[40]

Thus an elitist Christianity that substituted the refinement of a philosophical tradition for the crude matter of Hebrew mythology penetrated the aristocratic and cultivated milieus of the Empire. Upon this Christianity of schoolmasters—the source of future Catholic theology—there would suddenly break a Christianity that was wild, fanatical and popular, and that would, on the basis of renunciation and sacrifice, elevate [*ériger*] the misery and resentment of the disinherited classes. Its program would inscribe itself in this remark (attributed to Jesus and hostile to the 'pneumatics'): "Blessed are the poor in spirit"[41].

The Pistis Sophia

A late text (from the third century), the *Pistis Sophia* was a passably muddled, esoteric novel in which the remarks seem to reflect a concern with accommodating two antithetical notions: *pistis* (faith) and *gnosis* (knowledge). Leisegang summarizes it as follows:

> We are in the twelfth year after the resurrection of Jesus. Jesus recounts for his disciples, united on the Mount of Olives, his voyage across the world of the Eons and the Archons, whose power he had broken. In the course of his ascension he encountered Pistis Sophia, whose adventures he describes at great length. In the beginning, she dwelled in the thirteenth Eon; desire for the superior world of the light made her raise her eyes towards the light of the heights. She thus drew upon herself the hatred of the Archons of the Twelve Eons; it is necessary to understand by this reference the masters of the fixed heaven, who correspond to the twelve signs of the Zodiac. It was between this heaven and the domain of the light, in the intermediary place, beyond the world limited by the heaven of the stars, that Sophia lived. A false light attracted her towards the world and she became trapped in matter. Desperate, she addressed thirteen prayers of contrition to the light of the heights and implored that she be saved from the snares of her enemies. When she arrived at the ninth prayer of contrition, Jesus was sent into the chaotic world on the orders of the first mystery. He transported Sophia from Chaos to a place secluded from the world. Pistis Sophia then addressed to God a suite of hymns of thanks, because he had saved her from her distress. Finally, Jesus ascended again and led Pistis Sophia—that is to say,

the emanations of the Great Invisible—and their unengendered and their self-engendered and their engendered and their stars and their odd numbers and their archons and their powers and their lords and their archangels and their angels and their decans and their liturgies and all the dwellings of their spheres and all the orders of each one of them. And Jesus did not tell his disciples everything about the expansion [*extension*] of the emanations from the Treasury or their orders, and he did not tell them about the saviors of each order, and he did not tell them about the guardian who is at each of the doors to the Treasury of Light, and he did not tell them about the place of the Twin Savior who is the Child of the Child, and he did not tell them about the place of the three amens, the places in which the five trees grow, nor anything about the place or the expansion of the seven other amens—that is to say, the seven voices. And Jesus did not tell his disciples what kind are the five parasites, nor where they are placed; he did not tell them in which fashion the Great Light is deployed, nor in which place it is placed; he did not tell them about the location of the five regions, nor anything concerning the first commandment, but spoke to them only in general terms, teaching them that those things existed; he did not speak to them of their expansion or of the order of their places [...]. It is an engulfed world that reveals itself to us in this indefatigable enumeration of supra-terrestrial entities, celestial regions, and magic symbols; a world in which the first readers of the book must find themselves perfectly at ease among the Eons, decans, liturgies, archons, and angels, among the innumerable mysteries and their places.[42]

CHAPTER THIRTEEN

Marcus and the Hellenization of Jewish Hermeticism

Irenaeus vituperated the Hermeticist Marc (or Marcus) in his *Against Heresies*, which reveals his sympathy for the contemporary movement of the New Prophecy, many of whose followers perished in the pogroms at Lyon in 177. He mocked the favors lavished upon Marcus by the aristocracy—by "the ladies in robes bordered with purple"[1] (a privilege of the equestrian or even senatorial classes)—and his propensity for the pleasures of love. True or false, the anecdote that he relayed—so often plagiarized by Inquisitorial reports—conveys popular Christianity's reprobation of the 'sins of the flesh':

> A sad example of this occurred in the case of a certain Asiatic, one of our deacons, who had received him (Marcus) into his house. His wife, a woman of remarkable beauty, fell a victim both in mind and body to this magician, and for a long time, travelled about with him. At last, when, with no small difficulty, the brethren had converted her, she spent her whole time in the exercise of public confession, weeping over and lamenting the defilement which she had received from this magician.[2]

Well versed in *gematria*—interpretation based upon the numbering of the Hebrew letters—Marcus belonged to the Jewish milieus of Palestine or the Diaspora. He frequented Alexandria, where he was influenced by

Philo, Basilides, and Carpocrates; Asia Minor, which was the birthplace of Elchasaitism and so-called 'Montanism'; and Gaul, where Irenaeus fought against him.

Marcus renewed ties with the feminine nature of the Spirit (Achamoth or Sophia). This was the meaning of the rite of initiation that he practiced, although Irenaeus's report does not exclude an erotic usage of prophecy, such as that taken up by the faithful of Montanus: "He [Marcus] devotes himself especially to women, and those such as are well-bred, and elegantly attired [...] by addressing them in such seductive words as these: [...] 'Establish the germ of light in thy nuptial chamber. Receive from me a spouse, and become receptive of him, while thou art received by him. Behold Charis has descended upon thee open thy mouth and prophesy'"[3]. It is pleasing to recall here the original identity of the *pneuma* and the *sperma*, and the orgiastic character of the vocal modulations ascribed to the prophetesses of the past.

According to the *Elenchos*, Marcus reproduced the miracles that the tales of Montanist propaganda had diffused concerning Jesus, who went from being an *Angelos-Christos* to a Zorro for the poor. Before the faithful, he transformed water into wine and poured it into a small cup that he decanted into a large one, which was miraculously filled to the brim. His priestesses then administered the beverage in the guise of communion.

When the Church of the fourth century unleashed its polemic against the New Prophecy and its puritanism (which was called 'Encratism'), it calumniously maintained the confusion between Montanism—which accorded certain sacerdotal functions to devoted women, who were sanctified by their virginity—and the cult of Marcus, in which women incarnated the spirit that impregnated bodies through love, a practice that the Church perceived only in terms of 'license', 'debauchery', and 'fornication'.

Due to some kind of natural curse, fanaticism never resists the temptation to expound—and thereby to save from annihilation—the doctrines that are the objects of its execration. Irenaeus thus provided precise information about the teachings of Marcus, which were the meeting point between Pythagorean mysticism and Jewish Kabbalah.

The *Sige* of which Basilides spoke (the Silence of the Nothing-God) had, according to Marcus, deposited in himself, as in a womb, the germ of the Tetrad or Quaternary. In Hebrew, the Tetrad or Quaternary is called *Kolorbas*, which the heresiologues transformed into a certain Colorbases, a disciple of Marcus.

The Tetrad, an emanation of the Ineffable God, descended from the invisible places in the form of a woman. She revealed to Him her proper essence and the genesis of the All. Leisegang writes[4]:

> In the beginning, when the Apator—inconceivable, without essence, neither male nor female—wanted to render its ungraspable nature graspable and its invisible nature visible, it opened its mouth and emitted the Word (*Logos*), which was equal to itself. The *Logos* placed itself before Apator and showed Apator its essence, because it was the visible manifestation of the Invisible. The pronunciation of the name took place in the following manner. It said the first word of its name, this being:
>
> A P X H
> 1 2 3 4
>
> It was composed of four letters. Then he pronounced the second word, which was also formed from four letters. Then came the third, which contained ten letters. The following one contained twelve. The pronunciation of the whole name included thirty letters and four words. Each of these elements had its particular letters, its particular character, its particular pronunciation, its particular aspect, and none of them knew the figure of the word in which it was only an element, nor even the pronunciation of its neighbor; through its own sound, it imagined itself pronouncing the All. Each of them took the sound that was its own for the All, when in fact it was only a part of the All, and the sound did not cease to resonate until, in its emission, it had reached the last letter of the last element. After that the restoration of the All took place, when the All became a single letter and heard a single and self-same emission of the voice; according to the Marcusians, the image of this pronunciation was represented by the [']Amen['] that we say together. The sounds formed the substanceless and unbegotten Eon; they were the forms that the Lord called angels and that uninterruptedly see the face of the Father. The common and expressible names of the letter-elements are

the Eons, *Logoi*, Roots, *Spermata*, Pleromas and Fruits. As for their individual and particular names, they were—according to Marcus—contained in the name of the *Ekklēsia*. The last sign of the last letter of these elements made its own voice heard; the sound of this voice went out and engendered— in the image of the letters—its own elements; it is from them that the things of our world were made, before engendering those things that came after them. The letter itself, the sound of which followed the echo from below, was reprised on high by its own syllable so as to complete the entire name; as for the sound, it remained below, as if thrown away. The element itself, from which the sign descended with its pronunciation, was composed of thirty letters, and each of these thirty letters contained in itself other letters, thanks to which the name of each letter was determined; and these last letters were, in their turn, designated by other letters, and so on, with the result that their multitude extended to infinity, because each one was spelled in its turn with letters. The following example will make what I mean better understood: the letter $\Lambda = \Delta$ E Λ T A, which contains five letters: Δ, E, Λ, T, and A. These letters, in their turn, are written by means of other letters, and so on. Thus, if the structure of the Delta already breaks down into an infinity of parts, each letter engendering others in its turn and relaying still others, then the ocean of letters of this primordial Element will be even vaster. And if a unique letter is in fact infinite, you will see the abyss full of the letters of the entire name that—following the *Sige* of Marcus—composes the Propator. The Propator, aware of its incomprehensibility, gave to the elements that Marcus also called Eons the faculty of making each letter re-echo its own pronunciation, a single one being incapable of expressing the All.

Then came the evocation of the Naked Truth, in which each part of the body corresponded to letters, which were themselves twins of the twelve signs of the Zodiac, the twelve planets, the twelve hours, and the twelve masters (the Archons) of the entities or tutelary powers (*daimon*). Leisegang writes:

After having revealed this, the Tetractys said to him: I want to show you Aletheia herself; because I have made her descend from the dwellings on high so that you can see her naked and so that you can remark her beauty, so that you can even hear her speak and so that you can admire her wisdom. Look on high:

her head Α Ω
her neck Β Ψ
her shoulders and her hands Γ Χ
her bosom Δ Φ
her midriff Ε Γ
her belly Ζ Τ
her genitalia Η Σ
her thighs Θ Ρ
her knees Ι Π
her legs Κ Ο
her ankles Λ Ξ
her feet Μ Ν

This ancient tradition, which probably arose from the Jewish milieu in Alexandria in the first century, clarifies the remark reprised in the Apocalypse attributed to John: "'I am the Alpha and the Omega', says the Lord God, 'who is and who was and who is to come, the Almighty'"[5]. (Note that Dubourg has indicated the Hebrew origin of the formula 'The One who has been, is, will be': "Hebrew verbs are not conjugated in the past, present or future [...] but in the accomplished or the unaccomplished"[6]. For example, the accomplished form of the verb 'to say' *MR*, means: he says/has said/will say, completely, absolutely; while the unaccomplished form, *Y'MR*, means it is/was/will be in the process of being said.)

The entirety of the correspondences between the letters and the Eons constituted the Pleroma. By grasping an eon in its totality, magic allowed action upon the universe. (Note that Manuscript 44 at Nag Hammadi contains an invocation based upon vowels. The 'symphonia' or song of the seven vowels—each of which represented a planet—allowed one to express, through the various possible combinations, the harmony of the celestial spheres, and to exert action upon the stars. Charles Fourier later expounded a similar conception. The universe conceived as language gave meaning to Kabbalistic and magical investigations.)

By annexing the *Logos* Jesus, the syncretism of Marcus defined itself as a Christianity and perhaps revealed the reason why (towards the end of the first century or at the beginning of the second) there was a consensus in Alexandria and Antioch between the schools of Satornilus, Cerinthus, Peter, James, Thomas, and Saul regarding the secret name of the Messiah—the biblical Joshua who was set up as a symbol of revised Judaism.

The Hellenized version of Marcusian syncretism probably referred back to the same calculations that intrigued the esoteric circles whose tone was set by Essenism (cf. the horoscope of the Messiah and the interpretations of the letter *WAW* or *Episemon*, the sixth in the Hebrew alphabet). Leisegang writes:

> When the Tetractys said these words, Aletheia looked at him and opened her mouth to pronounce a word (*Logos*). This Word became a name and the name was that which we know and say: Christ Jesus. Once this name was pronounced, she immediately returned to a profound silence. As Marcus expected her to say more, the Tetractys advanced to say: ["]Do you consider the Word that you have heard from the mouth of Aletheia to be insignificant? This is not a matter of a name that you have long known and believed yourself to possess. You have only known the sound; you have not known all of its virtue. Because ΙΗΣΟΥΣ is a name honored by all; it is composed of six letters and it is invoked by all of the appeals["].
>
> The three primordial elements, which compose the three pairs of powers (*Pater* and *Aletheia*, *Logos* and *Zoe*, *Anthropos* and *Ekklēsia*) that together yield the number six, and from which proceed the twenty-four letters, if one multiplies them by four (that is to say, by the *Logos* of the Ineffable Tetrad), yield the same number as the letters do—that is to say, twenty-four. These twenty-four elements belong to the Unnamable. They are carried by the six powers so as to produce the resemblance of the Invisible. The images of the images of these elements are the three doubled letters Ξ Ψ Z that count double, as six letters. If, in accordance with this similarity, one adds them to the twenty-four letters, one obtains the number thirty. As the fruit of this calculation and this economy, there appears in the resemblance of an image the one who, after six days, climbed the mountain as the fourth and became

the sixth, and who descended again and was retained in the Hebdomad, being himself the Ogdoad and possessing in himself the complete number of the elements. This number was revealed by the descent of the dove when it came to be baptized. The dove is the omega = 800 and the alpha = 1, because its numeric value is 801.

It is for the same reason that Moses said that man was formed on the sixth day (the name ΙΗΣΟΥΣ is composed of six letters); this is also the reason why the salutary economy of the Passion took place on the sixth day; the Passion was the preparation by which the last man appeared for the regeneration of the first. The beginning and the end of this economy of salvation was the sixth hour, the hour at which he was nailed to the wood. The Perfect Nous, knowing that the number six contains in itself the virtue of creation and regeneration, manifested to the sons of the light, by way of the *episemon* that appeared in him, the regeneration that is worked by him [...].

As for Jesus, here is his ineffable origin: from the first Tetrad, Mother of All, came the second Tetrad in the form of a daughter; thus the Ogdoad was formed, and from it came the Decade. This was the origin of the number eighteen. Thus the Decade, come to join with the Ogdoad and multiplying it by 10, would engender the number 80, and the number 80, multiplied again by 10, produces the number 800, with the result that the total of the letters, going from the Ogdoad to the Decade, is 8, 80, 800, which is Jesus, because the name Jesus has the numerical value of 888:

10 + 8 + 200 + 70 + 400 + 200 = 888.[7]

CHAPTER FOURTEEN

Carpocrates, Epiphanius, and the Tradition of Simon of Samaria

Going against the Christian current, which was generally ascetic and was propagated in the second century by Gnostic esotericism and by the *pistis* of the New Prophecy, the teachings of Carpocrates and his son Epiphanius inscribed themselves in a line of life that only Simon of Samaria had known how to trace out amidst the tormented gloom of the era.

Carpocrates' biography remains obscure. Origen confused him with Harpocrates—son of Isis and Osiris—who is often represented in the magic papyruses seated on a lotus and is regarded as being the male principle that penetrates the feminine principle in order to impregnate her with his light. Carpocrates taught at Alexandria and wed Alexandreia. Their son, Epiphanius, who died at the age of 17 in 138, was interred on his island of birth, Cephalonia. Around 155 or 156, a philosopher named Marcellina taught the doctrines of the father and the son in Rome.

Clement of Alexandria had the merit of retranscribing a short extract by Epiphanius on the subject of justice:

> This is what he says, then, in the book *Concerning Righteousness*: "The righteousness of God is a kind of universal fairness and equality. There is equality in the heaven which is stretched out in all directions and contains the entire earth in its circle. The night reveals equally all the stars. The

light of the sun, which is the cause of the daytime and the father of light, God pours out from above upon the earth in equal measure on all who have power to see. For all see alike. There is no distinction between rich and poor, people and governor, stupid and clever, female and male, free men and slaves. Even the irrational animals are not accorded any different treatment; but in just the same way God pours out from above sunlight equally upon all the animals. He establishes his righteousness to both good and bad by seeing that none is able to get more than his share and to deprive his neighbour, so that he has twice the light his neighbour has. The sun causes food to grow for all living beings alike; the universal righteousness is given to all equally. In this respect there is no difference between the entire species of oxen and any individual oxen, between the species of pigs and particular pigs, between the species of sheep and particular sheep, and so on with all the rest. In them the universality of God's fairness is manifest. Furthermore all plants of whatever sort are sown equally in the earth. Common nourishment grows for all beasts which feed on the earth's produce; to all it is alike. It is regulated by no law, but rather is harmoniously available to all through the gift of him who gives it and makes it to grow.

"And for birth there is no written law (for otherwise it would have been transcribed). All beings beget and give birth alike, having received by God's righteousness an innate equality. The Creator and Father of all with his own righteousness appointed this, just as he gave equally the eye to all to enable them to see. He did not make a distinction between female and male, rational and irrational, nor between anything and anything else at all; rather he shared out sight equally and universally. It was given to all alike by a single command. As the laws (he says) could not punish men who were ignorant of them, they taught men that they were transgressors. But the laws, by presupposing the existence of private property, cut up and destroyed the universal equality decreed by the divine law". As he does not understand the words of the apostle where he says "Through the law I knew sin", he says that the idea of Mine and Thine came into existence through the laws so that the earth and money were no longer put to common use. And so also with marriage. "For God has made vines for all to use in common, since they are not protected against sparrows and a thief; and similarly corn and the other fruits. But the abolition, contrary to divine law, of community of use and equality begat the thief of domestic animals and fruits.

"God made all things for man to be common property. He brought female to be with male and in the same way united all animals. He thus showed righteousness to be a universal fairness and equality. But those who have been born in this way have denied the universality which is the corollary of their birth and say, 'Let him who has taken one woman keep her', whereas all alike can have her, just as the other animals do".[1]

Epiphanius still taught in proper religious terms that, "With a view to the permanence of the race, he [God] has implanted in males a strong and ardent desire which neither law nor custom nor any of their restraint is able to destroy. For it is God's decree"[2].

Quoting from Epiphanius's *Concerning Righteousness*, Clement of Alexandria writes, "Consequently one must understand the saying 'You shall not covet' as if the lawgiver was making a jest, to which he added the even more comic words 'your neighbor's house'[3]. For he himself who gave the desire to sustain the race orders that it is to be suppressed, though he removes it from no other animals. And by the words 'your neighbor's house' he says something even more ludicrous, since he forces what should be common property to be treated as a private possession"[4].

Epiphanius's astonishingly modern text participated in a current of thought and behavior that was radically hostile to Stoic, Epicurean, and Christian morals.

Carpocrates and Epiphanius both belonged to a Greek milieu that rejected Judaism. In the same way that Simon of Samaria restored the spirit of the Pentateuch (and of Genesis in particular) to the body, Epiphanius mocked the biblical commandments and the notions of sin and guilt. The Law of Moses fomented crime for the same reason that prohibition engenders transgression.

Thereafter, quotations from Paul were subjected to the kind of revisions that were typical of the heresiologues, who added canonical extracts to them in order to change into disagreements within Christianity those doctrines that in fact had nothing to do with Christianity but that nevertheless incorporated the Messiah Joshua (as well as Serapis, Seth, Abrasax, and Harpocrates) into their own syncretisms. Or, alternatively, these quotations were made to refer back to a Paul who was different from the image of him that Marcion and his successive manipulators presented—that is to say, to a Saul/Paul whose teachings justified the use of the name Simon, with which he was saddled by the Elchasaites living under the rule of Trajan.

Written when Epiphanius was fifteen or sixteen years old, the work of this young man, whom Jacques Lacarrière[5] called the Gnostic Rimbaud, linked social equality to the free exercise of desire. His critique of property surpassed the Rousseauist conception, and one would have to wait until Charles Fourier and the radicalism of individual anarchy—with its principle 'We only group ourselves according to affinities'—for an echo of the precocious genius of Epiphanius of Cephalonia.

I do not see why Marcellina, a disciple of Carpocrates and Epiphanius who taught in Rome around 160, would have decorated her school with "images of the philosophers of the world; that is to say, with the images of Pythagoras, and Plato, and Aristotle", as Irenaeus claimed[6], unless this claim was simply an occasion for the Bishop of Lyon to condemn those Christians who preferred Greek philosophy to the Bible.

On the other hand, it is probable that the community founded on the liberty of desire drew the idea that "the soul must be thoroughly tested before death" from Pythagorean theory, because, "for Epiphanius, desire was the expression of the first will of God and nature"[7]. And according to Simon of Samaria, since desire was identified with fire (the principle of creation and the principle of passion), there was nothing in the unity of the macrocosm and the microcosm that could limit it.

Epiphanius applied his conception of justice to mankind, the animals and the plants. Living beings perpetuate themselves by changing form. Irenaeus interpreted this theory, which rendered everything strange and odious to him, in terms of magic and metempsychosis:

> They practise also magical arts and incantations; philters, also, and love-potions; and have recourse to familiar spirits, dream-sending demons, and other abominations, declaring that they possess power to rule over, even now, the princes and formers of this world; and not only them, but also all things that are in it. [...]. So unbridled is their madness, that they declare

they have in their power all things which are irreligious and impious, and are at liberty to practise them; for they maintain that things are good or evil, simply in virtue of human opinion. They deem it necessary, therefore, that by means of transmigration from body to body, souls should experience of every kind of life as well as every kind of action [...] in order that, as their writings express it, their souls, having made trial of every kind of life, may, at their departure, not be wanting in any particular.[8]

A line by Irenaeus does not seem to be troubling: "We are saved, indeed, by means of faith and love; but all other things, while in their nature indifferent, are reckoned by the opinion of men—some good and some evil, there being nothing really evil by nature"[9].

According to Simon's *Megale Apophasis*, faith in oneself and love led to the Great Power, which resided in each person and moved the world. What is astonishing is the fact that, in a letter by Paul, the theme of faith and love gives birth to an enthusiastic development that jars with the misogyny and ascetic harshness that are confirmed everywhere else in the epistolary works of the man who succeeded Moses and stole from him the title of Apostle.

If I speak in the tongues of men and of angels, but have not love, I am a noisy gong or a clanging cymbal. And if I have prophetic powers, and understand all mysteries and all knowledge [*gnosis*], and if I have all faith, so as to remove mountains, but have not love, I am nothing. If I give away all I have [to the hungry], and if I deliver up my body [as a slave] to be burned, but have not love, I gain nothing.

Love is patient and kind; love does not envy or boast; it is not arrogant or rude. It does not insist on its own way; it is not irritable or resentful; it does not rejoice at wrongdoing, but rejoices with the truth. Love bears all things, hopes all things, endures all things.

Love never ends. (First Epistle to the Corinthians 13: 1–8).[10]

Which anti-Marcionite, coming to the potluck of Paul's epistles, took this fragment of Carpocratic doctrine and inserted it into a Christian perspective?

CHAPTER FIFTEEN

The New Prophecy and the Development of Popular Christianity

Born under the pressure of the Zealot guerrilla war and the struggle against Greco-Roman oppression, the messianism of the first century pertained exclusively to a Judaism that was on the road to reformation, one that was hostile to the Sadducees and the Pharisees.

The sects that speculated on the secret name of the Messiah only agreed on Joshua in the 80s and 90s. They developed a philosophical and esoteric doctrine that was hardly propitious for broad distribution. The Elchasaite Christians, who aroused the suspicions of the governor of Bithynia, Pliny the Younger, no doubt offered the first example of a Christianity established in more open milieus. They practiced social aid to widows, orphans, and the disinherited; and, imitating the prescriptions honored in the Phariseean communities, they prayed to and celebrated the God-Messiah (*christo quasi Deo*, in the words of a letter written by Pliny[1]).

Their numerical strength had not yet aroused the distrust of the authorities beyond Bithynia, the region nearby Phrygia, where the cults of Attis and Mithras remained dominant. In Bithynia there grew the first de-Judaicized and exoteric Christianity, a mass Christianity of the kind that stimulated the Saint-Sulpicean imaginations of people like Sienkiewicz and *tutti quanti*[2], who, an age later, revived the martyrs of the New Prophecy so as to hurl them into Nero's lion's den.

It is worth insisting on the point that the Church behaved towards the various Christianities from which it issued in a manner reminiscent of Stalin, who excluded from history all of the first Bolsheviks in order to set Lenin up as a holy apostle. 'True' Christianity—the one that gave a historical existence to Jesus; invented Mary, Joseph, the Child, the popular agitator, the enemy of the Jews, and the good thief put to death under the reign of Tiberius; grouped together the apostles of rival churches, finally uniting into a great mass movement; and mentioned Pontius Pilate for the first time—also engendered new thinkers, including Tertullian, who, having been placed under the names 'Phrygian heresy', 'Montanism', 'Pepuzianism', and 'Encratism', would be thunderously expelled from the Church in the fourth century.

At a time when the Marcionite Churches were brandishing the authority of the Apostle Paul on the basis of programmatic letters and clashing with the traditional Judeo-Christian communities, the Christianity preached by the prophet Montanus was achieving success in Phrygia and, soon after, in North Africa, Palestine, and Asia Minor. It then turned towards Rome and won over Gaul.

Montanus addressed himself to the disinherited—to slaves, artisans and rich people who had renounced their goods—and not to the exegetes who were well versed in the interpretation of mythological writings or to the biblical rats who nibbled on words in order to nourish their ascendency over a handful of disciples.

The important thing was no longer *gnosis*, knowledge, the learning that disentangled the obscure paths leading to salvation, but rather faith, *pistis*, the feeling of belonging to the army of the Christ, of being disposed to sacrifice one's life for him as he had sacrificed his life for the benefit of all, regardless of the nation or social class to which they belonged.

The movement that was propagated under the name New Prophecy countersigned the birth of a genuinely modern Christianity stripped of its Judaism, a Christianity that rejected Gnostic intellectualism and instead taught the principles that survived up until the decline of

Catholicism and Protestantism: sacrifice, the renunciation of the goods of this world, voluntary poverty, the taste for martyrdom, the consecration of suffering, chastity, virginity, abstinence, and misogyny, the execration of pleasure, and the repression of desire.

Although variously received according to the region and the Church—the Marcionites and the *pneumatics* scorned it, while the bishops tolerated by the imperial power dreaded its ostentatious pretensions to martyrdom—the New Prophecy attracted a large membership and, for the very first time in the history of Christianity, organized a powerful federation of Churches under which the rival bishoprics of Cephas, James, Thomas, Clement, and Saul/Paul, and even certain fringes of Naassenism and Sethianism, were subsumed. This was the evangelical Christianity that was subsequently dreamed about by the millenarians and apostolics who struggled against the Church of Rome—which, having been born in the corruption of temporal power, would remain in a state of power and corruption.

Around 160, the prophet Montanus, in whom Christ was supposedly incarnated, preached the good word in Phrygia and Mysia. Two prophetesses, Prisca (or Priscilla) and Maximilla, assisted him, which was an innovation that flagrantly contradicted Judeo-Christianity and Marcionism.

The New Prophecy announced the end of time. It was a millenarianism to which Irenaeus and Hermas were receptive. Asceticism was erected as its rule of conduct. The faithful—invited to repent, to fast, and to purify themselves of their sins—would inaugurate the New Jerusalem, which was destined to be concretized in two market towns of which all traces have been lost: Pepuza and Tynion.

Montanus' syncretism drew abundantly from the great competing religion, that of Attis. From this epoch came communion through bread and wine that were identified with the flesh and blood of the Messiah—a rite that was comparable to one that was used in the rituals of Attis. For the voluntary castration of the priest of Cybele-Attis were substituted the castration of desire, abstinence, and the virtue of virginity, to which some believers showed themselves to be so attached that they preferred torture to their renunciation.

Their provocative taste for martyrdom soon attracted the aggressive ardors of the crowds—always disposed to let off steam at the expense of the weak and of those who were resigned to their fates—and civil servants who were delighted to furnish distractions from their plundering and their abuses of authority.

Around 166 or 167, the pogroms in Smyrna involved the death of a bishop named Polycarp. Polycarp—the putative author of a letter from the Church of Smyrna to the community of Philomelium (in Phrygia), who was consequently suspected of adhering to the New Prophecy—was thereafter celebrated in *The Martyrdom of Polycarp*. But Eusebius of Caesarea, revealing the proceedings of the Church of Smyrna, took care to add an anti-Montanist interpolation to it, as Campenhause has demonstrated.[3]

The New Prophecy dominated Carthage, where Tertullian would shine, and Lyon, where Irenaeus defended its millenarianism and asceticism. In Rome the New Prophecy enjoyed the favor of at least one bishop, the future pope Eleuterus. Several pogroms that indiscriminately massacred Jews and Christians decimated the adherents to the New Prophecy in Lyon and Vienna in 177 and in Palestine in 178. Tertullian would sing the praises of the martyrs of Scilla who were lynched in 180. The persecutions that the new Christians attracted—as a lightning rod attracts lightning—in turn engendered in explicitly anti-Semitic mindsets everywhere a desire to perpetrate massacres that were not just encouraged by the sly consent of procurators playing the role of Pontius Pilate washing his hands, but were directly ordered by the imperial power.

The Christians' quest for martyrdom repulsed their persecutors. Did not Tertullian report, in a protest that was addressed to the proconsul Scapula—*Ad Scapulam*, 5.1, from 212 or 213—that in 185 the proconsul of Asia, Arrius Antoninus, encountered a group of Christians carrying knotted cords around their necks and asking to be executed? The proconsul sent them back, telling them that if they wanted to commit suicide, there were cliffs and precipices from which they could throw themselves.[4]

This ostentatious propensity for death sanctified by torments aroused the prudent reprobation of the bishops, the community leaders who wanted to negotiate for freedom of worship, and even simple Christians who believed that their continence and privation were sufficient guarantees of happiness in the beyond. These same reservations were expressed in the middle of the third century—when Novatian's movement revived the New Prophecy in its most extreme aspects—and in the fourth century, when the Donatists and the Circumcellions excommunicated the *lapsi*, the priests who had recanted by arguing that a living priest was better than a dead one when it came to propagating the faith.

The New Prophecy thus encountered the hostility of certain leaders of *Ekklēsia*. The Episcope of Anchiale, in Thrace, took measures against its adepts in 177, while the persecution was raging in Lyon. A certain Thémison produced against the new Christianity an *Epistola ad omnes ecclesia*, which Rufinus hastened to interpret as a definite reference to Catholicism. (In reality, Montanism founded the first actually popular ecclesial universality, a *catholicon* that was no longer elitist, as Marcion's had been.)

The bishop Melito of Sardis also stood up against the prophetic rage of Montanism in *On the Christian Life and the Prophets*. He had the best reasons in the world for doing so, because, in the manner of Justin, he addressed to the emperors apologies and appeals on the behalf of a religion for which he solicited tolerance. One could also cite in this context Theophilus of Antioch and Athenagoras.

Around 195, Apollonius of Ephesus, a personal enemy of Tertullian, affirmed that "Montanus and his crazy female prophetesses" were hanged[5] (this is hardly surprising) and that "we show that these first prophetesses themselves, as soon as they were filled with the Spirit, abandoned their husbands" (which sounds more like an allegation made by Eusebius)[6].

According to Runciman, "In the sixth century congregations of Montanists burnt themselves alive in their churches rather than suffer persecution at the hands of Justinian. In the eighth century the remnants of the sect perished in a similar holocaust"[7].

Reduced to the status of a marginal sect by 331, christened the 'Phrygian heresy', 'Montanism', and even 'Pepuzianism' (by Basil of Caesarea, Epiphanius of Salamis, the codex of Theodosianus, and Augustine of Hippo, who borrowed the term from Epiphanius), the New Prophecy formed the foundations of Greco-Roman Christianity. It is ironic that the New Prophecy's extreme masochism furnished the history of the Church with a substantial portion of its official martyrology.

The Catholics thus appropriated Blandina and her companions from Lyon. *The Martyrdom of Polycarp*, which exalted the torture of the faithful, who were thus assured of eternal bliss, made use of Montanist propaganda. In the third century, two works achieved a remarkable popular success: *The Martyrdom of Montanus and Lucius* and *The Passion of Saints Perpetua and Felicity*, the latter of which took the form of a letter to the (Montanist) Church of Carthage and recounted the torture of two virgins put to death in 203 under Septimius Severus, who prohibited all proselytism among Jews and Christians.

The martyrdom of the Montanist Perpetua inspired a vision, which was attributed to her and was supposed to harden the convictions of future victims. In it, the author evoked a *refrigerium*, a place of preservation, in which the martyr, refreshed and cleansed of his wounds, waited for the dawn of his glory and sometimes manifested himself to the living in order to exhort them to religious duty. The *refrigerium*—in which the tortured person, endowed with a new body, prepared to shine at the side of the God thanks to an imminent ascension—would much later give birth to the idea of purgatory.

It is more than probable that the original versions of the *Acts* of Andrew, Pilate, Paul and Thecla, Peter, and other apostles emanated from the 'propaganda services' of the New Prophecy. Many would be submitted to revisions in an easily predictable manner.

Prediction-making, which was an activity little valued by clergymen who aspired to exercise their priesthood with the benediction of the State, was always at risk of being put to abusive uses. The seer arrogated to himself the right to change the Law and the laws, since God had spoken through his mouth.

If one can believe Epiphanius of Salamis's *Panarion* (iv. 48. 11,9), Montanus proclaimed: "Neither angel nor messenger, but I the Lord, God the Father, have come"[8]. Montanus clearly marked a rupture with the conception of a Messiah who claimed to be the *Angelos-Christos*, the messenger-angel of God. (Between his two 'Marys' [Priscilla and Maximilia], Montanus concretized in human form the personage of Jesus, who had until then been abstract—a secret and sacred name, an angel descended from the heavens and resurrected in the beyond in order to assure the salvation of all through his sacrifice.)

This remark attributed to Montanus, which disavowed Judeo-Christianity and Marcionism, involved the human character of Jesus and his nature as a divine being—as a spirit capable of reincarnating himself in other prophets.

Tertullian was not mistaken: it is the man possessed by the spirit who can pardon, and not the Church: "'the Church', it is true, will forgive sins: but (it will be) the Church of the Spirit, by means of a spiritual man; not the Church which consists of a number of bishops" (*De pudicitia*, chapter 21: 17)[9]. This was competition that the Catholic Church could not tolerate. It claimed to unite in itself the temporality of the Son and the incarnation of the spirit that spoke through the Church's voice, proffering truths (orthodoxies) and condemning to death the prophets who succeeded each other from the ninth to the seventeenth centuries.

Nevertheless, the New Prophecy contented itself with following, to the letter, the Apostle, who up until the second century was the *only* apostle (in 220, Tertullian still knew no authority other than Paul). And the first Letter to the Corinthians (14: 3–5) prescribed prophecy bluntly: "the one who prophesies speaks to people for their upbuilding and encouragement and consolation. The one who speaks in a tongue builds up himself, but the one who prophesies builds up the church. Now I want you all to speak in tongues, but even more to prophesy. The one who prophesies is greater than the one who speaks in tongues".

The New Prophecy accorded to whoever spoke by the Spirit "the full power of renewing traditional eschatological conceptions from top to bottom"[10].

Prophecy was incorporated into the practices of the majority of Christian communities. It was prescribed by the *Didachē*. It reappeared in the seventeenth century in Pietist sects, which willingly identified themselves with primitive Christianity. Priscilla, practicing ecstasy, foreshadowed Mechthild of Magdeburg, Beatrice of Nazareth, Hadewijch of Antwerp, and Teresa of Ávila when she affirmed that the Christ had visited her and slept near her, at Pepuza, taking the form of fire and penetrating her with his wisdom.

The New Prophecy was also concerned with millenarianism, the imminence of the end of time, and the instauration of the kingdom of God on earth. Tertullian of Carthage and Irenaeus of Lyon were its ardent defenders. Montanus was the Holy Spirit descended to the earth. The Montanists' "so-called prophetess, Maximilla, says, 'After me there will be no prophet more, but the consummation'" (*Panarion*, ii. 48. 2,4)[11].

In each strain of millenarianism, the same scenario was reproduced: "The New Jerusalem will descend from the heavens to Pepuza. The Montanists received exceptional promises that would be kept at the End of Days. Due to the impending end, ethical demands took on an exceptionally acute character"[12].

For Tertullian, to avoid martyrdom was to cling to a world condemned to impending destruction. "Seek not to die on bridal beds, nor in miscarriages, nor in soft fevers", he wrote in *De fuga*, "but to die the martyr's death, that He may be glorified who has suffered for you"[13].

In sum, did not the tortures inflicted by the mob or by the justice system logically culminate in an existence from which asceticism prescribed the removal of all pleasure?

Tertullian, an adept and philosopher of the new current, laid the foundations for a new Christian morality with which Catholicism compromised but which Calvinism, and Protestantism in general, tried desperately to promote. Respectful of the abstinence extolled by its adversary, Marcion, the New Prophecy nevertheless gave a completely different meaning to asceticism. The Marcionites and the supporters of the idea of a bad world created by a crazy God refused pleasure, procreation, and any food that wasn't frugal so as to avoid ratifying a work that they denigrated. The Christians of the New Prophecy rejected neither the world nor the flesh; they wanted only wanted to purify those things and themselves, so that that the Spirit would descend to and reside upon the earth without the hindrances of materiality.

Long fasts eschewed the pleasures of terrestrial nourishment and exalted spiritual communion. The refusal of amorous relations did not pursue the objective of extinguishing the race of men, as it did among the Gnostics who were 'beyond the world'; it rather limited pleasure to procreative coitus in the manner of the Essenes. "It is not permitted, after believing, to know even a second marriage, differentiated though it be, to be sure, from the work of adultery and fornication by the nuptial and dotal tablets" (Tertullian, *De pudicitia*)[14]. The hatred of women shared by Tertullian, Epiphanius, Augustine, and the master thinkers of the Church was accompanied by the worship of virginity. The idea of Mary, virgin and mother of the Christ, certainly drew from the legends of Montanist propaganda.

(Note the following with respect to the hatred of women. The *Elenchos* (book 5, chapter 3) says: "they allege that the work of swine and dogs is the intercourse of the woman with a man"[15]. Tertullian: "*You* are the devil's gateway: *you* are the unsealer of that (forbidden) tree: *you* are the first deserter of the divine law: *you* are she who persuaded him whom the devil was not valiant enough to attack. *You* destroyed so easily God's image, man. On account of *your* desert—that is, death—even the Son of God had to die. And do you think about adorning yourself over and above your tunics of skins?"[16])

Montanism also preached (for the first time in the history of the Christianity) the resurrection of the body, which Saul/Paul had so oddly borrowed from the Pharisees. In his *De resurrectione carnis*, Tertullian says: "there is nobody who lives so much in accordance with the flesh as they who deny the resurrection of the flesh [...]. It is a shrewd saying which the Paraclete utters concerning these persons by the mouth of the prophetess Prisca: 'They are carnal, and yet they hate the flesh'"[17]. By dying, the martyrs exchanged their torn bodies for bodies of glory that would enter the divine cohort of saints, the veritable celestial Church.

Both virginal *and* penetrated by the Spirit, the prophetesses of Montanus aroused the reprobation of many community leaders. Tertullian insisted on celebrating their chastity in *De exhortatione castitatis*; the author of the *Elenchos* (around 230) reproached the new Christians for "letting themselves be guided by weak women [*femmelettes*]"[18]; and Origen, who pushed abnegation to the point of self-castration, referred the same Christians back to the Apostle Paul, who constituted their supreme authority—that polymorphous Paul, first erected against Marcion, his inventor, and then against the anti-Marcionites: "Women, the Apostle said, must keep quiet in the ecclesial communities[19]. Here is a prescription that the disciples of the women—those who let themselves be instructed by Priscilla and Maximilia—have not obeyed"[20].

(Note that Priscilla believed that the Epistle to the Laodiceans, a text from 160 or 170 that was originally Marcionite and placed under the name of Paul, was authentic.)

The New Prophecy and the Christian Philosophers of the Second Century

The New Prophecy threw the paving stone of faith into the pond of the many Christian Gnosticisms. *Pistis*, which brought the exalted crowds to undergo ordeals and to experience fervent convictions of which polytheism knew nothing, exercised the same kind of fascination for the Greco-Roman mindset that Judaism had done previously and that, since the last war of the Jews, xenophobia had condemned.

'True' Christianity swept away the theological arguments from the Gnostic systems. The fabrication of texts redesigned the personage of the Christ Jesus, giving him the realism of everyday existence. This fabrication reduced speculations about the *Angelos-Christos* to a secondary plane and bluntly mocked the intellectual Christians who had been diverted from the study of the Jews and their Scriptures and who had thrown themselves into Greek mythology and Platonic scholasticism.

Justin the Apologist, Irenaeus of Lyon, the author of *The Pastor*, and Tertullian all launched a philosophical offensive—implicitly supported by the army of the Christ, which scorned death in the name of the Living Spirit—against what Irenaeus called "so-called gnosis".

Justin the Apologist

Although his death roughly coincided with the birth of the New Prophecy, Justin belonged to a Hellenized and anti-Marcionite Christianity that was characterized by the search for martyrdom, the recuperation of the Jewish Scriptures, the care that it took to invite the State to recognize this religion (now purged of a Semitism that was odious to the Greeks and Romans), and a Church whose pacifist and non-violent ideals did not contravene public order.

Born around 100 in Flavia Neapolis [Nablus], in Samaria, Justin was initiated into philosophy and, in particular, Platonism and Stoicism. He founded schools at which he taught a Christianity that had broken with Essenean Judaism without rejecting the texts of the Scriptures.

Drafted around 135, after the defeat of Bar Kokhba and during the wave of anti-Semitic hysteria that followed it, Justin's *Dialogue with Trypho the Jew* affirmed that—the Christians having freed a truth from the Scriptures that the Jews no longer understood—the Bible by all rights belonged to the Churches of the Christ. (At the same time, a *Diatribe Against the Jews* by Apollonius Molon and *On the Jews* by Philo of Byblos were circulating.)

Though his Messiah was still related to the *Angelos-Christos* of Judeo-Christianity and Marcionism, Justin rejected Marcion's aggressive dualism. Justin's Good God confronted not the Demiurge who had created the world but the Adversary, the fallen angel, the bloody rebel raised against the Divine Order: Satan the tempter.

Justin's schools were celebrated in Asia Minor and Rome. He wrote a lampoon of Marcion that has been lost. Tatian, his disciple, discovered in the New Prophecy the application of Justin's lessons: one must follow the example of the Christ through the purity of one's mores and through self-sacrifice taken to the point of martyrdom.

Among the first followers of the new religion, Justin laid the bases for its recognition by the central State (it is possible in this regard that the morbid extremism of the Montanists displeased him, just as it was repugnant to Melito of Sardis, but it is also true that Tertullian, another apologist, found nothing distressing in it). Justin published his *First Apology*, which was addressed to Antoninus Pius, his sons, and the Roman Senate. Several years later, around 154, he reiterated his points in a *Second Apology of Justin Martyr*, which was addressed to the Roman Senate. (Note that these *Apologies* reflected the new political stance of the Churches. A federation, with Rome at its head, could reassure the State with the prospect of a replacement religion—a solution in which Christianity could be substituted for Rome's weakening polytheism and the solar cult of the emperors. Thus, Quadratus of Athens wrote to Hadrian (Emperor from 117 to 138 CE), Aristides and Justin wrote to Antoninus Pius (138–61), and Melito of Sardis and Apollinaris Claudius of Hierapolis wrote to Marcus Aurelius (161–80). Did not Athenagoras of Athens declare in his *Embassy for the Christians* (177–8) that "the Empire and Christianity have grown side by side. The prince has nothing to fear, but everything to gain by the conversion of the Empire"[21]?)

But these efforts were in vain. The Greeks and Romans did not care to distinguish Christians from Jews, or Justin's friends from the multitude of sects—Sethians, Cainites, Nazarenes, Elchasaites, Marcionites, Judeo-Christians, Valentinians, and anti-Marcionites—which all supported the idea of a crucified and resuscitated Messiah in whose name were excluded as idolatries the other cults that Rome liberally tolerated in the name of economic imperatives.

Religious fanaticism appeared particularly odious to the Greeks and Romans. They had a clear interest in searching it out in Palestine. Did not Deuteronomy (17: 12–3) enjoin that "the man who acts presumptuously by not obeying the priest who stands to minister there before the LORD your God, or the judge, that man shall die. So you shall purge the evil from Israel"?

What, therefore, did Justin ask of the Emperor? For the help of the State against those who were contemptuous of the Holy Spirit—by which one meant the partisans of Simon of Samaria and all those who could be identified with them. Ammianus Marcellinus would have been able to write in the second century what he established in the fourth: "no wild beasts are so hostile to men as Christian sects in general are to one another"[22].

Intolerance—such was still the reproach that Celsus, in his *True Discourse* (178–80), addressed to the people he found indistinguishable (Jews and Christians): to the sectarians of the crucified Serpent, to those of the God with the head of a donkey (Seth), and to those of a magician named Jesus.

The laurels of the martyr with which Justin found himself encumbered were as necessary to his fanaticism as was the taste for death celebrated by Tertullian and the Christians of the New Prophecy. During an acrimonious quarrel between Justin and the cynical philosopher

Crescens, the latter challenged him to extend his scorn for existence to its logical conclusion. The conflict became inflamed and a trial ensued. Crescens found an ally in the prefect Junius Rusticus, a Stoic philosopher who had initiated Marcus Aurelius into the doctrine of Epictetus. The polemic ended dramatically with Justin's decapitation in 165.

A dialogue, which has been preserved, played on the meanings of 'gnosis'—science, learning, and knowledge.

> The prefect [Rusticus] says to Justin, "Hearken, you who are called learned, and think that you know true doctrines; if you are scourged and beheaded, do you believe you will ascend into heaven?" [...] Justin said, "I do not suppose it, but I know and am fully persuaded of it".[23]

In his pamphlet *Philosophies for Sale*, Lucian of Samosata, a contemporary of Justin, scornfully refused to cite the Christians. Nevertheless, it is certain that this author had the Christians of the New Prophecy in mind when he ironically pointed out the following in a passage from his satire *The Death of Peregrinus* (quoted by Rougier in his *Celse contre les chrétiens*): "The poor wretches have convinced themselves, first and foremost, that they are going to be immortal and live for all time, in consequence of which they despise death and even willingly give themselves into custody, most of them"[24].

Goaded by the solicitations of their victims' collective masochism, the crowds devoted themselves enthusiastically to the bloody outbursts by which they temporarily freed themselves from the repressions and inhibitions from which they suffered. In these early cases, the victims did not succumb to the legal proceedings initiated by Antoninus the Pious or Marcus Aurelius. The twenty-three-year-long reign of Antoninus was among the least bloody in Roman history and was preserved in memory due precisely to the *suavitas morum* (the gentleness of the morals of the Emperor). Despite his excusable repugnance for sanctified morbidity, Marcus Aurelius did not depart from the principles instituted by Trajan: do not seek out the disciples of the Christ, and only punish them if, when denounced, they refuse obedience to the Emperor and the offerings of the traditional cults.

Hermas and The Pastor

In Rome, around the middle of the second century, there circulated under the name of *The Pastor* a collection of texts collated in the manner of a novel, the author of which called himself Hermas. Held in great esteem by Christians for three centuries, it would be excluded from the canon by Pope Gelasius' decree at the end of the fifth century.

A didactic work of Judeo-Christian inspiration, *The Pastor* presents itself as a revelation. (Its author refers to the now-lost apocalypse of *Eldat and Modat*.) It contains five visions—the last of which is actually an apocalypse—twelve precepts, and ten parables. Its spirit, still close to the Essenean *Manual of Discipline* and *The Damascus Document*, brought together Nazarenism and the New Prophecy-in-gestation, without succumbing to Marcionite influence. Its dualism has nothing in common with the 'two Gods'. It refers to the two spirits of *The Rule of the Community*: "The two spirits, then, when dwelling in the same habitation, are at discord with each other, and are troublesome to that man in whom they dwell"[25].

An embarrassment to the Catholic Church, *The Pastor* presented a Christian panorama that was completely different from the fanciful statements of the official history.

Hermas knew nothing of a historical Jesus and didn't even know the name 'Jesus'. He knew nothing of Mary, Joseph, Pilate, and their associates.

> The visions name the Son of God once, in a formula: "For the Lord has sworn by His glory", which doubles another one: "For the Lord hath sworn by His Son" (6, 8, 4), which is suspect as a result.[26]

The Son of God was the Spirit, the Great Archangel, sometimes named Michael.

Though Hermas and his associates resided in Rome, they never (and for good reason) heard anyone speak of the canonical Gospels, nor of Matthew, Luke, Mark, or John. Hermas's only references were to the Bible, the one that Marcion called the 'Old Testament'. If *The Pastor* spoke of apostles, it did so in the sense of itinerant missionaries who propagated the Christian doctrine: the book distinguishes them from the *didaskaloi*—that is, those who taught (this was the era of the *Didachē*, which was inspired by the Epistle of Barnabas).

In 150 Hermas had no knowledge of a monarchal episcopacy, *a fortiori* of the 'Ancient Pope', who according to the historians then reigned over the Church's destiny. "The farsighted [*presbytes*] and the overseers [*épiscopes*] were synonymous for him".[27] Moreover, Hermas denounced the ambitious caste of the priests: in one of his visions, he compares them to poisoning apothecaries and, in the ninth parable, to venomous reptiles.

As in Essenism and in Phariseean practice, the Church was identified by Hermas with a community tasked with protecting widows, orphans, and the poor. It appeared to him as an old woman, and he appealed for her rejuvenation through the purification of the faithful.

Purity of mores and the necessity of a penitence that washed the soul of its sins constituted the core of Hermas' Christian doctrine, wherein the old Essenean tradition married the movement of the New Prophecy at the moment of its birth.

Chastity is exalted in a scene that prefigures the adventures of Parsifal. Hermas resists the temptation of women who cajole and solicit his love. He does well in this, because—once he has triumphed in the test—it is revealed to him that 'virginal natures' were concealed beneath the appearance of seductresses. "'And these virgins, who are they?' 'They are holy spirits'".[28] Thus the virgin martyrs of the New Prophecy acceded to their reality as saints, clothed, beyond the torments of death, in resplendent bodies and haloed by virtue. Through a pleasing recurrence of things, the Italian painters of the Renaissance (painting their mistresses in ecstasy for the churches) returned them to their native sensuality. (We know, for example, that Filippo Lippi's Madonnas represented the pretty nun whom he seduced and who abandoned the God of her convent for the God of love, the revelation of which haloed her.)

In accord with the future rigor of Tertullian and the new Christianity, Hermas rebelled against those who judged sins of the flesh to be of little importance. Nevertheless, his asceticism was opposed to the spirit of Marcion and his doctrine of the two Gods: "First of all, believe that there is one God [...]. Have faith therefore in Him, and fear Him; and fearing Him, exercise self-control"[29]. Faith (*pistis*) had the upper hand over *gnosis* (knowledge). On the other hand, if there existed a possibility of salvation through works, through good acts, in no case did Hermas refer to a redemption accomplished through Jesus. In addition, questions of penitence and redemption were settled between the sinner and God, without the intervention of the priest. The faithful was he who, living in fear of displeasing the God of Goodness, banished earthly pleasures and nourishments from his existence: "adultery is committed not only by those who pollute their flesh, but by those who imitate the heathen in their actions"[30]. Calvin did not say anything different.

Irenaeus of Lyon

Around 180, Irenaeus, the bishop of a Christian community in Lyon, wrote a work against other Christians—principally the Marcionites and Valentinians—in which he attacked *gnosis* and the pursuit of salvation through knowledge. He related the entirety of these doctrines back to a unique source: the radicalism of Simon of Samaria.

His attempt corresponded to the New Prophecy's rejection of philosophical elitism, esotericism, and even magical practices that were disseminated in the name of the Messiah by a cultural class against which was opposed the faith of the simple believers, who were little interested in speculative quibbles and who adhered to an austere existence and a constant aspiration for martyrdom in order to assure their posthumous bliss.

Three years later, in Lyon and Vienna, pogroms put to death both Jews and the new Christians. The Marcionite, Valentinian, and Marcusian Gnostics in all probability escaped because of their connections with the well-to-do classes (the 'dames of the purple-bordered robes', disciples of Marcus).

In Irenaeus' desire to purge the Churches of the outrageous influence that anti-Semitism had accorded Greek philosophy, he wrote—not *Against Heresies*, which was a later work in Latin that suggested that its author [still identified as Irenaeus] spoke in the name of a Catholic Church and a well-established orthodoxy—but *On the Detection and Overthrow of the So-Called Gnosis*[31].

Irenaeus opposed blind faith, the *pistis* of the simple people who followed the law of the Christ without asking any questions, to the abstract developments of the Gnostics, which, by virtue of his polemical conventions, he relayed in the form of a tissue of absurdities. His was a proto-Pascalian profession of faith, one that inspired the "Blessed are the poor in spirit" line that the authors of the Gospels attributed to Jesus[32]:

> It is therefore better and more profitable to belong to the simple and unlettered class, and by means of love to attain to nearness to God, than, by imagining ourselves learned and skilful, to be found [among those who are] blasphemous against their own God, inasmuch as they conjure up another God as the Father.[33]

Irenaeus had two good reasons for attacking Marcion and Gnosticism. A partisan of the unification of the Churches who was resolved to confer supreme authority upon a Roman bishop, he perceived the antithetical character of ecclesial monarchism, on the one hand, and the belief in two Gods (one ungraspable, the other despicable), on the other.

Secondly, Irenaeus was the author of an *Epideixis*[34] in which the Christian doctrine was explicated on the basis of the prophetic texts of the Bible—the same ones that Marcion had rejected as immoral and incoherent.

It was apparently Irenaeus's love for the prophetic tradition that drew him to the Christianity of the New Prophecy and to the supposed incarnation of Christ in Phrygia, an event that set off a wave of conversions all across the Empire. In support of such a hypothesis about Irenaeus, it is fitting to recall that Tertullian mentioned a bishop of Rome who was a partisan of the Montanist current, and we know that Irenaeus intervened in favor of the new faith at the side of Eleuterus, who was a bishop of one of the churches of Rome between 170 and 190.

Annexed by Catholicism due to his hostility to *gnosis* and his defense of the monarchal principle in the Church, Irenaeus suffered the same fate as Origen, who was revised and corrected by Rufinus. The *Epideixis* disappeared. Irenaeus's millenarianism, which was shared by Hermas and the New Prophecy, was eradicated from his work. It took the discovery of a manuscript in the nineteenth century to reestablish the millenarian 'heresy' of this bishop, who had been sanctified by the Church at the cost of several instances of censorship.

The works of Irenaeus were recopied, revised, and stuffed full of interpolations (including quotations from canonical Gospels), while Tertullian, who was particularly erudite, knew of no other Gospel than the 'Good Word' of Paul. Of the original text of the *Refutation* there remain only Greek fragments of citations collected by the author of the *Elenchos* and by other notorious forgers: Eusebius of Caesarea, Epiphanius of Salamis, and Theodoret of Cyrus.

Tertullian, Philosopher of the New Prophecy
Born around 160 in Carthage, the aristocratic Tertullian had a classical education. Breaking off his studies of rhetoric, philosophy, and the law, he devoted himself to dissipation in his youth, only to suddenly renounce it (perhaps around 190) and convert to Christianity, which for the first time was spreading on a large scale.

"We are but of yesterday", Tertullian wrote in 197, "and we have filled every place among you—cities, islands, fortresses, towns, market-places, the very camp, tribes, companies, palace, senate, forum,—and we have left nothing to you but the temples of your gods"[35].

While persecutions most often took the form of anti-Jewish pogroms—Tertullian himself took care to separate the wheat from the chaff in his *Adversus judaeos*—proconsul Vigellius Saturninus decapitated eighteen Romanized Africans and Christians in the small town of Scillium in 180.

Tertullian was inflamed by the New Prophecy. "Repentance, men understand, so far as nature is able, to be an emotion of the mind arising from disgust at some *previously cherished* worse sentiment: that kind of men *I mean* which even we ourselves were in days gone by—blind, without the Lord's light", he moaned[36]. This was why he was only in the world "to weep and make outcries unto the Lord your God"[37].

Tertullian's militant asceticism led him to conclude that "the poets are fools, when they describe the gods with human passions and stories"[38] and to condemn the philosophers who become "patriarchs of heretics"[39]. He admired Justin, Tatian, Theophilus of Antioch, and Irenaeus, whom he imitated in a series of polemics against Marcion and the Valentinians.

Note that the New Prophecy professed a fanatical asceticism, albeit one different in character from that of Marcion, for whom pleasure seeking was a concession to the bad work of the Demiurge. "For this leads me to remark of Marcion's god", Tertullian wrote in his *Adversus Marcionem*, "that in reproaching marriage as an evil and unchaste thing, he is really prejudicing the cause of that very sanctity which he seems to serve"[40]. If women had some importance in Montanist revelation—to the point that the author of the *Elenchos* mocked the Montanists' "respect for the divagations of the weak women who indoctrinate them"[41]—this was at the cost of a frankly professed chastity and an emphasis on inviolable virginity (the martyrs preferred death to defloration). A spiritual movement *par excellence*, founded on the repression of desire, the New Prophecy responded to the entreaties of Tertullian: "by parsimony of the flesh you will gain the Spirit" (*De exhortatione castitatis*)[42].

Tertullian extolled martyrdom (*"the blood of Christians is seed"*)[43]; condemned second marriages (in a polemic against the Carthaginian painter Hermogenes, who defended the eternity of matter, Tertullian reproached him for having married several times); appealed to continence; and scorned women and the pleasures of love.

Note that the taste for martyrdom was the doctrine that provoked hysterical adhesion to Montanism, while also causing its eventual decline and its growing discredit. Did not Tertullian proclaim in his *De fuga* "seek not to die on bridal beds, nor in miscarriages, nor in soft fevers, but to die the martyr's death, that He may be glorified who has suffered for you?"[44]

Associating wealth with luxury and debauchery, the New Prophecy directly attacked the part of the clergy that subsisted on tithes from the faithful and that easily reconciled the duties of faith with the compromises associated with having to live in a society. This was why Tertullian, like the author of the *Elenchos*, rejected Callixtus, one of the principal bishops of Rome (his name was later given to a set of catacombs), whom they both reproached for his laxity.

The Church did not lack arguments for condemning Tertullian. But the importance of his apologetic works prompted Catholicism to set him aside by other means. His biographers insinuated that he adopted Montanist views only at a late stage, meaning that he had become senile (which is a thesis that the vigor of his thought and style unfortunately does not accredit). A lampoon of the heresies was even attributed to him, one in which anti-Gnosticism was placed next to critiques of Montanism!

CHAPTER SIXTEEN

Tatian and the Fabrication of the New Testament

Born in Syria around 120, Tatian posthumously became one of the founders of the Church due to his extremism in matters of asceticism. Irenaeus attacked him because, "like Marcion and Saturninus, he declared that marriage was nothing else than corruption and fornication. But his denial of Adam's salvation was an opinion due entirely to himself"[1].

A convert to Christianity and a disciple of Justin in Rome, Tatian was exposed to attacks by Crescens, Justin's accuser. Teaching Christianity in Rome around 172–3, he professed the anti-Marcionism of his master and transmitted it to his disciple, Rhodon. Then he left for the East and founded schools while the New Prophecy took off. It seems that he died at the end of that decade.

Tatian's only known work belongs to the genre of Apologetics. His *Address to the Greeks* opposed Christianity to Greek philosophy in general and to Stoicism in particular. In it he developed ideas shared by Tertullian and the new popular current. His profession of monotheistic faith contradicted the accusations of dualism that were often made against him by the Catholics. On the other hand, his idea of the Christ had not evolved beyond that of Justin: "For the heavenly Logos, a spirit emanating from the Father and a Logos from the Logos-power, in imitation of the Father who begot Him made man an image of immortality, so that, as incorruption is with God, in like manner, man, sharing in a part of God, might have the immortal principle also. The Logos, too, before the creation of men, was the Framer of angels"[2]. The Holy Spirit was called the Minister of God who had suffered.

Tatian's essay *On Perfection, According to the Savior* is lost, but Clement of Alexandria picked out of it an absolute condemnation of marriage that surpassed the Montanist spirit. The Church profited by erecting Tatian as the leader of a phantom heresy called Encratism, in which were grouped together—thanks to the Church's fourth-century struggle against the Donatists and the Circumcellions—the supporters of an excessive moral rigor.

No doubt there was another reason for the Church's animosity towards Tatian. Deschner cites him as one of the copyists who reworked the letters of Paul and conferred on them a stylistic unity[3].

The growth of popular Christianity engendered a general revival of Jewish *midrashim*, translated somehow or other by the Judeo-Christians: it was now a matter of de-Judaicizing them and explaining them rationally to the general public. Tatian has been credited with harmonizing, in addition to Paul's letters, the many propagandistic texts that presented themselves as being the Gospel preached by 'the' Apostle (at that time there was only one).

Nevertheless, neither Irenaeus, Tertullian, nor Clement of Alexandria mentioned the *Diatessaron euaggelion*, which would remain the dogmatic work *par excellence* of the Syrian Christian churches until the fifth century, when it was replaced by the four Gospels of the Catholic Church. A fourteen-line-long Greek fragment recovered at Dura-Europos dates from 230 at the latest. It proposed placing the fragments of the Gospels attributed to Mark, Luke, and Matthew end to end. Was this an attempt at *Diatessaron* [harmonization] and, if so, was it the one undertaken by Tatian? How come Tertullian, an admirer of Tatian, did not mention it? As for the fragments by Irenaeus, they were altered too much to offer serious testimony concerning the canonical Gospels in the second century.[4]

The Canonical Gospels

What aspect did Christianity present at the end of the second century? Although the Greeks and Romans did not distinguish it from Judaism and were confused about the differences between the sectarians of Jesus, the Sethians, the Naassenes, the Barbelites, and other messianists, the New Prophecy established in the urban milieu a popular Christianity that attracted slaves, a fraction of the plebes, and the petite bourgeois, as well as a fringe of the aristocracy, which until then had been broadly receptive to Gnostic doctrines and philosophical Christianity.

If the importance accorded to faith, to life lived according to the Christ, to asceticism, to the refusal of riches, and to the vocation of martyrdom reduced Gnosticism to a marginal status (even as Christianity exploited it in the genesis of its theology), Gnosticism still troubled a good number of bishops and heads of communities who, since the establishment of Trajan's conventions (which were renewed by Hadrian), had been integrated into public life and who, careful to avoid any scandal, already carried themselves as if they were the future ecclesiastical bureaucrats of the triumphant Church. The ardor and fanaticism of the poor Christians disturbed the lax bishops of the second century, who formed a proto-Catholic current, or, more precisely, who were chosen in the fourth, fifth, and sixth centuries to be the representatives of a backdated orthodoxy.

Ecclesiastical reluctance concerning Gnosticism grew, especially as the numbers of *lapsi* increased due to the persecutions of the third century, whereas Montanist intransigence was perpetuated among the partisans of Novatian and, much later, Donatus.

The *midrashim* of the Elchasaite and Judeo-Christian Churches conferred a legitimacy upon particular and often rival churches: the churches of Thomas, Simon-Peter, James, Saul-Paul, Clement, Philip, Matthias, and so on. The unity imposed by the great movement of the New Prophecy collated diverse writings that had been translated several times from Hebrew or Aramaic, while also being revised and forged along the way. This incongruous ensemble then gave birth to a propaganda-literature adapted to the working-class nature of the movement. Anti-Semitism, miraculous fables, and the exaltation of poverty and sacrifice gradually composed a

Jesus who conformed more closely to the plebian mindset. The apostles—initially witnesses of the Lord whose mythical authority supported this or that community—thenceforth formed a unified cohort tasked with propagating the Christian law that was substituted for Mosaic law.

The apostles who were set up as saints and martyrs served as models for the exaltation of the Christians of Carthage, Scillium, Lyon, Vienna, and Rome.

The Acts circulated, telling of the marvelous adventures, deaths and ascensions of Peter, Paul, Barnabas, Philip, Andrew, and James, who were the heroes of a saga dominated by Joshua and who were cut from the same cloth as the Christians who caused scandals and perished for their faith.

Justin[5] and Tertullian[6] mentioned the *Acts of Pilate*. (Augmented in the fifth century by a description of hell, the *Acts* became, in the eighth century, the *Gospel of Nicomedes*, in which the legends of Joseph of Arimathea and the Grail appeared. The *Acts* was originally a Montanist or pre-Montanist text that was excluded from the canon.) Considered a saint and martyr in Syria and Egypt, Pilate still belonged to a catalogue of dramatic works in which the *Angelos-Christos* lived a brief terrestrial existence in a specific historical context.

The *Acts of Pilate* contained materials that, in the hands of copyists who were less exalted and more careful with historical probability, were put to use in the fabrication of the canonical Gospels:

> It was the sixth hour; darkness covered the entire world until the ninth hour. The sun was obscured: the veil of the temple went from on high to down below, and split in two. Jesus cried in a loud voice: My Father, Abba, Adasch, Ephkidron, Adonai, Sabel, Louel, Eloei, Elemas, Ablakanei, Orioth, Mioth, Ouaoth, Soun, Perineth, Jothat.[7]

The names mentioned by Jesus, which identified him with a magician or a thaumaturge, corresponded to the Eons of power, many of which figured upon the *abraxas* or talismans of magic rituals.[8]

Tertullian's narrative in his *Apology* merits being quoted at length here because, by effacing the thaumaturgical aspects, it composed a more sober version that was nevertheless very different than that retained by the Catholic canon. The Christ was still the *Angelos-Christos*, but he was prey to a terrestrial drama that was perfectly comprehensible to those of the faithful who were headed towards ordeals and a radiant heavenly resurrection.

> That which has come forth out of God is at once God and the Son of God, and the two are one. In this way also, as He is Spirit of Spirit and God of God, He is made a second in manner of existence—in position, not in nature; and He did not withdraw from the original source, but went forth. This ray of God, then, as it was always foretold in ancient times, descending into a certain virgin, and made flesh in her womb, is in His birth God and man united. The flesh formed by the Spirit is nourished, grows up to manhood, speaks, teaches, works, and is the Christ. Receive meanwhile this fable, if you choose to call it so—it is like some of your own—while we go on to show how Christ's claims are proved, and who the parties are with you by whom such fables have been set agoing to overthrow the truth, which they resemble. The Jews, too, were well aware that Christ was coming, as those to whom the prophets spake. Nay, even now His advent is expected by them; nor is there any other contention between them and us, than that they believe the advent has not yet occurred. For two comings of Christ having been revealed to us: a first, which has been fulfilled in the lowliness of a human lot; a second, which impends over the world, now near its close, in all the majesty of Deity unveiled; and, by misunderstanding the first, they have concluded that the second—which, as matter of more manifest prediction, they set their hopes on—is the only one. It was the merited punishment of their sin not to understand the Lord's first advent: for if they had, they would have believed; and if they had believed, they would have obtained salvation. They themselves read how it is written of them that they are deprived of wisdom and understanding—of the use of eyes and ears. As, then, under the force of their pre-judgment, they had convinced themselves from His lowly guise that Christ was no more than man, it followed from that, as a necessary consequence, that they should hold Him a magician from the powers which He displayed—expelling devils from men by a word, restoring vision to the blind, cleansing the leprous,

reinvigorating the paralytic, summoning the dead to life again, making the very elements of nature obey Him, stilling the storms and walking on the sea; proving that He was the Logos of God, that primordial first-begotten Word, accompanied by power and reason, and based on Spirit—that He who was now doing all things by His word, and He who had done that of old, were one and the same. But the Jews were so exasperated by His teaching, by which their rulers and chiefs were convicted of the truth, chiefly because so many turned aside to Him, that at last they brought Him before Pontius Pilate, at that time Roman governor of Syria; and, by the violence of their outcries against Him, extorted a sentence giving Him up to them to be crucified. He Himself had predicted this; which, however, would have signified little had not the prophets of old done it as well. And yet, nailed upon the cross, He exhibited many notable signs, by which His death was distinguished from all others. At His own free-will, He with a word dismissed from Him His spirit, anticipating the executioner's work. In the same hour, too, the light of day was withdrawn, when the sun at the very time was in his meridian blaze. Those who were not aware that this had been predicted about Christ, no doubt thought it an eclipse. You yourselves have the account of the world-portent still in your archives. Then, when His body was taken down from the cross and placed in a sepulchre, the Jews in their eager watchfulness surrounded it with a large military guard, lest, as He had predicted His resurrection from the dead on the third day, His disciples might remove by stealth His body, and deceive even the incredulous. But, lo, on the third day there a was a sudden shock of earthquake, and the stone which sealed the sepulchre was rolled away, and the guard fled off in terror: without a single disciple near, the grave was found empty of all but the clothes of the buried One. But nevertheless, the leaders of the Jews, whom it nearly concerned both to spread abroad a lie, and keep back a people tributary and submissive to them from the faith, gave it out that the body of Christ had been stolen by His followers. For the Lord, you see, did not go forth into the public gaze, lest the wicked should be delivered from their error; that faith also, destined to a great reward, might hold its ground in difficulty. But He spent forty days with some of His disciples down in Galilee, a region of Judea, instructing them in the doctrines they were to teach to others. Thereafter, having given them commission to preach the gospel through the world, He was encompassed with a cloud and taken up to heaven,—a fact more certain far than the assertions of your Proculi concerning Romulus. All these things Pilate did to Christ; and now in fact a Christian in his own convictions, he sent word of Him to the reigning Cæsar, who was at the time Tiberius.[9]

Note that there's no doubt that the historical staging of the trial of Jesus the agitator was drawn from the Christian legend of Pilate. The events recounted here by Tertullian come under the headings of cosmic dramaturgy and hierophany.

Yes, and the Cæsars too would have believed on Christ, if either the Cæsars had not been necessary for the world, or if Christians could have been Cæsars. His disciples also, spreading over the world, did as their Divine Master bade them; and after suffering greatly themselves from the persecutions of the Jews, and with no unwilling heart, as having faith undoubting in the truth, at last by Nero's cruel sword sowed the seed of Christian blood at Rome. Yes, and we shall prove that even your own gods are effective witnesses for Christ. It is a great matter if, to give you faith in Christians, I can bring forward the authority of the very beings on account of whom you refuse them credit. Thus far we have carried out the plan we laid down. We have set forth this origin of our sect and name, with this account of the Founder of Christianity. Let no one henceforth charge us with infamous wickedness; let no one think that it is otherwise than we have represented, for none may give a false account of his religion. For in the very fact that he says he worships another god than he really does, he is guilty of denying the object of his worship, and transferring his worship and homage to another; and, in the transference, he ceases to worship the god he has repudiated. We say, and before all men we say, and torn and bleeding under your tortures, we cry out, "We worship God through Christ". Count Christ a man, if you please; by Him and in Him God would be known and be adored. If the Jews object, we answer that Moses, who was but a man, taught them their religion; against the Greeks we urge that Orpheus at Pieria, Musæus at Athens, Melampus at Argos, Trophonius in Bœotia, imposed religious rites [...].[10]

Contemporaneously with the spread of the Gnostic Gospels (which represented the persistence of an older Christianity and were discovered at Nag Hammadi), fantastical narratives similar to the ones that Tertullian decanted for the use of the Greeks and Romans continued to ascribe to Jesus the traits of a historical person who was quite similar to Apollonius of Tyana, though not without recalling that he remained God in the very reality of his human adventure. For the new Christian wave, Jesus was not a pure spirit. Such a belief, among others, founded a passage in the canonical Gospel attributed to Luke (24: 36–43).

In brief, these were the polemics and ideas of the second century that—by recuperating and explicating Jewish and Essenean speculations about the Messiah, and by making additions and corrections to the novels about Jesus—ended up producing the Jesus who made people forget about Joshua (although only belatedly: in 240 Origen was still emphasizing the omnipresence of Moses' warrior).

Upon all of those who glimpsed in the growing power of Christianity the possibility of enhancing their own power was imposed the necessity of ordering and harmonizing the acts, letters, apocalypses, and Gospels that were as numerous as the rival communities.

This was the epoch in which Celsus, in his *True Discourse* (written around 180), mocked the multitude of Christian prophets, their rivalries, and their lack of scruple in fabricating texts and in making multiple revisions to the old ones. (Tertullian showed where the shoe pinched when he wrote with some irritation: "Nor shall we hear it said of us from any quarter, that we have of our own mind fashioned our own materials"[11].) Each Church placed its Gospel or sacred text under the name of a 'founding father' or apostle.

The majority of them are unknown. Nevertheless, one can cite Tatian and a certain Leucius Charinus. Tertullian attributed the Acts of Paul, which included the narrative of Paul's martyrdom and the love that young Thecla felt for him, to the zeal of an Eastern priest who had dedicated a veritable cult to the Apostle (the text enjoyed great popular success in its Greek, Latin, Coptic, Syrian, Armenian, Slavic, and Arabic versions). The Acts of Paul stimulated Montanist fervor, as did the Gospel of Bartholomew, in which Jesus says, as if addressing Montanus:

"salvation to you, my twin, second Christ"[12].

On the other hand, the Epistle of James, which was of Elchasaite origin, attacked Paul heatedly.

Over the course of the cascading translations, the misreading of the Hebrew and Aramaic texts gave rise to incoherencies and peculiarities that were all the more perceptible in the apocryphal and canonical Gospels that abounded in quotations from the Hebrew mythologies.

The *Epistula apostolorum*, which probably issued from Asia Minor or Egypt in the second half of the second century, appears to be an attempt at syncretism that insists on the miracles and resurrection of Jesus. An apocalypse was inscribed in the millenarian preoccupations of Montanism: in the *Epistula*, Jesus responds to questions about the dates of the *parousia* [second coming] and the resurrection. There are elements of the text that it has in common with the Gospel attributed to John, the Apocalypse of Peter, the Epistle of Barnabas, and Hermas's *The Pastor*. In the same spirit, but without the millenarian allusions, the Acts of the Apostles, which was retained as canonical, reconciled the competing views of Paul and Simon-Peter in a historical novel. It corrected the *Epistula*, which, in the Montanist line, attacks the bishops and priests (who are accused of having misled the people of God) after championing "Saul, which being interpreted is Paul"[13].

Ninety-four texts of Christian propaganda were produced between the second and ninth centuries. Twenty-seven of them were retained in the formation of the neo-testamentary corpus and defined the Catholic Holy Scriptures. These 'gospels truths' emerged from a melting pot[14] in which armies of copyists battled to prune and remodel second- and third-hand materials with adjustments that were demanded by the polemics of the time, in order to end up with a dogmatic corpus that the imperial, pontifical and inquisitorial authorities would place beyond contestation. (Note what Celsus said: "Certain of the Christian believers, like persons who in a fit of drunkenness lay violent hands upon themselves, have corrupted the Gospel from its original integrity, to a threefold, and fourfold, and many-fold degree, and have remodeled it, so that they might be able to answer objections"[15].) If we are to judge from the pusillanimity with which today's historians approach the question, arguments from authority evidently remain efficacious. In fact, however, with the exception of several phrases from the Pauline letters, all of the texts of the New Testament are fakes—historical falsifications that covered for quite real struggles that took place over many epochs—just like the *Letters of the Jews sent to the Overseas Brothers at the time of Jesus*, in which Jews from the year 30 congratulate themselves on having crucified the Messiah. (In 1348 these *Letters* provided the inhabitants of Ulm with an excellent pretext for putting an end to the 'Jewry' of the city.[16])

Nevertheless, no one is unaware that the manuscript called *Sinaiticus*, which contained important fragments of the Gospels that were later chosen as canonical, belonged to a batch of fifty manuscripts that Eusebius of Caesarea, a sycophant of Constantine, transcribed around 331 under the orders of the Emperor, who desired to unify autocratically the emerging Catholic tradition by distributing copies of these manuscripts to the principal Churches of the Empire. They were also subjected to further modifications, as the Abbot Bergier emphasized in his *Dictionary of Theology*: "Men truly knowledgeable in matters of exegesis, and especially [the] sincere [ones], recognize that the text of the New Testament was not set before the end of the sixth century".

Jesus had been an Angel-Messiah, then an agitator put to death despite the Christian Pontius Pilate and because of the Jews. From the exoteric background provided by Montanism, Jesus—God and Man, as in the doctrines of Tertullian—emerged and was then seized and remodeled by anti-Montanist reactionaries.

Catholicism issued from the victory and the vengeance of the *lapsi*, the priests who, through fear of torture, abjured their faith during the successive persecutions of the third century. Against the Montanist principles of Novatian and, later, of Donatus, these priests set up a conciliatory Jesus, less intransigent and less imbued with asceticism than the Messiah of Tertullian, Clement, and Origen.

The critique of sources, which waited until the end of the twentieth century before it timidly got going, has demonstrated, through examinations of the Messiah's words, the various stages in the transformation of the biblical Joshua into Jesus of Nazareth.

When a community or Church needed to affirm its cohesion it gave itself rules that it founded on an older authority. It thus borrowed from the Bible or the *midrashim* remarks (*logia*) that it attributed to the Lord, the spiritual master of the faithful, who was much later identified with Joshua/Jesus.

> The statement, "It is more blessed to give than to receive"—presented in the Acts of the Apostles (20: 35) as a *logion* of Jesus—was in fact a Jewish maxim originally. One also finds it in the *Didachē* (1:5), but it isn't certain that this text recognizes in it the status of the word of the Lord [...]. The Church adopted the Jewish precepts by adapting them to its needs and by transforming them into the *logia* of Jesus.[17]

By Hellenizing themselves, the various Christianities of the second century also referred to Greek fables and philosophical precepts.

The *logia*, which were also inspired by the 'wisdom' of Solomon and Jesus the Son of Sira, inscribed themselves in the perspective of Gnostic Christianity. Jerome, citing a *logion* from the *Gospels of the Hebrews* in his *In prophetam Ezechielem commentarius*, wrote, "It is placed among the greatest sins 'if a man have grieved the spirit of his brother'"[18], which was in fact a banal moral commandment that he himself placed into the mouth of Jesus. The remark consequently played a role in Gnosticism, as a passage from Hermas makes clear: sadness is a vice because it chases away the Holy Spirit, who inhabits the human soul. The spirit of the brother is not the *animus*, but the *pneuma*.

> One can find other theological reasons that lead to the transformation of ancient words and the elaboration of new *logia*: for example, on the occasion of the controversy that took place with respect to the renewal of the pardons accorded to sinners after their conversion to Christianity [...] an argument that was based on the content of a *logion* could only acquire more weight.[19]

In fact, great controversy was born from the rigor and intransigence of the New Prophecy. It was against it that the redactors of the Gospels that were placed under the names of Matthew and Luke attributed these remarks to Jesus: "if he [your brother] sins against you seven times in the day, and turns to you seven times, saying 'I repent', you must forgive him" (Gospel attributed to Luke 17: 4). See also the staged episode that insists on the pardon merited by apostate priests, despite the opinions of Novatian and Donatus: "Then Peter came up and said to him, 'Lord, how often will my brother sin against me, and I forgive him? As many as seven times?' Jesus said to him, 'I do not say to you seven times, but seventy-seven times'" (Gospel attributed to Matthew 18: 21–2)[20].

The popular expansion of Christianity in the Greco-Roman Empire, under the impetus of Montanus and Tertullian, resulted in the anecdotal translation of Gnostic speculations, in the [genre of] apologue, and in the staging of the *logia*. The New Prophecy propagated imagery that the Catholic Church—in a marked contrast with Protestant reluctance on this point—has always encouraged among the 'simple of spirit'.

A passage from the Epistle of Barnabas shows the origin of the sponge of vinegar presented to Jesus on the cross:

> The Epistle of Barnabas testifies to another (quite simple) manner of according the authority of the Lord's word to some statement. In two instances in the text, the citation of a *logion* of the Lord concludes an exegetical debate.
>
> In the first passage, the author asks the following question in the context of a discussion of the meaning of the Jewish sacrificial rites (Epistle of Barnabas 7: 11): "But why is it that they place the wool in the midst of thorns? It is a type of Jesus set before the view of the Church. (They place the wool among thorns), that any one who wishes to bear it away may find it necessary to suffer much, because the thorn is formidable, and thus obtain it only as the result of suffering". And the author goes on to say, in the style of the *logia* of Jesus that were formulated in the first person and by beginning the following phrase with the expression φησιν ('he said'): "Those who wish to behold Me, and lay hold of My kingdom, must through tribulation and suffering obtain me".
>
> As Barnabas gave a typological significance to the entirety of the rite, such a remark by Jesus can be 'freed' from the Jewish model without particular effort.
>
> Another passage (Epistle of Barnabas 7: 4–5) offers a second example of this kind of method: "'And let all the priests alone eat the inwards,

unwashed with vinegar'. Wherefore?" And Barnabas now makes the Lord intervene in person, to give a response to his question: "Because to me, who am to offer my flesh for the sins of my new people, ye are to give gall with vinegar to drink: eat ye alone, while the people fast and mourn in sackcloth and ashes".[21]

Thus the three Gospels called synoptic were laboriously composed, harmonized (to some extent), and placed under the names of three unknowns: Mark, of which there was a secret version that Harnack attributes to Marcion; Matthew, which perhaps derived from the now-lost Gospel of Pseudo-Matthew; and Luke, which was written by a stylist, a professional writer such as Leucius Charinus or Tatian. (Note that it seems established that the Gospel attributed to John was originally a Christian Gnostic—if not a Naassenean or Sethian—text. According to I. Bel's book *Christian Papyri* (London, 1935)[22], the oldest fragments date from the years 125–65.) The 'unquestionable truth' of the synoptic Gospels eclipsed a great number of 'secret' Gospels (*apocrypha* in Greek), to the point that the Church imposed on the word 'apocrypha' the meaning 'false, falsified'.

The writings discovered at Nag Hammadi make no references to the synoptic Gospels, and the Jesus attested to by several texts was only an Angel-Messiah. But it would be important to the Church of the fourth century, in its struggles against Arius and Donatus, to situate the person of the Messiah Jesus historically so that he no longer appeared as the 'second Christ' (like Montanus) and so that his divine nature was 'consubstantially' mixed with the human nature of a prophet of whom the Church of Rome would set itself up as the universal legatee through a direct line of descent from the twelve apostles—especially Paul, the Roman citizen, and Peter, the first 'pope' of the Latin New Jerusalem.

CHAPTER SEVENTEEN

Three Local Christianities: Edessa and Bardaisan, Alexandria and Origen, Antioch and Paul of Samosata

While the New Prophecy, for the first time and despite the dissent of a minority of the bishops, concretized the project of a Christianity that attempted the conquest of the Greco-Roman Empire and ended up unifying the rival churches, there were three cities in which the oldest Judeo-Christian traditions guarded their particularities and perpetuated their privileges as ancient communities.

Such was the case with Edessa, Alexandria, and Antioch, the fortresses of Esseno-Nazarenism.

Bardaisan of Edessa

Starting from the first century, Edessa was a hub of Christian expansion.

"The structure of the archaic Christianity of Edessa", Drijvers writes, "shows the existence of varied groups with diverse opinions that fought against and complained about each other"[1].

Established in Edessa in the first century—at the same time that it was agitating spirits in Alexandria, Antioch, and Ephesus—was a system of beliefs that derived from Essenism and that engendered, on the foundation of local particularities, Churches that obeyed their own laws and doctrines.

The community or *Ekklēsia* of Edessa was placed—no doubt due to the missionary activity of some disciple of Thomas—under the patronage of Jude or Thomas, fancifully elected a 'witness' of the Lord.

This organization had to orient itself in the current of the second century according to the *logia* that were attributed to Joshua/Jesus and supposedly compiled by Matthias or Thomas. The Churches of Edessa perpetuated a Judeo-Christianity of the Elchasaite type and no doubt evolved towards anti-Semitism without, it seems, tipping over into either Marcionism or Montanism.

The first building in Edessa intended for meetings of the believers and taking the name 'church' was constructed in 201. It was destroyed shortly afterwards by a flood, which might be taken as a sign of a singular carelessness on the part of the tutelary God.[2]

Around 180, one of the Churches, led by Bishop Palut, attempted to impose its authority on all Christians. His adepts called themselves 'Palutians'. The struggles for precedence among the diverse Churches of Edessa lasted until the fifth century, when the Palutian faction secured power for itself and, rallying to the theses of Nicaea, embraced Catholicism. This faction consequently hastened to label as heretical the Churches that had shown hostility towards it in the past.

Such was the fate of the work of Bardaisan (or Bar Daysan), who offered an original example of the many syncretisms whose successive stratifications composed the Christianity of the first four centuries.

Born in Edessa in 144 or 155, Bardaisan belonged to the aristocracy and received a serious philosophical education before converting to the new religion in 180. (For a time he adhered to the Valentinian school.) His vast learning also embraced astrology, ethnology, and history. With his son Harmodius, he composed some 150 hymns in honor of the Syrian churches.

His *Dialogue on Destiny* and his *Book of the Laws of Countries*, from which his disciple Philip compiled his teachings, did not escape the destruction ordered by the Church, although Eusebius did authorize the citation of a few extracts.[3]

When Caracalla dealt a mortal blow to the independence of Edessa in 216, Bardaisan went into exile and reached Armenia, where, according to Moses of Chorene, he pursued historical research and worked for the propagation of Christianity. His teachings thereafter accorded an increasingly prominent position to the idea of liberty.

One cannot exclude the possibility of an encounter between Bardaisan and an Indian ambassador sent by the Emperor Heliogabalus around 218. Bardaisan is believed to have died in 222, leaving behind disciples and Christian communities that continued to exist until the fifth century.

Bardaisan's philosophical Christianity situated itself at an equal distance from the New Prophecy—the ascetic rigor and fantastic masochism of which he rejected—and from an ecclesial current that aimed at making itself into a recognized authority in the social order of Rome.

If he took up from the Valentinian Theodotus the trinitarian conception—Father, Son, and *Pneuma*-Spirit (or *Sophia*)—that triumphed at Nicaea, Bardaisan was opposed to Marcion and he rejected the idea of a demiurgical creation. According to Bardaisan, the world must have been the work of a Good God because, despite its imperfections, salvation remained a possibility available to mankind. Thus Ephrem the Syrian was wrong to accuse Bardaisan of having influenced Mani, the founder of the Manichean religion. If the Bardaisanites excluded from their canon the two epistles of Paul to the Corinthians, this was undoubtedly due to Marcionism, which presented versions that predated the Catholic corrections.

Bardaisan did not divide men into three classes—hylics, psychics, and *pneumatics*—in the way that significant strands of Gnostic opinion in the second century did. He instead distinguished in each person three levels in the ladder of consciousness: the *soma*, the *psyche*, and the *pneuma*. Through the Christ, God provided the model of a gradual elevation that traced out the path of salvation.

The Bardaisanites obviously knew nothing of the canonical Gospels, but referred to the *Acts of Thomas* and the *logia* that composed the Gospel attributed to the mythical apostle of Edessa.

Drijvers detects in the Bardaisanites the influence of Philo of Alexandria, an influence that was transmitted by Jewish milieus that were well established in Edessa[4]. The Essenean and Judeo-Christian doctrine of the two paths, Light and Darkness, left traces in Bardaisan's conception of liberty.

This conception was based on a spirit of divine origin, which, united with the soul, descended through the seven spheres of the planets (the Hebdomad) in order to implant itself in the human body at the moment of birth. Because the soul was subjected to the influence of planetary forces, which it must coax during its future ascension, the hour of birth determined the course of the person's existence and distributed fortune and misfortune within it.

In his goodness, God nevertheless permitted man to escape from the unavoidable. United with the soul, the spirit arrogated for itself the privilege of influencing circumstances. Knowledge of the horoscope intervened in salvation in a decisive manner. Adam made bad use of this gift and did not authorize his soul to return to the place of its divine origin, which Bardaisan called the "nuptial chamber of Light"[5]. (Note that the Gospel attributed to Philip, which dates from the same era, evokes relations between redemption and the *koinon* or 'nuptial chamber' in which the union with the Pleroma—the Divine Totality or the Ogdoad—takes place. The soul, the spirit, and the body give birth to a quite piquant anecdotal translation of this process: "There were three who always walked with the Lord: Mary, his mother, and her sister, and Magdalene, the one who was called his companion. His sister and his mother and his companion were each a Mary" (section 32)[6].)

The coming of the Christ—still conceived of as an *Angelos-Christos*, not as the historical founder of a religion—unveiled the soul's path to salvation, the means of untangling obscurity and darkness in order to vanquish the influence of the planets and assure the soul's final redemption. Here Bardaisan expounded the theory of free will, which would prove to be the warhorse of future Catholicism.

As the envoy of God, Jesus fulfilled no other mission than indicating, through the sacrifice of his flesh, the salvational path and the *gnosis* that taught one how to escape the obscure chaos of the body. Not an extreme asceticism, as was required by the New Prophecy, but a sacrificial exercise that elevated the spirit and that—united with the breath of the soul—held the power to vanquish the conspiracy [*conjuration*] of the planetary injunctions in order to return to the light. He who identified with the Christ modified the astrological laws and increased his own power over the macrocosm. Such were the teachings of Bardaisan. It was the thought of Simon of Samaria, albeit inverted by its *antiphysis* [rejection of nature] and denatured by the Christlike example. It was a thought that, even when Christianized, did not remain any less unacceptable to ecclesial authority, since Bardaisan entrusted the work of redemption to each individual person, without assigning a supportive role to any Church.

Audi

If one believes Michael the Syrian, the Archdeacon Audi (or Audie) belonged to the Bardaisanite community at the end of the third or the beginning of the fourth century. In order to legitimate his authority, he produced apocalypses and the Acts of the Apostles, which the Constantinian Church—adopting the political line of the 'Palutians'—would condemn as 'apocryphal'.

Gregory Bar Hebraeus, an Arab theologian in the seventh century, attributed to Audi ninety-four 'apocalypses' (revelations). The Bardaisanite doctrine of the descent and resurrection of the Spirit confronting the planetary Eons shows through from beneath the scornful and anecdotal reduction that Bar Hebraeus imposed on Audi's ideas: "[Audi claimed] that the Christ descended to all of the firmaments and that their inhabitants did not know him, and that his body was celestial, and that he was injured by the lance, and that he was not injured, that he was hung from the wood and that he was not hung"[7].

Audi's conception was not essentially different from that of Arius, the contemporaneous quarrel about whom greatly irritated the emerging tyranny of the Catholic, Apostolic, and Roman Church. Audi rejected the decisions made in Nicaea. Exiled to Scythia, he would propagate his Christianity among the Goths.[8]

Origen of Alexandria

The fate reserved for Origen and his work reveals the falsification that was accomplished by the Church after the Constantinian turn. An authentic Christian martyr and a philosopher in the service of faith, he was condemned for heresy because, despite the revisions of his doctrine, his Christology was still that of an Angel-Messiah, and because his Jesus found its source in Joshua. He also sympathized with the New Prophecy, and he devoted himself to asceticism with a disconcerting rigor that authorized him to scorn the apostate clergy of his era—the heritage of which the Constantinian Church would claim for itself.

Origen's work was reduced, as if by chance, to tiny fragments, which were contained in several large volumes (so great was the zeal of Rufinus and other guardians of orthodoxy to reconstitute it and to rectify it according to the correct dogmatic line).

Born around 185 to Christian parents in Alexandria, the city of all the doctrines, Origen was in his adolescence when his father, Leonides, was subjected to torture in 201 before perishing during the persecutions of the New Prophecy.

Origen was initiated into Neo-Platonist philosophy, which he tried to reconcile with Christianity. A disciple of Clement of Alexandria, he combated the work of Celsus, the *True Discourse*, which was directed against the new religion. In Rome he met Hippolytus, a bishop and philosopher, to whom the *Elenchos* is sometimes attributed. In the same way that Hippolytus, like Tertullian and the Montanists in this regard, vituperated the laxity of a fellow bishop of Rome (in Hippolytus's case it was Callixtus, whom many historians have without any ado taken for a pope), Origen, who succeeded Clement as the head of the Christian *didaskale* of Alexandria, came into conflict with a bishop named Demetrius. Origen pushed the concern for chastity to the point of self-castration in order to resist, in no uncertain terms, the temptations of the flesh. Forced into exile in Caesarea in 231, he died from tortures inflicted around 254, during the Decian persecution of Christians.

Origen was received badly by the clerical party of the *lapsi* and, a century after his death, incurred the wrath of Epiphanius of Salamis because he had been officially condemned by Emperor Justinian I at the second Council of Constantinople in 553.

The Church reproached Origen for having neglected the historical character of Jesus-Christ, which had probably been invented too recently to make it into Origen's writings, notwithstanding Rufinus's efforts to amend, expurgate, and correct everything in those writings that did not agree with that dogma.

Interpreting the Bible in an allegorical sense, Origen identified the Christ with an eternal *Logos* named Joshua, who had returned to the Father without ceasing to be present in the spirit of the Christians. His commentaries on Jesus, son of Nun, explain that "'God gave the name that is above every name' to our Lord and Savior Jesus Christ. For this 'name that is above every name' is Jesus. [...] And because this is 'the name above every name', for many generations it was given to no one"[9]. And Origen recalled the first mention of Jesus. It is found in Exodus: "God summoned Jesus and sent him to fight against Amalek"[10].

In her preface to the *Homilies on Joshua*, Annie Jaubert emphasizes the importance of the typology of Joshua: "this typology constituted itself precisely in opposition to Judaism. No one being greater for the Jews than Moses, prophet and legislator, the Christians had to prove that the Old Testament, through the person of Jesus Nave, had already manifested the superiority of Jesus over Moses"[11].

How can we not infer from such reasoning the appearance, at the beginning of the second century, of Jesus as the mythical founder of Christianity, as a double of Moses whom the Greco-Roman 'remake'[12] set up as a Montanist agitator and then as the founder of the Roman Church?

In fact, Origen preserved a Christianity whose spirit was originally formed in Alexandria, in the circles of Essenean, Nazarenean, Philonian, and Elchasaitean speculations. Like Clement, he remained a Gnostic in the sense that, for him, knowledge unveiled to consciousness what the faith of the New Prophecy unveiled to the body—that is, a purification in which access to salvation resided. In exchange for purification, God, in the infinity of his love, afforded a universal redemption in which the demons and the Devil himself could be saved.

Despite the calumnies of the so-called 'Church Fathers', the least limited of whom admired his erudition, Origen's ideas would be perpetuated in the works of Pseudo-Dionysius the Areopagite, Gregory of Nyssa, Johannes Scotus Eriugena, and even Hildegard of Bingen and Eckhardt.

Paul of Samosata, Bishop of Antioch

At the beginning of the fourth century, in Edessa, King Abgar—converted to the religion that had recently been recognized by the State—circulated personal letters addressed to Jesus-Christ, to which Abgar himself had obligingly responded. Abgar thereby revived to his own advantage the operation engaged in by the Church in order to attribute to Jesus, Paul, and Peter the status of historical personages. Later rejected as crude fakes, these letters differed from the New Testament only in their excessive degree of improbability.

Like all of the potentates touched by the commercialism [*affairisme*] of Rome, King Abgar used Catholicism as an instrument of power. He reorganized the clergy of the city, conferred upon them a monarchal form, transformed the temples into churches and the traditional festivals into consecrations of the saints, and marked out the space and time of the city on a religious basis, just as the Church undertook to do at the level of the *Imperium Romanum*.[13]

Paul of Samosata, the bishop of Antioch in 260, anticipated King Abgar's reforms by fifty years. To the title of leader of the Church of Antioch, he added those of Governor of the Syrian province of Commagene and Secretary of Finances to Queen Zenobia of Palmyra.

A personage of the first rank in the region, Paul of Samosata was on the best of terms with Zenobia, and favored a Syrian nationalism that aroused the suspicions of Rome and encouraged a revolt by his peers and ecclesiastical rivals. A synod united in Antioch deposed him in 268.

Paul of Samosata's doctrine illustrates the zone of uncertainty in which the debate concerning the nature of the Christ was still stuck. For Paul, God had engendered the *Logos* that could be called the Son. The *Logos* inspired Moses and the prophets, and then also Jesus, who was only a man when the *Logos* entered him during his baptism and transformed him into a perfect being. From then on he accomplished miracles, triumphing over the sin in himself and in all men, with the result that his death redeemed and saved all of humanity. He pre-existed and judged the living and the dead.

Ironically, the synod that deposed Paul of Samosata would reject the term *homoousios* (consubstantial), by which he designated the identity of God and the Christ. This was the same quality that the Church imposed in the fourth century as the one and only Trinitarian truth.

Paul's conception of the Trinity, it is true, took a personal turn that was hardly compatible with the idea that the Church would forge in the fourth century. According to Leontius of Byzantium, "he gave the name of Father to God, who created all things; the name of Son to himself, who was purely a man; and Spirit to the grace that was the result of the apostles"[14].

Theodore of Mopsuestia attributed to Paul of Samosata a remark whose echoes still reverberated a thousand years later among the Amauricians and the partisans of the Free Spirit: "I do not desire the Christ because he was made God, but because such as he was made, I was made, since this godliness is found in my nature"[15].

The enemies of Paul of Samosata did not lie in an exaggerated fashion when they affirmed that the psalms that were sung in Antioch were sung less in honor of God than of Paul himself. Paul accorded a place to women in religious offices, but nothing permits one to affirm that he did so in a significantly different manner from the Montanists and their virginal prophetesses.

The heresiologues detected his influence in the Nestorianism of the fifth century and in the Paulician movement that struggled against Byzantium in the eighth century.

CHAPTER EIGHTEEN

Novatian, the Apostate Clergy, and the Anti-Montanist Reaction

The breath of popular Christianity fanned the pyres in which the faithful were consumed, and the resentment of crowds that were accustomed to pogroms and to hunting for Jews was likewise nourished. According to its custom, imperial power imputed responsibility for these disorders not to the executioners but to the victims. The State's official persecutions replaced cunningly fomented instances of lynching, which indiscriminately struck all of the partisans of a God who was hostile to the other divinities.

In 202—contrary to the wishes of his wife, Julia Mamaea, who was favorable to the new religion (or so it is said)—Septimius Severus promulgated an edict that prohibited Jewish and Christian proselytism. The death of the Emperor suspended this repression; it was revived under Maximinus and then disappeared again, although not without being sporadically rekindled in the flames of the pogroms. One such pogrom exploded in Cappadocia at the instigation of the governor. The 249 pogrom in Alexandria inspired increased rigor on the part of Decius, who dreamed of restoring the ancient religious values and of reinvigorating the unity of the Empire through the annihilation of the Jews and the Christians. A comparable project revolved in the heads that the influential bishops managed to keep on their shoulders. Little by little a new doctrine was formed, a realistic and political form of Christianity: Catholicism.

One of the small number of victims of the trials that began in 250, the philosopher Origen, an adept of Montanist asceticism, died following prolonged torture.

A ruling promulgated against the Christians by Valerian in 257 suggested that they need not repudiate their worship, but that they must make sacrifices to the ancient Gods. The edict of tolerance issued by Gallienus reestablished the peace in 260. Nevertheless, the idea of a national religion continued to make headway. Emperor Aurelian, imbued with a desire to revive the brilliance of Rome through the radiance of a universal belief, revived the old monotheism of the *Sol invictus*—the cult of the Sun King—to suit himself. Death prevented him from restoring an authority that ecclesial propaganda soon after recuperated: it identified Jesus-Christ with the unconquered Sun. Under the ferule of bishops who were attached to their prerogatives and who were always on the lookout for potential compromises that might advance their power, the austere Christianity of the Essenes, the Nazarenes, the Gnostics, the Marcionites and the New Prophecy prepared to prostitute itself devotedly to the State.

After Gallienus' edict, the police and the governors tolerated the exercise of Christianity. But the truce was brutally interrupted so as to make room for the last and bloodiest of the repressions—that of Diocletian, who from 303 to 305 pursued both Christians and Manicheans in a senseless fury. Those who abjured—and they were many—were left untroubled.

The edict of tolerance issued by Galerius in 311 suffered a brief interruption under Maximinus, but the latter was vanquished in 313 by Licinius, whose victory announced the triumph of Christianity as the religion of the State.

Eusebius of Caesarea, a sycophant of the Emperor who assured his credit with the court through cunning and flattery, had good reason for exalting the faith and the firmness of the martyrs, whom he estimated as numbering in the tens of thousands. Frend, a historian of persecutions, has counted between 2,500 and 3,000 victims in the East and 500 in the West over the course of more than a century[1]. (The catacombs of the Via Latina date from the years 320–50 or 350–70. Contrary to the assertions of the Saint Sulpician legends, no known Christian sarcophagus predates the third century.) Priests and bishops close to Rome abjured more willingly than did those in the East, who were in solidarity with the local Churches, whose hostility to Roman power would not easily be placated. This hostility kindled Donatism and Arianism, and subsequently provoked the schism of Byzantium.

Eusebius's hyperbolic cult of the martyr makes one think of Stalin, who combined the glorification of Bolshevism with the massacre of its survivors. Who worked most effectively for the triumph of Eusebius and of the clerical bureaucracy, the fishnet of which would fall over the entire world? The *lapsi*, the apostates, the backsliders. And as for authentic Christianity, the party of the New Prophecy, the only legitimate holder of the laurels of the martyrs: under the name Montanism, it would be cast into the dustbin of 'heretical perversion'.

From the beginning of the third century, tension grew between the fervent Christians, who were more attached to faith than to life, and the bishops, whose sense of reality preferred an apostate priest to a dead one. Refusing torment, the renegade made use of his leisure—for the greater glory of the Church, of course—to exploit the work of the martyrs for edifying ends. This was an old argument in which principle ceded place to necessity. The delirious masochism of the Christians of the second century had certainly offered levelheaded spirits several reasons to calm down and to reprove excessive offerings to death. This was all very well, but the 'party of the bishops', which was scorned by Hermas, Origen, and Tertullian, also applied itself in this period—even as Rome was intensifying its repressions—to the safeguarding of an ecclesiastical power whose moderation was doubly useful: it guarded against the fury of the state, on the one hand, and it condemned an asceticism that was clearly incompatible with Greco-Roman license, on the other.

Tertullian had already stigmatized the laxity of certain bishops, as well as their taste for power. "Episcopatus semulatio schismatum mater est", he wrote in his *On Baptism*: "Emulation of the episcopal office is the mother of schisms"[2].

Callixtus, one of the principal bishops of Rome between 217 and 222, attracted the reprobation of another bishop, Hippolytus, who is sometimes identified as the author of the *Elenchos*. Accused of laxity because he ordained remarried priests (Tertullian and Montanism prohibited remarriage), Callixtus was a heretic in the eyes of the author of the *Elenchos*: "For he who is in the habit of attending the congregation of any one else, and is called a Christian, should he commit any transgression; the sin, they say, is not reckoned unto him, provided only he hurries off *and attaches himself* to the school of Calli[x]tus"[3]. The school of Callixtus—whom historians have long taken to be a pope and whose name was given to certain catacombs—was, according to the *Elenchos* (book 9, chapter 7), in the hands of the accomplices of abortion: "Whence women, reputed believers, began to resort to drugs for producing sterility, and to gird themselves round, so as to expel what was being conceived"[4].

Pseudo-Hippolytus did not hesitate to situate Callixtus in the line of the Elchasaitism that had been born in the third year of Trajan's rule (around 100); a certain Alcibiades possessed the Elchasaites' sacred book. 'Heresy'—as it appeared here and as it would later be codified—at first delineated a category to which anything that opposed or contested the bishop's authority was slanderously consigned. Assassinated during a riot in 222, Callixtus suffered the thunderous displeasure of the *Elenchos*. But his 'lax' policies would eventually open the doors of holiness for him. The dictionaries consecrated Callixtus as the sixth Pope of Rome, even though the papacy did not appear until the seventh century.

Around 250, Cyprian, the Bishop of Carthage—the area in which Tertullian and the New Prophecy were dominant—set himself up as the defender of the lapsi. His doctrine, expounded in an essay called *On the Unity of the Church*, indirectly laid the political foundations for Catholicism. For Cyprian, every legitimate bishop was the inheritor of "the throne of Peter"[5] and had the right to combat anyone who contested him. This right was the principle that most often founded accusations of heresy. The expression "the throne of Peter", which was intended to reinforce local power, was attacked by Stephen, the Bishop of Rome around 254–7: this foreshadowed the conflict in the fourth century between Rome, which monopolized "the throne of Peter" and accredited the execution of Simon-Peter in the imperial city, and the Churches that were firmly established in the East.

Against ecclesial *Realpolitik*, Novatian attempted to revive the ardors of Montanist faith. Ordained a bishop in 249, he did not escape the quarrels over precedence that set the various community leaders against each other. After the execution of Bishop Fabian, Novatian took control of a part of the Roman clergy and extolled a rigor that was strengthened by asceticism and the duties of faith. Indignant about the large number of faithful people and priests who abjured by agreeing to make sacrifices to the Emperor or by buying certificates of abjuration, Novatian refused to readmit into the community those guilty of renunciation. In opposition to another bishop of Rome named Cornelius, who was a partisan of moderation, Novatian nurtured a penitential movement and assured himself of the support of many Churches. He himself ordained other bishops who rallied to his ideas.

Novatian's doctrine emanated directly from the New Prophecy. In *On the Advantages of Chastity*, he implored the members of the "virgin church" to remain pure in order to keep a place of welcome for the Holy Spirit[6]. Tertullian did not say anything different. The influence of Origen was discernible in Novatian's text *On Jewish Food*, in which he perceived in the dishes condemned by the biblical texts an allegorical description of the vices.

Novatian's enemies, Cornelius of Rome and Cyprian of Carthage, held in esteem a treatise later called *On the Trinity*, although the word *trinitas* did not appear in it. This treatise expounded upon the unity of the Father and the Son. Because the Son of God became man, he could lead humanity to eternal salvation. After the Constantinian turn, such speculations were invoked in support of an escalating conflict: the one between the local Churches, which were close to the faithful and attentive to matters of faith, and the centralized and bureaucratized Church of Rome and its emperor.[7]

CHAPTER NINETEEN

Arianism and the Church of Rome

The Council of Nicaea, convened on the orders of Constantine in 325, marked the official births of orthodoxy and, consequently, of heresy. At that time, the dogma that took centuries to make precise its immutable truths arrogated for itself the privilege of a rectitude that people like Eusebius, Epiphanius, Augustine, Jerome, and their cohorts extended back into the past—as far back as Jesus, the chosen founder of Catholic invariance.

The Church pushed cynicism to the point of claiming for itself a Christianity that condemned the following successive manifestations as heresies: Nazarenism, Elchasaitism, Marcionism, anti-Marcionism, Christian Gnosticism, and the New Prophecy.

In the third century the notion of *hairesis*—questionable choices, subject to polemic—became a weapon by means of which the bishops defended their privileges against all contestation. In the hands of emperors and then popes, heresy was legally defined as a form of high treason. When the popes uprooted from the declining Empire the ecclesial authority that they had arrogated for themselves, they perpetuated the old Roman legislation that had formerly been used against the Jews and the Christians, who had been defined as 'rebels' against the State and as 'perverts' contravening moral order.

By imposing himself as Emperor by divine right, Constantine

successfully led a political enterprise in which his predecessors had fared only poorly. The party of collaborators, which the Christian *lapsi* had formed, met the aims of Constantine, who—having vanquished Maximinus and Licinius—wanted to consolidate the unity of the Empire. Nourished by the conception of an ecclesial monarchism that erected Rome as the New Jerusalem, national interests [*la raison d'État*] presided over the birth of Catholicism, the triumph of which remained burdened by the memory of the Christianities that had founded it and that it treated as bastards and abortions.

The polemics of the first three centuries concerned freedom of choice. The Council of Nicaea defined religious truth and, from then on, sustained the permanence of the lie: the forgery of Gospels, the falsification of writings, the destruction of heterodox works, and the fabrication of an official history to which the majority of scholars and historians still subscribe today.

Constantine was touched by grace? Come on! I borrow the following lines from a Catholic historian, Henri Guillemin: "Constantine did not believe in 'Jesus-Christ' in any sense; he was a pagan, and he only converted (if he ever did so) upon his death in 337. When he ordered the meeting at Nicaea in 325 he was only being shrewd, a realist, and 'pragmatic'. When faced with the growing numerical importance in his Empire of the sectarians of 'Krestos', he drew from this fact the consequences that imposed themselves concerning the well-being of his government"[1].

At the Emperor's deathbed was to be found the true father of Catholicism: Eusebius of Caesarea.

Eusebius of Caesarea
In his commentary on Eusebius of Caesarea's *Life of Constantine*, Jacob Burckhardt describes Eusebius as the "first thoroughly dishonest and unfair historian of ancient times"[2].

To understand the necessity that caused Eusebius to fabricate a *Church History*, canonical texts, and a direct line of descent from the apostles out of the scattered pieces of a three-centuries-old puzzle, it is fitting to recall that he was, above all, the first theorist to "introduce a rational conception of imperial power into the interior of a coherent ideology and metaphysics"[3].

For Eusebius, Jacques Jarry writes, "the terrestrial kingdom was in the image of the celestial kingdom". The task of the sovereign was that of the *Logos*: to make the law rule over the here below. "Carrying the image of the celestial kingdom, eyes fixed on heaven, he led and governed mortals on the model of an archetype that was fortified by the imitation of the monarchal power of the *Logos*".[4]

Eusebius's history of the Church logically had to lead to the theology that he had developed, and that theology was nothing other than the justification of the power of Constantine—the incarnation of the *Logos* by the grace of God, whom he was duty-bound to serve:

> God the Father, whom he called the Supreme Emperor, had certainly created the world. After creating it, he enclosed it in the reins of divine wisdom by making it submit to the constraints of time and the cycle of the years. But he entrusted this world, once created, to his only son, the Word. Eusebius of Caesarea made him "the eminent moderator of the world", the "common conserver of all things"; the Cosmos produced him so that he could govern it; "God entrusted him with the reins of this universe". "He received from the infinitely good Father a hereditary role"; "he rules what is inside as well as outside of the vault of heaven", and he imposes harmonization on all things.
>
> The *Logos* is thus the governor of the Cosmos, the one who maintains order in creation. It makes a harmony among all things, added Eusebius of Caesarea. He [the Son] was not a viceroy totally exterior to the ensemble that he governed. He was like the soul and spirit of the world. Eusebius of Caesarea described his functions in a characteristic passage: "The Divine Word", he said, "is not composed of parts and is not constituted from contraries, but is simple and indivisible. In a body, the parts and members, the viscera and the intestines, are multiple in their assemblage, but a single soul, a single spirit, indivisible and incorporeal, is spread throughout the ensemble; likewise, in the universe, the world itself is one, everything being combined from multiple parts, but the Divine Word, endowed with an immense and all-powerful force, also single, deployed throughout the universe,

does not stray here and there, but spreads through all things and is the cause of all that happens therein".[5]

Theology thenceforth loaned its privileged framework to the defense of ecclesial politics and imperial power, which were always in solidarity despite their violent rivalries. Theology thus seized upon two doctrines that offered neither novelty nor anything religiously shocking: Donatism and Arianism. The first inscribed itself in the line of the New Prophecy and Novatian; the second revived Gnostic-Christian speculations concerning the relations between God and his Messiah.

Arius

Although his name was invested with a glory that was propagated through the artifice of an alleged Arian party, neither Arius's life nor his works justified the celebrity with which he was rewarded. Born in Libya or Alexandria around 260, he studied with Lucian of Antioch and lived in Alexandria, where Peter, the bishop of the city (executed in 311), mentioned him for the first time. He belonged to the category of priests who eagerly awaited honors and preeminence. A partisan of Meletius of Lycopolis, a rival of the deceased Peter, Arius acceded to the priesthood under Achilles, the successor to the martyred bishop, and was then elevated in rank under the bishopric of someone named Alexander. Extolling asceticism, Arius grew in popularity among the faithful, who were still receptive to the old influence of Montanism, an influence that was renewed by Novatian.

In 318, Arius opposed his bishop, reproaching him for having attributed an equal eternity to the Father and the Son in a sermon. For Arius, the Son was neither eternal nor equal to the Father. The Son was created according to the same principle as all other things and only received his divine nature when he was invested with his mission as savior on earth. The first opinion resembled Jewish, Essenean, and Nazarenean Gnosticism, according to which Adam, or the new Adam set up as the redeemer Messiah, was the co-creator of the world. The second revived Montanism: the Messiah was a man, sharing in the vicissitudes of common human existence, but the Divine Spirit was incarnated in Him at His birth, since

He also was the son of *Sophia* or Mary. The two opinions were part of the evolution of the Christianity of the first two centuries.

A synod of a hundred bishops, convened around 318 or 319, excluded Arius and his partisans from the Christian community; he was refused communion, which marked belonging to the congregation. He left Alexandria and went to Nicomedia, where he enjoyed the support of Bishop Eusebius, despite having written a verse and prose pamphlet called *Thalia* (the Banquet) that enjoyed great popular success. Bishop Alexander responded to these developments in a detailed report on the quarrel. The hostility of Licinius towards the Christians and his war against Constantine relegated these debates to a secondary level of consideration, but once he was master of the Empire (after the defeat of Licinius), Constantine triumphantly acceded to double sovereignty (spiritual and temporal) and—at the request of Arius's friends—convened a council at Nicaea, not far from Nicomedia.

In 325, Constantine—circumscribed by his councilor Hosius of Cordova, who had been won over to the party of Bishop Alexander—convinced three hundred bishops to adopt positions opposed to those of Arius.

The Nicene Creed resulted from an imperial opinion that was hostile to Arius's theory, according to which "God existed when the Son did not", and which maintained that "he [the Son] didn't exist before birth"[6]. The credo proclaimed "We believe in one Lord, Jesus Christ, | the only Son of God, | eternally begotten of the Father, | God from God, Light from Light, | true God from true God, | begotten, not made, | of one Being with the Father"[7]—the last line of which translates the Greek term *homoiousios* [consubstantial].

Arius obeyed and renounced his doctrine. In 328 Eusebius of Nicomedia and Theognis of Nicaea, exiled along with their friend Arius, regained their positions. In 335 the synod of Tyre rehabilitated Arius. Constantine, whose sole desire in excluding them had been to assure the unity of the young universal Church, was preparing to reintegrate Arius into the clergy of Alexandria when the unfortunate protestor died in 336. (Note that the official Christian version of his death shot at him the last arrow of polemical elegance by propagating the rumor that he had died unexpectedly while satisfying an urgent need [to defecate]. The abbot François-André-Adrien Pluquet, following other heresiologues, rejoiced in this brilliant proof of divine wrath[8].)

From this shallow quarrel—in which the authority of the Emperor, elevated to the dignity of *pontifex maximus* (sovereign pontiff), was the only important factor—the theologians drew an enormous jumble of implications that were as thunderous as they were empty. Underneath the quibbling of the Arian party, the size of which was artificially swelled by its enemies in order to lend significance to what was actually trivial, there raged a power struggle between Rome and the Eastern Churches, and an unceasing combat between the West and Byzantium.

From a speculative point of view, it was easy to brandish the reproach of dualism—nay, even Marcion's concept of 'two Gods'—against Bishop Alexander and his thesis of the 'Eternal God, Eternal Son'. The credo of Nicaea recognized a single God in order to parry Marcionism, which the Manichean religion would claim for itself.

After the death of Constantine I, reconciliation seemed to prevail. Nevertheless, quite soon after that, his successor, Constans, supported the party of Nicaea, while in the East Constantine II gave his support to the Arians. After the death of Constans in 350, Constantine II, by intervening in several councils, attempted to Arianize the West and to hunt down Arius's enemies.

The sudden victory of Arianism gave birth to dissent, however. Three factions emerged. The Anomeans affirmed that the Son was dissimilar (*anomoios*) to the Father; the semi-Arians (or *homoiousians*) stated that the Son shared the same substance (*homoiousios*) as the Father; and the homoians believed that the Son was like (*homoios*) the Father.

In fact, such doctrinal positions were only pawns on the chessboard of rival influences. Valens, Emperor from 364 to 378, was inclined in favor of the *homoians*; Gratian and Theodosius I defended Nicaea. (Note that Theodosius imposed on all Christians an orthodox faith to which he brought a repressive firmness that thenceforth prevented deviations from the interests of national security [*la raison d'État*]. In a strict sense, he was the founder of Catholic orthodoxy.) The decrees of 380 and 381 condemned Arianism, chased its partisans from the Church, and foreshadowed many executions—these were the first victims of orthodoxy before Priscillian. In 381, the Council of Constantinople reaffirmed the credo of Nicaea and condemned the semi-Arians (the *homoiousians*).

With the emergence of a State religion, the *episcopatus aemulatio*—the quest for Episcopal honors (which Tertullian mocked and labeled the "mother of schisms")—was more easily pursued because the destiny of the martyr was no longer to be feared.

Born in Cilicia around 300, Aëtius was a rhetorician based in Antioch. He was a disciple of Arius before he founded the Anomean party and created his own doctrine by detecting a dissimilarity between the Father and the Son, in the latter of whom was incarnated the *Logos* or Holy Spirit. A friend of Emperor Gallus, Aëtius exploited certain opportunities to secure the triumph of his views, but his fate was ultimately a tragic one. Condemned to exile upon the fall of Gallus (354), he aroused the reprobation of the Councils of Ancyra (358) and Constantinople (360). Summoned by Emperor Julian and made a bishop, he ended his duties upon the death of Julian, the last tolerant emperor (the one whom the Church named the Apostate because he wanted to restore religious freedom). Aëtius participated in the revolt of Procopius (a cousin of Julian), barely escaped capital punishment, and died soon thereafter in Constantinople, where his secretary, Eunomius, developed a doctrine according to which the Father and the Son, though dissimilar in essence, were united by the same will.

Athanasius, Alexander's successor, combated the theses of Arius and Aëtius, reinforced the Nicene party, and invented the Arian party in his *Orations Against the Arians*; he portrayed Arianism as a power that threatened faith and Arius himself as the very spirit of heresy.

From such theological hyperbole—beneath which were played out banal power struggles between the notables of Rome, Alexandria, Antioch, and Constantinople—burst forth an Arian missionary vocation that almost carried off the laurels of orthodoxy by winning the sympathy of the new rival powers in Rome.

Constantine had condemned Arius only because he wished to protect the unity of the Church and the unity of the Empire. Arius had threatened stability and order only to a limited extent, in the sense that his influence did not garner the support of the vast majority of the people.

Constantine was not unaware, however, that, when he exiled Arius, he was condemning his own principal enemy, Athanasius, to the same fate. Constantine II—amid the uncertainty in which orthodoxy was still situated—likewise kept Athanasius and Aëtius at arm's length. Everything could have capsized at any moment. Weakened by the edict of tolerance issued by Emperor Julian (361–3), both parties nonetheless experienced a victory of sorts. The Nicaeans won the West, while the Anomean missionaries converted the Goths, who, after invading Spain and North Africa, imposed Arianism on those regions. As for Byzantium, whose hostility toward Rome only continued to increase, it gave to its schism a theological pretext by rejecting the post-Nicaea formula that was born in Spain during the seventh century: "The Holy Spirit proceeds from the Father *and* the Son". This quarrel became known as *Filioque* ('and of the Son').

The rivalries between Arian, anti-Arian, and pseudo-Arian factions rallied a good number of individuals who were in search of social advancement or who were animated by straightforward opportunism. (Note that the schismatic Lucifer, the Bishop of Cagliari in Sardinia, laid the grounds for an anti-Arian Church, which served his interests.) Was not Acacius, a bishop and the successor of Eusebius of Caesarea, successively Arian under Constans, Nicaean under Jovian, and Anomean under Valens? Such was the case with many.

More interesting was Aerius, the priest of Pontus, who was ordained by Eustathius the Bishop of Sebaste, with whom he came into conflict and whom he reproached for abandoning the ascetic conduct to which he had subscribed before attaining the dignity of office.

Aerius became part of the current opposed to Nicaea and to the establishment of State control over religion by advancing the view that no difference in rank between priests and bishops should exist. He condemned the ostentation of the ceremonies that were multiplied by the Church and judged prayers for the dead—which were a source of revenue for the clergy—to be useless. Finally, according to him, Easter did away with all Jewish superstitions. Epiphanius of Salamis—who deployed a tactic (that is to say, intentional confusion) that was popular among the inquisitors of the Middle Ages—associated Aerius with the Arians, to whom he thus imputed feelings of hostility towards the Church hierarchy.

CHAPTER TWENTY

Donatus and the Circumcellions

From the moment that Constantine agreed to support the Christian communities in 313, he took hold of the Church and treated it as an instrument of State power. He accorded to the bishops whom he recognized the license to enact sentences under imperial protection. His patronage of large-scale construction projects (Saint Peter's Basilica, the Basilica of Saint John Lateran, and the Basilica of Saint Agnes in Rome; the Church of the Holy Sepulcher in Jerusalem)—which honored a faith that he openly mocked before it served to consolidate his own absolutism—aroused the reprobation of a popular Christianity that had been imbued with asceticism and martyrdom since the end of the second century.

An old dispute opposed the party of the torture victims—the Christians who remained unshakeable in their convictions even when faced with their executioners—and the party of the *lapsi* and the *traditores*, the renegades and the traitors, who were more numerous and, due to their pragmatism, better positioned to accede to the clerical offices that were now conferred by the State.

It was in Carthage, the bastion of Tertullianism, that the most significant incident erupted; it was precipitated by an anti-Montanist offensive that was directed by a corrupt clergy.

During the brief (303–5) but cruel persecutions launched by

Diocletian, the majority of the clergy abjured. A small group of priests from Abitina (Tunisia), imprisoned in advance of being tortured, denounced the *traditores*. They proclaimed that only those who, following their example, remained loyal to the faith would reach paradise. Their intransigence irritated the clergy of Carthage and, in particular, the Archdeacon Caecilianus (Caecilian), who was later accused of preventing other Christians from bringing food and comfort to prisoners.[1]

When Caecilian succeeded the bishop of Carthage, who died in 311, the majority of the faithful reacted with indignation. A young bishop named Donatus Magnus led the protests.

Born in Numidia, Donatus had already attracted attention as a young bishop in Casa Nigra by demanding, at the conclusion of the persecutions, a new baptism for the lapsed clergy members. Taking up these entreaties, a council of seventy bishops met in 312, deposed Caecilian, and replaced him with Majorinus, the chaplain of Lucilla (a rich Spaniard who had been executed under the reign of Caecilian).

That same year, Constantine crushed his rival, Maxentius, and seized North Africa, which had until then been ruled by the deposed Emperor. On the recommendation of the Roman clergy, in which apostasy was dominant, Constantine restored Caecilian to his position, allotted him an important subsidy, and exempted from all taxes the clergy who obeyed the reinstated renegade.

Nevertheless, upon the death of Majorinus, Donatus succeeded him with the consent of the enemies of Caecilian, who sent the Emperor a list of the crimes imputed to Majorinus' protégé. Donatus went to Rome to plead his legitimacy, but Miltiades, the Bishop of Rome (whom Constantine consulted because of his African origins), sided against him, which caused Donatus to be condemned by the Emperor.

Principally concerned with unifying his empire, Constantine moved from threats to conciliation. In 321 he repealed the decree of exile that had been imposed on Donatus, whose influence was continuing to grow. In 336, within a territory that today stretches from Tunisia to East Algeria, 270 Donatist bishops controlled communities in which the lax party of Caecilian was in the minority. In Egypt the Donatist bishop Meletius enjoyed great popular support.

Donatus would no doubt have benefited from the tacit tolerance of imperial power if the peasant revolt of the Circumcellions had not been grafted onto his movement and thereby formed its working-class wing.

In 346, a commando group of Circumcellions attacked the commission sent to North Africa by the Emperor. Despite their disapproval of this action, Donatus and his principal partisans were exiled to Gaul, where the bishop of Casa Nigra died in 355.

The Circumcellion movement allied to religious fanaticism (which was hostile to the laxity of the wealthy) the demands of the disinherited of the countryside: laborers, shepherds, slaves, and poor peasants. Their name came from *circum cellas*: those who roam around the cells (*cellae*).

They called themselves 'saints' and 'athletes' (*agonists*), which were terms that originated in Essenism and Judeo-Christianity. Armed with clubs (each of which was called Israel), the Circumcellions attacked functionaries and the owners of large properties and liberated slaves, to whom they entrusted the task of treating their former masters in the manner in which they themselves had been treated in servitude. They combated the Devil in the person of his representatives: terrestrial property-owners, tax collectors, magistrates, and anti-Donatist priests. They acted under the leadership of two men, Axido and Fasir, 'sanctorum duces' (the Captains of the Saints), who, according to Optatus (340), "made property owners and creditors tremble"[2]. The Circumcellions supported the cult of the martyrs and opposed the sanctification achieved through asceticism to the idle and hedonistic existence of the rich.

Disavowed by the Donatists, the Circumcellions did not resist the imperial army and ended up being massacred around 348.

Nevertheless, Donatism survived until 429. It rejected the principal demands of the Circumcellions, which would so often be reprised by the various millenarian movements: the reign of the saints; universal equality under the sole power of God; moratoria on debts; judgments and executions of the rich; and the suppression of slavery.

Donatus, who from the outset cautioned against the zeal of the Circumcellions in their hunt for apostates, approved of their suppression but did not recover his credit with the Emperor.

The party of the *lapsi* and the morally lax regained the upper hand.

Optatus attacked his adversaries in *Against the Donatists*. From 399 to 415, Augustine of Hippo undertook to chase them out of Carthage. They were outlawed in 411.

In one of history's many ironies, Donatism disappeared in 429, at the same time as Roman colonization was being swept away by the invasion of the Vandals, who imposed as the new State religion the very Arianism that had previously been condemned as heretical.

The social and political elements that had assured the success of Donatism also led to its downfall. The nationalistic demands of Numidia and Mauritania ensured support for Donatus's anti-Roman stance and his project of creating an African Catholic Church. At least according to Optatus's *Against the Donatists*[3], when Donatus asked "What has the Emperor to do with the Church?", his response was doubly articulated. His Church—outside of which "there was no salvation" (the same of course being true for the Church of Rome)—refused to submit to the imperial power of an emperor who was at once the head of State and the leader of the clergy. He defended the principle of national Churches, independent of a central power.

Donatus contested the preeminence of temporal power over spiritual power, and this matched the views of the papacy starting from the seventh century. Augustine, an enemy of Donatism and a partisan of spiritual preeminence, was not being naïve when he borrowed from the Donatist theologian Ticonius the doctrine of the two cities (the terrestrial city and the city of God).

On the other hand, Donatus's Montanism and Tertullianism went against the attempts of the Church of Rome to reconcile itself with a Latin aristocracy that was little inclined to either asceticism or Puritanism. His Church claimed to be the 'Virgin Church' of Tertullian, in opposition to the temporal Church of the *lapsi*. It was a 'closed garden', a refuge for the long-suffering people of God, a place in which priests who had perjured themselves could have no part.

The Donatists did not grant—and here one finds again the arguments of the *Elenchos* against Callixtus, the Bishop of Rome—that a dignitary who had relinquished his celestial existence in order to save his terrestrial life had the right to pursue his ministry. The sacraments administered by such a bishop were devoid of value. The sacred character of the episcopal function could not accommodate abuses of authority. The clergy of Rome, in which the *lapsi* were in the majority, disagreed. For them, any bishop was invested with the right to administer the sacraments, even if, as a man, he had shown himself unworthy of the sacredness that he distributed. This was an endemic conflict, and one that—from a certain angle—clarified the very notion of heresy. Provided that he did not put aside dogma (and therefore remained an obedient son), a priest, bishop, or pope could surrender himself to debauchery and infamy without losing the grace that the Church bestowed upon him. But if he practiced virtue by contravening orthodoxy in his discourse, he incurred damnation both in the beyond and in the here below.

Augustine formulated his doctrine concerning the nature of the Church and the sacraments in opposition to Donatus. Not only did he appeal for police repression of individuals and groups that strayed from Catholic orthodoxy, he also made precise the point that the sacraments acted *ex opere operato*[4], through the sacred character of the Church officials.

CHAPTER TWENTY-ONE

The Spirituals,
Also Called Messalians or Euchites

Unlike Arianism, Donatism, and Monophysism—which, being born from rivalries between nations and Churches, might better be characterized as schisms than as heresies—the movement of the 'Spirituals', who were called Messalians or Euchites by their adversaries, was only superficially Christian. Beneath this surface was expressed the common people's taste for life, a taste that was easily diverted by neglect, by a leveling and destructive asceticism, and by religious or political fanaticism.

By combating the rigor of the New Prophecy as it was perpetuated by Novatian, Donatus, and the Circumcellions, the Church of Rome exercised a political wisdom of which many popes showed themselves to be worthy heirs. Though it was protected by its status as an unrivaled religion, Catholicism did not win the game outright. Only a minority of the Greco-Roman aristocracy was willing to banish from its everyday life the pleasures of the bed, the table, or even the bloody games of the circus. Unlike the 'Virgin Church' dear to Tertullian and Donatus, the Catholic, Apostolic, and Roman Church required strict obedience to its authority and its representatives only on the part of those who administered the sacraments and the absolution of sin. In all the accommodations that were thereby rendered possible—and the specifications of Augustine of Hippo soon came to clarify things—nothing prevented a Roman citizen inclined towards hedonism from embracing Catholicism.

Moreover, the priests, bishops, and popes only put the brakes on their habitual lasciviousness after the sixteenth century; that is, after the cold shower of the Reformation, which washed away the stains of Catholicism from primitive Christianity—from the true Western Christianity, which was anti-Semitic and puritanical (which was, in other words, the New Prophecy).

But the anti-Montanism of the Church also expressed the voice of wisdom. The trinity—by virtue of which the Church (no less than the Spirit) mediated between God and the Son, the latter of whom was incarnated in the weakness and corruption of human and terrestrial nature—fulfilled a primordial function: it avoided any confrontation with dualism and it set right the balance between good and evil, oppression and revolt, repression and relief. The reverse of Puritanism, Messalianism represented unbridled licentiousness. In this sense, it constituted the continuation of anti-Montanism.

In his *Hymns Against the Heresies*, which were composed in Edessa between 363 and 373, Ephrem the Syrian spoke of people who gave themselves up to a free morality under the cover of devotion. They called themselves *pneumatikoi*, 'Spirituals'. Their adversaries called them the 'Messalians' (from the Syrian word *mṣallyānā*, 'those who pray') or 'Euchites' (from the Greek *euchitai*).

Epiphanius of Salamis mentions their presence in Antioch around 376 or 377. He describes them as vagabonds who refused to possess any goods and slept in the streets of the town—as men and women mixing together, rejecting all forms of work, and contenting themselves with begging and praying.

Their founder was Adelphius, but other names were linked to a current that was scattered everywhere, that perpetuated itself only belatedly, and that (one can plausibly conjecture) rallied together a great number of people who were drawn to it more by ephemeral sensual pleasure than by the prize of a hypothetical beyond—indeed, this current never ceased to trace its furrows beneath a prudent semblance of religious obligation. Dadoes, Sabas, Hermas, Symeon, and Eustathius of Edessa have been mentioned by Photius, Michael the Syrian, Bar Hebraeus, and Philoxenus of Mabbug.

In the 380s, Flavian, the patriarch of Antioch, persecuted the Spirituals and chased them into the provinces of Lycaonia and Pamphylia, where the bishops condemned them around 388. In 390, Flavian of Antioch went further by anathematizing all of the Messalians, despite Adelphius's attempts to defend their cause.

The persecution of the Spirituals was extended into Armenia. Letoios, bishop of Melitene, ordered the burning of monasteries into which the Messalian doctrine had penetrated. (The recidivists were condemned to having the hollows of their knees sliced open.[1])

Around 405, Atticus, the patriarch of Byzantium, insisted on the necessity of expelling the Messalians. Nestorius was later associated with the same struggle. In 428 the imperial police were tasked with intervening against the Spirituals and making them outlaws. In 431 the Council of Ephesus ratified the measures that had previously been taken (without great success, it would appear).

In the second half of the fifth century the Spirituals united around Lampetius, a priest ordained around 460 by Alypius, the Bishop of Caesarea of Cappadocia. According to Theodore Bar Konai, Lampetius founded monasteries—located in the mountainous region between Cilicia and Isauria—where men and women lived a joyous life. (Note that, in the third and fourth centuries, the various ascetic Christianities condemned women who lived with bishops, priests, or deacons, and also those who exercised sacramental functions under the name 'Agapete', *agapetai*, 'the darlings'. The Celtic tradition, which was relatively favorable to women, introduced the Agapetes into the new Christian cults of Ireland and Britain, in which, during the sixth century, there still existed female hosts (*cohospitae*) in the monasteries who conferred the sacraments without having to renounce their feminine charms. The Arthurian legends often evoke these women.[2] Around 150, *The Pastor* by Hermas gave an allegorical meaning to their double nature as libertines and holy 'virgins'.)

There were other such monasteries in Egypt, where Lampetius enjoyed the protection of Alphius, the Bishop of Rhinocolura (El'Arich, near the Palestinian border). How could they not revive the memory of Carpocrates in Alexandria? But the patriarch of El'Arich, acting either out of indifference or sympathy, was content to demand an oral repudiation of their errors from these 'uncultivated' people.

The actions taken at the beginning of the sixth century by the patriarch of Antioch, along his refutation of a work by Lampetius titled *Testament*, demonstrate the persistence of the movement, which was also being fought by the Monophysite Churches of Syria.

Spirituals could be found in Constantinople towards the end of the sixth century. They were grouped around a moneychanger named Marcian, from whom, according to Maximus the Confessor, came the name 'Marcianites'[3]. Photius, the author of a ninth-century study of the Messalians, spoke of contemporary heretics with whom he had to deal.

In its most radical aspects, the Spirituals' doctrine was devoted to justifying the practice of a freedom that guaranteed them the feeling of having attained perfection and impeccability.

The Church principally reproached them for their scorn of the sacraments and the ecclesiastical hierarchy. Men and women lived in the streets or in monasteries, were animated by the grace of having vanquished the demon that was within them, and therefore acted with the assent of the angels and the Spirit.

In the remarks reported by their adversaries we can discern elements of a philosophy that aimed especially at justifying the pleasures of the way of life that they had chosen.

The fall of Adam had introduced into every person, from birth, a demon that dominated him and pushed him towards evil. Baptism and the sacraments remained inoperative in the face of such a presence. Only prayer—and here it was a question not of the Church's prayers but rather of continual and assiduous incantations—had the power to chase away the demon. Prayer had to be accompanied by a severe asceticism, of a duration that sometimes extended to three years. It culminated in a state of impassive equanimity—*apatheia*—that realized the union with the Spirit. The Spiritual thus recovered Adam before the Fall or, if you prefer, the Christ, who was—according to Origen, Paul of Samosata, Donatus, and Nestorius—the form of man assumed by the *Logos*. (Note that certain Messalians were passed off as Nestorians or Monophysites, before being denounced and chased away.)

According to the testimonies collected by John of Damascus in the late seventh or early eighth century, the expulsion of the demon and the union with the Spirit evoked the orgasm of amorous union. The Spirit, which is similar to fire, made man into a new being; it recreated him because "fire is the demiurge", because fire is the ardor of desire and the Great Power of life, as it was for Simon of Samaria.

The Spiritual was thereafter invested with the gift of prophecy; he was similar to the Christ and did not sin in whatever he did. The recourse to fasting, asceticism, mortification of the flesh, discipline, and the instruction of the soul fell into disuse.

Lampetius laughed at the monks whom he saw delivering themselves up to abstinence and penitential clothing, because they thereby showed that they had not acceded to perfection. Nevertheless, the Anthony-and-Macarius[4] crew spared no effort in the daily struggle against the demon of lust that the Master of the Altar Piece from Isenheim would express with so much pictorial felicity[5].

Lampetius himself lived in pleasure, dressed in delicate clothes and unveiled to his disciples the path to perfection, which was not without its charms. "Bring me a beautiful young woman", he said, "and I will show you what holiness is"[6].

Proclaiming themselves to be blessed and happy, the Spirituals inverted the project of holiness that had been pushed to extremes by the Montanists and that the anti-Montanist Church exhibited in the enclosures of ascetic monasticism, in its hyperbolic martyrology, and in its calendar, in which Catholic martyrs replaced the *daimon* that, according to the Gnostics, governed every day. (Note that in Alexandria in 415, ascetic Catholic monks let off steam by flaying alive the beautiful Hypatia, a philosopher and brilliant mathematician.) Furthermore, the Spirituals' pre-Adamite Christ embodied everything that could possibly displease a Church, an institution without which, if one can judge from the singular path to salvation that they pursued, they managed to do very well.

Practicing a sovereign freedom, the Spirituals rejected work, which they held to be a shameful activity. They advised against giving alms to the poor and needy so as to reserve for themselves—the truly poor in spirit who had rediscovered the purity of Adam and could therefore wed Eve in complete Edenic innocence—the resources that their bodies needed to sustain themselves.

Borborites, Coddians, Stratiotics, Phemionites

The heresiologues harbored a clear propensity to multiply, under a variety of names, the opinions that contravened their own doctrines or those of the Church of Rome. They intended to demonstrate by this profusion the extent of the confusion and incoherence that would reign from the moment their views were set aside. It seems that the movement of the Spirituals was thus fragmented into many names, such as 'Stratiotics', 'Phemionites' and 'Coddians' (from the Syrian word *codda*, 'platters', which designated 'those who eat apart').

The term 'Borborite' merits some attention. Victor Magnien recalls that the *borboros* (or 'quagmire') symbolized the impure life in which the uninitiated dwelled[7]. Plotinus identified the Borborites with the third category distinguished by a number of Gnostics: the Hylics, the prisoners of matter.

The Borborites were condemned by a codex issued by Theodosius II. According to Philostorgius, Aetius was reduced to silence by a Borborite[8].

Ecclesiastical opinion gave to 'Borborite' the meaning 'dirty, filthy, uncultivated'. In 480 Lazarus of Pharb spoke of people who were "ignorant and mocked all beliefs". He said that one could apply the following proverb to them: "For the bride of the swine, a bath of drain-water"[9].

Was this controversy really a question of uninitiated people submitting to the perfect Spirituals and striving through total destitution to attain the revelation of the Spirit, from which absolute freedom proceeded? Or did the term 'Borborite' simply designate the vast majority of those beings who, tormented by the difficulties of existence, seized hold of the smallest of pleasures without preoccupying themselves with belief in any other divinity than straightforward good or bad luck?

CHAPTER TWENTY-TWO

Monophysites and Dyophysites

Two doctrines stood out from the tormented landscape of ecclesiastical rivalries, from the quarrels of the Churches struggling for recognition of their authority and preeminence. They corresponded to the two poles of imperial power: Rome and Byzantium, on the one hand, and Alexandria, the cradle of Hellenized Christianity, on the other.

Monophysism was more a schism than a heresy. Born in Alexandria, this doctrine was not innovative but used old speculations on the nature of the Messiah in order to differentiate itself from the doctrines promulgated in Rome. After the Council of Chalcedon, which was held in 451, the Eastern Churches seized hold of Monophysism in order to constitute their dogma, which is still honored by the Coptics of Egypt, the Jacobites of Syria, and the Armenian churches. To understand the rise of Monophysism, one must also take account of the longstanding animosity between Alexandria and Antioch, the latter being the city in which the communities devoted to James and Simon-Peter had been established since the end of the first century. The judgment of Tertullian, "Episcopatus aemulatio schismatum mater est"[1], was verified once again.

By rejecting Arius, the Church of Rome had defined, through the Nicene Creed, the rudiments of Catholic dogma: the Christ was God; he formed a single substance with the Father; although he was created for all eternity by the Father, he was incarnated through his descent to earth and thereby became a man entirely apart from other men. This was the position of Tertullian and, for Rome, it was the one that most advantageously defined the role of the Church—as a spiritual and temporal power, and as the union of the celestial and temporal kingdoms. The Church had been founded by God and by 'Jesus, put to death under Pontius Pilate'. Its two principal apostles, Peter and Paul, were martyred in Rome, which was thereby designated the legitimate site of the 'Holy See'.

Arianism, originating in Alexandria, established a subordinate relationship between God, the creator of all things, and the Son, created as any man is but invested with the divine *Logos*. "Did you have a son before he was born?" Arius asked of mothers[2], and his question, ironically aimed at the Mother Church, attacked the pretensions of ecclesiastic Rome ['the eternal city'] to divine permanence.

It was in Alexandria that Cyril, a disciple of Athanasius (Arius's enemy), led a revolt against Rome. This revolt was grafted onto one of the specious quarrels in which Alexandria and Antioch had been engaged for centuries.

There was a single substance common to the Father, the Son, and the *Logos* (or the Spirit). But what was the nature, the *physis*, of the Jesus who was both a man entirely apart and the God of all eternity?

For the party of Antioch, there were two natures in the Messiah: one divine and one human. Such was the opinion of Theodore of Mopsuestia (350–428), Theodoret of Cyprus, and Nestorius, the Patriarch of Constantinople. That's wrong, retorted the party of Alexandria. To admit two natures was to recognize two Messiahs, two people: one the eternal *Logos*; the other a historical individual. Monophysites, or the supporters of a single nature, thenceforth joined the ranks of those who combated the Antiochians or Dyophysites, who distinguished between two natures.

Paradoxically, Monophysism derived from the hostility manifested towards Arius by Athanasius of Alexandria, who insisted on the single nature of the God *Logos* incarnate. Around 370, Apollinaris of Laodicea (Latakia, in Syria), desiring to pursue the struggle against Arianism, insisted on Athanasius's thesis and thus provoked the animosity of Epiphanius of Salamis, the hunter of heretics and the sworn enemy of Origen.

In 374, Epiphanius denounced Apollinaris to Damasus, the Bishop of

Rome: Apollinaris was condemned by a synod.

In 381, while the ecumenical council of Constantinople anathematized both Arianism and Apollinaris's theses, an adversary of Apollinaris named Diodorus of Tarsus (an Antiochian) took a position that was opposed to the latter doctrine. Diodorus decreed that the most important things about the Christ were his human nature, his suffering, and his exemplary sacrifice. He counted two natures in this Messiah, who, in thus being used as a pretext, was tossed from one side to the other on the waves of a theology of power: the Word or *Logos*, then the Son of God, and then Jesus the man, the son of Mary. Theodore of Mopsuestia subsequently developed Diodorus's theory.

The difficulty faced by the clerics who tried to legitimate their authority by fortifying it with 'divine truths' concerned precisely the way in which they transformed into concrete realities the purely speculative arguments that Judeo-Christian Gnosticism had advanced at the very limits of coherence: God drew from His eternal essence a *Logos* (or image) whose spark (or reflection) left its imprint in human matter. From this Divine Wisdom—*Sophia* or Mary, the feminine Spirit—was born (always from the same virginal essence) a Messiah, a savior, a redeemer, who assumed the body of a man, knew the miserable lot of mortals, and, through His exemplary sacrifice, ascended towards His Father while also showing men the path to salvation and the rising path of the divine that was inside them. What spoiled and complicated the metaphysical purity of such a construction was the will or the necessity to introduce into it a temporal power, a legal authority.

The apologues of *Sophia*, the virgin, and Prunikos, the prostitute, contented themselves with allegorically expressing the descent of the Spirit into matter and the deplorable fate that was imposed upon it by the 'malediction of the flesh'. But there was no mention of parthenogenesis by a young Jewish bride who gave birth to God after welcoming a dove!

In 423, when Theodosius II named the Antiochian Nestorius as the patriarch of Constantinople, popular Greek Christianity adopted the custom of celebrating Mary as the mother of God, thereby dressing up in fashionable clothes one of the commonly invoked ancient Goddesses. She was called *Theotokos*. (Note that, in the fourth and fifth centuries, the custom of offering cakes to Ceres became Christianized. The new Christians who dedicated to Mary the offerings that had previously been reserved for her Roman archetype were called 'Collyridians', a word derived from the Greek *collyres*, 'little cakes'. Epiphanius unleashed his fury against them, no doubt due partly to his misogyny, but also because he suspected that the old fertility rites remained intact beneath this Christian facade.)

Nestorius (381–451), the Bishop of Byzantium from 428–31, claimed for himself the Dyophysite school of Antioch. His disciples held him, Theodore of Mopsuestia, and Diodorus of Tarsus to be the 'three great lights of the Church'. His political realism persuaded him to vehemently persecute the 'heretics', particularly the Messalians, and to follow the Antiochian tradition of historical exegesis rather than the allegorical tradition of Alexandria. Nevertheless, he clashed with the general sentiment of the Greek Catholics by rejecting the expression 'mother of God' (*Theotokos*) and choosing instead *Anthropotokos* or *Christotokos* ('mother of Man' or 'mother of the Christ').

Cyril of Alexandria, an adversary of Nestorius and a partisan of Apollinaris of Laodicea, quickly counter-attacked: "if the God-inspired Scriptures call Him God, as God Incarnate and made Flesh, and it be not possible in any other way to be Incarnate, save through the birth of a woman, how is she not Mother of God, who bare Him?"[3]

In 431, the Emperor convened a council at Ephesus. Through a maneuver that revealed the obedience of theological argumentation to political imperatives, the partisans of Cyril, arriving first, obtained the condemnation of Nestorius. Mary triumphed as the *Theotokos*, the mother of God, and Nestorius was deposed. Although the Nestorians responded at a counter-council in 436 by deposing Cyril, the patriarch of Byzantium was banished to Petra—then in Upper Egypt—where he died. His collected works were burned by imperial order. A copy of his *Bazaar of Heracleides* escaped destruction, however. In this text he proclaimed that God could neither have been born from a woman nor have died on the cross. This was a thesis that was commonly accepted by the Christian Gnostics of the second century and that the Church later condemned under the name 'Docetism'.

Nestorius's fall caused the ruination of the Dyophysites Diodorus of Tarsus and Theodore of Mopsuestia, who—having been held to be orthodox in their own era—were posthumously placed in the camp of the heretics. Diodorus nevertheless deployed great ingenuity in explaining that the *Logos* had built a temple for itself in Mary's uterus. This temple was Jesus the man—headed for birth and suffering—while the divine *Logos* for its part escaped the influence of a human destiny.

Theodore likewise insisted on the conjoining, in a single person, of a man, completely human, with the *Logos*-Son, perfect in its divinity and consubstantial with the Father.

In 489, Emperor Zeno banned the school of Edessa, in which Nestorianism enjoyed great popularity. The persecution chased away the Nestorians, whose Churches spread all over the East, from Samarkand and Tartary to India and even China. They have continued to exist to the present day; they conserve the idea that the Holy Spirit proceeded from the Father and not, as the Byzantine Church affirmed, from the Son. The West has retained only traces of these doctrines, which were condemned under the name 'Adoptionism' and associated with Felix of Urgell and Elipand, the Bishop of Toledo, the latter of whom was excommunicated by the Council of Frankfurt in the eighth century for maintaining that God had adopted Jesus the man in order to deposit his *Logos* inside him.

In its will to maintain the unity of a Church of which it remained the true master, imperial power sought to reconcile the partisans of Cyril and Nestorius in the first half of the fifth century.

Did not Eutyches, the Archimandrite of a monastery in Constantinople, try to unite these points of view in the following formula: in Jesus there were two natures that only formed a single one after the union with the *Logos* had been accomplished?[4]

In 451 Emperor Marcian convened a new council in Chalcedon, not far from Byzantium. Its decision was that the Christ had been one person with two natures. The Monophysites, hurt by the attribution of two natures, were dismayed; the Dyophysites, for whom 'one person' was unacceptable, were dissatisfied. The Council also excluded Eutyches. The Egyptians felt betrayed. They declared: "We would be killed if we counter-signed the text of Leo" (i.e. the Bishop of Rome, who seemed to have envisioned two natures in his *Tome*). "We would prefer to die at the hands of the Emperor and the Council than at those of our followers"[5]. Their prudence with respect to confronting their faithful was only too well justified. The Council had scarcely deposed Dioscorus, the Monophysite bishop of Alexandria, when his Council-mandated successor Proterius was lynched by a mob.

The Monophysite schism affected Egypt, half of Palestine, Syria, Ethiopia, the South of Arabia, and Georgia, thereby outlining an anti-Chalcedonian front of Churches. The Churches of Armenia, which were not represented at the Council, became Monophysite in the sixth century.

In the East there subsisted a pro-Chalcedonian party: the Melchites, who professed opinions hostile to Monophysism. Emperor Justinian tried to reconcile them with the Monophysites. After kidnapping Vigilius, the Bishop of Rome (a 'Pope', as some have subsequently called him), Justinian kept him prisoner for seven years, until he obtained from him a Monophysite 'capitulation'.

The Syrian monk Jacob Baradaeus (500–78) founded new Monophysite Churches all through the East. The Churches in Syria preserved his memory by calling themselves Jacobites. These were orthodox Churches that hunted down heretics with the help, as everywhere else, of their thinkers: Severus of Antioch, Jacob of Serugh, Philoxenus of Mabbug, John of Tella, and Theodore of Arabia.

In the wake of Monophysism came the sect of the *Agnoetae* (the 'ignorant'), which was founded by Themistius, the Deacon of Alexandria, who, preoccupied with the intellect of Jesus, established a distinction between the omniscience of God (which was in Jesus, but in an unconscious state) and Jesus's comprehension, which barely surpassed the understanding shared by other men. Driven by rival powers, speculation on this question gave the decision of the Council of Chalcedon a certain originality: there were in fact two natures but only one person in Jesus. But Themistius did not occupy a significant position in the Church and Monophysism was already quite satisfactory to the Coptic Churches, which were independent of the Archbishopric of Rome (which became the papacy) and which, on the Byzantine side of things, were therefore assured of a relative peace.

Eulogius, the Greek Orthodox Patriarch of Alexandria (580–607), and Pope Gregory I (590–604) both condemned Themistius.

The quarrel over the nature(s) of the Christ suggested to Julian, the Bishop of Halicarnassus, the opinion that, because Jesus was not entirely human, his body remained incorruptible and inaccessible to suffering. Combated by the Monophysite Severus of Antioch, chased from his Episcopal See, and condemned, along with his partisans, under the barbaric label *Aphthartodocetes*, Julian took refuge in Alexandria in 518.[6]

A sectarian of Julian of Halicarnassus, Gaianus—enthroned in place of Theodosius (a supporter of Severus) in 535—united his partisans, or 'Gaianites', in a faction within which he was held to embody the spirit of Paul of Samosata. Communion was given in his name, and the women baptized their own children in the sea by invoking the name of Gaianus, who did not consider it beneath him to pass himself off as the 'second Christ' or to appear at Mass in His person.[7]

CHAPTER TWENTY-THREE

Pelagius and Augustine, or the Conception of Free Will and Predestination

By way of Augustine of Hippo, who fought against them, the doctrines of Pelagius enriched Catholic dogma—then in the process of formation—with two clarifications whose importance was due to the power that they conferred upon the Church of Rome and to the incessant quarrels that they kept alive over the course of the centuries.

Augustine's battles marked the beginning of the requirement to baptize children, who were held to be impure at birth, and the advent of the theory of predestination—later on judged to be heretical, but without triggering the impossible condemnation of one of the principal 'fathers' of Catholicism—which he fabricated in order use it against his old enemy, Pelagius.

Pelagius (340?–429?), who was born in Britain or Ireland, no doubt retained traces of a Celtic freedom of spirit when he reached Rome around 400. A little before the 410 fall of Rome and its sacking by the Goths, who had converted to Arianism, Pelagius and his disciple Celestius left for Carthage, where Pelagius's brilliant mind and rhetorical talents won him the friendship of Augustine of Hippo, the bishop of the city. But Augustine's authoritarianism quickly ceased to tolerate the uncertainty to which Pelagius's ideas gave rise concerning the function of the Church, which was an institution over which the master of Carthage intended to establish an absolute hegemony. (Note that Augustine did not hesitate to retrieve from Ticonius, who was a partisan of a type of Donatism that he anathematized, the theory of a City of God that was both superior to the terrestrial city and imbued with imperial power—power that was at that point slipping away from the Roman Empire.)

Pelagius took refuge in Palestine, where another Catholic doctrinarian, Jerome—alerted by Augustine's emissaries—persecuted him and charged his doctrine with Manichaeism, which was Catholicism's religious rival and was being repressed everywhere with great violence. (Note that Augustine was himself a renegade from Manichaeism. He subsequently turned his vehemence against his former co-religionists by calling down upon them the rigors of the law. It was from him that came the justifications for the bloody repression that would afflict the Manicheans and, later on, the Paulicians, the Bogomils, and the Cathars.)

Acquitted by the Synod of Jerusalem in 415, Pelagius and Celestius were excommunicated two years later by Pope Innocent I. At first, Zosimus, Innocent's successor, showed some sympathy towards Pelagius, but he soon pulled himself together and definitively condemned him at the Council of Carthage in 418.

The stakes of this dispute involved powerful interests.

To better understand Pelagius's teachings and Augustine's attitude towards them, it is fitting to situate the latter within the anti-Montanist reaction that the 'lax' practices of the ecclesiastic majorities in the West had stirred up.

If the Church managed to reconcile itself with Greco-Roman hedonism by exiling puritanical rigor to the monasteries, if it held the sacrificial perfection of the Christ to be an ideal that was difficult to reach, then it also acquiesced (without too much difficulty) to the depraved morals of many priests and faithful people—so long, at least, as the Church's authority and sacramental function were still publicly privileged.

The Spirituals or 'Messalians' weren't the only ones to turn away from the duplicity of the Church and to use several hastily Christianized arguments to cover for their quite commonplace decision to follow their sexual impulses and to pursue the pleasures of existence without being overly preoccupied with either obedience or guilt.

Around 380 a certain Helvidius—apparently a disciple of Auxentius (an Arian Bishop of Milan and the predecessor of Ambrose)—drew down upon himself the thunderbolts of Jerome (344?–420) for having mocked the virginity of Mary and for maintaining that she must have had other children because the canonical Gospels mention the brothers of the Lord [that is to say, James, Joseph, Simon, and Judas[1]]. Jerome fervently attempted to demonstrate that these brothers were only Jesus's cousins. But this involved getting far too tangled up with the word 'brother', which—in the traditions of Essenism and Nazarenism—means 'witness', which in turn became *martus* in Greek and 'martyr' in French [and English, too]. For Judeo-Christians, 'brother' or 'witness' only meant one who partook of the same sacrifices as did the 'Servant of the Lord' celebrated by the Book of Isaiah.

But Helvidius's remarks were less concerned with promoting historical exegesis than with dispensing with virginity's alleged superiority to amorous relations. This was why he rejected Tertullian, Montanus, and all of the Christianity of the New Prophecy.

A similar doctrine can be found in the thought of Jovinian, a disciple of Ambrose, the Bishop of Milan. In Rome, where he enjoyed a large audience, Jovinian made ironic comments about Mary's virginity. He argued that such a birth made Jesus a fantastical being: the *Angelos-Christos* invoked by the Gnostics and Manicheans who'd been condemned by the Church. Jovinian set up in opposition to the hypocritical asceticism of the faithful a healthy inclination towards the pleasures of the table, love, and the benefits of life, which were real instances of the grace accorded by divine goodness. For Jovinian, the purification of baptism was sufficient to wash away all sin and to protect oneself against the traps set by a demon who was eager to spoil and corrupt the gifts of God.

Condemned by Pope Siricius and the Council of Milan, which had been convened in 390 at Ambrose's request, Jovinian was exiled by imperial proscription.

Among the fiercest of Jovinian's adversaries were Jerome, a supporter of Marian virginity and the author of *Against Jovinian*; the no-less misogynistic Augustine; and Pelagius.

What separated Pelagius from the puritanical Augustine? A certain concept of human dignity. Pelagius did not share Augustine's notion of the fundamental ignominy of mankind, which the Bishop of Carthage had brilliantly summarized in the following finding: "Inter faesces et urinam nascimur" ("We are born between feces and urine").

Pelagius's austerity was related to that of Seneca and the atheistic moralists of the nineteenth century—nay, even to that of the freethinkers who denounced the debauchery of the clergy. Pelagius estimated that mankind had access to a force of will that was sufficient to attain virtue and goodness. There was no need for divine aid or the mediation of the Church if one wished to follow the ethical rules that were prescribed everywhere. All virtues resided in a germinal form in each individual; it was sufficient to bring these seeds to fruition if one wished to combat the temptations of evil.

One could not trace out the roads of public morality any better than by avoiding the detour of the Church.

According to Pelagius, the Church—now reduced to its smallest possible role—only intervened through the sacraments, which guaranteed the salvation of the soul once terrestrial life had accomplished its destiny according to the precepts of moral law.

Our freedom, by Pelagius's account, was as total as that of Adam and Eve before they misused it and condemned themselves to the Fall. By learning the privileges of moral will from infancy, men could obey God's designs. Baptism (which was not given to children at the time) simply affixed the Church's seal, as if it were a passport to eternal beatitude.

Many citizens of the Empire—among them those who prized moral rigor or Stoic or Epicurean philosophy—practiced such principles without needing to give them a Christian coloration. Even among the Catholics, Theophronius of Cappadocia maintained both that God's omniscience covered everything that was going to happen and (on the other hand) that God did not *positively* know all this as an accomplished fact, thus leaving to mankind the freedom to act beyond all determinations. For Theophronius, it was a question of reconciling, on the one hand, the absolute power of God and, on the other, human freedom, which the Church—called upon to extricate itself from Augustinian predestination—would call 'free will'.

And so, at the same time as Pelagius was reminding his followers of the principles of secular morality, Augustine (foreseeing the decline of imperial unity and its stranglehold on the West) was preparing for the advent of a pontifical authority that would sprinkle the entire world with traps, the tangled links of which both the City of God and the terrestrial city would endlessly tighten.

Augustine launched a doctrinal war machine against Pelagius. To the freedom defended by his adversary Augustine opposed a theory that Calvinism and Jansenism would later regurgitate: predestination.

The fate of mankind was traced out for all eternity by God, who, as absolute master, decided upon the salvation or damnation of His creatures. This was an appalling doctrine that, condemning human beings to fear and trembling, drained away their pride and abandoned them, gasping, to the consolations of a Church that constantly reminded them of their own indignity.

To break the Pelagians' excessive confidence in mankind, Pope Honorius subjected them and the philosopher Julian of Eclanum to the penalties prescribed for heretics. It is believed that Pelagius and Celestius died in exile shortly thereafter.

Another effect of the doctrine of predestination was to highlight an obvious fact that was even more embarrassing to the Church than freedom being left completely in the hands of mankind. If the fate of each being was determined according to the whims of God, what good was there in worrying about the protections of the Church, the priests, and the sacraments? It would take Thomas Aquinas's laborious arguments to endow the all-powerful divinity with the freedom to choose salvation or damnation for His creatures in the conscious and willful manner known among mortal men as 'free will'.

Augustine never incurred the least reprobation; he had done too much for the grandeur and enrichment of the Church to be at risk of censure. But in 475 the Council of Arles condemned as a heretic someone named Lucidus, who espoused the idea that, the freedom of mankind having been annihilated by the fall into sin, each person's destiny was controlled by a predestination decided upon by God, and that, by virtue of this predestination, each person's destiny led irremediably to either damnation or eternal life.

The amplified role of original sin and the impurity imputed to newborn infants supplied the Church's dogma with a response that aimed at annihilating Pelagian hopes of perfecting mankind. The Montanists, in their horror of nature and life, were the first (although such a revulsion had already animated Essenean zeal) to recommend the baptism of infants, at a time when the custom was not widespread. Augustine held up to mankind, which according to Pelagius was capable of elevating itself towards virtue, a very different portrait from that painted by Pelagius: man was a sickly creature, imbecilic, prey to all the temptations of the flesh and quite unable to resist them. Why? Because the original stain of Adam's sin had marked him from his birth. Only baptism cleansed him of this infamy, which the Church could not tolerate when it welcomed the faithful into its sanctuary.

Once the baptism of children had been established as a necessity, the newborn was devoted to the Catholic faith from the very first hours of its life. Children who weren't baptized would die like animals; unbaptized adults lived amidst errors and an innocence that they had rejected. A profitable market in penitence and redemption—the latter purchased by gifts, emoluments, alms, and submission—took root in the Augustinian doctrine of the intrinsic weakness of the body and the mind.

No one had sufficient force of character to successfully resist all temptation. If one estimated oneself capable of evading all the demoniac ruses of nature, then one committed the sin of pride. And so man, that miserable and negligible being, succumbed to sin because Rome had authorized him to redeem himself, to regain his salvation—not in the works of Augustine but in the comforting heart of the Church. The skillful organization of responsibility and free will subsequently established a calculus of salvation and damnation that facilitated the sale of indulgences and absolutions.

Augustine is rightly credited for his role here, as long as one excuses his doctrinal lapses into the darkness of the concept of predestination.

CHAPTER TWENTY-FOUR

Priscillian of Ávila

Among the letters falsely attributed to Cyprian, the Bishop of Carthage who was executed in 258, there is one—emanating from Novatian's partisans (that is to say, from the Christians loyal to the New Prophecy and hostile to the *lapsi*)—that attests to the presence in Spain of Christian communities of the Montanist tendency, the ardor of which Novatian had revived in the fire of imperial persecution.

In 254, an African council that was convened under the aegis of Cyprian had lent its support to the Novatians who, in the Spanish cities of Lleida, León, and Astorga, rejected those ministers who were suspected of having abjured during Decius's repressions.

But with the Constantinian turn, the Catholic ecclesial faction that had acceded to power recognized the authority of the perjured priests and collaborators. (See the example of Bishop Caecilian, the enemy of Donatus in Carthage.[1]) A century later, Bishop Pacianus of Barcelona denounced excessive penitential discipline and the rigor of the priest or bishop named Sympronianus.[2]

Priscillian's intervention is evidence of the persistence of a Christian tradition with which Catholicism confirmed its break because of its political aims. The execution of Priscillian put a bloody mark on an archaic Christianity that had been sacrificed to national interests [*la raison d'État*].

Through the unanswerable argument of the sword, Catholicism cut itself off from a Christianity that haunted it continually during the long funeral procession of the Waldensians, the Apostolics, the Flagellants, and the Spiritual Franciscans, right up to the emergence of a Reformation in which the spirits of Montanus and Tertullian were reincarnated in the founding fathers of modern capitalism.

Born around 340 to a well-to-do and probably senatorial Roman family based in Gallaecia, Priscillian was in his thirties when he joined a Christian current that was traditionally ascetic, millenarian, and ever on the lookout for the second coming of the Christ.

Priscillian soon clashed with the representatives of Rome and the new tendency. Among the clerical functionaries of the Emperor, two dignitaries—Ithacius, Bishop of Ossonoba (Faro), and his metropolitan, Hydatius of Emerita Augusta (Mérida)—accused Priscillian of imposing on his followers a personal oath of loyalty. These functionaries inflamed the Council of Saragossa, which in 380 brought together twenty-six bishops from Spain and Portugal, and two from South Gaul. What was the precise accusation? That Priscillian, who was well versed in biblical exegesis, had referred to texts other than the canonical ones, which had been imposed only recently. But the progress of Manichaeism, the great religion in competition with Catholicism, also gave the 'Romans' an opportunity to conflate things that were in fact unrelated (a strategy typical of such polemics). Priscillian, a perfect ascetic, had declared his support for clerical celibacy. This was all that was needed for his enemies to associate him with the disciples of Mani, against whom this neo-Novatian [Priscillian] had actually been engaged in a prolonged struggle.

That same year, Priscillian was chosen to be the Bishop of Ávila. This angered Hydatius, who rapidly obtained both the support of Ambrose, the Bishop of Milan and a future saint, and an imperial ruling that ordered the deposition of Priscillian and the banishment of the other "pseudo-Bishops and Manicheans".

Soon afterwards, Priscillian, two friendly bishops, and three women from his congregation went to Rome via Aquitaine to plead their case and to prove their religious orthodoxy. They expressed a wish to be judged not by a civilian tribunal but by ecclesiastical authorities.

Ambrose refused to give them an audience in Milan. Addressing themselves to Macedonius, Ambrose's adversary, they managed—through his intervention—to meet with Emperor Gratian, who was originally from Spain. Gratian was convinced by their arguments and restored Priscillian and his friend, Bishop Instantius, to their positions.

Ithacius reacted by going to Trier, where he made an appeal to Gratian. But in August 380 Gratian was assassinated by a rival—another Spaniard, Magnus Maximus, who, in spite of being acclaimed 'Augustus', was refused legitimate recognition, which left him vulnerable to the uncertainties attendant upon usurpation.

Impelled by his desire to reconcile the various sympathies of the unitary and Roman Church, Magnus Maximus took hold of the trial as if it were a political tool and convened a synod in Bordeaux so as to settle the question as if he were a veritable sovereign pontiff. His hatred of Gratian made him determined to demonstrate that, unlike his predecessor, he would tolerate neither polytheism nor heresy. Priscillian, who was summoned to Trier with his friends, confronted the bishops of Spain and Gaul, who had previously been favorable to Maximus's decisions.

With the exception (it is said) of Martin of Tours, all of the members of the synod condemned the Bishop of Ávila, who, having reproached the Manicheans during his combat with them for their recourse to magic, was now himself accused of Manichaeism and sorcery. He confessed under torture to having magical powers, to taking a role in demonic assemblies, and to customarily praying in the nude. The repressive tradition of the Church attempted to identify (in the popular imagination) Manichaeism and, later, Valdeism with rites of sorcery, which easily kindled the pyres of fear and hatred.

Because the iniquity of the trial of Priscillian had aroused the reprobation of Martin of Tours and perhaps also that of Siricius (a timid man who aspired to the papacy), Priscillian was given a second chance. But this opportunity ended abruptly with the decapitation in Trier between 385 and 387 of six people (Priscillian among them) who were charged with "magic and immorality". Received with indignation by the Christian communities, this news elicited a few belated regrets from Ambrose of Milan. The remains of Priscillian, repatriated to Gallaecia around 396, were the objects of the kind of veneration usually reserved for martyrs of the faith.

As the death of their leader did not weaken the Priscillians, Emperor Honorius issued a ruling against them in 408. In 561 or 563, the Council of Braga judged it useful to anathematize seventeen 'errors' that were imputed to Priscillian.

It is difficult to disentangle the Priscillian doctrine from the calumnies that the Church has intermixed with it over the centuries. Its basis derived from the Christianity that was dominant from the second half of the second century to the end of the fourth, and that the Church condemned under the names Montanism, Encratism, Novatianism, and Origenism. Priscillianism was therefore unacquainted with the compiled Gospels, which had been canonically enriched with arguments hostile to Arius and ascetic rigor. Priscillianism brought together clerics and lay people in assemblies in which asceticism and the cult of virginity were exalted. If the comparable state of the Pietist congregations of the seventeenth century is anything to go by, it is probable that ecstasies, illuminations, prophecies, and other forms of religious hysteria common to Puritanism were manifested in Priscillianism.

The Nicene conception of the Trinity did not affect either Spain or the working-class strata of Christianity. "Long after Nicaea, a very archaic view of and a similar experience with the Trinity continued to be dominant"[3].

According to Priscillian, Christian asceticism partook of the presence of the Christ-God. As in the prescriptions of Tertullian, one dreamed of exhausting the body in order to nurture the Spirit within it. As in Justin's argument against Trypho, the Christ was nothing other than the divine *Logos*. The presence of God resulted more from personal experience than from rational reflection. In and of itself, the revelation of the existence of the God-Christ permitted mankind to attain a state of perfection through the exercise of rigor. And Priscillian spoke of a *nova nativitas*, a new birth. Was it not his legacy that was welcomed by Spanish Catholicism, which—from Dominic to Queipo de Llano, by way of Ignatius of Loyola and the *genius loci*[4] Teresa of Ávila—furbished the weapons (intended to be used against life) known as *Viva la muerte*[5] and *Perinde ac cadaver*[6]?

Was it necessary to exclude the recourse to astrology, if not magic, from a teaching that was founded on the imitation of the Christ and that conferred *quies, libertas, unitas*[7]?

"The Priscillianist heretics", Pope Gregory stated, "think that all men are born under a conjunction of stars. And, in support of their error, they appeal to the fact that a new star appeared when Our Lord showed himself in the flesh"[8]. Perhaps the notion of a new birth gave rise to astrological speculations that were similar to those made by Bardaisan of Edessa. As for magic, its practice was fairly widespread in the Christian milieus, as is attested by the *abraxas* or talismans on which the Christ replaced Seth, Ophis, Mithras, Serapis, or Abrasax. The cult of the saints itself served as a supplement to invocations in which the sign of the cross was substituted for the song of the seven vowels and for the gestures that translated their diverse expressions.

To describe Priscillian as the first victim of Catholic orthodoxy and of the universal jurisdiction adopted in matters of heresy—which is how historians have typically seen him—is to forget the massacres of the Arians and the Donatists. The novelty of Priscillian's death in fact resides in the iniquity of the trial and in the arguments made against the accused. In fact, at Trier, the curtain was raised on a long series of staged events in which the accused—condemned in advance by the judgment of the Church—passed under the parodic sign of 'justice' and entered the flaming circle of expiatory sacrifice, a circle by means of which the clergy imposed upon sinners the dogma of their own purity and divine power.

CHAPTER TWENTY-FIVE

Paulicians and Bogomils

The Paulicians
Despite its idiosyncrasies, the Armenian Christianity of the fourth century presented the same sort of landscape as did the cities of Latium and Greece, if not those of the entire Empire: an old Christianity of an ascetic spirit; an increasingly well-organized pro-Roman clerical party; Marcionite communities; local Churches like those founded by Paul of Samosata; and archaic cults that were Christianized or that included the Christ in their ecumenism: Naassenes, Barbelites, Sethians, Valentinians, and sometimes all of these beliefs confounded together. (Contrary to what the majority of historians have claimed, and as shown by the sepulcher of the Aurelii.)

In Armenia the pro-Roman faction tried to rid itself of Montanist Christianity, the Marcionite Churches, and the schools of Bardaisan. Epiphanius, who was responsible for keeping track of the movements that resisted Roman Catholicism, mentioned a sect founded by a certain Peter of Kaphar Barucha that he designated 'the Archontics'. Its doctrine was propagated by Eutactus of Satala and was a syncretism of Marcionism and Barbelism. It took from Marcionism its anti-Semitism and a dualism according to which the Demiurge—the creator of an odious universe—was none other than Sabaoth, the God of the Jews, who resided in the seventh heaven and governed the Hebdomad. To rejoin its original Mother, the soul had to elevate itself to the eighth heaven (Ogdoad). We do not know by which type of ecstatic practice the union of the adept with Ogdoad was established, but it was no doubt induced with the aid incantations intended to avoid the traps set by the henchmen of the abominable Sabaoth[1]. The Archontics did not bother with baptism or the other sacraments.

After 325 the monarchs embraced Catholicism out of complacency and diplomacy and then imposed it on their subjects. The Roman clerical faction then took hold of the key posts and repressed all of the isolated pockets of resistance. The latter were soon afterwards listed in the catalogues of heresy, which were the identification files that inquisitorial police officers used up until the eighteenth century.

The Paulicians, who appeared in the middle of the seventh century in Armenia (the province that lay between Asia Minor and the Byzantine Empire), seem to have come from Samosata, from which they were driven by persecution. Fleeing Armenia and the combined zeal of the Church and the princes, they found refuge near Koloneia, which was under the suzerainty of the Arab caliphate. A little after 630, the Arabs rapidly seized the Byzantine provinces in North Africa, Egypt, Palestine, and Syria; they then threatened Byzantium, which was fractured by internal struggles.

Although Petrus Siculus believed that the Paulician movement stretched back to Paul of Samosata, it is more credible to link it with Paul the Armenian, who consolidated it from 699 to 718.

The Paulicians were dualists but did not adhere to the Manichean religion. Their doctrine instead looked back to archaic Gnostic Christianity, which was now adapted to the Paulicians' status as an embattled minority.

Peasants grouped together in 'free' agrarian communities—note that the Paulician communalist model played a role in the 820–24 peasant uprisings led by Thomas the Slav in Asia Minor—the Paulicians became soldiers in order to resist any power that might seek to indenture them. A good God supported their faith; the other God, a God of Evil, was identified with Byzantine authority, which was intent on annihilating them. They did not bother with the sacraments, practicing neither baptism, communion, penitence nor marriage. They rejected fasting and Catholicism's feast days. They execrated the cross (an instrument of torture and death), the worship of the saints, and icons, which they saw as perpetuating superstitious practices.

The Paulicians' Jesus was an *Angelos-Christos*. In the Old Testament they saw the work of the Demiurge. As for priests, they judged them to be useless, harmful, and corrupt, and they did not fail to kill them if the occasion presented itself.

They themselves had no clergy members, but they placed their trust in pastors who were tasked with preaching and in the *didachoi* (teachers) who explained the sacred texts. Without tipping over into Marcion's asceticism, the Paulicians aligned themselves with his primitive Christianity, which venerated the Apostle Paul and rejected the authority of Peter.

The Paulicians began to be persecuted after their establishment in Koloneia, where the bishop decimated them with the Emperor's consent. The first leader of their community, an Armenian named Constantine, died at the stake in 682. His successor, Simeon, suffered the same fate in 688. But the Paulicians, who fled to Episparis in response, found among the Arabs a tolerance that the Catholics cruelly lacked. Under the influence of their new leader, Paul the Armenian, their doctrine—a form of Christianity that had been common in 140 (apart from its perhaps belated refusal of baptism)—took on a coloration that was more clearly hostile to the clergy and to Catholicism.

From then on, their history blended into the atrocious war that Byzantium waged against them.

Nevertheless, the Empire, which from 726 to 843 was ravaged by a conflict over the status of icons, turned its rage from away the Paulicians in order to focus it on the hostile factions that the icons conflict had set against one another. (Note that the quarrel over these images merely aggravated an endemic social conflict in which two factions confronted one another: the Blues, who had aristocratic leanings, and the Greens, who were mostly artisans and often favored heterodoxy.)

In the spirit of Nestorius, the Iconoclasts did not tolerate the figuration of the principal divinities. Unlike the Paulicians, however, they venerated the cross and had no sympathy for indications of heresy. The worst persecutions of the Paulicians in fact took place on the initiative of the iconoclast Leon V (813–23). They continued under Theodora, who reestablished the cult of the images.

Exterminated in Byzantium, the Paulicians sought the help of the Arab emirs. Some of the Paulicians enlisted with the Islamic troops that were harassing the imperial city. In 843 a punitive Byzantium expedition triggered a rebellion led by an officer named Karbeas, whose father, a Paulician, had been impaled. He commanded a group of 5,000 men and founded an independent state in Tephrike, where he made use of the benevolent aid of the emirs of Melitene and Tarsus.

With his militia of soldier-peasants, Karbeas broke the offensive launched by Petronas, brother of the Empress Theodora, in 856. Two years later he defeated the army of Michael III. In 860, raids against Nicaea and Ephesus attested to the power of Tephrike. Killed in battle in 863, Karbeas was replaced by Chrysocheir, who had previously been denounced by the patriarch and heresiologue Photius.

The intervention of an ambassador, Petrus Siculus, who had been sent among the Paulicians by Emperor Basil I, was less an attempt at reconciliation than a pre-war reconnaissance mission. Because although the Emperor's forces were defeated at Tephrike in 870 or 871, Chrysocheir's death in battle in 872 brought about the demise of Tephrike, which was subsequently sacked by the Byzantines. The priests—inquisitors long before there was an Inquisition—organized the systematic massacre of the Paulicians, whether they were men, women, or children. The escapees took refuge in the Balkans and Thrace, where, between 1081 and 1118, Alexius I Comnenus undertook to eradicate them.

In the Arab armies that seized Constantinople in 1453 there were Paulician Christians whose hatred of the oppressive Empire fueled their spirit of vengeance.

In 1717 there was still a Christian community in Philippopolis that venerated the Apostle Paul and recognized the authority of Rome due to that community's hostility towards the Orthodox Church. Such a community still exists today under the name 'Uniates'[2].

The Bogomils

"This, then, is what happened in the land of Bulgaria. In the reign of the good Christian Tsar Peter there was a priest called Bogomil, 'worthy of God's compassion', but in reality Bogunemil, 'unworthy of God's compassion', who started for the first time to preach heresy in the country of Bulgaria"[3]. Thus begins[4] the *Sermon Against the Heretics, by the Unworthy Priest Cosmas*[5], a precious source of details concerning the movement that carried the name of its founder.

The one who called himself, with self-satisfied servility, "the unworthy priest" seized upon the terms that were used in a letter sent by Theophylact, the Patriarch of Byzantium, to King Peter of Bulgaria (who died 969). This letter anathematized the representatives "of a resurgent ancient heresy, Manichaeism mixed with Paulicianism"[6].

In its particularity, and without exactly reviving the Manichean religion, Bogomilism played the role of a hub between the Paulician communities, the distant inheritors of Marcion, and the Catharist beliefs that, starting in the eleventh century, reached the Rhine Valley, Cologne, Flanders, Champagne, Northern Italy, and Provence.

Initially governed by a propertied Boyar aristocracy and founded upon a Slavic rural commune, Bulgaria became feudalized in the ninth and tenth centuries. Under the influence of the neighboring Byzantine Empire, its princes adopted Catholicism and, as elsewhere, imposed it on their subjects. Nothing is more false than the notion that there was a spontaneous conversion of the people to the doctrines of Rome and Byzantium. The Nazarene, Elchasaite, Marcionite, Valentinian, Montanist, and Tertullianist Christianities had all inspired the adhesion of growing numbers of the faithful, whereas Catholicism was always propagated by the high and mighty deploying the persuasive point of a temporal sword. From 325 onwards, Catholicism ceased to be Christian, as Christianity ceased to be Jewish after 135. And Catholicism would deal with the adepts of voluntary poverty who followed Peter Waldo or Michael of Cesena, with the Apostolics who dreamed of reviving the Christianity of the New Prophecy, and with the Protestants (who, taking up the baton of the abhorred Church, justified in their turn the massacre of the Anabaptists and other dissidents) even more severely than it had dealt with the Jews.

Colonized by the Byzantine clergy, Bulgaria was covered with monasteries and saw descend upon the peasantry "monastic vermin" who subsisted on the work of rural communities.

The doctrine of Bogomil did not bother with Manichean complexities. It professed a moderate dualism, in conformity with the [socioeconomic] forces that were in play and the interests that were at stake.

In Bogomilism, God created the universe—that is to say, the seven heavens and the four elements (fire, air, water, and earth). God (a resurgence of the plural God Elohim) reigned harmoniously over a cohort of angels until one of them, Satanael, rebelled and was thrown to earth. Satanael separated the earth from the waters, thereby creating—under the essentially divine light of the sun—the material universe and mankind. Satanael included in the human body an angelic fragment, with the result that the duality of good and evil was incarnated in each person.

God sent the angel Christ—still an *Angelos-Christos*—to aid humanity. Satanael ordered that he be crucified, but the Messiah was resurrected, confounded his adversary, and sent him to hell, thereby exiling him from earth—which he ceaselessly tried to reconquer in order to finish his malevolent work. Satanael had allies who were wholly devoted to restoring his privileges: that is, the kings, the priests, the rich, and the Church. Thus Bogomilism rediscovered in dualism the subversive ferment that had been propagated by the Paulicians, who were similarly attached to the independence and autarky of rural communities.

Hostile to the frequentation of churches, the Bogomils called Saint Sophia the residence of demons. They derided baptism: if water possessed such power, they remarked, then all of the animals, and especially the fish, were baptized and therefore without sin. The rites of bread and wine were an absurd symbolism.

Without tilting into the excesses of asceticism, the Bogomils criticized the dissolute existence of the priests who summoned others to sanctify their souls, as Cosmas reported:

> Even if priests whose faith is sound lead idle lives, as you say when you condemn them, they still do not blaspheme the divinity as you do. [...] The heretics who hear these words answer us, "If you are sanctified, as you

claim, why do you not live as you are bidden to? As Paul says in his epistle to Timothy, 'Now a bishop must be above reproach, the husband of one wife, temperate, sober, dignified, hospitable, an apt teacher, no drunkard, not violent but gentle, not quarrelsome, and no lover of money. He must manage his household well' [...]. Now we see that you are not like this; priests act quite otherwise. They get drunk, they commit robbery and have other hidden vices, and nobody forbids them to do these evil deeds [...]".[7]

Cosmas specified that the Bogomils "teach their followers not to obey their masters; they scorn the rich, they hate the Tsars, they ridicule their superiors, they reproach the boyars, they believe that God looks in horror on those who labour for the Tsar, and advise every serf not to work for his master"[8]. (Note that Cosmas retorted: "It is the wisdom of God which says that 'emperors and lords have been instituted by God' [Prov. 8: 15–8]"[9].)

Like the Paulicians, the Bogomils mocked saints, icons, and relics, which were sources of profitable commerce. In the cross they saw a simple piece of wood that they called "the enemy of God". To them the miracles of the Christ were fables that had at the very least to be interpreted symbolically. (Note that in the seventeenth century the Englishman Thomas Woolston died in prison for espousing this very thesis.)

Rejecting the Old Testament, which was the work of Satanael, the Bogomils preferred a version of the Gospel attributed to John that was true to its ancient form as a Gnostic text.

Old-time Gnosticism also put its stamp on the Bogomils' two-tiered organization: there were the Perfect Ones, or Christians, who were the active and intellectual kernel (those who save), and the believers, who were peasants and bourgeois for whom *pistis* sufficed.

Consolamentum was what the Bogomils called a form of initiation in which the neophyte acceded to a state of perfection by having a copy of the Gospel attributed to John placed on his or her head as a sign of the assembly's assent.

The Perfect Ones ate no meat, preached, did not work, and collected no tithes. All of the believers received the *consolamentum* on their deathbeds or at an advanced age.

Who was Bogomil? A Macedonian priest who was initially loyal to the Church of Byzantium and Rome. Revolted by the situation of the peasants—who were the victims of war, the Boyars and the clergy—he broke with Catholicism and preached in the region of Skopje and in Thrace.

Cosmas opposed Bogomil by repeating the official doctrine. "Even if priests whose faith is sound lead idle lives, as you say when you condemn them, they still do not blaspheme the divinity as you do", he said. "Priests are honoured by God". And he asked, "Do you see, heretics, that you are commanded to hold priests in honour, even if they are wicked?"[10]

Concerning the miseries of the world, Cosmas furnished a simple and ecumenically convincing explanation, one that satisfied the Hebrew religion, the papacy, and Calvin: "Each among us must wonder [...] if it wasn't because of him that God put war on the earth"[11]. Such was not the opinion of Bogomil and his partisans, who were becoming increasingly numerous.

Events provided Bogomilism with a national and social basis for existence. In 1018 Emperor Basil II brought the existence of the Bulgarian kingdom to an end and crushed the nation under the yoke of Byzantine authority. Under the cover of peasant uprisings, to which the nobility and the towns now lent their aid, the Bogomil influence focused the resistance to the Empire. That influence infiltrated the cities, crossed the frontiers, and reached into Byzantium, despite constant and cruel persecution.

Euthymius Zigabenus[12], who pursued the Bogomils with pure clerical hatred, called them *Fundagiagites*—that is, "carriers of beggar's bags", "truly impious people who serve the devil in secret"[13]. Euthymius's diatribes were still nourishing the zeal of the persecutor Alexis Comnenus in the twelfth century.

In the twelfth century the Bogomil movement was established in Byzantium. Anna Comnena, daughter of the Emperor, left behind a narrative that provides an enlightening account of how one of the town's Perfect Ones was captured and put to death in 1111.

[The Emperor] had some of the Bogomils brought to the palace and all proclaimed a certain Basil as the teacher and chief representative of the

Bogomilian heresy. Of these, one Diblatius was kept in prison, and as he would not confess when questioned, he was subjected to torture and then informed against the man called Basil, and the disciples he had chosen. Accordingly the Emperor entrusted several men with the search for him. And Satanael's arch-satrap, Basil, was brought to light, in monk's habit, with a withered countenance, clean shaven and tall of stature. The Emperor, wishing to elicit his inmost thoughts by compulsion under the disguise of persuasion, at once invited the man on some righteous pretext. And he even rose from his chair to greet him, and made him sit by him and share his table, and threw out his whole fishing-line and fixed various baits on the hooks for this voracious whale to devour. And he made this monk, who was so many-sided in wickedness, swallow all the poison he offered him by pretending that he wished to become his disciple, and not he only, but probably his brother, the Sebastocrator Isaac, also; he pretended too to value all the words he spoke as if they came from a divine voice and to defer to him in all things, provided only that the villain Basil would effect his soul's salvation. "Most reverend father", he would say (for the Emperor rubbed sweets on the rim of the cup so that this demoniac should vomit forth his black thoughts), "I admire thee for thy virtue, and beseech thee to teach me the new doctrines thy Reverence has introduced, as those of our Churches are practically worthless and do not bring anybody to virtue". But the monk at first put on airs and he, that was really an ass, dragged about the lion's skin with him everywhere and shied at the Emperor's words, and yet was puffed up with his praises, for the Emperor even had him at his table. And in all this the Emperor's cousin [...] the Sebastocrator, aided and abetted him in the play; and finally Basil spued [sic] out the dogmas of his heresy. And how was this done? A curtain divided the women's apartments from the room where the two Emperors sat with the wretch who blurted out and openly declared all he had in his soul; whilst a secretary sitting on the inner side of the curtain committed his words to writing. And the nonsense-monger seemed to be the teacher while the Emperor pretended to be the pupil, and the secretary wrote down his doctrines. And that man, stricken of God, spun together all that horrible stuff and did not shun any abominable dogma, but even despised our theology and misrepresented all our ecclesiastical administration. And as for the churches, woe is me! he called our sacred churches the temples of devils, and our consecration of the body and blood of our one and greatest High Priest and Victim he considered and condemned as worthless. And what followed? the Emperor threw off his disguise and drew the curtain aside; and the whole senate was gathered together and the military contingent mustered, and the elders of the church were present too. The episcopal throne of the Queen of Cities was at that time occupied by that most blessed of patriarchs, Lord Nicholas, the Grammarian. Then the execrable doctrines were read out, and proof was impossible to attack. And the defendant did not deny anything, but immediately bared his head and proceeded to counter-demonstrations and professed himself willing to undergo fire, scourging and a thousand deaths. For these erring Bogomils believe that they can bear any suffering without feeling pain, as the angels forsooth will pluck them out of the fire. And although all . . . and reproached him for his impiety, even those whom he had involved in his own ruin, he remained the same Basil, an inflexible and very brave Bogomil. And although he was threatened with burning and other tortures he clung fast to his demon and embraced his Satanael. After he was consigned to prison the Emperor frequently sent for him and frequently exhorted him to forswear his impiety, but all the Emperor's exhortations left him unchanged. [...]

[A]ll the members of the holy synod and the chief monks, as well as the patriarch of that time, Nicholas, decreed that Basil who was the heresiarch and quite unrepentant, deserved to be burnt. The Emperor was of the same opinion and after conversing with him several times and recognizing that the man was mischievous and would not abandon his heresy, he finally had an immense pyre built in the Hippodrome. A very large trench was dug and a quantity of wood, all tall trees piled up together, made the structure look like a mountain. When the pile was lighted, a great crowd slowly collected on the floor and steps of the circus in eager expectation of what was to happen. On the opposite side a cross was fixed and the impious man was given a choice, for if he dreaded the fire and changed his mind, and walked to the cross, then he should be delivered from burning. A number of heretics were there watching their leader Basil. He shewed himself contemptuous of all punishment and threats, and while he was still at a distance from the fire he began to laugh and talk marvels, saying that angels would snatch him from the middle of the fire, and he proceeded to chant these words of David's, "It shall not come nigh thee; only with thine eyes shalt thou behold". But when the crowd stood aside and allowed him to have a free view of that terrifying sight, the burning pyre (for even at a good distance he could feel the fire, and saw the flames rising high and as it were thundering and shooting out sparks of fire which rose to the top of the stone obelisk which stands in the centre of the Hippodrome), then the bold fellow seemed to flinch from the fire and be disturbed. For as if wholly desperate, he constantly turned away his eyes and clapped his hands and beat his thigh. And yet in spite of being thus affected by the mere sight he was adamant. For the fire did not soften his iron will, nor did the messages sent by the Emperor subdue him. [...] [W]hile he was talking marvels and boasting that he would be seen unharmed in the middle of the fire, they took his cloak and said, "Now let us see whether the fire will touch your garments", and they threw it right into the middle of the pyre. But Basil was so uplifted by the demon that was deluding him that he said, "Look at my cloak floating up to the sky!" Then they "recognizing the web from the edge", took him and pushed him, clothes, shoes and all, into the middle of the pyre. And the flames, as if deeply enraged against him, ate the impious man up, without any odour arising or even a fresh appearance of smoke, only one thin smoky line could be seen in the midst of the flames. For even the elements are excited against the impious [...].[14]

The execution of Basil and a great number of his partisans did not hinder the progress of Bogomilism. In 1167 another Perfect One left Byzantium for Italy and France, so as to unite the assemblies there: the West knew him as 'Pope Nikita'.

Despite the extermination-politics of the Serbian and Bosnian princes, the missionary activity of Bogomilism continued to multiply its Churches: they included the Bulgarian Church, the Church of Dragovitia (Thrace), the Greek Church, the Patarene Church (Bosnia), and the Church of Philadelphia (Romania). Bogomilism found popular support among those who had reacted against Rome's prohibition of the use of native languages in the liturgy, but also among fighters for independence.

The Bosnian Church, which for a time was recognized by the princes, was subjected to new persecutions from 1443 to 1461, and, due to its hatred of Catholicism, turned more willingly towards the Turks. "This was why, when Bosnia fell under Ottoman domination, a great number of its inhabitants adopted the Muslim religion".[15]

Meanwhile, the adepts from Bulgaria, who were called *bougres*[16], tried to establish—in opposition to Rome—impossible peaceful communities, from Milan to Languedoc, and from Cologne to Flanders and Orleans. These were fraternal and little inclined to martyrdom.

CHAPTER TWENTY-SIX

Christs and Reformers:
Popular Resistance to the Institutional Church

The Church—by confirming the personal and temporal authority of the lax and collaborationist priests and bishops, against whom Tertullian, Hippolytus, Clement of Alexandria, Origen, Novatian, Donatus, and those faithful to popular Christianity had rebelled—set loose on the world a horde of clerics who were most often greedy and unscrupulous, and whose mission was to circumscribe kings, lords and worldly owners.

Gregory of Tours's claimed that his intention in writing his *Historia Francorum* [*History of the Franks*] was to present a damning assessment of clerical morals in sixth-century Gaul. The clerics and dignitaries in question were, with rare exceptions, letches, thieves, and murderers, and, when it came to extracting the greatest possible profit from the artisans and peasants, they rivaled the secular masters of the earth in their violence and deception. While the Bishop of Tours's purely formal reprobation relieved his own bad conscience—he lamented at great length the fact that conditions had not permitted him to remedy a state of affairs that he deplored from the bottom of his heart—the lay people, monks and priests who *were* sensitive to the misery of their parishioners threw themselves into a sacred mission of which the Church, in their eyes, had shown itself to be unworthy. Their interventions ended up inspiring a reformist politics in Rome, but not until the eleventh century. The goals of this reform movement—the restriction of the priests to celibacy and the suppression of both the sale of sacraments and the purchasing of ecclesiastical offices—also responded to a desire to free the Church, the parishes and the monasteries from their dependence upon monarchs and nobles, who were the masters of ecclesiastical appointments at all levels. The idea that ordination did not relieve priests of the duty to lead exemplary and 'apostolic' lives only entered Roman thinking at the Council of Trent, which was held after the success of the moralistic campaign of the Reformation.

The Christ of Bourges

In his chronicle for the year 591, Gregory, the Bishop of Tours, reported that an inhabitant of Bourges, finding himself exhausted in a forest, experienced a kind of trauma or ecstasy when he saw himself suddenly surrounded by a swarm of flies or wasps[1]. (Note that this same phenomenon was mentioned in the revelation of the peasant from Vertus. [See below.])

Living in a state of shock for two years, this man finally reached the Arles region, where, dressed in animal hides, he lived like a hermit and devoted all his time to prayer. At the end of a long period of asceticism, he claimed that he was invested with the supernatural gifts of healing and prophecy.

Wandering through the Cévennes and Gévaudan, he presented himself as the reincarnation of Christ and blessed his companion with the name 'Mary'.

Gregory attributed to a demon the exceptional powers that this man demonstrated and that drew to him a growing number of partisans. The man distributed to the poor the gold, money, and clothing with which his wealthy believers had honored him.

The chronicler accused him of having formed an armed band that, under his guidance, pillaged the towns and killed the bishops. Aurelius, the Bishop of Puy—before whom this army of Christ had emerged—sent to him an ambassador who assassinated him through treacherous means. His partisans were massacred or dispersed; Mary, on being subjected to torture, confessed that this Christ had resorted to diabolical proceedings in order to assure his control over the people.

Gregory himself admitted to having met several of these saints of the Last Days, who awakened a fleeting hope among people whose miserable lot in the midst of war, pillage, torture, famine, epidemics, and death quite naturally disposed them to sedition, which was in this instance additionally supported by the apostolic seal of the divine[2].

Adalbert

In 744, Winfrid (later sanctified under the name Boniface), acting with the approval of Pope Zacharias and the Frankish Kings Pepin and Carloman, united in Soissons a synod that was intended to break the popular movement of the monk named Adalbert.[3]

A wandering preacher, self-avowed monk, and practitioner of voluntary poverty, Adalbert was assailed by the Bishop of Soissons, who had prohibited him from preaching in the churches.

In the countryside Adalbert had erected crosses, at the foot of which he addressed crowds that were seduced by his remarks. Soon his followers built little chapels, then churches, in which he could preach.

To those who heard him, he affirmed that he had been invested with divine grace from the womb of his mother. In the manner of Mary, and just as the Gospels of the childhood of Jesus had reported, she had brought him into the world through her right side, thereby designating him as the second Messiah. Adalbert's privileged relationship with God was expressed in a prayer that Boniface transcribed for the Pope. In it, Adalbert evoked the support of the angels, thanks to whom he had obtained—for himself and for his faithful—the grace of being fulfilled in his desires. Like King Abgar, Adalbert kept a personal letter from Jesus, from which he derived his teachings.

The synodal report noted with disdain that the simple people and the women had abandoned the priests and the bishops to follow Adalbert instead. He seems to have been the object of a form of worship that competed with the traditional trade in relics, because his followers treasured the fingernail clippings and locks of hair with which he rewarded them.

Arrested and condemned by the synod of Soissons in 744, Adalbert managed to escape. The following year another synod—presided over by Boniface and King Carloman—excommunicated him, but without appreciable results. That same year, a synod in Rome of twenty-four bishops presided over by Pope Zacharias himself decided to declare that Adalbert was insane, no doubt because of the difficulty of cracking down on a man who was so popular and whose disciples had continued to grow in number. We know nothing of his end, but in 746 an ambassador of King Pepin, who was close to the Pope, attested to the persistent vogue for this particular Christ in Northern France.

Leuthard

The Bogomil missionaries, who were Slavic or Byzantine merchants, began to propagate their doctrine in Germany, France, and Italy around 1000. Leuthard, who was a farmer from Vertus, a village in the province of Champagne, wasn't so much one the first manifestations of Catharism as he was part of the tradition of wandering messiahs and prophets.

One day, Leuthard returned from the fields after having an illumination. (Note that Raoul Glauber[4] attributed to Leuthard, just as Gregory of Tours did with the Messiah of Bourges, the experience of seeing an aura of bees—a phenomenon that sometimes appeared in folklore and in fairy tales.) Leuthard decided to leave his wife and to break the church's crucifix. With a sudden eloquence that was nourished by the feeling that he possessed the word of God, he preached a return to the apostolic virtues. He enjoined his many adepts to cease paying tithes and to place no faith in the Old Testament.

Arrested in 1004 and taken before Bishop Gebuin II of Châlons (who was an educated and cunning man), Leuthard became aware of the vanity of his enterprise. He now found himself alone and facing cleverly contrived accusations of insanity. He threw himself into a well that same year.

Leuthard's rejections of the cross, the Old Testament, and marriage—as well as his more commonplace condemnations of the Church and tithes—do not suggest to us the influence, even in a confused form, of Bogomilism. Especially so because, less than a century later, peasants in the Châlons region were accused of Catharism. But it is true that, around 1025, the Italian Gundulf openly preached Bogomilism.

Éon de l'Étoile, or Eudo de Stella

Eudo was originally from Loudéac in Brittany, and he may have been the son of minor nobility. He preached in the name of Christ against the priests and monks in 1145 or so, at the same time that Bernard of Clairvaux was hastening to bring greater dignity and a more holy appearance to the monastic orders and to the clergy. Eudo lived in a community that was supposedly quite large, and exalted asceticism and the evangelic life.

His faithful called him the Lord of Lords. At a time when the myth of an immanent justice nourished the hopes of the disinherited, Eudo had come to judge the living and the dead. Chroniclers have mocked his completely personal interpretation of the exorcism formula—"Per eum qui venturus est judicare vivos et mortuos"[5]—which according to him meant: "By *Eudo* who has come to judge the living and the dead" [emphasis added]. But how was he any different from the Jewish, Gnostic, and Judeo-Christian exegetes of the Bible? Wasn't this how the famous evangelic truths ended up being written on the basis of the Hebrew and Aramaic *midrashim*?

In the forests in which his partisans took refuge, as if in a new 'desert', Eudo founded a Church with archbishops and bishops to whom he gave such names as Wisdom, Knowledge, and Judgment, each of which terms was endowed with a particular Gnostic connotation. (Note that a systematic study, in the manner of Robert Graves, of all the Christian mythologies would demonstrate the progress—perhaps even the migration, recreation, reoccurrence and transformation—of certain fundamental themes.)

While Brittany, ravaged by famine in 1144 and 1145, was prey to pillage and brigandage, the partisans of Eudo assured their own subsistence by conducting raids that destroyed churches and monasteries.

According to William of Newburgh, Eudo and his faithful lived in luxury, were magnificently dressed, and enjoyed a state of "perfect joy"[6] —an expression that perhaps suggests the distant influence of the Bogomils or Cathars. But one must keep in mind that William drafted his chronicle fifty years after the events he describes.

Like Paul of Samosata or Gaianus, Eudo celebrated Mass in his own name. An even more curious trait: he possessed a scepter in the shape of a Y. The two branches of the fork, when raised towards heaven, meant that two thirds of the world belonged to God and one third belonged to Eudo. The proportion was inverted in the contrary movement, which conferred upon Eudo an almost absolute power over the world, which had also been the dream of the Marcosians, of Simon of Samaria, and of the Barbelites. There were echoes here of ancient trinitarian conceptions that were no doubt unknown to the gentleman from Brittany.

In a case of smugness prevailing over the quest for a richer life, Eudo confronted the representatives of the Church who met in Rouen in 1148. Incarcerated in the archbishop's prison, he perished there from hunger and ill treatment. His partisans were arrested and burned at the stake.

Two Reformers: Peter of Bruys and Henry of Lausanne

While the new towns were using insurrection to try to win an independence that was refused them by the secular lords and prince-bishops—who were the objects of growing popular hatred because, while residing in the city and giving free rein to their dissolute morality and their general rapacity, they publicly insulted the principles of holiness recommended by the Church—preachers wandered around France, where small farmers and artisans were particularly well disposed to receive their messages. Two figures, targeted by ecclesiastic repression, stand out from the others, who remain unknown. (These others included various independent preachers, communalist agitators, Bogomil missionaries, and Cathars, who denounced those clerics and monks enjoying the privileges of Rome, and who tracked the movements of the heretic-hunters who were bankrolled by the Church).

Around 1105, Peter of Bruys, an old Provençal priest, traveled the south of France preaching, especially on the eastern side of the Rhône. He called for the destruction of churches, because one could pray just as well in an inn or a stable. He burned crosses, the instrument of the martyrdom of Christ, whose symbolism accorded all too perfectly with the cruel oppression of the Church.

For Peter of Bruys, the dead had no need of prayer. Of what value were sacraments administered by priests who were generally unworthy, and why was faith not sufficient to assure the salvation of believers, who were so badly served by the clergy of Rome?

Not content with encouraging the traditional refusal to pay tithes (which sufficed in itself to bring about accusations of heresy), Peter of Bruys denounced the market in penitence and indulgences.

He thereby attracted the animosity of the authorities in Cluny, where Bernard of Clairvaux moralized to the clergy about the respect and obedience that were due to them, while at the same time inciting them *ad capiendos vulpes* (to capture the foxes of heresy). The Council of Toulouse condemned Peter's doctrine in 1119, no doubt because of the agitation that he had fomented. It is believed that he met his disciple and successor, Henry of Lausanne, in the course of this agitation.

Peter of Bruys perished around 1126 in an ambush near the Abbey of Saint-Gilles, where he had preached. A faction probably incited by the authorities in Cluny seized and lynched him, before throwing his body onto a pyre. (Note that the cross sculpted on the tympanum of the Cathedral, which was then under construction, was erected in defiance of Peter's partisans, who denounced the cross's morbid and mortifying character.)

Several years later, Peter the Venerable, Abbot of Cluny, distributed a treatise against the Petrobrusians[7] that justified the repression of the doctrines adopted by Henry of Lausanne, around whom the partisans of Peter had rallied. The Councils of Pisa (1134) and Lateran (1139) made that condemnation official.

Henry of Lausanne, who died around 1148 and was also known as Henry of Le Mans, founded his agitation on the communalist struggles that opposed the cities to both the Church and the land-owning aristocracy, which was often hostile to the emerging bourgeoisie. His doctrine, which was perfectly coherent, mixed ideas promulgated by Peter of Bruys with elements derived from Bogomilism. It prepared the way for both Catharism and the movement that competed with it (the Waldensians).

Henry of Lausanne's origins remain obscure. A monk or a hermit, he was highly cultured; Bernard of Clairvaux called him *litteratus*. Perhaps he preached in Lausanne against the general corruption of the clergy and in the Petrobrusian spirit that opposed the *Ekklēsia*—identified with the community of believers—to the Roman Church. In 1116 the accuracy of Henry's predictions in Le Mans troubled Bishop Hildebert of Lavardin, who prohibited him from preaching. Henry ignored him and enjoyed, it seems, a considerable role in the government of the city. It is probable that the bishops at first tolerated some of Henry's reforms. While Pope Innocent III had recommended elevating the moral status of prostitutes and sparing them from contempt, Henry persuaded them to cut their hair, burn their rich clothes, and rid themselves of their jewelry. His sect offered them outfits, and its adepts married these 'impure' women who had no dowries. In place of marriage, the celebration, as Henry prescribed it, consisted solely in the mutual consent and sincere union of the participants' hearts.

A documented break with the misogyny maintained by the Church was part of this courtly current, which even today is only superficially studied but which was certainly noticed by the court of Champagne, at which Andreas Capellanus contrasted it with the practices in the Languedoc, where the freedom of women was translated into the juridical as well as the social domain. (Note that Capellanus's *De amore*, written in two parts around 1185, exalted women and carnal love in one part while exhibiting the worst aspects of misogyny in the other.)

Henry's exaltation of apostolic virtues did not tip over into ascetic rigor, because he—unlike the Cathars—estimated that the flesh merited neither an excess of dignity nor an excess of indignity.

In 1116, chased from the town or having left it voluntarily (it is hard to be sure), Henry traveled through Poitou, Bordeaux, and the region of Albi. No doubt he participated in the agitation in Toulouse, where it is possible that an encounter with Peter of Bruys radicalized his evangelic doctrine. In 1119 the Council of Toulouse excoriated Henry's 'errors'. It seems that, at the same time, his partisans were sacking churches, demolishing altars, burning crosses, and roughing up the Church's representatives.

Arrested by the Archbishop of Arles, Henry was brought before the Council of Pisa. Confronted by Bernard of Clairvaux, Henry feigned acceptance of his arguments and agreed to enter Cîteaux Abbey so as to avoid prison and even the pyre.

He soon escaped and returned to Provence. If we are to believe the words of Bernard of Clairvaux, who was resolved to finish off the

Henricians, Toulouse lived under the influence of this reformer. It is certainly true that the authorities there did not discourage the anti-Roman movement, which was widely popular and from which Catharism undoubtedly benefitted. We don't know whether Henry eventually fell into the hands of Cardinal Alberic, a papal legatee who had sworn to bring about Henry's downfall. His trail goes cold in 1144.

Around 1135 a community in Liège claimed to follow Henrician doctrines: rejection of the baptism of infants and prayers for the dead, and refusal of the sacrament of marriage in favor of the union of hearts.

Like the Bogomils, Henry was inclined to reject the Old Testament. His condemnation of the ornamental luxury of the churches—which Bernard of Clairvaux also condemned—foreshadowed the voluntary poverty of the Waldensians.

CHAPTER TWENTY-SEVEN

The Communalist Prophets

The eleventh century brought to the Western populations of Europe a slight amelioration of their condition, which demographic growth soon rendered precarious. While the development of the cities introduced the air of liberty into the confined atmosphere of an agrarian system that was socially frozen according to the three orders of Ratherius of Verona (soldiers, priests, and farmers), the economic growth of the towns began, little by little, to absorb the surplus of laborers coming there from the countryside.

Proliferating numbers of beggars, fermenting riots that were easily manipulated in the most diverse ways, were forces held in reserve that the lords, archbishops, guild leaders, and popular agitators learned to use for their own ends. The violence of these riots struck the masters as well as the rebels against the status quo and the Jews, the latter of whom were scapegoats for all kinds of fantastical resentments.

The First Crusade, which was launched in 1095 at the instigation of Pope Urban II (whose motivations included a desire to relocate to the conquered countries the overabundance of underprivileged people, ruined nobles, and other individuals whose fate was a matter of uncertainty), suddenly discovered in the designs of God and the Pope something that sanctified ambition, greed, and the need for bloody desublimation.

The influx of poor people into the towns posed a dilemma for the Church: how could it Christianize people reduced to the state of wild, starving dogs by extolling the holiness of the poor, even as the high clergy lived in opulence?

Norman Cohn notes:

> Insurrections occurred chiefly in episcopal cities. Unlike a lay prince, a bishop was a resident ruler in his city and was naturally concerned to keep his authority over the subjects in whose midst he lived. Moreover the attitude of the Church towards economic matters was profoundly conservative; in trade it could for a long time see nothing but usury and in merchants nothing but dangerous innovators whose designs ought to be firmly thwarted. The burghers for their part, if once they decided to break a bishop's power, were quite capable of killing him, setting fire to his cathedral and fighting off any of his vassals who might try to avenge him. And although in all this their aims usually remained severely limited and entirely material, it was only to be expected that some of these risings should be accompanied by an outcry against unworthy priests. When the lower strata of urban society were involved such protests tended in fact to rise shrilly enough.[1]

The Patarin Movement

The reforms undertaken by the Clunisian monk Hildebrand, who was made pope under the name Gregory VII, attempted to promote the moralization of the clergy in such a way as to enable the Christianization of the masses. At the same time that it sought to liberate the Church from the temporal control of the Emperor of Germany and the great feudal lords, Gregorian reform clashed with the privileges of ecclesiastic dignitaries, prince-bishops, archbishops, bishops, and even priests who had arrogated to themselves an excessive authority over rural communities and parishes.

"The purity of the life that the heretics preached became the second great goal of Gregory VII, who insisted on the personal dignity of the priests who performed the sacramental duties".[2]

The Patarin movement in Milan and Florence provided Gregory's reforms with a popular basis, in which voluntary poverty was proposed as the model for an apostolic life and which organized the communities of the faithful according to a mode of solidarity and mutual aid that was quite similar to that of the synagogues and churches of the second century.

The name 'Patarin' probably derived from the neighborhood of Pataria in Milan, which was inhabited by food resellers and dealers in second-hand items. The Patarins—notwithstanding the widespread confusion of *cathari* with *patari*—had nothing in common with the Cathars, who were not preoccupied with the reform of the Church or even really with adhesion to Christianity.

In 1057 Guido, the Archbishop of Milan, condemned the Patarin movement. Social insurrection was battering the authority of the men of the Church, and this with the consent of the Pope, whose political wager was that communal liberties would break the power of the feudal bishops. Nevertheless, "the union of the Pope and the Patarins was a union of means and not ends"[3].

The bourgeoisie and the weavers, who animated the movement and were in tactical solidarity with the reformers, demanded liberties that the Church began to restrict from the moment it ceased to require the assistance of these allies.

The *pataria* spread rapidly to Tuscany. They continued to exist until the 1110s in Florence and the 1120s in Orvieto and the region of Trier. The reaction to them was nevertheless speedy. In Milan, the Patarins were massacred in 1075 after being accused of arson.

The case of Ramihrdus of Cambrai was exemplary in this regard. In 1077 an insurrection by members of the bourgeoisie and the weavers forced the bishop to enfranchise the town. The priest Ramihrdus, who was close to the weavers (they propagated the most radical demands and doctrines), proclaimed that he would not receive communion from any abbot or bishop who thirsted after power and gain. Accused of heresy and burned alive, Ramihrdus had the posthumous consolation of being honored as a martyr by Gregory VII.[4]

In order to compete with the reformers who were too audacious in their demands, the hermits of Cîteaux, under the leadership of Robert of Molesme, founded ascetic and voluntarily impoverished groups that renounced all personal property. "To possess the smallest amount of money was, for them, a flagrant infraction of this principle and a 'grave' sin".[5]

In the same way, Robert of Arbrissel and his nomadic penitents defended from within the heart of the Church one of the themes of the anti-clerical reformers: mankind only used the riches of which God remained the unique owner. But were not Rome, the churches, and the abbeys instituted as the depositories of God's presence? Twenty-five years after its establishment, Cîteaux was a rich monastery with a doctrine centered on the poor. The papacy did not hesitate to render unto the Church what belonged to God, whose glory it kept alive.

Tanchelm of Antwerp

Even when stripped of the calumnies of the Archbishop of Utrecht, the figure of Tanchelm differs from Ramihrdus and the Patarin movement in many respects. Tanchelm's first steps towards power were nevertheless part of the framework of pontifical reforms to which Robert II, the Count of Flanders, was attached; Tanchelm may have been the Count's registrar or notary. He certainly took advantage of a conflict between the Count and the Archbishop of Utrecht in order to rouse the people of Antwerp against a corrupted clergy. Anecdote has it that the cohabitation of a priest named Hilduin with his niece incited Tanchelm to fulminate against the ecclesiastic hierarchy.

Tanchelm went to Rome, where Pascal II, the pope from 1099 to 1118, influenced his views. He then preached an anti-clerical doctrine — as well as the refusal to pay tithes and the rejection of sacraments delivered by unworthy priests — in Antwerp, Utrecht, Bruges, and Zeeland.

To the Church of the clerics Tanchelm opposed the Church of the simple people, whose guide he proclaimed himself to be in the name of the Spirit that was incarnated in him. It is hardly probable that, having denounced the "brothel of the Church", he surrendered himself to public debauchery, as was claimed by Norbert of Xanten (upon whom sanctity was bestowed following his campaign against Tanchelm). On the other hand, the fact that Tanchelm married a wooden figure of the Virgin Mary and favored marriages 'according to the heart' reveals a conception that may have been influenced by Bogomilism—that is, if one supposes that a formally worked out ideology was necessary to justify a practice that was in any case commonplace among the working classes.

A communalist prophet, Tanchelm governed the city in the name of God, surrounded himself with an armed ceremonial guard that was devoted to him, and gave an increasing number of sermons in a state of hysteria proper to this genre of ritual. One of his friends, the blacksmith Manasse, led a brotherhood of twelve men that recalled the apostles.

In a prelude to the Archbishop of Utrecht's offensive, a priest stabbed Tanchelm in 1115. His adepts retained power in Antwerp until the armed forces and the predictions of Norbert of Xanten (who also preached apostolic poverty, but within the framework of orthodoxy) combined to assure the clergy's control over the town, whose history is marked by continuous revolt against the Church.

Under the patronage of the Divine Spirit, Tanchelm united the functions of a tribune and the mission of an apostle. The demand for freedom, exalted by the movement for municipal independence, was spontaneously wedded to a renewal of the Christian community—a renewal that was hostile to the wealth and the useless pomp of the Church, and that identified true apostolic practice with poverty, fraternity, and solidarity organized through works of mutual aid and help for the starving. Around 1250 in Antwerp, William Cornelius, a kind of 'worker priest' close to the weavers of the time, reprised the idea that the goods of the rich and the clergy belonged to those whom poverty had sanctified.

Arnold of Brescia

Another communalist tribune and reformer, but one who did not make explicit references to Christ and the apostles, Arnold (born in Brescia around 1100) was a condottiere whose aspirations oscillated between a taste for power and a sincere attachment to the freedoms of the most disadvantaged.

After studying in Milan, where he was affected by the Patarin movement, and then in Bologna, Arnold left for Paris to receive instruction by Abelard.

In 1129, having become head of the canons regular in Milan, Arnold gained a popular audience by extolling an evangelic asceticism that was the precise opposite of the oppressive hedonism of the clergy (which he considered to be highly regrettable). He condemned the ownership of property by priests and demanded more rigorous reforms. He therefore quickly came into conflict with the bishop of the town. Condemned by the Council of Lateran in 1139—even though he did not profess the ideas of either Peter of Bruys or Henry of Lausanne—Arnold was banished.

Living as a refugee in France, where he remained close to Abelard, he incurred the threats of Bernard of Clairvaux, who pursued a vendetta against him. In the face of Bernard's persecution, Arnold left for Constance, from which he also had to flee after being denounced by an underhanded epistle from the holy reformer [Bernard]. But the troubles in Rome suddenly offered him the opportunity to put his ideas into practice.

Upon the death of Innocent II (1143) a conflict of succession broke out; it was doubled by a schism caused by an Antipope, Anacletus II. The Roman bourgeoisie soon profited from these events by demanding the recognition of its rights. A crowd lynched Pope Lucius II. Arnold survived as a mediator. He dealt with Eugene III, the successor to Lucius, and reestablished him in his functions, but did not succeed in keeping him under his control. In fact, the new Pope estimated that it would be more prudent to take refuge in Viterbo.

His hands now free, Arnold openly declared that he wished to destroy the power of the Church. His sermons preached the secularization of the clergy's goods, the confiscation of the riches of the bishops and cardinals, and the abolition of their temporal power. The spiritual leader of the Roman revolution, he demanded a communal republic that excluded government by the papacy. His program caused history the inconvenience of anticipating Garibaldi's program by eight centuries.

On 15 July 1148 Eugene III—quite powerless to shake Arnold's power so long as the tribune's politics didn't tip over into indecision and delay—hurled an anathema upon Arnold. Arnold was mistaken when he appealed for help from Emperor Frederick, who was little inclined to tolerate the instauration of a popular and republican government in Rome. His own partisans were divided on the merits of such an appeal. In 1155 Arnold left Rome and fell into the hands of Frederick Barbarossa, who, cutting across Tuscany, extended his tyrannical claws towards Rome. From then on, everything played out very quickly. As the price of a tactical reconciliation between Barbarossa and Rome, Arnold was delivered over to Pope Adrian IV, who hastened to hang and burn him.

The Arnoldians, sometimes called the 'poor of Lombardy', sought refuge in France, where they were joined by the partisans of Henry of Lausanne and Peter of Bruys. Several years later, Peter Waldo revived the dream of a reform that implied a return to the evangelic community—historically speaking, the community of the second century, the one that Christian mythology and its sectarians backdated to Jesus and his apostles in an idyllic Palestine.

Hugo Speroni

Even if the presence of a particularly eloquent tribune or agitator gave a specific character to demands for reform, the majority of communalist insurrections mixed together pell-mell demands for independence, appeals for commercial freedoms, and condemnations of the dignitaries of the Catholic Church.

Discreet as it was, the work of Hugo Speroni, a jurist from Piacenza, was no less indicative of the popularity of ideas that have traditionally been characterized as heretical and presented as the emanations of small groups that were marginal or minoritarian. In 1177, at the same time as Peter Waldo was sowing trouble in Lyon, Hugo Speroni led the struggle with equal brio on the political and religious fronts.

Speroni emphasized the importance of interiority and the intimate conviction of faith—the latter of which was sufficient in itself—and he rejected the Church and its sacramental arsenal. He rediscovered Pelagius's perspective when he assured his followers that infants were born without sin and were therefore saved, even if they happened to die without having been baptized. The true Christian had no need to pass through the sacrifice of redemption in order to become chosen. The morally obstinate practice of virtue was sufficient to fulfill the conditions of salvation. The right of the pure or perfect ones to unite according to the desires of their hearts—without submitting to the ecclesiastical ritual of marriage—derived from this conviction.[6]

CHAPTER TWENTY-EIGHT

Philosophy Against the Church

The elaboration of a theological system that justified the diverse privileges of the Church was nourished by Greek philosophy, from which Justin, Valentine, and Clement of Alexandria solicited aid as they sought to place the monotheism of the Hebrew Creator-God on a rational basis. Although interminable theological controversies had, over the course of the centuries, germinated in the uniquely Catholic manure of the trinity, predestination, free will, and grace, and had occasionally given rise to accusations of heresy (as in the cases of Abelard and Gilbert of Poitiers), these controversies did not exceed the framework of orthodoxy and, in any case, did not threaten the foundations of the faith that was propagated under Rome's supervision.

Gnostic, Platonic, Aristotelian, and Plotinian speculations—often badly digested by the Roman doctrine—caused the ecclesiastic body to vomit more than once and threatened to empty it of its substance. This philosophy, which the Church intended to treat as *ancilla theologiae*[1], as the servant of the Church, inherited the same weapons (designed to combat the closed system of dogma) that market rationality and the free circulation of goods deployed against the conservatism of agrarian structures. Philosophy also was founded on the aspiration to plenitude and emancipation that the body suggested to thought—that is, to people with particularly sensitive natures.

Sooner or later, the terrestrial economy had to absorb the celestial economy, and reject the sacred like excrement.

In 531, in Ephesus, the Monophysites produced works directed against their adversaries that were attributed to a certain Dionysius the Areopagite, whom the official history (that is, the history according to Rome) had been passing off as an epigone of Paul and as one of the bishops of Athens. The Archbishop of Ephesus disputed the author's authenticity. In fact, all the evidence suggests that the author was an Alexandrian philosopher of Gnostic inspiration who wrote during the second half of the fifth century. By a singular destiny, and perhaps because they furnished the powerful Monophysite Churches with arguments, the works of Pseudo-Dionysius the Areopagite were preserved, and they fed both a number of mystical visions and the conception known as pantheism, in which God, being everywhere, was effectively nowhere.

In the doctrine of Pseudo-Dionysius, God unknowingly manifested Himself by means of a series of emanations that came from spiritual natures or from the angels with material natures that composed the world. The essence of all things, God gave substance to all that existed.

God did not know evil, because evil possessed neither substance nor creative power but resided only in the lack of perfection in living creatures. It fell to each person to realize their ascension towards the *pleroma* [the totality] of the good according to the ladder of perfection and the destiny of all things, which was to return to the primordial unity. The soul united with the one who could only be known through a state of innocence and by means of "knowledge beyond all knowledge"[2]. This is what Nicholas of Cusa called "erudite ignorance". The partisans of the Free Spirit later claimed to possess an innocence in which knowing and non-knowing coincided in order to justify the impeccability of their unhindered lives.

John Scotus Eriugena

Around the middle of the ninth century, the theories of Pseudo-Dionysius inspired a philosopher of such brilliance that he seduced Charles the Bald, who was thenceforth resolved to protect this thinker against any possible constraints upon his intellectual freedom.

Born in Ireland or Scotland around 810, John Scotus Eriugena was around thirty years old when Charles the Bald invited him to teach grammar and dialectics at the palatial school of Quierzy, near Laon. The philosopher's *De praedestinatione*, written in 851 at the request of Hincmar, the Bishop of Reims (who was then engaged in an argument with Gottschalk), drew the condemnation of the Council of Valencia in 855, but without prejudicial consequences for its author.

Charles the Bald begged Eriugena to translate the works of Gregory of Nyssa, Maximus the Confessor, and Pseudo-Dionysius from Greek into Latin. Composed between 862 and 866, and written in the form of a dialogue between master and disciple (a dialogue in which the ideas of Amalric of Bena and David of Dinant were reconciled), Eriugena's *De divisione naturae* was condemned in 1210 at the Council of Paris, following the Amalrician agitations. Pope Honorius I ordered the burning of all copies of the text in 1225. In 1681 the Oxford edition still merited an entry in the Inquisitorial Index. John himself died around 877.

His system excluded theological speculation. According to his *De praedestinatione*, "the true philosophy is the true religion and the true religion is the true philosophy"[3].

"Universal nature", he tells us, "is divided into four categories: the being who is not created and who creates; the being who is created and who creates; the being who is created and does not create; and the being who is not created and does not create. The first and last of these categories are related to God; they are only different in our understanding, following which we consider God to be the principle or final goal of the world"[4]. Such are the main ideas in his system.

According to Scotus Eriugena, "two intellectual methods lead to God: one is the road of negation (άρνηση), which makes a clean sweep of all our representations of the divinity; the other is the road of affirmation (επιβεβαίωση), which applies to God all of our intellectual conceptions (with no exceptions), all of our qualities, and even all of our faults. These two methods, far from being mutually exclusive, form a single method that consists in conceiving of God as the being above all essence, all goodness, all wisdom, and all divinity, as the nothingness inaccessible to intelligence—

with respect to which negation is truer than affirmation and which remains unknown even to itself"[5].

The infinite being reveals himself by means of 'theophanies'—that is to say, through the series of creatures who emanate from him. These are accessible to intelligence, "in the same way that light, to become perceptible to the eye, must scatter itself into the air". It is not by virtue of a sudden movement of his nature that God created what exists: "to be, to think and to act are confounded for him in a single and self-same state. God created all things, which signifies nothing other than: God is in all things. Of him alone can one say that he exists; the world only exists insofar as it participates in the being of God"[6].

"Mankind finds itself among the supreme causes, an intellectual notion eternally conceived by divine thought. Mankind was made in the image of God and was destined to be the mediator between God and his creatures, the place of union of the creatures in a single and self-same unity. If mankind had not sinned, the division of the sexes would not have been produced: mankind would have remained in the primitive unity of its nature. Moreover, the world would not have been separated in him from paradise; that is to say, he would have spiritually inhabited it in the unity of his essence; the heavens and the earth would not have been separated in him, because all of his being would have been heavenly and without any corporeal element. Without the fall, he would have enjoyed the plenitude of being and would have reproduced in the manner of the angels.

"Nothing of what exists would have fallen into nothingness; the end of the fall of nature is the departure point for its rising"[7].

"Here-below, mankind possesses in itself two elements that compose universal nature, spirit and matter; he reconciles within himself the two opposed extremities of creation. He is the mediator between God and the world, the point at which all creatures—spiritual as well as material—are brought together in a single unity. Human nature lost nothing of its primitive purity through the fact of the fall; it has conserved it completely. It isn't in this nature that evil is seated, but in the perverse movements of our free will. Like any primary idea, this nature enjoys an imperishable beauty; evil only resides in the accident, in individual will. The image of God continues to exist in the human soul"[8].

It is through human intelligence that the return of the creation to God takes place. Exterior objects, conceived by us, pass into our nature and are united with it. They find in it the first causes, to which they return through the effect of our thought, which glimpses the eternal essence in passing phenomena and identifies itself intellectually with God. Thus the visible creatures ascend with us in God. "The Word is the principle and the final goal of the world; at the end of time it recovers the infinite multiplicity of its own being, now come back to itself in its original unity", or, to employ the allegorical language that reduces the facts of Christian revelation to the status of symbols and images of this evolution of the divine being: "Christ rose into the heavens in an invisible manner in the hearts of those who elevate themselves to him through contemplation"[9].

["]Physical death is the beginning of the return of mankind to God. On the one side, matter vanishes without leaving any traces; on the other side, all the divisions that were successively issued from the divine unity and that co-exist in the human soul come back together. The first stage of this universal unification is the return of mankind to the primitive state of his nature, such as it existed in heaven, without the division of the sexes. Resurrected Christ preceded us to the paradise of human nature unified with itself, in which all creatures are one"[10]. All men indistinctly return to the unity of human nature, because this nature is the communal property of all. But here a triple distinction is established. Those who were elevated during their lives as high as the contemplation of the divine being will be elevated above the unity of their heavenly nature, to the point of deification; those who did not surpass the ordinary level of terrestrial existence will remain in the state of glorified human nature; and those who yielded to the "irrational movements of perverse desire" will fall into eternal torment, without their human nature— which formed the foundation of their being—attaining its ideal bliss through their suffering. Individual consciousness alone will be the seat of suffering.

"After the annihilation of this world there will be no malice, no death, no misery. Divine goodness will absorb malice; eternal life will absorb death; and bliss will absorb misery. Evil will end; it will have no reality in itself because God will not know it"[11]. All of Scotus Eriugena's treatise on predestination is dedicated to the exposition of this same idea. Eternal suffering is absolutely condemned by the logic of his system.

David of Dinant

At the Council of Paris of 1210, Peter of Corbeil (the Archbishop of Sens), and Peter of Nemours (the Bishop of Paris) all had excellent reasons for sending the Amalricians to the pyre and for pell-mell condemning Amalric of Bena, Aristotle, and David of Dinant. Ideas did not seriously threaten the foundations of faith so long as they only circulated within the inner circles devoted to scholastic quarrels. But when they served as pretexts or justifications for a natural lack of faith or for the frightened hostility that clerical politics provoked among their opponents, they soon acquired an importance of which their authors were sometimes unaware.

It is difficult to represent the doctrine of Dinant with precision, because we now only have quotations from his work. Nevertheless, he seems to have advanced a formula that still scandalized religious milieus when it appeared under Spinoza's name in the seventeenth century: *Deus sive natura* ("God is nothing other than nature")[12].

According to the *Chronicle of the Monk of Loudun*, Dinant was born in the Meuse Valley. He lived in the family circle of Pope Innocent III and was an intelligent politician, jurist and man of learning.

The *Compilatio de novo spiritu*, attributed to Albertus Magnus (Albert the Great), specified that Dinant fled France at the time of the Council of 1210 because "he would have been punished if he had been caught"[13].

Albert quotes extracts from Dinant's *Liber de tomis sive divisionibus*, also known as *Liber atomorum*.

According to David, everything is simultaneously matter, spirit, and God. These three terms formed a unique substance in which the indivisible components of the body, the intellect, and the soul (that is to say, matter, spirit and God) had their source.

In Jundt's opinion[14], David would have known about a work written by Avicebron (an Arab philosopher and contemporary of Avicenna) called *Fons vitae* (*The Fountain of Life*), which supported the thesis of a material substance endowed with varying modes of expression that ranged from the simple to the complex.

Such metaphysical subtleties were obviously of less interest than the conclusion, to which many people subscribed even when they could neither read nor argue: namely, that there is only terrestrial life, and that it falls to each person to construct his or her destiny within it. This was the lesson propagated by the Amalricians.

Thomas Scoto and Herman of Rijswijk[15]

The name Thomas Scoto would have completely disappeared from history (carefully purified by the Church) if it hadn't appeared in the writings of the clerical executioners who perpetuated the memories of their victims. The Inquisitor Alvarus Pelagius (Álvaro Pelayo) granted him a note in his *Collyrium contra haereses*, published in 1344.

First a Dominican and then a Franciscan, Thomas Scoto taught at the school in Lisbon that studied papal decretals in the first half of the fourteenth century.

After having a dispute with him in Lisbon, Pelagius threw Scoto in prison and then, in all probability, had him burned.

What doctrine can be gleaned from the inquisitor's accusations? Contrary to the belief that there was no atheism in the Middle Ages, Scoto's conception suggested the thesis of an eternal and uncreated world. The soul was annihilated at death. Scoto rejected the sacraments, the virginity of Mary, the miracles of the Christ, His divine nature, and the authority of the Church. Four centuries before Isaac Pererius, Scoto held that mankind existed before Adam. He estimated that the world would be better governed by philosophers than by theologians, and had little respect for people like Augustine of Hippo and Bernard of Clairvaux.

Is it excessive to conjecture that Thomas Scoto is only one example among many other thinkers whose dangerous opinions prudence dictated should not be published? Pelagius noted one of those dangerous opinions: "There have been three deceivers in the world, to wit: Moses, who deceived the Jews; Christ, who deceived the Christians; and Mahommed, who deceived the Saracens"[16]. This was the celebrated title of a book [*De tribus impostoribus*] attributed to Frederick II or to his chancellor, Peter of the Vineyard, of which no trace has been found—other, that is, than an allegedly reprinted edition from the end of the seventeenth century (thanks to a priest named Meslier[17]). Whether it was real or fake, this text cast a scandalous shadow from the thirteenth to the seventeenth century, due to the concision with which it summarized an opinion that many people professed secretly or that was held by people connected to the universities and among the wandering or Goliard clerics, but which was prevented from being discussed openly by the omnipresent suspicions of the clergy.

At the beginning of the sixteenth century—years before the appearance of Geoffroy Vallée, Lucilio Vanini, and Giordano Bruno[18]—another Free Spirit, Herman of Rijswijk, was placed on the pyre in 1512 as a recidivist, having already escaped from the prison to which a trial had condemned him in 1502. Herman's works, which have since disappeared, affirmed that the world had existed for all eternity and did not begin with creation, "which was an invention of the foolish Moses". Herman denounced the "farcical gospels". Faced with the inquisitor, a notary, and witnesses, he added to the accusations against him: "I was born a Christian, but I am not a Christian, any because the Christians are utterly stupid"[19]. All of these men—from David of Dinant to Herman of Rijswijk, passing through Thomas Scoto—enable us to conjecture that these were neither the first nor the only atheists before the Renaissance, which inflicted on the Church of Rome in particular and on religion in general injuries that no scar tissue would ever heal.[20]

CHAPTER TWENTY-NINE

The Cathars

The flickering lights of Marcion have projected the most diverse shadows onto the world and onto history. The fanatical founder of a Church of which he claimed to be the master, Marcion imprinted on the ecclesiastic party—which was in fact among his adversaries—the political will thanks to which Christianity was shaped and reshaped by temporal exigencies until it fitted the Constantinian mold. Mani, who came from an Elchasaite milieu, was also influenced by Marcion. Whereas Marcionite Churches failed because they made untenably paradoxical claims to missionary authority within a universe that they also characterized as irredeemably evil, Mani made his way through the old Persian dualism, which was better disposed to receive him than was the Greco-Roman propensity to market rationality and national self-interest (which was easily conquered by monotheism).

The Paulicians and the Bogomils formed other branches that grew in parallel with a dualism that was rooted in the separation of mankind from itself. This dualism separated out light from darkness, good from evil, and the spiritual from the material, thereby representing the fractured unity of human life—of a life that was born from nature and that aspired to rediscover in nature a new, peaceful and creative alliance.

The Cathar movement, such as it was propagated in Northern Italy, Provence, the Rhineland region, Flanders, and Champagne, was originally fostered by Bogomil missionaries. The heretic hunters were not mistaken when they called them 'Bulgari' [*bougres*]—that is to say, Bulgarians (the *Song of the Albigensian Crusade*, v. 18, calls the Cathars "those from Bulgaria"[1]). The term 'Cathar', which came from the Greek word *catharos* ('pure'), became *Ketzer* ('heretic') in German. Flanders knew them from the beginning as the 'piffles' and in Gaul they were called 'the weavers'—a reference to a guild that was driven to take action against tyranny and to spread ideas of liberty.[2]

Catharism manifested itself in the current of the twelfth century as a new syncretism, assimilating several Christian notions and texts, but on a basis absolutely distinct from Christianity and *a fortiori* from the Catholicism of Rome.

The First Bogomil Missionaries

Singular though it was, the case of Leuthard of Vertus suggests the presence in France of Bogomil missionaries: wandering merchants, pilgrims, itinerant day laborers or Goliards, who were active all over Western Europe. Other isolated sectarians met in Ravenna and Mainz.

Around 1018, an important group that was well established in the working-class milieus of Aquitaine rejected the cross, baptism, marriage and the consumption of animal flesh. Around 1022, the population of Toulouse showed itself receptive to their influence—whence came the city's reputation for being the old nest of heretics that Petrus Valium claimed it was: *Tolosa tota dolosa*[3].

In 1022 the Orléans affair exploded.[4] The nobles and priests of the Church of the Holy Cross, including a familiar of King Robert and the confessor of Queen Constance, professed Bogomil opinions, perhaps having been influenced by an Italian missionary. They held that matter was impure and they rejected marriage, the pleasures of love, baptism, communion, confession, prayer, the ecclesiastic hierarchy, and the material existence of the Christ ("We were not there and we cannot judge if it is true", they said in their confessions). Through the laying-on of hands they purified the believer of his or her sins. The Holy Spirit would then descend on him or her, and from then on his or her soul would be elevated and delivered from suffering.

Having been denounced to King Robert, this group was placed on the pyre on 28 December 1022, in line with the penalty reserved by customary right for sorcerers. The chroniclers of the time assured their readers that the condemned went to their deaths laughing.

In 1025, in the dioceses of Châlons and Arras, an Italian named Gundulf aroused the enthusiasm of the disinherited and the weaver-workers by preaching a doctrine in which were mixed together various social themes, Bogomilism, and the reforms announced by Henry of Lausanne and Peter of Bruys.[5]

For Gundulf it was absurd to impose baptism on newborns whose reason was insufficiently enlightened to accede to evangelic life. Unworthy priests had no right to the privileges that their responsibilities conferred upon them. The Eucharist was merely a "vile negotium", a "vile business": how could Christ share his body of flesh (now become bread) with so many faithful? Faith had little regard for the facts: the Churches were only masses of stones, and the cross and the ecclesiastic hierarchy with its bells and songs merited no attention at all.

Marriage had no importance: one only had to make love without being saddled with an aggressive concupiscence (this position was absolutely opposed to Catharism, but it did, on the other hand, ratify the emerging and ephemeral privileges of women, which were expressed in a watered-down form by courtly love).

The apostolic life consisted in living from the work of one's own hands, in not hating anyone, and in loving all of one's fellows. Gerard I, the Bishop of Cambrai and an intelligent man who favored reform of the Church, preferred to turn a blind eye and, refusing to repress Gundulf, "converted him to the Church".

And yet in the same era, Terry, a hermit living in a grotto near Corbigny in the Nevers region, made similar remarks and was burned, along with two women from among his faithful.[6]

In Italy, whence some of the agitators originally came, Bogomilism had put down roots and engendered specific doctrines. In 1028 a community of some thirty people belonging to the nobility and centered around the Countess of Orte met at the Château de Montfort. They formed an ascetic group whose aspiration to an evangelic Christianity assimilated the teachings of Bogomil and foreshadowed Catharism.

In their doctrines, Christ was not God but the Soul of man, the beloved of God. The hidden meaning of the Bible (note that their recognition of the Old Testament distinguished them from the teachings of the Bogomils and Cathars) and the revelation of the Holy Spirit presided over the regeneration of each person. The new man, disapproving of all that came from this world, discovered in his own virginity his most elevated ideal: the doctrine of the 'pure love' ("If he is married, he should consider his wife to be his mother or his sister, and dream that humanity, like the bees, will perpetuate itself without sin"). This same doctrine was proposed in different variations by the Benedictine Monials of the thirteenth century, the erotica of the troubadours, and the Cathars.

> All goods must be placed in common; one must not eat meat; one must fast and pray constantly, *vicissim*[7], day and night. One must mortify oneself in order to be forgiven and, as soon as natural death approaches, one must let oneself be finished off by one's companions so as to achieve martyrdom and holiness.[8]

(Note that this prescription was the same as the Cathars' voluntary death or *endura*.)

When the Archbishop of Milan, Ariberto, undertook to pursue these people, they offered no resistance, confessed their faith, and—obliged to choose between adoration of the cross and the pyre—willingly threw themselves into the flames, assured of another world that would liberate them from the miserable imperfections of terrestrial existence.

Adepts of similar beliefs showed up near Verona, Ravenna, and Venice. Gerard Sagredo, the Bishop of Csanád from 1037 to 1046, remarked that they had many brothers in faith in Greece. They scorned the Church, the priests, and their rites, and they mocked the resurrection of the flesh.

Between 1043 and 1048 the agitation spread to the region of Châlons—not far from Vertus, where Leuthard had previously sowed trouble. At the time of the Council of Rheims (1049) there were mysterious assemblies of peasants who refused marriage and the pleasures of love. They practiced the laying-on of hands and refused to kill animals.

In 1051, in Goslar, the Emperor condemned to the gallows those Lorraine peasants who had refused to kill the chickens that the bishop of the town had presented to them as a test of their beliefs.

For almost a century, no document attested to the perpetuation of Bogomilism, which was shaped by local interpretations during its propagation in Western Europe. Either its adherents prudently availed themselves of the protections of clandestinity, or the communalist insurrections gave to their demands a less religious aspect.

It wasn't until the 1140s that Byzantium's persecution of Bogomilism pushed towards the West a new wave of believers, who were often identified with the Manicheans. No doubt the deplorable outcome of the Second Crusade returned to their homes Crusaders who had become disillusioned and who, since their stay in Byzantium, had become carriers of a new faith in which the powerful were identified with Satan's henchmen.

The Second Wave of Bogomil Preaching

Towards the end of the first half of the twelfth century, the *novi haeretici*[9] appeared everywhere and in force. The name 'Cathar' was only applied to them after 1163. The preachers, surrounded by their partisans, were replaced by schools, organizations and Churches.

In 1143, in Cologne, there were many people who led the apostolic life, gloried in possessing nothing, worked with their hands, and punctuated with periods of fasting and prayer an existence that was in conformity with the true Church, which was assuredly not that of the rich prelates. The first abominable pyres were lit for them in Cologne and Bonn.

At the same time, two brothers from the village of Bussy—Evrard and Clement—who propagated ideas of reform and purification were delivered over to Guibert of Nogent, who had them lynched and burned by his henchmen.[10]

In Périgord, around 1147, the *novi haeretici* easily seduced nobles, clerics, monks, nuns, peasants, and weavers. "In scarcely two years, the Cathar movement controlled the areas from the Rhine to the Pyrenees [...]. The spark lit in the East now became a powerful flame".[11]

The former partisans of Henry of Lausanne rallied to a Cathar bishop who preached in the region of Albi. In the north, Champagne had a Cathar bishop at Mont-Aimé. The gravedigger Marcus, converted to the new faith, preached in Lombardy. Wandering missionaries reached Naples and England, where, around 1162, adepts were quickly put to death. On 5 August 1163, several Cathars were burned in Cologne in front of the Jewish cemetery, at the instigation of Canon Eckbert. The scholar Hildegard of Bingen did not fail to denounce them.

With the development of a veritable Church, internal dissidence and polemics increased. Western Bogomilism was grafted onto an ensemble of social demands and an agenda of apostolic reform as moral practice took precedence over dogmatic questions. The gap grew wider between a Christian current of egalitarian evangelism and a dualist religion that had nothing in common with the Montanist Christianity that was being propagated by the currents of voluntary poverty.

The intervention circa 1167 of Nicetas, the Bogomil Bishop of the Church of Byzantium (who was close to Marcus, the deacon of the Italian Cathars), imprinted a more extreme dualism on the movement as a whole: Satan, the master of an execrable world, was a divinity parallel to the God of Goodness. The beliefs in which the majority of the Cathar communities recognized themselves thereafter composed a doctrine that was irreconcilable with the principles of Christianity. More than a heresy, Catharism displayed itself to Rome with the magnitude of a competing religion, of a regeneration of Manichaeism.

Nevertheless, rivalries and schisms multiplied within Catharism. The notion that the purity of ideas and rites depended on moral purity provided a weapon in struggles for power. The Cathars of Florence rejected Garattus, a candidate for the Lombard bishopric, as well as his doctrine, because he had been caught in the company of a 'star of the Shepherd'[12]. The star that Lucifer brought down with him in his fall was thought to be a prostitute.

Furthermore, in 1178 certain bishops of Toulouse and the Aran Valley professed their Christian faith and disavowed the belief in two divinities.

Such internal dissensions underhandedly introduced into the movement a ferment of desperation, the power of which, as Arno Borst has shown, attracted all social classes:

The archbishops of Bordeaux, Narbonne and Bourges were seriously threatened by Catharism. In the environs of Albi, Toulouse and Carcassonne, in Gascony, the Cathars were so numerous that the alarmed Count of Toulouse was driven to intervene in 1177. The Cathars appeared in the north of France, in Burgundy, and in Flanders, as well as in Nevers, Vézelay, Auxerre, Troyes, Besançon, Metz, Reims, Soissons, Roanne, Arras and other towns. In Spain they were still rare, but one found them in England around 1210. In Germany one encountered them all along the Rhine—in the archdioceses in particular, but also in the bishoprics along the Danube (in Passau and Vienna). But their paradise was the north of Italy, the walled-in worlds of the cities of Milan, Udine, Como and Viterbo. Towns, out-lying areas, villages and castles were filled with them. Everything that, nearby or from afar, had been more or less favorable to the birth of Cathar ecumenism now found itself implicated, to its great astonishment, in a universal conspiracy against the Catholic Church. Every social stratum was touched by the Cathar missions. The severity of Cathar morality attracted the ruling classes: noble and princely patrons, knights, and rich and cultivated people everywhere were drawn to it. Priests and monks received the new sacred teachings and put them into practice. But these milieus were not engaged in spreading those particular teachings because, at that moment, evangelic morality was no longer the Cathars' fundamental preoccupation: Bogomil dogma had surpassed it in prominence. The simple rationality of that dogma particularly touched the lower classes. A gravedigger who daily experienced the destruction of matter preached in Italy. His principal theme: the Demon created the flesh. Men of letters and weavers, workers belonging to sedentary or meditative professions, followed the ruling classes; laborers both skilled and unskilled fell into step. A proletarian intellectualism took hold of Bogomil teachings. But despite the 'elective affinities' that united the laboring classes with the most elevated layers of society, this was not a proletarian movement. It remained disparate in its social structure, and in 1125 it was still unclear who would succeed in imposing themselves: the high or the low, the adepts of a simple Christianity or those of Bogomil dualism.

The Cathars' situation on the economic plane also rested on a contradiction. They certainly extolled apostolic poverty. Each 'Perfect One', upon his entrance into the sect, had to give his fortune and his goods to the Cathar

Church and satisfy his needs through the work of his own hands. The adept was poor, no doubt, but the Church was rich. In 1162 in Flanders, and in 1163 in Cologne, it offered to Catholic prelates the spectacle of a Church corrupted by money; in 1177, in the south of France, it swam in riches.

In Rimini, as in Béziers, the Cathars offered loans. Mobs crowded around them *pro subsidiis temporalibus*[13]. And the heretics, who were themselves merchants, conducted both their business affairs and affairs of the soul in public places (and at the same time). They collected gifts for their Church. They did not prohibit their adepts from loaning money with interest—the rich believers relieved their consciences with large offerings. A conflict once again arose between the exigencies of Western evangelic morality and the financial necessities of a Church founded on a well-defined dogma; profiting from the confused situation that created these Catharist contradictions, a precocious capitalism was instaurated.

The Cathars' political position was unclear. In the south of France especially, the ascetics who scorned the world were soon supported by the nobles, and, at the beginning of the thirteenth century, almost all of the barons were adepts. Count Raymond VI of Toulouse (1194 to 1222) and Raymond-Roger of Foix (1188–1223) were examples of this tendency. Their wives supported the Cathar Church. An elderly aristocrat, Pontius of Rodelle, explained to Foulques, the Catholic Bishop of Toulouse: ["]The Cathars are our parents; they live among us. Why must we persecute them?["] But it wasn't just the severe and impressive morality of the Cathars that seduced the nobility. The nobility in Provence was poor and the Cathars were the enemies of the Catholic Church, whose riches came from the lords. The Cathars did not have a political program, but they became an instrument of politics when they offered to ally themselves with the Count of Toulouse against Paris. The Pope was not completely wrong when he reproached them—what a powerful person does is always done well. Here enthusiastic honor and bad faith stood side by side; here material interests served to shape piety and renunciation.[14]

The first popular and Christian reaction that rose up against Catharism would have furnished a highly effective army—if the Church hadn't disavowed and rejected it as heretical. Born around 1173 and centered around a merchant named Peter Waldes or Waldo, the Waldensian current advocated fidelity to Catholic dogma and, at the same time, the necessity of reforming ecclesiastic morals. The popes had left it too late and missed a crucial opportunity by the time they moved to combat the Cathars on the terrain of voluntary poverty.

When the Cathars reproached the Spanish Bishop of Osma, Diego de Acebo, for preaching amidst splendor, he chose to confront them from beneath a facade of poverty and humility. Dominic de Guzmán and his Dominican order adopted a similar tactic. The paltry results of this approach augured the inevitable recourse to a final solution.

The assassination of the papal legatee Pierre of Castelnau in 1208 by sympathizers of the Count of Toulouse and the Cathars quickly provided justification for appending to the crucifix the indispensible extension of the sword.

Cîteaux[15] preached this new Crusade. The conflict that opposed King Philip Augustus to his vassal, the Count of Toulouse, added to political interests hopes of profit and plunder, which were more easily obtained at home than in the Saracen regions.

The End of Catharism

The violence of the Crusade against the Albigensians put the Church in a position of strength, buying it time to craftily enact reforms from which it would later be able gradually to distance itself. How could people [i.e. the Cathars] so sensitive to the delights of the beyond—where the Good God reigned—not be resigned to encountering the brutes of the North? Even when their resistance was organized, the Cathars carried within themselves the seeds of their own defeat. Their goodness was founded on a renunciation of self; their love was founded on abstinence. What strength could they draw from pleasures that were not of this world?

The Cathars did not tire of dogmatic quarrels, even as the prospect of extermination loomed over them. Around 1230, John of Lugio composed a vast work in Latin in which he tried to revive the Christian tradition by finding a philosophical justification for Catharism.

In Italy, the towns won over by Catharism were by turns protected or repressed according to political about-faces that, breaking or renewing alliances, incited Emperor Frederick II to either to fire up the pyres or to extinguish them.

Languedoc succumbed to its attackers in the blood (most often mixed together) of the Cathars, the Catholics, and the peasants who still practiced the old agrarian cults, as well as in that of those who declined to believe in any dogma whatsoever. But the Church that was carried to victory by the French version of the *Reconquista* fell into the hands of the kingdom that was decorated by the *fleur-de-lis*. For two centuries the Church paid the price for its success by indenturing itself to French temporal power.

Frederick II, anticipating all Roman initiatives, soon gave the force of law to the ordinances of the Council of Lateran. He decreed death by fire for all the Cathars. For him, heresy was a crime against the State; he held anyone who dared to contest his decisions to be heretical, as if he were the Pope.

Rome made use of the Dominicans, those thugs dressed in monks' habits. Languedoc particularly execrated their founder, Dominic, and his acolyte, Peter of Verona (known as the Martyr), whom the hardliners among the heretics succeeded in executing. In 1231 the Inquisition finally began to function. It took on and legalized the work of the heretic-hunters, who had previously acted more or less on their own initiative, as had Robert the Bulgarian[16] and Konrad von Marburg, torturers who organized huge burnings everywhere they went.

Around 1244, with the fall of the bastion of Montségur, Catharism received its deathblow. It thenceforth perpetuated itself clandestinely, but not without prompting renewals of repression in 1295 (when the pyre ended Peire Autier's campaign of agitation) and in 1321 (when Pastor Guillaume Bélibaste fell into the hands of the Inquisition and perished in fire). In 1340 the pyre was lit at Carcassonne for the last Cathars. They survived up until 1322 in the areas around Florence, until 1340 in Sicily, 1388 in Sienna, and 1412 in Turin. (Note that the 'black Manichaeism' of sorcery, which triggered hysteria between the fourteenth and sixteenth centuries, and which was associated with regressions in the freedom of women and the freedom to love, suggested a continuation of Catharism without Cathars. Identifying the Waldensians and the Perfect Ones with sorcerers—one spoke of the 'vauderie'[17] of Arras—the Church reclaimed the principle of purity and, in its way, pursued the combat of the angels against the forces of evil: that is, against marginal people, Jews, and 'inferior' races, all of whom were considered sectarians of the Devil.)

Dualism and Asceticism

Despite their diversity, the various local Catharisms (including Albigensianism, which was swelled by the Crusade and incorrectly presented as the entirety of the movement) shared certain common traits, which were principally linked to dualism and to the ascetic rigor that characterized the first Greco-Roman strain of Christianity.

It is customary to recognize in these various Catharisms two modes of dualism. One (somewhat attenuated) version conceived of a single God who had created all things, including the angel Satanael, who repudiated his native goodness, corrupted himself, and formed a corrupted world out of material existence. The human soul, proceeding from these two primordial angelic natures, made use (through free will) of the faculty of choosing between good and evil, and thereby opted either for salvation or damnation.

This doctrine was propagated in milieus that were attached to a certain Christian formalism.

Absolute dualism, on the other hand, broke more deliberately with Christianity and, like Marcionism, recognized two antagonistic powers. The material world was the work of a Bad God. The Good God engendered an incorruptible universe—that of spirits or the Spirit.

The theory of the *Angelos-Christos* resurged in Catharism. The Christ, the angel of God, only possessed a spiritual body.

In his *Book of the Two Principles*, John of Lugio argued for the co-eternal character of the perfect world—the domain of the God of Goodness—and the bad world governed by Satan. The idea that Satan forced God to reveal the evil that was in Him in the forms of the Will to Justice and the Power to Punish proceeded curiously—perhaps influenced by the Kabalistic Jewish milieus or by the Passagians—from the Jewish Gnosticism of an Essene faction. (Note that the Passagians were a Judaicized sect that appeared in Lombardy and was condemned at the Council of Verona in 1184. Hostile to the sacraments and the Church, this sect believed that circumcision was indispensible for salvation.)

Like Marcionism, Catharism professed an absolute refusal of nature, which was identified with evil, perversion, and death. Beneath the surface of an apparent respect for life—which enjoined them from killing other men or animals, forbade them from thieving or committing acts of violence, and taught them more generally to conduct themselves as fundamentally good people (traits that one also found among apostolic preachers such as Gundulf)—the Cathars scorned the pleasures of existence. At the heart of a civilization in which the privileges of love and women were only timidly asserted, the Cathars condemned all amorous relations as a mortal sin. Even marriage was a *jurata fornicatio*[18]. Women were to be fearfully avoided. Some Cathars estimated that Satan inhabited the bodies of pregnant women.[19] Such an extreme rigor was not without its reversals or excesses. It seems that the Catharist Bishop Philip hazarded the idea—reprised by the Beghards of the Free Spirit—that "there is no sin below the waist"[20].

It is true that the Catharist believers were not subject to the constraints of the puritanism that was imposed on the Perfect Ones, and that they had the right to get married.

The Perfect Ones refused to swear, take oaths, or sit on tribunals, because human justice was essentially diabolical. It was not permitted for the Perfect Ones to carry arms, eat meat, or enjoy the least sensual pleasure.

The *consolamentum*, the principal ceremony and a legacy of Bogomilism, absolved one of all sin and initiated one into the order of the Perfect Ones.

The *endura* (the fast that was sometimes prolonged until death) was a form of suicide. Contrary to Catholic assertions, it was never made the object of an obligation or an incentive, but it did possess a certain attraction for people who were little disposed to discover the charms of the here-below.

Few Cathar texts other than the *Liber de duobus principiis* [*Book of Two Principles*] by John of Lugio and the *Interrogatio Johannis* [*The*

Questions of John], a Gospel of Bogomil origin, have survived. Other writings circulated and were echoed in the *Summa de catharis* [*Summa on the Cathars*] by Raneiro Sacchoni, an apostate Cathar. Fables that composed a veritable mythology translated the teachings of the Perfect Ones into colorful narratives (a dragon carries off angels in the folds of its tail; a battle in a glass sky that breaks under the weight of demons; the theme of *golem* animated by Lucifer. . .). Their influence on folklore has yet to be studied.

CHAPTER THIRTY

The Waldensians and the Adepts of Voluntary Poverty

The Waldensian movement illustrates both the opportunity lost by Rome in its struggles against the Cathars and the subversive effects of the urban pauperization that was exploited by the 'apostolic' reformers. Few records exist that clarify the figure of the movement's founder, a rich merchant from Lyon named Peter Waldo, Waldo, or Valdes (perhaps *de la Vallée* [of the valley]).

Legend has it that he received a warning from heaven while listening to a minstrel singing the *Life of Saint Alexius*. He made gifts of all his belongings in order to devote himself to voluntary poverty and evangelism, as was prescribed by the canonical text attributed to Matthew (19: 21): "Jesus said to him, 'If you would be perfect, go, sell what you possess and give to the poor'".

Around 1170, men and women assembled around Waldo and began to preach voluntary poverty within the strict framework of Catholic orthodoxy—without any possible collusion with Catharism, with the *pataria* (who were explicitly anti-clerical), or *a fortiori* with the Henricians, Petrobrusians or 'apostolics'.

The conflict began when Guichard—Archbishop of Lyon from 1165 to 1181—intent on guarding his privileges, prohibited the group from preaching. Waldo was summoned to Rome, where the Pope, scalded by the radicalism of the Patarins and attempting to support the archbishop, enjoined Waldo to preach only at the request of the clergy. Waldo ignored him. He was excommunicated and chased from Lyon by its next Archbishop, John of Canterbury, which was an error all the more unpardonable because, according to Thouzellier, Waldo had signed (at a regional synod held in Lyon in 1180) a profession of faith in which he confirmed his devotion to Roman Catholicism[1].

Between 1181 and 1184 there circulated a *Liber antihaeresis* that clearly opposed the true Christianity of the Waldensians to the non-Christian teachings of the Cathars. The partisans of Waldo were nevertheless summoned to Verona in 1184 and condemned as "pertinaces and schismatics" by a scornful decree that identified them with other heretics[2]. The repressive machine thereafter set in motion continued to massacre them until the seventeenth century with all the refinements of cruelty that tyrants usually reserve for their closest friends. Thouzellier dates the death of Peter Waldo to between 1206 and 1210; that of Gonnet to between 1205 and 1206[3].

The rapid expansion of the movement easily conquered Northern Italy, where Patarins and Cathars shared the loyalty of the population, which was unanimously hostile to the Roman clergy.

In 1205 Waldo probably witnessed the schism between the Italian and French branches of the movement. Preserving Waldo's doctrine, Giovanni di Ronco led the 'Poor of Lombardy'[4]. This group, sometimes known as the Roncolists, experienced further schisms. The 'del Prato' group that formed in Milan soon drew closer to Catholicism.

The main traditionalist sect in Italy recommended manual labor and recognized private property. In their practice if not in their doctrine, the Roncolists sometimes resembled popular Catharism. Italian Waldensianism soon gained the support of the *humiliati*, a kind of Patarin group that was very active in the workers' milieu (principally in the explicitly subversive class of the weavers). Innocent III was sufficiently canny to lend his support to these 'honest workers' in June 1201.[5] During the religious conference held at Pamiers that brought together the various French Waldensians (who were sometimes known as 'Leonists'), the organization and the certified orthodoxy of the *humiliati* influenced the schism of Durand of Huesca, who, after joining the party of Rome, founded the Order of the Poor Catholics and engaged in a crusade of apostolic virtue against the Cathars that was followed two years later, in 1209, by a more effective and better-armed crusade that was intended to propagate the truth in a forceful fashion. (Note that the *Opusculum contra haereticos* has been attributed to Durand of Huesca's companion, Ermangaudus.)

The Waldensian community continues to exist today, despite secular persecutions. It formed a distinctive Church among the Protestant currents.

The rupture with the Church of Rome gave Waldensian doctrine a more resolutely critical content. In the name of a practice that conformed with the morality of primitive Christianity, the Waldensians entered the ranks of the reformers.

According to them, the Church of Rome had become corrupt after Pope Sylvester [314–35]. They were indignant about the Cistercian philosopher Alain de Lille, for whom bad priests fulfilled their sacred roles perfectly well so long as they followed the rites. For Waldo's disciples, the validity of the sacraments depended on the inward purity of the priest who administered them.

They rejected the baptism of infants for the same reason that the Henricians and Petrobrusians did. They fought the sale of indulgences, founded penitence on personal contrition, and only consented to confess to men who were fundamentally good. For them the Mass, or communion through bread and wine, was meaningless unless it was administered in commemoration of the Last Supper, the meal that united Jesus and his friends.

The Waldensians estimated, as did Paul in his Epistle to the Corinthians, that it was better to marry than to burn with concupiscent ardor, and that, if there was to be a marriage, it should at least be founded on the mutual inclinations of the spouses.

Unlike the Cathars, the Waldensians recognized women as possessing the same rights as men. They denied the existence of purgatory, and they also held the widely accepted view that hell existed on earth and that—what with the conspiratorial conjunction of war, famine, poverty, massacres, and torture—there was no need of anywhere else for the infliction of these ravages.

The morals of the Waldensians approximated to the customs of the Cathars, but without tipping over into misogyny and a complete horror of sex. The Waldensians prohibited oaths, because they had only to answer to God. They condemned war and certain judicial practices, particularly corporeal punishment and the death penalty. Nevertheless, the remarks made by the Waldensian Raymond-Roger, the Count of Foix—who insisted to Bishop Jacques Fournier that "it is permitted to the secular power to execute or mutilate malefactors because without that there can be no peace and security among men"[6]—suggest that, had one or other of them been triumphant, both Catharism and Waldensianism would quickly have accommodated themselves to the cruel penal repressions of the period.

While Waldensianism was endlessly reborn from the pyres that were everywhere lit to annihilate it, and while it managed to spread to Provence, Languedoc, and Italy, and to reach Liège, Trier, Metz, Strasbourg, Mainz, and the Rhineland before touching Bavaria and Austria, pontifical power discovered in one adept of voluntary poverty an opportunity to recuperate—under the Church's control—the enterprise prematurely launched by Peter Waldo. Exalting a virtue that he knew to be fallible (forgiveness for failing to live up to it had to be purchased through the ecclesiastic market in redemption), Francis of Assisi (1182–25) proposed a syncretic order in which orthodoxy would preside over vows of poverty and act in defense of a universal fraternity (which now included the animals that the Cathars refused to kill).

In 1209 Innocent III approved the founding of an order [the Franciscans] in which both men and women were active (as was also the case with the Waldensians). Another ruling—one that was specifically devoted to lay people living in the world, even to those who were married—guaranteed a Catholic presence among the disadvantaged and 'dangerous' classes in the urban milieus.

Engaged on the side of the Dominicans in the crusade against the Cathars—in which their leniency was intended to temper the rigor of their 'brother preachers'—the Franciscans found the Waldensian heresy that they had hastily swallowed difficult to digest.

The observance of voluntary poverty very rapidly caused a divergence between the 'Conventuals', who maintained a respect for pontifical decisions, and the 'Spirituals', whose scorn for terrestrial goods increasingly came into conflict with an ecclesial politics that had been seduced by the solicitations of mercantile development and by the call to 'Get Rich'.

In 1254 a Spiritual from Pisa named Gerardo di Borgo San Donnino was inspired by the millenarian theories of Joachim of Fiore and, in his *Introduction to the Eternal Gospel*, predicted the imminent disappearance of the Roman Church and the advent of a Spiritual Church—the latter being in gestation within Franciscanism. Gerardo died after eighteen years of incarceration in harsh conditions, without ever repudiating his convictions.

He found disciples in Peter-John Olivi (1248–98), whose *Postilla in apocalypsim* announced the replacement of the Church of the Flesh (Rome) by the Church of the Spirit, and in Ubertino of Casale (approximately 1259–1320), who preached in Perugia against the Pope and the monarchy, and who called the Church "Babylon, the great whore who destroys humanity and poisons it, delivering it up to the pleasures of the flesh, and to pride and avarice"[7].

Forced into exile to escape the resentment of Pope John XXII, who strove to decimate the party of the Spirituals, Ubertino of Casale—when he served as an Inquisitor in Tuscany, in the valley of Spoleto, and in the region of Ancona—still cracked down on the Free Spirit, which seduced a dissident group within the Spirituals (that is say, the Fraticelles).

Within the diversity of forms taken by the doctrine of voluntary poverty, Beghardism and the movement of the *Pastoureaux* [the shepherd boys] responded in diametrically opposed ways to the social problems caused by the growing pauperization of the towns and the countryside, but they shared a refusal of Waldensianism.

While the Beghards and Beguines rapidly distanced themselves from the Catholicism from which they had originally emanated and became devoted to the teachings of the Free Spirit, the crusade of the *Pastoureaux*—with its pillaging and anti-Semitism—was part of the same tradition as the raids against Islam that the papacy had encouraged under the name 'Crusades'. In a predictable return of certain enthusiasms that was caused by the Crusaders' failure and disarray, the movement of the *Pastoureaux* turned the weapons of purification (which had previously been aimed at Muslims) against priests and 'bad Christians'. Norman Cohn reports in *The Pursuit of the Millennium*[8]:

> At Easter 1251 three men began to preach the crusade in Picardy and within a few days their summons had spread to Brabant, Flanders and Hainaut—lands beyond the frontiers of the French kingdom, but where the masses were still as hungry for a messiah [...]. One of these men was a renegade monk called Jacob, who was said to have come from Hungary and was known as the 'Master of Hungary'. He was a thin, pale, bearded ascetic of some sixty years of age, a man of commanding bearing and able to speak with great eloquence in French, German and Latin. He claimed that the Virgin Mary, surrounded by a host of angels, had appeared to him and had given him a letter—which he always carried in his hand, as Peter the Hermit is said to have carried a similar document. According to Jacob, the letter summoned all shepherds to help King Louis to free the Holy Sepulchre. God, he proclaimed, was displeased with the pride and ostentation of the French knights and had chosen the lowly to carry out his work. It was to shepherds that the glad tidings of the Nativity had first been made known and it was through shepherds that the Lord was now about to manifest his power and glory.
>
> Shepherds and cowherds—young men, boys and girls alike—deserted their flocks and, without taking leave of their parents, gathered under the strange banners on which the miraculous visitation of the Virgin was portrayed. Before long thieves, prostitutes, outlaws, apostate monks and murderers joined them; and these elements provided the leaders. But many of these newcomers too dressed as shepherds and all alike became known as the *Pastoureaux*. Soon there was an army which—though the contemporary estimate of 60,000 need not be taken seriously—must certainly have numbered many thousands. It was divided into fifty companies; these marched separately, armed with pitchforks, hatchets, daggers, pikes carried aloft as they entered towns and villages, so as to intimidate the authorities. When they ran short of provisions they took what they needed by force; but much was given freely for—as emerges from many different accounts—people revered the *Pastoureaux* as holy men.

[...] Surrounded by an armed guard, Jacob preached against the clergy, attacking the Mendicants as hypocrites and vagabonds, the Cistercians as lovers of land and property, the Premonstratensians as proud and gluttonous, the canons regular as half-secular fast-breakers [...]. His followers were taught to regard the sacraments with contempt and to see in their own gatherings the sole embodiment of truth. For himself he claimed that he could not only see visions but could heal the sick—and people brought their sick to be touched by him. He declared that food and wine set before his men never grew less, but rather increased as they were eaten and drunk (again the 'messianic banquet'!) He promised that when the crusaders arrived at the sea the water would roll back before them and they would march dryshod to the Holy Land. On the strength of his miraculous powers he arrogated to himself the right to grant absolution from every kind of sin. If a man and a woman amongst his followers wished to marry he would perform the ceremony; and if they wished to part he would divorce them with equal ease. He was said to have married eleven men to one woman—an arrangement reminiscent of Tanchelm and which suggests that Jacob, too, saw himself as a 'living Christ' requiring 'disciples' and a 'Virgin Mary'. And Jacob's bodyguard behaved exactly like Tanchelm's. If anyone contradicted the leader he was at once struck down. The murder of a priest was regarded as particularly praiseworthy; according to Jacob it could be atoned for by a drink of wine. It is not surprising that the clergy watched the spread of this movement with horror.

Jacob's army went first to Amiens, where it met with an enthusiastic reception. The burghers put their food and drink at the disposal of the crusaders, calling them the holiest of men. Jacob made such a favorable impression that they begged him to help himself to their belongings. Some knelt down before him 'as though he had been the Body of Christ'. After Amiens the army split up into two groups. One of these marched on Rouen, where it was able to disperse a synod which was meeting there under the Archbishop. The other group proceeded to Paris. There Jacob so fascinated the Queen Mother Blanche that she loaded him with presents and left him free to do whatever he would. Jacob now dressed as a bishop, preached in churches, sprinkled holy water after some strange rite of his own. Meanwhile while the *Pastoureaux* in the city began to attack the clergy, putting many to the sword and drowning many in the Seine. The students of the University—who of course were also clerics, though in minor orders—would have been massacred if the bridge had not been closed in time.

When the *Pastoureaux* left Paris they moved in a number of bands, each under the leadership of a 'Master', who, as they passed through towns and villages, blessed the crowds. At Tours the crusaders again attacked the clergy, especially Dominican and Franciscan friars, whom they dragged and whipped through the streets. The Dominicans' church was looted, the Franciscan friary was attacked and broken into. The old contempt for sacraments administered by unworthy hands showed itself: the host was seized and, amidst insults, thrown on to the street. All this was done with the approval and support of the populace. At Orleans similar scenes occurred. Here the Bishop had the gates closed against the oncoming horde, but the burghers deliberately disobeyed him and admitted the *Pastoureaux* into the town. Jacob preached in public, and a scholar from the cathedral school who dared to oppose him was struck down with an axe. The *Pastoureaux* rushed to the houses where the priests and monks had hidden themselves, stormed them and burned many to the ground. Many clergy, including teachers at the University, and many burghers were struck down or drowned in the Loire. The remaining clergy were forced out of the town. When the *Pastoureaux* left the town the Bishop, enraged at the reception that had been accorded them, put Orleans under interdict. It was indeed the opinion of contemporaries that the *Pastoureaux* owed their prestige very largely to their habit of killing and despoiling priests. When the clergy tried to protest or resist they found no support amongst the populace. It is understandable that some clerics, observing the activities of the *Pastoureaux*, felt that the Church had never been in greater danger.

At Bourges the fortunes of the *Pastoureaux* began to change. Here too the burghers, disobeying their Archbishop, admitted as many of the horde as the town could hold; the rest remaining encamped outside. Jacob preached this time against the Jews and sent his men to destroy the Sacred Rolls. The crusaders also pillaged houses throughout the town, taking gold and silver where they found it and raping any woman they could lay hands on. If the clergy were not molested it was only because they remained in hiding. By this time the Queen Mother had realised what sort of movement this was and had outlawed all those taking part in it. When this news reached Bourges many *Pastoureaux* deserted. At length, one day when Jacob was thundering against the laxity of the clergy and calling upon the townsfolk to turn against them, someone in the crowd dared to contradict him. Jacob rushed at the man with a sword and killed him; but this was too much for the burghers, who in their turn took up arms and chased the unruly visitors from the town.

Now it was the turn of the *Pastoureaux* to suffer violence. Jacob was pursued by mounted burghers and cut to pieces. Many of his followers were captured by the royal officials at Bourges and hanged. Bands of survivors made their way to Marseilles and to Aigues Mortes, where they hoped to embark for the Holy Land; but both towns had received warnings from Bourges and the *Pastoureaux* were caught and hanged. A final band reached Bordeaux but only to be met there by English forces under the Governor of Gascony, Simon de Montfort, and dispersed. Their leader, attempting to embark for the East, was recognised by some sailors and drowned. One of his lieutenants fled to England and having landed at Shoreham collected a following of some hundreds of peasants and shepherds. When the news of these happenings reached King Henry III he was sufficiently alarmed to issue instructions for the suppression of the movement to sheriffs throughout the kingdom. But very soon the whole movement disintegrated, even the apostle at Shoreham being torn to pieces by his own followers. Once everything was over rumours sprang up on all sides. It was said that the movement had been a plot of the Sultan's, who had paid Jacob to bring him Christian men and youths as slaves. Jacob and other leaders were said to have been Mahometans who had won ascendancy over Christians by means of black magic. But there were also those who believed that at the time of its suppression the movement of the *Pastoureaux* had broached only the first part of its programme. These people said that the leaders of the *Pastoureaux* had intended to massacre first all priests and monks, then all knights and nobles; and when all authority had been overthrown, to spread their teaching throughout the world.

Less than a century later, the fear and resentment aroused by those who had been rendered destitute by the Crusades (as Jacob and his

Pastoureaux had been, hence their rage and vindictiveness) secretly fuelled the hatred that fell upon other inheritors of the legacy of the Crusades. But this time it was the privileged factions, the bankers of the French state, who were burned alive by bankrupted account holders in front of Notre-Dame in Paris in 1310. Characterized as heretics and sorcerers, the Templars were thrown into the same inferno as the other servants—humble and powerful alike—of a power that no longer perceived the utility of their services and that opportunely disposed of the witnesses to its turpitude.

CHAPTER THIRTY-ONE

The Movement of the Free Spirit

In opposition to the religious system that captured beings and things so as to 'bind' [*relier*] them (in accordance with the meaning of *religio*) to a temporal power that drew its justification from a heavenly transcendence, the 'Movement of the Free Spirit' (active from the thirteenth to the seventeenth centuries) designates an ensemble of options that were more individual than collective and were determined to privilege relations with the earth, the body, desire, and the flux of life that nature ceaselessly regenerates.

Only the theses of Simon of Samaria, reported by the *Elenchos*, shared these aspirations, which discover in natural irreligion the raw materials of desires that must be refined in order for them to attain a veritable humanity.

The conception of a relational unity with nature—perfectible on earth and in the individual, attained not through the paths of asceticism and renunciation but, on the contrary, through pleasure in oneself and in others—escaped from the syzygy of orthodoxy and heterodoxy.

In its radical form the attitude labeled 'Free Spirit' by the Inquisitors, who struggled in their efforts to define it, did not fit easily into their taxonomy of heresies. It belonged instead to the project of the total man—a project as old in its hopes as are the wanderings of a mankind that has been separated from itself by an economy that exploits it.

Infiltrating the Catholic convents, the Beguine convents, and the Franciscan orders, as well as seducing the clergy attached to Christianity or to Catholicism, the spirit of freedom took on aspects that conformed more closely with the dominant discourse; the refinement of desire was replaced by the passing fancies of those who, identifying themselves with God, wanted to satisfy themselves in the ways that are common to all tyrants.

The Amalricians[1]

The ecclesiastic concern with identifying behaviors that escaped the control of the Catholic Church with a particular heresy resulted in the grouping together, under the name Amalricians (that is, the disciples of Amalric of Bena), various clerics, many of whom were parish priests in villages situated not far from Paris (Vieux-Corbeil, La Celle, Ursines, Lorris, and Saint-Cloud).

Originally from Bena, near Chartres, Master Amalric taught in Paris, where one of his assertions stirred up controversy at the heart of the university. In 1204 his thesis that all Christians were members of Christ and had actually suffered the torture of the cross with him were submitted to the Pope, who condemned it. Amalric abjured his faith and died around 1207. Struck down by a simple pontifical reprobation, Amalric's conception was not, in itself, particularly subversive. And yet it became so because it translated into theological jargon the concrete reality lived by ordinary people, the reality that was quite brutally evoked by the Amalricians put on trial in 1210 and 1211: if Christ died for the sins of humanity, then each person was exempted from having to pay off his or her sins a second time through suffering, renunciation, contrition, guilt, penitence, and submission to the Church.

Ten of the accused perished on the pyre; four were condemned to prison in perpetuity. In 1211 Master Godin, cleric of Amiens, was burned for having propagated Amalrician ideas[2], which the Fourth Council of Lateran (1215) condemned as "not so much heretical as insane"[3]. A revealing formula: beyond heresy, the negative province of orthodoxy's own territory, there existed only what was 'beyond sense'.

Among the eighty victims executed by fire in Strasbourg in 1215, there were Waldensians and Cathars who were accused of affirming that "the grossest sins are permitted and are in accordance with nature"[4].

In 1216 there appeared in Alsace and Thuringia "a new and shameful heresy": "Its supporters were convinced that it was permissible, and in conformity with nature, to eat meat and other foodstuffs any day and in any season, and even to indulge in every kind of sensual pleasure without being obliged to expiate it"[5].

An unknown person was burned in Troyes in 1220 for claiming that the Holy Spirit was incarnated within him. He shared the conviction of the knight who fought against Thomas Aquinas and declared to him: "If Saint Peter was saved, I will be too, because the same spirit lives in him and in me".

It's worth recalling that, at a time when the comportment of the majority of people was affected by neither the mixture of terror and controlled hope that was propagated by the Church of Rome, nor by the ascetic rigor that was extolled by the Cistercian missionaries, the Cathars, and the Waldensians, most people rallied instead around the popular and summary credo: 'Enjoy life and mock everything else'.

The Goliards (wandering clerics) mocked the Church, parodied the evangelical texts, and sang the Mass of the God Bacchus: "Introibo ad altare Bacchi, ad Deum qui laetificat cor hominis"[6].

In the eleventh century, Guibert of Nogent (1053–1124) vituperated a noble who was unconcerned with religion. This nobleman, who was titled the Count Jean de Soissons and was a friend of the Jews (and note that Guibert had written a work called *On the Incarnation Against the Jews*), treated the Passion of the Christ as if it was a lie; he affirmed that he only frequented the church to amuse himself by watching the beautiful women who came there to pass the night. According to the Count, there was no sin in making love. On the point of death, he declared to his confessor: "You want, I can see, that I should give my goods to parasites—that is to say, to the priests. They will get only a pittance"[7].

In the thirteenth century, speaking of students who were contemporaries of Amalric, Petrus Comestor wrote: "In eating and drinking they have no equals. They are ravenous at [the] table, but far from devout at

Mass. At work, they yawn; at a banquet, they fear no one. They abhor thinking about the sacred books, but they love seeing the wine sparkling in their glass and swallow it down undaunted"[8].

This assessment, which was in fact applicable to all strata of society, only ended up authenticating (from certain points of view) the native weakness of mankind and ratifying the Church's resolution to shoulder and absolve mankind's sins in exchange for gratuities and obedience.

The Waldensians and Cathars, who did without the Church's services, were formidable competition, but what could one say of people who pushed insolence as far as proclaiming that each person had the right to follow his or her own desires, without bearing anything else in mind and without experiencing the least guilt?

What did John, a priest from Ursines, teach his parishioners? That God made everything, evil as well as good. What was the good of worrying when both evil and good emanated from God?

A certain Garnier de Rochefort summarized the Amalrician doctrine in his *Contra Amaurianos*. In this work he makes clear that, according to the Amalricians, whoever understands that God accomplished everything by Himself can make love without sinning. God being in each person, attaining inward revelation is all that is required in order for one to behave according to His intentions in whatever one does. Such was the pantheism that—once its philosophical implications became clear—led to the condemnation of Scotus Eriugena, David of Dinant, and Aristotle in 1215.

William the Goldsmith, who was designated the group's master thinker, advanced the notion that, "five years from now, all men will be Spirituals, and they all be able to say: 'I am the Holy Spirit' and 'Before Abraham was, I was', just as Christ was able to say, 'I am the son of God' and 'Before Abraham was born, I was'"[9].

For the first time, it seemed, the doctrine of Joachim of Fiore had found its subversive uses.

In his *Philippide*, William the Breton indicated the point—i.e. the beginning of the thirteenth century—at which the time of the saints announced by Joachim coincided with a freedom of spirit that was identical to the consciousness that each person could have of the divine presence acting within him or her and tracing out the path of perfection and impeccability (note that the idea of the *Sophia* or divine spark enclosed in each person was, after more than a millennium, still connected to Gnosticism):

> They thus said that the sacraments of the New Testament came to an end in our epoch, and that the period of the Holy Spirit had started, in which there was no place for confession, baptism, Eucharist and the other guarantees of salvation. Henceforth, there would be no salvation except by the inward grace of the Holy Spirit, with no outward works. And they thought of the virtue of charity in such a broad sense that they ensured that every act regarded as a sin ceased to be so if it was performed out of charity. This is why they devoted themselves, in the name of charity, to debauchery, adultery and all the other pleasures of the body. And they promised impunity [penitence was unnecessary] to the women with whom they sinned and to the simple people whom they misled, preaching that God is a being of goodness and not a judge.[10]

A sermon by Johannes Teutonicus, the Abbot of Saint-Victor in Paris from 1203 to 1229, emphasized the traits that were most shocking to Christians and Catholics:

> Look at these profane novelties, propagated by people who are disciples of Epicurus rather than Christ. With fearsome treachery, they are secretly committed to spreading the belief that one can sin with impunity. They are convinced that there is no sin, and that, therefore, there is no one who ought to be punished by God for having offended. Although outwardly, on their faces and in their speech, they can affect an air of piety, inwardly, in their spirit and their secret works, they reject virtue.[11]
>
> An accumulation of the most extreme folly and the most shameless lies: they neither fear nor blush to assert that they are God! Infinite extravagance! Abominable presumption! They call God the adulterous man, the companion of other men's beds, the being defiled by all kinds of infamy, the receptacle of all crimes. This surpasses the aberrations of the gentiles, who lied more modestly when they claimed that the greatest of their princes

would become gods after their death. Assuredly, anyone who could say "God does not exist" is talking raving nonsense. But the individual who claims "I am God" is even more insane.

Oh, let us hope at least that such a plague does not pollute this city, the source of all learning and the true flower of wisdom![12]

If pantheism could be summarized by the formula *Deus sive natura* [God or nature], the Free Spirit implied the identification *Deus sive homo* [God or man]. The question 'What God and what omnipotence?' required a preliminary clarification: 'What behavioral choices should the justified individual follow?'

Wasn't the sovereigns' and princes' thirst for power authorized and legitimated by divine will? There was an oft-discerned tendency in the Free Spirit to certify a similar power—or something that was claimed to be such—by way of self-deification. A radically different tendency was expressed, however, by the doctrines of 'pure love' or 'refined love'.

'Fin amor'

Hadewijch of Antwerp—whose exegetes, more concerned with religion than with history, have improperly added her to their pantheon of the devout—mentioned in her "List of Perfect Ones" the Beguine Aleydis, who was condemned to the pyre by Robert le Bougre[13] because of her concept of 'just love'. Unlike the Waldensians burned at Cambrai in 1236 by that sinister hunter of heretics, Aleydis was alleged to have professed Amalrician ideas, which were to be found in the towns along the Rhine (Cologne, Mainz, and Strasbourg) and in the northern cities (Valenciennes, Amiens, Cambrai, Tournai, Brussels, and Antwerp).

The doctrine of pure love (which, fifty years later, Marguerite Porete identified with the life force through which human nature liberated itself from its alienation from nature [*sa dénaturation*] in order to blend itself with the will of a Good God) haunted the poems and visions of Hadewijch of Antwerp and several Cistercian Monials in the North, without it being possible to say for sure whether pure love was spiritual ecstasy—an *amor extaticus*—an exaltation of amorous pleasure, or, as in the diverse variants of Tantrism, a combination of the two.

The bawdiness of the times, from which only a segment of the bourgeoisie and a few defenders of clerical austerity escaped, was engaged in to an equal extent in cottages, convents, castles and churches (as is attested to by various fables, literary works, and historical chronicles). The typical obstacles to such bawdiness were feelings of guilt, contrition, and remorse, which fed the coffers of penitential redemption and the market in indulgences.

The union with the Spirit or, in its Christian form, the Christ—alias the *pneuma* or *Sophia*—was revealed in the eyes of the adepts of the Free Spirit as being identical to the union of man and woman, to the *koinos* [the shared-in-common] that was evoked by the Hermetic writings of Asclepius and by the Gospel attributed to Philip. Amorous pleasure, identified with a finally renewed unity between the body and the spirit, regenerated the Adamite state, the state of innocence in which there existed neither sin nor guilt. This is why, from the poorest people to the aristocracy, the Free Spirit gained support—support that, to the great disappointment of the inquisitorial police, was most often undetectable, because the supporters of the Free Spirit, unconcerned with sacrifice, behaved prudently and, with rare exceptions, neither preached nor issued propaganda.

The New Spirit in Swabia

A text titled *Determinatio de novo spiritio*, attributed to Albert the Great and intended for use by the Inquisitors, sounded the alarm about a contemporary tendency that, though neither Catharist nor Waldensian, did not (for all that) present any less of a threat to religion, be that in Rome or elsewhere.

Albert's denunciation implicated several convents in the Ries the region neighboring Augsburg, Nördlingen, Olmütz, and Tübingen.

In 1245, after the first Council of Lyon, the Bishop of Olmütz deplored the presence in his diocese of wandering agitators of both genders, dressed like religious people but hostile to the ecclesiastic hierarchy and espousing the idea that God should be served in absolute freedom.[14]

Such reformers, who were closer to courtly ideas than to Cistercian asceticism, easily won over to their teachings a number of ecclesial communities that had been split between guilty debauchery and puritanical hysteria.

Did they not offer the peace of the heart and the grace of the spirit to the amorous inclination that brought naturally passionate men and women towards each other?

Among the articles in the list of charges set out by Albert, many left no doubt about the loudly proclaimed innocence of those relations that the Church, the various ascetic heterodoxies, and lay morality saddled with guilt.

> Man can be united with God in such a way that he no longer sins, whatever he does.
>
> According to them, there are no angels apart from human virtues, no demons except men's sins and vices. There is no hell. All creation is God in his plenitude. The angels would not have fallen if they had behaved as they should have in their union with Lucifer.[15]
>
> Man united with God, as they claim to be, is not bound to accord honor or respect to the saints, or to observe fasts and similar things on the day of the Lord.
>
> Whoever is united with God can assuage his carnal desire with impunity and in any way, with either sex, and even by inverting the roles.
>
> There is no need to believe in the Resurrection. [...][16]
>
> They assert that, during the elevation of the Host, they are themselves elevated; whether they are seated or standing, it is to themselves that they address the signs of reverence, but they perform all the usual gestures in order not to scandalize others.
>
> People hinder and retard their perfection and their good qualities when they indulge in fasting, flagellation, discipline, vigils and similar things.
>
> It is not right to take part in work, but it is good to taste the sweetness of the Lord in leisure.[17] Prayers have no validity when they are under the yoke of manual labor.[18] [...]
>
> Those of them who want to become perfect do not have to think about the Passion of the Christ.
>
> There is no need to feel concern, neither sorrow nor bitterness, at faults committed and days wasted. Suffering of this sort retards their access to a fuller grace.

In their view, the blood of good men like themselves, or of others who had achieved a similar level of completeness, ought to be venerated in the same way as the body and blood of Christ on the altar. They are convinced that freedom, evil, rest and bodily well-being create in man a place and habitation for the Holy Spirit.[19]

They say that Christ knows them carnally, that a woman can become God, that a mother of five children can be a virgin[20], that one of them had suckled the baby Jesus with his mother until she was exhausted and faint.[21]

Love was at the center of the debate that agitated the most advanced minds of the twelfth and thirteenth centuries. The privileged place of women—recognized for the first time in history—posed the question of the refinement of morals, of an approach to sexuality that was confined neither to the banal rule of repression (with its morbid and mortiferous visions) nor to desublimation (with its procession of rapes and cruelties). The *dolce stil nuovo* and the erotica of the troubadours, so uncertain in their daily practices, suggest a preoccupation that the end of the twentieth century has barely begun to rediscover and that was mythologically sketched out by Dante's path of initiation to Beatrice[22]. It is therefore fitting to strip away the theological clutter and falsifications that encumber the works of Hadewijch of Antwerp and Marguerite Porete, works that the religious prejudices of the scholars have remained content to conceal beneath a moth-eaten cover of mysticism.

Marguerite Porete[23]

Originally from Hainault, Marguerite Porete probably belonged to a comfortable and cultivated milieu, perhaps the court of Bourgogne. She was a resident of Mons, where the Countess Philippa de Hainault—the daughter of Guillaume d'Avesnes—was considered to be a refined spirit, attached to courtly ideas.

Perhaps Marguerite was a Beguine before breaking with the entirety of the clergy: "Beguines will say that I am in error, [as do] priests, clerics and preachers, Augustinians and Carmelites, and the Minor friars"[24].

At the end of the 1290s her work on "the person of refined love" was burned at Valenciennes on the orders of Gui II de Colmieu (Guido of Collemezzo), the Bishop of Cambrai from 1296 to 1306, who prohibited the author from circulating further books or doctrines.

Nevertheless, she relapsed and—as a provocation or in innocence?—sent a copy of a book entitled *The Mirror of Simple Souls* to the bishop of Châlons-sur-Marne. Denounced to the Inquisition, she appeared in 1307 before Guillaume Humbert, the Inquisitor General of France, who was the confessor of Philip the Fair and the future accomplice of Philippe de Marigny in the extermination proceedings conducted against the Templars.

Marguerite refused to take an oath, not in the manner of the Waldensians or the Cathars but because "the free soul does not respond to anyone if it does not want to"[25].

On 11 April 1310 she was judged to be a heretic and a recidivist. Fifteen extracts from her book, which was condemned, were subsequently used in the redaction of the *Ad nostrum* that—at the time of the 1311 Council of Vienne—listed the principal charges against the Beghards and Beguines who were sullied by the Free Spirit. She was delivered to the flames in Paris on 1 June 1310. Her companion or lover, Guion de Cressonaert, a cleric of the Cambrian diocese who called himself the angel of Philadelphia, was apprehended and condemned to prison in perpetuity for having tried to save her. (Note that, in the name 'angel of Philadelphia', there may have been a reference to the Church of Philadelphia, one of the Bogomil Churches still active in the Balkans.)

The text of *The Mirror of Simple Souls*, which is preserved in the library of the Condé Museum in Chantilly and has been published by Romana Guarnieri[26], reveals the presence of some stylistically trite interpolations. The orthodoxy of these interpolations presented an advantage over the (lost) original, in that they facilitated the book's circulation during subsequent periods in which the mystical speculations of people like Jan van Ruysbroeck and Gerhardt Groote were removing the subversive character of Marguerite's propositions.

On the other hand, it is undeniable that the most audacious theses of *The Mirror* reflect a mindset that was common in Germany and even in the region of Langres, where the Franciscan Inquisitor Nicholas of Lyra, one of Porete's accusers, fulminated against heretics who, by advocating the notion that one need not listen to the prophets but simply live freely according to the needs of the flesh, "propagated their own impurities under the cloak of devotion"[27].

Marguerite did not identify God with nature such as it reigns in the wild state of mankind and the animals, but with a refinement of human nature that, stripped of its envelope [*sa gangue*], accedes to a state of perfection or purity comparable to that of the philosopher's stone.

In spite of being stuffed with interpolations prescribed by the orthodox milieus, the text of *The Mirror* is one of the rare testimonies of the Free Spirit that—perhaps because of the canonical revisions made to it—was spared from the Church's destructive zeal. In its initial iteration, moreover, Marguerite's doctrine did not differ from the mysticism of Eckhart, Beatrice of Nazareth, or Mechthild of Magdeburg: "the soul touched by grace is without sin"[28]. According to the *scala perfectionis* [the scale of perfection], seven initiatory graces lead the *pneuma* to the enjoyment of God, the remanence of the seven planets of the Hebdomad, beyond which begins the Ogdoad or Pleroma.

Annihilated in God, the soul loses its will, its desires, and its essence, and identities itself with the totality, with the Pleroma. Here Porete went beyond the limits of ecstatic love, of the beatific vision into which the mystics sank. For the effusion that she described, which was established in the enjoyment of God, conferred freedom upon the love that was the divine presence of life, acting in the multiplicity of its desires.

> And also, why should such souls scruple to take what they need when necessity demands it? It would be a loss of innocence for these souls, and troubling to the peace in which the soul has drawn back from all things. Who should scruple to take what he needs from the four elements, taking light from the sky, heat from fire, dew from water and support from the earth? We take the service of the four elements in all the ways that Nature has needs, without the reproach of Reason; these gracious elements are made by God, like all other things; and thus such souls use all things made and created of which Nature has need, in the same peace of heart as they use the earth on which they walk.[29]

One has to create a nature in which the God of goodness is reincarnated after being obliterated by the avatar of the Demiurge Ialdabaoth, who perpetuated the God of the Roman Church, which Marguerite called the Small Church. The one who, through the grace of love, incorporates into himself the manifestation of such a God possesses the *Megale Dynamis* of which Simon of Samaria spoke. It falls to this person to develop it so as to found a new Edenic innocence on earth.

To the antiphysis of Catholicism Marguerite opposed a rehabilitation of the state of nature before the fall—before the intervention of sin and guilt. To awaken in oneself the sleeping God was to emancipate oneself from all social constraints in order to give to desire the freedoms of nature.

To describe Porete as a quietist is to read her with the spectacles of a theologian. A horror of sexuality was successfully propagated everywhere in the seventeenth century, but in the thirteenth century this horror was a mere dead letter and the topic of vain chatter in the sermons of clerics who were openly living with their lovers and enjoying sexual freedom. The terrible, grimacing face of sin only truly began to impose itself in the fifteenth century, as a result of the market in death and promotional morbidity. Unlike Teresa of Ávila, Antoinette Bourignon, and Jeanne-Marie Bouvier de la Motte Guyon[30], Porete pressed into the annihilation of the soul a reinvention of the body, on which love conferred the mark of its omnipotence.

Heilwige Bloemardinne[31]

Marguerite's doctrine and 'fin amor' were illustrated in Brussels in the first years of the fourteenth century by the mysterious preeminence of a woman whose reputation held in check an Inquisition that was, it is true, often discouraged by the liberal politics of the opulent cities.

Of Heilwige Bloemardinne[32] there remain only the popular legend of a thaumaturge revered by the people and the notables, a few biographical references, and the pages that her enemies devoted to her.

The daughter of an alderman named Guillaume Bloemart (he died sometime between 1283 and 1287) and a member of a family that was among the most influential in Brussels, Heilwige must have been born between 1250 and 1260 or between 1283 and 1287; her death certificate carries the date 23 August 1335.

While he was still a parish priest at St. Gudula, the mystic Jan van Ruysbroeck—later suspected of harboring Free Spirit sympathies by Jean Charlier de Gerson—engaged in a lively polemic against Heilwige. Tradition tells us that such animosity forced her to flee Brussels under popular pressure, and to seek refuge in Groenendael Abbey (Vaux-Vert), in which she passed the rest of life.

In his biography of Jan van Ruysbroeck, Henry Pomerius[33] collected the testimonies of Jan van Schoonhoven, Ruysbroeck's companion and successor:

> In Brussels, when the servant of God [Ruysbroeck] was a secular priest there, there was a woman of perverse beliefs, whom the people called Bloemardinne. She had acquired such a reputation that when she approached the altar to take Holy Communion, she was popularly believed to be flanked on each side by seraphim.
>
> She had written much on the spirit of freedom and on the most infamous carnal love, which she called seraphic love. Her many disciples, who shared her beliefs, venerated her as the originator of a new doctrine.
>
> It was said that when she wrote or taught she sat in a chair made of silver.[34] After her death the chair was said to have been offered to the duchess of Brabant, in the belief that it was still imbued with Bloemardinne's thought. Similarly, the maimed touched her dead body in the belief that they might thereby be healed.
>
> Being a man of true piety, he [Ruysbroeck] suffered to see error so widespread, and he rose once again against the perversity of this doctrine and, though her followers were very numerous, he unmasked writings which, under the guise of truth, contained nothing but heresies, which Bloemardinne, contemptuous of our faith, had for so long attributed to divine inspiration. In this, he demonstrated both wisdom and courage, showing himself unafraid of the difficulties placed in his way by Bloemardinne's followers, and refusing to allow himself to be taken in by the look and smell of truth of these false doctrines. I can attest from personal experience that these wicked writings were, to begin with, clothed in a veil of truth, to such an extent that

no one could have revealed the seed of error in them without grace and the aid of Him who teaches all truth.[35]

Though he didn't name her, Bloemardinne was the one who affirmed the unity of carnal and seraphic love, which was rejected by Ruysbroeck in *The Adornment of Spiritual Marriages*:

> But to them they are exalted above all the choirs of saints and angels and above all rewards, which can be merited in any way. And therefore they say that they can never grow more virtuous, that they can never deserve a greater reward and that they can never commit a sin. For they live without will, and they have relinquished to God their spirit devoted to repose and idleness; they are one with God and have been reduced to nothing themselves. And therefore they may freely consent to the desires of nature, for they have attained innocence, and laws do not apply to them. Henceforth, if nature is inclined to do what gives satisfaction, and if, in order to resist it, [the] idleness of their spirits must be in some way diverted or hindered, they obey the instincts of nature, so that their spirits' idleness will remain unhindered. Thus, they pay no attention to fasting or saints' days, or to any commandment or precept whatever, save for the sake of men's opinion: for in all things they live their lives without conscience.[36]

William Cornelius of Antwerp, Voluntarily Poor Man and Adept of the Free Spirit

When they were not oppressing the people in the name of a power emanating from Rome, the members of the lower clergy willingly made common cause with the oppressed. William Cornelius seems to had have a reputation among the agitated population of weavers in Antwerp as a man of integrity whose advice was valued because he was less concerned with the Church's interests than with the lot of the simple people whom the Church wanted to rule. His title 'Master' appears in the deed of a gift from the chaplain of the church of Notre-Dame of Antwerp in 1243. According to his slanderer, Thomas de Cantimpré, William benefited from a prebend that he later renounced in order to found a movement of voluntary poverty.

Cornelius added to Waldensian asceticism a program that sought to reform the sale of indulgences. Working against oppression by the dominant class, he also propagated the idea that poverty washes away all sin. The official charges against him summarized his doctrine as follows:

> The indulgences of prelates do not help souls.[37]
> No one can give alms [if they deduct them] from their own surplus.[38]
> No rich man can be saved, and all the rich are miserly.[39]
> It is permissible to take from the rich and give to the poor.[40]
> No poor person can be damned, for they will all be saved.
> There is no hell after Judgment Day.[41]
> As rust is consumed by fire, so all sin is consumed by poverty and annulled in the eyes of God.[42]
> Simple fornication is not a sin for those who live in poverty.[43]
> There are only three mortal sins: envy, avarice and ostentatious prodigality[44]; and also having one's wife when she is pregnant.[45]
> That which is called sin against nature is not a sin.[46]
> No man should take his wife more three times a week.[47]

The last article calls for a remark. To the freedom in matters of sexual relations that prevailed among the weavers, Cornelius attempted to add respect for women, which was the very principle of the refinement of love. As against the misogyny shared by the bourgeoisie and its fabliaux, he proposed a code of courtesy in which women were neither the objects of rape nor spiritualized subjects. The state of poverty, voluntary or otherwise, accorded them the right to give themselves to whoever pleased them (the crime characterized as 'fornication' by the clerical police) and to refuse if they judged it good to do so. This parish priest thereby made himself the spokesman of the female workers—the same ones whose miserable existence was evoked by Chrétien de Troyes—who were exhausted by labor at the workshops to the point of occasionally regarding as inopportune the constant solicitations of men infatuated with their own virile prowess.

Such ideas, which were propagated from 1240 to the end of the thirteenth century in Antwerp and Brabant, illuminated the writings of Hadewijch and her international group, which she called "The New Ones" (*De Nuwen*).

Around 1243, Cornelius' agitation took advantage of a conflict that set the people of Antwerp against the bishops of Cambrai (to which Antwerp was subordinate), who were accused of corruption and tyranny.

At the instigation of the Dominicans, who reproached him for his lack of zeal in the struggle against heresy, Guyard of Laon, a bishop of Cambrai, resolved in 1248 to crack down on William's partisans. On 23 June sickness overtook Guyard at the Abbey of Affligem, where he died on 16 September. Bishop Nicholas of Fontaines, who succeeded him in 1249, organized and personally financed the repression.

William's natural death—around 1253—did not discourage the ardor of his partisans. Nor did Nicholas of Fontaines succeed in doing so, even when, in 1257, he exhumed and burned the body of the man who was a priest-worker before there were priest-workers properly speaking. In 1280 the Dominicans were still roaming the Brabant, where Duke John ordered his subjects and officers to put themselves at their service whenever they required it.

CHAPTER THIRTY-TWO

Beghards and Beguines

Around the end of the twelfth century, associations that were both religious and secular were founded, most often on the initiative of magistrates or rich bourgeois. The members of these associations, designated by the names 'Beghards' and 'Beguines', lived in communitarian houses called 'beguinages'.

Founded as a public service to contain the increase of poor people in the towns, which drained the surplus of manpower from the countryside, these communities were independent of all monastic orders and were placed under the exclusive control of the local bishops. The influx of beggars of both genders continued to increase, especially in northern towns such as Liège, where the first such establishments started up between 1180 and 1184 (and were therefore contemporaneous with the initiatives of Peter Waldo in Lyon), Tienen (1202), Valenciennes (1212), Douai (1219), Ghent (1227), and Antwerp (1230). In 1250 there were more than 1,000 adherents in Paris and Cambrai, and 2,000 in Cologne.

Mixing together individual and communitarian interests, the current of the Free Spirit caused ripples in the beguinages, which Jundt paints in an idyllic tableau:

> In France and Germany the Beguines lived in great numbers in the same house, whereas in Belgium their habitation recalls to us less a cloister than

one of our modern workers' cities: they were composed (and are still composed today) of a series of small houses, each of which held no more than two or three Beguines; at the center a church and a hospital for aged or sick sisters was erected; close by one found a cemetery. The type of life led by these women occupied a space between the monastic and the profane. They renounced neither the society of men nor terrestrial affairs and occupations; they made vows of chastity and obedience, but not in an absolute manner like those in the religious orders; they retained the right to leave the association when they wished and to get married [...].

It wasn't long before there were imitators. Brotherhoods of artisans, most often of weavers, were formed in their image in the various towns where they had their establishments. Called Beghards by the people, the members of these eminently secular associations enjoyed the same independence as the Beguines; they devoted their lives to manual labor and the exercise of piety, and thus attracted the favor of the people.

The progress of these two religious societies did not fail to create enemies, especially among the secular clergy, whose jealousy they aroused. The parish priests received a certain sum per year to indemnify them for the losses caused by the presence of priests who were specially attached to these associations; one even gave them a portion of the price of a burial when some rich bourgeois—and such cases were not rare—demanded to be buried in the cemetery adjoining the establishment; as for the religious orders, they could only lose out to pious foundations that deprived them not only of the support of many members, but also of important donations.[1]

The spirit of freedom spread like wildfire within communities of men and women who were less preoccupied with theological quarrels than with the two great themes that were debated in the thirteenth century (the relevance of which themes was demonstrated on a daily basis): the meaning of poverty and the practice of love, the latter of which aspired to raise itself from brutal satisfaction to the art of pleasure. Where were such pressing questions of utility and pleasure more likely to receive responses than in these places of refuge and encounter, in which Beghards and Beguines learned—through a beneficial idleness and under the pretext of good works—to live according to their preferences?

From 1244 onwards, the Archbishop of Mainz set himself against the abuses that the young Beguines were making of their freedom. Monastic communities and parish priests cast a disapproving eye on the impetuous zeal of beguinages that, by offering their aid free of charge, deprived them of profitable business. The Pope initially intervened to defend the Beghard communities from the plundering and the legal actions initiated by the local clergy, but local condemnations multiplied rapidly. In 1258 the Synod of Fritzlar condemned the wandering Beguines and Beghards who begged to cries of "Brod durch Gott"[2] and who preached in secret underground places[3].

In 1307, at the Synod of Cologne, Bishop Heinrich II of Virneburg enumerated the charges against them.[4] Among them one found such commonly-made remarks as "Simple fornication is not a sin" and "Those who are led by the Spirit of God are no longer subject to the law, for the law is not imposed on the just, on those who live without sin"[5].

In 1311 Pope Clement V was disturbed by the progress of the Free Spirit in Italy and everywhere else. At the Council of Vienne, which took place that same year, he launched against those invoke "the freedom of spirit, which means the freedom to do anything they like"[6] two decrees: *Ad nostrum qui desideranter* and *Cum de quibusdam mulieribus*[7], the combination of which formed the *Clementines* and thereafter served as an inquisitorial guide for the systematic persecution of the Beghards and Beguines, a persecution which dragged to the pyre a number of good Catholics who were devoted to the struggle against pauperization. The adepts of the Free Spirit meanwhile simply adjured if they needed to, for the simple reason that sacrifice or martyrdom did not enter into their aspirations.

The Communities in Cologne and Swidnica
Walter of Holland, the author of *De novem rupibus spiritualibus*[8], a text that is lost today but which Mosheim consulted in the eighteenth century, founded in Cologne a group that met in a place called 'Paradise'. According to the chronicler William of Egmont, a couple represented Jesus and Mary. After a ceremony conducted by Christ dressed up in precious clothes, a nude preacher invited the assembly to undress and to celebrate

their re-found Edenic innocence with a banquet, which was followed by the pleasures of love.

In the manner of the *homines intelligentiae*[9] who were active a century later in Brussels, an initiatory ceremony based on 'refined love' expressed the unity of the body and the spirit through the identification of amorous ecstasy with the incarnated Spirit, which removed sin and guilt. (Note that this was another instance of the Gnostic *pneuma* being identified with the *sperma*.) As among the Barbelites and Messalians, courtesy and the refinement of pleasure—in order to be practiced with a good conscience—followed the paths of hierogamy and a rudimentary form of psychoanalysis, in which God the Father, the Son, and his mother (virgin and wife, both traditional factors in castration and repression) suddenly give their unreserved consent to the essential quest for love.

The persecution led by Bishop Heinrich II of Virneburg sent Walter to the pyre in 1323. William of Egmont counted fifty victims who were burned or drowned in the Rhine.

Another community existed at that time, however. It survived until 1335, which indicates both the popular expansion of the movement and the ineffectiveness of the attempts that were made to repress it.

Indeed, in 1335 a certain John of Brünn[10], who lived with his brother Albert in a Beghard community in Cologne for twenty years, adjured and avoided the pyre by rallying to the Dominican order. In his confession to Gallus Neuhaus, the Inquisitor of Prague, he revealed the singular practices of the Free Spirit in the ecclesiastical lower-orders.

The association was divided into two classes: the neophytes and the Perfect Ones. The first group, after having all of their goods and clothes taken away and given to the second, begged and learned how to renounce their own willpower, in order to allow themselves to be penetrated by divine plenitude. They devoted themselves to jobs that constrained them and were repugnant to them so that they could better break the body by the power of the mind. Once they no longer had a conscience—with the result that they stole and killed with impunity and with neither scruples nor remorse (note that they called such killings 'sending them back to eternity')—they acceded to the state of perfection and lived in luxury and pleasure. They made love with Beguines or adepts, whom they recognized (as the Messalians had) from their use of codes and signs (tickling the palm of the hand, touching the end of the nose)—unless they simply declared "Fac mihi caritatem" ("Give me charity"), since they excelled at giving a pleasantly sensual meaning to ritualized formulas.

For twenty-five years a community of Beguines or Monials functioned at Swidnica, in Silesia, on a model identical to that of Cologne. Denunciations made by mistreated novices attracted the attention of the Inquisitor Johannes Schwenlenfeld (who in 1314 died, as many functionaries of his type did, under the blows of an anonymous avenger). The facts revealed by an inquest in 1332 brought to light practices quite similar to those that were reported in the eighteenth century by Diderot's *The Religious* and attested to by the cadavers of newborns frequently discovered in old monasteries. Such practices take on a certain significance here only because of the doctrine of spiritual freedom that was invoked to justify them. Here was the same annihilation of the will among novices who were reduced to slavery and subjected to the caprices of 'Marthas', or mistresses; the same state of impeccability and absolute license among the Perfect Ones, who dressed in the most beautiful finery and passed [*coulant*] their days in luxury and debauchery. Gertrude of Civitatis, the head of the community, stated: "If God has created everything, then I have shared in his creation, I created everything with him. And I am God with God, and I am Christ, and I am more than these"[11].

The 'Marthas' of Swidnica often visited other convents or communities. Their presence was attested to in Strasbourg, where their teachings chimed with a sermon falsely attributed to Eckhart—the *Sister Catherine Treatise*—that described the diverse stages of the initiation of a novice acceding to the Free Spirit and to an Adamite innocence wherein 'Everything is permitted'.

Wandering Beghards and Beguines

The trials of the Beghards and Beguines who propagated the doctrine of absolute freedom or, in the manner of Marguerite Porete, the art of refined love provide an indication of how far this current—whose meaning the Church failed to understand, even as it sought its eradication—had travelled.

The majority of the condemned had either succumbed to the temptations of presumption and played the role of prophet or Christ in a sensual apostolate, or they had aroused the suspicions of the inquisitorial functionaries—of the monks and the priests who were always ready to make the first move so as to avoid condemnation by the religious police themselves—because their partisans were too numerous

While Bloemardinne's popularity and her reputation for holiness discouraged the inquisitors in Brussels and chased away Ruysbroeck, a post-Eckhartian treatise titled *Meester Eckhart en de onbekende leer* (*Master Eckhart and the Unknown Teachings*) attested to the presence of identical preoccupations in Holland. Soon after, Gerhard Groote and his Modern Devotion movement strove to oppose to the Free Spirit a doctrine that was simultaneously reduced to pure intellectual speculation and strictly confined within the limits of dogma. In 1380 Groote denounced Bartholomew, an Augustinian partisan of the Free Spirit; he also exhumed and burned the body of Matthew of Gouda, who had affirmed that he had "more reasons than Christ to be called God"[12].

In 1336 three Beguines "of high spirit" who were arrested in Magdeburg hastened to abjure "their errors and horrible blasphemies" and were set free. That same year, a certain Constantine was burned in Erfurt. In 1339 three Beghards "professing the crudest pantheism" were sent to prison in perpetuity in Konstanz. Others were arrested in Nuremburg and Regensburg (1340), and then in Würzburg (1342); Hermann Küchener suffered the penalty of fire in Nuremburg in 1342 for professing his belief in a return to the prelapsarian innocence of Adam.

The theologian Jordan von Quedlinburg composed a work that attempted to refute the Beghards of the Free Spirit. Romana Guarnieri has selected important extracts from it[13].

The Inquisitor Schadelant sent Berthold von Rohrbach, who was accused of having preached the theses of the Free Spirit in Franconia, to the pyre at Spire in 1356.

In spite of being overshadowed by the Spanish Inquisition, which often became a gigantic pogrom, the German Inquisition exercised a bureaucratic ferocity worse than that seen anywhere else. It kindled the largest number of pyres and it operated its procedural machinery with the greatest efficiency. It was also in Germany—once the flames of heresy had been extinguished—that women, men, and children accused of sorcery took up the slack for the Beghards and wandering prophets. In this regard the Frenchmen Henry Boguet and Pierre de Rosteguy de Lancre, pursuing the demons of their morbid fantasies, gave their German colleagues a run for their money.

The execution of the Beguine Metza von Westenhove in 1366 was of a particularly odious character. Having been condemned fifty years earlier for advocating the freedom to act according to one's desires, she was judged to be a recidivist at an advanced age and was offered up as a sacrifice during a welcoming festival for a prince that was organized by the city of Strasbourg.

The case of John Hartmann[14], who was known as the Spinner or the Weaver and who was arrested and burned in Erfurt in 1367, illustrates the behavior of certain adepts of the Free Spirit—behavior that reminds one of the conceptions of Donatien Alphonse François de Sade.

The state of perfection and self-deification to which John had acceded—by way of the preliminaries of asceticism and revelation—prescribed that he unreservedly follow the caprices, desires, and passions that God (that is to say, he himself and nature) had inspired in him. He coveted a woman? He seduced or raped her. A valuable item? He appropriated it. The owner objected? He sent him back 'into eternity', which was also where the money that had been spent and the pleasures that it had offered would go. And John had this peremptory formula: "It would be better for the whole earth to perish than for him to renounce an action to which his nature urges him"[15].

That same year [1367], Walter Kerling, Hartmann's accuser, sent seven other Beghards to the pyre at Nordhausen in Thuringia.

In France, the troubles of the great peasant revolt and the war with England gave the wandering preachers greater scope to evade the nets of the heretic-hunters. It seems that, in Paris, the numerical importance of the Beghards and Beguines known under the name 'Turlupins' (in the Netherlands and England they were called 'Lollards') drew down upon them the repression of 1372. Mosheim supposed that many came from Germany, fleeing the persecutions[16]. The Inquisitor of Ile-de-France,

Jacques de More, killed the Turlupins along with Jeanne Dabenton, their prophetess. The pyre also consumed the body of a friend of hers who had died shortly before in prison. Some Turlupins reached Savoy, where the Pope engaged Count Amadeus to crack down on them there, and then in Switzerland. An adept of the Free Spirit was burned at Bremgarten, near Bern.

> According to [Jean Charlier de] Gerson, the sect still had representatives in his era, but they fled the populous localities and hid themselves in overlooked and deserted places.
>
> Gerson preserved the fundamental points of their doctrine for us. They taught that a man, when he had achieved peace and tranquility of the spirit, was relieved of the requirement to observe the divine laws; that it was not necessary to blush at anything that was given to us by nature; and that it was through nudity that we returned to the state of innocence of the first men and attained the supreme degree of bliss in the here-below. "These Epicureans, dressed in the tunics of Christ, introduced themselves among the women by simulating a profound devotion; little by little they won their confidence and did not delay in making them the playthings of their passions". Abolishing all decency, not only in their language but also in their relations with each other, they conducted secret meetings in which they tried to represent the innocence of Paradise in the manner of the heretics of Cologne. In several passages Gerson sets them into relation with Joachim of Fiore. It is probable that they based their principle of spiritual freedom on the theory of the three ages, and it is beyond doubt that one of the five prophetesses who was charged with announcing the beginning of the era of the Holy Spirit was seized in Lyon in 1423.[17]

While Gerhard Groote was launching the mystical and orthodox movement of the New Devotion in Holland, Germany intensified its persecution of the Beghards. On 26 January 1381, Conrad Kannler, brought before the inquisitorial tribunal at Eichstädt, expounded upon his conception of the Free Spirit: "It exists when all remorse of conscience ceases and man can no longer sin [...]. I am one with God and God is one with me"[18]. He insisted on the legitimacy of satisfying his passions, whatever they were, on the condition that the desire assumed an irresistible character.[19] Thus it was that the Fraticelles and, later on, the *Alumbrados* of Spain recommended to men and women that they sleep nude, side by side, and remain chaste as long as possible, in order to lead their passion to the point at which it could no longer contain itself.

The group founded by Nicholas of Basle placed itself in the line of the Free Spirit, Joachimite millenarianism, and the various Christs of the eleventh century.[20]

Considering himself to be infallible on account of being the incarnation of God, Nicholas availed himself of all rights and powers. As the holder of an authority that he deemed superior to that of the Pope, he had the power to release his disciples from all other forms of obedience and from the state of sin and guilt. To be venerated by him granted them the state of Edenic innocence. In this sense Nicholas can be said to have founded a libertarian theocracy, if that isn't too glaring an oxymoron.

Having been enthroned by Nicholas, some of his disciples enjoyed analogous prerogatives. Martin of Mainz, a monk originally from the Abbey of Reichenau in the diocese of Konstanz, thus acquired the privilege, conferred on him by his God and sovereign pontiff [Nicholas], of liberating his disciples from submission to anyone—Church, lord, or master—other than himself. He was burned in 1393. The 'sovereign pontiff' mounted the pyre himself in 1395 (in Vienna) with two Beghards who were his apostles. Several disciples of Martin of Mainz (the name of his brotherhood, the 'Friends of God', recalled Marguerite Porete's expression "The true friends of God"), were executed in Heidelberg during those same years.

While inquisitorial zeal led the partisans of the Free Spirit—Beghards and lay people alike—to become increasingly cautious, the doctrine progressed in England, where Walter Hilton denounced the "errors of false spiritual freedom and false mystic illuminism" in his *Scala perfectionis*[21].

England was favorable to the reforms of John Wycliffe (1320–87), who, without exactly participating in the Beghardist heresy, gave his support to voluntary poverty, denied that the clergy had the right to possess temporal goods, and skillfully entered into the schemes of the Regent of England, the Duke of Lancaster, who was hostile to the papacy.

A schismatic, Wycliffe added to the quarrels between the popes and the anti-popes a nationalistic note from which the future Anglican Church profited in the sixteenth century. Nevertheless, in 1415, thirty years after his death, the Council of Konstanz ordered that his body be exhumed and burned.

The Lollards, who were English Beghards, found in Wycliffe's reforms strong grounds for their social struggles, which distinguished them from the individualistic demands of the Free Spirit. Nevertheless, the tendency towards individualism manifested itself here and there, even if it did not present the same radicalism as it did in the large European cities.

John Cobham—who was a disciple of Wycliffe, a lord and aristocrat close to the King, and a protector of the Lollards, who were tracked by Bishop Arundel—was accused of heresy in 1413. His confession of faith recalled his loyalty to the King and denounced the Roman Pope, who was characterized as the Antichrist. Condemned to death, Cobham managed to escape and led an army of Lollards whose voluntary poverty and impeccability kept alive both the egalitarianism of John Ball and German Beghardism.

Captured and then condemned to be hanged and burned, Cobham left behind many disciples whose activities hastened the instauration of Protestantism in England, and also that of the popularity of a certain 'spiritual freedom' that was extolled by the Familists and Ranters of the seventeenth century.[22]

It is hard to say whether it is fitting to link Cobham's movement with the activities of Paul Crawer, who was burned in Scotland in 1433 for having propagated Adamite ideas similar to those of the *pikarti* [Picards] and the Men of Intelligence.

The End of the Beghards and Beguines
Gregory XI, sensitive to the grievances that were formulated by those Beghards and Beguines who remained faithful to the strict orthodoxy of their semi-religious order, brought some moderation to the zeal of the inquisitors. In 1394 Pope Boniface IX annulled Gregory's reservations and concessions in order to have done with the heresy as quickly as possible.

John Wasmod of Hamburg, Inquisitor of Mainz and then Rector of the University of Heidelberg, seconded Boniface's enterprise by writing a *Tractatus contra hereticos beckhardos, lulhardos et swestriones*[23], which is rich in information about those still-flourishing communities.

Nothing would thenceforth restrain the action of the Inquisitors. In 1402 two partisans of the Free Spirit, Wilhelm and Bernard, perished on the pyre; the first in Lübeck, the second in Wismar. In Mainz, at around the same time, several heretics who preferred to abjure their doctrines rather than submit to torture were seized. The Inquisition's last victims from among the partisans of the Free Spirit lived around the middle of the fifteenth century. Around 1430 someone named Burkard was burned with his companions in Zurich; in the canton of Uri the same penalty was inflicted on a certain Brother Charles, who had created many relationships within the populations in these regions. Konstanz, Ulm, and several towns in Württemberg inflicted similar tortures; in other localities the heretics abjured and underwent penitence.[24]

In 1457 the Archbishop of Mainz incriminated a Beghard named Bosehans, who was judged guilty of distributing heretical books. A poorly indexed literature circulated, often attributing seditious writings to orthodox authors. (Note that *The Mirror of Simple Souls* was attributed to Mary of Hungary; the *Sister Catherine Treatise* to Eckhart; and the *Buch von geistlicher Armut*[25] to Tauler. These mistakes increased due to the speed of the printing press, which was invented at roughly the same time.)

The death on the pyre of the Beghard Hans Becker, a 'laicus indoctus'[26] who was burned along with his books in Mainz in 1458, may have been the last execution of a Beghard. Preaching was thenceforth nourished by social demands, while appeals for the moralization of the Church paved the way for the Reformation. But the Free Spirit continued to exist in a clandestinity that was dictated by prudence. It reappeared in broad daylight with the Spiritual Libertines combated by Luther and Calvin, and among the Ranters, who were hostile to Cromwell.

Matthias von Kemnat, relating the execution of a Beghard in Mainz in 1453 in his *Chronik Friedrich I*, still thought it worth addressing a warning to his readers: "Guard against the hermits who live in the woods, the Beghards and Lollards, because they are filled with heresies; guard against the articles of faith that they profess and that are such that simple people cannot hear them without danger"[27].

At the end of the fifteenth century the satirical poet Sebastian Brandt mocked the scandalous comportment of the Beguines in *The Ship of Fools*. His contemporary Johann Geiler von Kaysersberg, a preacher from Strasbourg, objected to the 'people of the Free Spirit', but he estimated that they lived far off in woods and valleys that were unknown to other people, as if they had rediscovered in nature the freedom that would have been denied them in the towns that were harshly controlled by the clergy. Was that estimation a dream, a regret, or an ironic vision? In any event, Wilhelm Fraenger[28] related the imaginary world of Jerome [Hieronymus] Bosch[29], who painted the storms and frenzies of internal landscapes while at his peaceful retreat at Hertogenbosch, to the teachings of the Free Spirit.

CHAPTER THIRTY-THREE

The Millenarians

What the Jewish, Essenean, and Christianized apocalypses (or 'revelations') all expressed, via the adventures of God, was the historical myth of a Golden Age. The Greco-Roman mindset, which was disappointed by the disorder of the emperors and which adorned an ideal and universal republic with every possible virtue, conceived of that Golden Age—with a mixture of regret and hopefulness—as being both in the past and destined to return.

In those 'revelations' the creator God, originally imperceptible and inaccessible, approached His creatures and, as their epiphany grew, manifested Himself in order to separate the just and loyal from the bad and wicked—the result being that, after the latter were annihilated, He would then descend to the earth and, together with the saints and the elect, build a kingdom that would last a thousand years.

The allegedly 'Catholic' Constantinian Church accommodated itself poorly to millenarianism, a doctrine that had previously and collectively been accepted by a Hellenized Christianity that aspired to the triumph, not of an ecclesial authority, but of the *Ekklēsia* or the community of the faithful. Justin the Apologist, Irenaeus of Lyon, Tertullian, and Origen were all convinced millenarians. This conception persisted discreetly up until the twelfth century, in spite of the misgivings of the clergy—the exclusive holders of salvation who controlled access to the kingdom of the saints.

Joachim of Fiore

With the renewal of the social and political forms of the twelfth century there was sketched out a consciousness of a history that was in progress but that was still enclosed within the cyclical forms of myth. The revolutionary process of market expansion—which also incited philosophy to free itself from the tutelage of theology—injected into the very heart of the language of God the venom [*venin*] of becoming [*devenir*], a venom that would eventually kill off that language altogether.

The idea of an Eden that was uprooted to the beyond and inscribed in a human future expressed, to a greater or lesser extent, and at the heart of a theocentric cosmos, the same hopes for the future that would be sung (to the point of loss of voice and life) by the ideologies of the revolutions still to come.

Ironically, such a project was born in the brain of a monk who was far from being inclined to sow trouble in the ecclesiastic universe. The theories of Joachim of Fiore posed a danger to the Church only because of the interpretations of those theories to which the turmoil of the age gave rise.

In the ninth century Bishop Ratherius of Verona founded upon the balance of three orders the conservative society that produced the agrarian economy: the *oratores*, the monks and priests; the *armatores*, the soldiers; and the *laboratores*, the workers who fed those who protected them on earth and in the name of heaven.

Everything happened as if the commercial growth of the towns—an arrow shot in the direction of the modernity of capital—was making the cyclical and static representation of Ratherius veer into the spirit of Joachim, flattening and stretching that representation out according to a linear unfolding that was ordered into three ages.

The *Book of Concord of the New and Old Testaments*, written around 1180, put forth a sampling of formulas, none of which was in itself threatening to the Church. But the meaning and direction of these formulas—sharpened as they were by history—cut like a knife into the adipose flesh of Roman power.

> The first period was that of knowledge; the second that of understanding, and the third will be the period of complete intelligence.[1] The first was

servile obedience, the second filial servitude, and the third will be freedom. The first was affliction, the second action, and the third will be contemplation. The first was fear, the second faith, and the third will be love. The first was the age of slaves, the second the age of sons, and the third will be the age of friends. The first was the age of old people, the second of young people, and the third will be an age of children. The first was spent in starlight, the second in the dawn, and the third will be in the full light of day. The first was winter, the second the beginning of spring, and the third will be summer. The first bore nettles, the second roses, and the third will bear lilies. The first gave us grass, the second spices, and the third will give us wheat. The first gave us water, the second wine, and the third will give us oil. The first relates to Septuagesima, the second to Quadragesima, and the third will be Easter. The first age therefore relates to the Father, who is the author of all things, the second to the Son, who deigned to take on our filth, and the third will be the age of the Holy Spirit, of whom the apostle said, "Where the Spirit of the Lord is, there is freedom".[2]

The explosive mix of the Joachimite component, on the one hand, and historical evolution, on the other, found a detonator in the form of the precise date that the Calabrian monk assigned to the advent of the Third Age. Joachim counted forty-two generations of thirty years—1,260 years in total—from Adam to Jesus. As the same period of time had to pass again, starting from the birth of the Christ, the new era had to begin at the dawn of 1260. Great troubles and the unleashing of the Antichrist would be the obvious prelude to the birth of a paradisiacal world in which the saints would joyfully anticipate the return of Christ.

Beneath the archaism of these cyclical calculations lay a subtle political design. Joachim foresaw the growing importance of the mendicant orders, which were a veritable war machine that the Church set in opposition to the progress of the Waldensinian heresy and the voluntarily impoverished reformers. It was of the latter's preeminence that Joachim thought when he announced the reign of the saints. But it was the Franciscans—the order whose practices most closely approximated apostolic austerity—who succumbed most easily to the seductions of millenarianism.

With the rule of the elect in the Joachimite Third Age, the reign of the Church would be abolished. There would no longer be Father, nor Son, nor rites, nor sacrifices, nor sacraments, but just one single law: the *lex libertatis*[3]. The Amalricians—even simple reformers such as Peter of Bruys and Henry of Lausanne—had already predisposed the Joachimite spirit to a social and individual practice that was radically hostile both to Rome and, in the best of cases, to the very essence of religion, which is the exile of the self. Indeed, when one was faced with the imminence of a paradisiacal nature into which God would be dissolved, and when the ecclesiastic barrier that prohibited access to the conjoined pleasures of the world and oneself was broken, how could one prevent abstract concepts from retaking bodily form?

Previously sterilized by theological and philosophical speculation, certain words began to recover their vitality. In the notion of 'perfection' germinated the refusal of all guilt; 'contemplation' became the illumination of the God of desire that each person carried inside him- or herself; 'charity' was elevated to the art of erotic courtesy; 'love' was the effusion of lovers; and 'freedom' at the very least evoked the freedom of nature and, in its strongest forms, indicated the surpassing of the unfortunate coupling of divine tyranny with an oppressed and violated nature.

Joachimism

Joachim's writings met with immediate success among the literate. Among the Amalricians condemned in 1210, William the Goldsmith and Master Godin of Amiens had already drawn out the subversive implications of the imminence of the Third Age. If Waldensianism and Catharism knew nothing about these implications, the 'spiritual' faction that was born from divisions within the Franciscan order perceived in the rule of the saints the emergence of a society inspired by the voluntary poverty that Francis of Assisi had so cleverly snatched from Waldo's disciples, the Cathars, and the apostolic preachers.

The date 1260, foreseen by Joachim as the inauguration of the new era, exploded into multiple social, political, and religious fragments. The shock waves that assailed the accumulation of the centuries that had been built up by the passage of time came without a meaningful expiration date attached, since Eden ended up being repeatedly deferred. The non-appearance of the millennium had no other consequences than the revision of the prophetic calculus.

Two widely distributed works that were drafted in the second half of the thirteenth century demonstrate the impact of Joachimism on the political rivalry between Rome and the emperors of Germany. The *Abbatis Joachim Florensis scriptum super Esaiam prophetam*[4] (the manuscript of which was later printed in Venice in 1517) and the *Interpraetatio praeclara abbatis Joachim in Hieremian prophetam*[5] (printed in Venice in 1525) had fixed 1260 as the end date of the affliction of the Holy City. The German Emperor, Frederick II, would be the whip held in the hands of God and was destined to punish the sinful Church. The Roman *Imperium* being ravaged by the Saracens, who in their turn would be destroyed by the Mongols and the Tartars, would lead the world to the brink of annihilation. Thereafter, as a backlash, the rule of peace and the era of the just would finally come to pass. (Note that, in the nineteenth century, at a moment when ideological language had supplanted its religious counterpart, such was the conception of the anarchist Ernest Coeurderoy in his *Hurrah!!! ou la révolution par les cosaques* (*Hurrah, or the Revolution of the Cossacks*)[6].)

The elitism of the Spirituals discovered nourishment appropriate to their chiliastic pretensions in the theories of Joachim of Fiore. In 1254 a Spiritual from Pisa, Gerardo of Borgo San Donnino, radicalized and popularized Joachimite ideas in his *Introductorium in evangelium aeternum*[7]. Insisting on the fateful year 1260, he predicted the disappearance of the Roman Church and the advent of a spiritual Church, one that was already germinating within Franciscanism. The condemnation of the book in 1255 incriminated the Abbot from Fiore, who was thenceforth suspected of heresy. Condemned to perpetual imprisonment, Gerardo of Borgo San Donnino died, after eighteen years of incarceration in harsh conditions, without having disowned his ideas.[8]

Joachimism was revived again, and more vividly, among the Spirituals, who took up the old program of reform and were increasingly opposed to the commercialized wheeler-dealer politics of Rome. A radical faction, on the boundary between Franciscanism and the Free Spirit, was born from the Spiritual current; the Church condemned it under the name 'Fraticelles'.

Finally, there appeared an egalitarian social movement—egalitarian, that is, if one stripped away the anti-Semitic resentment of the *Pastoureaux* and the morbid comportment of the flagellants—in which God constituted less a religious referent than a principle of government that excluded the Church and the princes in the name of a new and classless society.

Gerard Segarelli

In the Italian towns the political and social struggle most often responded to the tangle of quarrels between the Guelphs, who were allies of Rome, and the Ghibellines, who were partisans of the Emperor of Germany. Revolutionary millenarianism and the will to purge the Church of its corruption (which Savonarola was still demanding in 1491) were involved in virtually all of these tumults, which broke out on a monthly, if not weekly, basis.

In the Joachimite year of 1260, in Parma, which was at that point ravaged by famine and internecine wars, a shopkeeper named Gerard Segarelli—renewing the gesture of Peter Waldo—sold his goods to the profit of the poor and decided to promote a community of the faithful in which the apostolic virtues of Christ and his apostles would be revived.

Illuminated and, no doubt, shaped by the hysteria that was shared by preachers and tribunes of all types, Segarelli soon took on the role of a popular and picturesque Messiah in Parma, although he failed to denounce as lies and calumnies most of the ludicrous traits that the Franciscan Salimbene di Adam imputed to him. (Note that, in his *Chronicle*, Salimbene confessed the motives that lay behind his harsh invective: "And the Parmese, my own fellow citizens, men and women, gave more, more liberally, to these men than they did to the Minorites and the Preachers"[9].) Segarelli enjoyed the benevolent protection of Bishop Opizo, who may have been motivated less by solicitude than by an aversion to the official beggars who made up the Dominicans (universally detested for their base police work) and the Franciscans (who were often charged with hypocrisy).

Rallying the flagellants to his ecumenism, Segarelli traveled through the town to cries of "Penitenziagite!", the popular form of "Poenitentiam agite!" ("Do penitence!")[10].

With the aid of an elderly Franciscan called Robert, who was known as Fra Glutto (Glutton), Segarelli organized a brotherhood to which thronged disciples who were described by Salimbene as "rascals, seducers, deceivers, thieves, and fornicators" who "neither work nor pray" and "spent every day running through the cities seeking out women"[11]. In vain did the Council of Lyon of 1274 order them to dissolve or rally to one of the orders recognized by Rome.

Strengthened by their large numbers and their growing audience, the Segarellists sent out missionaries—wandering apostles who were often confused with the Beghards, with whom they shared a devotion to voluntary poverty and the impeccability that that devotion guaranteed.

'The spirit of freedom' was not without influence on Segarellism, despite the latter's exhortations to penitence. The prophet himself made assurances that the life of the poor was the true life of the apostles: it "is free and the most perfect of lives . . . [consisting in] freedom in adoring God, freedom in the [marital] vow, freedom in the relations between man and woman"[12].

One practice that has been attributed to Segarelli and his disciples is that of the 'white martyr'. Recommended by the very orthodox Robert of Abrissel, it consisted in a couple going to bed nude and interlaced, but resisting the natural solicitations of love. The current of the Free Spirit gave to the exercise a more human meaning by changing it into a patient refinement of desire, which could not be satisfied until it had become irresistible. It is probable that certain apostles of Segarelli were more inclined towards the latter version of this practice, which was thereby denuded of excessive rigor.

Salimbene was surprised that Segarelli refused to assume the role of community leader, even though he was the object of a great veneration. Sincerely devoted to the myth of Christ, he held that it would detract from his holiness if he governed rather than glowed. He could not avoid all forms of temporal power, however.

Guidone Putagi, who was the brother of the Podestà of Bologna, took control of the government of the congregation and presided over it for many years, even though his ostentatious way of life deviated from evangelic requirements.

A schism was declared. It degenerated into an armed struggle in which each camp argued over Segarelli, a most unfortunate God who tried to use his successive incarnations in an attempt to be present once again at the birth of a new Church.

Guidone's partisans won the battle, but he soon afterwards left the brotherhood and rallied to the Order of the Templars. (Note that his joining the Templars left the way open to various hypotheses concerning the open-mindedness of those future victims of King Philip the Fair and Pope Clement V. Merchants and bankers two centuries ahead of their time, the Templars were open to receiving ideas and pleasures that were cynically camouflaged by the exemplary reputations of these soldiers and businessmen, who were thought to be above suspicion.)

In 1286, Pope Honorius IV condemned the Segarellist apostolics and prohibited believers from receiving them or from giving them alms that ought to have gone into the Vatican's coffers.

A year later, the Council of Würzburg enjoined the faithful to no longer welcome or feed the wandering apostolics who dressed in extravagant clothing and were called *leccatores, ghiottoni,* or *scrocconi*—that is to say, 'gluttons'[13].

According to Salimbene, Segarelli became increasingly eccentric. Three of his disciples, having been accused of debauchery, were hanged in Bologna in order to plant doubts about their much-trumpeted holy calling.

Thrown into prison, Segarelli owed his salvation to the Bishop of Parma, who offered him refuge in his house. Nevertheless, a new bull issued in 1290 by Pope Nicolas IV restarted the repression. In 1294, on the authority of the Inquisition, two men and two women who were members of the congregation were put on the pyre. That same year, in order to catch off-guard an institution [the Inquisition] that was unanimously abhorred, even by the civil power and by several ecclesiastic authorities, the Bishop of Parma arrested [and eventually released] the prophet [Segarelli] whose downfall Rome had sworn to bring about and whom it had condemned to perpetual imprisonment.

This gambit did not take into account the tenacity of the Inquisitorial police. The pursuits engaged in by the Inquisition led to Gerard Segarelli being condemned to death, forty years after his divine revelation. With him perished many of his partisans, including Stefano, one of his principal evangelists.

Among those who contemplated the prophet in his tunic of flames on 18 July 1300 was one of his partisans, Fra Dolcino of Novara, who later brought to Joachimism the modern form of a social and peasant-based revolution, and thereby inaugurated a tradition that continued to exist until the decline of colonialism in the twentieth century.

The Guillelmites

At the same as Segarelli was agitating Parma and attracting the hostility of a Church that was obsessed with the accumulation of capital, a millenarian group founded in Milan claimed for women the privilege of guiding humanity as a whole towards the Third Age and the egalitarian kingdom.

In the prophetic year 1260, a young widow and her son arrived in Milan. Guglielma, said to be from Bohemia, seems to have been the daughter of Constance, wife of the king of Bohemia. Nothing authenticates such parentage other than the declaration of one of her disciples, Andreas Saramita, who had been to see Constance in the hope of recovering a debt. Guglielma's exemplary piety rapidly attracted followers, whose numbers increased as her reputation as a thaumaturge grew and as miraculous instances of her healing powers multiplied. The worship of this saint was soon drawn into the whirlwind of fashionable messianic ideas. Her sectarians let it be understood that she had been chosen to convert the Jews and the Saracens, and to instaurate the universality of the Christian faith.

Around 1276 a gilded legend maintained that Guglielma was the incarnation of the Holy Spirit, whom Joachim of Fiore had claimed was the harbinger of Third Age. She would be the incarnation of the third person in the Trinity as Christ had been the incarnation of the second in the body of a man. If we are to believe two of her more zealous partisans—

Andreas Saramita, a noblewoman from Milan, and Sister Maifreda da Pirovano, an *umiliata*[14] in the ancient convent of Biassono who belonged to the powerful Visconti family—her nature was at once divine and natural. Guglielma had the prudence to openly contest this claim, which was subject to Inquisitorial approval, but, with or without her consent, her role as saint implicated her in the double signification of millenarianism and the feminine preeminence that continued to disturb the Church from the Cistercian Monials to Hadewijch and Porete.

When Guglielma died on 24 August 1281 she left her goods to the Cistercian community of Chiaravalle, near Milan, where she was buried with a great display of piety. The cult organized in her honor did profitable business. A month after the transfer of her remains, Andreas Saramita exhumed the body with great pomp. He washed it with wine and water, and preserved this precious mix as a cream for the healing of the sick. Maifreda used it for the healing of pilgrims; she also instaurated specific ceremonies for the anniversary of Guglielma's death and the transfer of the remains of the saint. The Abbey, whose prestige grew year by year, attracted the favor of generous donors. One of them, Giaccobe da Novati, a nobleman from Milan, bequeathed to it all of his goods and offered his powerful protection to the Guillelmites.

Nothing more was needed for the group to claim that it constituted the kernel of a new Church—that it marked the advent of the reign of the saints. Andreas, the spiritual son of Guglielma, devoted himself to defining a new dogma. The Archangel Raphael had announced to the blessed Constance that the Holy Spirit had been incarnated in her; he had chosen feminine form because, in masculine form, he would have perished like Christ did, and the entire world would have perished with him. The grave at Chiaravalle was elevated to the glory of the Holy Sepulcher; rites were prescribed and communion was held there.

From time to time Guglielma appeared to the faithful in the form of a dove. The Gospels were replaced by Andreas's writings, which imitated Paul's Epistles. Maifreda, the author of litanies and prayers, prophesied the second coming of Guglielma and the end of the traditional papacy. She herself would become the pope. She worked to form a college of cardinals composed exclusively of women. She gave her benediction, celebrated Mass, consecrated the Host, and gave communion to the faithful while sumptuously dressed.

The support of a number of rich Milanese, including the Visconti family, in all probability explains the slowness and hesitancy of the Inquisition. It was disquieted by the Guillelmites in 1284, but contented itself with a simple admonition. The inquiries of 1295 and 1296 were not followed up on. However, when Maifreda revived the millenarian threat by announcing the coming of the Holy Spirit on the Pentecost of 1300, the Church decided to intervene against a hotbed of agitation that had consolidated a front of apostolics, Fraticelles, Dolcinians, and heterodox Beghards.

Among the Guillelmites who were arrested, four or five were condemned as recidivists. On 23 August 1300, Sister Giaccoba dei Bassani mounted the pyre. In September it was the turn of Andreas Saramita and Maifreda. Lighter penalties were given to the others. Guglielma's remains were exhumed and burned. Thus ended a schism that had opposed the patriarchal Church with a feminine one and that had given a gynecratic character to millenarian hopes. It wasn't until the writings of Guillaume Postel in the sixteenth century that the idea of salvation through women would reappear.

Dolcino of Novara

In Dolcino were incarnated both the millenarian aspirations of the urban areas and the old collectivist dream of the peasant commune. This pairing governed the archaic and modern meanings of economic, political, and social revolution up until the twentieth century. Remarkable for his intelligence, courage, and sincerity, Dolcino offered the next seven centuries of history one of the first and noblest revolutionary figures to have contemplated the instauration of a new society.

Originally from the region of Novara, Dolcino was the son of a certain Giulio, who was either a priest based in Trento in the Ossola valley or a hermit from Prato near Novara. Another priest, Agosto, who was attached to the church of St Agnes in Vercelli, took charge of Dolcino's education and entrusted him to a pedagogue named Sione. His brilliant mind attracted animosity. A calumnious imputation accused him of stealing from his protector, driving him from Vercelli. Perhaps he then joined a wandering group of Apostolics, Fraticelles, or Beghards—adepts of Segarelli. His prestige and eloquence rallied to him a large number of partisans. Carried to the head of the Segarellist movement a month after the prophet's execution, he drafted a new version of Joachimite doctrine.

In this version, the past was divided into three periods. The first covered the centuries of the Old Testament; the second extended from the coming of Christ to Pope Sylvester and passed under the sign of penitence; the third ran from Sylvester to Segarelli and was marked by the decadence of a Church that no reform had succeeded in saving—neither that of Benedict nor the attempts of Dominic or Francis of Assisi. The fourth period, inaugurated in 1260, led up to the annihilation of the corrupt Church, the end of the monks and the priests, and the triumph of the poor and humble, who were the sole carriers of the Holy Spirit and the future creators of a new fraternal and egalitarian society.

Like all the prophets, Dolcino made the error of fixing a precise date—in his case it was three years hence, i.e. in 1303—for the universal upheaval from which would burst forth the light of the terrestrial kingdom. Politically, Dolcino placed his bets on Frederick II, an enemy of the papacy upon whom it fell to accomplish the designs of divine justice.

In accordance with both the Apocalypse attributed to John and Bogomilist tradition, Dolcino identified the angels of the seven Churches: Sylvester for Pergamum, Benedict for Ephesus, Dominic for Laodicea, Francis for Sardis, Segarelli for Thyatira, and Dolcino himself for Philadelphia. (Note that, at the same time, Guion de Cressonaert, a friend of Marguerite Porete, also called himself the angel of Philadelphia[15].)

The course of events contradicted Dolcino's short-term prophecies. Boniface VIII died in 1303 on the orders of Philip the Fair, King of France and a victim of the brutalities to which the Pope had subjected Nogaret and Colonna. Frederick did not manifest himself and the new Pope, Benedict XI, was chased from Rome by Colonna's faction, took refuge in Perugia, and did nothing to temper the zeal of the Inquisitors against the Dolcinians.

A second epistle from Dolcino pushed back the date of the end of the Church of Rome by two or three years. In 1304 Benedict XI perished unexpectedly, no doubt with the aid of a poison; Frederick had no part in it. Clement V, an enemy of the Beghards of the Free Spirit, proclaimed his resolution to finish off the Dolcinian movement.

At the head of some 4,000 men, Dolcino—accompanied by his friend, the rich and beautiful Margaret of Trent—commanded a staff of such experienced men as Alberto of Cimega, Longino Cattaneo of Bergamo, Federigo of Novara, and Valderigo of Brescia. Dolcino then began a guerrilla campaign whose remarkable mobility baffled his enemies. It won Bologna and Modena and, from there, much of Northern Italy, and probably the regions around Bergamo, Brescia, Milan, and Como as well. He was arrested by the Inquisition on three occasions and escaped each time. He ended up establishing himself in the region neighboring Novara and Vercelli, where the peasant populations regrouped under his leadership into a veritable peasant revolt.

Milano Sola, a rich property owner from Borgo di Sesia, offered to shelter Dolcino, but the pressure brought to bear by the armies levied by the Holy See prompted him to search in the mountains of Valsesia for a better refuge. Mount Balmara and then, in 1305, the *Parete Calvo*[16] — both snowy and difficult-to-reach summits in the Italian Alps—hosted fortified camps for a population of fourteen hundred people, organized as a commune.

The partisans were called to establish around the couple formed by Dolcino and Margaret the basis for a new world in which goods necessary for survival would be collectivized, property would be abolished, and marriage—which reduced women to objects of appropriation—would be suppressed in the name of the 'union according to the heart'. Dolcino recommended the practice of couples refining—while nude—the gestures of love until irresistible desire accomplished the will of nature with an innocence that revoked all guilt.

Clement V likened the struggle against the Dolcinians to a crusade that was enriched by indulgences. Through threats and promises, the people of Valsesia were forced to belong to an association that was intended to block all aid to the besieged. Under the pressure of deprivation, Dolcino's partisans conducted raids and pillages that alienated the villagers who had initially favored their cause. The presence of enemy troops contributed to the increasingly insupportable misery and the cowardice that are typically found in such situations.

Nevertheless, Dolcino's audacity proved advantageous in this ostensibly disastrous situation. The Podestà of Varallo, who fell into the hands of the Dolcinians after trying to besiege the *Parete Calvo*, was exchanged along with his troops for an important shipment of supplies.

On 10 March 1306, after a year of cold and scarcity, the Dolcinians abandoned their mountain retreat, which, had they stayed there, would have doomed them to slow annihilation. They succeeded in taking up a new position on Mount Rubello, near the village of Triverio in the Vercelli region. Weakened and badly armed, their numbers did not exceed 1,000, but they nevertheless managed to defeat two offensives launched against them by the Bishop of Vercelli. Driven by famine, Dolcino provoked the enemy into fighting by throwing himself into a hazardous confrontation from which he emerged victorious. The prisoners he captured were exchanged for supplies.

By multiplying his Bulls of Crusade and promising tax reductions and advantages for all the religious orders, Clement V obtained military reinforcements from Lombardy, Piedmont, and the Count of Savoy. To the blockade of Dolcino's position, Clement V added catapults and armies of experienced mercenaries.

Dante Alighieri did not conceal his sympathy for Dolcino's guerrilla war while he was writing the *Divina Commedia* [*Divine Comedy*]. It put him on his guard against the tactic of falling back into an inhospitable climate and depriving one's forces of the advantages that assure the mobility of seasoned and well-fed troops. (Note that the three books of the *Divina Commedia* correspond to the three Joachimite ages. The three stages of the *Scala perfectionis*[17] pertained to both the alchemical process and the quest for 'refined love'.)

At the start of winter, a battle that turned to carnage saw the Dolcinians again emerge victorious. The blockade and the severity of the cold were, in the end, motivations for their heroism. But on 23 March 1307 the assault exhausted the last resistance.

Clement V showed his relief by giving prebends and fiscal compensation to the Crusaders. His resentment caused him to inflict the most odious punishments upon Dolcino, Margaret, and their friends. Dragged through the streets of Vercelli, they were—like many arrestees on the way to the pyre—dismembered alive with the aid of red-hot pincers. Witnesses recounted that Dolcino did not let out a single cry.

Bernard Gui, one of the most ignoble men ever produced by inquisitorial fanaticism, devoted his life to the pursuit of the remaining Dolcinians. They were burned in Toulouse in 1322, along with Pierre de Lugo, who was originally from Galicia; in Trent in 1332 and 1333; in Compostela, where the disciples of the Italian Dolcinian Richard were condemned at the instigation of Bernard Gui; in Prague around 1315; in Rieti in 1335, despite the objections of the municipal authorities, who refused to deliver the Dolcinians to the Inquisition; in England; in Padua around 1350; in Avignon, under John XXII; in Naples in 1372; and in Germany at the beginning of the fifteenth century.

Although it was led by the parish priest Guillaume Cale, the great French peasant revolt of 1358 was unencumbered by religious considerations. It had more to do with rioting and tumult than with a political strategy or a program of precise demands. The peasant movement led in England by John Ball in the second half of the thirteenth century enjoyed the sympathy of the Lollards, but—apart from Ball's preaching and his celebrated question, "When Adam delved and Eve span, Who was then the gentleman?"[18]—it had no religious connotations. The same is true of the revolt led by Watt Tyler[19] and of the many working-class insurrections that tore apart the great cities. Millenarianism, still imbued with the sacred spirit, did not reappear until the Anabaptists of Münster. It fascinated thinkers such as Tomasso Campanella and Wilhelm Weitling, a contemporary of Karl Marx. The great revolutionary movements later gave to millenarianism a more ideological than religious form. Nevertheless, it would be a mistake to underestimate the role of irrational and Joachimite faith in Nazi millenarianism[20]—that is to say, in that which was the very antithesis of projects for a classless society or an ecological paradise, both of which were brought to the fore by the successive waves of the burgeoning economy[21].

CHAPTER THIRTY-FOUR

The Flagellants

Stoicism taught that one should endure suffering; Judeo-Christianity taught one to love it. From punishment as a proof of divine love to the love of punishment was a mere step. Were not the markets in dereliction, death, and fear among the most profitable for the Church?

The appearance in Perugia around 1250 of the movement of the Flagellants was part of a series of events—the famine of 1250, the plague of 1259, the bloody struggle between the Guelphs and the Ghibellines—that was propitious for the nourishment of the sentiment that the misfortune of losing one's life entailed the consolation of involving the whole world in that loss. The Joachimite expiration date of 1260 once more catalyzed the tumult of passions that an impossible way of life easily directed towards the outlet of death.

At first encouraged by the Church, hysterical and collective self-punishment rapidly came—due to its pretensions to exclusivity—to threaten the clergy's privileges of dispensing affliction and consolation. The existence of hell on earth deprived the merchants of the beyond of all credit. Furthermore, the idea spread that surrendering oneself to outrages and torments of the flesh identified one with Christ and released one from all duties to the Church.

For a long time flagellation was among the self-punitive practices that the Church allowed. It expressed the commonplace scorn for terrestrial life and pleasure that was inherent in all religions, without for all that curtailing—as in the practices of the New Prophecy or the Cathars' *endura*—an existence that was denuded of attractions by the quest for a sanctifying ordeal.

It was in the crowded Italian towns that organised flagellant processions appeared for the first time. The movement was launched in 1260 by a hermit of Perugia and spread southwards to Rome and northwards to the Lombard cities with such rapidity that to contemporaries it appeared a sudden epidemic of remorse. Led usually by priests, masses of men, youths and boys marched day and night, with banners and burning candles, from town to town. And each time they came to a town they would arrange themselves in groups before the church and flog themselves for hours on end. The impact which this public penance made upon the general population was great. Criminals confessed, robbers returned their loot and usurers the interest on their loans, enemies were reconciled and feuds forgotten. Even the two warring parties which were dividing Italy, the Guelphs or supporters of the Pope and the Ghibellines or the supporters of the Emperor, for a moment lost some of their intransigence. Whole towns became involved in the movement—at Reggio the chief magistrate, the bishop and all the guilds took part. As the processions moved along they constantly increased in size, until they were many thousand strong. But if at times people of all classes would join in, it was the poor who persevered; so that in the latter stages of the movement they alone remained.

The circumstances under which this first outbreak of mass self-flagellation occurred are significant. Even by medieval standards, conditions in Italy at that moment were exceptionally hard. In 1258 there had been famine, in 1259 a serious outbreak of plague. Above all, incessant warfare between Guelph and Ghibelline had reduced the country to a state of the utmost misery and insecurity. The situation of the Guelph towns was particularly desperate, for their cause had just suffered a heavy blow when the Florentines were defeated at Montaperto, with fearful slaughter, by the Tuscan Ghibellines. Frederick II's son, Manfred, seemed well on the way to establishing his sway over the whole of Italy. It was not for nothing that the flagellant movement started in a Guelph city and flourished most amongst

Guelphs. Yet all these afflictions were felt to be but a prelude to a final and overwhelming catastrophe. A chronicler remarked that during the flagellant processions people behaved as though they feared that as a punishment for their sins God was about to destroy them all by earthquake and by fire from on high. It was in a world which seemed poised on the brink of the abyss that these penitents cried out, as they beat themselves and threw themselves upon their faces: "Holy Virgin take pity on us! Beg Jesus Christ to spare us!" and: "Mercy, mercy! Peace, peace!"—calling ceaselessly, we are told, until the fields and mountains seemed to echo with their prayers and musical instruments fell silent and love-songs died away.[1]

Though the sentiment that this was an intolerable existence often gave rise to the obscure desire for universal annihilation, the principle of hope also fought its way through: a phoenix reborn from the ashes. Thus the most diverse traits and people were mixed together in the flagellant movement: the refusal of the Church and the clergy; the divine freedom to which the most disadvantaged people (who suffered the most) acceded by right; and even those who—like the Beghards of Cologne, the Beguines of Swidnica and the former Messalians—overcame the ordeal of sorrow and entered the promised land of Edenic happiness; but also the resentment of the oppressed people who turned this way and that against the powerful and who, in their routine outbursts [*l'ordinaire sanie*] of cowardice and sadism, most frequently tortured and massacred Jewish men, women, and children.

In 1349, the Pope rejected the Flagellants: "most of them or their followers, beneath an appearance of piety, set their hands to cruel and impious works, shedding the blood of Jews, whom Christian piety accepts and sustains"[2].

In 1261 and 1262 the movement crossed the Alps, went up the Rhine, and spread in Southern Germany, where it took a turn that was more popular, more anti-clerical, and more faithful to Joachimite eschatology. The appeals to purity of soul and faith didn't fail to revive the anti-Semitic sentiments that had been cultivated by Emicho of Leiningen, the Master of Hungary, and by an anonymous person from Passau. (Note that, in the second half of the thirteenth century, there was a chronicle in which the author, a cleric from Passau, attributed all of the world's misfortunes to the Jews and heretics.)

If one participated in a procession of flagellants, the duration of which would have been thirty-three-and-a-half days (in memory of Christ's age), this was deemed sufficient to assure one of the impeccability of whatever one did, which obviously dispensed with the need for the Church and its sacraments. After 1262 the ongoing threat to clerical profitability justified the prohibition that was pronounced against these hysterical hordes, who exhibited their bloody wounds and pled Christ-like sorrows in the countryside and the towns in order to be able subsequently to devote themselves, without committing any sins, to couplings, libations, rape, and pillage.

The Black Plague of 1348–9 revived the propensity for merciful suffering, on which the Church of the fifteenth century would base its lucrative market in death. Possessed by a holy fury, groups of fifty to five hundred people paraded in successive waves in Germany, the Netherlands, and Hungary, exorcising through an exemplary expiation the just anger with which God overwhelmed his creatures. England, which was little interested in redemption obtained by way of a cynical one-upmanship in misfortune, rejected the Flagellants.

Repressed in Strasbourg in 1296, Bergamo in 1334, and Cremona in 1346, the Flagellants still managed to invade Bruges, Ghent, Tournai, and Dordrecht. The bishops sometimes tolerated them and tried in vain to temper their devastating zeal.

As the excess of horrors that accumulated during the 1350s elevated suffering to the dignity of a supreme good, millenarianism reappeared: it was the logical extension of the project of annihilation that God was in the middle of conducting with great conviction. A mysterious *Heavenly Letter*, which no doubt issued from Segarellism, announced the Lord's decision—as dictated to a prophet—to exterminate mankind. Angered by the unworthy conduct of His creatures and, in particular, the rich, God would only spare humanity in exchange for general repentance and contrition enlivened by the whip. One still had to receive clemency through the intercession of Mary. The egalitarianism of the adepts of voluntary poverty drove the nobility away from the movement, though the nobles sometimes gave in to penitential temptations. Didn't Clement VI prescribe the virtues of flagellation? Yes, but he retracted his support and, in 1349, he condemned the movement, with the result that the messianism of the artisans and peasants turned to confront the aristocracy, the bourgeoisie, and the clergy, the hedonism of which—judged to be contrary to the wishes of God—had aroused heavenly anger.

Anti-clericalism most often gave way to anti-Semitism. The pogroms made productive use of pent-up frustrations, which were unleashed upon marginal people who had been condemned to disgrace by the Church (which had made the Jews scapegoats when they ceased to fill up the coffers of the bishops and princes). The Jewish communities of Frankfurt, Mainz, Cologne, and Brussels were exterminated. (Note that, in 1146, Peter the Venerable, the abbot of the Benedictine Abbey of Cluny, had already remarked, "What good does it do to go to the end of the world [...] to combat the Saracens when we let live among us other infidels who are guiltier with respect to Christ than the Mohammedans?"[3])

Konrad Schmid led the millenarian flagellants in Thuringia. He revived the legend of the return of Frederick, the Emperor of the Last Days, to which Dolcino had imprudently given political credit.

Renewing the tradition of the itinerant Christ, Schmid demanded absolute submission to his person. He decreed that self-flagellation was the prelude to the birth of an Edenic age to come in 1369. The Inquisition hastened to seize Schmid and burn him in Nordhausen in 1368, one year in advance of the due date.

By reinforcing its repression, Rome attempted, as was its custom, to recuperate the movement to its own profit. The Spaniard Vincent Ferrier[4] took control of the penitents, who were severely boxed in and controlled; he won his sanctification by giving an orthodox coloration to the welts made by the whip. In this he was only partially successful.

From then on the Inquisition took the initiative. The pyres (principally in Germany) reduced to cinders some ninety flagellants in 1414; 300 of them in 1416; and a dozen in Nordhausen in 1446 and in Sondershausen in 1454. The last victims succumbed around 1480.

The Flagellants' doctrine was little concerned with theological subtleties. Konrad Schmid advocated a second baptism—a baptism of blood, which conferred personal salvation and rendered the Church, the clergy, and the sacraments superfluous. The refusal to pay tithes and the denunciation of the trade in indulgences were characteristic of all of the popular movements that the Church continually aroused against itself and against its clerical bureaucracy. The rejection of the cult of the saints and purgatory would be passed down to Martin Luther, as would, all things considered, anti-Semitism.

Domenico Savi (also known Meco del Sacco) was burned in 1344 in Ascoli; his doctrines attested to the penetration of Free Spirit ideas into even the destructive fury of the Flagellants. He taught the following theses, transcribed here in the spirit of the inquisitors who sent him to death:

> Shameless fondling, even taken as far as orgasm, is not a sin; men and women praying together in the darkness of the night do not commit sin, whatever else they do at the same time; women are permitted to flagellate themselves, for their sins, naked and in public; laymen also have the ability to absolve all sins.[5]

Nevertheless, the Church discovered in collective self-flagellation a way of exercising a form of control over populations, albeit one whose power the official history has always exaggerated. Catholicism only inspired a true devotion in the fifteenth century, on the eve of the schism that amputated half of its empire. Using the fear of death and the horror of a beyond that would perpetuate the atrocities of life on earth, Rome endlessly readjusted its control over subjects who were reduced to the condition of sinners.

The Dance of Death, which deployed an avenging and egalitarian imagery (since death spins all the social classes in its sinister round), celebrated the interminable festival of dead life. The only way out of such a life of suffering was to pay the parish priest (who lay in waiting ready to ambush the patient's final breath) for the 'last rites' that gave a life-saving meaning to sorrow. Many pardons were issued to those who underwent intense suffering, so long as they resigned themselves to honoring the payments that the Church collected at each and every moment of an existence that it subjected to its total control—from the cries of birth to the death rattles of the final agony. Ironically, from the fifteenth century onwards, the Church imposed itself in the guise of a mother, while death, which was depicted as a half-emaciated skeleton, took on the figure of Woman as understood by the patriarchy: an enemy in life, a friend in putrefaction.

CHAPTER THIRTY-FIVE

The Fraticelles

The name 'Fraticelles' (from the Italian *fraticelli*, sometimes translated in French as *frérots* ['kid brothers']) designated radical dissidents of the 'Spiritual' faction who, within the Franciscan order, were opposed to the 'Conventual' or orthodox wing: they adhered to the strict vocation of poverty, as prescribed by Francis of Assisi.

Although John XXII, in an instance of polemical malignance, deliberately misapplied the term 'Fraticelles' to all of the Spirituals, he never made the mistake of seriously attacking them, even though they were blemished by the same spirit of freedom as were the Beghards, Beguines, Apostolics, and Dolcinians.

Respectful of the original directives of Franciscanism, the Spirituals extolled—in addition to absolute poverty and the refusal of all ecclesial property—theses that were becoming more and more embarrassing to the Church, which was engaged in the whirlwind of business affairs and was already equipped with the modern financial power that at that point had barely set in motion the decline in political and spiritual authority that the Church would undergo in the twentieth century. Three men took the lead in the struggle against pontifical politics: Angelo Clareno (Pietro da Fossombrone), Peter John Olivi, and Ubertino of Casale. Angelo Clareno gave a historical account of the conflict in his *A Chronicle or History of the Seven Tribulations of the Order of Brothers Minor*.

According to him, Crescentius of Iesi—the general of the Order from 1244 to 1247 and the successor of Elias of Cortona—showed "the same avidity [that Elias had] for wealth and science, and the same aversion to poor convents scattered in solitude, which he changed into sumptuous monasteries; around him, the brothers chased after testaments [i.e. financial legacies], sued their debtors, attached themselves to schools of dialectics, and neglected prayer and Scripture in favor of the useless curiosities of Aristotle"[1]. Brother Bonadies, a jurisconsulate and the deputy of the general, "drank fraud and lied like water". He observed with a malevolent eye the growing sect of the Spirituals, "who [he thought] did not work according to the truth of the Gospel, scorned the rules of the order, believed themselves better than the others, lived in their own manner, related everything to the Spirit, and even wore cloaks that were too short"[2].

Innocent IV, then at war with Frederick II, gave Crescentius permission to pursue the dissidents and to eliminate "their occasions for schism and scandal in the order". The ascension of John of Parma to the head of the order restored power to the Spirituals for a time, but his sympathies for Joachimite theories and for the reforms of Segarelli gave the enemies of the austere Spirituals the opportunity to associate them with the 'libertarian' party of the Fraticelles.

After a period in exile in Armenia between 1290 and 1293, an autonomous group led by Liberatus (Peter of Macerata) and Angelo Clareno obtained the protection of Pope Celestine V and, in 1294, formed the *Pauperes heremitae domini Caelestini*[3]. This was all in vain, because Celestine's successor, Boniface VIII, had the liveliest interest in the temporal concerns of the Church. He condemned the Spirituals and threw into prison the poet Jacopo Benedetti, who—having converted to voluntary poverty after the accidental death of his wife (which did not prevent him from comparing women to serpents and Satan)—had joined Angelo Clareno's friends.

Liberatus and his adepts took refuge in Achaia, and then in Thessaly. Upon the death of Liberatus, Angelo Clareno became the head of the Spirituals and returned to Italy. One of his partisans, the physician and alchemist Arnaud of Villeneuve, convinced Clement V to reconcile the two rival tendencies.

Ubertino of Casale, the leader of the Spirituals in Tuscany, went to Avignon to confront the leaders of the Conventual faction, Bonagrazia of Bergamo and Raymond of Fronsac. It is worth recalling that Ubertino considered it prudent to avoid incurring any reproach for harboring sympathies for the Fraticelles—as an Inquisitor, he had in fact cracked down hard on the Franciscan partisans of the Free Spirit in the Spoleto region. Arnaud himself did not hold back from anathematizing a doctrine that was so contrary to religion. The conciliation ran aground, however, because the Conventual Franciscans were at that point unaware of the extent to which the progress of the economy was strengthening the power of the Roman Church and its then-uncertain control over nations and principalities.

The ascension of the formidable businessman John of Cahors to the pontificate under the name John XXII gave the signal for the repression to begin. The same reprobation fell upon the Spirituals, the Fraticelles, the Dolcinians, the Beghards, and the partisans of the Free Spirit, whom Clement V had condemned at the Council of Vienne in 1311.

The Pope ordered the sovereigns from whom the Spirituals had sought refuge to expel them as heretics. The bull *Sancta romana* officially bestowed on them the denomination 'Fraticelles' for the first time.

Arrested in Avignon and then freed, Angelo Clareno precipitously left for Italy, where, in 1318, he began rallying partisans to the notion that Christ and his disciples held no possessions. In 1322, at the Chapter of Perugia, he obtained the important support of Michael of Cesena, the general minister of the Franciscan order, who held the absolute destitution of Jesus and the apostles to be 'holy and Catholic' dogma. (Note that, in order to combat the thesis of the Spirituals by way of iconographic propaganda, the Church recommended that painters depict Jesus and the apostles as carrying purses for the collection of alms.)

This thesis directly challenged the interests of the Church, that tributary of capitalist development that was slowly freeing itself from the agrarian mode of production. One soon saw the Joachimite legend return in force, now rewritten and adapted for the people of the time. John XXII, the leader of the 'corporeal Church', was stigmatized as a 'mystical Antichrist'.

This Antichrist, scorning the reformers and their preoccupation with the misery of life, responded with a very shrewd maneuver.

While Francis of Assisi had prescribed that the Holy See should hold on to all of the order's property, the Pope decided to transfer it back to the Franciscans, entrusting them with a responsibility that transformed them into property owners whether they liked it or not. At the same time, his bull dated 12 November 1323, *Cum inter nonnullos*, condemned as heretical the theses of Michael of Cesena, who quickly took refuge with his friends under the auspices of Emperor Louis of Bavaria.

Angelo Clareno went into exile in Basilicata, where he continued to lead his party until his death in 1337.

The Spirituals remained active in the region of Naples, in Sicily (to which the Tuscan group of Henry of Ceva withdrew), and in Tabriz, Armenia.

It was among the Spiritual adepts of Monte Maiella that the Roman tribune Cola di Rienzi was welcomed after he was denounced by a papal bull.

In the eyes of the Church there no longer existed a single Franciscanism (that of the 'Observants'). The dissidents fell under the inquisitorial label 'Fraticelles of Opinion', with 'opinion' designating adherence to the theses of voluntary poverty.

Bernard Délicieux

On 7 May 1318 the first victims of Franciscan orthodoxy perished on the pyres of Marseille. That same year the Inquisition condemned to life imprisonment a rare—if not the only—public and openly declared adversary of the Catholic and Roman police.

Bernard Délicieux, who was born in Montpellier in 1260 and entered the Franciscan order in 1284, soon thereafter became the spokesman of the populations of Toulouse, Carcassonne, and Razès, which were indignant about the machinations of the Inquisition and the barbarity of the Dominicans. In Carcassonne he led a riot that seized the citadel and freed the heretics held in the official 'wall' or 'prison'.

His intention was in part to appeal to the justice of the King of France, who was more generous in matters of faith, but, having been implicated in a conspiracy (his involvement may have been faked in order to bring him down), he instead attracted Philip the Fair's displeasure. The King had the consuls of Carcassonne, Limoux, and Razès hanged; his despotism was hostile to the politics of communal autonomy. Having been reprieved in 1307, in 1313 Bernard fell into the net that had been patiently woven for him by inquisitorial vindictiveness. He was accused of attempting to poison the Pope, with the complicity of Arnaud of Villeneuve. The crudeness of the accusation may have elicited some reservations; he only escaped the pyre by dying in 1320 after two years of incarceration in the jail of God's executioners, whose infamy he had denounced. It was only in the sixteenth century, with the appearance of Sebastian Castellion, that a second voice in the world concert demanded the abrogation of the death penalty for crimes of belief.

Prous Boneta
In 1325 the Inquisition seized Prous Boneta, who was venerated by the Spirituals for her courage and humanity. Imprisoned in 1315 in Montpellier, she resolved soon after being freed to lend her help to the persecuted Spirituals, along with her sister Alissette.

In 1320 Prous had been gripped by visions similar to those of Hadewijch, Mechthild of Magdeburg, and Teresa of Ávila. She later had an ecstatic encounter with Christ. On Maundy Thursday in 1321 He had breathed His *pneuma* into her and promised her that she would give birth to the Holy Spirit, which would inaugurate the Third Age. According to her own version of Joachimism, Elijah was Francis of Assisi and Enoch was Olivi.

The power given to Christ by God ended from the moment that Olivi was invested with the Holy Spirit: the papacy would soon after cease to exist, and the sacraments and confession would fall into desuetude. Thenceforth, contrition would efface sin without the need for either penitence or priests.

Rising up as she did against the massacre of the Spirituals and the lepers, who were unjustly accused of poisoning water sources in 1321 and 1322, and whom she compared to the Innocents (the presumed victims of Herod), Prous Boneta presented all the traits of an ideal defendant in the eyes of Henry of Chamay, the Inquisitor of Carcassonne. She did not repudiate any of her convictions before the tribunal and was delivered to the flames in 1325.[4]

In Avignon, the celebrated troubadour Raimon de Cornet barely escaped the pyre in 1326. Jean de Roquetaillade (Juan de Rocatallada, better known to the alchemists as John of Rupescissa) also narrowly avoided such a fate. Professing Joachimite opinions, this friend of Arnaud of Villeneuve and the Spirituals compared the Church to a bird that is born without feathers and strips the plumage from all others so as to adorn itself through pride and tyranny.

As the trials of the Spirituals multiplied in number, the Free Spirit and libertarian behaviors were incriminated with an increasing frequency. This incrimination most often took the form of the commonplace calumny by which popes, ecclesiastic dignitaries, and inquisitors imputed their own debauchery and erotic fantasies to poor ascetics. The Spirituals had always fought the Fraticelles, and we have no grounds for suspecting that the martyrs of Franciscan fanaticism—such as Francesco of Pistoia, who was burned in Venice in 1337, John of Castillon and Francis of Arquata, who were executed in Avignon in 1354, and Fra Michele Berti, who was reduced to cinders in Florence in 1389—took libidinous liberties.

In 1317, John XXII definitively confirmed the dissolution of the dissident group[5], which was thereafter doomed to extermination. In one of those ironic developments that so often bring about the downfalls of infamous people, this Pope, who enjoyed the odor of burning bundles of sticks—he had the Bishop of Cahors (the Pope's hometown) skinned alive and burned—suddenly reiterated the doctrine of Pelagius regarding the innocence of newborns and the pointlessness of baptizing them. A council instructed him to keep silent concerning a matter that bore closely upon the Church's financial interests, which he had always vehemently defended. Alarmed at hearing such manifestly heretical remarks from his lips, the council's fathers deposed him and discreetly put him to death.

Bentivenga of Gubbio[6]

It fell to the members of the Franciscan Observance—an order that was invested from its beginning with inquisitorial missions, since the Franciscans were reputed to act with less ferocity than the Dominicans—to impose a final solution to what John XXII called the "pestilential plague of Fraticellianism".

Unlike the Spirituals who had broken with the practice of asceticism, the Fraticelles were most often confused with the Beghards and the Apostolics of Free Spirit. Such was the case with Bentivenga da Gubbio.

Bentivenga adhered to the apostolic group of Gerard Segarelli in Parma until the episcopal prohibition of 1281, which forced the adepts to disperse. He then joined the Minorites (note: the 'minor brothers' or Conventual Franciscans) and, in Umbria, rallied the partisans of Free Spirit, who seemed to be numerous in the region. Before his arrival there, there was grouped in Spoleto—around a certain Ottonello—a *congregatio libertatis*[7] that was combated by Giacomo da Bevagna, whom Clare of Montefalco would much later suspect of having a free spirit. Ottonello's influence was such that the Flagellants passing through the valley abandoned their procession in order to discover the effects of pleasure freed from suffering.

Conceitedness incited Bentivenga to expound his theories to Clare of Montefalco, who was subsequently sanctified. She delivered him to the Inquisition along with six other Minorites. Ubertino of Casale, who was part of the Spiritual current, had already taken Bentivenga to task in his *Arbor vitae crucifixae Jesu*[8]. He had reproached him for ideas "inspired by the devil to corrupt the spirit of simple people"[9]. He summarized those ideas in this way:

1. Apathy: an impious deception has appeared, inspired by the enemy, that corrupts the spirit of simple people, and maintains, under the pretext of serenity in the will of God, that they should remain unmoved by both the Passion of Christ and the suffering of their fellow man, and enjoy themselves, so to speak, in the sole pleasure of God, having no heed for the injury done to God nor the pain of their fellow man. And they say, "God leads everything to the best choice"[10].

2. Sinlessness: they say that men who have the grace of God and charity cannot sin. They assert that those who sin in any way have never had charity or the grace of God.
3. From the very true principle of the death of the Son—that we can do nothing good without grace—they infer that, whatever we do, everything is done by grace. For this reason, they say that eating and making love and other similar things represent no fault in us, because they are convinced that grace incites them to these things.[11]

In the summer of 1307 Bentivenga was condemned to life in prison.

Paolo Zoppo

In Rieti in 1334, the Inquisitor Simone da Spoleto began legal proceedings against a group of Fraticelles united around Paolo Zoppo. Robert of Arbrissel labeled "white martyrdom" the test that consisted in sleeping nude between two nude women and triumphing over the desire to make love. With a widow and her servant, Zoppo practiced a style of caress in which the delays imposed upon *amor extaticus*[12] were related to the tantric method of obtaining illumination through sexual tension. The *homines intelligentiae*[13] in Brussels and the *Alumbrados* or 'Illuminati' of Spain practiced the same method of delayed pleasure. Paolo Zoppo and his companions paid with life-long imprisonment for wanting to substitute the refinement of amorous pleasure and the celebration of women—creators of all joy—for the ordinary, cunning, and brutal debauchery of the convents.[14]

At the time of the trial in Rieti, it appeared that the Fraticelles envisioned electing a Pope who would be opposed to the 'Antichrist John XXII'. According to Francis Vanni of Assisi, Angelo Clareno himself recommended awarding the pontificate to Philip of Majorca.

In 1419, the Inquisitor Manfred of Vercelli reported that the 'Fraticelles of Opinion'—particularly numerous in Florence, Tuscany, and the region around Rome—were refusing to submit to Martin V because they had a pope of their own. In 1451, when Nicholas V tasked the Inquisition with proceeding against the Fraticelles who had taken refuge in Athens, he specially recommended the capture of their pope.

The Extermination Trial of the Fraticelles

Tasked by Martin V in 1418 and 1426, and by Eugene IV in 1432, with pitilessly pursuing the Fraticelles, James of the Marches, and John of Capistrano—both honored with the title of saint for their good inquisitorial services—burned thirty-six rebel residences and increased the number of book-burnings. The hatred that they aroused in the people was such that they had ceaselessly to protect themselves against assassination attempts.

In 1449 new pyres were lit in Florence. In 1452—also the year in which Girolamo Savonarola was born—James of the Marches published his *Dialogus contra fraticellos*, in which he recounted the extermination-trial at Maiolati.[15]

There had been a community of Fraticelles of Free Spirit in Maiolati ever since 1410 or 1420. A bell at the church carried the following inscription, which was dated 1429: "Brother Gabriel, Bishop of the Church of Philadelphia, parish priest and general minister of the minor brothers". (Note that, a century earlier, a friend of Marguerite Porete had called himself the angel of Philadelphia[16].)

The official report of the trial was inspired by the accusations that Epiphanius of Salamis had once made against the Barbelites (the Inquisitors also used them without scruple against the Waldensinians and the Cathars): men and women were meeting at night, chanting hymns,

> [and] extinguishing the candles and rushing to each other at random. The children issued from such commerce were brought before the assembly; they were passed hand-to-hand in a round until they died. The one in whose hands they died was elected the great pontiff. They burned one of the babies and threw the cinders into a vase, into which they poured wine; they made those who were being initiated into their brotherhood drink from it. They fought against the ownership of goods and believed that the faithful need not to engage with any magistrates and that the souls of the fortunate would only see God after the resurrection.[17]

Thus did Pierre Bayle recount the trial in his *Historical and Critical Dictionary*. As was his custom, he relayed the arguments of the prosecution and the defense. He did not follow a practice that was often used to justify the cruelest repressions and that the Inquisitors called the *barilotto*[18]. The propaganda that was skillfully conducted in order to discredit the unfortunate Fraticelles in the eyes of the pious exercised its ravages upon public opinion with a durable effect: for a long time afterward, popular language preserved the insulting expression 'Tu sei nato dal barilotto' (Italian for 'You were born from a barrel').

For all that, Bayle estimated that there was a strong probability that this Fraticellian community led a joyous life for thirty years and enjoyed a terrestrial existence that was as luxurious and luxuriant as possible, with the approval of the heavens and in the absence of the guilt that gnawed at the tormented hedonism of the powerful. At the time, the rage of the two holy inquisitors was only exacerbated. A great expiatory blaze illuminated the sinister depths of their consciences.[19]

In 1466 a group of Fraticelles who were arrested and tortured in Assisi confirmed—on the insistence of the inquisitors—the use of *barilotti* in Poli (near Tivoli), in Les Marches, and in Maiolati. This sect, known by the name 'The Truth' (which has anachronistically Freemasonic connotations), distributed pamphlets in which the ideas of the Free Spirit were expounded.[20]

As among the Beghards of Cologne, the solicitation to love was expressed by the formula *Fac mihi caritatem* ('Give me charity'), with *caritas* here returning to its original meaning of 'love of one's fellow man', *carus*, 'beloved'.

The Fraticelles then disappear from the Inquisition's registers, but a popular fable has it that, entrenched in deep valleys and forests, they continued to maintain the sort of fantastical convents that haunted the tormented imaginations of readers of the Marquis de Sade, Matthew Lewis, Ann Radcliffe, Horace Walpole, and the Gothic novel more generally.

CHAPTER THIRTY-SIX

The Eastern Reformers: The Hussites and Taborites

Rome discovered in Bohemia a source of considerable riches. Half the land belonged to the clergy, which—while exploiting it in the name of Christ—aroused a popular hatred more lively than that seen anywhere else, if that is possible.

In Prague in 1360, the ascetic reformer Jan Milíč denounced the corruption of the Church—the veritable incarnation of the Antichrist—and vainly exhorted priests to adopt the voluntary poverty that he characterized as evangelic.

Upon Milíč's death, his disciple Matthew of Janov pursued his reforms. He opposed the 'body of the Antichrist'—served up in the form of the Host during the communion of the corrupted Church—with the Eucharist of the *Ekklēsia*, the true Church of the faithful. The commensality of bread and wine, which Janov opposed to the abstract and mechanical ritual of clerical communion, explains the intensification of the eucharistic quarrels that took place in Bohemia during the Hussite, Taborite, and Adamite wars. (Note that the communion that used these two items at the same time was intended to be a symbol that was hostile to Catholicism, in which one communed using just one of them.)

Around 1380 the reformist doctrines of Wycliffe—which benefitted from England's sly hostility towards Roman power—began to spread.

Jan Hus[1], an admirer of Wycliffe, suddenly introduced a turn towards worldwide critique into his preaching, which until then had stayed within the limits of national concerns. The prestige attached to his position as Rector of the University of Prague conferred on his voice an import that caused it to resound all over Europe. His significance was demonstrated when John XXII dispatched to Prague emissaries whom he had charged with preaching a crusade against his personal enemy, the King of Naples, and with collecting the funds necessary to that enterprise by way of a promotional sale of indulgences. Hus rose up against the cynicism of this Pope in the name of the Holy Scriptures and condemned an attitude that he regarded as being unworthy of Christian teachings.

Hus was neither a heretic nor a revolutionary. He simply pushed honesty to the point of imprudence when he denounced the economic and financial politics of the Church. He also presumptuously counted on the support of King Wenceslas, who was indeed favorable to him but was nonetheless distracted from Hus's fate by more pressing concerns.

Having been excommunicated and summoned to the Council of Konstanz in 1414, Hus went there accompanied by his disciple, Jerome of Prague, and fortified by the safe conduct guaranteed him by Emperor Sigismund. Hus defended his thesis in front of the Council: the Christ was the leader of the Church, not the Pope. The council decided in his favor on one point: it "deposed Pope John XXIII for simony, murder, sodomy and fornication"—complaints that, all things considered, could have been made against most of the pontifical sovereigns[2]. (Note that, in the twentieth century, in order to efface the memory of a Pope who was far from being one of the worst, another was given the title 'John XXIII'.)

On the other hand, the ecclesiastic dignitaries would not allow their lucrative apostolic functions to be taken from them. Led by the French Cardinal Pierre d'Ailly (who, though a committed millenarian, was always attentive to his immediate interests), the Council Fathers excommunicated Jan and Jerome, and delivered them to the pyre in 1415. Emperor Sigismund, who had counseled Hus to retract his statements, had little desire to see the creation of an independent Bohemia, the demand for which he perceived beneath Hus's theological quarrels. This was a poor calculation on the part of the Council Fathers, because the executions of Hus and Jerome precipitated an insurrection.

Although King Wenceslas broke with the Hussites at the insistence of Pope Martin V and his brother, Emperor Sigismund, the Church of Bohemia passed over to secular control and was snatched away from Roman domination.

In July 1418, when Wenceslas excluded from the government of Prague the representatives of the working-class neighborhood of New Town, weavers, stone carvers, brewers, and peasants seized City Hall and defenestrated the new councilors. Under the pretext of hunting down the patrician families hostile to Jan Hus, the uprising made itself well and truly part of the tradition of communalist class struggles.

The guilds and artisanal confederations expelled the Catholics, expropriated the monasteries, and confiscated ecclesiastic riches to the profit of insurgent Prague. A division very quickly appeared between proletarian radicalism and the notables who had hastily converted to Hussism. A moderate party emerged, which, while close to the Catholics, nevertheless distinguished itself by communing through bread *and* wine—that is to say, using two items. Its members adopted the name 'Utraquists'.

In 1419 the radical wing of the Hussite movement organized itself on a resolutely autonomous basis. Located on a hill near the Castle of Bechyně, a group of partisans renamed the hill after Mount Tabor, a location that the canonical Gospel attributed to Matthew had made famous by identifying it as the place where Jesus had announced his return before being elevated to heaven.

The Taborites accorded to each person the right to interpret the Scriptures. They rejected purgatory, prayers for the dead, and the cults of the saints and the relics. Like the Waldensians, they refused to take oaths and were opposed to the death penalty. Once more there intermingled (as a result of working-class demands) the themes of voluntary poverty, egalitarian millenarianism, and, in an antagonistic manner, the thrust of the Free Spirit and the weight of fundamentalist fanaticism.

In 1420 the news that the fire of God was going to descend upon the towns and villages started a great exodus towards the mountains, where five Taborite cities were erected and received divine protection, because "they would not make a treaty with the Antichrist"[3].

To justify the massacre of sinners, the military commander Jan Capek took his stand on citations from the Old Testament: "Accursed be the man who withholds his sword from shedding the blood of the enemies of the Christ. Each believer must wash his hands in that blood"[4]. Some people, such as Petr Chelčický, who was faithful to the principle of pacifism, reacted against the hysteria of such remarks and denounced the ruses of Satan, who had cleverly suggested to the furious that they were angels tasked with purifying the world.

In March 1420 the truce between Sigismund and the moderate Hussites gave way to a merciless war in which the personality of the Chief Taborite, Jan Žižka, imposed itself. Žižka haloed himself with prophetic glory by crushing the German and Hungarian troops whose swords had supposedly received the benediction of Rome. It fell to him to instaurate the millennium and to prepare, through the kingdom of the saints, the return of Christ to earth. The social program had hardly changed: "All men will live together like brothers, none will be subjected to another"[5]. "All the lords, all the nobles and all the knights will be executed and exterminated in the forests as outlaws".[6] As often happens, the first victims of the purge were not external enemies but the radical wing of the Taborites: the 'Pikarti' [Picards], who were decimated by Žižka in the name of holy morality.

The collectivization of subsistence that was instaurated in the Taborite communities did not extend to organizing the production of goods, and so the Taborites were soon reduced to raiding and pillaging for their supplies. The plundering of the nobility and the clergy was followed by the exploitation of the peasants, who found themselves in a worse situation than they had experience under the regime of the lords.

In April 1421 Žižka annihilated the libertarian communities formed by the Picards and the Adamites. Their protests in favor of egalitarianism continued to spread, however, and they fomented peasant revolts in Burgundy and Germany, where the peasants' war became endemic.

In 1430 the Taborite armies attacked Leipzig, Bamberg, and Nuremburg. Their victories provoked uprisings against the patricians in Mainz, Konstanz, Weimar, and Stettin. But the moderate wing—the Utraquists—seceded and soon went over to the enemy. In 1434, at Liban, the Ultraquists of Bohemia defeated the Taborites. This was the beginning of a slow debacle that came to an end with the seizure of Mount Tabor in 1452. The majority of the survivors of the general massacre returned to peaceful ways and founded the community of the Moravian Brothers. For all that, the Taborite doctrine did not cease to spread: it continued to keep alive, in the towns and in the countryside, the flame of freedom that had found a decrepit world worthy of being set on fire.

Around 1460, when Bohemia had just emerged from a long civil war, two nobles demonstrated the extent to which expectations of the millennium remained alive. In addition to the usual chronological calculations of the *parousia* [the Second Coming], Janko and Livin von Wirsberg expounded a novel conception of God's relations with the world that he created. The Son of Man was preparing through his imminent return to save not only humanity but also God himself, who had been crippled since the beginning of time by the sins of mankind. It was to be delivered from his own suffering that God appealed to the Savior. The idea of a divinity that would be nothing without the men who created it thus pursued its course.

How was this new reign, destined to restore God to His power, to begin? With the extermination of the armed forces of the Antichrist: the Pope and his ministers, followed by all other adversaries. Only 14,000 people would survive to found the Spiritual Church. The 'sword' of this crusade would be formed by former Taborites, generally regrouped into bands of brigands. Jan van Batenburg would do precisely that after the disaster at Münster.[7]

Centered in Eger, this movement even had an influence on the Fraticelles of Italy. The year 1467, predicted to be the date of the return of the Christ in bloody majesty, prompted the Pope's legatee to act with determination. Janko escaped the consequent repression; Livin abjured in order to escape the pyre and died in the prison of the archbishop, in Regensburg.

CHAPTER THIRTY-SEVEN

The Men of Intelligence and the Picards of Bohemia

On 12 June 1411 Willem van Hildernissem of the Carmelite Order was called before the Inquisitor Henry of Selles, who was acting on behalf of the episcopal tribunal of Cambrai. Willem van Hildernissem was accused of playing an important role in a Free Spirit group known to Brussels by the name 'the Men of Intelligence' [*homines intelligentiae*][1]. Formerly a reader of Holy Scriptures at the Carmelite convent of Tienen, he had found an inspired ally in Gilles of Canter (Gilles the Cantor, Aegidius Cantor), a sexagenarian layman (probably the son of a noble family) who was dead by the time of the trial.

Everything seems to indicate that they shared an interest in the theories of Bloermardinne, whose memory remained more vivid than any inquisitor dared to imagine. Consequently, Henry of Selles—who was attached to the Abbey of Groenendael where Ruysbroeck, the enemy of Bloermardinne, had died in 1381—barely escaped a premeditated assassination attempt by the partisans of the *homines intelligentiae* at a ford crossing. Since he was not killed, a song ridiculing him circulated in Brussels.

The support that the group received from both the working class and the notables (their meetings were held in a tower owned by an alderman) was not irrelevant to the leniency of the judgment that was passed on them. Willem was allowed out after three years in prison, perhaps

477

because of a deal whereby he adjured and rejected the most subversive part of Gilles' doctrine.

The Joachimite connotations were immediately clear from the very name of the sect. The Third Age was to be that of the natural intelligence of beings and things, of an 'erudite ignorance' in which were joined the innocence of the child and the knowledge of the total man—a union of *gnosis* and *pistis*, with *pistis* meaning faith in oneself rather than faith in God. Gilles of Canter had said that one day the Holy Spirit inspired him and said to him: "You have arrived at the stage of a child of three years".

In the original, natural state of freedom, there was neither sin nor guilt, neither spiritual nor temporal authority. The Church, the laws, and the sacraments had no meaning; neither did penitence and redemption. The only important thing was the path to perfection on which amorous ecstasy produced the state of perfect humanity ('divinity' in religious language). The adepts of Gilles and Willem thus traveled—if they so desired—along an initiatory road marked by various degrees of amorous pleasure. But each person was free to remain chaste or to give him- or herself up to libertinage.

Well versed in the Holy Scriptures, Willem van Hildernissem was able to justify any behavior with appropriate quotations, because everything was desired by God.

In the 'paradise' in which the sectarians united without distinctions based on class or wealth, Gilles of Canter taught a way of making love "that was the one of Adam and Eve before the Fall". This was probably a form of delayed orgasm, without ejaculation, culminating in tantric illumination and the removal of the fear of possible pregnancy for the women.

The absence of fear and guilt, allied with an art of sexual pleasure that was authorized in all the domains of the most voluptuous quests, easily induced in the minds of the adepts the idea that they belonged to an elite, without comparison to the mass of their contemporaries who led absurd and frightened lives under the shepherd's crooks of the lords and the priests.

The prudence they employed during their trial and the laughable severity [i.e. the lightness] of the judgment that was passed against them indicate the skill with which the adepts succeeded in propagating their doctrines in complete safety: they enjoyed great favor in urban areas and the protection of the notables. Such were the doctrines that the 'Picards'[2]—who left Picardy to radicalize the Taborite revolution—attempted to implant in Bohemia.

The Picards, or the Adamites of Bohemia

Who were the Picards who, around 1418[3], flocked to Bohemia, where the Taborites had instaurated a kind of peasant collectivism? Contrary to the opinion that sees in the word *Picards* a translation of *begardi*, Enea Silvio Piccolomini gave it the meaning "Picard, who came originally from Belgian Gaul"[4]. The Free Spirit doctrine that they propagated suggests a close relationship with the *homines intelligentiae*, whose community in Brussels had been prosecuted by the Inquisition.

In the manner of the Anabaptists tramping towards Münster a century later, the Picards converged on Bohemia, where the Hussite insurrection sent out glimmers of freedom and provided a glimpse of the possibility of an existence lived in accordance with the teachings of Willem van Hildernissem and Gilles of Canter.

The Picardian doctrine took hold especially in the regions with weak Taborite influence, such as Žatec, Plzen, and Prague. It showed through in a diluted form in the closed field of the theological quarrels that surrounded Sigmund of Repan and, especially, Martin Huska, who was also known as 'Loquis' and who preached a kind of Dolcinianism that evoked the end of time and the reign of the saints. In the fashion of the times, Huska announced "a new kingdom of the saints on earth, [where] the good would have no more suffering"—because, he said, "if Christians would always have to suffer in this way, I would not want to be a servant of God"[5].

In February 1421 the chronicler Lawrence of Brezová denounced the progression of the Free Spirit among the Taborites: "On account of this heresy, alas, the brothers living at Tabor split into two fractions, one Picard and the other Taborite. The more faithful section, the Taborites, expelled more than 200 men and women infected with the Picard heresy"[6].

In the eighteenth century, Isaac de Beausobre[7] would attribute to the Picards the name 'Adamites', due to the Edenic innocence that they claimed for themselves. According to Lawrence of Brezová:

> As they went on their way through the forests and hills, some of them fell into such madness that men and women took off their clothes and went naked, saying that clothes had been adopted as a result of the sin committed by their first parents, but that they were in a state of innocence. By a similar madness, they imagined that they did not sin if one of the brothers had commerce with one of the sisters. And if the woman had a child, they said that she had conceived by the Holy Spirit. [Baptism does not exist, because] the children of parents living in sanctity [that is, as members of the community] are conceived without original mortal sin. . . . They pray to the God that they possess within themselves, saying: "Our Father, who art within us . . ."[8]

Aloof from Picardian radicalization, Martin Huska remained loyal to the apostolic tradition and was inspired by more moderate demands that would subsequently instaurate a religious modernism in matters of the Eucharist.

The autonomy of the Picardian community would last two months, from December 1420 to January 1421. Its spokesperson, Peter Kanis, who was seconded by men and women of the people such as Rohan the Blacksmith, Nicholas (also known as Moses), Adam, and Mary, preached in the taverns and celebrated free weddings based on love that the clergy and the Taborites called fornication or sexual license.

Soon enough, the persecutions of the Picards began. Nicholas of Pelhřimov published a treatise against Kanis as a prelude to the attack that, around mid-April, the military chief Jan Žižka launched against those expelled from Mount Tabor. Fifty prisoners, including Peter Kanis, were burned at Klokoty.

The survivors then organized their resistance under the leadership of Rohan the Blacksmith. On 20 April, after violent battles, Žižka crushed the Picards and sent twenty-five prisoners to the pyre. Others were executed in Prague.

On 21 October 1421 the partisans of Kanis, who had taken refuge in a forest outside of Bernatrice, succumbed and were exterminated, except for a single person who was spared so that he could give a report on the Picardian doctrine.[9] Before fleeing to the south, a small number of Adamites occupied the fortress of Ostrov for a while by conducting subsistence raids on the villages, which gave them a reputation for brigandage.

The terror by way of which Žižka's Taborites exempted themselves from the difficulties they faced made an expiatory victim of Martin Huska. Although Huska was no longer in solidarity with the Picards and had abjured, Žižka vowed that he would be burned in Prague, along with his friend Procope the One-Eyed. Frightened by the troubles in the capital, where Huska enjoyed a great deal of sympathy, the magistrates preferred to send their executioners to Rudnice. Huska and Procope were put to death there in a refinement of the tortures that the Inquisition wished to apply to the Taborite heretics, who were inspired by the very same God as the Picards.

CHAPTER THIRTY-EIGHT

The Victory of the Reformers and the Birth of the Protestant Churches

The so-called Reformation, which saw the emergence of schismatic Churches around Martin Luther and John Calvin, did not add anything particularly novel to the program of the reformers who, from the eleventh century onward, had fought against the temporal interests of the clergy and Rome. The commonly held view among historians—that Catholicism had previously had a firm hold on the people of Europe—is contradicted as soon as we look beyond the power of the laws that were imposed by the princes and the ecclesiastic hierarchy, along with the latter's grid of parishes, confessors, priests, inquisitors, and preachers who propagated guilt, a horror of sexuality, the Satanism of women, the omnipresent image of death, and a Hell directly inspired by the abuses of penal justice here on earth.

Fear of and hatred and scorn for the Constantinian Church never ceased to animate a wide range of social classes. Indifference and irreligion reigned in the disadvantaged milieus, where the beggars and supplicants deployed false piety in a cynical fashion. It was only the aspiration for a pre-Constantinian Christianity—ascetic, altruistic, loyal to voluntary poverty, inclined towards martyrdom, anti-clerical, and theocratic— that brought a religious coloration to the collectivist nostalgias of the fourth to the sixteenth centuries. The Catholic Church persecuted this Christianity on every occasion that it manifested itself, with the exception of a brief period in the eleventh century.

Attentive to the temporal prerogatives that, by way of material enrichment, conferred upon it a considerable power, the Catholic Church became increasingly distant from the *Ekklēsia*—the spiritual communities of the faithful—which pinned their hopes on the Waldensians, the adepts of voluntary poverty, Wycliffe's Lollards, the Hussites, the Taborites, and a crowd of agitators whose project of abolishing tithes guaranteed them a certain amount of success.

In the Church itself, voices were raised to clamor for new accords between the interests of God and the financial interests of a 'multinational' that claimed to be descended from the Zealot Simon (metamorphosed into Saint Peter).

"Our fat canons think they are quit in the sight of God if they sing in a clear voice in the choir an alleluiah or a response; they then return home to amuse themselves and sup well with their mummers and jugglers".[1] This diatribe was not written by Savonarola or Luther but by Anthony of Padua (1195–1231), who was an orthodox spirit but was nonetheless aware of the split between the faith of the poor and the Church of the rich. This Church, through its carelessness, failed to encourage the resignation of the disadvantaged, who were quite dumbfounded by the call to 'live as Christ did'.

Wycliffe, Hus, Savonarola, Luther, and Calvin did not pursue aims that were revolutionary, schismatic, or hostile to Catholicism. Their designs placed them in the political line of Gregory IX (when he took the side of Ramihrdus against the high clergy).

The development of the economic process gave Luther and Calvin a weapon that was finally capable of breaking the spiritual monopoly that the cynicism of the pontifical bureaucracy had discredited through the scandalous market in indulgences and through the priority that the bureaucracy gave to business affairs. The expansion of commerce, the growing independence of the banks, and the preindustrial artisanal enterprises established a state of mind that was favorable to the new reformers. The separation from Rome did not just signify the end of an odious hierarchy that intermixed financial interests with faith; it also implied the notion that belief properly belonged to the individual in his or her relationship with God, and that the management of capital constituted a domain separate from religion, albeit one governed by the imperatives of Christian morality. A Calvinist businessman's rigorous obedience to God accorded with his relentless search for profit because the latter—having banished crazy, hedonistic expenditure—underwrote an ascetic morality that was in conformity with the institution of Christianity. As Max Weber has shown, Protestantism discovered in the austerity of accumulation and the reproduction of capital a Puritanism that inspired a 'free' relationship between the sinner and the tutelary God who kept watch over the rate of profit. While Rome had looted [*pille*] and squandered [*gaspille*], the reformers economized and invested.

The concern with improving the morals of the clergy emerged too late to dam up the pious ethics of the reformers. The Council of Trent ran aground in its attempt to restore the authority of Catholicism in the northern regions—the cradle of the industrial revolution and the first bourgeois, parliamentary and democratic regimes.

Two Agitators at the Dawn of the Reformation: Hans Böhm and Girolamo Savonarola

"He was", Norman Cohn writes, "a shepherd and, in his spare time, a popular entertainer, drumming and piping in hostelries and in the market-place—whence the nickname, by which he is still known, of Drummer (or Piper) of Niklashausen"[2].

In one of history's many ironies, Hans Böhm was led to believe that the Italian Franciscan John of Capistrano was not a pitiless inquisitor or the author of the massacre of the Fraticelles in Maiolati, but rather a brother who, thirty years before those persecutions, had extolled repentance and the rejection of luxury in Germany. Since John of Capistrano had invited his listeners to take part in the bonfire of the vanities—in which the people set aside their beautiful clothes, their games of dice and cards, and their objects of pure enjoyment, on a day during Lent—this shepherd (Böhm) decided to burn his drum in front of the parish-church of Niklashausen and to start preaching.

Mary appeared to him and conveyed to him the order to propagate the Good Word, so that Niklashausen could be raised to the glory of a terrestrial Jerusalem. In the local church there was a statue of the Virgin, to which miraculous powers were attributed. The priest of the parish did not give his support to Böhm's project, which would have erected Niklashausen, not Rome, as the location selected by divine providence.

This little shepherd suddenly revealed himself to be endowed with extraordinary eloquence. He soon inferred from the fascination that he exercised upon the crowds and the diverse classes of society that God had endowed him with thaumaturgic powers. He preached the simplicity of morals, which was an ethical code that was strong enough to keep any soul out of hell. The bonfire of the vanities was to be followed by violent attacks on the corrupt clergy and the powerful.

He soon incited his listeners to refuse to pay taxes and tithes. He also demanded that the priests abandon their outrageous privileges and content themselves with whatever the people agreed to give them.

The Archbishop of Mainz, who until then had adopted a prudently reserved posture, plotted to bring an end to an agitation that was winning over a growing number of German regions.

In the words of Norman Cohn:

> In the end Böhm emerged as a social revolutionary, proclaiming the imminence of the egalitarian millennium based on Natural Law. In the coming Kingdom the use of wood, water and pasturage, the right to fish and hunt would be freely enjoyed by all, as they had been in olden times. Tributes of all kinds would be abolished forever. No rent or services would be owed to any lord, no taxes or duties to any prince. Distinctions of rank and status would cease to exist and nobody would have authority over anybody else. All would live together as brothers, everyone enjoying the same liberties and doing the same amount of work as everyone else. "Princes, ecclesiastical and secular alike, and counts and knights should only possess as much as common folk, then everyone would have enough. The time will have to come when princes and lords will work for their daily bread". And Böhm extended his attack beyond the local lords and princes to the very summit of society: "The Emperor is a scoundrel and the Pope is useless. It is the Emperor who gives the princes and counts and knights the right to levy taxes on the common people. Alas, poor devils that you are!"

No doubt Böhm's teaching appealed in different ways to different sections of the population. The demand for the overthrow of all rulers, great and small, probably appealed particularly to the urban proletariat; we know that the townsfolk did in fact come to Niklashausen, not only from Würzburg but from all over southern and central Germany. On the other hand in demanding that wood, water, pasturage, fishing and hunting should be free to all men, Böhm was voicing a very general aspiration of the peasants. The German peasants believed that these rights had in fact been theirs in olden time, until usurped by the nobility; this was one of the wrongs which they were always expecting the future 'Emperor Frederick' to undo. But above all it was the prestige of the preacher himself, as a miraculous being sent by God, which drew the tens of thousands into the Tauber valley. The common people, peasants and artisans alike, saw in him a supernatural protector and leader, such as the 'Emperor Frederick' was to have been: a saviour who could bestow on them individually the fulness of Divine Grace and who would lead them collectively into an earthly Paradise.

News of the wonderful happenings at Niklashausen passed rapidly from village to village in the neighbourhood and was carried further afield, too, by messengers who went out in all directions. Soon vast hordes of common folk of all ages and both sexes, and including whole families, were streaming towards Niklashausen. Not only the surrounding country but all parts of southern and central Germany were in commotion, from the Alps to the Rhineland and to Thuringia. Artisans deserted their workshops and peasants their fields, shepherds and shepherdesses abandoned their flocks and hastened—often still in the same clothes and carrying their picks and hammers and scythes—to hear and adore him who was now known as 'the Holy Youth'. These people greeted one another only as 'Brother' or 'Sister' and these greetings acquired the significance of a rallying-cry. Amongst the multitudes of simple, wildly excited folk there circulated fantastic rumours. What the *plebs pauperum* had believed of Jerusalem these believed of Niklashausen. There Paradise had literally descended upon the earth; and infinite riches were lying ready to be gathered by the faithful, who would share them out amongst themselves in brotherly love. Meanwhile the hordes—like the *Pastoureaux* and the Flagellants before them—advanced in long columns, bearing banners and singing songs of their own composition.[3]

Hans Böhm began to preach around 1474. Towards the end of March 1476, the pilgrimages that people made in order to hear him led to retaliatory measures on the part of the large towns. The municipal council of Nuremburg prohibited its inhabitants from going to Niklashausen. Würzburg closed its doors and armed its militias. On 12 July, the Prince-Bishop sent a squadron of cavalry to the holy city. Having been arrested, Hans Böhm was incarcerated in Würzburg, while a peasant, invested with a prophetic role in his turn, incited the people to march upon the episcopal city, where the walls would fall like those of Jericho. Forty millenarian liberators were killed. Hans Böhm was tried hastily and sent to the pyre, where it is said that he died singing hymns. The offerings deposited by pilgrims at the church of Niklashausen were confiscated. The Archbishop of Mainz, the Bishop of Würzburg, and the count in whose territory the church stood did not consider it beneath them to share the loot equitably amongst themselves. The cinders of the prophet, which were dispersed so that no cult could pay homage to him, did not fail to fill the air of the time with the seeds of a millenarian and reformational resurgence that would eventually break the reins of an all-powerful Rome.

Girolamo Savonarola
For Girolamo Savonarola, Joachimite prophecy, voluntary poverty, the asceticism of the Spirituals, and the political calculations of the communalist tribunes formed a conjunction of diverse ambitions that both elevated him to power and paved the way for his downfall.

Born in Ferrara in 1452, he distinguished himself from his contemporaries in the Dominican Order by his eloquence and his culture. As the Prior of the Monastery of San Marco in Florence he soon exercised upon the brilliant court of Lorenzo de' Medici a fascination that increased the appeal of purity, which is so frequently a factor in the decline of the enjoyment taken in guilty pleasures.

Giovanni Pico della Mirandola, whose philosophical theses were condemned by the Church, discerned an ally in this monk-prophet who, through his diatribes against the *luxuria* and *aviditas*[4] of the Pope and the clergy, added his voice to the popular anger concerning the despotism of Rome that had accumulated over the centuries.

Savonarola's millenarianism proved seductive at a time during which both large-scale reversals of fortune and quotidian misery suggested an imminent apocalypse. Savonarola shared with Dolcino the mistake of giving too precise a date in his prophecies. He announced terrible misfortunes for Italy. He was believed, because misfortune occurred every day. Death appeared even in the lines of the poems in which Lorenzo celebrated youth and beauty.

Against the vices and tyranny of the papacy, King Charles VIII of France brandished the "scourge of God, the vengeful sword"—the new Charlemagne, the new Frederick, the new king of a Third Age. Marsilio Ficino, a friend of literature and pleasure and a scholar who was well versed in Kabbalah, discerned in the monk [i.e. Savonarola] the acrid odor of a rigor that was as pernicious as the Sadean hedonism of the prelates and aristocrats.

After the death of Lorenzo de' Medici, who, at the end of a dissipated life, had supposedly asked Fra Girolamo to accept his confession, his son Piero de' Medici showed greater reserve—frank hostility, even—towards the one who now aspired to rule the lives of the Florentines.

Savonarola's appeals to voluntary poverty, which revived memories of the Fraticelles and the Spirituals, rallied to him the support of the disadvantaged classes. He soon after tipped over into the mystical Puritanism that all religious extremisms have in common.

The flight of Piero, the proclamation of the Florentine Republic in 1494, and the triumphal entry of King Charles VIII into the city granted Savonarola the power of a spiritual and temporal leader.

The new government of Florence, promoted as the New Jerusalem, finally marked the beginning of the Third Age, the prelude to the return of Christ to earth, and the mass conversion of the Turks and the Jews.

The hysteria inherent in the compulsion for virtue kindled in the town, which was renowned for the refinement of its arts, purifying flames that were known as 'bonfires of the vanities'. Onto these were thrown jewels, ornaments, books, paintings, and luxurious clothes.

Sandro Botticelli, the most sensual of the painters, succumbed to this destructive madness, to this rage in which life gets revenge for the scorn by which it has been overwhelmed by annihilating with a sinister joy all that has made life pleasant. Into this rage was mixed the legitimate resentment of the exploited, on whose backs pressed the weight of the luxury from which they were excluded. Savonarola's sermons, which flattered both the demands that he could not satisfy and the hatred to which he ascribed evangelical virtue, gradually alienated the aristocracy and the intellectuals from him, even as his promises of a new order remain dead letters politically.

The party of Rome regrouped its partisans. Pope Alexander VI, who was intelligent, brutal, and corrupt, excommunicated the monk and prohibited him from preaching. Savonarola ignored him. Having been arrested in his convent at San Marco, tortured, and charged with heresy (which his doctrine did not merit), he was—despite the effervescence of his partisans, the *Piagnoni* (a name that derived from the *Piagnona*, which was the bell in the convent of San Marco)[5]—hanged and burned with two of his disciples, Domenico da Pescia and Silvestro Maruff, on 23 May 1498.

The program for the renewal of the Church, which Savonarola had folded into the uncertain politics of the city, was expounded by Luther as a protest by all of Christianity against the ignominy of Catholicism—the religion soiled by the unworthiness of its priests. Luther had the prudence to remain in Germany, where the tradition of the emperors and princes who were hostile to Rome made the old principle *cuius regio, eius religio*[6] work in Lutheranism's favor.

From Heresy to the Religion of the State: Luther and Calvin

The Reformation of the Church triumphed with Luther and Calvin, but it triumphed outside of the Church and against it. What victories could those who dreamed of a renewal of faith and of freedom of belief hope to see from the new religions of the State?

Born in 1483 and dismissed as a student from the University of Erfurt in 1505, Luther was ordained as a priest in 1507. He attained the position of professor and preacher at the University of Wittenberg, due to the sympathies that he aroused in the Prince-Elector of Saxony.

A visit to Rome in 1511 revealed to him the state of cupidity and license that prevailed among the prelates and at the pontifical court. He was of course far from being the only one (nor was he the first) who was jealous of and vehemently indignant about the splendor and luxury of the Church.

The promotional sale of indulgences, which was begun in 1513 by Pope Leo X to finance the building of the St. Peter's Basilica, offered Luther an occasion to excite not only the discontent of the northern towns and of the regions heated by the agitation of Böhm and the Taborites, but also the discontent of the German princes, who were traditionally hostile to Rome and were soon thereafter (around 1520) alienated by the authoritarianism of the Catholic Emperor Charles V.

The archbishop of Mainz deputized the Dominican Johann Tetzel, a talented preacher who would absolve all sins if his price was paid, to collect funds from the sale of indulgences, which could allow someone "to fornicate with the Virgin Mary herself"[7].

After Tetzel's arrival in Wittenberg, a violent polemic set him in opposition to Luther, who had the double advantage of being on his own turf and able to express widely held opinions with all the tartness of popular language. With the glibness of a traveling salesman, Tetzel proposed to settle the debate with an ordeal of fire and water. "I laugh at your jackass braying", Luther retorted. "In place of water, I advise you to use the juice of the trailing vine and, in place of fire, the aroma of a roasted goose"[8]. The rough treatment that the people gave to Tetzel's emulators alarmed those in Rome who had been responsible for a marketing[9] operation that was founded on the redemption of sin, while the monk of Wittenberg—emboldened by his popularity—summarized in ninety-five articles his theses against the Roman clique. On 31 October 1517 he attached them to the walls of the Church of All Saints. Cardinal Cajetan, the apostolic nuncio, and the ecclesial hierarchy all tried and failed to get him to sign a retraction.

In 1520 the papal bull *Exsurge* condemned forty-one of Luther's propositions and ordered that his pamphlets be burned. Accompanied by his disciples, Luther went to the door of Wittenberg, where a pyre had been lighted, and, with great solemnity, threw into it both the papal bull and the writings of Luther's adversaries.

From Germany to England, by way of France and the Netherlands, the pyre of Wittenberg—which had symbolically consumed the power of Rome—inflamed public opinion. For the princes and kings, Catholicism was merely an instrument of political domination. None of them had any scruples about rejecting it if it hindered more than it helped. In 1527 Charles V, the loyal servant of the faith, subjected Rome to the most pitiless sacking and massacres that it had known since the days of the Visigoths. King Francis I of France, no less a good Catholic, burned Protestants but also helped the German reformers in their struggle against Charles V; he hated the Emperor so much that he did not hesitate to ally himself with Islam.

While politics had condemned Dolcino, the Spirituals and Savonarola, it saved Luther and his movement; it carried them to power by virtue of a force that, beneath the surface of religion and ideology, was beginning to appear in broad daylight as the veritable mode of the government of mankind: the economy.

Luther and Calvin ratified the obscure decrees of free enterprise, and even helped to crush peasant communalism and condemn the Free Spirit that was so resolutely irreconcilable with the economic controls exercised over the lives of men and women.

In 1521 Charles V summoned Luther to appear before the Diet of the Princes convened in Worms, in the Rhineland. Strengthened by the sympathy that his act of rebellion had aroused among the lords who were disinclined to grovel at the feet of the Emperor, Luther presented his profession of faith as if he were issuing a challenge. Foreseeing arrest, he then took refuge in Saxony, where the Elector—under the pretext of imprisoning him—protected him at his castle in Wartburg. There Luther translated the Bible into German and laid the basis for a new dogma.

In 1521 Thomas Müntzer, taking literally the freedoms claimed by Luther, joined the peasants in revolt and revived hopes of a Joachimite Third Age. Luther, in his 1525 pamphlet *Wider die Mordischen und Reubischen Rotten der Bawren*[10], called for the most pitiless repression, thereby removing the last misgivings of the German princes concerning his doctrine and co-signing the birth of Lutheranism as the religion of the State. In the space of five years, the heresiarch repeated in his own fashion the Constantinian operation of the Roman Church. He set himself up as the *pontifex maximus*[11] by lending the support of the bourgeoisie of free enterprise (which saw in enrichment a compensation for sacrifice and for obedience to a reasonable God) to the national and religious independence of the northern principalities and kingdoms.

John Calvin

The career of the heresiarch John Calvin ended with a *coup d'état*[11] whose success he himself assured. He was born in 1509 at Noyon, in Picardy, where his father, the prosecutor at the local chapter, had reserved for him a career in the Church. After studying at the Collège de Montaigu in Paris, as well as in Orléans and Bourges, he published a commentary on Seneca's *De clementia*.

Around 1533, he adopted the ideas of the Reformation. Suspected of having drafted the inaugural address made by his friend Nicolas Cop (the Rector of the University of Paris and a man deeply permeated by the Lutheran doctrine), he fled to Angoulême and then took refuge in Nérac with the help of Marguerite of Navarre, the sister of Francis I and a protector of the reforms.

In 1534 Calvin was in Basle, where he drafted the first version of *Institutes of the Christian Religion*. In 1536 Guillaume Farel, who was attempting to establish the Reformation in Geneva, invited Calvin to use his authority to win over the citizens, who were in no hurry to exchange a new religious truth for an old one about which they cared little. Calvin and Farel were both sanctioned by banishment in 1538. Calvin went to Strasbourg, where Martin Bucer had consolidated one of the bastions of Lutheranism. Returning to Geneva in 1541, Calvin thenceforth worked to establish his own power. Opposition rose against him from among the inhabitants of the city; it was founded as much on an awareness of belonging to a free state as on the repugnance that Calvinist austerity aroused among people who were naturally inclined to the joys of existence. Calvin worked patiently at breaking the opposition, stigmatizing under the name 'Libertines' the supporters of political liberties, who were led by Jacques Gruet, and vituperated under the name 'Spiritual Libertines' the faction constituted by Pocquet, Perceval and Quintin

Thierry. Following an iniquitous trial, Jacques Gruet was decapitated in 1547 for having defended the free choice of atheism and for fighting against the dictatorship of a Puritanism that would go on, in Northern Europe, to forge the Anglo-Saxon mindset that was illustrated by English Victorianism and by Americanism in its most deplorable sense.

To confirm the truth that God had enjoined him to impose and to share in inquisitorial barbarity, Calvin did not fail to send to the pyre the physician Michael Servetus [Miguel Serveto Conesa], who had taken refuge in Geneva in 1553.

CHAPTER THIRTY-NINE

The Dissidents from Lutheranism and Calvinism

In 1523 Luther published the treatise *That Jesus Christ Was Born a Jew*, which accused the papacy of having distanced the Jews from the truth faith. The Church had confined them to the practice of usury; it had calumnied them, "saying they must have Christian blood to wash away the Jewish stain, and I know not what nonsense"[1]. "If we really want to help them, we must be guided in our dealings with them not by papal law but by the law of Christian love".[2]

What became of such beautiful dispositions after the 'Constantinian' turn of the 'reformed' religion and after the appeal for a holy war against the peasants? In 1543, two pamphlets were published one after the other by the master of Wittenberg: *Against the Jews and Their Lies* and *Of the Unknowable Name*.

Jean Delumeau has judged it useful to provide some extracts[3] from writings that Hitler went on to have reprinted in millions of copies[4].

> "Now let me commend these Jews sincerely to whoever feels the desire to shelter and feed them, to honor them, to be fleeced, robbed, plundered, defamed, vilified, and cursed by them, and to suffer every evil at their hands—these venomous serpents and devil's children, who are the most vehement enemies of Christ our Lord and of us all. And if that is not enough, let him stuff them into his mouth, or crawl into their behind and worship this holy object. Then

let him boast of his mercy, then let him boast that he has strengthened the devil and his brood for further blaspheming our dear Lord and the precious blood with which we Christians are redeemed. Then he will be a perfect Christian, filled with the works of mercy for which Christ will reward him on the day of judgment, together with the Jews in the eternal fire of hell!"[5]

"When Judas Sharioth hanged himself, his intestines burst, and, as happens to the hanged, his bladder burst: perhaps the Jews had their servants there with gold and silver jugs and basins which caught the Judas-piss (as it is called) together with the rest of the holy things, thereafter they mixed it into the excrement and ate it among each other and drank it so that they developed such sharp eyes, so that they see such comments in the scripture, which neither Matthew nor Isaiah himself, nor all the angels, let alone we damned *Goyim* can see"[6]. "Did I not tell you earlier that a Jew is such a noble, precious jewel that God and all the angels dance when he farts?"[7]

"Observe all that the Jews have suffered for fifteen hundred years; there will be much worse for them in Hell [...]. They must tell us why [...] they are a people who are rejected by God, who are without a king, without prophets, without a temple; they can't give any other reason than their sins....". "Never has the anger of God manifested itself with more brilliance than it has against these people"[8].

"Set fire to their synagogues or schools and bury and cover with dirt whatever will not burn, so that no man will ever again see a stone or cinder of them". "They [should] be forbidden on pain of death to praise God, to give thanks, to pray, and to teach publicly among us and in our country"[9].

In 1523, when Luther advocated a degree of tolerance for the Jews, he also communicated prudent reservations about the notion of heresy—reservations that no doubt intimated to him his own destiny:

"If you want to extirpate heresy", Luther wrote in 1523, "above all you must know how to remove it from the heart and how to lead men to turn away from it through a profound movement of the will. The use of force will not exhaust heresy, but will reinforce it ... Because if, using force, one burns all the Jews and the heretics, one will neither convince nor convert a single one through such means"[10].

But after the violence of Th. Müntzer and the war of the peasants, and once the princes and towns had adhered in great numbers to the Reformation, Luther changed his tone, by virtue of another logic that was contrary to the first one: Protestantism is the return to Scripture, the removal of the "novelties"—the Roman "superstitions" as well as the "sacramentalism" of [Huldrych] Zwingli. Inversely, "the wickedness of the world" manifests itself as both "idolatry and heresy". The State could not tolerate these satanic aberrations. The Reformer thus judged the intervention of civil authority to be necessary in order to bring an end to such 'abominations' as the Mass. Under threats, the Chapter of the Collegiate Church of Wittenberg was forced to cease celebrating Mass on Christmas in 1524. Two years later Luther wrote to John, the new Elector of Saxony: "There must only be a single kind of preaching in each place"[11]. In 1527 he demanded that the Elector organize 'ecclesiastic visits' to his territory. Thenceforth, in the Lutheran countries, the State would control the organization of the Church, would break up religious deviances, and would oversee the preaching of the Gospels. The 'German mystical spiritualists', having been thus disappointed by Luther, had good sport reproaching him and the other reformers of the era for having substituted 'a new papacy'—a 'paper papacy' (the Bible)—for the Roman one. For Schwenckfeld, "Dr. Martin led us out of Egypt, through the Red Sea and into the wilderness, and there he left us to lose ourselves on the rough roads; yet he seeks to persuade everybody that we are already in the Promised Land"[12]. A little later, Weigel would reproach the 'Pope of Wittenberg' for having organized a new slavery and for persecuting visionaries.[13]

Like the popes whom he vilified, Luther was not above adopting the commonplace hypocrisy that, in order to serve powerful interests, one needed so as to suffocate with the left hand the morality that one caressed with the right. When Philip I, Landgrave of Hesse, asked Luther for authorization to get married a second time, the spiritual master, after equivocating, consented on the condition that the affair remained a secret. Philip sent a vat of Rhineland wine as payment for the indulgence. At least Pope Julius II paid Michelangelo with actual money, which he had extorted from the Catholics!

Calvin knew nothing of such weaknesses. He detested pleasure with a visceral hatred and his faith never tolerated the least lapse. Unlike Sebastian Castellion, who protested again the barbarity of the treatment of Michael Servetus (and who declared in his *Treatise of the Heretics* that "we see that there is hardly any sect—and today there are so many of them—that does not see the others as heretical, with the result that, if in one city or region you are esteemed to be truly loyal, in the next one you are esteemed to be heretical"[14]), Calvin—just a few month after he had Servetus assassinated—published a *Defense of the True Faith*, in which he declared:

> Our merciful ones, who take such great pleasure in letting heresies go unpunished [...], would like it if—out of a concern that the Church of God not be defamed for its excessive rigor—we were to authorize all of the errors [...]. [On the contrary,] God wants us to spare neither the towns nor the people, to the point that we must raze the walls and exterminate the memory of the inhabitants and burn everything as a sign of an even greater hatred, so that the infection does not spread any further.[15]

Theodore Beza raised the stakes even higher:

> Tyranny is a lesser evil than having a license such that each one acts according to his fancy, and it is better to have a tyrant—even a cruel one—than to have no prince at all, or to have one under whom each person is permitted to do what he wants [...]. Those who do not want the magistrate to mix himself up in religious affairs and, principally, to punish heretics, scorn what the Word of God expresses [...] and bring ruin and extreme destruction to the Church.[16]

> The ruler will be fully occupied in rendering the true religion secure by means of good and noble decrees against those who assail and resist it out of pure obstinacy, as we have seen done in our times in England, Denmark, Sweden, Scotland, and the greater part of Germany and Switzerland against the Papists, the Anabaptists and other heretics.[17]

Hans Denck

While the shadow of Lutheranism and Calvinism threatened to spread over the world an obscurantism that, when compared to Rome, had the deceptive advantages of 'reason' and 'freedom', Hans Denck was (along with Sebastian Castellion) among the rare, lucid and sincere men for whom human feelings had the upper hand over beliefs and ideologies that were always quick to suffocate those feelings beneath their sublime abstractions.

Denck was a member of no party other than his own; he had no ambition to govern others. To him, emancipating himself from all constraints appeared to be a sufficient task. Lutheran freedom did not accommodate itself to such license, which was indeed difficult to reconcile with any Church at all.

Born in 1500 in Habach, in Upper Bavaria, Denck entered the University of Ingolstadt at the age of seventeen. While pursuing his studies at Basle, he worked as a proofreader at a print shop and perfected his Latin, Greek, and Hebrew. He read Erasmus, was passionate about medieval mysticism, and adhered to the ideas of Thomas Müntzer. At the insistence of the Lutheran Johannes Oecolampadius, he was named Rector of the Saint Sebaldus School at Nuremberg when he was twenty-three. He got married and frequented milieus that can, without anachronism, be called libertarian.

Like other large preindustrial towns, Nuremberg oscillated in the backwash of the Reformation between Lutheran tyranny, disappointment with imperfect freedoms, and the old Catholic current in which the restless and the disenchanted ebbed and flowed. Indifference to the whole religious thing, which, notwithstanding compulsory ritual observances, had dominated the absolute reign of Catholicism, changed into cold and willful skepticism.

A number of strong spirits, including some among the clergy, no doubt shared the atheism of Thomas Scoto or Herman van Rijswijk but were insufficiently bold to proclaim it. Few indeed were those—such as Frederick II or the *condottiere* Federico da Montefeltro, whose casket bore an inscription that was destined to have a beautiful future: "Neither God nor master"[18]—who possessed the means of protecting their insolence. The multiplication of dogmatic truths and of parties of the 'true faith' was now opening the way for the contestation of the very existence of God.

The affair of the 'three Godless painters'[19] offered to the municipality [Nuremberg] the occasion to crack down on the party of the skeptics. The mocking banter that was opposed to religion had little difficulty in finding well-disposed ears among the people. It sharpened the language of the intellectuals and artists. The three implicated painters (the brothers Behaim, plus Georg Pencz) enjoyed the friendship of Hans Denck, whose independence of spirit had more than once irritated the Lutheran notables, particularly Andreas Osiander.

The council summoned Denck to appear and demanded of him a confession of faith that would wash away all suspicions. He complied, and in two successive texts expounded upon his doubts with a provocative sincerity.

Examining the belief system in which he had been educated, he came to see that it was a matter of a purely fictive faith, "because it had not triumphed over my spiritual poverty, my inclination to sin, my weakness and my unhealthy state [...]. I will not venture to claim that I now possess the faith that can be translated into life, although I see clearly that my lack of belief [in Christ] can no longer be maintained before God". And he added: "All believers are, at one moment or another, unbelievers. To become believers, they must let their passions and the terrestrial man die in such a fashion that it is no longer they who live, as they did when they lacked belief, but God who lives in them through the mediation of Christ"[20].

God's presence acting in man freed him from all constraints and all sin: such was the doctrine of those whom Calvin called the 'Spiritual Libertines'.

On 25 January 1525 Denck was condemned to banishment. Forced to leave his family and stripped of his university position, in June 1525 he took refuge among the Anabaptists of Saint-Gall, who were themselves victims of the hatred of the Lutherans. He would soon shock them with his conceptions of individual freedom. He wandered to Augsburg, where he stayed until October 1526 drafting *Wer die Wahre warlich lieb hat*[21]—a balance sheet of paradoxes, contradictions, and absurdities in the Bible—which brought him to the conclusion that quarrels over its interpretation had no shared meaning and that only the presence of God in each person (when the Spirit deigned to reveal that presence) mattered and served as a guide to existence through the spontaneity of the impulses that it engendered.

Lutheran hostility forced Denck into exile again. The same fate awaited him in Strasbourg, where Martin Bucer and Wolfgang Capito denounced him for subversive activities.

He was already worn out by his solitary combat when he arrived in Basle in September 1527. Oecolampadius was disposed to accord him asylum on the condition that he adjured. Denck wrote a kind of confession, mixing a few concessions (dictated by weariness) with opinions close to those of Caspar Schwenckfeld and his notion of the inward man. Oecolampadius became part of the tradition of inquisitorial deceptions by publishing this document three months after Denck's death in October 1527 under the title (misleading at the very least) *Protestation and Confession: Recantation.*

When Denck died from plague in Basle at the age of twenty-seven, he was about to publish *Von der Wahren Liebe*[22]. In it he insisted on the following theme: he who loves God and has God in his heart need not bother with institutions, which merely blind him.

In 1528 two of his texts, which appeared as the preface and the appendix to the *Theologia Deutsche*[23], made clear "that the creature is necessary to God and that the man deified by illumination, as well as Christ, enjoys union with Him"[24], which was an idea that the philosopher Jakob Böhme—another victim of the New [Protestant] Churches—developed in the seventeenth century.

The nineteenth century saw in Denck one of the pioneers of free thought. No doubt he influenced the lucid and tormented conscience of Kierkegaard. It seems that the combined hatred felt for him by the Protestants and the Catholics was caused by his impregnation with the Free Spirit, which was discernible in his thesis: "Where there is faith, there is no sin; where there is no sin, there resides divine virtue"[25].

Sebastian Franck

A philosopher and historian, Sebastian Franck belonged to the very small number of humanists who combined intelligence with an unfailing passion for tolerance and a respect for life.

Born at Donauwörth, in Swabia, in 1499, he enrolled at the University of Heidelberg, where he associated with Martin Bucer, the future master of Strasbourg. Despite his contacts with Luther after 1519, he began his ecclesiastic career in the Catholic Church, which he left around 1525. An evangelic preacher in the region of Nuremburg, he married Ottilie Behaim, sister of the godless painters Bartholomew and Sebald, who were disciples of Albrecht Dürer and Free Spirits to whom all forms of religion were repugnant.

Nevertheless, Franck took a position opposed to the justification through faith defended by Hans Denck—who was also a friend of the Behaims—and adopted a stance that conformed to Christian principles. But in 1529 he resigned from his ecclesiastic position, moved to Strasbourg, associated with Michael Servetus and Caspar Schwenckfeld, and gradually adopted the attitude of Denck, for whom convictions only had meaning when there was a coherence between ideas, on the one hand, and life experiences that were stripped of artifice and hypocrisy, on the other. Such was the spirit that animated Franck's masterpiece, *Chronica, Zeitbuch und Geschictbibel*[26], published in 1531. Erasmus took offense at his inclusion in the book as a heretic and denounced its author to the Council of Strasbourg; with Bucer's support he got Franck expelled from the city. Exposed to the hatred of Erasmus and the Lutherans, and condemned by Philip Melanchthon, Franck ended up as a printer in Ulm, the council of which rejected several demands for his expulsion, including one made by Luther's patron Philip of Hesse. Franck used his time there to publish several personal works and a treatise by Cornelius Agrippa before he was banished in 1530. Taking refuge in Basle, where he entered into a second marriage with the heiress of a great family of publishers, Franck did not cease publishing—his collection of proverbs enjoyed great popularity—and fighting for tolerance and the abolition of the death penalty. ("If the choice was given to me, I would much rather be in the condition of the many whom the world has condemned as heretical than among those whom it has canonized".[27]) He died in 1542, scarcely forty-three years old.

Hostile to all forms of ecclesiastic organization, he rejected the authority of the priests as well as that of the Scriptures. The Gospels, he said, had replaced pontifical authority with a *papieren Papst* (a paper Pope). That authority was the cause of all evils; he denounced it in a society dominated by the strength and power of the Prince. No war was just because all wars derived from the principle of appropriation. On the other hand, his pessimism hardly accorded any value to revolt. Closer to the Tao than to La Boétie[28], he contented himself with identifying God with a feeling of internal plenitude, in which he dreamed that brutality and the misery of an immutable world would be annihilated.

In the insurmountable and vain confrontation in which truths bitterly fought one another, tolerance represented the sole human virtue. ("Thus take from each sect what is good and leave the rest to the Devil".[29]) This was enough to bring down upon him the animosity of the majority of the humanists, ideologues and sectarians of his time, from the Catholics to the Anabaptists. On the other hand, Sebastian Castellion did everything he could to distribute his works, to which Valentin Weigel, Jakob Böhme, Dirck Coornhert, and the historian Gottfried Arnold all paid homage.

Karlstadt and Schwenckfeld

The rivalry for power that quickly opposed Luther to Andreas Rudolf Bodenstein, also known as Karlstadt, determined a rivalry of opinions that was even more subject to uncertainty than the dogma of the Protestants, which was uneasily cemented together through various controversies. The Constantinian Catholic Church can hardly be said to have proceeded otherwise, but its absolutism dealt with doubts at the point of a sword. When Luther, Calvin, and Henry VIII of England attempted a similar procedure, the historical conditions were very different. Beneath the surface predominance of the agrarian mode of production, the mole of mercantile expansion was at work. The progress of the values that were open to modernity guaranteed neither the stability of the divine order nor the immutable power of its ministers.

The defeat of the Roman Church, the power of which was only

imperfectly restored by the counter-offensive of the Council of Trent, thus prohibited the despotic pretensions of the popes of the Reformation from extending beyond local tyrannies that resisted contestation only ineffectively.

Unlike Denck, Müntzer, Storch, Hoffmann, and Schwenckfeld, Karlstadt did not have a doctrine properly speaking. He contented himself with mocking Luther, with dogging that conceited windbag whose shadow extended all over Europe.

Born around 1480, Karlstadt studied philosophy and theology in Erfurt (1499) and then in Cologne (1500). He became a professor of theology, exegete of the Bible, and doctor of law at the University of Sienna. Though interested in Luther's demands, he soon clashed with the man's intransigence, thanks to which the dogmatic interpretation of sacred texts had prevailed over the generosity of the heart's impulses. And was it not precisely this most sensitive—nay, sensual—part of man that had most ardently led the combat against the Roman clergy?

Karlstadt's meeting with Thomas Müntzer, whose revolutionary millenarianism both fascinated and frightened him, hastened this break with Luther, who chased Karlstadt from Wittenberg. Having taken refuge in Orlamünde, where he came out against the necessity of baptism and communion, he was expelled on the insistence of his old friend, who pursued him in hatred everywhere where he had the support of the princes. Karlstadt only found peace in the company of Zwingli, who founded a rival Protestant Church in Zurich and did not follow Luther. Karlstadt defended positions that were close to the ideas of Denck, estimating that sincere faith dispensed with the need for all spiritual authority. He was teaching at the University of Zurich when he died from the plague in 1541.

Freedom was the cause of the break between Luther and Caspar Schwenckfeld (1490–1561), whose sect experienced equally severe persecution under the Catholics and the Lutherans. In the line of Denck, Schwenckfeld rejected religious rites and the sacraments in favor of faith, wherein humanity founded its feeling of being in step with the designs of God. He put the accent on the inward man, whose mystical experiences partook of illumination. Certain Pietists later claimed his teachings.

Michael Servetus

A physician and humanist born around 1509 in Villanueva, Spain, Michael Servetus owed his dramatic end less to the audacity of his thought—which was more commonplace and less reckless than it might appear—than to a settling of accounts to which John Calvin's morbid authority ended up lowering itself. His medical studies at the University of Toulouse and the University of Paris induced in him, as was also the case with Rabelais, a certain skepticism in theological matters. The man who discovered the mechanisms behind the circulation of blood in the lungs experienced some difficulty in discerning clarity in the doctrine of the Trinity that was a part of the Constantinian arsenal and that had presided over the instauration of Catholicism as the religion of the State.

Anti-trinitarianism, popularized by Socinus [Fausto Paolo Sozzini] and his friends, responded less to a theological preoccupation than to a questioning of the Church that the took the form of deriding a principle that had never succeeded in getting itself out of trouble and whose mystical character had served to conceal the political necessity of maintaining—between God (the Father) and humankind (the Son)—the balancing act of the Spirit [i.e. the Church] that governed the temporal in the name of a heavenly mandate.

Servetus's *De trinitatis erroribus* (published in 1531)[30] supported Arius and the old Gnosticism, denying the existence of the Spirit—and thus of the Church—as a distinct being. According to Servetus, everything took place between the Logos, which was eternal, and the Son, who was not.

In 1553 the anonymous publication of Servetus' *Christianismi restitutio*[31] drew down upon him threats from the Inquisition. Arrested in Lyon and imprisoned, he had the good fortune to escape and the misfortune of going to Geneva—that is, near Calvin, with whom he had exchanged letters more than once. The *Restitutio* was an ironic take on Calvin's *Institutions* and it alarmed Calvin in the sense that Servetus therein adopted positions that closely approximated those of Anabaptism. But it was his freedom of morals and language in particular that ate away at Calvin like an insult to his majesty as a prophet. An unjust trial, which nobody regarded as credible because the grievances were so much more serious than the accusations that had been made against Jacques Gruet, succeeded where the Inquisition had failed and completed Rome's work. Servetus was burned alive on 27 October 1553.[32]

Sebastian Castellion

By the force of things, the Reformation was part of the desacralization inherent in the mercantile expansion that would, in the twentieth century, reduce the religions of the industrialized nations to supermarket junk. With its multiple sects, Protestantism marked the transition from a clerical theocracy—supported by a huge apparatus of popes and monarchs who ruled by virtue of divine right—to ideologies that were founded on a restrictive ethics; and so it oscillated between totalitarianisms of the nationalist or collectivist type and the demand for freedom that was underwritten by the development of the economy.

The importance of morality in the reformed religion extended the project of the reformers who, starting in the eleventh century and in the whirlwind of urban freedoms, had undertaken to moralize the Church. Even if the tyranny of dogmatic prescriptions was often succeeded by an *ethical* despotism, from the moment Protestantism achieved the predominant position in a given country or region, the absence of a sacred orthodoxy—a rectilinear perspective in which God was the point of departure and arrival—meant that one was no longer authorized to speak of heresies.

If Calvin treated Servetus like a heretic, this was because he estimated himself to be the equal of the Pope, elected by God and fixing in Geneva that New Jerusalem whose geography was perpetually fluctuating. In the debate between him and Sebastian Castellion, by contrast, Calvin's role as Puritan dictator took precedence: the controversy was no longer theological, but ideological. It challenged the inhumanity of the repressive discourse attributed to God.

Official history makes a lot of Erasmus—humanist and anti-Semite, intellectual and misogynist, defender of freedom and partisan of the death penalty for heretics, whom he occasionally denounced. But that history knows nothing about Guillaume Postel, who discerned in the emancipation of women the foundation of a humane society, nor anything of Castellion, who fought for tolerance.

Born in 1515 in Saint-Martin-du-Frêne—in the Bugey, where the influence of the Waldensinians continued to exist—Sebastian Castellion studied in Lyon and associated with humanists who had been seduced by the new ideas. The spectacle of the persecutions and his reading of Calvin's *Institutes of the Christian Religion* won him over to the Reformation. He left for Strasbourg, then Geneva, where Calvin offered him a professor's position in 1542. His *Sacred Dialogues* reflected his first hesitations regarding Calvin's growing authoritarianism. In this work he celebrated tolerance and remarked that "there is no one who more obstinately resists the truth than the great ones of this world"[33]. He soon left Geneva, having attracted the animosity of the man whom he had naively admonished for his sectarianism.

A reader of Greek at the University of Basle, he provided the first manifesto of free conscience in the preface to his translation of the Bible into Latin. Indignant at the execution of Servetus in 1553, which inspired him to write *Are the Heretics to be Persecuted?*[34], he developed a doctrine that was opposed to predestination, which Calvin used to justify his own crimes.

Published in 1562, Castellion's *Advice to a Desolate France* called for universal tolerance and for a refusal to "force consciences"[35]. It opposed the horrors and fanaticism of the wars undertaken for the greater glory of God. Rarely has a book been welcomed with such unanimous reprobation. Lutherans, Calvinists, Catholics, and humanists all judged the project of abolishing the death penalty for the crime of heresy to be criminal. Castellion's nephew and brother-in-law, who were guilty of having introduced the book into Geneva, had to take flight in order to save their lives. Up until his death on 29 September 1563, Castellion continued to send letters extolling freedom of thought all over Europe, to all those whom he regarded as capable of sharing his ideas and of spreading their effects.[36]

CHAPTER FORTY

The *Alumbrados* of Spain

Having previously been fairly discreet, the Inquisition was unleashed in Spain in 1492 and took up—under the mantle of defending a besieged faith—a gigantic genocidal project that was principally directed against the Jews, the systematic plundering of whom kept the coffers of the State well stocked. The power that the Inquisition had been given in recognition of the extraordinary services rendered during its mission to balance the accounts of the kingdom (whose conquest of American markets had in a certain sense been indirectly financed by the Jews) also allowed it to inflict on Spain the functionaries of this religious police force [i.e. of the Inquisition]—one with which Northern Europe had cancelled its contracts and which Renaissance Italy valued more for its activities beyond Italy's borders than for those it conducted within them.

Italian Catholicism accommodated itself to pleasures that were sooner or later seized by redemption, remorse, and contrition, without the intervention of a religious police force. The hedonism of a country inclined to luxury and passion erected more effectively than did the Council of Trent a natural barrier against the incursions of Reformation Puritanism, whose enticing program had already been presented there in the form of Savonarola's pre-Calvinist austerity.

Still stuck within the old agrarian structures in which the taste for life and liberty was expressed only by the insurrections of the *comuneros*[1], by several peasant revolts, and by the emerging wealth of the large towns, Spain retained the heritage of the ascetic masochism of Priscillian and Dominic de Guzmán (the leader of an order of divine killers whose fervor Ignatius of Loyola soon after revived by giving it a less brutal and more civilized turn).

With a zeal that was the envy of its German counterparts, the Inquisition lastingly prevented the establishment of Protestantism in Spain, although it did fail to contain it in Flanders (notwithstanding its perpetration of frightening massacres).

The Inquisition was nevertheless disconcerted when it discovered the existence of apparently quite numerous groups of people who devoted themselves to the freedoms of love by way of the paths of ecstasy, which popular language situated in the seventh heaven by way of strange references to the old Gnosticism and the Hebdomad.

Marcel Bataillon cites 1512 as the date of the first appearance of the qualifier *alumbrado*, which was applied to a Franciscan who was *"illuminated* by the darkness of Satan"[2].

In Toledo, where the influence of heterodox Sufis had secretly been perpetuated, the Inquisition hesitated to pursue Isabel de la Cruz, who had a reputation for holiness and around whom had formed a group whose teachings recalled those of Marguerite Porete. It wasn't until 23 September 1525 that Inquisitor General Alonso Manrique de Lara promulgated an edict against the *Alumbrados*, no doubt under the cover of a campaign against the Protestants, with whom they could only have been confused as a result of some malignity on the part of the Holy Office. Isabel de la Cruz was arrested in 1529 and condemned to life imprisonment. One of her disciples, the priest Juan López, mounted the pyre in Grenada one year later.

The chronicler Alfonso de Santa Cruz transcribed several articles from the charges at the trial in Toledo:

> They say that the love of God in man is God. . . .[3] [They] assert that ecstasy, or illumination, leads to such perfection that men can no longer sin, neither mortally nor venially, and that illumination makes them free and releases them from all authority, and that they are not answerable to anyone, even

God, as they have entrusted themselves to him.[4]

They call the host a bit of pastry, the cross a stick and genuflection idolatry. They regard the annihilation of their own will as the supreme glory. . . . They deny hell. . . .

Far from lamenting the Passion of Christ, they rejoice over it, and indulge in every sort of pleasure during Holy Week. They affirm that the Father was incarnate like the Son, and believe they can speak with this God neither more nor less than they can speak with the Corregidor of Escalona. When they want to remember Our Lady, they look at a women's face instead of contemplating an image. They called the conjugal act union with God. The sect centered around Isabel de La Cruz and a certain Father Alcázar.[5]

At the same time, a group of *Alumbrados* grew up around the *beata*[6] Francisca Hernández, who was originally from Canillas de Albaida, which is near Salamanca[7]. Around 1519 her court consisted of young clergymen: Bernardino Tovar, the Franciscan Gil Lopez, and the young theologian Antonio of Medrano, whose amorous relations with Francisca were denounced to the Inquisition, which condemned the lovers to live separately.

Relocated to Valladolid, Francisca lived first with Bernardino Tovar and then with the financier Pedro Cazalla. In the tradition of the *homines intelligentiae*, she founded an occult center named 'Paradise', in which the refinements of love conferred Edenic innocence upon the participants at the end of an initiation that intermixed chastity, libertinage, and all-encompassing passion.

Antonio of Medrano declared at his trial that, ever since he had known Francisca, God had given him the grace to no longer experience carnal desires, with the result that he could sleep with a woman in the same bed without harm to his soul. On the other hand, friar Francisco Ortiz affirmed: "After having had relations with her for about twenty days, I realized I had acquired more wisdom in Valladolid than if I had studied in Paris for twenty years. For it was not Paris but Paradise which was able to teach me this wisdom"[8].

Francisca Hernández seemed to have attained such a decree of holiness that continence was no longer necessary to her. The richest part of her teachings no doubt consisted in liberating her lovers and disciples from the feeling of guilt, which—along with the fear of pleasure—formed a vicious circle in which love was poisoned. The theologian Melchior Cano expressed Francisca's eruditely irreligious enterprise in an astonishingly modern formula: "To remove fear and to give assurance"[9].

It was precisely upon fear and anguish—the foundations of all religion—that the Inquisition played in order to annihilate *Alumbradismo*. Arrested in 1529, Francisca Hernández and her follower, María Ramirez, denounced—under the threat of torture and the *quemadero*[10]—Bernardino Tovar, his brother [Juan de Vergara], and fourteen other people. And, following the will of the inquisitorial tribunal, they denounced them not as *Alumbrados* but as Lutherans, a fact that, considering Luther and Calvin's hatred for the adepts of the Free Spirit, is not without piquancy.

In many regions of Spain, the *Alumbrados* represented such a force that the Church did not dare to attack them directly and preferred instead to identify them as Protestants, the condemnation of whom aroused fewer hesitations. They were so numerous in Seville that the Inquisition did not intervene there. "'The greater part of the city is infected', reported a letter of the period. 'There is not a duchess or a marquise, or any woman of high or low condition, who cannot be accused of some error of this heresy'"[11].

In the second half of the sixteenth century a group of *Alumbrados* were so imprudent as to contest the Church's teachings publicly. In 1578 the Dominican Alonso de la Fuente—while denouncing the *Alumbrados* from his pulpit at Llerena, in Extremadura—was interrupted by a woman who said: "Padre, the life they lead is better than yours, as is their doctrine". Her audacity, supported in all probability by a widespread sentiment within the region, prompted the immediate reaction of the Inquisition. Arrested and subjected to torture, she confessed the names of her companions.

Eight members of the secular clergy expounded their doctrine. Fernando Alvarez and Father Chamizo recommended that novices meditate on the wounds of the crucified Christ with such ardor that they become red in face, break out in a sweat, feel sorrow in their hearts, become nauseated, and end up experiencing an ecstasy in which, according to their expression, they would "become liquefied in the love of God". Porete had spoken of the 'annihilated soul' that signaled the kind of identification with God that Simon of Samaria had called *Megale Dynamis*, while the Beghard John of Brünn evoked the identity of the *pneuma* and the *sperma* in the fusion that left him *totaliter liquefactus*.

Rendered impeccable by orgasmic illumination, the *Alumbrados* acceded to the state of perfection and, having been plunged permanently into inward exaltation, were justified in following their desires and in rejecting the Church, its authority and its rites.

In addition to Alvarez and Chamizo, the latter of whom was reproached for having initiated thirty-four people into the heavenly pleasures, the community at Llerena included Juan Garcia, a clergyman from Almendralejo; the theologian Rodrigo Vasquez, a parish-priest in La Morera who affirmed: "If the Turks had been able to capture and govern Spain, we would all live as we liked"; Doctor Cristóbal Mejía, a clergyman from Cazalla; Pedro of Santa Maria, a sixty-three-year-old Franciscan from Valladolid; and Francisca de Mesa, a parish priest from Zafra who, speaking of the Passion of the Christ, asked: "What is the point of thinking about this man's death every day?"[12]

In Zafra, where the adepts united around the widow Lari Gómez, a shoemaker named Juan Bernal nourished his intention of presenting to the court a memorandum in defense of the *Alumbrados*.

The group had existed for four years when the Bishop of Salamanca, Francisco Soto y Salazar, took charge of the investigation into it, in 1578. When he died in Llerena on 21 June of that same year, rumors spread that the *Alumbrados* had poisoned him. The majority of them perished on the pyre.[13]

Such was the context in which the mystical exaltation of Juan de la Cruz and Teresa of Ávila took place. Initially suspected of *Alumbradismo*, they both hastened to furnish proofs of their perfect submission to the Church and channeled towards a morbid asceticism the carnal ecstasies that had previously haloed them with a divine grace.

CHAPTER FORTY-ONE

The Spiritual Libertines

At the same time as the Spanish Inquisition was worrying about people who didn't give a damn about Catholicism, Protestantism, the Church, or its reforms, and who lived in the quest for love and discovered in that quest the very meaning of their existence, Luther and Calvin were attempting—in the countries that were slowly being conquered by their glacial truths—to subdue the natural liberties that had authorized among the common people the spiritual liberties that were now being arrogated by the Reformers.

Eloi Pruystinck and the Eloisten[1]

With the development of the economy, Antwerp around 1520 was the scene for a new wave of individual initiative that pushed forward the audacity of private enterprise, the conversion of God into divine capital, and, at the same time, the propensity for luxury and the feeling of power that elevated the man of business to the status of the elect—nay, even that of the Demiurge.

At the beginning of the sixteenth century, when God—carved up by two factions that claimed exclusive ownership of Him—finally left an opening for humanity to emerge, a slate-roofer by the name of Eloi Pruystinck[2], who was supposedly an *illiteratus et mechanicus*[3] proletarian, agitated the working-class neighborhood of Saint-André.

A letter from David Joris[4] indicates that an encounter between them got the two men thinking about the following question: What, according to the God of goodness and freedom praised by the Reformation, is the best life (at least in the mind of Eloi)?

In February 1525, Pruystinck went to Wittenberg with the intention of persuading the man towards whom Europe had turned its eyes—Martin Luther, now entangled in his sudden glory—of the justness of his own convictions. Pruystinck confronted Philip Melanchthon in the presence of the master, who, scandalized by Eloi's libertarian opinions, sent a veritable letter of denunciation to the Protestants of Antwerp:

> I have heard how much your region is being agitated by minds full of error, who do all they can to impede the progress of Christian truth; I know that a devil incarnate has arrived among you, with the intention of leading you into error and distorting the true meaning of the Gospel so that you will fall into his darkness. So that you can avoid his traps more easily, I shall tell you some of his propositions: "Every man", according to him, "has the Holy Spirit; the Holy Spirit is nothing else but our reason.—Every man has faith; nature teaches me to do to my neighbor what I would have him do to me; to want to act thus is to have faith.—Everyone will have eternal life; there is neither hell, nor damnation; the flesh alone will be damned.—The law is violated by wicked desires, so long as the will does not give way to desire.—Whoever does not possess the Holy Spirit does not possess sin, either, because he does not possess reason". Everyone wants to be more learned than Luther, and to win their spurs at my expense. Once your devil had left my presence, he denied all these articles, although they had been shown to be his and although he had betrayed himself by defending several of them. Truthfully, he is unreliable and a liar, full of insolence and audacity, quite capable of both affirming and denying something, at the same time, not daring to argue any of the propositions he puts forward: the only reason he came here was so that he could boast that he had disputed with us. He energetically maintained that God's commandments are good, and that God did not wish sin to exist, to both of which I willingly agreed; but what he obstinately refused to admit is that God, while not willing sin, allows it to govern men. I have no doubt that he will tell you that I have said that sin is willed by God.[5]

Returning to Antwerp, Eloi did not cease to propagate his conception of a life inspired by a good God—by a God who was hostile to violence, punishment, and guilt, and whose grace bestowed Edenic innocence on those who followed their desires and their propensity for happiness. Eloi seems to have associated with the humanist Johann Campanus, a gentle man whose project—expounded under the title *On the Possibility of a Union of the Christians and the Turks* (1546)—in part inspired Pruystinck's ideas. (Note that, in 1530, Melanchthon refused any contact with Campanus and demanded that he be arrested. He was imprisoned for twenty years and then burned by Calvin after the Servetus affair.)

In February 1526 Eloi and nine of his friends were arrested for the crimes of heresy and reading forbidden books. The penal moderation that the Regent Margaret of Austria encouraged in the Netherlands explains the clemency of the judgment against them. Condemned to apologize and to wear a pectoral sign that designated him a heretic, Eloi—loyal to his principled refusal of martyrdom—simulated such perfect devotion that the magistrates dispensed with the defamatory mark.

A group formed around Eloi that became increasingly important. Dominick van Oucle, who was the "writer of all their books"[6], created their propaganda, which was distributed in Holland and Germany. Emanuel van Meteren revealed that among their many adepts were several bourgeois from Antwerp[7]—"the best, the richest and most highly regarded, who lived with the others joyously and in an epicurean manner". This chronicler deplored their "impious opinions, gratifying the world and the flesh, abusing and making fun of the Roman Catholic religion as well as the Protestants"[8].

Like the *homines intelligentiae* in Brussels a century earlier, the Eloisten became increasingly reckless, because the numbers of people who were indifferent to the war being conducted in the name of the Pope of Rome or the Pope of Wittenberg were increasing. In 1533 the Lutheran Michel Carnovianus, passing through Antwerp, wrote indignantly in a letter that he sent to Johann Hess about the 'Illuminati' in that city: "These men are far more perverse and obstinate than the Anabaptists"[9].

The winds of repression became more violent when "in 1531 Margaret of Austria ceded the regency of the Netherlands to her niece, Mary of Hungary, sister of Charles V, who determined, as she wrote to her brother, to pursue the heretics, 'whether or not they show repentance, with enough severity to root out their error in a single blow, with no other consideration except not to depopulate the provinces completely'"[10].

No doubt the frenzied persecution of the Anabaptists temporarily diverted the inquisitorial eye (in which the light of the pyres perpetually glimmered) away from the Eloisten. Nourishing as little sympathy for the adepts of Melchior Hoffmann as they did for any of the other henchman of the God of Justice, the Eloisten did not join the Anabaptist Münsterites who plotted to seize Antwerp's City Hall on 11 May 1535. They were therefore spared during the ghastly massacre that ensued, while the siege of Antwerp by the Duke of Gelderland (who was acting for the King of France and against Charles V) further deferred their fate.

The fatal blow came from Deventer, where Juliaan Ketel—a friend of David Joris—was tortured and denounced Cornelis van Lier, (a lord of Berchem, a village near Antwerp), his two brothers-in-law, the French jeweler Christopher Hérault (a companion of Eloi), and a 'slate-roofer'. When informed of these facts, the Governess Mary of Hungary demanded expeditious justice.

Other accusations, which were sneakily leaked to the public, proceeded from the Calvinist milieu.

In 1544 Vallérand Poulain (from Strasbourg) wrote to Calvin: "Our brothers from Valenciennes, who recently brought us some writings of the Quintinists, have returned.... I should be very pleased if you could take up arms against the Quintinists.... My brother Raymond writes that these horrors are spreading in Lower Germany now, a result of the actions of two individuals called David and Eloi. He has not yet sent me the account of their doctrine, which he promised me. As soon as he does, I will send it on to you"[11]. All the evidence suggests that the promised account was none other than the *Summa doctrinae*, which was published in Latin by Johann Joseph Ignaz von Döllinger. I provided the French translation in *The Movement of the Free Spirit*[12].

In July the police arrested Eloi, Christopher Hérault, John Davion (a rich bourgeois originally from Lille), Jan Dorhout (a poor salt-seller), Dominick van Oucle (the author of the pamphlets), the painter Heinrich

Smet, the engraver and sculptor Cornelis van den Bossche, and others.

A large number of Eloisten took flight and went to England, where some of them joined the Familists of Henry Niclaes. On 14 September 1544, Dominick van Oucle, having learned of the tortures to which Eloi had been subjected, took advantage of the absence of his guard and hanged himself in his cell. Eloi was burned on 25 October. His legend as an amiable dreamer and gentle Epicurean lived on into the nineteenth century in his neighborhood of Saint-André, where it was encountered by Georges Eeckhout[13]. Hérault and his companions were decapitated.

No doubt the Eloist movement survived clandestinely. The chroniclers no longer mentioned it, but in 1550 the existence of a group of men and women claiming for themselves the freedoms of love was indicated in the environs of Aalst in Flanders. In 1561 an attack on a convent of Dominicans near Bruges was attributed to this band. Then came the iconoclastic outburst of 1566.[14] The exploits of Jacob Gheeraerts (known as the Dutchman) were more reminiscent of the partisans of Battenberg[15] than of the peaceful Eloisten, but Eloi's doctrine does not give us grounds for thinking that the partisans of the sweetness of life would have allowed themselves to be slaughtered without putting up a fight.

The Eloist influence was discernible in the Familists, the Ranters, Dirck Coornhert, and the anti-clericalism that for a long time had a strong presence in the country [England] that Richard Payne Knight [1750–1824] assured his readers was, from the very beginning, devoted to the symbiotic cults of the Magna Mater.

Jacques Gruet

It is to the honor of Geneva that, corrupted though it was by dictatorship, there were citizens within its boundaries who, following a national tradition of liberty, were inclined to rise up against Calvin's theocratic pretentions and to claim the free disposition of self. Several enlightened bourgeois took it upon themselves to confront that fanatic, who was resolved to subject the city's entire population to his austere compulsions.

This revolt, which started off with mockery, revealed the existence of an atheistic and irreligious current that, due to the uncertain fate of the Reformation party, could still enjoy a degree of happy licentiousness.

Benoîte, the wife of Senator Pierre Ameaux, justified the luxuriance of her amorous life[16] by declaring that it was merely one of the fortunate effects of the "communion of the saints"[17].

Jacques Gruet, the leader of the opposition to Calvin, composed a pamphlet that evoked the theses of Thomas Scoto and Herman van Rijswijk. The autocrat ordered the destruction of this book but could not restrain himself from quoting extracts in his *Advice That Calvin Gave on the Procedure That Must Be Followed by the Senate of Geneva Concerning Gruet's Book.*

In 1547 Gruet tried to stir up the people of Geneva. He affixed a call for revolt to the walls of the city's principal church. Had he waited too long? Calvin obtained Gruet's arrest and that of his friends. The accused were decapitated, and Calvin continued to reign as the master of his citadel, throwing to the mercy of divine anger the enemies whom he enticed so as better to consume them or whom he denounced to magistrates—Catholic and Protestant alike—so that justice could be done.

Calvin labeled 'libertines' the friends of the political and religious liberties that he was in the process of suppressing. He gave the name 'Spiritual Libertines' to the faction that propagated among the humanists and the common people—who were both seduced by the modernity of the Reformation and repelled by its obscurantism—the doctrine of the free satisfaction of desire, which they propagated in line with the tradition of the Free Spirit.

Jacques Gruet rejected the existence of God and denied the existence of eternal life in the beyond, "saying of the law of God that it was worth nothing, just like the people who made it, and that the Gospel is only lies and that all of the Scriptures is a false and crazy doctrine"[18].

In an article on the Gruet affair, Berriot has published several remarks attributed to the incriminated pamphlet. He adds to them a letter [by Gruet] discovered at the time of his arrest. Concerning the pamphlet, Berriot writes:

> Moses is mocked in his "person" and in his "doctrine", as are all of the "patriarchs and prophets", who are characterized as "crazies, dreamers, fantastics": as for "their Scriptures", the author has only "detestation"! There is

no tenderness for the 'evangelists' and 'disciples', upon whom he inflicts the epithets: *"maraux*, scoundrels, apostates, oafs, *escervelés"*[19]. As for the Virgin Mary—by way of whom Jesus is attacked—she is ridiculed in her "honor" and in her "modesty", since she is described as a "bawd". [...] Nevertheless, it is Christ who is the target of the liveliest insults: the manuscript denies his "divinity" and contests both "his Passion" and his "resurrection"; Jesus of Nazareth, who is at first referred to in the pamphlet as "Nycollas de Molle", is defined as "a beggar, a liar, a lunatic, a seducer, a wicked man and a miserable, unhappy fantastic, [...] [as] a boor full of malignant presumption" whose "miracles [...] are only sorceries and antics" and whose hanging [from the cross] was "merited"; in brief, Christ, who *"cuidoit estre* [believed himself to be] the son of God" and who "was a hypocrite", who in fact "died miserably in his folly, a crazy *follastre*[20], a great drunk, a detestable traitor and a hanged wicked man"! The "Holy Spirit", which seems to be of little interest to the author, is the object only of a number of blasphemies, "intolerable" or "abominable", it is true; while "the [...] Scriptures, the Old as well as the New Testament", are the subject of many manuscript pages that express a veritable "detestation": "The Gospel [...] is only lies"; "all of the Scriptures are false and wicked and [...] have less meaning than Aesop's fables", since "they are a false and crazy doctrine". [...] Thus the author clearly vows "to mock all Christianity" and "all the Christians who have believed in [...] Jesus Christ and who now believe and would like to believe in him". Finally, he questions in a fundamental fashion "this law of God that is worth nothing"; he "blasphemes against the divine power and the essence of God" and, denying that God is "creator of the heavens and earth", he "renounces and abolishes all religion and divinity" so as to conclude that "God is nothing", that "men are similar to the beasts", and that "eternal life" doesn't exist!

Faced with such remarks, the historian of ideas certainly regrets not having access to the thirteen manuscript sheets that were publicly burned in 1550, as well as the original copy of the letter *Clarissime lector*[21] (which was found at the time of the arrest and of which Gruet, in 1547, denied paternity, but which he admitted that he had had in his possession and which he said he had gotten from Jean des Cordes), which has also disappeared (in the nineteenth century, it seems). [...] Through a fortunate turn of events, Jean-François Rocca—the secretary of the Consistory, later the archivist of

Geneva in 1768, and someone who knew of the Gruet affair through the *Letter* from La Monnoie that concerned *The Treatise of the Three Impostors*—had, while recounting the entirety of the trial in his *Collection of Manuscript Memoirs* concerning Geneva from 1526 to 1593, copied several pieces and transcribed the precious text of the *Clarissime lector* (which still existed at that point): a text to which explicit reference was made by both the interrogators of June 1547 and by Théodore de Bèze's *Vita Calvini*, as well as by Letter LXXVII from Calvin to [Pierre] Viret. [...] It is therefore in François Rocca's *Manuscript Memoirs*, deposited at the Geneva Historical Society, that one can find a copy of this document, which is so important to the history of Renaissance thought and which obviously merits quotation at length:

Very illustrious reader,

There are men of diverse opinions: one is a professor of literature [*litterarum professor*], another is a soldier [*bellicator*], another is in love with riches, another is a philosopher, another is a blacksmith. What do I seem to you, illustrious reader?

I do not know what men have said and written, but I believe that all that has been written with respect to divine power is falsehood, illusion and fantasy. . . . Several wise men say that man was created from the substance of the earth and that the first man was Adam. . . .

Truly, I myself think that the world is without beginning [*absque principio*] and that it will have no end [*necdam aliqua finis*]. In fact, who is the man who was able truly to describe the beginning of the world? None other than Moses, who described the first generation. And this same Moses wrote about what took place two thousand years before his own epoch: therefore, all that he wrote, he had in his mind, having no other authority than what he himself said and what he says was revealed to him. . . . Me, I deny his authority because many men have contested it [...]. He says that he saw God in the form of fire and that God presented himself to him in another form [...] [as] a voice [...]. Truly, I am in agreement with Aristotle, who wrote the following after reading the works of Moses: I am astonished to see this cuckold say a lot and prove nothing [*iste cornutus multa dicit, sed nihil probat*]!

This same Moses affirmed, as I have said, that his first narratives were revealed to him by God, which is something I do not know about [...]. After him came other men who invented still more [...] and added other fables and wrote them [...]—fables like Job, Isaiah and the other ancients. Then the moderns—such as Jerome, Ambrose, Bede, Scot, Aquinas and other barbarians [*barbari*]—invented other falsehoods [...]. Still others would come later [...].

Nevertheless, what dignity did their God have? It is a horrible thing to make man, to give him life, and then, after two hours and three days of it, to bring death to him [*est res nefanda facere hominem, dare illi vitam, post tandem alicui tempus vitae duarum horarum alteri trium dierum et postandem illi contribuere mortem*]. It is an improbable thing to create man and then break him [...]. Likewise, some say that the soul is in the body, while others say that it is a spirit: where does this spirit go when it leaves the body? If you respond to me ["]it remains in a certain place, waiting for the final advent["], then why does God not leave it in its own body, rather than changing its place? If you say ["]they are at rest, glorifying God, and the others are in Hell["], [then I will respond:] if they are in Hell then some essence would have appeared, and so nothing is known of these things with certitude! . . . Likewise, if it had so happened that some were resurrected from among the dead, like Lazarus and many others, I believe that they would have described something of the form of this other world. . . . But are these things invented for the pleasure of men, like those [stories of people] who sleep for a whole year?

And then the one whom one calls Christ, who claimed to be the Son of God: why did he suffer so badly during the Passion? If he had been the Son of God then he would have demonstrated the power that he said that God had. I do not believe that he was the Son of God but that he was a madman [*fantasticus*] who wanted to glorify himself, and that all the things that have been written on this subject are most certainly false [...].

Me, I believe that when a man is dead there is no more hope for life [*Hoc ideo credo quod, cum mortuus est homo, nulla altera expectatio vitae*].

Finally, we who are called Christians: do we not think that the Jews, the Turks, and those who live differently are condemned because they do not believe in Christ? Therefore, if truly there is only one God, a master of all things [*unus Deus actor omnium rerum*] who created mankind, why did he create such a great multitude only to make them perish [*quare creavit tantam magnam multitudinem et postea vellet ipsam periri facere*]? This is absurd: do you not see that all prosper, the Turks as well as the Christians? [...]

Nevertheless, as I said at the outset, there is a difference in the nature of men: some are bloodthirsty, others are peaceful; some are truly chaste where women are concerned, others are lustful. Whence could this difference have come? From the nature of the elements [*ex natura elementorum*].... While our moderns support the idea that this machine [*hanc fabricam*] is entirely governed by a single God, I think that the astrological philosophers are closer to the truth [*puto philosophos astrologos propinquiores esse veritati...*]. I truly think that everything is driven by the sun, the moon, and the stars, along with the four elements [*sole, luna et stellis, cum quatuor elementis*]. Nevertheless, if you ask me who made these things, since no one is their author [*nullus est author de iis*] I do not know how I would respond to you. But there are astronomers [...] such as Plato and Aristotle, and if you read them you will perceive the truth more closely [*sunt aliqui astronomi ... sicut Plato, Aristoteles quos, si leges, percipas proprius veritatem*]. ....[22]

(Note that in his *Scrutinium atheismi historico-aetiologicum* [1663], Theophilus Spizelius [also known as Gottlieb Spitzel] attributed to his contemporary, Theodore Simon, the following credo: "I believe in three things: the heavens, the earth, and the heavenly form. The earth is the nourishing mother of all things and the heavenly form contains all thought and all speech. Therefore eat, drink, and partake of pleasure, because God is nothing other than those things"[23].)

Quintin Thierry and His Friends

Around 1525, in Antwerp, while Eloi the Roofer was using the Scriptures to justify the search for the pleasures and charms of life, Coppin of Lille—known to us by way of Calvin's nasty allusions[24]—professed a similar teaching in his hometown. Not far from there, in Tournai, a tailor named Quintin Thierry (or Thiefry)[25] left his trade and his city to go to France, where a state of mind that was both detached from Catholic dogma and reticent with respect to Lutheranism was in the process of spreading. In any case, Quintin and his companion Bertrand des Moulins had little difficulty in rallying sympathy. Anthony Pocquet of Lille and Claude Perceval (who was undoubtedly originally from Rouen) assisted Quintin after the death of Bertrand des Moulins. In Paris, Quintin confronted Calvin, who later wrote a pamphlet that dwelled upon the necessity of 'putting him in his place'. Many artisans in the capital shared the opinions of the man from Tournai.

For his part, Pocquet went to Strasbourg where, using the double language of devotion, he deceived the Lutheran Bucer and obtained from him letters of recommendation addressed to Protestants in other countries. Nevertheless, starting in 1538, this same Bucer warned Queen Margaret of Navarre (the author of the gallant tales of the *Heptameron*)—who, regardless of what their opinions were, had been sheltering at her court in Nérac those innovators who were threatened by the politics of her brother, Francis I—about Pocquet.

Pocquet pushed insolence and provocation to the point of getting a meeting with Calvin, who, being less trusting than Bucer, did not accord him any recommendations.

The court of Navarre responded favorably, however, to a discourse that gave to ordinary terrestrial pleasures—which were practiced enthusiastically in this stratum of society—the very best celestial justifications. Had not Marguerite Porete's book *The Mirror of Simple Souls* been attributed to the 'Marguerite des marguerites'[26]?

Describing the small court at Nérac, Jundt has remarked that "One spoke a lot there, it is true, of inward piety, but one gaily surrendered to the pleasures of life"[27].

In 1543 Pocquet and Quintin received an attentive welcome at Margaret's court. There they developed the idea that there was no sin in devoting oneself to the sensual pleasures of love and that following the liberties of nature resulted precisely from the presence in each person of a God of universal goodness.

When Calvin's accusations—enclosed within his treatise *Against the Fantastic and Furious Sect of the Libertines Who Call Themselves Spirituals*—arrived in Nérac, they aroused only scorn and reprobation. Margaret expressed quite clearly the contempt in which she held this text, directed as it was "against herself and against her servants"[28]. She let the author know that she had no desire to have such a contemptible man anywhere near her.

But Calvin's insistence finally ended up alarming Margaret, whose sympathies for persons persecuted by her brother placed her in a difficult situation. It was advisable for her to avoid thunderbolts from Geneva even more assiduously than she did those that came from Rome.

Pocquet and Quintin returned to the Netherlands, where Calvin's henchmen—Vallérand Poulain and his friends—had not been idle. On 13 September 1542 Hughes Lescantelier—a brewer from Maire les Tournai—and Caso Hocq were decapitated in Valenciennes for supporting a "new sect called 'libertine'"[29].

Lescantelier had proclaimed his state of impeccability, while Hocq—rediscovering the theses of primitive Christianity—had explained that Christ did not die on the cross, but that he had simply abandoned his human appearance, which he'd taken on in order to manifest himself on earth.

In 1546 Quintin—having been denounced by Calvin to the Catholic authorities of Tournai, who drew their accusations from the pamphlet that Calvin had written—was arrested with many of his partisans, who were shoemakers, carpenters, and other such artisans. Quintin, who was apprehended because Calvin had said that he had rallied many ladies of the city to his sect, was hanged and burned. Three of his friends perished by the sword.

Quintin shared Jacques Gruet's contempt for the so-called apostles. Calvin was indignant: Quintin "had assigned an insulting epithet to each of the apostles in order to render them contemptible. And so he called Saint Paul 'broken pot' and, using his Picardian dialect, he called Saint John 'young idiot' [*josne sottelet*], Saint Peter a denier of God, and Saint Matthew a usurer"[30].

Quintin rejected all the forms of the Church, all of the rituals and sacraments. By dying on the cross after his descent to earth, God signified that He had abolished sin. From then on one needed only to follow one's inclinations, without being preoccupied with anything else. Quintin and his followers celebrated amorous passion, which offended Calvin with an intensity that revealed a great deal about his own conceptions about the matter:

> These wretches profane marriage, and men mingle with women like brute beasts, as their desires lead them. And they disguise their beastly defilement under the name of spiritual marriage: giving the name of spiritual impulse to the raging impetuosity that inflames a man like a bull and a woman like a bitch in heat.[31] And to leave no order among men, they create a similar confusion about possessions, saying that theirs is the communion of the saints, in which no one possesses anything of his own, but everyone takes what he can get.[32]

In the words of Auguste Jundt:

> Around 1546 their doctrine was taught in Rouen by an old Cordelier, who counted among his proselytes several ladies from noble families. He was put in prison the following year as a Protestant. Calvin, to whom his writings were communicated, refuted them in an epistle addressed to the Protestant community of Rouen. Once set free, the Cordelier published *The Shield of Defense* in response, to which Farel would oppose *The Sword of the Word* in 1550. In France, the last vestiges of the Spiritual Libertines met at Corbigny in the Nivernais; in 1559 Calvin wrote to the Protestants of this town to warn them of the heretics' machinations. A few rare signs indicated the continued presence of these heretics in the towns along the Rhine beyond Strasbourg. In a letter to Rudolf Gwalther, one of the theologians of Zurich, Pierre Viret, reported the existence of the sect in Lower Germany in 1544, and in the same year Calvin let it be understood that the heresy had partisans in Cologne. In 1545 the Walloon community of Wesel declared in its confession of faith that it rejected, among other errors, those of the Libertines.[33]

CHAPTER FORTY-TWO

The Anabaptists

If in the sixteenth century no religious movement endured as much combined hostility from the Catholics, the Protestants, and the temporal authorities as Anabaptism did, this was because it added to the religious discourse of egalitarian theocracy the old social dream in which nostalgia for a golden age provided weapons of hope to the desperate struggle against those who exploited and destroyed natural wealth.

In premonitions of the Third Age, the imminence of which fitted in with the crisis of the birth of modern capitalism, the proletarian demands of the towns mixed easily with both the peasants' aspirations for and the regrets concerning the old autarkic rural communes.

The specter of the millennium—whose agrarian fundamentalism would ultimately bring to the surface (in the antithetical ideologies of Bolshevism and fascism) the inhumanity inherent in the celestial mandate—engendered among both the partisans of the old order and the adepts of an anticipated new one a climate of endemic fear and hatred that paved the way for all sorts of cruel excesses.

Close to the Waldensian tradition, the peaceful Anabaptists incurred persecution to no less an extent than did those who extolled armed struggle. The peaceful ones nourished such dreams of martyrdom that they practically guided the executioner's hand. In Münster, where they instituted an equality that was assured by divine right, the partisans of armed struggle showed that the God of the little fathers of the people did not spare the children judged to be unworthy of his goodness.

Storch, Pfeiffer, and Müntzer

'Anabaptism' (at least in the writings of its enemies) designated an ensemble of independent groups that were governed by prophets or apostles who were armed with the sword and word of God. Their common traits recalled the demands of the reformers of the Middle Ages. They rejected the imposition of baptism on infants because it was generally administered by unworthy priests and because it did not follow from choices consciously made by individuals within the community of the faithful. In practice, baptism played a role among the Anabaptists—and especially among the Münsterians—similar to that played by party-membership cards among the old Stalinists of the twentieth century. It was a sign of election that authorized access to the egalitarian kingdom of the saints.

The absolute authority that the Anabaptists recognized in God, whose ministers they were, liberated them from obedience to spiritual and temporal authorities. In the German principalities, that divine authority expressed itself through an almost unanimous rejection of the prince-bishop and his allies. The collusion of the Catholic and Lutheran bigwigs reflected the discredited status of two religions that were judged to be irreconcilable with God's designs. Anabaptism in particular estimated itself to be the carrier of a new order. It needed to destroy the ramparts of the old tyrannies in order to impose the authoritarian reign of the saints. Such a project discovered its social ferment in the peasant wars and in the insurrections of the miners, weavers, and crowds of unemployed workers.

Peasant discontent had been a constant factor in history since the era of the Circumcellions and the Bagaudae[1]. The peasant uprisings led by Dolcino, Guillaume Cale, and John Ball punctuated this steady state of discontent with an energy that was intensified on each occasion that the economy undermined the closed system of the agrarian mode of production—the maternal paradise that was being ruined by the sordid exploitation of terrestrial and human nature—through the free circulation of goods.

From century to century—like sparks from a forge being hammered by a humanity condemned to Hell—there flew manifestoes, prophecies, and pamphlets such as *The Book of One Hundred Chapters*, which was written at the beginning of the sixteenth century by the "Revolutionary of the Upper Rhineland"[2].

Inspired by John Ball and the radical Taborites, this work expounded the demands for equality and justice that animated the revolt of the *Bundschuh*[3] and breathed life into the notion of freedom that Luther had celebrated and then disavowed.

Grouping together peasants, poor people from the villages and wandering mercenaries, the *Bundschuh* movement drew its name from its emblem, which was a peasant's laced buskin. (According to Maurice Pianzola, their flag was painted by Jerg Ratgeb[4].) Led by a man of the people, Joss Fritz, a forest ranger from the village of Lehen, this movement attempted to take Sélestat in 1493 and in 1502 imposed itself in the region of Speyer. The insurrection was crushed, but Joss Fritz managed to escape the repression and, in 1513 and then again in 1517, organized new conflagrations in Swabia and Alsace. His millenarian program was untroubled by theological considerations: he called for the extermination of the rich and the nobles, and for the establishment of an egalitarian and fraternal society. Aside from the patrician caste and the lords, the majority of the towns were receptive, and the current of sympathy aroused by the peasant wars expressed itself so strongly among the artists of the time that most official histories of art have opted to pass over them in silence. Pianzola alone has taken the time to consider these artists, in his study *Painters and Villains*[5].

These artists were Albrecht Dürer, Matthias Grünewald, the aforementioned Jerg Ratgeb (who was a painter and a military counselor to the armed peasants quartered at Pforzheim in 1526), the brothers Sebald and Barthel Beham (who had already been condemned for irreligion at a celebrated trial at Nuremberg), Lucas Cranach, Niklaus Manuel Deutsch, Urs Graf, Philip Dietmar (decapitated at Würzburg in 1525), and Tilman Riemenschneider (who was renowned for the never-equaled beauty of the hands of his figures and whose fingers were broken by the executioners at the time of the tortures in Würzburg in 1526).

It fell to Müntzer and his friends to give to the movement a type of religious carapace, which was more apt to stifle it than to protect it, because the spirit of sacrifice predisposed the movement more to martyrdom and expiatory defeat than to securing the victory of natural liberty.

Born in Stolberg (Thuringia) in 1488, Thomas Müntzer studied Greek, Latin, and Hebrew in the course of several brilliant years at the university, which destined him for the priesthood. He rallied to Luther's party soon thereafter, but he quit it no less rapidly when, having become the Pastor at Zwickau, not far from Bohemia, he met the weaver Nicholas Storch.

Influenced by the Taborite movement, Storch preached the imminence of the millenarian revolution. The saints or the Elect of the New Age would be the faithful who possessed in themselves the Spirit or the Living Christ. Müntzer adhered to Storch's views and gave them a more theological and sacrificial turn.

Stripped of his own will, a Storchian adept would expose himself—in the manner of Christ—to ordeals and suffering, which Müntzer called "the cross". Finally permitted a kind of resurrection, he received the Living Christ in himself, and the will of God then manifested itself through various interventions. Here the idea of the incarnated God, which was common among adepts of the Free Spirit, passed through the preliminary stage of the renunciation of life and along the access road to social purification, without which there could be no kingdom of the saints.

Like Savonarola, Müntzer rejected culture and erudition, and condemned reading, pleasure, and lust. His preaching against the Lutheran notables and the lechery of the bishops attracted the sympathies of the weavers and miners who had been reduced to poverty by inflation.

In April 1521 the municipal authorities chased him from the city. Storch unleashed an uprising that was quickly crushed. Müntzer traveled through Bohemia, got expelled from Prague, wandered in Germany, and in 1523 found himself the preacher of Allstedt in Thuringia, where—with the peasants, the copper-mine workers and the artisans from the town—he founded the League of the Elect, which prefigured the secular League of Communists that Marx dreamed would be the iron lance of the proletariat.

Invited to preach before Duke John of Saxony in July 1524, he predicted the harmonious and peaceful return of humanity to Christ, to nature, and to paradise. Was the sovereign—an open and tolerant spirit—seduced by Müntzer's eloquence and his program? He took time to reflect before summoning the prophet to Weimar for a meeting, at which he simply asked him to abstain from all prophetic declarations.

But when the former monk Heinrich Pfeiffer incited a revolt of the disinherited classes against the patrician oligarchy in Mühlhausen, Müntzer hastened to join him and to lend him the support of his association. The failure of the insurrection caused Müntzer to be chased from the city and convinced him to throw in his lot with the peasant movement. In a second audacious act, Pfeiffer succeeded in upending the municipal majority and in instaurating working-class power.

In April 1525 Müntzer hoisted at his church a white banner painted with a rainbow, which was the symbol of the divine law that haloes the earth. Müntzer then commenced an apocalyptic discourse whose hysterical ardor reflected a corresponding deficiency in the actual means required for the success of his efforts:

> If there are but three of you who, trusting in God, seek only his name and honour, you will not fear a hundred thousand.
> Now go at them, and at them, and at them! [...] The scoundrels are as dispirited as dogs.[6]

Pfeiffer refused to leave Mühlhausen. Storch, on the other hand, joined the peasant forces led by the Messiah of the Third Age.

Joss Fritz conducted guerrilla operations with his skillful and fast-moving forces. As for Müntzer, he put the fate of his army in the hands of the same God that Luther, from his side, had invoked in aid of the princes who were aiming to finish off the rabble. In Frankenhausen, 5,000 peasants—hoping until the last minute for a gesture from the Savior—allowed themselves to be massacred. The army of Luther and the princes lost eight mercenaries. Storch was killed while trying to extricate himself from the vise that the masters of heaven and earth were tightening around him. Thomas Müntzer and Heinrich Pfeiffer were decapitated on 27 May 1525 after being subjected to the customary tortures. The repression descended upon all of Germany. But if revolutionary Anabaptism ebbed in the countryside, it did so only to be reborn in a more rigorous form in the towns, where economic development progressed at the cost of a relentless exploitation of the proletariat.

Hut, Hubmaier, and Hutter

While the persecutions in the towns and countryside increased the numbers of pyres, gallows, and wheels of torture—which the works of Pieter Brueghel held up to a thoroughly tainted humanity as if they were judicial charges—the Anabaptist movement hesitated between the anemic pacifism of the Waldensians and the violence in which God (as ever) recognized His own.

Hans Hut, a native of Thuringia and a disciple of Müntzer, had no hesitation in announcing that Christ would descend to the earth in 1528 and that he would lend the sword of his justice to the re-baptized saints so that they could annihilate the parish priests, pastors, nobles and kings. The kingdom of God would be established in a shared community of goods and in the freedom of love.

Hut was captured in 1527 and died in prison—no doubt due to torture—leaving to others the task of seeing his program through: "Christ would return to earth and placed the two-edged sword of justice in the hands of the rebaptised Saints. The Saints would hold judgment on the priests and pastors for their false teachings and, above all, on the great ones of the earth for their persecutions; kings and nobles would be cast into chains"[7].

Hut wasn't the only one to substitute a God of resentment and radical purification for the God of the dominant forms of oppression. In 1528 the Anabaptists of Esslingen am Neckar and Ulm fomented social revolution under the banner of what the twentieth century now calls 'extremism'. (Note that the last monotheistic religion, Islam, rediscovered extremism during a similar clash between the decline of the agrarian system and the emergence of mercantile modernity.)

Unlike the doctrines of Hut and Müntzer, those of Balthasar Hubmaier (Pacimontanus in Latin) professed an absolute pacifism and a great spiritual awakening. The Pastor at Waldshut in Bavaria and a preacher at Regensburg Cathedral, he expounded the cause of Anabaptism in 1525. He became uneasy shortly thereafter and went to Zurich, whence he was chased away in 1526.

Taking refuge in Moravia, he rallied the sympathies of the inhabitants of Nikolsburg to his pacifist ideals. He gained the protection of the lords of Lichtenstein. He founded a print shop, from which came tracts that popularized the new faith. His adepts were estimated to number around twelve thousand people.

Around 1527 Hans Amon, the leader of the Anabaptists in Lower Austria, provoked a schism within Hubmaier's community. Amon contended that believers should possess nothing of their own, in contrast to the more moderate view that Menno Simons—following the doctrinal line traced out by Hubmaier—would subsequently adopt.

Moravia soon experienced the backwash of the repressive wave that was engulfing Germany. Since Vienna had summoned him to appear and to answer for his religious options, Hubmaier—who refused to retract his remarks—was delivered to the inquisitors by his protectors, the lords of Lichtenstein. He was burned on 10 March 1528.

Hans Amon took refuge with his disciples in Slavkov, better known as Austerlitz. There, in 1523, he faced the dissidence of a faction—inheritors of the line of the *Pikarti* or Adamites—who intended to live in accordance with free sex, even free love.

Jakob Hutter, a native of Moos in South Tyrol, was invited to lead this community. He banished those who had enriched themselves. Threatened with arrest, he left Moravia for Tyrol, where he was executed in February 1536.

Under the name 'Hutterites', the Moravian Anabaptist community known in Slovakia as the 'Habans'—from the Hebrew *ha banim*, 'the true children of God', which is what the Anabaptists called themselves—passed on the fundamental teachings of the Waldensians that had been adopted by Anabaptism: the rejection of private property; the refusal to pay duties and taxes (which was justified by the argument that the State used this money to finance armed conflicts); the popular election of the preacher who led the community; baptism being left to the decision of adults; the refusal to bear arms; and the condemnation of war and the death penalty. All this was quite sufficient to arouse against them the lasting animosity of the temporal and spiritual authorities.

Around the middle of the sixteenth century, there were nearly 70,000 adepts in Moravia. Incited by the Jesuits, the Catholic authorities chased them from the country. The adepts' refusal to fight during the Thirty Years' War resulted in their dispersal. They went to Transylvania, Poland, Southern Russia and—starting in the eighteenth century—the United States.

Meanwhile, the doctrines of the Mennonites (see below) dissuaded the faithful from following up on their ambition to establish on earth an egalitarian kingdom of 'each for God and God for all'.

Melchior Hoffmann

The path taken by Melchior Hoffmann traced itself out indecisively between the aggressiveness of Müntzer and Hut and the pacifism of Hubmaier. Born around 1495 in Schwäbisch Hall, Hoffmann was enthusiastic about the mystical works of Tauler and the writings of Luther, whom he defended at Valmiera until his expulsion from the town in 1523. At Tartu, in Estonia, he preached against the use of images and in 1525 he inspired an iconoclastic riot, in the course of which the crowd prevented his arrest.

Hoffmann's obstinacy in predicting the end of time attracted the hostility of the Lutherans, one of whom (Sylvester Tegetmeyer) forced Hoffmann to leave Tartu. In Stockholm, where he got married, Hoffmann fixed 1533 as the advent of the era of the saints. Exiled by King Gustav Vasa, he fled to Lübeck with his wife and children. Then he went to Magdeburg, where the Lutheran Nicolaus von Amsdorf demanded his expulsion. Welcomed in Holstein, he was flushed out by the intrigues of Luther, whose zeal in persecuting dissidents was the envy of the inquisitors. Summoned by Duke Christian to present himself at a public confrontation in Flensburg, Hoffmann responded as follows (not without a degree of arrogance) to the question of who his partisans were: "I do not recognize any adherents. I hold myself upright and only in the Word of God. Each person does the same"[8].

Chased out of Denmark, Hoffmann took refuge at Frise [in France]—where he encountered Karlstadt—and then went to Strasbourg. In 1529 he published there his *Dialogues* concerning the quarrels of Flensburg. He associated with Caspar Schwenckfeld and produced many prophetic texts. Then Hoffmann joined the Anabaptists and intervened at the Council at Strasbourg so that a church might be assigned to them. This had the effect of fuelling the fires of repression. Hoffmann was once again forced into exile. He founded an Anabaptist community in Frise, while Luther raged against those whom (drawing upon Hoffmann's first name) he called 'Melchiorites'. Luther's words had the force of a guillotine blade. In 1531 a man named Volkertszoon and eight other Melchiorites were decapitated at The Hague. Stirred by the ardor of their martyrdom, Hoffmann preached in Hesse and Frise, where, around 1532, Obbe Philips became his disciple.

Amid the incessant blaze of the violence, Hoffmann suddenly proposed (in his *Commentary on the Epistle to the Romans*) a peaceful conception of Anabaptism that prohibited all recourse to weapons—persuaded as he now was that the redemption of humanity would come from those who preached in the desert.

He had scarcely appeased the notables and the property owners when a pamphlet in which he addressed prayers neither to Christ nor to the Holy-Spirit but to God alone displeased the Protestant clergy, who, like all priests and ministers, were quick to take offense at the notion that one might address oneself to the master of the heavens without first referring to the masters of the earth. Bucer, the Pope of Strasbourg, had him arrested.

Hoffmann's biographers have claimed that this was an error from the point of view of maintaining order, since his growing influence had increasingly served to counterbalance the directives of Anabaptism's insurrectional tendency—a tendency which was growing in Holland and which would soon inspire a wave of urban revolts that, although they ran aground in Amsterdam, Antwerp, and Lübeck, did prove successful in Münster.

After the crushing of the Münsterites, during which his disciple Rothman was among those who perished, the conditions of Hoffmann's detention became more severe. Only the hope of dragging a public retraction out of him—which both Bucer and Capito tried to do—saved him from capital punishment. He died in 1543 without ever having lost his eloquence, his naivety, or his faith in the imminence of a terrestrial Jerusalem.

The majority of Hoffmann's disciples found themselves at the center of the Münsterian powder keg, which was an ironic development considering Hoffman's pacifism. But it is true that, for close to a century, Anabaptism expressed in theological terms an endemic insurrectional impulse whose violence often got lost in those countries that were dominated by Catholicism and its religious wars. Like Hans Denck, who wryly lamented that God had not permitted him to believe in God, the Anabaptists substituted for the God of the feudal lords a collectivist God who was elected by the members of the party. In this sense Münster offered a beautiful example of the kind of divine collectivism that was headed for a terrible future in which God would be deposed by the State—an entity that, once it had achieved self-sufficiency, would no longer feel the need to invoke a heavenly phantom in order to perpetuate its reign of terror on earth.[9]

The Münsterites

North-west Germany at the beginning of the sixteenth century consisted in the main of a number of petty ecclesiastical states, each with a prince-bishop as its sovereign. Usually such a state was torn by fierce social conflicts. The government of the state was in the hands of the prince-bishop and of the chapter of the diocese, which elected him and to a large extent controlled his policy. The members of the chapter were recruited solely from the local aristocracy—a coat of arms with at least four quarterings was commonly an indispensable qualification—and they often chose one of their own number as bishop. This group of aristocratic clerics was subject to no control by any higher authority; in the regional diet they were powerfully represented and could always rely on the support of the knighthood. They therefore tended to govern solely in the interest of their own class and of the clergy of the diocese. In an ecclesiastical state the clergy were not only very numerous—in the bishopric of Münster there were some thirty ecclesiastical centres, including four monasteries, seven convents, ten churches, a cathedral and of course the chapter itself—but also highly privileged. Members of the chapter enjoyed rich prebends and canonries. The monks were permitted to carry on secular trades and handicrafts. Above all, the clergy as a whole were almost entirely exempt from taxation.[10]

In 1531 Chaplain Bernt Rothmann was converted to Lutheranism at Münster. He enjoyed the support of the guilds and that of a rich textile manufacturer named Knipperdollinck. Seduced by the prophetic inspiration of Melchior Hoffmann, Rothmann preached the imminence of "messianic sorrows" that would herald the birth of a new era in 1533 (the fifteenth centenary of the death of Christ).

Upon the death of the bishop, the guilds opened the town to Protestant pastors. Having been hunted everywhere, the Anabaptists came there as if to the Promised Land.

In 1531, Sebastian Franck summarized the Fifth Epistle attributed to Clement thus:

> A little later Nimrod began to reign, and then anyone who was successful dominated his neighbor. And they began to divide the world and to quarrel about questions of property. Then one began to distinguish Mine from Yours. Finally the people became savage, like wild beasts. Each one wanted to be more beautiful and better than the others, and in fact hoped to become their master. But God had made all things to be held in common, as today we still enjoy the air, fire, the rain and the sun in common; a few thievish and tyrannical men cannot appropriate and jealously keep these things for themselves.[11]

The theme of the Fifth Epistle was a favorite of Rothmann, whose popularity was growing with the influx of unemployed Dutch workers, whom the rich Lutherans could not see wandering the streets of the city, permeated with holiness, without shuddering.

Melchior Hoffmann's imprisonment in Strasbourg weakened the pacifist faction and favored the efflorescence of prophets and apostles who were more willing to brandish the torch of Münster. Among the latter, the baker Jan Matthys of Haarlem and Jan Bockelson (also known as John of Leyden) set themselves up as spokesmen for a crowd that believed that God was readying Himself to impose a new egalitarian law.

In February 1534 a veritable hysteria for conversion seized the city. The streets were filled with ecstatic people professing their obedience to the eternal Father, to whom they delivered the city hall without encountering any opposition. Lutherans and Catholics took flight while the voices of Rothmann, Matthys, and Bockelson proclaimed Münster the New Jerusalem.

The goods of the banished Lutherans and Catholics were confiscated and used to enrich communal funds. Even as a decree was being issued that imposed the death penalty on those who balked at consenting to be re-baptized, the Bishop of Münster was organizing the siege of the town and alerting the princes and municipal councils so that the hordes that were marching in anticipation of the egalitarian millennium could be intercepted and massacred.

After the death of Matthys, who was killed during a sortie that a divine order enjoined him to attempt, Bockelson imposed a collectivist regime and a theocratic dictatorship under which all opposition was held to be high treason.

Each person was paid by the municipal power, and communal meals in the refectories covered the needs of all under the auspices of fraternal communion. Since private property was a sin, it was mandated that the doors of all houses be kept open. The executions of 'heretics'—presided over by 'the King of the Final Days'—went on and on in an atmosphere of terror, to which was soon added famine. Like all paradises based on obedience to heaven or to governments, the reign of the perfect ones turned into Hell.[12]

The millenarian revolution collapsed into horror. After the town was recaptured, the terror that had been imposed by the Anabaptists meant that the dream of these collectivists of God was effaced with a ferocity that exceeded even the fear that they had inspired. John of Leyden, Knipperdollinck, and their friend Krechting were dismembered by red-hot pincers while still alive, and yet they died without letting out a single cry, thus producing an eternal silence that expressed the inhumanity of the consensual pairing of oppressor and oppressed that continues to reign under the inappropriate name of 'human history'.

Pacifists and Terrorists: Menno Simons and Battenberg

The annihilation of Münster enraged the hardliners at the same time as the pacifism of Hubmaier and the elderly Hoffmann was restoring Anabaptism to the path of sweet resignation. God once again found the odor of sanctity in the very fetidity of his carnivorous breath.

Although they were persecuted just as fiercely as the Münsterites, the disciples of Menno Simons (1496–1560)—known as 'Mennonites'—professed a resolutely nonviolent doctrine that was stripped of collectivist demands. In 1537 the tendency inspired by Hubmaier came under the control of Simons, who organized it and founded one of the many Protestant Churches still in vogue today in Holland, the United States, and Canada.

By contrast, the guerilla war led by John of Battenberg (born in 1495 in Gelderland) marked a transitional stage between the disaster at Münster and the mass arrival of Iconoclasts in the Southern Netherlands and in Northern France.

Abandoning his functions as the Mayor of Steenwijk in the Overijssel, John of Battenberg rallied the insurrectional wing of the Anabaptists and, in 1535—during a tumult caused by the sect—seized Oldeklooster, a monastery in the Bolsward region.

That same year, he founded with the survivors of Münster the group known as *Zwaardgeesten*, 'The Spirits of the Sword'. Identifying himself with Isaiah and as being tasked with preparing the return of Christ to earth, Battenberg called for the destruction of the churches, preached polygamy and the community of goods, prescribed divorce when one party to a marriage refused to practice confession, and exhorted his followers to use their swords to exterminate anyone who didn't share his opinions.

In 1536 the Congress of Bocholt tried in vain to reconcile the Münsterites, the partisans of Battenberg, and the sectarians of David Joris. The pacifists carried the day and Battenberg's appeal for armed struggle was judged to be premature.

Arrested in 1537 in Vilvoorde near Brussels, Battenberg died on the pyre in 1538, leaving Zeylmaker, Appelman, and Mickers at the head of the *Zwaardgeesten*. Attacks on monasteries and churches increased; pillaging was carried out in Alkmaar (1538), Utrecht (1541), the Overijssel, Frise, Brabant, Leyden, and in the surroundings of Münster, where the Battenbergian Peter Van Ork was burned in 1544. Despite the execution of Appelman in Leyden that same year, anti-clerical action intensified in Frise (1549), in Aalst (1550)—where a group of insurgents practiced sexual freedom—in Leyden (1552), and in Courtrai (1553).

The sacking of churches and the assassination of their ministers met with popular approval because, as Marcus van Vaernewyck wrote in his *Memoirs of a Ghentian Patrician on the Religious Troubles in Flanders*, "there was no lack of people who did not like priests, and they gladly applauded the priests' troubles and disasters" and wanted to "hang their balls in the air"[13].

The Iconoclasts

Even after the disappearance of the leaders of the Battenbergist party, Anabaptist uprisings did not cease to inflame the Netherlands and Northern France. But their social and political motivations ended up predominating—and this in an increasingly obvious manner—over their religious character. The national struggle undertaken in the Netherlands against Spanish domination created a heterogeneous front in which the most diverse interests tried to unite within the general discontent, which lacked a shared program. The nobles uneasily tolerated the restrictions imposed on their regional privileges by the absolutism of Philip II; the bourgeoisie balked at paying taxes to fund a war that was hindering its growth; and even the clergy feared having its hands tied by a State power that the Inquisition wielded with a self-interested fervor. And as for that "dangerous animal called the people"—to use the words of Antoine Perrenot de Granvelle, the chief counselor to Margaret of Parma, regent in the Netherlands—its sole recourse was to topple both those who ruled over it and the symbols of its oppression (that is to say, almost the entirety of what surrounded it).

The social violence was doubly advantageous for the political designs of the various contenders for power: for example, it elevated William of Orange to the status of royalty and sustained his legend as the liberator of the northern provinces. Through the repression that the social violence incurred, and once victory had been assured, he was legitimated in the eyes of the princes, who were impatient to cage the wild beasts after having let them roar for a while.

The discontent seems to have started in Saint-Omer in 1566. (Note that, as early as 1562, two Calvinist weavers who had been led to the pyre in Valenciennes were liberated by rioters. In 1564 the people forced open the doors of the prisons in Bruges and Brussels.) The troubles spread to the north. On 13 August 1566, in Bailleul, the crowd destroyed the cloister, burned the crosses and the sacerdotal habits, and brought down the tabernacles. The sacking lasted eight months and spread to Armentières, Menen, Hondschoote (which was so constant in its resolution that the commissars of the Duke of Alba, who were later tasked with enforcing penal sanctions, steered clear of the area), Tournai (where several magistrates embraced the party of the Iconoclasts), a part of Artois, Brabant, Utrecht, Zeeland, and Amsterdam. In Antwerp the houses of the rich were pillaged after the third day of the uprising.

On 5 April 1566, taking the surge of the iconoclasts as their pretext, Catholics and Calvinists joined together to address to the Regent Margaret of Parma a remonstrance directed against the Inquisition and the "bad counselors to the King" that was known as the 'Compromise of the Nobles'. In this covenant, the Catholics and Calvinists coupled their rejection of absolutism with a promise to restore order. They adorned themselves, as if it were an escutcheon, with the epithet 'beggars', which a minister had applied to them in an insulting manner and which the destroyers of cathedrals adopted at every opportunity.

On 25 August 1566 Margaret of Parma feigned to give in. She decreed the suppression of the Inquisition, freedom for the Protestant religion, and amnesty for the nobles accused of conspiracy. The latter hastened to suppress the riots and intervened in the consistories to calm the peoples' spirits. William of Orange marched on Antwerp and the Count of Egmont attempted to restore order in Flanders, where the number of rebels was estimated to be 60,000 out of a total of 200,000 inhabitants.

Reassured by the guarantees of freedom offered to their ministries, the Calvinist preachers condemned the iconoclastic party, whose ardor was undiminished. At first, those whom one called the 'howlers' [*hurlus*] in Northern France refrained from killing and from carrying off ecclesiastical goods, which were generally destroyed on the spot. They prided themselves on the total destruction of some 400 churches.

After concentrating the Spanish troops, Margaret went on the offensive in December 1566. She annulled the decisions that had been dictated to her by the necessity of playing for time, and she sent the army into Armentières, Tournai, and Valenciennes, where it brought to a satisfactory conclusion the repression upon which the feudal lords had embarked.

William of Orange and Hendrik van Brederode fled to the northern provinces, where an open guerrilla war was being fought against Spain. The expeditious justice meted out by the Duke of Alba, who was acting as Philip II's envoy, did not spare Iconoclasts, Catholics, Calvinists, or nobles who were judged to have been disloyal. (The Counts of Egmont and Horn were decapitated in 1568.)

In the southern provinces, the 'Beggars' harassed their Spanish enemies on two fronts. They fought on land, in the forests of Hainaut and Artois. In Flanders, they fought under Jean Camerlynck (who was originally from Hondschoote), the preacher Jan Michiels, and Jacob van Heule (the latter of whom was the son of a rich family from Bruges). They also fought on the seas; the 'Sea Beggars' attacked Spanish ships with the aid of small, light boats. These guerrillas profited from the benevolence of Elizabeth I of England and the aid of William of Orange, who tried (in vain) to make them submit to his authority. On 1 April 1572 the seizure of the port of Brill and the subsequent occupation of Vlissingen marked a decisive stage in the liberation of Holland. Alba, who failed in his attempt to recapture it, was recalled to Spain the following year. The movement of the 'Beggars' fell beneath the blows of William of Orange and, in the South, was only able to launch inconsequential political conspiracies.

The last flare-up of revolutionary Anabaptism embraced the regions of Cleves and Wesel in Westphalia in 1567. A shoemaker named Jan

Willemsen, leading 300 adepts (among whom were survivors of Münster), founded the *n*th version of the New Jerusalem, to which Adamite sexual practices lent a little spiciness. Polygamy was prescribed and the Messiah Willemsen married twenty-one chosen ones. The community of goods did not require an economy of production; the saints lived off of raids and pillaging, and attacked the homes of priests and nobles. They lasted a dozen years before being crushed by punitive expeditions.[14]

CHAPTER FORTY-THREE

The Individualist Messiahs: David Joris, Nicholas Frey, Henry Niclaes

David Joris

Among the wandering preachers whom the Reformation and the free interpretation of sacred texts set in motion along Europe's roads, David Joris distinguished himself more through the singularity of his destiny than through the originality of his thought. Pursued by the hatred of Catholics, Lutherans, Calvinists, Mennonites, and Münsterians, this man—upon whose head there was a price wherever he went—ended his life peacefully in Basel, shielded by the outward appearance of a notable, of an orthodox adept of Protestant doctrines bearing the honorable title 'John of Bruges'.

Born in Bruges—or perhaps in Delft or, less probably, in Ghent—in 1501, he was named David after the role traditionally played by his father, Georgius, in the literary societies that portrayed the sacred mysteries. After a career as a glass engraver in Delft, he traveled through the Netherlands, France, and England in his capacity as a merchant. He frequently visited Antwerp, where he engaged in polemics with Eloi Pruystinck, founder of a Free Spirit group.

In 1524 he wedded Dirckgen Willems in Delft. In 1528 his enthusiasm for the Reformation and his hostility towards the Roman clergy earned him public torture and a three-year term of banishment. He then adhered to the most persecuted of the sects (the Anabaptists), went to

Strasbourg in 1535, and declared his opposition to the violence of the Münsterites. Quite anomalously, his megalomania never led him to renounce the ideals of tolerance and pacifism.

A vision he had of the prophetess Anneke Esaiasdochter (also known as Anna Jansz) suddenly revealed to him his eschatological mission. Identifying himself with the biblical David, whom his father had so often played on the boards of the local theater, he preached renunciation, asceticism, and the advent of the millennium. The increasing numbers of his partisans soon began to trouble the temporal powers, which took repressive measures against him. Like all those elected by God, David discerned in the threats that loomed on the horizon the very ordeals that traditionally announced the birth of a new era. He wrote to the court of Holland, to Philip of Hesse, and to the Emperor, soliciting their support for the Davidian royalty that God had enjoined him to found.

In 1539, when Menno Simons denounced her as a false prophet, Anneke Esaiasdochter was burned at Delft. Having been condemned to exile, Joris clandestinely visited Holland, Frise, and Belgium. After the death of John of Battenberg, many of the Battenbergian terrorists joined his party, in which non-violence created an increasing amount of space for certain Free Spirit ideas, particularly for Adamism—that is, for the necessity of recovering Edenic innocence.

Although he was hunted everywhere in Europe, David Joris devoted himself to frenetic activity with the aim of getting himself recognized as a Messiah. He went to Oldenburg and Strasbourg, where he encountered the moderate wing of the Anabaptists, whom he irritated by obstinately demanding their obedience. In 1542 his most important work, *The Book of Miracles* (*T'Wonder-Boeck*), was published.

David denied the Bible its self-avowed status as the only true Book. Mystical experience took priority over Scripture because only revelation illuminated the presence of God in each person. Identifying the body of man with the temple of God, David—in the first edition of his book—depicted "the last Adam or the new ecclesiastical man" and "the fiancée of Christ, the renewal of all things" in engravings that were judged to be 'obscene'. A note spelled out the idea that the attractiveness of the young woman (or the Eve) of the era of the saints symbolized "the bliss, life and voluptuousness of the spirit". Amorous coupling once again discovered in spiritual androgyny a basis for its natural legitimacy. The secret life joyously led by David after his retreat to Basel involved using religious discourse to remove shame and guilt.

Jundt quotes many extracts from David's *Wonder-Boeck*.

God is absolute, without beginning, a light beyond all light, a depthless abyss, the eternal origin of all that exists, an endless end. He remains unchanging and impassive, incomprehensible and silent, reposing on the foundation of his own being, like a rock or a mountain of gold. Essence without essence, he does not manifest himself in his absoluteness; he does not think about himself, nor does he express what he is, as his grandeur, length, size and depth surpass all human conception; everything is annihilated in comparison with him. And yet he is the supreme activity; he is the eternal essence and lives in all objects. It is not outside of ourselves that we must look for him, but inside ourselves, because he is the Spirit; he is the infinite light of eternal justice, wisdom, truth and reason; he is the Lord of this very light, substance, life and intelligence that enlighten the intimate thoughts within the hearts of believers and thanks to which we are able to distinguish the objects of the visible world: holy and pure essence, of perfect beauty and innocence.

The eternal and hidden God is obliged to manifest his unknowable essence through his Word of justice, in the power of his eternal wisdom and truth; in his Word he actualizes the potential that he has to know himself. In his Word, he lets escape outside of himself, and creates in visible form, his Sons and Daughters in conformity with his own manner of being, and they are destined to possess in all truth his Spirit and essence, as the eternal lights of the new heavens. God knows himself in the Word, which is the image of his divine splendor, of his Spirit, and of his substance, insofar as it is inclined towards the world of the creatures. He expresses in himself all that exists—he expresses his holy creatures, who are equal to him, who are his Sons and Daughters. In this way, God begins to exist in concrete form in his creatures; his creation has its eternal origin in himself and continues indefinitely by means of the Son—that is to say, by means of the divine intelligence and the distinctions that this intelligence establishes in the absolute essence. Everything that emanates from God is and remains God; God resides in everything, him alone and none other. In these emanations towards us, God has received in Christ the many denominations, by means of which we try, stammering, to express his essence. This emanation does not exhaust the divine essence: similar to a fountain that flows without interruption, the Spirit of God overflows from every direction and lets the plenitude of his being, strength, life, and intelligence escape beyond him.

When a person is elevated to the perfection of the life of the Spirit, for him there is no longer any difference between good and evil, life and death, fall and rising. The members of the body fulfill quite different functions and yet are equally necessary to it: it is likewise unnecessary to say that one thing is not as good as another, because all things are equally good in the eyes of God and it isn't possible to make them otherwise or better. To scorn anything would be to scorn God in his work. It is only for us that there are different degrees of beauty, faith, spirituality and holiness: for God and in God there is neither augmentation nor diminution; he remains immutable in his essence and has always been so. If someone—following the example of the Pharisees—wants to make his external life appear to be irreproachable so as to seem just and good in the eyes of mankind, he only worsens the actual state of corruption in which he finds himself; because he is scorning the work and life of God in doing so, he in fact damns his soul through his own justice and his own wisdom. No: to be blamed and condemned on earth is to be justified and sanctified in heaven. What one in the here-below calls ugly and corrupt is beautiful and praiseworthy to the Lord, because what pleases men displeases God; what they call good, he calls evil; what they consider to be pure and holy, he considers impure and execrable. In the same way that light follows darkness, and day is born from night, it is necessary that faith manifests itself through incredulity, hope through despair, love through hate and envy, kindness of the heart through cunning, simplicity through duplicity, innocence through shamelessness, frankness through dissimulation, the spirit through the flesh, the truth through the lie, and heavenly essence through terrestrial essence; and so it is necessary to place oneself above the judgment of men (whether they blame you or they praise you), to act in complete freedom, to accomplish good through evil with a total independence, to reach what is imperishable through what is perishable, and to let what is luminous and pure manifest itself in its purity through what is impure.

Mankind must completely abandon itself to God's direction and do what he commands—women as well as men. God only acts from eternity in eternity; everything that exists is his work. It follows that all that is, must be, and that all that does not exist, must not. God in his goodness has made everything good. We therefore live without being concerned about anything, because we are free from all evil; we reside and live in the good. We abstain from finding anything bad, because all God's works are good. If someone does us wrong, we do not get carried away: do we get irritated with the stone against which we stub our toe? In the same way that a flute does not play itself but is played by the breath of a person, mankind does not act by itself but by God, who made it and who speaks through it and manifests himself through it. Mankind is the property of God; the unique goal of its existence is to glorify its Creator; it must therefore not seek its own glory in anything but must attribute all glory to God and to Christ, according to the terms of the Scriptures. Each must be content with the destiny that has been assigned to him; mankind must obey without murmuring appeals to its Creator, must be ready to follow God anywhere he pleases to lead it, and must let God make of it what he wants. Doesn't the potter have the right to give the clay the form that suits it? The Eternal will break all resistance from his creatures with his iron scepter, as easily as the potter smashes in anger the vase that he has fashioned. The man to whom these truths appear too lofty must not reject them simply because he does not understand them; he must receive and accept them in complete submission and keep quiet about what exceeds his understanding. Otherwise, according to the Scriptures, he risks blaspheming God in his ignorance.

Born-again people need no longer desire, seek and marry a woman according to [the demands of] the flesh, as if they were mere men, subjected to their sinful natures. They can instead (according to the inward Spirit) desire, seek and marry the heavenly substance, whose beauty is eternal and whose glory is imperishable; they must in their intelligence conceive the splendor and the purity of the divine essence—the unalterable satisfaction that God experiences in himself—and they must let all the rest follow its regular course, according to the good will of God. A man must not devote himself to a woman, and a woman should not devote herself to a man: the elect must devote themselves exclusively to the Lord. It is not that men and women must cease to procreate, which would be contrary to the plan and will of God: here it is a question of the marriages of the angels, of celestial weddings, which according to the words of Jeremiah 31 have long since been prepared for the children of God: a woman will surround a man and unite with him; she will become a man with him, flesh of his flesh, bone of his bone. It isn't of a single woman whom the prophet speaks, but of seven women united into one: the Fiancée of Christ who resides in seven communities. Seven women, yes, seven communities—understand me well!—must voluntarily humble themselves before one man who is Christ, and they will be called his wives. Many communities give to Christ the names of Lord, Husband and King, but they are not his wives and his body: as long as they have not become his wives, he will not be their husband and their life. Christ lives for God and the community lives for Christ—that is to say, woman lives for man, but man does not live for woman. In fact, man was not created for woman, but woman was created for man. Woman is deprived of liberty, vigor and will; she is placed under the power of man, not under the protection and power of God. Such were Adam and Eve, whose image we carry in our nature: they were two souls, originally united in a single body. That unity was broken: man carries in himself the substance of the heavens; woman the substance of the earth. This is why it is necessary for woman to become man, according to the Scriptures—so that the substance foreign to the divine being disappears. Then man will be an angel before the face of God, and man and woman together will again become equal to the Creator. Whosoever is not found in this state of heavenly marriage will be cursed.[1]

Jundt concludes: "David Joris thus founded the legitimacy of polygamy—or, rather, that of elective affinity—on the metaphysical principle of the re-composition of the integrity of human nature through the union of the sexes in a single being"[2].

The unfortunate turn of events that he experienced gave David Joris the feeling that it was best to live an existence that accorded with the will of the Lord, but one that was also less bitter than that of a Messiah, sect leader, apostle, or exile. His mother was decapitated at Delft. In

Deventer his friend and publisher, Juriaen Ketel, died on the scaffold; his confessions led to the death of Eloi Pruystinck of Antwerp and to the execution of his 'libertine' friends. Filled with hatred, Menno Simons pursued Joris, denouncing his hypocrisy and the debaucheries that he had perpetrated under the cover of perfection.

A polemic with Jan Łaski in Frise, wherein his authority as prophet was smashed, motivated David Joris to withdraw to Basel, where he moved in 1544 with his family, which included his son-in-law Nikolaas Meyndertsz van Blesdijk, who was a defector from the Mennonites. There in Basel, under the name John of Bruges, Joris presented himself as a Lutheran who had been persecuted by papists.

Having become a respectable citizen thanks to the money that his disciples had sent him, Joris continued to send numerous letters of millenarian hope to his partisans, some of whom lived as far away as Denmark. He justified his retreat by referring to the flight of Christ to Egypt. No doubt he also found good reasons for his disciples to live in voluntary poverty, even as he himself lived in opulence off of the funds of his sect.

He also used his credit as a public figure in Basel to fight openly in favor of tolerance. He defended Michael Servetus and united in friendship with Schwenckfeld and Castellion. Towards the end of his life he quarreled with his son-in-law Blesdijk, who went from being an unconditional friend to an enemy. David Joris died on 25 August 1556 and was interred with great pomp at the Church of Saint Leonard in Basel.

Approximately two and a half years later, following family quarrels in which Blesdijk was involved, Joris's identity was brutally revealed. This caused a scandal in the city. His family and friends anxiously protested their innocence. They affirmed that they knew nothing of David's doctrines, whose far-from-orthodox aspects were condemned by Blesdijk in a pamphlet. They publicly adjured.

On 13 May 1559 David's exhumed body and his books were thrown on the pyre. As late as the seventeenth century, partisans of David Joris continued to exist in Holstein, surrounded by polemics and calumny. David found a defender in Gottfried Arnold, who attempted to rehabilitate him in his *Unparteiische Kirchen und Ketzerhistorie*[3].

Nicholas Frey

The cases of Nicholas Frey (also known as Claus or Klaus Frey) and Henry VIII of England make for a piquant comparison. While the sword of justice overcame one and served the other, the same divine will conferred the seal of its absolutism upon their very personal choices in matters of conjugal and private affairs.

Nicholas Frey was originally from Bad Windsheim in Bavaria, where he was a trader in furs. When the Reformation came to this town he became one of the most zealous partisans of the new ideas, but a short time later he allied himself with the Anabaptists in the countryside and received a second baptism, which proved to be the occasion for trouble in his native town. He was imprisoned and then released when he promised to change his conduct. But when the authorities demanded that he publicly retract his errors, he preferred to flee rather than submit to this humiliation. Thus, after fifteen years of marriage, he left his wife, Katherine, with whom he had eight children, and headed towards Nuremburg. Taking advantage of the hospitality that he was offered in this town by one of its most pious and respected citizens, he won over to his doctrines the sister of his host—a woman named Elisabeth—and engaged with her in what he called a spiritual and celestial marriage. Katherine, the abandoned wife, arrived a little later in Nuremburg and encouraged her husband to return with her to their native town. In response, Frey mistreated her and chased her away. Later on he wrote about this subject to his spiritual sister or, as he called her, his conjugal sister, Elisabeth: "I have seen in the Trinity that I must break the head of my first wife, so that the prophecies of the Old and New Testaments may be fulfilled.[4] Is it not in fact said that the seed of the woman will break the head of the serpent? My first wife is the serpent or demon spoken of by the Scriptures; as far as you are concerned, you are the woman whose seed must break her head. To become a disciple of Christ, I must hate women, children, home and homeland. If I have crushed the serpent of disbelief, this is because I was forced to do so, because it isn't me who did it, but God who lives inside me and in whom I live". Obliged to leave Nuremburg, Frey went to Strasbourg in 1532; Elisabeth joined him soon thereafter. Their imprudent schemes and poorly concealed relations with the other sectarians in the locality soon attracted the attention of the authorities. They were imprisoned. Informed of the presence of her husband in Strasbourg, Katherine went there and beseeched him to return with her to Windsheim. Frey was inflexible. Seeing his obstinacy, the magistrate condemned him on 19 May 1534 to be drowned as a bigamist, which took place three days later at the Pont du Corbeau.

According to Capito[5], he had to confess that he'd made the following errors:

1. The general practice of the sacraments and the rites of the church come from the devil—so he says, although he allowed himself to be baptized a second time.
2. All scripture foretold of him, his old wife and his new love, so that Els[beth]'s seed came from scripture, whereas his wife's seed was anchored in earthly things, and although he was a man, he also was the spiritual seed, and must trample what is carnal, that is, his wife.
3. In Saul we see that his wife was the head of the empire of unbelief, whereas his new sister Elisabeth was David, and taking the place of David she was anointed by God and the Holy Spirit for the eternal kingdom of the faith, 1 Samuel 22. According to the spiritual meaning, he, Claus Frey, was Jonathan and made an eternal pact with David (that is, Elisabeth) according to the Spirit. This bothered Saul (his rightful wife), and she hurled the spear of evil words, calling him a scoundrel and Elisabeth a whore.
4. The right and perfect work was for him, as a faithful man, to leave his former wife and take another.
5. The belief in justification and Christian love of one's neighbour consisted in Elisabeth's persistent love for him. That was the work of God, to improve the good, pious man, and thus faith was a very different thing from that taught by the above-named preachers.
6. His Elisabeth could rightly be called the mother of all believers, for she was the beginning of correct Christian faith.
7. His Elisabeth had, like Mary, given birth to Christ, thus she must reveal the image of Christ, and if Christ was the head of the church, there must be a maker, and she calls herself that and may say the

Magnificat with the Virgin Mary: "My soul magnifies the Lord and my spirit rejoices in God, my salvation". And everyone should put his faith in him, and he will become apparent in his fruit and from what happened to her.

8. He alone was the head of the church, in whom Christ had perfected everything, and there would be no other to perfect it.
9. He was Christ according to the Word, and his flesh the brother of Christ.
10. He was sent by God to bear the image of Christ, and in these last days all secrets of God would be revealed, for just as Moses had borne the image of God, he must bear the image of Christ, and be a forerunner to the faithful.
11. Through him all things must be corrected that have been corrupted since the birth of Christ; he was the tool to give God his glory.
12. Elisabeth states that God revealed this to her in his august school and indicated it to her in her heart through the Holy Spirit, that is, at the foot of Christ's cross, where she had betaken herself.
13. The common preachers were only workers in the rough, who gave the stone a rough outline and cleared the area, but were unable to build anything, etc.
14. The preachers of God were thieves of honour and seducers; they must not be believed when they say we are all sinners and when they teach that we must not do what is perfect, that is, that he must not leave his wife and children.[6]

Henry Niclaes and the Familists

Founded in 1540 by Henry Niclaes [also known as Henry Nicholis or Hendrik Niclaes], the Family of Love—often wrongly defined as an Anabaptist sect—intended to reestablish the original human community in all its innocence. Its organization included a bishop, whose authority was supported by twelve sages and by four classes of priests. All gave their personal belongings to the sect, which included quite a large number of believers—principally in the Netherlands and England, where their existence was still attested to in the seventeenth century.

Born in 1502, Henry Niclaes claimed to have had his first visions at the age of nine while attending courses at a Latin school. He worked for his family's business from the age of twelve and took it over upon the death of his father. After being arrested in 1529 for his adherence to Lutheranism, he went to Amsterdam, where he stayed for nine years before being suspected of Anabaptism. In 1541 he lived in Emden, where he engaged in a flourishing trade in wool. He frequently traveled to Antwerp, where his friend, the printer Christopher Plantin, had inspired several of his texts.

At the age of fifty-nine, new prophetic visions and the publicity that he gave them caused him to be tortured by the authorities. He fled to the Kampen in Overijssel and then to London, which must have been a temporary exile because we know that Niclaes opportunely saved Plantin from ruin by transporting to Cologne the typographical materials that those who accused the printer of heresy had threatened to seize. Dissent within the Family of Love darkened his final years. He died in 1580. Nippold[7] attributed to him fifty pamphlets that were distributed clandestinely.

Niclaes's doctrines preached love, tolerance, and mutual respect, and rejected the God of justice in favor of a God of goodness. From millenarianism he retained the pretense that he was acting as the mediator of divine revelation and as the herald of a new era in which antagonism among men would disappear.

His principal disciple was his servant, Hendrik Jansen, known as Barrefelt (no doubt because he was born in Barneveld). Around the time of his break with Niclaes in 1573 he took the name Hiel, which in Hebrew means 'one life in God'. Having gained the friendship of Christopher Plantin, Hiel began to prophesy on his own—possibly in England, where the Family of Love would continue to exist for more than a century. Many of its adepts joined the Ranters. Hiel's religious doctrine was related to that of Hans Denck.

> "The Father made himself human with us in accordance with the inward man and constructed us in accordance with the inward man in a Spirit with him. The soul of man is not a creature, but a part of the uncreated God". And he also called himself "a man whom God resurrected from among the

dead, whom he filled and anointed with the Holy Spirit; a man enlightened by the Spirit of the celestial truth and by the veritable light of the perfect essence; a man deified with God in the spirit of his divine love and transformed into the being of God". According to him, Christ is merely "the image of the being on the right side of the Father"; he must no longer be envisioned as a historical personage but rather as a "condition" shared by all those who live in union with God. From this metaphysical principle he deduced that sin no longer exists in the hearts of the born-again: he and his disciples "only said in their prayers the first three parts of the Sunday oration, because, for them, they did not sin insofar as they were born from God". He deduced from this idea both the uselessness and the unimportance of religious ceremonies: "the Lovers live and die without either baptism or the sacraments", or, rather, they considered the baptism of infants to be a valueless act that some were free to neglect while others were free to practice it. They thereby distinguished themselves from the Anabaptists, to whom it is no doubt fitting nonetheless to link them historically. Henry Niclaes founded his doctrine on the theory of the three ages: "Moses only preached hope, Christ only taught faith, but Niclaes announced the love that unites all. The first entered the square in front of the temple, the second entered the sanctuary, and the third entered into the Holy of Holies".[8]

The Puritan John Knewstub said of Henry Niclaes: "[He] turns religion upside down. He buildeth heaven here upon earth; he maketh God man and man God". "[For his disciples, according to Christopher Hill,] heaven was when men laugh and are merry, hell was sorrow, grief and pain".[9]

Johannes Torrentius
Born in Amsterdam in 1589, Johannes Torrentius [Johannes van der Beeck]—who was charged with Anabaptism and with adhering to the ideas of David Joris and the Family of Love—was thought in Holland (which was comparatively liberal, or which had at the very least been liberated from Catholicism) to be an accursed painter. A painter of still lifes and of supposedly erotic images, he attempted to illustrate the hedonism celebrated by seventeenth-century Dutch painting with (perhaps) less reservation than Jan Steen did.

A member of an Adamite group[10] that practiced the pleasures of love and the table, he was arrested and subjected to torture. He denied all participation in the sect, but the 'scandalous' character of his works earned him twenty years in prison.

Having been freed due to the entreaties of the Austrian ambassador, he took refuge in England. His return to Amsterdam inspired new persecutions from the Protestants, and these continued until his death in 1640. The government ordered that all his paintings be collected and burned by an executioner.[11]

CHAPTER FORTY-FOUR

Ironists and Skeptics

The fact that *The Discourse on Voluntary Servitude*[1] — the most radical work of (at the very least) the sixteenth century — positioned itself outside the terrain of theology is a useful indication of the extent to which the discourse of God had fallen into disuse. Religious language, over which the Church and the various other orthodoxies claimed to exercise control, ceded its place to an ideological language by means of which the changing economy — which was engaged in transforming the yesterday's liberties into tomorrow's constraints — smothered the blazes that it was also constantly igniting.

If it is true that 'He who controls meaning controls the world', ecclesiastical power — which had been unable to conceive of any other revolt against itself than that of those who were outside of all meaning (the senseless, the crazy) — began, from the Renaissance onwards, to lose those means of persuasion and terror that somehow or other had bolstered the dogma around which the spirits (if not the hearts) of beings and things had gravitated.

The mockery and irony that whipped the austere and unhealthy ass of religion were not, of course, born from the tumults of the sixteenth century. The difference here was that they had previously been formulated in spoken words rather than in writing. Penal history teems with such reports as the one that Jundt relays in his study of popular pantheism:

In 1359 the town council forever banished a certain Claushorn (surnamed Engelbrecht), the school director Selden, and Cüntzelin of Atzenheim because they had rapped on a wooden chair and three-legged stool and said, "Here is God; we would like to break his foot", and because they had erased the black points with which their dice were marked and said, "Here is God, we would like to burst his eyes". One of them even threw his knife at the sky and cried out, "I would like to strike God with my knife".[2]

The formidable network of awakening and dumbing-down that the printing press spread out over the towns and the countryside had placed in everybody's hands the two Testaments—both of which were stuffed full of incoherencies, absurdities, and infamies—through which God had manifested his uncertain presence in society. By emphasizing the inconsistencies in the Bible, Hans Denck left it up to each individual to devote (or indeed not to devote) him- or herself to the convictions of a faith that was personal and deprived of reason. A little later, those whom the Church called "strong-minded people" (because they threatened the power of its Spirit) began to use writing to convey a sense of irony that was capable of dissolving the authority of a Book that had for centuries crushed terrestrial and voluptuous life beneath its weight of guilt, fear, ferocity, and contempt.

Much in this mixture of audacity and pusillanimity is still only poorly known.

Valentin Weigel

In spite of his comparatively weak attachment to violence, Valentin Weigel (1533–88) seems highly reminiscent of the parish priest Jean Meslier. A Lutheran pastor in Zschopau, Weigel led an existence that was seemingly devoid of remarkable features. After his death, however, it was revealed that he'd written a book, *Libellus de vita beata non in particularibus ab extra quaerenda, sed in summo bono intra nos ipsos possidenda*[3]—partially published in Halle in 1609—in which he limited the sacred texts solely to the Revelations attributed to John, which was in turn summarized by the name of the Beast, whose number [666] nourished visions of the Third Age. Weigel considered Luther, the Pope,

Zwingli, and others to be Antichrists, and he considered the pastorate to be perfectly useless. Each man possessed in himself the divine spark that—embracing both the body and the soul—rendered the Scriptures, grace, the clergy, theology, and all historical religion null and void. The knowledge of God proceeded neither from the Bible nor from the sacraments, but from an inward conviction that no one could restrain.

Dirck Volckertszoon Coornhert

A polemicist, writer, engraver, and humanist, Dirck Coornhert was among the principal representatives of the Renaissance in Holland. Versatile and courageous—and this in a country in which Protestant intransigence had succeeded Catholic intolerance—he led, in the face of persecution, a ceaseless campaign in favor of religious freedoms and against the imposition of the death penalty in cases of heresy. A precursor of freethinking, he entrusted to each person the task of relying upon his or her own conscience and of founding secular morality on respect for others and on a form of Stoicism. His belief in the perfectibility of mankind brought down upon him charges of 'Pelagianism'—a term that in the sixteenth century had already largely fallen into disuse.

Born in Amsterdam in 1522, Coornhert was educated in the Catholic faith, which he never abjured, even when William of Orange took power. He especially kept to his evangelic principles. He traveled to Spain and Portugal, became familiar with biblical exegesis, and learned music and engraving. After his return to Amsterdam, he got married in 1540 and then moved to Haarlem, where he became a professional engraver. Around 1544 he discovered the works of Luther, Calvin, and Menno Simons. In 1550 he wrote *Comedie van de Rijke Man*, and shortly thereafter translated Boethius' *De consolatione philosophiae*[4]. Coornhert associated with Henry Niclaes, the founder of the Family of Love, with whom he later quarreled, though not without maintaining a certain nostalgia for an idyllic original community. He was also enthusiastic about Sebastian Franck and the mystical fragments of the *Theologia Deutsch*. In 1560 Coornhert took exception to Calvin and Menno. Two years later, Calvin threw at him his *Response to a Certain Dutchman Who, under the Guise of Making the Christians Completely Spiritual, Permits Them to Pollute their Bodies through Idolatry*[5]. In response to other texts by Coornhert concerning free will, Calvin was on his guard against "this man who pushes impiety to the extreme".

A notary at the court of Holland, Coornhert succeeding in arousing the suspicions of both the Catholics and the Protestants. Following the riots of the Iconoclasts, in which his role has not been clearly established, he was imprisoned at The Hague in 1567. He devoted his detention to writing short texts and pamphlets; he escaped in 1568 and, despite the hostility of the Protestants, served as a secret agent for the Prince of Orange until 1572. He returned to Haarlem and was tasked with producing a report on the 'Beggars' led by Lumey. He denounced their brutalities and abuses of power, thereby attracting their hatred. Coornhert hid himself in Leyden, then Xanten. When Requesens, the Governor of the Netherlands, announced a general pardon in 1574, Coornhert was excluded from it. He didn't hesitate to address himself to Philip II in the hope of recovering his confiscated goods, whence came the reputation (by which he was dogged) for 'playing all the angles'.

When Coornhert returned to Holland, Protestant hostility towards him had grown and he did nothing to attenuate it. He defended the Catholic minority, which was oppressed in Holland; he produced many appeals for tolerance; he declared himself opposed to the death penalty for dissidents of all stripes; and he translated the writings of Sebastian Castellion. It was only because of the influence of William of Orange that Coornhert was not condemned to life in prison. Having been chased from Haarlem in 1585 he went to Emden, where he published a work of Stoic inspiration in 1586. Banished from Delft after a stay of three months, he sought refuge in Gouda and died there on 29 October 1590.

In Coornhert one sees the passage from Christian morality to a secular morality enriched by such notions as tolerance and freedom of spirit. The influence of the mystics, as well as that of Denck, appeared in his language, which was stripped of sacred references and which instead exhorted his readers to have respect for all individuals. Finally, his idea that mankind could attain perfection through a constant effort of will that, if it was sufficiently strong, would render mankind incapable of sin resembled Pelagius's theses and not—as Coornhert was sometimes charged—the doctrines of the Spiritual Libertines.

Bernardino Ochino

Over the course of his life, the humanist Bernardino Ochino (1487–1564) adhered to nearly all of the religions and doctrines of his time. He did not wait for the signs of old age before affirming that the unique value of life (with all its vicissitudes) is to be found in terrestrial favors and flavors. Born in Sienna in the Oca neighborhood (from which he drew his name), he entered the Franciscan order and became a Capuchin preacher. He met Juan de Valdés and allowed himself be seduced by Luther's ideas. Ochino broke with Catholicism and went to Geneva, where he tested Calvin's repugnance for tolerant spirits. Ochino then went to Augsburg, Strasbourg, and Canterbury, where he vituperated the Pope. He wrote *The Labyrinth of Free Will or, to Speak Truly, Servile Will and the Means of Getting Out of It*. He distanced himself from all belief systems and professed a discreet atheism that he allied to a Rabelaisian quest for pleasure. Authorship of *The Book of the Three Impostors* was at the time attributed to him, albeit probably falsely. This text has also been imputed to other adventurers of his type, the influence of whom ought really to be studied more closely. One such was Simon de Neufville (from Hainaut), who died in Padua in 1530. Simon was a disciple of the skeptic Christophe de Longueil, who was himself the teacher of Étienne Dolet.

At the age of sixty, Ochino wed a young woman. His *Dialogi XXX*, which celebrated the merits of polygamy, caused his expulsion from Zurich in 1563. He took refuge in Poland and then in Slavkov (Austerlitz) in Moravia, where he succumbed to the plague in 1565.[6]

Noël Journet

Originally a schoolteacher from Suzanne, nearby Attigny, Noël Journet was among the disciples of Dirck Coornhert, whom he met during a visit to the Netherlands. Journet placed himself in the line of Hans Denck through his attention to inconsistencies and absurdities in the Bible. The publication of his commentaries drew down upon him the denunciations of the Calvinists, who had him burned, along with his work, at Metz on 29 June 1582.[7]

Pastor Jean de Chassanion considered it worth refuting those commentaries. He thereby added his own name to the annals of infamous informers, while also adding Journet's name to the annals of Reason's misfortunes.

The Refutation of the Strange Errors and Horrible Blasphemies Against God and the Holy Scriptures and the Holy Prophets and Apostles Made by a Certain Miserable Person Who for Such Impieties Was Justly Condemned to Die and Who Was Burned in the City of Metz on 29 June, the Year of Our Lord MDLXXXII, by Jean de Chassanion, Minister of the Reformed Church of Metz quoted the following statements, among others:

> Moses was an enemy of humankind, a captain of murderers and brigands. He gave the order to his people to sack the place when they entered Canaan, to kill the women and all the male children whom the downfall of the Madianites had spared; Moses also only preserved the virginal girls (Numbers 31: 17–8; Deuteronomy 7: 2).
>
> Jacob was a deceiver. He notably used striped sticks to influence the color of lambs, and thereby to increase his portion of the livestock (Genesis 30: 37–42).
>
> Moses cannot have written the Pentateuch, given that his own death is related at the end of it (Deuteronomy 34).
>
> Deuteronomy was drafted in the land of Canaan, because it says (4:47) that the children of Israel possessed the land of the two Amorean kings *beyond* the Jordan.

Other affirmations even more surely brought the sanctions of the judicial system down upon him. He declared that the magistrates were all "tyrants and thieves", that the great ones [*les tailles*] were "true tyrants", and that "a woman no longer married according to her tastes can take another husband so as to avoid bawdiness"[8].

Geoffroy Vallée

Geoffroy Vallée owed both his renown and his premature death to a pamphlet titled *The Beatitude of the Christians, or the Scourge of Faith* and published in 1573. Born in Orléans around 1550, the 'beautiful Valley'—

as his libertine friends called him—allied his search for the pleasures of existence with a taste for publicly critiquing the things that hindered and perverted those pleasures. He was sufficiently imprudent as to put his name to a pamphlet that was directed not only against all religions but against all religious beliefs, which according to him were invariably founded on fear. Sometimes distributed under the title *De arte nihil credendi*[9], this text was accused of committing divine high treason. Arrested on the orders of the Provost-Marshal Nicolas Rapin, Vallée soon after benefited from the support and friendship of the libertine aristocracy, although this was not enough to save him. This was the same libertine aristocracy that in the seventeenth century boasted among its numbers such people as Jacques Vallée Des Barreaux (who was Geoffroy's great-nephew), Claude Le Petit, Bélurgey, Théophile de Viau, Blot, and Cyrano de Bergerac—free spirits who often drove to despair those who issued prohibitions against the simple aspiration to live well.

The defense at Geoffroy's trial—adopting an old argument of the Church—invoked the 'senseless' character of the writing and of its author. Rapin would have been inclined to be relatively lenient if the Bishop of Nevers, Armand Sorbin, hadn't personally intervened to demand the young man's execution. On 9 February 1574, the twenty-four-year-old Geoffroy Vallée was hanged and then burned. The Jesuit François Garasse later rejoiced at the "beautiful sacrifice to God at the Place de Grève, where he [Geoffroy] was burned half-alive"[10].

Geoffroy Vallée was dedicated to the execration of "this religious faith, since they want lodged within it all that we are, for all of our lives; even when we die they sing the Credo to us". He successively examined the Catholic faith, "from which comes all evil" and which forged the fear of the devil and created executioners, and the faith of the Huguenots, with their "false intelligence [and] their fears and baton blows, which you cannot be saved without heeding". The faiths of the Anabaptists and the libertines fared little better. Not even atheism found a place in his heart, because "I enjoy my sensual pleasures without God; in God I have only torment". Atheism did not reject the fear that was inherent in all beliefs. "All the religions", he wrote, with great lucidity, "have removed from man the ecstasy of the body in order to make him ever more miserable".

In sum, the important thing wasn't believing or not believing, but being without fear: "He who is in fear, whatever that fear is, cannot be happy". One must therefore banish the fear that is inherent in all of the faiths in order to have "reason in one's head, without seeking it outside oneself or in the sword"[11]. Here Vallée attained a radicalism of which the libertines of the seventeenth century, the atheists of the eighteenth century, and the freethinkers of the nineteenth and twentieth centuries were ignorant. (Note that the interest of such humanists as Paracelsus, Heinrich Cornelius Agrippa von Nettesheim, Guillaume Postel, Tommaso Campanella, Giordano Bruno, and Lucio Vanini is greater than that of the history of philosophy.)

CHAPTER FORTY-FIVE

Levelers, Diggers, and Ranters

By decapitating King Charles (1649), the English Revolution removed God from public affairs. Cromwell's instauration of a new republic that proved to be profitable to the interests of small landowners and to those of the bourgeoisie revived with the breath of freedom the fire of working-class insurrection that had continued to smolder since the days of John Ball. The legends of Robin Hood the beloved brigand had illustrated more clearly in England than anywhere else the widely held view that, all things considered, to rob the rich in order to soften the misfortunes of the poor was to reestablish the natural obligations of solidarity.

The development of Protestantism as the ideology of emergent modern capitalism broke the old structure of the religious myth, at the same time as the barriers and enclosures that been erected everywhere by feudalism and by the predominance of the agrarian economy were giving way to the free circulation of commodities. Despite the fact that it remained inflexible in its principle of indenturing its followers to the masters of the heavens and the earth, religion was now advancing towards the status of an ideology—in which capacity it would be diminished and marginalized by nationalism, liberalism, socialism, fascism, and communism. Opening itself up to the bourgeois virtue of formal tolerance— and doing so despite the preferences of the high and mighty—the Protestant religion increased the diversity of the sects that were like so many chains enclosed in a single ring, with each being forged in a divine spirit of guilt and repressed pleasure.

Such was the vengeance of the Judeo-Christian religions: stripped of the weapons of divine justice and theocratic language, they imbued the ideologies that were most hostile to their playacting rituals with the odors of sacrifice, sin, mortifying compulsion, and voluntary servitude.

Levelers and Diggers

Just as "the old world" was—according to Gerrard Winstanley's formula—"running up like parchment in the fire"[1], the Levelers and the Diggers were inscribing themselves less in a religious current than in the framework of social and economic revolution[2].

The favors done to small landowners by Cromwell led to increases in the price of land rent, which condemned tenant farmers to hiring themselves out as day laborers or shepherds. Starting in 1649, the Levelers, under the leadership of John Lilburne (1614–57), formed the left wing of Cromwell's troops.

> Whilst food prices reached famine levels, the Levellers demanded re-election of Agitators and recall of the General Council of the Army. "We were before ruled by King, Lords and Commons, now by a General, a Court Martial and House of Commons; and we pray you what is the difference?" At the end of March [1649], Lilburne, [Richard] Overton, [William] Walwyn and [Thomas] Prince were arrested. A Leveller pamphlet, *More Light Shining in Buckinghamshire*, appealed to the soldiers "to stand everyone in his place, to oppose all tyranny whatsoever", particularly that of lawyers enclosing lords of manors [*sic*] and the Army Grandees who have rejected social reform and have done nothing for the poor.
>
> Next month mutinies broke out in the Army when men who refused to volunteer for service in Ireland were demobilized without payment of arrears—exactly what had driven the Army to revolt two years earlier, though then with the acquiescence of the generals. In May more serious revolts broke out among troops in Oxfordshire, Wiltshire and Buckinghamshire, and there were rumours of civilian support from the South-west, the old Clubmen area. Cromwell and [Thomas] Fairfax, acting with great vigour

and determination, overwhelmingly defeated the mutinous regiments at Burford on 14 May. The period of crisis for the military régime was over. Frightened conservatives rallied to its support, as the lesser evil. Oxford University and the City of London hastened to honour Fairfax and Cromwell. The sermon preached on the latter occasion appropriately denounced those who aspired to remove their neighbour's landmark. Leveler conspiracies continued [...]: but none of them offered a serious threat to the régime so long as the repeatedly purged Army remained securely under the control of its generals.

Nevertheless, the early months of 1649 had been a terrifying time for the men of property. It was for some time not so obvious to contemporaries as it is to us that the defeat at Burford had been final and decisive. As late as November 1649 Ralph Josselin tells us that men feared to travel because of danger from robbers, and the rich even felt insecure in their own houses. Poor people, he added the following month, "were never more regardless of God than nowadays".[3]

Isolated from the political scene, in which they figured less on account of their popular support than because of the democratic aspirations that animated their speeches and manifestoes, the Levelers revealed, by withdrawing from politics, the presence of rural agitators who were engaged in struggles against the local powers and who were determined to establish the collective ownership of farm lands. This latter movement—that of the Diggers—was characterized by a clear rejection of religious obedience.

In April 1649, in Walton-on-Thames, "the church [was] invaded by a group of six soldiers" who "announced that the Sabbath, tithes, [religious] ministers, magistrates and the Bible were all abolished".[4] Not far from there, day laborers were attempting to dig the fallow lands, thereby signifying their seizure of the commons. They chose Sunday in a deliberate attempt to annul the administration of time that the Church had arrogated to itself since the sixth century.

With the Diggers, the social revolution joined up with the tradition of the incendiaries who had annihilated God in his temples and in the bodies of his ministers. Ever since 1630, England had been experiencing a wave of church destruction that extended the previous century's upsurge of iconoclasm in the Netherlands. But this later movement was more consequential because the Bible was also quite frequently condemned to the fires or was otherwise execrated. As Clement Writer, a draper from Worcester, wrote in his *Fides divina* (1657): "No testimony that is fallible and liable to error can possibly be a divine testimony"[5].

The ranks of the Diggers grew rapidly around Gerrard Winstanley, a small merchant who had fallen on hard times and become a salaried farmer at Walton-on-Thames.

A vision enjoined him to spread the news that "the earth should be made a common treasury of livelihood to whole mankind, without respect of persons"[6]. Winstanley's agitation advanced to the south and center of England, where the Diggers dug, added manure to, and seeded the communal fallow lands. While Winstanley produced many pamphlets between 1649 and 1650, John Lilburne, the leaders of the Levelers, condemned "the erroneous tenets of the poor Diggers" and "repudiated any idea of abolishing property"[7].

> For Winstanley Jesus Christ was the Head Leveller. Winstanley's thought incorporates many Leveller ideas: it goes beyond them, beyond the vision of the small proprietor, in its hostility to private property as such.

> In the beginning of time the great creator, Reason, made the earth to be a common treasury, to preserve beasts, birds, fishes and man, the lord that was to govern this creation . . . Not one word was spoken in the beginning that one branch of mankind should rule over another . . . But . . . selfish imaginations . . . did set up one man to teach and rule over another. And thereby . . . man was brought into bondage, and became a greater slave to such of his own kind than the beasts of the field were to him. And hereupon the earth . . . was hedged into enclosures by the teachers and rulers, and the others were made . . . slaves. And that earth that is within this Creation made a common storehouse for all, is bought and sold and kept in the hands of a few, whereby the great Creator is mightily dishonoured, as if he were a respecter of persons, delighting in the comfortable livelihood of some and rejoicing in the

miserable poverty and straits of others. From the beginning it was not so . . .

Winstanley told lords of manors that

> . . . the power of enclosing land and owning property was brought into the creation by your ancestors by the sword; which first did murder their fellow creatures, men, and after plunder or steal away their land, and left this land successively to you, their children. And therefore, though you did not kill or thieve, yet you hold that cursed thing in your hand by the power of the sword; and so you justify the wicked deeds of your fathers, and that sin of your fathers shall be visited upon the head of you and your children to the third and fourth generation, and longer too, till your bloody and thieving power be rooted out of the land.

Winstanley extended the Leveller justification of political democracy to economic democracy:

> The poorest man hath as true a title and just right to the land as the richest man . . . True freedom lies in the free enjoyment of the earth . . . If the common people have no more freedom in England but only to live among their elder brothers and work for them for hire, what freedom then have they in England more than we can have in Turkey or France?

Winstanley transcended the Leveller theory of the Norman Yoke, that all we need is to get back to the laws of the free Anglo-Saxons. "The best laws that England hath", he declared, "are yokes and manacles, tying one sort of people to another". "All laws that are not grounded upon equity and reason, not giving a universal freedom to all but respecting persons, ought . . . to be cut off with the King's head". But England's rulers had not completed the Revolution [...].

Winstanley must have been expressing the opinions of many disappointed radicals when he wrote in 1652:

> Therefore, you Army of England's Commonwealth, look to it! The

enemy could not beat you in the field, but they may be too hard for you by policy in counsel if you do not stick close to see common freedom established. For if so be that kingly authority be set up in your laws again, King Charles hath conquered you and your posterity by policy, and won the field of you, though you seemingly have cut off his head.[8]

Winstanley went even further when he demanded the suppression of prisons and emphasized that all laws must be corrective rather than punitive. He was, before the philosophers, one of the first to demand that reason be substituted for divine providence (which had been especially profitable to the exploiters) in the governance of societies.

"What is the reason", Winstanley asked, "that most people are so ignorant of their freedoms, and so few fit to be chosen commonwealth's officers? Because", he replied, "the old kingly clergy . . . are continually distilling their blind principles into the people, and do thereby nurse up ignorance in them". Many of them had taught that Charles I was the Lord's Anointed. Priests

> lay claim to heaven after they are dead, and yet they require their heaven in this world too, and grumble mightily against the people that will not give them a large temporal maintenance. And yet they tell the poor people that they must be content with their poverty, and they shall have their heaven hereafter. But why may not we have our heaven here (that is, a comfortable livelihood in the earth) and heaven hereafter too, as well as you? . . . While men are gazing up to heaven, imagining after a happiness or fearing a hell after they are dead, their eyes are put out, that they see not what is their birthrights, and what is to be done by them here on earth while they are living.

A traditional Christian, who "thinks God is in the heavens above the skies, and so prays to that God which he imagines to be there and everywhere, . . . worships his own imagination, which is the devil", "Your Saviour must be a power within you, to deliver you from that bondage within; the outward Christ or the outward God are but men Saviours". Winstanley himself came to use the word Reason in preference to God, "because I have been held under darkness by that word, as I see many people are". We must be careful "lest we dishonour the Lord in making him the author of the creatures' misery", as hell-fire preachers do. Winstanley spoke of their God in terms which came near to William Blake's Nobodaddy—unless we are to suppose he held a completely Manichean dualism, which is unlikely. Winstanley told "priests and zealous professors" that they worshipped the devil. He spoke of "the God Devil". "The outward Christ, or the outward God . . . sometimes proves devils". He told his opponents in Kingston court that "that God whom you serve, and which did entitle you lords, knights, gentlemen and landlords, is covetousness". This God gave men a claim to private property in land. He "appointed the people to pay tithes to the clergy". It is this God-Devil that the state church worships. "We will neither come to church nor serve their God".[9]

Close to the partisans of Jakob Böhme, who began to appear in England around 1640, Winstanley refused to venerate any other Christ than the symbol of the resurrection of man in himself. Eden was humanity seeking to reconstruct the innocent conditions that had been destroyed by covetousness and appropriation. But if Winstanley believed that sin was a lucrative invention of the clergy's, he never adopted the views of the Ranters, who revoked sin in the name of pleasure and the natural liberties that it founded.

During the punitive expeditions that were launched against the Diggers, many sects—for example the Seekers and the Quakers—exploited their popularity but did not adopt their subversive practices. These sects thereby acceded rapidly to the status of Churches, thanks to their tolerance of those who threatened neither the foundations of religion nor the established order.

The Ranters
Luther and Calvin removed from sin the insurance policy that the Roman Church had attached to it by means of confession and redemption. For the creature who was exposed to the libidinous temptations of the Evil One, sin became an even more daunting prospect once it could no longer be offset by the payment of a licensing fee.

In the tradition of the Free Spirit, the Ranters affirmed an absolute rejection of all guilt by way of affirming an imprescriptible right to enjoy the benefits of existence.

> At one Ranter meeting of which we have a (hostile) report, the mixed company met at a tavern, sang blasphemous songs to the well-known tunes of metrical psalms and partook of a communal feast. One of them tore off a piece of beef, saying "This is the flesh of Christ, take and eat"[10]. Another threw a cup of ale into the chimney corner, saying "There is the blood of Christ". Clarkson called a tavern the house of God; sack was divinity. Even a Puritan enemy expresses what is almost a grudging admiration for the high spirits of the Ranters' dionysiac orgies: "they are the merriest of all devils for extempore lascivious songs, . . . for healths, music, downright bawdry and dancing".[11]

Spontaneously rediscovering the pleasantries that had gotten three joyful mercenaries banished from Strasbourg in 1359, a Ranter affirmed: "If I should worship the sun or the moon, or that pewter pot on the table, nobody has anything to do with it"[12]. Captain Francis Freeman, a great lover of ribald songs, declared that he saw God in a table and a candlestick.

Captain Underhill restored theological speculation to its terrestrial origins and meanings with as much lucidity as humor when he explained that "the Spirit had sent into him the witness of free grace, while he was in the moderate enjoyment of the creature called tobacco"[13].

Some Ranters denied the existence of Christ or, affirming themselves to be Christ or God, joyously permitted themselves all forms of license.

If God existed, Jacob Bauthumley proclaimed, He was in Bauthumley himself and in

> every living thing [...]: "man and beast, fish and fowl, and every green thing, from the highest cedar to the ivy on the wall". "He does not exist outside the creatures". God is in "this dog, this tobacco pipe, he is me and I am him" [...].[14]

A similar spirit animated Christopher Smart's poetic work *Jubilate Agno* in the eighteenth century[15].

Active between 1649 and 1651, the Ranters were not constituted as organized groups, and none of them took the title of leader or guru. They contented themselves with leading joyous lives and with possessing clear consciences. It is unfortunate that a Scottish peasant named Jack was hanged in 1656 for denying the existence of heaven, hell, God, and the Christ, since the Ranters—what with their taste for the pleasures of terrestrial existence—made it their duty to avoid martyrdom by offering prompt retractions of their statements.

Abiezer Coppe

Originally from Warwick, Coppe was a student at Oxford and then a preacher in the army. He was thirty when he gained his reputation as a Ranter. In 1649 he published *Some Sweet Sips of Some Spirituall Wine* and, with the same taste for alliteration, *A Fiery Flying Roll.*

Here there was no deceitful prophecy dictated by God. The message emanated from "my most excellent majesty and eternal glory (in me) . . . who am universal love, and whose service is perfect freedom and pure libertinism". Coppe proclaimed: "sin and transgression is finished and ended", because God, "that mighty Leveller", prepares to "lay the Mountains low"[16].

Coppe was at first on the radical wing of the Levelers. He called for cutting "the neck of horrid pride", which was the cause of all spilled blood. Bishops, kings, lords, and the great ones of this world would have to disappear so that "parity, equality, community" could assure the reign of "universal love, universal peace, and perfect freedom"[17].

"The betrayal of the Levelers"—as Christopher Hill calls it—accentuated for Coppe the feeling of a necessary unity between individual pleasure, on the one hand, and a unified struggle against the powerful, on the other. He recounted how, standing in the middle of the street, he used to hurl contempt at men and women of high social rank, taking exception to coaches and their occupants. "Hide not thyself from thine own flesh", he wrote, "from a cripple, a rogue, a beggar, . . . a whoremonger, a thief, etc., he's thine own flesh"[18].

Addressing himself to the rich, he threatened them:

Thou hast many bags of money, and behold I (the Lord) come as a thief in the night, with my sword drawn in my hand, and like a thief as I am—I say deliver your purse, deliver sirrah! deliver or I'll cut thy throat!

I say (once more) deliver, deliver my money ... to rogues, thieves, whores and cutpurses, who are flesh of thy flesh, and every whit as good as thyself in mine eye, who are ready to starve in plaguey gaols and nasty dungeons ...

The plague of God is in your purses, barns, houses, horses, murrain will take your hogs (O ye fat swine of the earth) who shall shortly go to the knife and be hung up in the roof, except - - - -

Did you not see my hand, this last year, stretched out?

You did not see.

My hand is stretched out still - - - -

Your gold and silver, though you can't see it, is cankered ...

The rust of your silver, I say, shall eat your flesh as it were fire. ... Have ALL THINGS common, or else the plague of God will rot and consume all that you have.[19]

At the same time, however, Coppe perceived in the happiness of serving his pleasures a guarantee of peace and a protection against violence: "Not by the sword; we (holily) scorn to fight for any thing; we had as lief be dead drunk every day of the week, and lie with whores i'th marketplace; and account them as good actions as taking the poor abused enslaved ploughman's money from him"[20].

In 1650 Parliament condemned *A Fiery Flying Roll*—which was judged to be full of "many horrid blasphemies"[21]—to the flames and sent Coppe himself to prison in Newgate. In exchange for his release, he drafted a partial retraction and then wrote another, more complete one, the mischievous reservations of which suggest that it was less than fully sincere.

(Note that Coppe, like Jacques Gruet and Noël Journet, did not deny himself of the pleasures of irony here. He wrote: "God forbids killing, but tells Abraham to slay his son; [he forbids] adultery, but tells Hosea to take a wife of whoredoms". He proclaimed that it is "the community which is sinful", but added, "if flesh of my flesh be ready to perish, . . . [and] if I have bread it shall or should be his". Forced to recognize the notion of sin, he declared that "[t]he laying of nets, traps and snares for the feet of our neighbours is a sin, whether men imagine it to be so or no; and so is the not undoing of heavy burdens, the not letting the oppressed go free, the not healing every yoke, and the not dealing of bread to the hungry . . . whether men imagine it to be so or no"[22].)

After the Restoration, prudence enjoined Coppe to change his name. He became a physician and was a respected figure in the small town of Barnes, in Surrey. He had sufficient sense of humor to have himself buried in the cemetery of the local parish church.

Lawrence Clarkson

A wandering preacher who was born in Preston and raised as a Puritan, Clarkson very quickly acquired an equal repugnance for all of the sects, as well as for the clerical profession: "Thousands better than your parish priests have saluted the gallows. It is more commendable to take a purse by the highway than compel any of the parish to maintain such that seek their ruin, whose doctrine is poisonable to their consciences"[23].

Having been a Leveler in 1647, he rallied to the Ranters and maintained that, God being "in all living things and in all matter", all action came "from him [i.e. from God]" and that nothing, not even "the crucifixion of Christ", was a sin in his eyes[24]. There is neither heaven nor hell beyond mankind. He publicly declared: "I really believed no Moses, Prophets, Christ or Apostles". "[T]here is no such act as drunkenness, adultery and theft in God. . . . Sin hath its conception only in the imagination . . . What act soever is done by thee in light and love, is light and lovely, though it be that act called adultery . . . No matter what Scripture, saints or churches say, if that within thee do not condemn thee, thou shalt not be condemned"[25].

"None", he wrote, "can be free from sin till in purity it can be acted as no sin, for I judged that pure to me which to a dark understanding was impure"[26].

Clarkson lived joyously in sweetness and love, "travel[ed] the country with Mrs. Star", sought adventure with other women—but was "careful for moneys for my wife"—and amused himself at an assembly of Ranters where "Dr Paget's maid stripped herself naked and skipped"[27].

When arrested in 1650, he asserted his rights as "a freeborn subject". He was condemned to exile and then subsequently pardoned, no doubt following a retraction. From then on he settled down and studied magic and astrology in order to join Muggleton's sect[28], which is one of the many groups that has continued to exist in the mists of millenarianism and apocalypse.

Jacob Bauthumley

A shoemaker like Böhme, Bauthumley was arrested by the authorities in 1650 for having published *The Light and Dark Sides of God*. "The book was condemned as blasphemous, and Bauthumley was bored through the tongue".[29] John Milton admired him and shared many of ideas.[30]

According to Bauthumley, the light of God manifested itself through its presence in every creature and every thing:

> "Not the least flower or herb in the field but there is the divine being by which it is that which it is; and as that departs out of it, so it comes to nothing, and so it is to-day clothed by God, and to-morrow cast into the oven". "All the creatures in the world . . . are but one entire being". "Nothing that partakes of the divine nature, or is of God, but is God". God cannot love one man more than another: all are alike to him. God "as really and substantially dwells in the flesh of other men and creatures as well as in the man Christ". Where God dwells is "all the heaven I look ever to enjoy". "Sin is properly the dark side of God, which is a mere privation of light". "God is no more provoked by sin to wrath than he is allured to blessing by my holiness". [...] "The reason why we call some men wicked and some godly is not any thing in the man, but as the divine being appears more gloriously in them. . . . . According to the counsel of his will, they did no more that crucified Christ, than they that did embrace him".[31]

Bauthumley denied the existence of hell and the personification of Satan. The resurrection was a purely inward act and did not take place in the beyond.

Like Coppe, he "ended as a respectable citizen of his native [town] Leicester", where he worked as a bookseller.[32]

Thomas Webbe

The Rector of Langley Burhill, Webbe seems to have made a solemn promise not to "accept tithes from his parishioners"[33]. His popularity, having already been guaranteed by a step that no Church would have tolerated, was greatly increased when he proclaimed from the pulpit that he hoped "that he would live long enough to see 'no such thing as a parsonage or minister in England'". The French parish priest Jean Meslier had taken the sensible precaution of dying before he made similar remarks publicly available.

During the 1650s "[a] group around him was alleged to have formed 'a Babel of profaneness and community'"[34]. An admirer of Coppe, he said a remarkable thing in a letter to Joseph Salmon: "the Lord grant that we may know the worth of hell, that we may for ever scorn heaven".

In 1650, the notables—looking to get rid of him—charged him with "adultery, [which was] then liable to the death sentence". He was acquitted. He "claimed [according to a witness] to 'live above ordinances, and that it was lawful for him to lie with any woman'". The following witticism was attributed to him: "there's no heaven but women, nor no hell save marriage". His enemies managed to get him banished.

Coppin, Pordage, and Tany

Richard Coppin was from the moderate wing of the Ranters; he was satisfied with a pantheism in which theology predominated over the refusal of social and moral imperatives.

> "God is all in one, and so is in everyone", he wrote in *Divine Teachings*. "The same all which is in me, is in thee; the same God which dwells in one dwells in another, even in all; and in the same fullness as he is in one, he is in everyone".[35]

Resurrection consisted of leaving the grave—which was in us and in the Scriptures—in order to be reborn as "[t]he new man [who] sinneth not"[36].

Coppin refused the Church in the name of his own experiences of the Lord. Referring to "the act of 1650 [that] abolished compulsory Sunday church attendance", he spoke of "the anti-christian law of compelling men to church"[37]. Coppin was arrested in 1655 and condemned to six months in prison.

John Pordage, a disciple of Jakob Böhme who was the curate at Reading and then the Rector of Bradfield, attracted the attention of the authorities in 1655 by propagating the opinions of the Ranters. He "den[ied] the historical Christ", believed in the presence of God "in every man", refused the notion of sin, held marriage to be a harmful institution, and announced the imminent disappearance of "Parliament, [the] magistra[cy], the government in England", and all of "the higher powers", which "he cared no more for [...] than for the dust beneath his feet"[38].

His friend Thomas Tany, known as Theaureaujohn, estimated that "man could not lose his salvation". But he also went further and maintained that "all religion was 'a lie, a cheat, a deceit, for there is but one truth, and that is love'". He furthermore demanded that "common lands should lands should return to the common people". In 1654 Tany made an exemplary and unusually audacious gesture. In a beautifully concise work of criticism, he "burnt the Bible in St George's Fields 'because the people say it is the Word of God, and it is not'"[39].

CHAPTER FORTY-SIX

The Jansenists

While Holland and England—both of which were won over to the formal freedoms of the bourgeois revolution—were giving birth to a multitude of sects whose language (though still drawing upon theological artifices) concealed their ideological character to a rapidly diminishing extent, the Catholic countries, which were prey to the intense troubles of the Counter-Reformation, once again found in monarchal and pontifical absolutism the guarantee of a Catholicism that was thereby restored to its full temporal and spiritual powers.

Indulging in a Constantinian parody of the divine right of kings, Louis XIV persisted in concealing beneath the pomp of a Church in which Bossuet enjoyed the company of people like Lully[1] a tormented pusillanimity that was corroded by the acidity of prestige. The sun with which he, following the example of other mediocrities, claimed to have crowned himself[2] dispensed its light only to the courtiers of literature and the arts, who were apt to dilute their genius in the artifices of panegyric. But obscurantism did not spare free spirits such as Cyrano de Bergerac, the peasants suffering from famine and the rapacity of the tax collectors, or the Protestants who were condemned to the galleys by the thousands[3]. This was the reign of the bigots, who threw the poet Claude Le Petit upon the pyre for having celebrated the art of fucking while the sovereign himself was warming the bed of his extramarital couplings with insincere remorse.

The quarrel of Jansenism thus inscribed itself within both an archaic framework of theological disputation and a political tradition in which the temporal masters claimed the right to legislate in spiritual matters.

Michael Baius

Born in 1515 in Meslin-l'Évêque in the Hainaut region, Michael Baius (or de Bay) was a doctor at the University of Louvain. He was a fervent Catholic who combated the Lutheranism and Calvinism that, by taking their stand on Scripture (which Protestantism set up as the supreme authority), had become widespread in the Netherlands.

Along with his friend Jean Hessels, Baius set against Calvin—who held that irremediably sinful mankind was entirely in the hands of a capricious God—a softened version of the predestinarian doctrine that dated back to Augustine of Hippo. For Baius, nature was originally good but eminently corruptible. Adam sinned freely and, through his sin, lost the control that he had once exercised over his senses. Mankind had ever since felt the attractions of concupiscence so intensely that it had been unable to resist them.

Calvin drew from the Augustinian notion of predestination the idea that, being saved or damned by God's will alone, the human creature had no other choice but to assume the burden of his misery through a constant torment in which all pleasure was obscenely discordant. But predestination also opened the way for the argument that everything was permitted because God had made a mockery of all human endeavors. Baius, who could hardly be suspected of licentiousness or debauchery, partially reconciled theological free will with the desperate mortification to which devout Protestants had dedicated themselves.

Baius and Hessels's conceptions did not initially shock either the Cardinal of Granville—who was then the Governor of the Netherlands—or the papacy, since the two theologians had participated in the Council of Trent.

Even when Pius V reacted in a Papal Bull that condemned seventy-three of the propositions advanced by Baius, the latter (whose name hadn't actually been mentioned) remained the Chancellor of the University of Louvain and submitted a retraction in good grace.

Among his adepts were Jacques Janson, a theologian from Louvrain, and Cornelius Jansenius, the Bishop of Ypres, both whom pledged to cleanse Baius's reputation of suspicions of heterodoxy that they regarded as being unmerited.

The Jesuit Leonardus Lessius meanwhile revived the quarrel over predestination within those milieus that always eagerly awaited theological speculations, to which they attributed great public importance (even though the majority of the people—already sufficiently encumbered by the constraints of Mass, the sacraments, and ecclesiastic rituals—could easily do without them).

Lessius estimated that sinners did not lose their means of acceding to the eternal life of the heavens. He agreed with the Spanish Jesuit Luis de Molina (1536–1600) that divine foreknowledge did not hinder mankind's free will in its choice between good and evil.

In the wooden language of theology, what expressed the discord between the theses expounded by Molina in *The Concordance of Grace and Free Will*, on the one hand, and Jansenism, on the other, if it wasn't the conflict between the Christian presence that governed the world at the cost of certain necessary compromises and an eremitic Christianity that, in retreat from the social world, awaited the feverish and anguished arrival of an intransigent God? In Molière's depiction of the situation, it was Tartuffe against the misanthrope of Port-Royal[4].

Cornelius Jansenius

Born in 1585 near Leerdam in Holland, Cornelius Jansenius (also known as Jansen) studied at Utrecht and Louvain, where his teacher was Baius's disciple Jacques Janson. Jansenius was friends with Jean Duvergier de Hauranne, the future Abbot of Saint Cyran. He devoted himself passionately to the study of Augustine of Hippo and his theses against Pelagianism. After a stay in France he returned to Louvain; he believed that he had discovered in Augustine's philosophy arguments that would properly rehabilitate Baius. It is not easy to discern the motive that prompted him to brave pontifical thunderbolts and the opposition of the powerful Jesuit party. His affection for Jacques Janson? The hope of shining in the reflected light of faraway pyres? A moral rigor that corresponded to his taste for asceticism and that led him to condemn the discreet license of the confessors who mixed devotion with the perfume of the boudoir and who practiced a theological variant of psychoanalysis long before there was such thing as psychoanalysis?

"The further I advance", Jansenius wrote to Duvergier de Hauranne, "the more the affair frightens me [...]. I do not dare to say what I think about predestination and grace for fear that, when everything is ready and matured, what has happened to the others will happen to me" (i.e. that he would be condemned[5].

Jansenius was thoughtful enough to die from the plague in Ypres shortly after sending to Pope Urban VIII a letter in which declared himself disposed to approve, improve or retract his statements "according to what will be prescribed by the voice of thunder that comes from the clouds of the Apostolic See"[6].

His posthumous work, the *Augustinus*, published in 1640, was condemned by Urban VIII two years later.

Father d'Avrigny summarized Jansenius's doctrine in his *Chronological and Dogmatic Memoirs*:

> That, since the fall of Adam, pleasure has been the unique spring that moves the heart of man. That this pleasure is unavoidable when it is coming and invincible once it has come. If this pleasure is celestial, it brings virtue; if it is terrestrial, it causes vice; and the will necessarily finds itself led by the stronger of the two. These two delights, the author says, are like the two plates on a balancing scale; one cannot rise without the other descending. Thus, irresistibly but voluntarily, man does good or evil according to whether he is dominated by grace or cupidity.[7]

Here is proof—as if proof were needed—that all religious controversies have ultimately had their roots in the tormented attitudes of individuals being confronted by the pleasures of a life that has been denied to them by the mandates of heaven and the Spirit (the dreadful abstractions of the earth and the body, respectively).

The Church's obsessive fears were caused not by the scandalous licenses to which the pious Jansenius was improbably given access by the implications of his argument, but by the personal determination that was attributed to him and that, were it to be directed against the most devout asceticism, would deprive dogma and clergymen of any utility in the government of beings and things.

Jansenism moreover quite rapidly took shape from within a Calvinism that had been transplanted into a society that had still not delegated its powers to free enterprise or to a divinely sanctified devotion to money.

Jean-Ambroise Duvergier de Hauranne, the Abbot of Saint-Cyran, who had long been influenced by Baius's ideas, saw it as his mission to propagate the doctrines of his friend Jansenius. His rigor was more pleasing than the enjoyment of pleasures that were chilled by feelings of remorse, which had led to the complacency that comes with always being disappointed. He won the sympathies of the Arnauld family, especially Pascal and Nicole, and their support served to maintain the monastery of Port-Royal and to set it up as the bastion of Jansenism.

When Duvergier died in 1643, the 'Great Arnauld' succeeded him and took over the leadership of the movement, which he treated as if it were a family affair. It is worth dwelling a little on this clan, which brandished before the court of France and the Church of Rome a theological arsenal whose firepower seemed to derive from the unpleasant relations that divided the members of a community that was as holy as it was tormented.

The Arnauld Family

Originally from Herment in Puy-de-Dôme, Antoine Arnauld (1560–1619) was born to a Protestant father whom the St Bartholomew's Day Massacre of 1572 convinced to convert to Catholicism. Antoine settled in Paris in 1577 and professed disdain for military glory and the quest for royal favors. Instead he made religion his field of battle. From him descended a breed of lawyers and scholars whose puritanical rigor, taste for authority, paradoxical propensity for revolt, and solid business sense would have veered towards Calvinism had Jansenism not furnished better opportunities for worldly success.

After he'd attended the University of Paris and received a law degree from Bourges (where he studied under Cujas), Antoine Arnauld was admitted to the bar and applied himself ardently to producing anti-Jesuit polemics. Her served as the Procurator General for Catherine de' Medici in Paris. A Gallican and a nationalist, he mocked the Jesuits' "blind obedience to a Spanish General", defended the University of Paris against them, and was opposed to their return after Jean Châtel's attack on Henry IV caused them to be banished from France.

Antoine's wife Catherine Marion (who became a nun at Port-Royal in 1641) gave birth to twenty children, among whom were Catherine, Jacqueline-Marie-Angélique, Jeanne-Catherine-Agnès (the author of a collection of letters), Anne, Marie, and Madeleine, who belonged to the Abbey, as did Robert and Antoine, the twentieth child, who became known as the 'Great Arnauld'. Henri Arnauld became the Bishop of Angers, thereby providing his family—which was always at the frontiers of heresy—with the security of his orthodoxy.

The Great Arnauld was born in 1612, the last child of Catherine Marion. He was seven years old when his brutal and tyrannical father died. The boy was educated either by his mother or, more likely, by Jean Duvergier de Hauranne, the celebrated Abbot and spiritual director of Saint-Cyran who presided over the affairs of Port-Royal. Yet the world seduced young Antoine: he was attracted by jurisprudence, he frequented the literary circles of Madame de Rambouillet, he became affected in his manner, and he imitated Vincent Voiture. Nonetheless, his fate had been decided: he belonged to theology. Enrolled at the Sorbonne in 1633, he studied Augustine under Duvergier's spiritual direction. The older man, for whom "nothing was as dangerous as knowledge", imposed on the younger such ordeals as fasting twice a week, praying, and reading the Holy Scriptures on bended knee.

The young man was ordained as a priest and then entered Port-Royal a year later (in 1641), resolving to "flee the conversations of the world as if they were poisoned air". It is said that he loved mystery so much that he denounced as false a thesis that he judged to be too intelligible. *On Frequent Communion*, which was published in the year of Duvergier's death (1643), brought Arnauld to the head of the Jansenist current and aroused the hatred of the Jesuits. In response, he wrote *The Moral Theology of the Jesuits*, which furnished Blaise Pascal with material for his *Provincial*

Letters. The Jesuits responded to Arnauld so vociferously that he had to go into hiding. Restored to grace in 1669, the Great Arnauld became friends with Nicolas Boileau-Despréaux and Jean Racine. He also violently attacked Calvinism, on this point joining with his brother Henri, the Bishop of Angers, who applauded the revocation of the Edict of Nantes.

When internal politics took a hostile turn at Port-Royal, the Great Arnauld fled to Mons, Tournai, and then Brussels, where he died in 1694. A letter from his friend the Abbot of La Trappe demonstrates the esteem in which he was held: "At last, Monsieur Arnauld is dead. After pushing his career as far as he could, it had to come to an end. Whatever else one says, these questions are now closed"[8]. To Abbot Bremond, he was "a theological machine gun in perpetual movement, but completely devoid of inner life"[9]. It took little time to see that Arnauld's grandeur in fact resulted from an accumulation of pettiness.

A similar tissue of gossip and eloquent refusals of the world animated the life of Robert, known as Arnauld d'Andilly. His *Memoirs*, which were published posthumously in 1734, served his own glory more than that of the God he claimed to venerate: "I have never had a single ambition, because I have had too many of them". The empire of the absolute nevertheless agreed with his taste for intrigue and influence peddling. A madrigal that he offered in the manner of the *Guirlande de Julie*[10] showed that he had little difficulty in wedding gallantry to devotion. Devurgier made Robert his universal legatee on the condition that he retire to Port-Royal. Robert then used all sorts of pretexts to delay the date of his retirement. He tried to become a private tutor to the Dauphin. Towards this end, he published *Stanzas on Diverse Christian Truths* in 1642; he wrote a poem on the life of the Christ that was published in 1634; and in 1680 he produced his *Letters*, in which he took care to include endorsements from the Jesuits. All in vain. The charge that he so coveted eluded him and disappointment finally drove him to Port-Royal, where he also hastened to send six of his daughters (out of his fifteen children). The noise generated by his retirement, which had been being orchestrated for so long, made him a celebrated person and Jansenism fashionable.

In 1664 the dispersal of the community caused Robert to go into exile in Pomponne, where one of his sons lived. He had been an appalling father and he seemed execrable to his daughter-in-law, who saw him die in 1674 without experiencing the slightest displeasure. He had translated Augustine's *Confessions*, the works of Saint Teresa, and Flavius Josephus's *Jewish Antiquities*.

Antoine's second daughter, Jacqueline-Marie-Angélique (b. 1591), was of a completely different nature. In her brutal frankness she departed from the caution displayed by Robert and the Great Arnauld, both of whom were far closer to Tartuffe than to Molière's Misanthrope. She was intelligent and lively and preferred the prospect of marriage to life in the Abbey, which was imposed on her from the age of seven. "You would like me to be a nun", she said. "I would quite like that, but on the condition that I am the Abbess". She made her profession of faith at the age of nine, but not without specifying that she "felt free in front of men, and committed to God". Her involuntary vocation was always a source of horror to her: "I was cursed when men, not God, made me the Abbess and when the monks of the Cîteaux Abbey consecrated me at the age of eleven". Her father had to remain on the other side of a grill when she visited him. When he treated her in response as if she were a parricidal monster, she stated: "My parents made me a nun at the age of nine, when I did not want to be one; today they want me to damn myself by not observing my own rules".

As one after another of her sisters entered Port-Royal, she became a fervent believer, as if overcome by a somber and desperate ecstasy. Named Abbess in 1642, she wedded herself to the cause of Jansenism and did not hesitate to treat Pope Innocent X as a deceiver when he condemned the five propositions of *Augustinus* in 1653. God was the weapon of her vengeance against the men who had banished her from the world. This passionate woman, whose intelligence and sad but fiery sensuality merited a destiny better suited to her hopes, died in 1661 while Pope Alexander was busy promulgating new condemnations of Jansenism in a formulary that the clergy were obliged to sign.

The Jansenists were lauded by a current of popular opinion that was motivated less by religious conviction than by hatred of the Jesuits. It applauded their rebellion against Rome and their insolence in the face of a monarch who was as vain as he was petty, and who was haunted by his military defeats.

Reduced to silence by the threat of corporal punishment issued by Louis XIV, the Jansenists went to Holland, from which they continued to pour out pamphlets. A Jansenist Church founded in the Netherlands continued to exist until the nineteenth century. The fight was taken up in France by Pasquier Quesnel, but the condemnation of his propositions in 1713 by the Papal Bull *Unigenitus*[11] confirmed the end of a movement that died out due to the general decline of theology—the decline, that is, of the language of God.

Stripped of its celestial supporting arguments, the moral rigor of the Jansenists revealed the effects of its repressions in hysterical manifestations that produced neither religious homilies nor political speeches. The burial of Deacon François de Pâris (a model of Jansenist fervor) in the cemetery at Saint-Médard in Paris brought about convulsive outbursts and miraculous recoveries at the graveside that exhilarated Parisians. An edict prohibiting convulsion-inducing assemblies gave rise to the following celebrated inscription: "In the name of the King, do not make miracles at this place". In 1787 Bonjour—the parish-priest of Fareins, near Trévoux, who continued the tradition of the convulsionists—crucified his mistress on the cross of his church in the hope of producing new miraculous recoveries.

From the Great Arnauld to Bonjour, Jansenism fulfilled the destiny that modernity had reserved for the heresies: to become sects at the same time as the Churches and the thunderbolts that Jansenius had seen come crackling from the Holy See were beginning to enter the spectacle of ideology, wherein—subverted by the great apparatuses of the State and their violations of consciousness—they endured an increasingly marginal existence until, one day, they only appeared (aside from the occasional Sunday visit to church) in folkloric rites concerning births, weddings, and deaths.

CHAPTER FORTY-SEVEN

Pietists, Visionaries, and Quietists

The Pietists

Born from the preaching of the Lutheran pastor Philipp Jakob Spener (1635–1705), Pietism was part of the tradition of Hans Denck, for whom faith—or its absence, because only personal conviction was important— had nothing to do with sacraments, priests, or pastors, nor even with the allegedly sacred texts.

Under German and English Pietism there also smoldered the thought of Jakob Böhme (1575–1624), the shoemaker from Görlitz (in Silesia), whose doctrine was part of the Hermetic tradition and was centered around the subtle alchemy of individual experience.

Without entering into an analysis of Pietism's rich and dense belief structure, it is important to emphasize the point at which Pietism's God— who was effectively dissolved into nature—annihilated the very idea of God more perfectly than did atheism, which was content to reduce God to a social function that was present everywhere in the exercise of power and authority qua the abstract government of beings and things. If, for Böhme, the symbols of the divine still wore the tattered rags of theology (Christ, the Trinity, grace), they were no less surely symbols of a life associated—as in the thought of Marguerite Porete and Simon of Samaria— with an eternal flux in which the 'amorous' conjunction created the beings and things that mankind re-created in its turn.

The universe manifested itself at every instant in the inseparable coupling of material energy with energetic matter, in the desire in which the androgyny of interlaced lovers and the *mysterium magnum*[1] of pleasure and creation rejoiced.

The radical wing of Pietism expressed—most often through the vehicles of visions, revelations, and apocalypses—the feeling of a diffuse sexuality in search of an experience in which the unity of the individual and the world would be accomplished.

It so happens that the very vehicle of these visions drove the illuminatus into a matrix of political interests in which his or her ambition to rule the future attracted the condemnation (if not worse) of the authorities.

Johann Albrecht Adelgrief had a sad life. The seven angels who had mandated him to reform the conduct of the world's rulers did not prevent him from being burned at Königsberg in 1636. Czar Peter, also known as Peter the Great, proceeded in the same manner against the unfortunate Quirinus Kuhlmann, who was condemned to the pyre in Moscow in 1689.

The theosophical alchemist Paul Felgenhauer spent a large part of his life either in prison or, due to successive banishments, wandering Europe. His *Dawn of Wisdom*, in which the Aurora and the *Sophia* dear to Böhme reappeared, fixed at some time in his own century [the seventeenth] the beginning of the millennium. It never came. Paul Nagel foresaw the collapse of the papacy in March 1623 with the same certainty.

Other Pietists, such as the worker Elias Eller (1690–1750), guaranteed his prophetic announcements on matters of destiny with a greater degree of skill. Eller seduced a rich widow while seeking work in Elberfeld. Together they founded the Communion of Ronsdorf, a Pietist community in which prayer and exaltation propelled faith in the divine presence well beyond the domes of the temples and beyond all the other places that were "contaminated by papist or Protestant [*parpaillots*] cockroaches".

Anna von Büchel, the daughter of a baker, plunged her adepts into ecstasy through luxuriant visions in which she conducted intimate dialogues with Jesus Christ. Since Elias Eller was taking the carnal place of Jesus in her heart, her husband took offense and accused her of perpetrating a hoax and of making sacrifices to Satan. Eller got him locked up as a lunatic and married the prophetess, whose revelations he recorded in a work titled *Hirtentasche* (*The Shepherd's Sack*).

Figured as the Mother and Father of Zion, this couple undertook to contrive the rebirth of Jesus in Anna's womb. The first child appeared in the unfortunate form of a girl. A second, male this time, died soon thereafter, seemingly indifferent to his forthcoming triumphs. Anna succumbed in her turn.

Elias Eller entered into a third marriage. His adepts were numerous in Rehmsdorf, where he was named mayor. He died in 1750, well liked by the citizens. We do not know whether he actually lived in harmony with his desires or merely in a cunningly calculated mix of holiness, honorability, and libertinage.

Johann Wilhelm Petersen (1649–1727) was inspired by Jakob Böhme and Valentin Weigel. He provided his pious communities with the effervescence of millenarian preaching and the exaltation of visionaries (such as himself) who catechized the crowds. His religious ardor sometimes took on the colors of mystical sensuality.

> Assuredly the Spirit of prophecy was not partial to anyone in particular. There was a swarm of clairvoyants who fluttered around the leaders of the sect: Madeleine Elrich, Christine-Regina Bader, Adélaïde Schwartz and Anne-Marguerite Jahn. As in any well-regulated troupe, each had her role: Anna-Maria was the 'Pietist singer', while Anne-Eve Jacob was 'the sucker of blood'. There were other stars who, naturally, had more important roles. Johann Wilhelm Petersen had the privilege of receiving divine illuminations, and he also had the advantage of being married to Eleonore von Merlau, who had visions of her own. She composed works that the celebrated Pietist published under his own name. Guillaume Postel also had some influence on Petersen's thought. Petersen referred as well to a book by an English countess, whose name he did not mention and who composed *De principiis philosophiae antiquissimae et recentissimae*[2], which is a work that is not without depth and which was inspired by Jewish Kabbalah.
>
> According to Petersen, when the reign of a thousand years had established itself in heaven and on earth, the Jews would convert and, on returning to Palestine, reestablish their ancient kingdom. Petersen refrained from

setting the date of the second coming of Jesus Christ. One observes, moreover, that the 'end of this age' did not designate a universal conflagration but rather the 'end of the current age'. Contrary to a certain tradition, the woman of the Revelations who would give birth (Chapter 12) was the Jewish nation, which would give birth to Christ despite the efforts of the infernal Dragon (the monster that would be killed by Saint Michael, the protecting angel of Israel). Rosamunde Juliane von der Asseburg was one of the leading dancers in the ballet troupe of Pietist Sibyls. Leibniz judged her visions to be quite respectable, on a par with those of Saint Hildegard [of Bingen], Saint Bridget [of Sweden], Saint Mechtilde [of Hackeborn] and other holy ladies. Leibniz was also the publisher of several of Petersen's works. Madame Petersen had a considerable influence in both England and Germany.[3]

For Johann Georg Gichtel and Eva von Buttlar, the *Sophia* of Böhme and the ancient Gnostics was illustrated by two figures (less antithetical than they might at first appear): the future Eve and the current Eve—that is to say, femininity in-itself as a distant princess and femininity for-itself as a proximate and tumultuous sensuality (this doubling of figures was also seen in certain portrayals of the exalted Pietist 'suckers of blood' and in the *pneuma* that was identical with *sperma*).

Serge Hutin devotes several pages to Gichtel in his study of *The English Disciples of Jakob Böhme*.

Johann-Georg Gichtel (1638–1710), the son of a counselor to the court of Regensburg, had displayed mystical tendencies since his childhood. As an adolescent he wanted, in imitation of Christ, "to annihilate" his carnal self: renouncing all pleasure, he vowed perpetual virginity. A Lutheran by upbringing, he was rapidly disappointed by the dryness of official Protestantism and turned towards the Catholic religion, which soon disappointed him as well. This young man who was sinking deeper and deeper into a solitary and exalted devotion was also a passionate student who spent entire nights immersed in Greek, the sacred Eastern languages, and theology. He successfully enrolled in the College of Theology at the University of Strasbourg but subsequently had to give in to his tutors, who compelled him to follow his father and become a magistrate. Notwithstanding his personal preferences he became a lawyer at the imperial High Court of Speyer. But this important function did not monopolize his attention for long: fleeing from pressing feminine solicitations, Gichtel returned to his native town in great haste. Enrolled in the bar at Regensburg, he happened—while at a library—to meet Baron Justinian Ernst von Weltz; the two men became close friends on the spot. Weltz (1621–68) was a rich illuminatus who wanted to found a missionary society—the *Christerbauliche Jesusgesellschaft*[4]—whose objectives would be the realization of Christian unity and the conversion of the entire world to the Gospel. He associated with Gichtel and together they submitted their project to the Evangelical Assembly of the Lutheran Church. At first the Assembly welcomed the proposal and the Baron deposited in a bank in Nuremberg the then-enormous sum of 30,000 *riksdalers*. But the theologians quite quickly manifested their disapproval when they became aware of the nebulous and chimerical character of the project. To disencumber themselves of these two associates, who had begun to create a scandal in the Rhineland, the apostolic delegates from Mainz proposed to them that they go and convert the Indians of South America. Weltz and Gichtel went to Holland but then refused at the last minute to get on the boat.

Having left the Baron and returned to Regensburg, Gichtel experienced after fervent prayers an "illumination" that put him in direct contact with the Divinity. Submitting himself in advance to all the ordeals that Christ would have him undergo, he abandoned himself completely to the superior "Will" that had "annihilated" his own. Losing all sense of prudence, he publicly denied the necessity of outward worship—in which he now saw a daunting obstacle to the soul's inward communion with God—and, even more maladroitly, he violently expelled the pastors from the town. The pastors brought him before the tribunals as "seditious" as an "enthusiast" and an "Anabaptist". Gichtel was at first imprisoned in Nuremberg and then languished for three weeks in a somber dungeon in Regensburg. Condemned for "anti-social heresy", he was excommunicated, excluded from the sacraments and from all the ceremonies of the Lutheran Church, and was even sentenced to be executed. After the intervention of the burgomaster of the city, however, his death sentence was commuted to perpetual banishment. Deprived of his position, his goods, and his status as a citizen, the visionary was chased from Regensburg in February 1655.

At first Gichtel wandered through southern Germany, where charitable people provisionally housed him. Then he went to Vienna, where he had influential relatives, and obtained a position at the imperial court, at which he was assailed with many worldly temptations (riches, honors, and so on). Seeing how he was favored in the capital, his persecutors in Regensburg became afraid and restored his fortune to him. But Gichtel, having made the irrevocable resolution to renounce all the goods of this world, vowed extreme poverty: he gave his money to his eldest sister (who quickly squandered it), abandoned his official functions, gave up his luxurious clothing for a coarse frock made of leather, and left for Holland on foot.

After being detained in Zwolle by the Lutheran authorities, who suspected him of being an Anabaptist, Gichtel established himself in Amsterdam, where he was thenceforth forced to live off subsidies from various protectors—his religious convictions having expressly prohibited him from plying any trade whatsoever.

In 1669 he became "the spiritual husband of the Virgin Sophia". She manifested herself to him, became his 'wife', revealed to him the final explication of all things, and enjoined him to institute the "priesthood of Melchizedek"—to found the "New Church", the Church of the Last Dispensation. All books had to be rejected, with the exceptions of the Bible (when interpreted theosophically) and the works of Jakob Böhme. After this great "illumination", Gichtel united around him a small group of disciples who desired to live—according to his own example and the model of Christ—a life of perfect purity. This was the community of the Brothers of the Angelic Life, a small sect that still subsists secretly in Germany.

According to Gichtel, the Reformation had destroyed Catholicism without substituting anything better in its place. A *true* Reformation would therefore have to be instituted, and this Reformation would have to consist precisely in putting the theosophy of Jakob Böhme into practice. [...]

To put this new dispensation into practice, Gichtel established the "priesthood of Melchizedek"—a community of "saints", "Brothers of the Angelic Life", and "soldiers of Christ". These brothers and sisters (women were admitted into the community with rights equal to those of the men) would have to strive to return to the state of *angelic perfection* lost by Adam at the Fall. It would thus be possible for them to regain the primitive androgyny of man: "... in heaven, there are neither men nor women".

Seeking to free themselves from all human imperfections by leading lives of contemplation and continuous prayer, they had to imitate the perfect existence of Christ in all points.

"And [Christ] also taught us", Gichtel said, "that when we want to be his, we should likewise renounce all earthy will, take up our cross and follow him, which teaching is found not only among the disciples, but among all Christians in common. The first Christians *practiced* this commandment and thereby testified that they loved Christ and upheld His law".[5]

In the consecration of Melchizedek, Gichtel's frenzied asceticism rediscovered the Essenism that had been the original, true Christianity.

In the same way that the priests of the Old Testament had to keep themselves pure, holy, immaculate, and chaste in order to perform their worship, the priests of Melchizedek of the New Alliance—so that they did not arouse the Anger of God, and so that they could stand before God in the Sanctuary— demanded similar sacrifices but even more vehemently, because complete divine service required a total renunciation of terrestrial love.[6]

Unlike the Stylites and the Anchorites, whose repression of sexuality was allied to a hatred of the self (they called sexuality the absolute evil of Satan), Gichtel extracted from his libidinal energy—which was transmuted into mystical visions—not the horrors of diabolical temptation but rather a kind of ravishing succubus, which was none other than the *Sophia* of the Gnostics and Böhme. Gichtel himself recounted the dazzling nature of his ethereal orgasms.

"Then I saw in the heart a bright white light, around the heart a thick serpent, three times around like a chain wound; and in the midst of the serpent appeared Jesus in a bright light in the form he is described in John's Apoc. 1: 13–5".

"Now if the soul lingers with its dear bride in the rosegarden and collects and holds beautiful flowers and aphorisms [...] in its heart, so the dear bride takes her dear wooer, the soul, together out of the whole body.

"[...] There it sees a fiery globe—see the third figure and observe the majestic wondereye of Jakob Böhme—and immerses it in the fiery ocean—as has happened to me also in five days five times, when I was praying in the evening; there I saw that it was crystalline blue like the bright heaven in the middle, but was a fiery water, which plays over the soul as a fiery small wave; the lovely task and perception I cannot express"[7].

"[...] after a black cloud appeared a white one followed, and out of it came the noble, heavenly Virgin Sophia of Jesus [...]—his loyal companion and friend whom he [Gichtel] had loved until then without knowing her. And she appeared to him in his spirit, face to face; God had thus sent . . . his eternal Word Jesus in virginal form, to serve him [Gichtel] as consort and wife. . . . O how lovingly she embraced his soul! No woman frolicked more affectionately with her husband than Sophia did with his soul. And what he experienced in the course this union he equally desired that other souls should enjoy, because words cannot express the inexpressible sweetness, even if it were permitted. . . ."[8]

In his correspondence with Colonel Kirchberger[9], Louis-Claude de Saint-Martin evoked the love of Gichtel and his Sophia. Quoting from that correspondence, Sarane Alexandrian[10] explains the following:

"Sophia, his dear divine Sophia, whom he loved so well, and had never seen, came on Christmas-day, 1673, and made him her first visit; he, in the third principle, saw this shining heavenly virgin. On this occasion she accepted him for her husband, and the marriage was consummated in ineffable delight". Married to Sophia (who "gave him to hope for a spiritual progeniture"), living with her "in the luminous ground within", Gichtel engaged in daily conversations with her: "Sophia had also a central language, without words, without vibration or air, which was like no human language; nevertheless, he understood it as well as his mother tongue". Through revelations concerning the soul and nature, she directed him to publish the works of Jakob Böhme.

Raadt, a scholar who was associated with Gichtel, fell in love with Sophia and imposed "spiritual circumcision" on himself and his wife so as to merit seeing this entity. "She allowed some rays of her image to fall on the earthy qualities of their souls". Around Gichtel was soon formed the Society of the Thirty—all lovers of Sophia and beneficiaries of her favors—which caused him to remark "how the astral spirit is desirous of the nuptial couch of Sophia". Dissent appeared among the Thirty in 1682, but a young wholesaler from Frankfurt named Uberfeld, who later published Gichtel's letters, went and met with him and decided to remain as a disciple. "On his arrival, Sophia manifested herself to the two friends together, in the third principle, in the most glorious manner". Uberfeld took Sophia as his wife and "he was raised to the sublimest degrees".

It was confirmed that Sophia, the immaterial wife, was polygamous, sharing herself among all her chosen ones, on the condition that they were initiated: no soul, not even a good one, could entirely possess Sophia. She could even be the celestial spouse of a woman, since the first vision that the English mystic Jane Leade had was one in which Sophia manifested herself physically. Saint-Martin said of the wedding of Gichtel and Sophia: "Everything bears the stamp of truth. If I were near you, I could give you a story of a marriage in which the same way was followed with me, though under different forms, ending in the same result".[11]

At the same time, in France, Nicolas-Pierre-Henri de Montfaucon de Villars—in his *Count of Gabalis*, published in 1670—was approaching *cum grano salis*[12] the problem of libertine relations with beings issued from the mysteries of nature rather than from the heavens: "the Fairest amongst them all, is Loathsom, in respect of the Homeliest *Sylphide*". The air, water, fire, and earth were full of superb creatures whose favors were enjoyed by the initiate. "They require Men but to abstain from *Women*, whose Defects they cannot abide; and [...] they permit us to Love amongst them, as many as we please"[13].

In *The Amorous Devil* (1772), and in the same gallant manner, Jacques Cazotte treated ideas that had already been in fashion among the Gnostics and the Alexandrine Hermeticists, and that the Byzantine monk Michael Psellos had expounded in the eleventh century in his *Peri energeias daimonon*[14].

While Gichtel extinguished the excesses of repressed sexuality by way of esoteric couplings, other Pietists married the heavens to the earth in less disembodied—if not less spiritual—weddings.

In Germany, colleges of piety multiplied; these were congregations in which religious hysteria made use of an audience that was ready to let loose unreservedly. Such assemblies survive in great numbers in the Churches and sects of the United States, where television has successfully exhibited the neurotic disorders of ecstasy.

Founded by Eva von Buttlar, the Christian and Philadelphian Society ascribed to Böhme and Gichtel's Sophia the traits of a terrestrial and generous sensuality. Von Buttlar herself had wed a French refugee, a dance professor at Eisenbach. She left him to throw herself into Pietism. Having founded an association in which piety would excite her passionate nature, she got herself recognized as the Sophia—at once the New Eve and an incarnation of the Holy Spirit. The heavens, over which she ruled, granted her two lovers. She named one 'God the Father' and the other 'God the Son'. She believed that marriage was a sin and preached the holiness of love freely given and received. In November 1704, in the name of maintaining public order, the Lutherans got the police to disrupt the paradise in which Eva von Buttlar and her adepts had practiced what Charles Fourier would much later on characterize as the teachings of God.

The counts of Wittgenstein opened their domains to all those whose beliefs condemned them to persecution. Eva took refuge there, but her crime appeared inexpiable. Sophia and 'God the Father' were condemned to death but managed to escape from the authorities. They no doubt consoled themselves about their lost paradise in a prudently clandestine fashion.

At the beginning of the eighteenth century, Pietism moved on to the *Aufklärung*[15]. Two workers—the Kohler brothers, Christian and Hieronymus—mixed apocalyptic diatribes together with the first signs of a proletarian insurrection that they announced for Christmas Day 1748. One was executed, the other imprisoned. They prefigured Wilhelm Weitling, a contemporary of the young Marx, who mocked Weitling's archaisms. Weitling proposed a general insurrection of the proletariat, the iron lance of which—constituted by criminals released from prison and transformed by their divine mission—would introduce into the cadaver of the old world the ferment of an egalitarian millennium. It is not certain that such a beautiful project would have produced more gruesome results than the quite rational program of the Communist parties.

Ernst Christoph Hochmann von Hochenau (1670–1721), a wandering preacher who was persecuted everywhere he went, also found asylum in the domains of the counts of Wittgenstein. From there he led the fight for tolerance and the abolition of the death penalty.

The radical Pietist Gottfried Arnold was the first to approach the history of the Church and the various heresies in a spirit that was disengaged from theological (if not religious) prejudices. For Arnold, the sincerity of one's convictions took precedence over doctrine, and none of the many available opinions and practices was to be condemned as long as they did not threaten the lives or the dignity of individuals. The human meaning that slowly revoked the heavenly obedience that was required by the various religions could not, perhaps, have been expressed any better than it was by Hölderlin: his 'Diotima'[16] was a sensual and amorous Sophia, and she exorcised the torments of a Pietist education by attributing to the marvelous designs of childhood the poetic source that creates and re-creates the world.

The Quietists

The Church of Rome reserved for monastic communities the pursuit of contemplation and the privilege of assuring (through the use of prayer) a direct line of communication between God and humanity. The path of the world could therefore be pursued under the ferule of the spiritual and temporal powers without the ardors of faith being able to claim at any inopportune moment to be able to move institutional mountains.

The people were not happy to be feeding these congregations of loafers, which in return for the care of souls made money in the form of corvées, taxes, and tithes. The people later demonstrated their displeasure by joyously sacking the abbeys and monasteries.

By expelling the monastic orders, the Reformation authorized those who sought for themselves the luxury of communing with God without having to worry about providing for their own terrestrial subsistence.

During the seventeenth century, the form of visionary Pietism known in Catholic countries as 'Quietism' elicited the reprobation of both Rome and the governmental authorities.

Antoinette Bourignon de la Porte (1616–80), an inhabitant of Lille, was distinguished very early in her life by a form of devotion that was extreme but still characterized by a strictly Catholic obedience. A sudden illumination persuaded her to confer the light of divine inspiration upon the world.

She condemned the external forms of organized religion in the name of the powerful movements of the soul. Leszek Kołakowski has noted Antoinette's "disgust for her mother—which appeared during her childhood—and later her hatred for women and her obsessive fear of sexual matters"[17].

Bourignon's speculations on the original androgyny of human beings were not without their piquant aspects:

> The human being had in his belly a vessel from which small eggs were born and another vessel full of a liquor that would make these eggs fecund. And when this man became excited by the love of his God, the desire that he had for other creatures to praise him [i.e. God], to love and adore this great majesty, was spread—by the fire of the love of God—over one or several of these eggs with inconceivable delights; and this egg or eggs, made fecund, then exited from the man through a canal in the form of an egg. Shortly thereafter there hatched out from this egg a perfect man. There will thus be in eternal life a holy and endless procreation quite different from that which sin has introduced by means of women. By means of this holy procreation, and in conformity with the new discoveries of anatomy, God will form men by drawing from the flanks of Adam the viscera that contain the eggs that women possess and from which men are still born today.[18]

Serge Hutin comments:

> This womb was ripped out of Adam during the bipartition (caused by the Fall) of the original androgyny.
>
> These considerations were tied to a highly original Christology: the Word was engendered by Adam when he was in the hermaphroditic state of innocence. The work of Jesus in his terrestrial incarnation was to teach mankind the means by which it could recover the favor of God and return to its prelapasarian state of perfection.

To be saved one had to detach oneself completely from terrestrial things, and to become aware of the fact that they had disappeared and that God alone remained (the person having been annihilated in Him). The only qualification required for teaching the Truth is therefore a perfect union of the soul with God.

Antoinette Bourignon thus described the birth—after the end of this world—of the *New Jerusalem*, the celestial dwelling of the just. She also showed how the earth would be transformed after the Last Judgment into an infernal prison in which the individual wills of the damned would be given over to a merciless struggle. Divine mercy would finally triumph and deliver the damned, however.[19]

Traveling the world so as to propagate her vision of an inward and purely spiritualized reality, Antoinette Bourignon was able to escape the fates of her friend Quirinus Kuhlmann (1651–80) and her contemporary Simon Morin (1623–63), both of whom were executed for their beliefs.

A visionary and a self-avowed reincarnation of the Messiah, Simon Morin had the misfortune of living under the rule of a devout king, to whom he was denounced by a mediocre writer named Jean Desmarets, Sieur de Saint-Sorlin. The latter pretended to join the ranks of Morin's proselytes, obtained from Morin an exposition of his chiliastic doctrine, and delivered this exposition to the authorities. Louis XIV had Morin burned along with his writings in 1663. Morin had published his *Thoughts of Simon Morin* in 1647.

As for Quirinus Kuhlmann, Paul Vulliaud has summarized his destiny in a few words: "The pyre was his throne"[20].

At the age of eighteen and at the end of a serious illness, Kuhlmann had a vision of God, who entrusted him with the mission of revealing his message to all the nations. Kuhlmann then left Breslau, his native town, and traveled through Germany and Holland, where he became enthusiastic about the works of Jakob Böhme.

According to Serge Hutin,

in Amsterdam Kuhlmann came to know another young visionary, Johannes Rothe, who was as fanatical as he was. They both joined the community of the 'Angelic Brothers' [the Brothers of the Angelic Life], but then quickly came into conflict with Gichtel and founded their own society.

After Rothe's arrest Kuhlmann led a wandering existence, traveling aimlessly according to his prophetic 'inspirations'. In 1675 he went to Lübeck. He wanted to go to Rome to dethrone the Pope but finally embarked for Smyrna, where he proclaimed the imminence of the definitive Reformation. Persuaded that he would be its craftsman and that the 'spiritual kingdom' would at first be established in the East, he went to Constantinople, where he tried in vain—using the Dutch ambassador as an intermediary—to obtain an audience with the great vizier (1678). He then went to Switzerland, England (he visited London in 1679 and translated his books into English), France (he was in Paris in 1681), and Germany.

He finally left for Russia with the goal of establishing the 'Kingdom of God' there. He took two wives, frequented the strangest Russian sects, and attempted to convert the Muscovites to his mission. Peter the Great had him imprisoned as a dangerous heretic and conspirator, and on 4 October 1689 Kuhlmann and his friend Conrad Nordermann were burned alive in Moscow.[21]

Pierre Poiret (1646–1719) was in a sense situated at the hinge between the first and second generations of Quietism. Born in Metz, he was a Calvinist minister in Heidelberg and Zweibrücken. His reading of texts by Tauler, Thomas à Kempis, and, especially, Antoinette Bourignon converted him to Quietism, which reduced existence to the pure contemplation of an inward God and the ecstasies of the depthless soul. His desire to meet Bourignon led him to Amsterdam and then to Hamburg. He eventually became her disciple and stayed with her until her death in 1680. Persecuted by the Lutherans, he went to Rijnsburg, a place near Leyden, where he died in 1719. He published the works of Antoinette Bourignon, as well as those of Jeanne-Marie Bouvier de La Motte-Guyon—better known as Madame Guyon—who lent Quietism a degree of respectability.

Madame Guyon

In 1675 the Spanish priest Miguel de Molinos (1628–96) published *The Spiritual Guide Which Disentangles the Soul*. Having been well received within Catholic milieus, the book was suddenly condemned as Quietist and, in 1679, Pope Innocent XI pushed cruelty as far as throwing its author into the prison of the Holy Office, where he eventually died. The sole crime committed by the unfortunate Molinos was that he brought back to the surface the still-threatening memories of the *Alumbrados* of the sixteenth century, even though he attributed to them a great spirituality. Molinos advocated maintaining the soul and the body in a state of total inaction so that God could express himself in each person without encountering the obstacles of conscience and moral imperatives. Molinos excluded from his argument the notion that the faithful should break with the observance of religious duties, but he conferred so many privileges upon the annihilation of the soul in ecstasy that the functions of the Church, the sacraments, and works of piety were greatly reduced.

The Bishop of Naples, who was Molinos's principal accuser, claimed that the people who pursued divine quests did so in order to revoke his personal authority and to follow their inclinations freely. And there was no doubt some truth in this, given that the satisfactions of nature excel at providing those who would thwart them with justifications for doing so.

Molinos's doctrine found echoes in France, where Jeanne-Marie Bouvier de La Motte, the widow of a certain Guyon, recommended the annihilation of the soul to the point that all prayer disappeared, except for the entreaty: "Thy will be done!"

Violently attacked by Bossuet, Madame Guyon obtained the protection of Fénelon, the Bishop of Cambrai. She did not repudiate any of her opinions, even when she was condemned to prison and then sent into exile. Fénelon abjured when he was accused of following Molinos by Pope Innocent XII.

Like the 'Guérinets' (the adepts of the parish priest Guérin, of whom Racine spoke in his *Brief History of Port-Royal*[22]), neither Madame Guyon nor Fénelon used the illumination that they acquired through prayer to take any Jesuitical liberties with asceticism. But it is probable that the simple people made better use of the divine graces and ecstasies that are so common in love. Songs that lampooned the Quietists circulated at this time. One of their refrains related the miraculous effects of devotion:

> As for my body, I abandon it to you,
> My soul being my only care.
> When the soul gives itself to God
> One can leave one's body to one's friend.

It is certain that the virtuous Bossuet, wearing his cassock, was then enjoying the charming perils and disgraces of love with Mademoiselle de Mauléon. In a society that was being suffocated by the devout party and by the prudishness of a pitiful monarchy, the pleasures of the senses had to be exalted in the metaphorical shadow of the confessional, since it was dangerous to rally to the joyous revolt of such libertines as Saint-Pavin, Blot, Claude Le Petit, and Cyrano de Bergerac.

CHAPTER FORTY-EIGHT

The End of the Divine Right

In the profusion of its diverse tendencies, the triumph of Protestantism—in which the economic mechanisms that chaotically governed historical evolution burst the skin of the God that had clothed them with his myth—put an end to the need for repressive orthodoxy and, consequently, for the existence of 'heresy'.

The sects had given to the Greek word *hairesis* the neutral meaning of 'choice' or 'option'. They then entered the currents of opinion that, following Destutt de Tracy and Benjamin Constant, became known as 'ideologies'[1]. The decapitation of Louis XVI, a monarch by virtue of divine right, removed from God the ecclesiastical head at which—like those of a monstrous cephalopod—had been articulated the secular arms that were tasked with imposing God's writs of mandamus. The French Revolution deprived the Church of its penal authority; until then, princes and priests had been the intermediaries that imposed its laws.

The jubilation that brought down the churches and monasteries around the end of the eighteenth century began to express itself openly in works in which the derision of sacred things underlined the fact that religion merited less the death blows that were being inflicted by philosophical reason than casual gibes and taunts. The execution of the knight de la Barre was a reminder that the Church was still capable of biting cruelly, but this was the last persecution that was required by civil law's obedience to religious power.

Nevertheless, if Diderot only received a short jail sentence as punishment for his insolence, the anti-religious thinkers of the early eighteenth century still had the keenest interest in being careful and circumspect.

The case of Jean Meslier is too well known to be discussed at length here.[2] Let us recall that this parish priest from Étrépigny lived the life of a man who fulfilled the duties of his position (although he did have a disagreement with the lord of the town and a forbidden love affair with his own servant). His *Testament*, which was discovered after his death, removed God from society and from the universe as a whole by dragging him out of it, along with hierarchical power and the exploitation of man by his fellow man (the latter pair being the foundation of God's fantastical existence). The text was mutilated by Voltaire and only later distributed in unabridged form, but Meslier's celebrity preceded the publication of his work thanks to his celebrated formula: "Humanity will only be happy when the last priest has been hanged with the guts of the last prince"[3].

Thomas Woolston

Both the humorous irreverence and the misfortune of Thomas Woolston proceeded from a misunderstanding. Despite its corrosive humor, his book *A Discourse on the Miracles of Our Saviour* grew out of a serious desire to demonstrate the degree to which the Scriptures had a merely allegorical meaning. Such had already been the opinion of Origen, Denck, and Weigel, and it is today the view of those theologians who are appalled by the everyday derision to which the religion of present-day commodity consumption is subjected.

Born in Northampton in 1669 and educated at Cambridge, Woolston became renowned as an erudite and punctilious man of the Church. His Latin dissertation on a letter from Pontius Pilate to Tiberius about Jesus called into question the authenticity of a document that, like many such documents, had been fabricated with a view to authenticating the historical Jesus.

Another of his works insisted on the necessity of interpreting ostensibly sacred texts in an allegorical sense. Intervening in the quarrel between Anthony Collins and the theologians concerning the foundations of Christianity, he wrote an ironic work titled *The Moderator Between an Infidel and an Apostate* [1725].

Published in 1727, his *A Discourse on the Miracles of Our Saviour* led to a quarrel with his friends and exposed him to the persecutions of all the religious minds of the day (conformist or otherwise). Condemned to a year in prison and hit with a fine that he could not pay, he aroused the democratic sentiments of a number of his fellow citizens. Samuel Clarke solicited his release in the name of the freedom of thought claimed by England. The authorities consented, on the condition that Woolston refrain from publishing anything shocking. He refused to exchange repudiation for liberty, which he held to be the spring of natural rights. He died on 27 January 1733, saying: "This is a struggle which all men must go through, and which I bear not only patiently but willingly"[4].

He addressed an acerbic dedication to his prosecutor, the Bishop of London; it rendered homage to him "with as much justice as you are due, because of the prosecution that you have wisely brought against the *Moderator*, as against a nonbeliever who here renders to you his very humble thanks, and who declares himself to be an admirer of your zeal, wisdom and conduct"[5].

His Second *Discourse on the Miracles our Saviour* ridiculed the Scriptures. He was astonished that Jesus-Christ had permitted demons to enter a herd of pigs and to cause destruction. "Where was the Goodness and Justice of his so doing?"[6] With respect to the healing of a woman who had lost some blood, he remarked: "And what if we had been told of the *Popes* curing an *Hemorrhage* like this before us? What would *Protestants* have said to it? Why, 'that a foolish, credulous, and superstitious Woman had fancy'd herself cured of some slight Indisposition; and the crafty *Pope* and his Adherents, aspiring after popular Applause, magnified the presumed Cure into a Miracle'"[7].

He added: "I am charmed that it is not said in the Gospels that he [Jesus] had taken money from these brave people, for having exercised his trade as a fortune teller; had this been said, our doctors would not have failed to found upon such an example a right to demand tithes, salaries and pensions as payment for their divinations"[8].

Woolston ridiculed the story of Jesus cursing a fig tree—which dried up overnight in consequence—without taking the interests of the thus-wronged owner into account. He mocked the resurrection and the fact that Jesus appealed to Lazarus in a loud voice, "as if he had been as deaf as a dead Man"[9]. Like Jacques Gruet, Thomas Scoto, and Herman van Rijswick, Woolston characterized the Savior "as [an] impostor full of deceit"[10].

Woolston's caustic spirit could hardly assail the authority that the Constantinian Church had invested in the mythical Jesus-Christ without also taking aim at all the truths that had been so quick to send to the pyre or prison-house those who declined to bow down before them. Woolston defended the memory of Servetus against Calvin. His refusal of a freedom whose price would have been enslavement to received ideas rested on a model of dignity that struggled for tolerance—and this at a time when many others (among them Voltaire) were content to raise their voices only when the danger had passed and when their personal glory was not at risk.

Woolston's spirit, liberated from qualms about having faith in God outside of any established Church, sharpened itself on Holbach's *Portable Theology* and, especially, on the works of the Abbot Henri-Joseph Du Laurens (1719–97), whose *Godfather Matthew, or the Diversity of the Human Spirit*[11] was among the most amusing of the texts that ridiculed religious prejudices. (Note that one of his characters says the following, which conveys a large part of the mystery of faith: "You have taken a great step towards mystical love if you have previously exercised all the faculties of your soul in the soul of a lover".)

The Book of the Three Impostors

A mythic book if there ever was one, *De tribus impostoribus*[12] haunted the imaginations of the Middle Ages and the Renaissance before offering bibliophiles occasions for research and for passionate quarrels.

If ever there existed such a manuscript, circulated hand to hand with all the attractions of peril and prohibition, its contents probably added nothing to the thesis that its title proposes with such pleasing concision:

three impostors have led the world—Moses, Jesus, and Mohammed. Is it really necessary to seek out authors for such a formula when its obviousness would have imposed itself sooner or later—if only furtively—on anyone who was disturbed by the chaos and the conflicts that were afflicting society and the order of things? Goliards, ribald students, shameless priests, bishops, and popes who were less concerned with faith than with prestige, peasants being tyrannized by the aristocracy, bourgeois who got entangled in financial crimes, workers, and unemployed people seeking day and night for a little food and money in the streets, women who were scorned or treated like Satan's creatures—who did not at one time or another spit upon those holy figures who were everywhere set up like bloody totems of monotheism and its ministers?

Even a moderately exhaustive study of the history of Western mindsets from the fourth to the eighteenth centuries would indicate the degree to which religious belief—perhaps more so within certain orthodoxies than in many heretical engagements—was generally just a prudent or comfortable cover beneath which the torments and fleeting satisfactions of passion were given free rein. (Note that, in 1470, a police ordinance in Nuremberg concerning foreign beggars conceded to them permission to exercise their trade on the condition that they knew how to recite the Pater Noster, the Ave Maria, the Credo, and the Ten Commandments.)

In the preface to his reprint of *De tribus impostoribus*, Gerhardt Bartsch retraces the history of this text, which, in all probability, existed as a short statement of its provocative assertion before acceding to the typographical reality of a book[13].

Abu Tahir al-Jannabi, a philosopher belonging to the Qarmatian current that from the ninth to the tenth centuries rejected and ridiculed the credibility of Islam and Mohammed, said: "In this world, three individuals have corrupted mankind: a shepherd [Moses], a physician [Jesus] and a camel-driver [Mohammed]. And this camel-driver was the worst conjuror, the worst prestidigitator of the three"[14]. This idea, which was adopted by Abu'l Walid Muhammad Ibn Rushd (better known as Averroes), suggested to the West the existence of a work that proved to be as elusive as the opinion that it expressed: the *Liber de tribus impostoribus, sive Tractatus de vanitate religionum* (the *Book of the Three Impostors*, *or the Inanity of the Religions)*.[15] (In the words of Averroes: "The Jewish religion was a law for children; the Christian religion a law which it was impossible to follow; and the Mahometan religion a law in favor of swine"[16].)

A professor at the Sorbonne and an admirer of Aristotle, Master Simon of Tournai (1130–1301) proclaimed—without, it seems, being unduly disturbed by this fact—that "the Jews were seduced by Moses, the Christians by Jesus, and the Gentiles by Mohammed"[17].

The scholar Bernard de La Monnoye, who was among the first to study this question, cited the accusation made by Pope Gregory IX against the Holy Roman Emperor Frederick II, for whom religion was a mere instrument of domination. For a long time the book *[De tribus impostoribus]* appeared to have come from his Frederick's pen, or from that of his chancellor, Pietro della Vigna, though there was no proof of either hypothesis.

According to Alvarus Pelagius, Thomas Scoto denounced the imposture of the prophets. Herman van Rijswick referred to it in his confession. Putative authors were not hard to come by: Arnaldus de Villa Nova, Michel Servetus, Jacques Gruet, Fausto Longiano (whose *Temple of the Truth,* now lost, dismissed all the religions), Jeannin de Solcia, the Canon of Bergamo (who, under the name Javinus de Solcia, was condemned by Pope Pius II on 14 November 1459 for affirming that the three impostors "governed the world according to their fancy"[18]), and all of the following: Ochino, Campanella, Poggio, Cardan, Pompanacius, and even Spinoza. (Note that I have found no trace in the works of Antoine-Gaspard Couillard of the remark that was denounced by Fernand Drujon: "Jesus-Christ founded his religion on idiots".)

Studying the printed copy dated 1598, which he found at the Library of Vienna, Bartsch established that it had in fact been back-dated. Without presupposing the existence of an earlier copy in manuscript, he confirmed Presser's thesis that the book—published around 1753—was in fact the work of Johannes Joachim Müller (1661–1733), the grandson of the theologian Johannes Müller (1598–1672), who was in turn the author of a study titled *Atheismus devictus*[19]. Having been taught about the existence of this mythic book, Johannes Joachim undertook to give it a reality, and—not without a degree of mischievousness—fixed its date of publication as 1598, the date of his grandfather's birth.

In its modern version, *De tribus impostoribus* contains allusions to the Jesuits and sets the 'eternal truths' of each religion against those of the others. It emphasizes the incoherencies of the sacred texts and reaches the following conclusion: that there is no other God than nature, and no other religion than the laws of nature.

Matthias Knützen

A poet of atheism and of the struggle against religious obscurantism, Matthias Knützen (1646–74) played an exemplary and impassioned role in the history of the emancipation of mankind under the *Ancien Régime*. His theses inspired the French encyclopedists, even though—with the exception of Jacques-André Naigeon—they were resolved not to mention him.

Born in 1646 in Oldenswort, in Holstein, he was the son of an organist. Upon the death of his parents, he was welcomed to the Altstädtisches Gymnasium by Pastor Fabricius, who took care of his education but failed—or so it seems—to inculcate in the boy an obedience to the austere morals that were thought to be pleasing to God. His studies of theology in Königsberg ended up winning him over to atheism.

At the age of twenty-one he returned to his hometown without much of a desire to preach there. In 1668 he enrolled at the University of Copenhagen, where he wrote the now-lost *De lacrimis Christi*[20]. On returning to Oldenswort, he scandalized the good people of the town by taking the floor in front of an assembly of peasants in Tönning and calling for rebellion against the Protestantism of the pastors and the absolutism of the princes. He was banished by the city council in 1673 and took refuge at Krempen (in Denmark), where he resumed his diatribes against the wealth of the consistories. After being chased out of Krempen he traveled through Germany, where he publicly preached atheism and called for a struggle against the aristocracy. On 5 September 1674 he deposited at the principal church of Jena the manuscript of *Gespräch zwischen einem Gastgeber und drei Gästen ungleicher Religion* and the Latin text *Amicus amicis amica!*[21]. These anonymous pamphlets, which were also sent to the principal authorities, aroused a great deal of excitement in the city.

Knützen narrowly escaped the subsequent repression and went to Coburg, where he distributed and diligently recopied his *Amicus*. He did the same in Nuremberg. He returned to Jena under the pseudonym 'Matthias Donner'. He spread rumors about an international sect, the 'Conscientarians', of which he was the initiator. This sect was solely the product of his will to propagate individual freedom and to revolt against all forms of power. His pamphlets—which were clandestinely printed by his disciples, the existence of whom he was probably unaware—made it into France, where they were among the first texts to open a breach in the feudal citadel against which the French Revolution would one day hurl itself. There is no trace of him after 1674, and the common view is that he died in Italy. One of his letters, falsely date-lined Rome, was published in French by Maturinus Veyssière La Croze's *Entretiens sur divers sujets d'histoire* in Cologne in 1711.

"Above all", Knützen wrote in *Amicus amicis amica!*, "we deny God, and we hurl him down from his heights, rejecting the temple and all of its priests. What suffices for us, the Conscientarians, is the science, not of one, but of the greatest number [...]. The consciousness that nature, the benevolent mother of the humble people, has accorded to all men, in place of the [various] Bibles"[22].

The Fall of God

Just as Knützen had wanted, the French Revolution hurled God down to earth, where He was in his death throes for two centuries and lived on in the spirit of the great political ideologies that supplanted the European religions. At the end of the twentieth century, the collapse of both the religions and the political ideologies wholly discredited the last residues of celestial thought (regardless of whether those residues were sacred or profane, theistic or atheistic, religious or secular).

The decline of intellectualized conceptions of the living—conceptions that ultimately turned against life—was completed in the midst of an indifference that contrasted with the fury that had once characterized the critique of those conceptions. The hatred felt towards the 'calotte-wearers' [*les calotins*]—which was expressed through the sacking of churches and monasteries in both the towns and the countryside, and which turned out to be a prelude to the Revolution—was confirmed in law by the Civil Constitution of the Clergy, an act of bureaucratization that marked the end of religious power over the citizenry and its replacement by secular governmental repression.

Enacted in 1790 by the French Revolution, the Civil Constitution of the Clergy had only a few points in common with the relatively limited provisions that subjected the ministers of the Anglican Church to royal power. More than just the prerogatives of the Pope, it was the supremacy of religion itself that was revoked. The refusal of Roman authority proceeded from the destruction of the divine rights of kings.

Supported by the new exigencies of the economy, philosophy triumphed over a 'religious obscurantism' which nonetheless continued to haunt it and which perpetuated in apparently enlightened mindsets the cruel stupidity that tore the individual away from what was most alive in order to identify him or her with the frozen truths of science, politics, sociology, ethics, and ethnic groups. The flag replaced the cross and was then burned in its turn. Although the collapse of Jacobinism and Bonapartism gave the Church of the nineteenth century considerable power, the decline of Catholicism and Protestantism—both of which were worn away by social modernity—continued. At the dawn of the twenty-first century, they survive only as a kind of folklore that gets recounted on Sundays.

In the towns as well as in the countryside, the first months of the revolutionary effervescence decided the fate of the clergy. The Church dignitaries, who were closer to the aristocracy than to the people, shared in the discredit of the *Ancien Régime*. Some of them opted prudently for conciliation. Others, espousing the convictions of their parishioners, took pride in representing them at the National Assembly. From their zeal came the image of 'Citizen Jesus', which demonstrated the astonishing capacity of religious values to adapt to circumstances, even to the point of developing a theology of liberation.

Some dignitaries refused to swear allegiance to the Civil Constitution, preferring exile or clandestinity. Others made pledges and then betrayed them at opportune moments, and still others took high-risk careers as local-government officers. Their discomfort with the new law grew as

Jacobinite centralism began to displease the provinces and the countryside and to incite liberal insurrections and Catholic peasant revolts.

After eight months of silence, Pope Pius VI condemned the Civil Constitution as "composed of principles derived from heresy", "heretical in many of its decrees", and "sacrilegious and schismatic" in others[23]. His effigy was hanged and burned in the Tuileries Garden soon thereafter. Nevertheless, the parish priests gained in political stature what they had lost in sanctified virtue. Those who, in the manner of Jacques Roux, took the side of the Enragés succumbed to Jacobin persecution. Refractory priests were pursued, and those who swore allegiance were held to be hypocrites. The high clergy maneuvered skillfully in order to safeguard their privileges. In a symbol of the two centuries that were to come, Charles Maurice de Talleyrand-Périgord (1754–1838)—a statesman and diplomat who was sufficiently unscrupulous as to take the oath and to consecrate other bishops who did the same—survived the Revolution, Bonapartism, Empire, the Restoration, and the monarchy through the use of skillful mimicry.

His exemplary modernity, his art of chipping away at the sacred in accordance with political necessity, presaged the destiny of Christianity itself, which was condemned to become domesticated before it finally succumbed to the generalized indifference that market society propagated at the end of the twentieth century.

AFTERWORD TO THE ENGLISH EDITION

Beyond religion, which, right up until the final disillusionment, was the heart of a heartless world

Dedicated to the Iranian women who burn their hijabs[1]

> You want to build ideal cities
> Destroy the monstrosities first
> Governments, barracks, cathedrals
> Which are just so many absurdities to us.
>
> Charles d'Avray[2]

By some kind of cosmic alchemy, unknown to us, the human being finds him- or herself the possessor of an exceptional creative power. While the other species only possess the genius of adaptation, men and women discover that nature has bestowed upon them an exceptional privilege—that of evolving through self-creation and by recreating the world as a whole.

Isn't this the height of absurdity? Humanity, the builder of its own destiny, renounces its creative genius in order to delegate it to the Gods that humanity has itself invented.

A halt, a stasis, has deflected away from its natural evolution the process of humanization that ought to be taking place in a symbiosis between humanity and its environment. The advanced level of development that was once attained is attested to by the 35,000 years of civilization that preceded the advent of the agricultural-market civilization that has been ours for nearly 10,000 years.

To what phenomenon must we impute such a change of orientation? Undeniably, to the appearance and expansion of an economic, social, political, and existential system that is founded on the conjoined exploitation of terrestrial and human nature.

From Lucy[3] (3,500,000 years ago) to Lascaux[4] (15,500 years ago), collectivities that gathered crops and occasionally went hunting managed to live without wars or major conflicts. An alliance with the environment provided them with food and with materials from which their technology [*technique*] derived ceaselessly perfected tools. Artistic productions of an astounding refinement permit us to suppose that they led relatively gentle lives, free from the frenzy of hard work. In these egalitarian societies, we note a great abundance of female statues and portraits, which leads one to suppose that the creative work of women—bringing children into the world and, especially, mothering the nourishing earth—haloed them with a distinctive benevolence.

Over the course of several millennia—for reasons that are the subject of controversy—the process of humanization was in a sense suspended, or put on hold, by a system of dehumanization that first affected its own producers.

Thus does the self-alienated human—the *homo œconomicus*, the economized human—find itself today brutally confronted with the extinction of its own species and with that of all other living species. Neither religion nor ideology is any longer able to conceal the devastating results of the senseless war against nature.

The passage from a hunter-gatherer economy to an agricultural-market one took place during the transition from the Paleolithic era to the Neolithic, when intensive agriculture and livestock farming took hold and led to the settling down of the populations. There was a profound change in mentalities, behaviors, and morals. The new economic structure modified the structures of the collectivities and the psychologies of the individuals who composed them.

A hierarchy of masters and slaves abolished the reign of equality, fraternity and mutual aid. The exploitation and plundering of natural resources cut short the symbiosis between human beings and their environment.

The rape of Mother Earth presided over violence against women, which, perpetrated with impunity by an arrogant patriarchy, passed itself off as a glorious accomplishment.

It is this male power, which today is in dire straits, that the ongoing revolt of women has made ridiculous by compelling it to bite the dust. This particular battle, which is also that of a more general emancipation, has clarified something obvious: that contempt for and fear of femininity will dominate until we have abolished the dogma of antiphysis—of anti-nature—that is the pivot of market civilization.

Let no one speak to us of an ontological curse or the innate weakness of mankind. Predatory rape—the legitimation of which annuls mutual aid and creative autonomy—belongs to a historically datable period. It quite simply inaugurates the history made by and against us.

Baptized the 'agricultural revolution', this takeover by the City-State [*coup d'État-Cité*] consecrated the private appropriation of land and the mistreatment of nature. It multiplied the number of towns, which were governed by tyrants and which struggled against each other. The imposture that identified freedom of living with a license to oppress, to kill, to pillage, to ransack, to exploit, was only instituted six or seven thousand years before 'our' era began.

Having suppressed the mutual aid that linked free individuals to one another in prehistoric societies, the enslavement of terrestrial nature and human nature needed to link slaves, not to each together, but to a divine master who enchained them all.

Such is the origin of the various religions. They are the instruments of power. Belief becomes a policy of the State from the moment that it becomes a slave of the State.

* * *

The Gods are the shame of the human race. While life has spread us out over the earth by endowing us with the exceptional ability to create ourselves by recreating the world, we have accepted a historical upheaval that has denatured our evolution. Religion is the crooked reality that makes us walk straight.

Brought to light by the French Revolution, the crumbling of the hierarchical pyramid of universal power has gradually undermined the preeminence and authority of religion. Social struggles have thrown the Gods into the trash bin. The decapitation of the monarchy and the

Ancien Régime have abandoned Judeo-Christian monotheism to a God without a head, to an acephalous God.

The industrial capitalism of the nineteenth century exulted in playing the role of Prometheus by claiming responsibility for a form of progress in which God no longer had a place. The historical motor of dechristianization, industrial capitalism has continued since then to further the deterioration of the Church. By promoting consumerism wherever it can, has capitalism not had had the audacity to place crucifixes and dildos—which are differentiated only by their respective sale prices—side by side in its supermarkets? The triumph of commercial hedonism has dealt more serious blows to the authority of religion than the ferocity of anti-clerical struggles ever managed to do.

Although Islamism and Calvinist evangelism continue to generate a great deal of spectacular hype, they are still fated to disappear, to be devoured by the economic system that originally gave birth to them.

It is striking to recall that both faiths were born within the old *agricultural enclosure* that was the cradle of market civilization. Europe gets from that enclosure a tradition of tyrannical regimes that—despite their differences, and up until the fall of the guillotine blade in 1793—were able to flatter themselves that they were heavenly and eternal.

The world beyond Europe is marked by an oriental despotism that remains intact in spite of the damage inflicted upon it by globalized consumerism. There still exists an agricultural structure that maintains the existence of archaic mentalities—patriarchy, misogyny, voluntary servitude, religious fanaticism, and contempt for nature. It is curious that the United States—so proud of its industrial progressivism—promulgates the same laws that, in the Islamic tyrannies, seek to control amorous behavior, to prohibit and punish freedom of desire[5].

This archaism paradoxically bestows a spurious modernity upon an evangelistic movement that has always served as the spiritual cover for the imperialism of the governments of North America. Who can forget the smallpox-infected blankets that the missionaries offered to the Native Americans in the hope of decimating them?[6]

Iran and the United States thus form a contentious couple, one that is united, in spite of itself and in the name of a mercilessly benevolent

God, by a common puritanism and the same cult of obedience, hypocrisy and predation.

Islam, whether in its Shiite or Sunni forms, owes its survival to the predominance of an agricultural economy, which conceives of petroleum deposits as products of the soil and stock market speculation as an effect of the geysers of those deposits. The great difference with the United States is that the Iranian women are burning their hijabs (which are the marks of their alienation), while a good number of American women are still saying 'grace' and going to church on Sunday[7]. No matter how powerful the supremacist and macho politics of the United States aspires to be, it cannot *by nature* withstand the blows of *insurgent women who assert through guerrilla tactics their will to live.*

The Promethean ambitions of nascent industrialization did not spare the Catholic branch of Christianity, the dead wood of which was all that remained after the great pruning of 1789. Catholicism was condemned from the moment the agricultural economy that had nourished it and guaranteed its longevity disappeared.

Protestantism showed itself to be more durable. It was the inheritor of the system of free exchange that, with the outbreak of communalist struggles in the eleventh and twelfth centuries in France, had begun the struggle against the feudal regime and its aristocratic tyranny. It was a struggle endowed with merely formal liberties.

During the era in which capitalism was spreading through banking institutions, Calvin insisted on the heavenly character of progress. As Max Weber has demonstrated[8], Calvin saw progress as a divine intervention. The hand that God places on a man's shoulder can be removed unexpectedly, thereby deciding the success or failure of his enterprises. The fortunate man arouses the respect that is due to God's elect; the unfortunate one attracts the condemnation and scorn that are typically incurred by the damned. This worship of financial success, which was viewed as a resounding proof of divine approval, ended up taking a particularly potent form: the "little man of egotistical calculations"[9], who supplants the man of unified societies wherever exploitation reigns. If the *self-made man*[10] infests the entire world with his pestilence, this is because he exudes the *sanctified fear* of success and failure—and this to the point that it starts to appear reasonable to attribute the spread of pandemics to Puritanism and to the spirit of guilt inherent in capitalism.

The principles of asceticism, sacrifice, and renunciation proceed from the transformation of the life force into a work force, an entity that has been regarded as being of public utility ever since the appearance of the City-States (which subsequently became nations and empires). After staggering through the mists of profit-making, however, capitalism reached the point at which—under the auspices of the Marshall Plan—it was supposed to give money to the countries that were devastated by the war, to colonize Europe by proposing a state of well being (a *welfare state*[11]) that would be within easy reach (or almost so) for all the stock markets. Capitalism became subject to a contradiction that is simultaneously saving and sinking it.

What sticks in the throat of Islam is the same bone of consumerism that suffocated the so-called Soviet (actually Russian) empire. Greedy and falsified though it is, market hedonism has eviscerated what remained of religion. While the pauperization of the people both accelerates and threatens the profitability of the consumer sector, capitalism plays its cards right and obtains new profits by way of financial speculation. Although the neon lights of the Edens of cheap rubbish are gradually fading, the attractions of pleasure, readily available in the supermarkets, continue to dominate consumers' mentalities to the point that they forget that their pleasures and their freedom must be paid for on the way out, at the cash register.

The spiritual and angelic cover provided by ascetic capitalism is in shreds. Evangelical militancy tries in vain to patch it up, with or without the aid of the CIA's sewing needles. To the universal hatred and scorn aroused by the imperialist polices of the United States are added jubilatory denunciations of *Calvinist hypocrisy, which preaches moral hygiene in the cesspools of the profits that it reaps.*

By setting itself up as the religious adversary of Islam, Calvinist Protestantism has injected its venom into the veins of the secularism that is cheerfully glorified in France. Fortunately, Protestantism cannot escape the global garrote that is tightening around it and that is making it both a victim and an executioner. The last residue of the debacle of

Judeo-Christianity, Calvinist Protestantism is an instrument that even an economy that is trying to profit from its own death throes can no longer use.

We have reached such a level of ridiculous confusion that the sermons of Leftist militants who advocate *degrowth* and an ethic of frugality are actually providing aid and comfort (in spite of their authors' best intentions) to the globalized mafias that appeal for abstinence in order to alleviate the collapse of the real economy and to reinforce the virtual one.

Now that everything is collapsing, we can see clearly that humanity has been disavowed. Thanks to an absurd choice, Being has been sacrificed in the name of Having—of the Having that ends up degrading itself by transforming into deserts both the earth and its inhabitants.

Voltaire's cry, "Crush the loathsome thing!"[12] has always expressed a religious wish, if one may say so! To crush a religion is to see it immediately reappear thanks to the pain that waters it and the suffering that it inflicts. It is only when life flourishes that religious credulity perishes like a withered shoot, wilting away and ending up in the herbarium of folklore.

There are no revolts in cemeteries, but there are revolts that abolish cemeteries. It will be a social and existential uprising that produces the clean sweep that will consign the various religions to the past.

Nevertheless, the *nausea*[13] that today affects all of the believers in God as well as the believers in Mankind demands more than just the promise of evacuation. Why should we want to tear out the "heart of a heartless world"[14] that religion has artificially caused to beat, when a turn imposed upon history allows us to perform a Hegelian surpassing of religion—that is, to resolve its contradictions by refusing heavenly obedience and by preserving the links between mutual aid and solidarity?

Revolutions have until now only been made halfway. They have neglected something obvious: that, as Saint-Just observed, social change that does not radically change the everyday lives of men and women digs its own grave[15]. If the jubilations of insurgent peoples do not attain a consciousness of the need for the kind of self-managed organization that will assure their permanence, they will sink into the depths of traditional lamentations.

Commercial civilization is toppling over into nothingness, but it also understands that its fragility will not be able to drag us down with it. We have in us and for us a world in which the will to live is everywhere spreading its blazing unrest. The radicalism of some is enough to annul the alienation of a great many people. Because if stupidity is contagious, intelligence is empathetic. The former wastes away; the latter is reborn and shines out. The imposture of the Gods and masters no longer obscures the era of the creators[16]. To allow renatured freedoms to govern us is to protect ourselves from *all* forms of government.

We only dream of life and its festivals—let's make them real!

Raoul Vaneigem
——21 September 2022

Notes

TRANSLATOR'S INTRODUCTION

1. Raoul Vaneigem, *Le Mouvement du libre-esprit: Généralités et témoignages sur les affleurements de la vie à la surface du Moyen Âge, de la Renaissance et, incidemment, de notre époque* (Paris: Ramsay, 1986).

2. Raoul Vaneigem, *The Movement of the Free Spirit: General Considerations and Firsthand Testimony Concerning Some Brief Flowerings of Life in the Middle Ages, the Renaissance and, Incidentally, Our Own Time*, trans. Randall Cherry and Ian Patterson (New York: Zone Books, 1994).

3. Béatrice Delvaux and Catherine Makereel, "Les Racines élémentaires de Raoul Vaneigem: 'L'humanité meurt pour que survive une économie où l'argent fou tourne en rond'", *Le Soir*, 14 Nov. 2020.

4. Vaneigem, *The Movement of the Free Spirit*, 12–3.

5. Ibid.

6. Ibid. 10.

7. Ibid. 13.

8. Norman Cohn, *The Pursuit of the Millennium: Revolutionary Messianism in Medieval and Reformation Europe and Its Bearing on Modern Totalitarian Movements* (2nd edn., New York: Harper & Brothers, 1961), xiii–xv.

9. Greil Marcus, *Lipstick Traces: A Secret History of the Twentieth Century* (Cambridge: Harvard University Press, 1989), 91.

10. Revised and expanded edition (New York: Oxford University Press, 1970).

11. Ibid. 205–6.

12. Ibid.

13. Guy Debord, *La Société du spectacle* (Paris: Buchet-Chastel, 1967). Here I quote from Donald Nicholson-Smith's translation, *The Society of the Spectacle* (New York: Zone Books, 1995), 101–2.

14. Internationale Lettriste, "Les Cathares Avaient Raison", *Potlatch: Bulletin d'information du groupe français de l'Internationale lettriste*, 5 (20 July 1954).

15. Neither does Norman Cohn. In the Foreword to the 1970 edition of his book, he writes that, if there is "some acquaintance with the sociology of religion", "one is unlikely to imagine that all medieval 'heresy' was of one kind, reflecting the same kind of discontent and appealing to the same segments of society" (12).

16. Vaneigem, *The Movement of the Free Spirit*, op. cit. 9.

17. Vaneigem, preface to reprint of *Le Mouvement du libre-esprit: Généralités et témoignages sur les affleurements de la vie à la surface du Moyen Âge, de la Renaissance et, incidemment, de notre époque* (Paris: L'Or des fous editeur, 2005).

18. Ibid.

AUTHOR'S FOREWORD

1. *Translator's note*. Convened by Pope John XXIII and held in Rome between 1962 and 1965, this council was intended to update the Catholic Church in order to meet the needs of an increasingly secular world.

2. *Translator's note*. Latin for 'the final argument'.

3. *Translator's note*. On 1 July 1766, François-Jean Lefebvre de la Barre, a young French nobleman, was tortured, beheaded, and burned, allegedly because he insulted a Roman Catholic procession and damaged a crucifix.

4. In the 1990s, the hostility—sometimes sly, sometimes openly declared—of the Catholic, Protestant, and Jewish establishments towards a novelist who'd been condemned to death for impiety by Islamic fanaticism speaks volumes about the democratic sincerity and spirit of tolerance allegedly possessed by these diverse sectarians of the 'true God', who are quite fortunately deprived of the aid of State terrorism. [*Translator's note*. Note that in August 2022, while this translation of Vaneigem's book was being prepared for publication, Salman Rushdie, the author of *The Satanic Verses*, was attacked and seriously injured at a public event in western New York.]

5. This numbering of the centuries is an arbitrary system that accredits an alleged

Messiah and thus still recalls the extravagant appropriation of time by the Church.

6. *Translator's note.* English in original.

7. *Translator's note.* Latin in original, meaning 'willingly or unwillingly'.

8. *Translator's note.* A concept developed by Wilhelm Reich in *Charakteranalyse: Technik und Grundlagen für studierende und praktizierende Analytiker*, first published in German (Vienna: Im Selbstverlage des Verfassers, 1933) and then revised and published in English as *Character Analysis*, trans. Vincent R. Carfagno (New York: Farrar, Straus, and Giroux, 1946).

9. *Translator's note.* Cf. the concept of "repressive desublimation" in Herbert Marcuse, *One-Dimensional Man* (Boston: Beacon Press, 1964).

10. *Translator's note.* Denis Diderot, reviewing the Salon of 1767, reprinted in Denis Diderot, *Ruines et paysages: Salons de 1767*, ed. Michel Delon, Else Marie Bulkdahl, Annette Lorenceau (Paris: Hermann, 2008).

11. *Translator's note.* In the works of François Rabelais (1483–1553), Physis is joyful and unashamed, and Antiphysis is hateful and destructive.

12. *Translator's note.* The first volume of this work (*The Criminal History of Christianity*) was published in 1986 (Reinbek: Rowohlt Verlag). A total of ten volumes were published before the author's passing in 2014.

13. *Translator's note.* An anonymous song from the nineteenth century, sung by the French anarchist Ravachol (François Claudius Koenigstein) before his execution in 1892.

14. *Translator's note.* The Order of Lenin was established by the Central Executive Committee on 6 Apr. 1930. It was the highest civilian decoration awarded by the Soviet Union.

15. *Translator's note.* First published between 1926 and 1947, this immense work was intended to further the aims of the Communist Party and the Soviet State. It was extensively revised in the 1950s.

16. *Translator's note.* A fictional character created in 1919 by Johnston McCulley, Zorro was a masked vigilante who defended working-class and Native American peoples against corrupt governmental officials and businessmen.

17. *Translator's note.* Vaneigem's *Traité de savoir-vivre a l'usage des jeunes générations* (Paris: Gallimard, 1967), translated as *The Revolution of Everyday Life* by Donald Nicholson-Smith (Oakland: PM Press, 2012); *Le Livre des plaisirs* (Paris: Encre, 1979), translated as *The Book of Pleasures* by John Fullerton (London: Pending Press, 1983), and *Adresse aux vivants sur la mort qui les gouverne* (Paris: Seghers, 1990), not yet translated into English.

18. *Translator's note. Le Mouvement du libre-esprit: Généralites et témoignages sur les affleurements de la vie à la surface du Moyen-Age, de la Renaissance, et, incidemment, de notre époque* (Paris: Editions Ramsey, 1986), translated by Randall Cherry and Ian Patterson as *The Movement of the Free Spirit: General Considerations and Firsthand Testimony Concerning Some Brief Flowerings of Life in the Middle Ages, the Renaissance, and, Incidentally, Our Own Time* (New York: Zone Books, 1994). Note the latter's rendering of the apostil that Vaneigem mentions here: "If it is true that the test of a book's intelligence is what it can offer toward the pleasure of living better, let me say, right from the start, that there is no such intention in my study of the movement of the Free Spirit. Not until that glad hour when we are at last rid of our delusions about the science of the experts, and are content simply to choose among pleasures, can we face the unknown with a lucid, passionate gaze" (12).

19. *Translator's note.* An allusion to the title of Friedrich Nietzsche's book *Die fröhliche Wissenschaft (The Gay Science)*, published in 1882. Also found in Rabelais's *Gargantua and Pantagruel* (1532–4), this phrase refers to the skills required for writing good poetry.

A NATION SACRIFICED TO HISTORY

1. *Translator's note.* That is to say, as the 'Chosen People'.

2. *Translator's note.* Latin for 'in its essential or universal form or nature'.

3. Marcel Simon, *Le Judaïsme et le christianisme antique: D'Antiochus Épiphane à Constantin* (Paris: 1968), 49.

4. Jean Hadot, *Histoire des religions* (Brussels: Presses universitaires de Bruxelles, 1980), 14.

5. Ibid. 27.

6. Charles C. Torrey, "Certainly Pseudo-Ezekiel", *Journal of Biblical Literature*, 53/4 (1934): 291–320.

7. *Translator's note.* All quotations from the Bible will be taken from *The Holy Bible: English Standard Version* (London: HarperCollins, 2016).

8. Bernard Dubourg, *L'Invention de Jésus* (Paris: Gallimard, 1987), i. 251–60.

9. Yigael Yadin, *The Ben Sira Scroll from Masada* (Jerusalem: The Israel Exploration Society and the Shrine of the Book, 1965); Theophil Middendorp, *Die Stellung Jesu Ben Siras zwischen Judentum und Hellenismus* (E. J. Brill: Leiden, 1973).

10. *Translator's note. The Wisdom of Ben Sira*, trans. Patrick W. Skehan (New York: Doubleday, 1987), p. 262 (xv. 1).

11. *Translator's note.* Ibid. (xv. 2–3)

12. Flavius Josephus, *Antiquitiés judaiques* (Paris, 1929), 13. 45. [*Translator's note.* Flavius Josephus, "Antiquities of the Jews", in *The Complete Works of Flavius Josephus*, trans. William Whiston (London: T. Nelson and Sons, 1854), p. 216 (book 8, chapter 2).]

13. *Translator's note. The Wisdom of Solomon in the Revised Version*, ed. J. A. F. Gregg (Cambridge: Cambridge University Press, 1909), p. 71 (vii. 19–20).

14. Émile Puech, "(11QPsAp^a): Un rituel d'exorcismes. Essai de reconstruction", *Revue de Qumran*, 14/55 (1990).

15. *Translator's note.* From Vaneigem's French.

DIASPORA AND ANTI-SEMITISM

1. *Translator's note.* Cf. W. Roscher, "The Status of the Jews in the Middle Ages Considered from the Standpoint of Commercial Policy", *Historia Judaica*, 6 (Apr. 1944): "According to Strabo it was not easy to discover a place in the entire world where Jews were not to be found and which was not ruled [financially] by them" (17).

2. Josy Eisenberg, *Une histoire du peuple juif* (Paris: Fayard, 1974), 174. [*Translator's note.* Cf. the account given by Philo, *The Works of Philo Judæus*, trans. Charles Duke Yonge (London: G. Bell, 1855), in which Agrippa says the following: "Concerning the holy city [...] [it] is my native country, and the metropolis, not only of the one country of Judæa, but also of many, by reason of the colonies which it has sent out from time to time into the bordering districts of Egypt, Phœnicia, Syria in general, and [...] the greater part of Asia Minor as far as Bithynia [...]. And in the same manner into Europe, into Thessaly, and Boeotia, and Macedonia" (iv. 161).]

3. Eisenberg, *Une histoire du peuple juif*, 163.

4. *Translator's note.* Cassius Dio, *Roman History*, trans. Earnest Cary (London: William Heinemann, 1914), iii. 127.

5. *Translator's note.* Cf. Talmud, Yevamot 63b, commentary by Rabbi Eliezer ("He who does not engage in propagation of the race is as though he sheds blood") and Rabbi Yaakov ("as though he has diminished the Divine Image"), quoted by Joshua E. London, "Jewish Family Values", in *Public Policy and Social Issues: Jewish Sources and Perspectives*, ed. Marshall Jordan Breger (Westport, CT: Praeger, 2003), 231 n. 9.

6. Eisenberg, *Une Histoire du peuple juif*, 165. [*Translator's note.* Flavius Josephus, "Against Apion", in *The Complete Works of Flavius Josephus*, p. 822 (book 2, chapter 40).]

7. Theodor Mommsen, *Histoire romaine*, trans. C. A. Alexandre, 8 vols. (Paris: Librairie A. Franck, 1863–72). [*Translator's note.* Originally published in German as *Römische Geschichte*, 8 vols. (Leipzig: Reimer & Hirzel, 1854–6).]

NOTES

8. *Translator's note.* Letter of Claudius, in *Select Papyri*, ed. A. S. Hunt and G. C. Edgar (Cambridge, MA: Harvard University Press, 1934), ii. 87.

9. Karlheinz Deschner, *Kriminalgeschicte des Christentums* (Hamburg: Rowohlt Verlag, 1986–2008), i. 125.

10. *Translator's note.* "Origen Against Celsus", trans. Frederick Crombie, in *The Ante-Nicene Fathers: Translations of The Writings of the Fathers down to A.D. 325*, ed. Alexander Roberts, James Donaldson, and A. Cleveland Coxe (New York: Charles Scribner's Sons, 1913), vol. iv, pp. 635–6 (book 7, chapter 62).

11. Marcel Simon, *Recherches d'histoire judéo-chrétienne* (Paris: Mouton & Co., 1962); see also Marcel Simon, "La polémique anti-juive de S. Jean Chrysostome et le mouvement judaïsant d'Antioch", in Édouard Dumont et al., *Mélanges Franz Cumont* (Bruxelles: L'Institut de philologie et d'histoire orientales et slaves, 1936).

12. *Translator's note.* Cf. the discussion of the Sicarii in Flavius Josephus, "The Wars of the Jews, or, the History of the Destruction of Jerusalem", in *The Complete Works of Flavius Josephus*, pp. 623–5 (book 2, chapter 13).

13. *Translator's note. Horace Satires and Epistles; Perseus Satires*, trans. Niall Rudd (London: Penguin, 2005), 34 (Satire 1.9).

14. Petronius, *Satyricon*, 371.

15. Molly Whittaker, *Jews and Christians: Graeco-Roman Views* (Cambridge: Cambridge University Press, 1984), 82.

16. *Translator's note.* Pliny the Elder, *The Natural History of Pliny*, trans. John Bostock and Henry T. Riley (London: Henry G. Bohn, 1855), vol. iii, p. 176 (book 13, chapter 9).

17. *Translator's note.* Quoted by Flavius Josephus, in "Against Apion", p. 803 (book 1).

18. *Translator's note. Martial Epigrams*, trans. Walter C. A. Ker (London: William Heinemann, 1925), vol i, p. 443 (7.30).

19. *Translator's note.* Tacitus, *The Histories*, trans. W. Hamilton Fyfe (Oxford: Clarendon Press, 1912), vol. i, p. 207 (5.5).

20. *Translator's note.* Ibid. vol. i, p. 216 (5.13).

21. *Translator's note.* From Vaneigem's French.

22. David Rokeah, *Jews, Pagans, and Christians in Conflict* (Jerusalem: The Magnus Press, 1982), 210.

23. Eisenberg, op. cit. 179. [*Translator's note.* Philostratus, *Life of Apollonius of Tyana*, ed. and trans. F. C. Conybeare (Cambridge, MA: Harvard University Press, 1912) vol. i, p. 541 (5.33).]

24. Deschner, op. cit. 117 sq.

THE JUDEAN SECTS

1. Dubourg, *L'Invention de Jésus*, i. 266.

2. Marcel Simon, *Les Sectes juives au temps de Jésus* (Paris: Presses universitaires de France, 1960); E. M. Laperrousaz, *L'Attente du messie en Palestine à la veille et au début de l'ère chrétienne* (Paris: A. et J. Picard, 1982).

3. Flavius Josephus, *Antiquités judaiques*, book 17, chapter 10. [*Translator's note.* "Antiquities of the Jews" in *The Complete Works of Flavius Josephus*, p. 476.]

4. Flavius Josephus, *La Guerre des juifs*, trans. Pierre Savinel and Pierre Vidal-Naquet (Paris: Éditions de Minuit, 1977), book 2, chapter 4. [*Translator's note.* "The War of the Jews", p. 611.]

5. *Translator's note.* 2 Samuel, 24: 2: "Go through all the tribes of Israel, from Dan to Beersheba, and number the people, that I may know the number of the people".

6. Flavius Josephus, *La Guerre des juifs*, book 2, chapter 8. [*Translator's note.* "The War of the Jews", in *The Complete Works of Flavius Josephus*, p. 614.]

7. Flavius Josephus, *Antiquités judaiques*, book 12, chapter 10. [*Translator's note.* "Antiquities of the Jews", p. 476. The textual interpolation here appears in Whiston's translation.]

8. *Translator's note.* "The War of the Jews", p. 483 (book 18, chapter 1).

9. *Translator's note.* Ibid. pp. 483-4 (book 18, chapter 1).

10. Flavius Josephus, *La Guerre des juifs*, book 18, chapter 1. [*Translator's note.* "The War of the Jews", pp. 484-5.]

11. *Translator's note.* See Acts 21: 20.

12. *Translator's note.* This is why he sometimes refers to himself in the third person.

13. *Translator's note.* In Jeroboam. Cf. I Kings 12: 28.

14. Flavius Josephus, *La Guerre des juifs*, book 4, chapter 1. [*Translator's note.* "The War of the Jews", pp. 674-5.]

15. Yadin, *The Ben Sira Scroll from Masada*, op. cit.

16. *Translator's note.* This French word can mean a two-sided coin—a 'doubloon'—or a typographic double.

THE MEN OF THE COMMUNITY, OR THE ESSENES

1. André Dupont-Sommer, *Les écrits esséniens découverts près de la mer Morte* (Paris: Payot, 1980), 408; Hadot, op. cit. 35.

2. Jean Marquès-Rivière, *Histoire des sectes et des sociétés secrètes* (Paris, 1972), 92.

3. Jean-Claude Picard, "Histoire des bienheureux du temps de Jérémie",

in *Pseudépigraphes de l'Ancien Testament et manuscrits de la mer Morte*, ed. Marc Philonenko (Presses universitaries de France, 1967), 34.

4. *Translator's note.* Also known as *War Rule*, *Rule of War* and the *War Scroll*.

5. Félicien de Saulcy, *Dictionnaire des antiquités bibliques, traitant de l'archéologie sacrée, des monuments hébraïques de toutes les époques* (Paris: Migne, 1859).

6. Jean Doresse, *Les livres secrets des gnostiques d'Egypte* (Paris: Plon, 1958–9), ii. 328.

7. Dubourg, *L'invention de Jésus*, op. cit. ii.

8. *Translator's note.* "Commentary on Habakkuk (1QpHab)", in, *The Dead Sea Scrolls in English*, trans. Geza Vermes (3rd edn., Sheffield: JSOT Press, 1987), 284. The textual emendations here are Vermes's.

9. Jean-Marc Rosenstiehl (ed.), *L'Apocalypse d'Élie* (Paris: Librairie Orientaliste, 1972), 69.

10. *Pseudépigraphes de l'Ancien Testament et manuscrits de la mer Morte*, ed. Marc Philonenko (Paris: Presses universitaries de France, 1967), vol. i.

11. *Translator's note.* Note well that excerpts from "The Preaching of Peter" only appear in Clement of Alexandria's *Stromata*, while the *Kerygmata Petrou* (*The Sermons of Peter*) are another name for the Homilies attributed to Clement of Rome (the *Clementine Homilies*).

12. Annie Jaubert, *La Date de la Cène: Calendrier biblique et liturgie chrétienne* (Paris: Lecoffre, 1957).

13. Franco Michelini Tocci, *I manoscritti del mar Morto* (Bari: Laterza, 1967).

14. Jean Duhaime, "Étude comparative de 4QM^a FGG. *1–3* et *1QM*", *Revue de Qumrân*, 14/55 (Aug. 1990).

15. *Translator's note.* Pliny the Elder, *The Natural History of Pliny*, trans. John Bostock and Henry T. Riley (London: Henry G. Bohn, 1855), vol. i, p. 431 (book 5, chapter 15).

16. Bernard de Montfaucon, *Lettres pour et contre, sur la fameuse question, si les solitaires, appelés Therapeutes, dont a parlé Philon le Juif, etaient chrétiens* (Paris, 1712).

17. Dupont-Sommer, *Les écrits esséniens*, op. cit. 16. [*Translator's note.* Translated from the French as quoted by Vaneigem.]

18. *Translator's note.* *The Complete Book of Enoch: Standard English Version*, ed. and trans. Jay Winter (Winter Publications, 2015), book 2, chapter 2.

19. *Translator's note.* From Vaneigem's French.

20. Philonenko, op. cit.

21. *Translator's note.* I have been unable to find this passage in "The Rule Annex",

ed. A. Dupont-Sommer and trans. G. Vermes, *The Essene Writings from Qumran* (Oxford: Basil Blackwell, 1961), and have therefore translated it from Vaneigem's French.

22. Marc Philonenko, *Les Interpolations chrétiennes des testaments des douze patriarches et les manuscrits de Quomrân* (Paris: Presses universitaires de France, 1960), 31.

23. Ibid. 20. [*Translator's note*. "Benjamin" in *The Testaments of the Twelve Patriarchs*, trans. R. H. Charles (London: Adam and Charles Black, 1908), 214 (chapter 10). The textual emendations here are Charles's.]

24. Joseph A. Fitzmyer, "The Qumran Scrolls and the New Testament after Forty Years", *Revue de Qumrân*, 13/49–52 (Oct.1988), 613.

25. *Translator's note*. *The Complete Book of Enoch*, book 2, chapter 2.

26. *Translator's note*. Ibid.

27. Marc Philonenko, *Les Interpolations chrétiennes*, 29. [*Translator's note*. "Joseph", in *The Testaments of the Twelve Patriarchs*, trans. R. H. Charles (London: Adam and Charles Black, 1908), 194 (chapter 18). The emendation here is Charles's.]

28. *Translator's note*. From Vaneigem's French.

29. Dupont-Sommer, op. cit. 377. [*Translator's note*. Note that Dupont-Sommer cites "Isaiah, 3, 9, 12".]

30. *Translator's note*. From Vaneigem's French.

31. Dupont-Sommer, op. cit. 373. [*Translator's note*. See Isaiah 61: 1.]

32. Id., *Observations sur le Manuel de discipline decouvert près de la mer Morte* (Paris: Librairie Adrien-Maisonneuve, 1951).

33. *Translator's note*. Unable to find these passages in *The Book of Enoch*, trans. R. H. Charles (London: SPCK, 1917), I have translated them from Vaneigem's French.

34. *Translator's note*. "The Community Rule (1Qs)", in *The Dead Sea Scrolls in English*, 77.

35. Dupont-Sommer, op. cit. 384. [*Translator's note*. "The Community Rule", 67.]

36. J. L. Teicher, "The Teaching of the Pre-Pauline Church in the Dead Sea Scrolls", *Journal of Jewish Studies*, 3/3 (1952).

37. Dupont-Sommer, *Les écrits esséniens*, op. cit. 235.

38. *Translator's note*. Matthew 16: 18.

39. *Translator's note*. "The Community Rule", 78.

40. *The Rule of War*, 11, 6–8; Picard, "Histoire des bienheureux du temps de Jérémie", op. cit. 4. [*Translator's note*. "The Community Rule", 78–9.]

41. Dupont-Sommer, *Observations*, 24. [*Translator's note*. "The Community Rule", 69.]

42. *Translator's note*. "According to Shahrastani, Arius borrowed his doctrine of a

Messiah Angel from the ancient sect of Maqaribe (= Magharia), plausibly identified with the Essenes". William H. Brownlee, "Messianic Motifs of Qumran and the New Testament", *New Testament Studies*, 3/3 (May 1957), 195–210.

43. *Translator's note.* From Vaneigem's French.

44. Jarl E. Fossum, "The Name of God and the Angel of the Lord: The Origins of the Idea of Intermediation in Gnosticism", Diss. (Utrecht University, 1982), 154.

45. *Translator's note.* From Vaneigem's French.

46. *Translator's note.* From Vaneigem's French.

47. D. Barthélemy and J. T. Milik, *Discoveries in the Judean Desert, I Qumran Cave 1* (Oxford: Clarendon Press, 1955).

48. *Translator's note.* Source unknown, translated from Vaneigem's French.

49. Mario Erbetta, *Gli apocrifi del Nuovo Testamento* (Turin: Marietti, 1966–81), vol. iii.

THE BAPTIST MOVEMENT OF THE SAMARITAN MESSIAH DUSIS/DOSITHEOS

1. J. Massingberd Ford, "Can We Exclude Samaritan Influence from Qumran?", *Revue de Qumrân*, 6/21 (Feb. 1967), 109 sq.

2. Stanley Isser, *The Dositheans: A Samaritan Sect in Late Antiquity* (Leiden: E. J. Brill, 1976); Thomas Caldwell, "Dositheos Samaritanus", *Kairos*, 4 (1962), 105 sq; R. McL. Wilson, "Simon, Dositheus and the Dead Sea Scroll", *Zeitschrift für Religions- und Geistesgeschichte*, 9/1 (1957).

3. Eduard Vilmar, *Abulfathi annales samaritani* (Gotha: Perthes, 1865).

4. Fossum, "The Name of God and the Angel of the Lord", 37.

5. Ibid. 36 and 37.

6. Ibid. 48. [*Translator's note.* From Vaneigem's French.]

7. Michael Goulder, "The Two Roots of the Christian Myth", in *The Myth of God Incarnate*, ed. John Hick (London: SCM Press, 1977).

8. *Translator's note.* The *Kitāb Al-Tarīkh of Abū 'l-Fath*, ed. and trans. Paul Stenhouse (Sydney: Mandelbaum Trust, University of Sydney, 1985), 224.

9. Oscar Cullmann, *Le Problème littéraire et historique du roman pseudo-Clémentin: Étude sur le rapport entre le gnosticisme et le judéo-christianisme* (Félix Alcan: Paris 1930), 184. [*Translator's note.* Note well the different phrasing of this passage found in the *Clementine Homilies*; see homily 17, chapter 4, trans. James Donaldson, in *The Ante-Nicene Fathers: Translations of The Writings of the Fathers down to A.D. 325*, ed. Alexander Roberts, James Donaldson, and A. Cleveland Coxe, (Buffalo, NY: Christian Literature Publishing Co., 1886), vol. viii, pp. 318–9: "For the framer of the world was

known to Adam whom He had made, and to Enoch who pleased him, and to Noah who was seen to be just by Him; likewise to Abraham, and Isaac, and Jacob; also to Moses, and the people, and the whole world. But Jesus, the teacher of Peter himself, came and said, 'No one knew the Father except the Son'".]

10. Vilmar, op. cit. 160.

11. Quoted by Fossum, op. cit. 245. [*Translator's note.* This was the last of the ten plagues that God brought down upon the Egyptians. It is still part of modern Jewish celebrations of the Passover.]

12. Ibid. 39.

SIMON OF SAMARIA AND GNOSTIC RADICALISM

1. *Translator's note.* In what follows, all quotations from the *Elenchos* are taken from Hippolytus, "The Refutation of All Heresies", trans. J. H. MacMahon, in *The Ante-Nicene Fathers: Translations of The Writings of the Fathers down to A.D. 325*, ed. Alexander Roberts, James Donaldson, and A. Cleveland Coxe (New York: Charles Scribner's Sons, 1888), vol. v. At various points MacMahon draws attention in his editorial notes to biblical quotations within the text of the "Refutation". At such moments I have, unless otherwise indicated, substituted in the equivalent verse as rendered in the English Standard Version and supplied the verse reference in an endnote. As for Vaneigem, his source is Hippolytus, *Philosophumena, ou, Réfutation de toutes les hérésies*, trans A. Siouville (Paris: Rieder, 1928).

2. Jean-Marie A. Salles-Dabadie, *Recherches sur Simon le Mage: L'Apophasis Megalè* (Paris: J. Gabalda et Cie, 1969), 10.

3. Ibid. 15. [*Translator's note.* "The Refutation of All Heresies", p. 75 (book 6, chapter 4).]

4. Ibid. [*Translator's note.* Ibid.]

5. Ibid. [*Translator's note.* Ibid.]

6. Ibid. 21. [*Translator's note.* Ibid. p. 76 (book 6, chapter 7).]

7. Salles-Dabadie, *Recherches sur Simon le Mage*, 25.

8. Ibid. [*Translator's note.* "The Refutation of All Heresies", p. 77 (book 6, chapter 9).]

9. Ibid. 27–9. [*Translator's note.* "The Refutation of All Heresies", pp. 77–8 (book 6, chapter 9).]

10. *Translator's note.* Homer, *The Odyssey*, trans. Robert Fagles (New York, Penguin Books, 1996).

11. *Translator's note.* MacMahon notes the reference here to Isaiah 2: 4: "they shall beat their swords into ploughshares, | and their spears into pruning hooks".

12. Salles-Dabadie, *Recherches sur Simon le Mage*, 33. [*Translator's note.* "The

Refutation of All Heresies", p. 78 (book 6, chapter 11).]

13. Ibid. 35. [*Translator's note.* "The Refutation of All Heresies", p. 79 (book 6, chapter 12).]

14. Ibid. 35–7. [*Translator's note.* Ibid. 79.]

15. *Translator's note.* "The First Apology of Justin", trans. Marcus Dods and George Reith, in *The Ante-Nicene Fathers: The Writings of the Fathers down to A.D. 325*, ed. Alexander Roberts, James Donaldson, and A. Cleveland Coxe (Buffalo, NY: Christian Literature Publishing Company, 1887), i. 171.

16. Fossum, op. cit. 160.

17. Jacques Annequin, *Recherches sur l'acte magique et ses represéntations (Ier et IIe siècles après J. C.)* (Paris: Les Belles Lettres, 1979), 16.

18. Ibid. 17.

19. Ibid. [*Translator's note.* Mishnah Chagigah 2:1, in *Hebraic Literature: Translations from the Talmud, Midrashim and Kabbala*, ed. and trans. Maurice H. Harris (New York: Tudor Publishing, 1943), 61.]

20. *Translator's note.* From Vaneigem's French.

21. Jacques Ménard (ed.), *Les Textes de Nag Hammadi: Colloque du Centre d'histoire des religions, Strasbourg, 23–25 octobre 1974* (Leiden: E. J. Brill, 1975), 127 and 128. [*Translator's note.* "Asclepius 21–29", trans. James Brashler, Peter A. Dirkse and Douglas M. Parrott, in *The Nag Hammadi Library in English*, ed. James M. Robinson (rev. edn., San Francisco: 1990), 332.]

22. [*Translator's note.* "A time will come [when] darkness will be preferred to light and death will be preferred to life" ("Asclepius 21–29", 334–5.]

23. Irenaeus, *Contre les hérésies: Mise en lumière et réfutation de la prétendue 'Connaissance'*, trans. François Sagnard (Paris: Éditions du Cerf, 1979–82), book 1, chapter 31: 2 [*Translator's note.* Irenaeus, "Against Heresies", trans. Alexander Roberts and William Rambaut, in *The Ante-Nicene Fathers*, i. 358. Originally written in Greek around 180, the *Elenchos kai anatropē tēs pseudōnymou gnōseōs* (literally *On the Detection and Overthrow of the So-Called Gnosis*) was later translated into Latin as *Adversus haereses (Against Heresies)*.]

24. Jean-Marie Sevrin, "Les noces spirituelles dans l'Evangile selon Philippe", *Museon*, 87/1–2 (1974), 157. [*Translator's note.* Translated from the French as quoted by Vaneigem.]

25. Armand Delatte, *Études sur la magie grecque* (Louvain: Fontemoing, 1914), xviii, 75.

26. W. Köller, *Archiv für Religionswissenschaft*, 8 (1915), 229.

27. Irenaeus, op. cit. book 1, chapter 24: 1–2.

28. Robert McQueen Grant, *Gnosticism and Early Christianity* (New York: Columbia University Press, 1959), 15–7.

29. Michel Tardieu, "Le Titre du deuxième écrit du Codex VI", *Museon*, 87 (1974), 530.

30. *Translator's note*. I have been unable to locate the precise hymn quoted here, but it is similar to part of the Nag Hammadi text "The Thunder, Perfect Mind" that has come to be called The Hymn of Isis, ed. Douglas M. Parrott and trans. George W. MacRae, in *The Nag Hammadi Library in English*: "I am the < mother > and the daughter. | I am the members of my mother. | I am the barren one and many are her sons. | I am she whose wedding is great, and I have not taken a husband. | I am the midwife and she who does not bear. | I am the solace of my labor pains. | I am the bride and the bridegroom, and it is my husband who begot me. | I am the mother of my father and the sister of my husband, and he is my offspring. | I am the slave of him who prepared me. | I am the ruler of my offspring. But he is the one who begot me before the time on a birthday. | And he is my offspring [in] (due) time, | and my power is from him" (297–8). The textual emendations here are Parrott and MacRae's.

THE PHALLIC AND SYMBIOTIC CULTS

1. *Translator's note*: "fiery serpents" in the English Standard Version.

2. *Translator's note*: "fiery serpents" in the English Standard Version.

3. *Translator's note*: "to burn their sons and their daughters in the fire" in the English Standard Version.

4. Walter Louis Dulière, *De la dyade à l'unité par la triade: Préhistoire de la religion biblique, l'avenir du divin* (Paris: A. Maisonneuve, 1965), 76.

5. *Translator's note*. Avodah Zara, 22 b, trans. Rabbi Adin Even-Israel Steinsaltz in *Koren Talmud Bavli: The Noé Edition*, xxxii: *Avoda Zara Horayot* (Jerusalem: Koren Publishers, 2017).

6. Walter Louis Dulière, *De la dyade à l'unité par la triade*, op. cit. [*Translator's note*. Translated from the French as quoted by Vaneigem.]

7. Ibid.

8. Jacques Matter, *Histoire critique du gnosticisme: Et de son influence sur les sectes religieuses et philosophiques des six premiers siècles de l'ère chrétienne* (Paris: Levrault, 1828), ii. 53.

9. *Translator's note*. "Origen Against Celsus", p. 587 (book 6, chapter 30).

10. Fossum, op. cit. 268.

11. Quoted by Hans Leisegang, *Die Gnosis* (Stuttgart: Kröner, 1941), translated by Jean Gouillard as *La Gnose* (Paris: Payot, 1951), 81.

12. Delatte, op. cit. 78.

13. *Translator's note.* Greek for 'the all is one'.

14. *Translator's note.* Cf. Deuteronomy, 33: 17.

15. *Translator's note.* "The Refutation of All Heresies", p. 57 (book 5, chapter 4). The internal quotation is from Genesis 2: 10.

16. *Translator's note.* In MacMahon's translation of the "Refutation", this name is spelled Edem. It is a principle, not the name of the garden.

17. Leisegang, op. cit. 100. [*Translator's note.* Leisegang's final quotation here is from the *Elenchos*, book 5, chapter 9 ("The Refutation of All Heresies", p. 57).]

18. *Elenchos*, book 5, chapter 1. [*Translator's note.* "The Refutation of All Heresies", p. 48 (book 5, chapter 1).]

19. *Translator's note.* "The Refutation of All Heresies", p. 48 (book 5, chapter 2).

20. *Translator's note.* Here and elsewhere in passages from the "Refutation of All Heresies", "he says" refers to an actual or hypothetical member of the heretical sect in question.

21. Leisegang, op. cit. 103. [*Translator's note.* "The Refutation of All Heresies", p. 64 (book 5, chapter 12).]

22. *Translator's note.* "The Refutation of All Heresies", p. 47

23. *Translator's note.* Translated from Vaneigem's French.

24. Serge Hutin, *Les Gnostiques* (Paris: Presses universitaires de France, 1978).

25. Antoine Dupont-Sommer, *La doctrine gnostique de la lettre 'wâw' d'après une lamelle araméene inédite* (Paris: Librairie Orientaliste Paul Geuther, 1946).

26. *Translator's note.* "The Refutation of All Heresies", p. 62.

27. Leisegang, op. cit. 104.

28. Following Leisegang, op. cit. 101.

29. *Translator's note.* The next seven blocks of indented quotations are taken from "The Refutation of All Heresies", pp. 62–3 (book 5, chapter 11).

30. *Translator's note.* In the version of the *Elenchos* used by Vaneigem, "Virgin" is substituted for "rod".

31. *Translator's note.* Genesis 33: 10.

32. *Translator's note.* Genesis 10: 9.

33. *Translator's note.* John 1: 1–4.

34. *Translator's note.* For the internal quotation here I have substituted in Homer, *The*

Odyssey, trans. Robert Fagles (New York: Penguin Books, 1996), 5.204–7.

35. *Translator's note.* "Refutation of All Heresies", pp. 60–1.

36. *Translator's note.* From Vaneigem's French, since I have been unable to trace this passage in MacMahon's translation of the "Refutation of All Heresies". Vaneigem gives as a reference *"Elenchos,* V, 16, 14–16".

37. *Translator's note.* "In that day the LORD with his hard and great and strong sword will punish Leviathan the fleeing serpent, Leviathan the twisting serpent, and he will slay the dragon that is in the sea".

38. *Translator's note.* The Panarion *of Epiphanius of Salamis: Book I (Sects 1–46),* trans. Frank Williams (2nd edn., Leiden: Brill, 2009), p. 265–6.

39. *Translator's note.* "Tractate I", in *Priscillian of Avila: The Complete Works,* ed. and trans. Marco Conti (Oxford: Oxford University Press, 2010), 63.

40. *Translator's note.* "Refutation of All Heresies", pp. 70–2 (book 5, chapter 21). Translation slightly modified: a few spelling mistakes have been corrected.

41. *Translator's note.* The seven other names are missing from the manuscript.

42. *Translator's note.* In the version of the *Elenchos* used by Vaneigem, Leviathan is replaced by Kanithan.

43. *Translator's note.* Genesis 2: 8.

44. *Translator's note.* In the version of the *Elenchos* used by Vaneigem, "spirit" is replaced by *"pneuma".*

45. *Translator's note.* Genesis 1: 28.

46. *Translator's note.* MacMahon notes here the similarity to Psalm 118: 19. In the English Standard Version: "Open to me the gates of righteousness, that I may enter through them and give thanks to the LORD".

47. *Translator's note.* Psalm 118: 20.

48. *Translator's note.* Psalm 110: 1.

49. *Translator's note.* The closing bracket here is my correction.

50. *Translator's note.* In the version of the *Elenchos* used by Vaneigem, Venus is replaced by Aphrodite.

51. *Translator's note.* Genesis 2: 16–7.

52. *Translator's note.* MacMahon notes the similarity to John 19: 26. In the English Standard Version: "Woman, behold, your son!"

53. "The Refutation of All Heresies", p. 72 (book 5, chapter 21).

54. *Translator's note.* "Eden" in Leisegang's original text.

55. *Translator's note.* "Eden" in Leisegang's original text.

56. *Translator's note.* Friedrich Nietzsche, *Also sprach Zarathustra* (1885), translated by Thomas Common as *Thus Spake Zarathustra* (London: G. Allen & Unwin, 1911): "Let man fear woman when she loveth: then maketh she every sacrifice, and everything else she regardeth as worthless. Let man fear woman when she hateth: for man in his innermost soul is merely evil; woman, however, is mean" (76).

57. *Translator's note.* "Eden" in Leisegang's original text.

58. *Translator's note.* "Eden" in Leisegang's original text.

59. *Translator's note.* "Eden" in Leisegang's original text.

60. Leisegang, op. cit. 115.

61. *Translator's note.* Isaiah 44: 6. I have substituted in here the verse as rendered in the English Standard Version.

62. *Translator's note. The* Panarion *of Epiphanius of Salamis: Book I*, p. 85.

63. *Translator's note.* Ibid.

64. *Translator's note.* The love feast.

65. *Translator's note. The* Panarion *of Epiphanius of Salamis: Book I*, p. 93–4.

66. *Translator's note.* "The Gospel of Thomas (II ,2)", trans. Thomas O. Lambdin, in *The Nag Hammadi Library in English*, 133.

67. Robert Graves, *La Déesse blanche: Un mythe poétique expliqué par l'histoire*, trans. Guy Trévoux (Paris: Éditions du Rocher, 1979). [*Translator's note.* This book was originally published in English in 1948 as *The White Goddess: A Historical Grammar of Poetic Myth.*]

68. Leisegang, op. cit. 133.

69. Ibid. 135 and 136.

70. *Translator's note. The* Panarion *of Epiphanius of Salamis: Book I*, p. 94.

71. *Translator's note. The* Panarion *of Epiphanius of Salamis: Book I*, p. 94.

72. *Translator's note. The* Panarion *of Epiphanius of Salamis: Book I*, p. 95.

73. *Translator's note.* The word 'Aeon' is used in the French version: "l'Archonte qui a créé l'Aeon".

74. *Translator's note.* "On Marriage (*Stromateis*, III)", in *The Library of Christian Classics*, ii: *Alexandrian Christianity: Selected Translations of Clement and Origen*, ed. and trans. John Ernest Leonard Oulton and Henry Chadwick (Philadelphia: Westminster Press, 1954), pp. 61, 83, 70 (book 3, chapter 4: 45; book 3, chapter 13: 92; and book 3, chapter 9: 66, respectively). Ellipses separating these passages are mine.

75. *Translator's note. The* Panarion *of Epiphanius of Salamis: Book I*, p. 88.

76. *Translator's note. The* Panarion *of Epiphanius of Salamis: Book I*, p. 91.

77. *Translator's note.* "Others are not ashamed to speak of a 'Gospel of Eve'. For they sow <their stunted> crop in her name because, supposedly, she obtained the food of knowledge by revelation from the serpent which spoke to her" (*The* Panarion *of Epiphanius of Salamis: Book I*, p. 92 (ii. 26. 2,6).

78. *Translator's note.* These are the Good God and Barbelo, the latter hardened and diminished by the loss of her power, respectively.

79. *The* Panarion *of Epiphanius of Salamis: Book I*, p. 92.

THREE ESSENO-CHRISTIAN CHRISTS

1. Fossum, op. cit. 297.

2. Ibid. 307. [*Translator's note.* According to the English Standard Edition, the texts of Colossians 1: 15 and 1: 18 read "He is the image of the invisible God" and "he is the head of the body, the church", respectively.]

3. Joseph. A. Fitzmyer, "The Contribution of Qumran Aramaic to the Study of the New Testament", *New Testament Studies*, 20/4 (July 1974), 391.

4. Fossum, op. cit. 290.

5. Ibid. 312.

6. Ibid.

7. John D. Turner, "Sethian Gnosticism: A Literary History", in *Nag Hammadi, Gnosticism, and Early Christianity*, ed. Charles W. Hedrick and Robert Hodgson, Jr. (Peabody, MA: Hendrickson Publishers, 1988), 55–86.

8. Henri-Charles Puech, *Les Nouveaux écrits gnostiques découverts en Haute-Egypte (premier inventaire et essai d'identification)* (Boston: Byzantine Institute, 1950), 127; Michel Tardieu, "Les livres mis sous le nom de Seth et les séthiens de l'hérésiologie", in *Gnosis and Gnosticism: Papers Read at the Seventh International Conference on Patristic Studies (Oxford, September 8th-13th 1975)*, ed. Martin Krause (Leiden: E. J. Brill, 1977).

9. Gedaliahu G. Stroumsa, "Aher: A Gnostic", in *Rediscovery of Gnosticism: Proceedings of the International Conference on Gnosticism at Yale, New Haven, Connecticut, March 28–31, 1978*, ed. Bentley Layton (Leiden: E. J. Brill, 1986), vol. ii.

10. *Translator's note.* The next three blocks of quoted material come from "The Refutation of All Heresies", pp. 65–6 (book 5, chapter 14).

11. *Translator's note.* MacMahon suggests Psalm 29: 3. In the English Standard Version: "The voice of the LORD is over the waters; the God of glory thunders, the LORD, over many waters".

12. Jean Doresse, *Les Livres secrets des gnostiques d'Égypte* (Paris: Libraire Plon, 1958), 211. [*Translator's note*. "Eugnostos the Blessed" (combining III,3 and V,1), trans. Douglas M. Parrott, in *The Nag Hammadi Library in English*. The interpolations here are Parrott's.]

13. *Rediscovery of Gnosticism*, op. cit. ii. 656.

14. Fitzmyer, "The Qumran Scrolls and the New Testament after Forty Years", op. cit. 619.

15. Jean Carmignac, "Le Document de Qumran sur Melkisédeq", *Revue de Qumrân*, 7/3 (Dec. 1970), 343 sq.

16. *Translator's note*. Cf. Luke 2: 10–1: "Fear not, for behold, I bring you good news of great joy that will be for all the people. For unto you is born this day in the city of David a Saviour, who is Christ the Lord".

17. Henry Corbin, "Nécessité de l'angélologie", in *L'Ange et l'homme* (Paris: A. Michel, 1978), 38. [*Translator's note*. The Complete Book of Enoch, op. cit. book 3, chapter 4.]

18. Ibid. 39.

19. André Vaillant, *Les Livre des secrets d'Hénoch*, Slavic text and French translation (Paris: Institut d'études slaves, 1976); Michael A. Knibb (ed.), *The Ethiopic Book of Enoch: A New Edition in the Light of the Aramaic Dead Sea Fragments* (Oxford: Clarendon Press, 1978), 2 vols.; R. H. Charles (trans.), *The Book of Enoch* (London: SPCK, 1917).

20. *Translator's note*. Hebrews 7: 15–6: "This becomes even more evident when another priest arises in the likeness of Melchizedek, who has become a priest, not on the basis of a legal requirement concerning bodily descent, but by the power of an indestructible life".

21. *Translator's note*. "The Testament of Levi", in *The Testaments of the Twelve Patriarchs*, trans. R. H. Charles (London: Adam and Charles Black, 1908), 62 (chapter 18).

22. Martin Werner, *Die Entstehung des christlichen Dogmas: Problemgeschichtlich dargestellt* (Bern: P. Haupt, 1953), 344.

23. *Translator's note*. Polygraphs are nonspecialized authors of historical texts.

24. Iosif Aronovič Kryvelev, *Le Christ: Mythe ou réalité?* (Moscow: *Social Sciences Today* Editorial Board, 1987).

25. *Translator's note*. "Letter 10, 96: Pliny to the Emperor Trajan", trans. William Harris, in *The Historians of Ancient Rome: An Anthology of the Major Writings*, ed. Ronald Mellor (2nd edn., New York: Routledge, 2004), 537.

26. Justin, *Dialogue avec le juif Tryphon*, 49. [*Translator's note*. In existing English-language translations this passage is considerably shorter: "But Christ—if He has

indeed been born, and exists anywhere—is unknown, and does not even know himself, and has no power until Elias come to anoint Him, and make Him manifest to all". "Dialogue of Justin, Philosopher and Martyr, with Trypho, a Jew", trans. Marcus Dods and George Reith, in *The Ante-Nicene Fathers*, vol. i, p. 199 (chapter 8).]

27. Marthe de Chambrun Ruspoli, *Le Retour du phénix* (Paris: Les Belles Lettres, 1982), 69.

28. Justin, op. cit. 48. [*Translator's note.* "Dialogue of Justin", p. 199 (chapter 8).]

29. Pierre de Labriolle, *La réaction païenne: Étude sur la polémique antichrétienne du 1er au IVe siècle* (Paris: L'Artisan du livre, 1934), 19. [*Translator's note.* Julian the Apostate, *Against the Galileans*, excerpted in Cyril of Alexandria, *Contra Julianum*, trans. Wilmer Cave Wright (1923) <https://www.tertullian.org/fathers/julian_apostate_galileans_1_text.htm>.]

30. *Translator's note.* German for 'cult legends'.

31. Hans von Soden, *Christentum und Kultur in der geschictlichen Entwicklung ihrer Beziehungen* (Tübingen: J. C. B. Mohr, 1933).

32. S. G. F. Brandon, *Jesus and the Zealots: A Study of the Political Factor in Primitive Christianity* (Manchester: Manchester University Press, 1967).

33. Robert Ambelain, *Jésus ou le mortel secret des templiers* (Paris: Robert Laffont, 1970).

34. Robert Graves, *La Déesse blanche*, op. cit. 66. [*Translator's note.* First published in English in 1948 as *The White Goddess*. Rather than translating the French translation back into English, I have quoted the original text (60).]

35. *Translator's note.* See Hyam Maccoby, *Revolution in Judaea: Jesus and the Jewish Resistance* (New York: Taplinger Publishing Company, 1981).

36. *Translator's note.* "The Refutation of All Heresies", p. 58.

37. *Translator's note.* Also known as *The Wisdom of Ben Sira*.

38. *Translator's note.* The *Wisdom of Ben Sira*, p. 262 (xv. 2–3).

39. Jacques Brill, *Lilith, ou, la mère obscure* (Paris: Payot, 1981).

40. Jean Doresse, *L'Evangile selon Thomas, ou les paroles secrètes de Jésus* (Paris: Librairie Plon, 1959).

41. Dubourg, *L'Invention du Jésus* (Paris: Gallimard, 1987), ii. 264.

42. *Translator's note.* "Gospel of the Hebrews", trans. Philipp Vielhauer and George Ogg, in *The Other Gospels: Non-Canonical Gospel Texts*, ed. Ron Cameron (Philadelphia: The Westminster Press, 1982), 85.

43. A. Dupont-Sommer, *La Doctrine gnostique de la lettre 'wâw' d'après une lamelle*

araméene inédite (Paris, 1961).

44. Leisegang, *La Gnose*, op. cit. 212. [*Translator's note*. In point of fact, it wasn't Ptolemy who wrote these words, but Irenaeus in his summary of the ideas held by Ptolemy's disciples. See Irenaeus, "Against Heresies", in *The Ante-Nicene Fathers*, vol. i, p. 318 (book 1, chapter 2: 6).]

45. Fossum, op. cit. 357.

46. *Translator's note*. Translated from Vaneigem's French.

47. Corbin, op. cit. 41.

48. *Translator's note*. From Vaneigem's French.

49. Dupont-Sommer, *Les écrits esséniens*, op. cit. 373. [*Translator's note*. Isaiah 61: 1.]

50. *Translator's note*. Isaiah 49: 1.

51. Cited by E. M. Laperrousaz, *Les manuscrits de la mer Morte* (Paris: Presses universitaires de France, 1961), 55. [*Translator's note*. I have been unable to locate this passage in the Book of Isaiah.]

52. Chambrun Ruspoli, op. cit. 79.

53. Hyam Maccoby, *Paul et l'invention du christianisme*, trans. Jean Gerber and Jean-Luc Allouche (Paris: Lieu commun, 1987), 60. [*Translator's note*. First published in English as Hyam Maccoby, *The Mythmaker: Paul and the Invention of Christianity* (New York: Harper & Row, 1986), 37.]

54. *Translator's note*. "The First Apology of Justin", p. 183.

55. *Translator's note*. Latin for 'for the greater glory of God'.

56. Dubourg, op. cit. ii. 46.

THE MESSIANIC SECTS OF JOSHUA/JESUS

1. Dubourg, *L'Invention de Jésus*, op. cit. ii. 157.

2. *Translator's note*. Epiphanius does not mention the Elchasaites at all; when he speaks of the people who "are neither Christians, Jews nor pagans" and who, "since they are just in the middle, [...] are nothing", he is referring to the Sampsaeans (*The* Panarion *of Epiphanius of Salamis: Books II and III. De Fide*, trans. Frank Williams (2nd edn., Leiden: Brill, 2013), p. 71 (iv. 53. 1,2)).

3. Gerard P. Luttikhuizen, *The Revelation of Elchasai: Investigations into the Evidence for a Mesopotamian Jewish Apocalypse of the Second Century and its Reception by Judeo-Christian Propagandists* (Tübingen: J. C. B. Mohr, 1985).

QUARRELS ABOUT PROPHETS AND APOSTLES

1. *Translator's note.* "Antiquities of the Jews", p. 491 (book 18, chapter 5). The second, third, and fourth interpolations here appear in Whiston's translation.

2. *Antiquitiés judaiques*, book 18, 116–8. [*Translator's note.* "Antiquities of the Jews", p. 491 (book 18, chapter 5).]

3. *Translator's note.* From Vaneigem's French.

4. *Translator's note.* From Vaneigem's French.

5. *Translator's note.* See John 1: 23.

6. *Translator's note.* "I will grant authority to my two witnesses" (Revelation 11: 3).

7. *Translator's note.* "Antiquities of the Jews", p. 539 (book 20, chapter 5).

8. *Translator's note.* Traditionally attributed to St. Luke the Evangelist.

9. Robert Eisenmann, *Maccabees, Zadokites, Christians and Qumran: A New Hypothesis of Qumran Origins* (Leiden: E. J. Brill, 1983).

10. *Translator's note.* "Antiquities of the Jews", p. 539 (book 20, chapter 5).

11. Henri Grégoire, Paul Orgels, Jacques Moreau, and André Maricq, *Les Persécutions dans l'empire romain* (Brussels: Palais des Académies, 1964).

12. *Translator's note.* "Acts of the Holy Apostle Thomas", trans. Alexander Walker, in *The Ante-Nicene Fathers*, vol viii.

13. *Translator's note.* Hermes Trismegistus, "<Discourse> of Hermes Trismegistus: Poimandres", in *Hermetica: The Greek Corpus Hermeticum and the Latin Asclepius in a New English Translation, with Notes and Introduction*, trans. Brian P. Copenhaver (Cambridge: Cambridge University Press, 1992): "But god immediately spoke a holy speech: 'Increase in increasing and multiply in multitude, all you creatures and craftworks, and let him <who> is mindful recognize that he is immortal, that desire is the cause of death, and let him recognize all that exists'" (4).

14. Jacques É. Ménard (ed. and trans.), *L'Evangile selon Thomas* (Leiden: E. J. Brill, 1975).

15. Grant, *Gnosticism and Early Christianity*, op. cit.

16. *Translator's note.* "The Gospel of Thomas (II ,2)", trans. Thomas O. Lambdin, in *The Nag Hammadi Library in English*: "These are the secret sayings which the living Jesus spoke and which Didymos Judas Thomas wrote down" (126).

17. Doresse, *L'Evangile selon Thomas*, op. cit.

18. *Translator's note.* Eusebius of Caesarea, "The Church History", trans. Arthur Cushman McGiffert, in *A Select Library of Nicene and Post-Nicene Fathers of the Christian Church: Second Series*, ed. Philip Schaff and Henry Wace (New York: Christian

Literature Publishing Company, 1890), vol. i, p. 104 (book 2, chapter 1: 4).

19. *Translator's note.* Ibid. (book 2, chapter 1: 2).

20. *Translator's note.* "The Stromata, or Miscellanies", trans. William Wilson, in *The Ante-Nicene Fathers*, ed. Alexander Roberts, James Donaldson, and A. Cleveland Coxe (New York: Charles Scribner's Sons, 1913), vol. ii, p. 301 (book 1, chapter 1). Note that this volume does not include an English translation of book 3.

21. Doresse, *L'Evangile selon Thomas*, op. cit. 88. [*Translator's note.* "The Gospel of Thomas (II ,2)", 127.]

22. Ibid. 31–5.

23. *Translator's note.* See 2 Corinthians 12: 4.

24. "The Refutation of All Heresies", p. 48.

25. *Translator's note.* Eusebius of Caesarea, "The Church History", p. 125 (book 2, chapter 23: 5).

26. *Translator's note.* Ibid. pp. 125–6 (book 2, chapter 23: 7 and 9).

27. *Translator's note.* "Antiquities of the Jews", p. 539.

28. Cullmann, op. cit. 82 and 83.

29. Ibid.

30. Ibid. 83.

31. *Translator's note.* "The Clementine Homilies", trans. Thomas Smith, in *The Ante-Nicene Fathers*, vol. viii, p. 236 (homily 2, chapter 38).

32. *Translator's note.* Ibid. p. 340 (homily 20, chapter 3).

33. Cited by Maccoby, *Paul et l'invention du christianisme*, op. cit. 260. [*Translator's note.* I have been unable to find this passage in either Maccoby or any other source.]

34. *Translator's note.* "The Clementine Homilies", p. 242 (homily 3, chapter 10).

35. *Translator's note.* Ibid. p. 232 (homily 2, chapter 18).

36. *Translator's note.* Galatians 2: 4.

37. *Translator's note.* Discovered by Samuel Stern in 1966 and studied by Shlomo Pines, this manuscript was eventually published as 'Abd al-Jabbār, *Critique of Christian Origins*, ed. and trans. Gabriel Said Reynolds and Samir Khalil Samir (Provo, UT: Brigham Young University Press, 2010).

38. Jean-Marc Rosenstiehl, "Le Portrait de l'Antichrist", in *Pseudépigraphes de l'ancien testament et manuscrits de la mer Morte*, i. 59. [*Translator's note.* I have been unable to locate this passage in Rosenstiehl's essay or any other source.]

39. *The* Panarion *of Epiphanius of Salamis: Book I*, p. 144.

40. Erbetta, *Gli apocrifi*, op. cit.

41. Cited by M. de Chambrun-Ruspoli, *Le Retour du Phénix*, op. cit. 165. [*Translator's note*. Morton Smith, *Clement of Alexandria and a Secret Gospel of Mark* (Cambridge, MA: Harvard University Press, 1973), 446.]

42. *Translator's note*. Deuteronomy 10: 16.

43. *Translator's note*. "The Epistle of Barnabas", in *The Apostolic Fathers*, trans. Joseph Barber Lightfoot and J. R. Harmer (London: Macmillan and Co., 1898), 281.

44. *Translator's note*. Ibid.

45. *Translator's note*. Hebrews 10: 10.

46. *Translator's note*. Hebrews 2: 7.

47. Prosper Alfaric, *Le problème de Jésus et les origines du christianisme* (Paris: Cercle Ernest-Renan, 1954), 21. [*Translator's note*. "Scourge" is an allusion to Hebrews 12: 6: "For the lord disciplines the ones he loves, and chastises every son whom he receives".]

48. Dubourg, op. cit. ii.149. [*Translator's note*. Cf. Frederick Nietzsche's characterization of Socrates as "the one who does not write" (*Twilight of the Idols*, trans. Duncan Large (Oxford: Oxford University Press, 2008)) and Jacques Derrida's comments on an image in which Socrates holds a stylus in *The Post Card: From Socrates to Freud and Beyond*, trans. Alan Bass (Chicago: University of Chicago Press, 1987)].

49. E. Mary Smallwood, *The Jews under Roman Rule from Pompey to Diocletian: A Study in Political Relations* (2nd edn., Leiden: E. J. Brill, 1976), 234.

50. Georges Ory, *Le Christ et Jésus* (Brussels: Éditions du Pavillon, 1968); Wayne A. Meeks, *The First Urban Christians: The Social World of the Apostle Paul* (New Haven: Yale University Press, 1983), 8.

51. *Translator's note*. Georges Ory, *Le Christ et Jésus* (Brussels: Éditions du Cercle d'Education Populaire, 1968).

52. Deschner, op. cit. iii. 99.

53. Dubourg, op. cit.

54. Deschner, op. cit. iii. 99.

55. Ibid. 100 and 101.

56. Ibid. 102.

57. Erbetta, op. cit.

58. *Translator's note*. Acts of the Apostles, 24: 14–5.

59. *Translator's note*. Note that the King James Version uses the word 'heresy' (derived from the Greek *hairèsis*): "after the way which they call heresy, so worship I the God of my fathers".

60. Jerome Murphy-O'Connor (ed.), *Paul and Qumran: Studies in New Testament*

Exegesis (London: Priory Press, 1968).

61. Dupont-Sommer, *Les écrits esséniens*, op. cit. 378 and 379.

62. *Translator's note.* From Vaneigem's French. But note well the translation of this line (iv. 3–4) in Philip R. Davies, *The Damascus Covenant: An Interpretation of the "Damascus Document"* (Sheffield: Journal for the Study of the Old Testament, 1983): "The sons of Zadok are the chosen ones of Israel, those 'called by name' who arise at the end of days" (241).

63. Cullmann, op. cit. 85.

64. *Translator's note. Horace Satires and Epistles; Perseus Satires*, trans. Niall Rudd (London: Penguin, 2005), 34 (Satire 1.9): "Do you want to affront the circumcised Jews?"

65. *Translator's note.* See 1 Timothy 1: 4.

66. Maccoby, op. cit. [*Translator's note.* See Maccoby, *The Mythmaker*, 195.]

67. *Translator's note.* Anthony C. Thiselton, *The First Epistle to the Corinthians: A Commentary on the Greek Text* (Grand Rapids, MI: William B. Eerdmans Publishing Company, 1997), 165, 231–2, translates this phrase as "the rulers of this world order".

68. *Translator's note.* In this passage, all interpolations apart from "known" (which is mine) are by Vaneigem.

69. Leisegang, 74.

70. *Translator's note.* See Colossians 2: 9.

71. *Translator's note.* See Galatians 4: 3.

72. *Translator's note.* The ellipsis is mine.

73. Elaine H. Pagels, *The Gnostic Gospels* (New York: Vintage Books, 1981), 15.

MARCION AND THE HELLENIZATION OF CHRISTIANITY

1. W. H. C. Frend, *Martyrdom and Persecution in the Early Church: A Study of a Conflict from the Maccabees to Donatus* (Oxford: Basil Blackwell, 1965), 222 sq.

2. Adolf von Harnack, *Marcion. Das Evangelium vom fremden Gott: Eine Monographie zur Geschichte der Grundlegung der katholischen* (Leipzig: J. C. Hinrichs, 1921).

3. *Translator's note.* Tertullian, "The Five Books Against Marcion", trans. Peter Holmes, in *The Ante-Nicene Fathers*, ed. Alexander Roberts, James Donaldson, and A. Cleveland Coxe (New York: Charles Scribner's Sons, 1918), vol. iii, p. 246 (book 5, chapter 17).

4. Hermann Raschke, *Die Werkstatt des Markusevangelisten: Eine neue Evangelientheorie* (Jena: E. Diedrichs, 1924).

5. Joseph Turmel, *Histoire des dogmes* (Paris: Rieder, 1931–6).

6. *Translator's note.* "Dialogue of Justin", op. cit. p. 219 (chapter 48). Note well Justin's response: "I know that the statement does appear to be paradoxical [...]. Now assuredly, Trypho, [...] [the proof] that this man is the Christ of God does not fail, though I be unable to prove that He existed formerly as Son of the Maker of all things, being God, and was born a man by the Virgin. But since I have certainly proved that this man is the Christ of God, whoever He be, even if I do not prove that He pre-existed, and submitted to be born a man of like passions with us, having a body, according to the Father's will; in this last matter alone is it just to say that I have erred, and not to deny that He is the Christ, though it should appear that He was born man of men, and [nothing more] is proved [than this], that He has become Christ by election". The emendations—but not the ellipses—here are by Dods and Reith.

7. Cited in Chambrun-Ruspoli, *Le Retour du phénix*, op. cit. 69. [*Translator's note.* The last sentence in this quotation does not appear in Dods and Reith's English translation.]

8. Leisegang, *La Gnose*, op. cit. 187 sq.

9. *Translator's note.* From Vaneigem's French.

10. Albert Huck, *Huck's Synopsis of the First Three Gospels*, ed. Ross L. Finney (Cincinnati: Jennings and Graham, 1907).

11. Turmel, op. cit.

12. *Translator's note.* From Vaneigem's French.

13. Deschner, iii.75. [*Translator's note.* From Vaneigem's translation of Deschner into French.]

THE INVENTORS OF A CHRISTIAN THEOLOGY

1. Eusebius of Caesarea, "Church History", p. 178 (book 4, chapter 7: 1–2).

2. Clement of Alexandria, *Les Stromates* (Paris, 1951), book 3, chapter 1: 1–3. [*Translator's note.* p. 40 (book 3, chapter 1: 1).]

3. *Translator's note.* "On Marriage (*Stromateis*, III)", pp. 40–1 (book 3, chapter 1: 2).

4. *Les Stromates*, book 3, chapter 1: 2–3 [*Translator's note.* "On Marriage (*Stromateis*, III)", p. 41.]

5. *Translator's note.* "The Stromata, or Miscellanies", pp. 423–4 (book 4, chapter 12).

6. *Translator's note.* "Who can bring a clean thing out of an unclean? | There is not one".

7. *Translator's note.* "The Stromata, or Miscellanies", p. 372 (book 2, chapter 19).

8. Leisegang, op. cit. 146.

9. *Elenchos*, book 7, chapter 20. [*Translator's note.* "The Refutation of All Heresies", p. 103 (book 7, chapter 8).]

10. Pseudo-Dionysius the Areopagite, "Théologie mystique", trans. Maurice de Gandillac, in *Oeuvres complètes* (Paris: Aubier, 1943). [*Translator's note.* "The Mystical Theology", in *The Works of Dionysius the Areopagite Part 1: Divine Names, Mystic Theology, Letters, &c.*, trans. John Parker (London, James Parker and Co., 1897), 136–7].

11. Irenaeus, op. cit. book 1, chapter 24. [*Translator's note.* Irenaeus, "Against Heresies", pp. 349–50 (book 1, chapter 24: 3–7). Apart from the first, the interpolations here are by Roberts and Rambaut.]

12. Campbell Bonner, *Studies in Magical Amulets, Chiefly Graeco-Egyptian* (Ann Arbor: University of Michigan Press, 1950).

13. Leisegang, op. cit. 171.

14. Ibid. 172.

15. Louis Rougier, *Celse contre les chrétiens: La réaction païenne sous l'empire romain* (Paris: Copernic, 1977), 13. [*Translator's note.* Letter of Hadrian to Servianus quoted in Ferdinand Gregorovius, *The Emperor Hadrian: A Picture of the Graeco-Roman World in His Time*, trans. Mary E. Robinson (London: Macmillan and Co., 1898). Gregorovius suggests that the "one God" is lucre.]

16. *Translator's note.* The Panarion *of Epiphanius of Salamis: Book I*, p. 170.

17. *Elenchos*, book 6, chapter 37. [*Translator's note.* "The Refutation of All Heresies", p. 93.]

18. *Elenchos*, book 6, chapter 32. [*Translator's note.* "The Refutation of All Heresies", p. 91.]

19. *Translator's note.* "The Stromata, or Miscellanies", p. 349 (book 2, chapter 3).

20. *Translator's note.* "The Treatise of the Resurrection (I, 4)", trans. Malcolm L. Peel, in *The Nag Hammadi Library in English*: "Do not think in part, O Rheginos, nor live in conformity with this flesh for the sake of unanimity, but flee from the divisions and the fetters, and already you have the resurrection" (56).

21. Clement of Alexandria, *Stromates*, book 3, chapter 7: 59. [*Translator's note.* "On Marriage (*Stromateis*, III)", p. 67.]

22. *Translator's note.* Quoted by Clement of Alexandria, "The Stromata, or Miscellanies", p. 425 (book 4, chapter 13).

23. *Elenchos* (book 8, chapter 7). [*Translator's note.* "The Refutation of All Heresies", p. 121.]

24. Cited by Leisegang, op. cit. 203 and 204.

25. Ptolemy, *Lettre à Flora*, ed. and trans. Gilles Quispel (Paris: Éditions du Cerf, 1949). [*Translator's note.* "Ptolemy's Epistle to Flora", in *The Gnostic Scriptures*, ed. and trans. Bentley Layton and David Brakke (2nd edn., New Haven: Yale University Press, 2021), p. 439 (33.3.1–33.3.2). The elision here is mine, but the bracketed interpolations are by the editors.]

26. *Translator's note.* Layton and Brakke here note the connection to Plato's *Timaeus*; see *Timaeus*, trans. Benjamin Jowett (Delhi: Lector House, 2019): 28c.

27. *Translator's note.* "Ptolemy's Epistle to Flora", pp. 443–5 (33.5.3–33.6.6). Bracketed interpolations are by Layton and Brakke unless otherwise indicated; elisions in square brackets are mine.

28. *Translator's note.* Exodus, 20: 13. I have substituted in here the verse as given in the English Standard Version.

29. *Translator's note.* Matthew 15: 4. I have substituted in here the verse as given in the English Standard Version.

30. *Translator's note.* This interpolation is taken from a footnote in Layton and Brakke's edition.

31. *Translator's note.* 1 Corinthians 5: 7. I have substituted in here the verse as given in the English Standard Version.

32. *Translator's note.* Exodus 20: 13–14. I have substituted in here the verses as given in the English Standard Version.

33. *Translator's note.* Exodus 21: 24. I have substituted in here the verse as given in the English Standard Version.

34. *Translator's note.* Matthew 5: 39. I have substituted in here the verse as given in the English Standard Version.

35. *Translator's note.* Ephesians 2: 15. I have substituted in here the verse as given in the English Standard Version.

36. *Translator's note.* Romans 7: 12. I have substituted in here the verse as given in the English Standard Version.

37. *Translator's note.* Matthew 19: 17. I have substituted in here the verse as given in the English Standard Version.

38. *Translator's note.* 1 Corinthians 8: 6. I have substituted in here the verse as given in the English Standard Version.

39. *Translator's note.* "Ptolemy's Epistle to Flora", pp. 445–7 (33.7.1–33.7.8). Bracketed interpolations are by Layton and Brakke unless otherwise indicated; elisions in square brackets are mine.

40. *Translator's note.* "Ptolemy's Epistle to Flora", p. 445 (33.7.9–33.7.10). The elision here is mine.

41. *Translator's note.* Matthew 5: 3.

42. Leisegang, 287–8.

MARCUS AND THE HELLENIZATION OF JEWISH HERMETICISM

1. *Translator's note.* I have not found anything like this passage in Irenaeus's text, but note well the following from Jerome's "Letter XXII. To Eustochium", trans. W. H. Fremantle, G. Lewis and W. G. Martley, in *A Select Library of Nicene and Post-Nicene Fathers of the Christian Church: Second Series*, ed. Philip Schaff and Henry Wace (New York: Christian Literature Company, 1893), vol. vi: "You may see many women widows before wedded, who try to conceal their miserable fall by a lying garb. [...] Their robes have but a narrow purple stripe, it is true" (27).

2. Irenaeus, book 1, chapter 13: 5. [*Translator's note.* Irenaeus, "Against Heresies", p. 335.]

3. Ibid. book 1, chapter 13 sq. [*Translator's note.* Ibid. p. 334 (book 1, chapter 13: 3).]

4. Leisegang, op. cit. 227 and 228.

5. *Translator's note.* Revelations 1: 8.

6. Dubourg, *L'invention de Jésus*, op. cit. 245.

7. Leisegang, op. cit. 227 and 228.

CARPOCRATES, EPIPHANIUS, AND THE TRADITION OF SIMON OF SAMARIA

1. *Translator's note.* "On Marriage (*Stromateis*, III)", pp. 43–4 (book 3, chapter 2: 6).

2. Ibid. p. 44 (book 3, chapter 2: 8).

3. *Translator's note.* Exodus 20: 17. I have substituted in here the verse as given in the English Standard Version.

4. Clement of Alexandria, *Stromates*, book 3, chapter 2: 9, and chapter 3: 9. [*Translator's note.* "On Marriage (*Stromateis*, III)", p. 44 (book 3, chapter 2: 9).]

5. *Translator's note.* Cf. Jacques Lacarrière, *Les Gnostiques* (Paris: Idées Gallimard, 1973). Translated into English by Nina Rootes as *The Gnostics* (London: Peter Owen Ltd., 1977).

6. Leisegang, op. cit. 180 and 181. [*Translator's note.* Irenaeus, "Against Heresies", p. 351 (book 1, chapter 25: 6).]

7. Leisegang, *La Gnose*, op. cit. 179.

8. Irenaeus, book 1, chapter 25. [*Translator's note.* Irenaeus, "Against Heresies", pp.

350–1 (book 1, chapter 25: 3–4).]

9. *Translator's note.* "Against Heresies", p. 351 (book 1, chapter 25: 5).

10. *Translator's note.* Interpolations by Vaneigem.

THE NEW PROPHECY AND THE DEVELOPMENT OF POPULAR CHRISTIANITY

1. *Translator's note.* "Letter 10, 96: Pliny to the Emperor Trajan", trans. William Harris, in *The Historians of Ancient Rome*, ed. Ronald Mellor: "They stated that the sum total of their error or misjudgment, had been coming to a meeting on a given day before dawn, and singing responsively a hymn to Christ as to God" (537).

2. *Translator's note.* Henryk Sienkiewicz (1846–1916), the author of *Quo Vadis*. *Tutti quanti* is Italian for 'all the rest'.

3. Frend, *Martyrdom and Persecution in the Early Church*, op. cit. 288.

4. Ibid. 293.

5. *Translator's note.* Eusebius of Caesarea, "The Church History", p. 232 (book 5, chapter 16: 13): "But by another kind of death Montanus and Maximilla are said to have died. For the report is that, incited by the spirit of frenzy, they both hung themselves".

6. Apollonius of Ephesus, quoted in Eusebius of Caesarea, *Histoire ecclésiatique* (Paris: Cerf, 1952–60). [*Translator's note.* Eusebius of Caesarea, "The Church History", p. 235 (book 5, chapter 18: 3).]

7. Steve Runciman, *Le manichéisme médiéval: L'Hérésie dualiste dans le christianisme*, trans. Simone Pétrement and Jacques Marty (Paris: Payot, 1972), 23. [*Translator's note.* Instead of translating Runciman from the French back into English, I have quoted from the original: *The Medieval Manichee: A Study of the Christian Dualist Heresy* (Cambridge: Cambridge University Press, 1947), 18.]

8. *Translator's note.* The Panarion *of Epiphanius of Salamis: Books II and III*, p. 17.

9. *Translator's note.* Tertullian, "On Modesty", trans. S. Thelwall, in *The Ante-Nicene Fathers*, vol. iv, p. 100.

10. Kurt Aland, "Augustin und der Montanismus", in *Kirchengeschichtliche Entwürfe: Alte Kirche, Reformation und Luthertum, Pietismus und Erweckungsbewegung* (Gütersloh: Gerd Mohn, 1960), 132.

11. *Translator's note.* The Panarion *of Epiphanius of Salamis: Books II and III*, p. 8.

12. Aland, op. cit. 126.

13. *Translator's note.* Tertullian, "De fuga in persecutione", trans. S. Thelwall, in *The Ante-Nicene Fathers*, vol. iv, p. 121 (paragraph 9).

14. *Translator's note.* Tertullian, "On Modesty", p. 75 (chapter 1).

15. *Translator's note.* "The Refutation of All Heresies", p. 55.

16. *Translator's note.* Tertullian, "On the Apparel of Women", trans. S. Thelwall, in *The Ante-Nicene Fathers*, vol. iv, p. 14 (book 1, chapter 1).

17. *Translator's note.* Tertullian, "On the Resurrection of the Flesh", trans. Peter Holmes, in *The Ante-Nicene Fathers*, vol. iii, p. 552 (chapter 11).

18. *Translator's note.* From Vaneigem's French.

19. *Translator's note.* 1 Corinthians 14: 33–4: "As in all churches of the saints, the women should keep silent in the churches. For they are not permitted to speak, but should be in submission, as the Law also says".

20. *Translator's note.* From Vaneigem's French.

21. *Translator's note.* The only English translation of this text—"A Plea for the Christians", trans. B. P. Pratten, in *The Ante-Nicene Fathers*, vol. ii—does not include this passage. I have therefore translated from Vaneigem's French.

22. Ammianus Marcellinus, quoted in Rougier, *Celse contre les chrétiens*, 13. [*Translator's note.* Ammianus Marcellinus, *The Roman History of Ammianus Marcellinus during the Reigns of the Emperors Constantius, Julian, Jovianus, Valentinian, and Valens*, trans. C. D. Yonge (London: G. Bell and Sons, Ltd, 1911), book 22, chapter 5.]

23. *Translator's note.* "The Martyrdom of Justin", trans. Marcus Dods, in *The Ante-Nicene Fathers*, vol. i, p. 306 (chapter 4).

24. Louis Rougier, *Celse contre les chrétiens* (Paris: Copernic, 1977), 13. [*Translator's note.* Lucian of Samosata, "The Passing of Peregrinus", trans. A. M. Harmon, in *Lucian* (Cambridge, MA: Harvard University Press, 1936), vol. v, p. 17 (paragraph 13).]

25. *Translator's note.* "The Pastor of Hermas", trans. F. Crombie, in *The Ante-Nicene Fathers*, vol. ii, p. 23 (book 2, commandment 5, chapter 1).

26. Stanislase Giet, "Un courant judéo-chrétien à Rome au milieu du IIe siècle", in *Aspects du judéo-christianisme: Colloque de Strasbourg, 23–25 avril 1964*, ed. Marcel Simon (Paris: Presses universitaires de France, 1965). [*Translator's note.* The internal quotations here are taken from "The Pastor of Hermas", op. cit. p. 11 (book 1, vision 2, chapter 2).]

27. Robert Joly, introduction to *Hermas. Le Pasteur*, trans. Robert Joly (Paris: Cerf, 1968), 41.

28. *Translator's note.* "The Pastor of Hermas", op. cit. p. 48 (book 3, similitude 9, chapter 13).

29. *Translator's note.* Ibid. p. 20 (book 2, commandment 1).

30. *Translator's note.* Ibid. p. 21 (book 2, commandment 4, chapter 1).

31. *Translator's note.* Cf. Chapter 6 of the present work.

32. *Translator's note.* Matthew 5: 3.

33. Quoted by Rougier, op. cit. 14. [*Translator's note.* Irenaeus, "Against Heresies", p. 397 (book, chapter 26: 1). The textual interpolation here is by Roberts and Rambaut.]

34. *Translator's note.* This is not the title of a work, but Aristotle's name for a type of oratory that is self-consciously literary and that seeks to praise some and blame others—in this case, *Against Heresies.*

35. Tertullian, *Apologétique*, ed. and trans. Jean-Pierre Waltzing (2nd edn., Paris: Les Belles Lettres, 1961), 37, 4. [*Translator's note.* Tertullian, "Apology", trans. S. Thelwall, in *The Ante-Nicene Fathers*, vol. iii, p. 45 (chapter 37).]

36. Id. *De Poenitentia*, 1.1. [*Translator's note.* Tertullian, "On Repentance", trans. S. Thelwall, in *The Ante-Nicene Fathers*, vol. iii, p. 657 (chapter 1).]

37. Ibid. 4. [*Translator's note.* Ibid. p. 664 (chapter 9).]

38. *Translator's note.* Tertullian, "The Soul's Testimony", trans. S. Thelwall, in *The Ante-Nicene Fathers*, vol. iii, p. 175 (chapter 1).

39. Tertullian, *De Anima*. [*Translator's note.* Tertullian, "A Treatise on the Soul", trans. Peter Holmes, in *The Ante-Nicene Fathers*, vol. iii, p. 183 (chapter 3).]

40. *Translator's note.* Tertullian, "The Five Books Against Marcion", op. cit. p. 294 (book 1, chapter 29).

41. *Translator's note.* From Vaneigem's French. But note the following from *Elenchos* (book 10, chapters 22 and 23, respectively): "The Phrygians, however, derive the principles of their heresy from a certain Montanus, and Priscilla, and Maximilla, and regard these wretched women as prophetesses"; and "But others of them [...] entertain similar opinions to those relating to the silly women *of the Phrygians*, and to Montanus" ("The Refutation of All Heresies", pp. 147–8).

42. *Translator's note.* Tertullian, "On Exhortation to Chastity", trans. S. Thelwall, in *The Ante-Nicene Fathers*, vol. iv, p. 56 (chapter 11).

43. *Translator's note.* Tertullian, "Apology", op. cit. p. 55 (chapter 50).

44. *Translator's note.* Tertullian, "De fuga in persecutione", p. 121 (paragraph 9).

TATIAN AND THE FABRICATION OF THE NEW TESTAMENT

1. Irenaeus, *Contre les hérésies*, op. cit. book 1, chapter 28: 1. [*Translator's note.* Irenaeus, "Against Heresies", p. 353.]

2. Tatian, *Oratio*, chapter 7. [*Translator's note.* Tatian, "Address of Tatian to the Greeks", trans. J. E. Ryland, in *The Ante-Nicene Fathers*, vol. ii, p. 67.]

3. Deschner, iii. 109.

4. "The Diatessaron of Tatian", trans. Hope W. Hogg in *The Ante-Nicene Fathers*, ed. Allan Menzies (5th edn., New York: Charles Scribner's Sons, 1906), vol. ix; Tatian, *Oratio ad Graecos and Fragments*, ed. and trans. Molly Whittaker (Oxford: Clarendon Press, 1982).

5. Louis Pautigny, *Justin: Apologies* (Paris: A. Picard, 1904), I, 35, 9–48, 3.

6. Tertullian, *Apologétique*, 21, 24.

7. *Acta Pilatis*, ed. and trans. Carlos Eugenio Revillout (Paris: 1913). [*Translator's note*. In "The Gospel of Nicodemus, or Acts of Pilate", in *The Apocryphal New Testament: Being the Apocryphal Gospels, Acts, Epistles, and Apostles*, trans. M. R. James (Oxford: Clarendon Press, 1924), this passage reads: "And it was about the sixth hour, and there was darkness over the land until the ninth hour, for the sun was darkened; and the veil of the temple was rent asunder in the midst. And Jesus called with a loud voice and said: Father, baddach ephkid rouel, which is interpreted: Into thy hands I commend my spirit" (104).]

8. Bonner, *Studies in Magical Amulets*, op. cit.

9. *Translator's note*. Tertullian, "Apology", pp. 34–5 (chapter 21).

10. Tertullian, *Apologétique*, chapter 21, p. 8 sq. [*Translator's note*. "Apology", pp. 35–6 (chapter 11).]

11. *Translator's note*. Tertullian, "Against the Valentinians", trans. Alexander Roberts, in *The Ante-Nicene Fathers*, vol. iii, p. 505 (chapter 5).

12. *Translator's note*. Unable to find this remark in "The Gospel of Bartholomew", trans. M. R. James, *The Apocryphal New Testament* (Oxford: Clarendon Press, 1924), I have translated it from Vaneigem's French.

13. *Translator's note*. "The Epistle of the Apostles", in *The Apocryphal New Testament*, 496.

14. *Translator's note*. The English phrase 'melting pot' is used in the original.

15. *Translator's note*. "Origen Against Celsus", p. 443 (book 2, chapter 28).

16. Erbetta, *Gli apocrifi*, op. cit. 139.

17. Éric Junod, "Créations romanesques et traditions ecclésiatiques dans les Actes apocryphes des apôtres", in *Genèse de l'écriture chrétienne*, ed. François Bovon and Helmut Koester (Turnhout: Brepols, 1991), 36. [*Translator's note*. The translation of the biblical verse here is taken from the English Standard Version.]

18. *Translator's note*. "The Gospel According to the Hebrews", commentary on Ezekiel 18: 7, in *The Apocryphal New Testament*, 5. Cf. Ezekiel 18: 5–9: "If a man is righteous and does what is just and right [...] [and] does not oppress anyone [...] he shall surely live,

declares the Lord GOD" (ellipses are mine.)

19. Junod, op. cit. 43.

20. Ibid. 43 and 44.

21. Ibid. [*Translator's note.* Quotations from Barnabas here taken from "The Epistle of Barnabas", trans. Alexander Roberts and James Donaldson, in *The Ante-Nicene Fathers*, vol. i, pp. 142 and 141 (chapter 7).]

22. *Translator's note.* Harold Idris Bell and Theodore Cressy Skeat, *Fragments of an Unknown Gospel and Other Early Christian Papyri* (London: Trustees of the British Museum, 1935).

THREE LOCAL CHRISTIANITIES

1. H. J. W. Drijvers, *Cults and Beliefs at Edessa* (Leiden: Brill, 1980), 194.

2. Ibid. 5 and 7.

3. *The Book of the Laws of Countries: Dialogue on Fate of Bardaisan of Edessa*, ed. and trans. H. J. W. Drijvers (Assen: Van Gorcum & Company, 1965).

4. Drijvers, *Cults and Beliefs at Edessa*, op. cit. p. 222.

5. Ibid. 219.

6. *Translator's note.* "The Gospel of Philip (*II*,3)", trans. Wesley W. Isenberg, in *The Nag Hammadi Library in English*, ed. James M. Robinson (San Francisco: Harper & Row, 1990), 145.

7. Éric Junod and Jean-Daniel Kaestli, *L'histoire des Actes apocryphes des apôtres du IIIe au IXe siècle: Le cas des Actes de Jean* (Geneva, Lausanne, and Neuchâtel: Cahiers de la Revue de théologie et de philosophie, 1982), 41.

8. Charles Puech, "Audianer", in *Reallexikon für Antike und Christentum: Sachwörterbuch zur Auseinandersetzung des Christentums mit der antiken Welt*, ed. Franz Joseph Dölger, Theodor Klauser, and Ernst Dassmann (Stuttgart: Hiersemann Verlag, 1950), 910 sq.

9. *Translator's note.* "Homily 1", in *Origen: Homilies on Joshua*, ed. Cynthia White and trans. Barbara J. Bruce (Washington, DC: Catholic University of America Press, 2002), 26.

10. *Translator's note.* Cf. Exodus 17: 9–10: "So Moses said to Joshua, 'Choose for us men, and go out and fight with Amalek. Tomorrow I will stand on the top of the hill with the staff of God in my hand'. So Joshua did as Moses told him, and fought with Amalek".

11. Annie Jaubert, preface to *Origène: Homélies sur Josué* (Paris: Éditions du Cerf, 1960).

12. *Translator's note.* English in original.

13. Drijvers, *Cults and Beliefs at Edessa*, 196.

14. Leontius of Byzantium, *De sectis*, 3. 3. [*Translator's note.* From Vaneigem's French.]

15. Theodore of Mopsuestia, *Une controverse avec les Macédoniens*, ed. and trans. François Nau (Paris: Firmin-Didot, 1913). [*Translator's note.* Translated from the French as quoted by Vaneigem. Note that in *Woodbrooke Studies*, vi: *Commentary of Theodore of Mopsuestia on the Lord's Prayer and on the Sacraments of Baptism and the Eucharist*, ed. and trans. Alphonse Mingana (Cambridge: W. Heffer and Sons Ltd., 1933), Theodore writes "An angel of Satan is Paul of Samosata, who asserted that Christ our Lord was a simple man and denied (the existence) before the worlds of the person of the Divinity of the Only Begotten" (40).]

NOVATIAN, THE APOSTATE CLERGY, AND THE ANTI-MONTANIST REACTION

1. Frend, *Martyrdom and Persecution in the Early Church*, op. cit.

2. *Translator's note.* Tertullian, "On Baptism", trans. S. Thelwall, in *The Ante-Nicene Fathers*, vol. iii, p. 677 (chapter 17).

3. *Translator's note.* "The Refutation of All Heresies", p. 131 (book 9, chapter 8).

4. Hippolytus, *Philosophumena ou réfutation de toutes les hérésies*, 194. [*Translator's note.* "The Refutation of All Heresies", p. 131.]

5. *Translator's note.* Cf. Cyprian of Carthage, "The Epistles of Cyprian", trans. Ernest Wallis, in *The Ante-Nicene Fathers*, vol. v, p. 544: "After such things as these, moreover, they still dare [...] to set sail and to bear letters from schismatic and profane persons to the throne of Peter" (epistle 54: 14).

6. *Translator's note.* "Novatian", in *Encyclopedia of Early Christianity*, ed. Everett Ferguson (2nd edn., New York: Taylor & Francis, 2013): "*On the Advantages of Chastity*, written after Novatian's consecration as bishop, calls the members of the 'virgin church' to remain pure as the dwelling place of the Holy Spirit".

7. Hermann Josef Vogt, *Coetus Sanctorum: Der Kirchenbegriff des Novatian und die Geschicte seiner Sonderkirche* (Bonn: P. Hanstein, 1968).

ARIANISM AND THE CHURCH OF ROME

1. Henri Guillemin, *L'Affaire Jésus* (Paris: Éditions du Seuil, 1982), 75.

2. Robert Louis Wilken, *Le Mythe des origines chrétiennes: Influence de l'histoire sur la foi*, trans. J. Chambert (Paris: Fayard, 1974), 58; originally published in English as *The*

Myth of Christian Beginnings: History's Impact on Belief (Garden City, NY: Doubleday, 1971). [*Translator's note*. Quoting Wilken's English rendering of Burckhardt.]

3. Jacques Jarry, *Hérésies et factions dans l'empire byzantin du IVe au VIIe siècle* (Cairo: Institut français d'archéologie orientale, 1968), 189.

4. Ibid. 192.

5. Ibid. 190 and 191. [*Translator's note*. Translated from the French as quoted by Vaneigem.]

6. *Translator's note*. From Vaneigem's French. Note well Epiphanius, *Panarion*, ii. 62. 8,1: "the blunderer Arius gets the notion that only the one, that is, only the Father, is called the '*true*' God, while the Son is God but not '*true* God'" (*The* Panarion *of Epiphanius of Salamis: Books II and III*, p. 129).

7. *Translator's note*. The Nicene Creed, in *The Book of Common Prayer and Administration of the Sacraments and Other Rites and Ceremonies of the Church; Together with the Psalter or Psalms of David; According to the Use of The Episcopal Church* (New York: Church Hymnal Corporation, 1979).

8. Abbé Pluquet, "Arianisme", in *Mémoires pour servir à l'histoire des égarements* (Besançon: Petit, 1817). [*Translator's note*. This work is also known under the title *Dictionnaire des hérésies, des erreurs et des schismes* (*Dictionary of Heresies, Errors and Schisms*) and seems to have been first published in 1762.]

DONATUS AND THE CIRCUMCELLIONS

1. *Acta Saturnini*, in *Patrologie latine*, ed. Jacques-Paul Migne (1844), 18, 8, 701.

2. Optatus (Bishop of Mileve), *Traité contre les donatistes*, ed. and trans. Mireille Labrousse (Paris: Éditions du Cerf, 1995). [*Translator's note. The Work of St. Optatus, Bishop of Milevis, Against the Donatists*, ed. and trans. O. R. Vassall-Phillips (London: Longmans, Green, and Company, 1917), book 3.4: "For when men of this sort were [...] wandering about in every place, and in their insanity called Axido and Fasir 'Captains of the Saints', no man could rest secure in his possessions. Written acknowledgements of indebtedness had lost their value. At that time no creditor was free to press his claim, and all were terrified by the letters of these fellows" (144).]

3. Ibid. book 3.3. [*Translator's note. The Work of St. Optatus*, 131.]

4. *Translator's note*. 'From the works performed', that is, from the sacrament itself.

THE SPIRITUALS, ALSO CALLED MESSALIANS OR EUCHITES

1. Runciman, *Le Manichéisme médiéval*, op. cit. 31.

2. *Translator's note.* Cf. the 'Castle Anthrax' scene in *Monty Python and the Holy Grail*, directed by Terry Gilliam and Terry Jones (1975), in which "eight-score blondes and brunettes, all between sixteen and nineteen-and-a-half", ask Sir Galahad to spank them and them let them perform oral sex on him. He is 'rescued' and carried off by force by Sir Lancelot, who calls Zoot, the leader of the Castle Anthrax, a "foul temptress" and threatens her with his sword.

3. Maximus the Confessor, *Scholia*, in *Opuscules*, ed. and trans. J. P. Migne, *Patrologie grecque*, 4, 3192b. [*Translator's note.* Cf. *Two Anonymous Sets of Scholia on Dionysius the Areopagite's* Heavenly Hierarchy, trans. Sergio La Porta (Louvain: Peeters, 2008)].

4. *Translator's note.* Anthony the Great and Macarius of Egypt lived in the fourth century and are considered saints by Catholic and Orthodox Churches.

5. *Translator's note.* The Isenheim Altarpiece is an altarpiece sculpted and painted by Niclaus of Haguenau and Matthias Grünewald between 1512 and 1516.

6. *Photius: Bibliothèque*, ed. René Henry (Paris: Société d'édition les belles lettres, 1960), 39.

7. Victor Magnien, *Les Mystères d'Éleusis* (Paris: Payot, 1938).

8. Philostorgius, *Epitome historiarum*, iii, in *Patrologie grecque*, lxv, 501–5.

9. Quoted by Runciman, op. cit. 34. [*Translator's note.* Runciman, *The Medieval Manichee*, op. cit. 41.]

MONOPHYSITES AND DYOPHYSITES

1. *Translator's note.* This Latin maxim, which appears in Tertullian's *De baptismo*, can be translated as, "Emulation of the episcopal office is the mother of schisms" (Tertullian, "On Baptism", p. 677 (chapter 17)).

2. *Translator's note.* From Vaneigem's French.

3. *Translator's note.* Cyril of Alexandria, *Scholia on the Incarnation of the Only-Begotten*, trans. P. E. Pusey (1881) <.https://www.tertullian.org/fathers/cyril_scholia_incarnation_01_text.htm>.

4. *Translator's note.* Yes, he did, and, as a result, he was condemned as a heretic by the Council of Chalcedon in 451.

5. *Sacrorum conciliorum nova et amplissima collectio*, ed. Giovanni Domenico Mansi (Florence and Venice, 1759), 7, 58–60. [*Translator's note.* From Vaneigem's French.]

6. W. H. C. Frend, *The Rise of the Monophysite Movement: Chapters in the History of the Church in the Fifth and Sixth Centuries* (Cambridge: Cambridge University Press, 1972).

7. Jarry, *Hérésies et factions dans l'empire byzantin du IVe au VIIe siècle*, op. cit. 82.

PELAGIUS AND AUGUSTINE

1. *Translator's note.* Matthew 13: 55.

PRISCILLIAN OF ÁVILA

1. *Translator's note.* In 311, Caecilian, a new bishop of Carthage, was consecrated by Felix, Bishop of Aptunga, who had allegedly repudiated his faith during the Diocletian Persecution of 303.

2. Henry Chadwick, *Priscillian of Avila: The Occult and the Charismatic in the Early Church* (Oxford: Clarendon Press, 1976).

3. A. B. J. M. Goosen, "Achtergronden van Priscillianus' christelijike ascese", Diss. (Nijmegen, 1976), 401.

4. *Translator's note.* Latin for 'the spirit of a place'.

5. *Translator's note.* 'Long live death' was the slogan of the Spanish fascists in the 1930s.

6. *Translator's note.* A shortening of *perinde ac si cadaver essent*, this is Latin for 'as obedient as a corpse', which was a slogan of the Jesuits. Cf. Jesuit *Constitutions* (1554), no. 547, quoted in Romanus Cessario, "Molina and Aquinas", in *A Companion to Luis de Molina*, ed. Matthias Kaufmann and Alexander Aichele (Leiden: Brill, 2014): "Let everyone persuade himself that those who live under obedience must let themselves be led and ruled by divine providence through their superiors, as if they were a corpse which allows itself to be carried here and there and treated in any way" (297 n. 22).

7. *Translator's note.* Latin for 'peace, freedom, unity'.

8. Cited in "Priscillian", in *Dictionnaire d'histoire et de géographie ecclésiastiques*, ed. Alfred Baudrillart et al. (Paris: Letouzey et Ané, 1912).

PAULICIANS AND BOGOMILS

1. Epiphanius, *Panarion*, i. 3.

2. *Translator's note.* Cf. the Eastern Catholic Churches.

3. *Translator's note.* "The Discourse of the Priest Cosmas Against Bogomils (after 972)", in *Christian Dualist Heresies in the Byzantine World c. 650–c. 1450*, ed. and trans. Janet Hamilton, Bernard Hamilton, and Yuri Stoyanov (Manchester: Manchester University Press, 1998), 116.

4. *Translator's note.* In point of fact, the text begins with the affirmations that "All the

commandments of Our Lord Jesus Christ are wonderful, dear to those who read them, since they were spoken for our salvation", and that "Our enemy the devil knows this, and [...] he has not ceased to try to entice all men from the faith [...]. But since he saw that all these sins cannot be compared with heresy", the devil "entered" a sequence of people: Arius, Sabellius, and Macedonius (115). In the words of the text's translators, "Th[is] list of earlier heretics resembles those found in other anti-heretical texts" (115 n.).

5. *Translator's note*. It is only in some manuscripts that the title of this work insists on Cosmas being 'unworthy'. Cf. Eirini Artemi's paper "The Heresy of Bogomils and Its Confrontation by the Serbian King Stefan Nemanja", *Nis and Byzantium*, 16 (2017), 71 n. 34.

6. Borislav Primov, *Les Bougres: Histoire du pope Bogomile et de ses adeptes*, trans. Monette Ribeyrol (Paris: Payot, 1975), 97. [*Translator's note*. From the French as quoted by Vaneigem.]

7. Martin Erbstösser, *Les Hérétiques au Moyen Âge* (Leipzig: Edition Leipzig, 1984), 51 and 52. [*Translator's note*. "The Discourse of the Priest Cosmas Against Bogomils", 121–2.]

8. Primov, op. cit. 120. [*Translator's note*. "The Discourse of the Priest Cosmas Against Bogomils", 132.]

9. *Translator's note*. "The Discourse of the Priest Cosmas Against Bogomils", 132. The interpolation here is by Hamilton, Hamilton, and Stoyanov.

10. Primov, 100. [*Translator's note*. "The Discourse of the Priest Cosmas Against Bogomils", 121–2.]

11. Primov, 100. [*Translator's note*. Unable to locate this sentence in "The Discourse of the Priest Cosmas Against Bogomils", I have translated it from the French as quoted by Vaneigem.]

12. *Translator's note*. A twelfth-century monk who compiled a work on heresy titled *The Doctrinal Armory of the Orthodox Faith* for Alexius I Comnenus.

13. Primov, op. cit. 157. [*Translator's note*. Translated from the French as quoted by Vaneigem.]

14. Primov, op. cit. 162–4. [*Translator's note*. *The Alexiad of the Princess Anna Comnena*, ed. and trans. Elizabeth A. S. Dawes (London: Kegan Paul, Trench, Trubner, and Company, Ltd., 1928), 412–4, 417–8.]

15. Primov, 180.

16. *Translator's note*. The online edition of the *Larousse dictionnaire de français* indicates that this word means "Bulgarian heretics said to engage in sodomy" (my translation).

CHRISTS AND REFORMERS

1. Gregory of Tours, *Historia francorum*, book 10, chapter 25. [*Translator's note*. Gregory Bishop of Tours, *History of the Franks*, ed. and trans. Ernest Brehaut (New York: Columbia University Press, 1916): "For a certain man of Bourges, as he himself told later, went into the deep woods to cut logs which he needed for a certain work and a swarm of flies surrounded him, as a result of which he was considered crazy for two years; whence it may be believed that they were a wickedness sent by the devil" (244).]

2. Ibid.

3. Jeffrey B. Russell, "Saint Boniface and the Eccentrics", *Church History*, 33/3 (Sept. 1964), 235–47.

4. *Translator's note*. A Benedictine monk who lived in the eleventh century.

5. *Translator's note*. Latin for 'By him who has come to judge the living and the dead'.

6. *Translator's note*. *The History of William of Newburgh*, trans. Joseph Stevenson (London, 1856; repr. Felinfach: Llanerch Publishers, 1996): "his adherents, free from anxiety and labour, seemed to be expensively apparelled, to banquet splendidly, and to live in perfect joy" (425).

7. *Translator's note*. 'Petrobrusian' is a contraction of 'Peter of Bruys'.

THE COMMUNALIST PROPHETS

1. Norman Cohn, *Les Fanatiques de l'apocalypse: Millénaristes révolutionnaires et anarchistes mystiques au Moyen Age*, trans. Simone Clémendot (Paris: Payot, 1983), 46. [*Translator's note*. This is the French translation of Norman Cohn, *The Pursuit of the Millennium: Revolutionary Millenarians and Mystical Anarchists of the Middle Ages* (rev. edn., New York: Oxford University Press, 1970), 48–9. Rather than translate Cohn back into English, I have quoted directly from the English-language original.]

2. Arno Borst, *Les Cathares*, trans. Charles Roy (Paris: Payot, 1974), 73.

3. Ibid. 73.

4. Ibid.

5. Tadeusz Manteuffel, *Naissance d'une hérésie: Les adeptes de la pauvreté volontaire au Moyen Âge* (Paris: Moulton, 1970), 29.

6. Ilarino da Milano, *L'eresia di Ugo Speroni nella confutazione del maestro Vacario* (Vatican City: Biblioteca apostolica Vaticana, 1945).

PHILOSOPHY AGAINST THE CHURCH

1. *Translator's note*. Latin for 'the servant of theology'.

2. Pseudo-Dionysius the Areopagite, *De theologia mystica*, 2.3. [*Translator's note.* "Théologie mystique", in *Oeuvres complètes*, trans. Maurice de Gandillac (Paris: Aubier, 1943).]

3. John Scotus Eriugena, *De pradestinatione*, i. 1. [*Translator's note.* The long passage full of quotations from Eriugena that follows this remark comes from Auguste Jundt, *Histoire du panthéisme populaire au Moyen Âge et au seizième siècle* (Strasbourg: Fischbach, 1875), 12. All translations of Eriugena made from the French as quoted by Vaneigem.]

4. John Scotus Eriugena, *De divisione naturae*, ii. 1.

5. Ibid. ii. 19.

6. Ibid. i. 74.

7. Ibid. v. 7.

8. Ibid. ii. 5.

9. Ibid. v. 20.

10. Ibid. v. 7.

11. Ibid. v. 25.

12. Gabriel Théry, *Autour du décret de 1210*, i: *David de Dinant: Étude sur son panthéisme matérialiste* (Kain: Le Saulchoir, 1925). [*Translator's note.* Most sources translate *Deus sive natura* as "God or nature".]

13. *Translator's note.* From Vaneigem's French.

14. Jundt, *Histoire du panthéisme*, op. cit.

15. *Translator's note.* Cf. Raoul Vaneigem, *Le Mouvement du libre-esprit: Généralités et témoignages sur les affleurements de la vie à la surface du Moyen Âge, de la Renaissance et, incidemment, de notre époque* (Paris: Ramsay, 1986), translated by Randall Cherry and Ian Patterson as Raoul Vaneigem, *The Movement of the Free Spirit: General Considerations and Firsthand Testimony Concerning Some Brief Flowerings of Life in the Middle Ages, the Renaissance and, Incidentally, Our Own Time* (New York: Zone Books, 1994), 178–80 and 195–7, respectively.

16. *Translator's note.* Alvarus Pelagius, *Collyrium fidei adversus haereses*, translation from J. F. Meirinhos, "Was There a Portuguese Averroism in the 14th Century? Alphonsus Dionisii and Thomas Scotus", paper given at the 12th SIEPM Congress, Palermo, 17–22 Sept. 2007 (published online: <http://ifilosofia.up.pt/inv/admins/meirinhos/docs/Meirinhos_averroism_14thCent_Portugal.pdf>).

17. *Translator's note.* Jean Meslier (1664–1729) was a French Catholic priest who authored an atheistic *Testament*, but this does not seem to have been the *The Three*

Impostors. Note that, in 2002, Vaneigem himself edited and wrote a preface for *L'Art de ne croire en rien suivi de Livre des trios imposteurs*, a volume published by Éditions Payot et Rivages (Rivages poche/Petite Bibliothèque) that offered a modern French version of Geoffroy Vallée's *L'Art de ne croire en rien*—also known as *La Béatitude des chrétiens ou le Fléau de la foi*—and a French translation of an edition of *De tribus impostoribus* that was published in 1598.

18. *Translator's note*. All of whom were burnt at the stake as heretics between 1574 and 1619.

19. *Translator's note*. Vaneigem, *Movement of the Free Spirit*, 196–7.

20. Vaneigem, *Movement of the Free Spirit*, op. cit; *Paul Frédéricq, Corpus documentarum inquisitionis hereticae pravitatis neerlandicae* (Ghent, 1889–1900), i. 452.

THE CATHARS

1. *Translator's note*. This phrase from the *Song of the Albigensian Crusade* is translated by Piotr Czarnecki in "If Not Bogomilism Than What? The Origins of Catharism in the Light of Sources", *Studia Ceranea*, 11 (2021), 60.

2. Claude Gaignebet and Jean-Dominique Lajoux, *Art profane et religion populaire au Moyen Âge* (Paris: Presses universitaires de France, 1985).

3. *Translator's note*. Punning Latin for 'Completely deceitful Toulouse'. Petrus Valium appears to be another name for Peter de Vaux-Sarnai.

4. *Translator's note*. The Seventh Council of Orléans, held in 1022 under Bishop Odolric, proceeded against the Manicheans.

5. Stefano, *Riformatori ed eretici del Medioevo* (Palermo: F. Ciuni, 1938), 347; Ilarino da Milano, *L'eresia di Ugo Speroni*, 68.

6. Louis Ellies Dupin, *Histoire des controverses et des matières ecclésiastiques traitées dans le XIIIe siècle* (Paris: Chez André Pralard, 1694; repr. 1842), chapter vi.

7. *Translator's note*. Latin for 'in turn' or 'again'.

8. Borst, *Les Cathares*, op. cit. 70.

9. *Translator's note*. Latin for 'new heretics', a phrase one finds in the works of Bernard of Clairvaux circa 1140.

10. Bernard Monod, *Le Moine Guibert et son temps (1053–1124)* (Paris: Hachette, 1905).

11. Borst, op. cit. 81.

12. *Translator's note*. The planet Venus is nicknamed 'the star of the Shepherd' because it can easily be seen at dawn, before the sun rises.

13. *Translator's note.* Latin for 'for temporary assistance'.

14. Borst, op. cit. 90–3.

15. *Translator's note.* That is to say, Arnaud Amalric, the Seventeen Abbot of Cîteaux, who is infamous for saying "Caedite eos. Novit enim Dominus qui sunt eius". ("Kill them all. For the Lord knoweth them that are His".)

16. *Translator's note.* A former heretic who 'converted' and became a member of the Dominican Order.

17. *Translator's note.* A term that refers both to Waldo (Valdes), the founder of the Waldensians, and to witchcraft. The 'Vauderie d'Arras' was a trial of alleged witches that took place in Arras, France between 1459 and 1461.

18. *Translator's note.* Latin for 'legalized fornication'.

19. Borst, 156.

20. *Translator's note.* From Vaneigem's French. See the citation from Anselm of Alessandria, *Tractatus de haereticis*, in James Edward Myers, "Morality Among Cathar Perfects and Believers in France and Italy, 1100–1300", MA Thesis (Western Michigan University, 1976): "Anselm of Alessandria recorded an incident concerning a specific Cathar perfect, Philip, who upon becoming a Cathar bishop '. . . after a short time knew two Cathar women, and so leaving the Cathars returned to the secular life with the women'" (38–9).

THE WALDENSIANS AND THE ADEPTS OF VOLUNTARY POVERTY

1. Christine Thouzellier, *Catharisme et valdéisme en Languedoc à la fin du XIIe et au début du XIIIe siècle* (Paris: Presses universitaires de France, 1966).

2. *Translator's note.* Pope Lucius III, *Ad abolendam diversam haeresium pravitatem* [*To Abolish Diverse Malignant Heresies*], in *Facts and Documents Illustrative of the History, Doctrine, and Rites of the Ancient Albigenses and Waldenses*, ed. and trans. S. R. Maitland (London: C.J.G. and F. Rivington, 1832): "we lay under a perpetual anathema the CATHARI, PATARINI, and those who falsely call themselves HUMILIATI, or POOR MEN OF LYONS" (177). For the description of the Waldensians as "pertinaces and schismatics", which does not appear in the papal bull in question, see Jean Gonnet, "La figure et l'œuvre de Vaudès dans la tradition historique et selon les dernières recherches", in *Vaudois languedociens et pauvres catholiques* (Toulouse: Éditions Privat, 1967), 92 and 95.

3. Thouzellier, op. cit. [*Translator's note.* Cf. Jean Gonnet, *Les vaudois du Moyen Âge* (Torino: Claudiana, 1974).]

4. *Translator's note.* The French branch called itself the Poor of Lyons.

5. *Translator's note.* See Brenda Bolton, "Innocent III's Treatment of the *Humiliati*", in *Popular Belief and Practice: Papers Read at the Ninth Summer Meeting and the Tenth Winter Meeting of the Ecclesiastical History Society*, ed. G. J. Cuming and Derek Baker (Cambridge: Cambridge University Press, 1972), 73–82.

6. *Translator's note.* "Raymond de Sainte-Foy, Deacon of the Vaudois Sect: Confession 3", trans. Nancy P. Stork <https://www.sjsu.edu/people/nancy.stork/jacquesfournier/Raymond-de-Sainte-Foy-FINAL.pdf>.

7. *Translator's note.* Vaneigem, *The Movement of the Free Spirit*, 79.

8. Cohn, *Les Fanatiques de l'apocalypse*, 98–102. [*Translator's note.* Vaneigem refers to the French translation of Norman Cohn's *The Pursuit of the Millennium*. Rather than translate Cohn back into English, I have directly quoted from the original (94–8). All ellipses are in conformity with Vaneigem's citations.]

THE MOVEMENT OF THE FREE SPIRIT

1. *Translator's note.* In Vaneigem, *The Movement of the Free Spirit*, op. cit. 95, these disciples of Amalric of Bena are called the Amaurians.

2. *Translator's note.* See Vaneigem, *The Movement of the Free Spirit*, 99. In an endnote, Vaneigem describes Godin as "a philosopher whose ideas are similar to those of David of Dinant and to pantheism, which, in its reduction of divinity to nature, is the atheism of the Middle Ages" (267 n. 40).

3. *Translator's note.* "The Twelfth General Council (Fourth Lateran Council, 1215)", in *Disciplinary Decrees of the General Councils: Text, Translation and Commentary*, ed. and trans. H. J. Schroeder (St. Louis: B. Herder, 1937), p. 242 (canon 2).

4. Johannes Nauclerus, *Chronica* (Cologne, 1544), 912. [*Translator's note.* This citation of Nauclerus also appears in Vaneigem, *The Movement of the Free Spirit*, op. cit. 100. Here and in each of the other cases in which I have used an endnote to indicate overlaps between *The Movement of the Free Spirit* and the present work, I have retained the translation that is offered in the former.]

5. Livarius Oliger, "De secta operitus libertatis, in Umbria seculo XIV. Disquistio et documenta", in *Storia e letteratura reccolta di studi et testi* (Rome: G. De Luca, 1943), 101. [*Translator's note.* See Vaneigem, *The Movement of the Free Spirit*, 100, where the above passage ends with the untranslated Latin phrase *nullo piaculo contracto*; 'no atonement contracted'.]

6. *Translator's note.* Latin for 'I will enter the altar of Bacchus, to the God who makes the heart of man happy'.

7. Bernard Monod, *Le Moine Guibert et son temps* (Paris: Hachette et cie, 1905), 202.

8. Ibid. [*Translator's note*. In Vaneigem, *The Movement of the Free Spirit*, 102, this quotation from Monod's book is followed by an endnote (264 n. 18) that refers the reader to Petrus Comestor, *Scholastica historia magistri Petri Comestoris sacre scripture seriem breuem nimis et expositam exponentis* (Paris, 1513–9). Note that Petrus Comestor (Pierre le Mangeur) means 'Peter the Eater'.]

9. Vaneigem, *Le Mouvement du libre-esprit*, op. cit. 103. [*Translator's note*. See Vaneigem, *The Movement of the Free Spirit*, 109, which refers the reader via an endnote (268 n. 46) to Garnius von Rochefort, "Contra Amaurianos", in *Beitrage zur Geschicte zur Philosophie und Theologie des Mittelalters*, ed. Clems Baeumker (Münster: Aschendorff, 1926), vol. xxiv.]

10. Ibid. [*Translator's note*. See Vaneigem, *The Movement of the Free Spirit*, 109–10, which refers the reader via an endnote (268 n. 47) to William the Breton, "Gesta Philippi Augusti", in *Oeuvres de Rigord et de Guillaume le Breton*, ed. H. François Delaborde (Paris: Renouard, 1882–5), vol. i. The textual interpolation in this passage also appears in *The Movement of the Free Spirit*.]

11. *Translator's note*. In Vaneigem, *The Movement of the Free Spirit*, 110–1, this passage includes an endnote by the author: "The criticism of hypocrisy relates to ordinary anticlericism, which could not tolerate priests using their sacred mission as a cover for their debauchery (acknowledged, admittedly, as sins). The Church cleverly turned this against the heretics—the 'foxes', as Bernard of Clairvaux called them, who had no alternatives beyond dissimulation or the stake" (269 n. 51).

12. Vaneigem, *Le Mouvement du libre-esprit*, 104–5. [*Translator's note*. In Vaneigem, *The Movement of the Free Spirit*, 110–1, this passage is followed by an endnote (269 n. 53) that refers the reader to Joseph de Guibert, *Documenta ecclesiastica christianae perfectionis studium spectantia* (Rome: Pontifical Gregorian University, 1931).]

13. *Translator's note*. Also known as Robert le Petit and Robert the Bulgarian (1173–1239), he was a former Cathar who returned to the ranks of Catholic orthodoxy.

14. Vaneigem, *Le Mouvement du libre-esprit*, 113. [*Translator's note*. See Vaneigem, *The Movement of the Free Spirit*, 116: "In 1245, after the first Council of Lyons, the Bishop of Olmtz complained of the presence in his diocese of wandering agitators of both sexes. Dressed as members of religious orders, but resolutely hostile to the ecclesiastical hierarchies, they spread the idea that God should be served in absolute freedom, outside of any rule or discipline". An endnote (273 n. 82) to this passage refers the reader to Herbert Grundmann, *Religiöse Bewegungen im Mittelalter* (Berlin: Ebering, 1935), 400.]

15. *Translator's note.* In Vaneigem, *The Movement of the Free Spirit*, 118, this sentence is followed by an endnote by the author: "Th[is] response indicates a desire on the part of the inquisitor to bring the accused back into the framework of Christian mythology. Belief in angels, devils, hell and the Fall is current only among those who do not recognize God in man" (274 n. 87).

16. *Translator's note.* Ibid. 119 includes a sentence that does not appear in the present work: "The good man need not confess his sins, however important they may be, but only tell them to another good man, or say in the presence of God, in secret, 'I have sinned'". In an endnote appended to this sentence, Vaneigem writes: "This proposition belongs to Catharism, not to the movement of the Free Spirit" (274 n. 88).

17. *Translator's note.* Ibid. includes an endnote by the author: "The idea of God as a God of justice and fear is rejected and realized instead as a principle of bounty and natural gratuity. This is the sentiment that Francis of Assisi tried to disseminate within the Church, and which his dissolute followers, the Fraticelli, attributed to nature" (274 n. 89).

18. *Translator's note.* Ibid. includes an endnote by the author: "Compare with the refusal of work in the group William of Saint-Amour describes" (278 n. 90).

19. *Translator's note.* Ibid. 120 includes an endnote by the author: "It is in the body as the site of pleasure and displeasure that the Holy Spirit, that is, God, is incarnate" (274 n. 95).

20. *Translator's note.* Ibid. includes an endnote by the author: "The Church tried to use the cult of the Virgin Mary to prevent the renewal of life expressed in the thirteenth century by the nascent (and temporary) supremacy of women. The patriarchal contempt for feminine existence was responsible for this. It is revealing that one of the most enthusiastic devotees of the Virgin, Jacopo of Todi, wrote fiercely misogynistic poems and, after the death of his wife, devoted himself to the cult of Mary, this mother purified to the point of virginity by divine adultery.

"That devotion to Mary was ridiculed from the thirteenth to the sixteenth century is confirmed by the constant repression that occurred during that period. Two cases, out of many, will illustrate this: on April 1, 1275, Mathilde Billarde 'for the vileness she uttered and the words against the Mother of God . . . was banished and placed into exile and pilloried at Tournai' (Frédéricq, *Corpus*, vol. 1, p. 140); and Jacob Acarin, from Chausé-Notre-Dame in Hainault was sentenced to three years in prison in 1451 for saying: 'Why be ashamed? Our Lady had no shame. She had feelings just like other people, for she was married as we are. Do you think she was a virgin? Nay' (*ibid.*, vol. 1, p. 231).

"An attempt at a feminine Church appeared after the death of Wilhelmina of

Bohemia (1282), venerated as an incarnation of the Holy Spirit, and founder of the group known as the Family of Love. The Church put an end to that competing enterprise, with its female hierarchy and its own rites, by burning the Wilhelminites" (274–5 n. 96).

21. Vaneigem, *Le Mouvement du libre-esprit*, 115–6. [*Translator's note.* This passage in *The Movement of the Free Spirit*, 120, is followed by an endnote by the author (275 n. 97): "Cited in Haupt, 'Beiträge'"—that is to say, in Herman Haupt, "Beiträge zur Geschichte der Sekte vom freien Geiste und des Beghartentums", *Zeitschrift für Kirchengeschichte*, 7 (1885). Vaneigem's endnote goes on to say: "The statements of the nuns and lay members of the New Spirit in Swabia—and perhaps in those convents 'that enjoyed the freedom of the Fraticelli'—is adequate demonstration of the source of those 'effusions of divine love' praised by devout commentators. Even if the intellectualism of figures such as Beatrice of Nazareth and Mechtild of Magdeburg (Mechtild of Magdeburg, *Offenbanungen der Schwester Mechtild von Magdeburg oder das fliessende Licht der Gottheit*, ed. Gall Morel [Regensburg: G. J. Manz, 1869]) transcends a vague sensual experience, there were, nonetheless, companions around them whom the movement of the Free Spirit had made God or Christ and who 'knew carnally' their female companions, simultaneously virgins and mothers, offering the milk of their ardor until they fainted". The square brackets within this quotation appear in Cherry and Patterson's translation.]

22. *Translator's note.* For the 'sweet new style', see Dante Alighieri, *Vita Nuova* (1295), and, for the path to Beatrice, *Divina Commedia* (1321).

23. *Translator's note.* Cf. Vaneigem, *The Movement of the Free Spirit*, 128–43.

24. Marguerite Porete, "Le miroir des simples âmes", in *Il movimento del libero spirito: Testi e documenti*, ed. Romana Guarnieri (Rome: Edizioni di storia e letteratura, 1965), 617. [*Translator's note.* See Vaneigem, *The Movement of the Free Spirit*, 129. The textual emendation here also appears in that volume.]

25. Vaneigem, *Le Mouvement du libre-esprit*, 127. [*Translator's note.* See Vaneigem, *The Movement of the Free Spirit*, 130, which refers the reader via an endnote (277 n. 116) to Guarnieri, *Il movimento del libero spirito*, 586.]

26. Guarnieri, op. cit.

27. Vaneigem, *Le Mouvement du libre-esprit*, 128. [*Translator's note.* See Vaneigem, *The Movement of the Free Spirit*, 131.]

28. *Translator's note.* See Vaneigem, *The Movement of the Free Spirit*, 131.

29. Vaneigem, *Le Mouvement du libre-esprit*, 129. [*Translator's note.* Vaneigem is quoting here from Marguerite Porete's *The Mirror of Simple Souls*. See *The Movement of the Free Spirit*, 132.]

30. *Translator's note.* Mystics of the sixteenth and seventeenth centuries.

31. *Translator's note.* Cf. Vaneigem, *The Movement of the Free Spirit*, 143–9.

32. *Translator's note.* Alternative spellings of her last name include Blomart, Bloermardinne, Bloemards, and Bloemaerts.

33. *Translator's note.* Born Hendrik Utenbogaerde and sometimes known as Henricus Pomerius (1382–1469). The title of his work about Ruysbroeck was *De origine monasterii Viridisvallis una cum vitis B. Joannis Rusbrochii primi prioris hujus monasterii et aliquot coaetaneorum ejus.*

34. *Translator's note.* This passage in Vaneigem, *The Movement of the Free Spirit*, 144 is followed by an endnote by the author: "The throne of silver recalls the magnificence of Walter [of Holland], and the silk garments that the nuns of Schweidnitz wore under their hair shirts. In the *Book of Two Men*, Rulmann Merswin also speaks of Beguines who 'before accomplishing the praise of God through the meditation of the senses, dressed themselves in wonderful clothes'. He describes, elsewhere, the alchemical magisterium in which the union of the king and the queen forms the androgynous egg, the site of sexual pleasure in which separations are abolished under the double symbol of the elixir of youth and the universal stone of transmutation" (278 n. 126).

35. *Translator's note.* Vaneigem, *The Movement of the Free Spirit*, 144–5, which refers the reader via an endnote (278 n. 127) to Paul Frédéricq, *Corpus documentorum inquisitionis haereticae pravitatis neerlandicae* (Ghent: Vuylsteke, 1889–1900) i. 186.

36. *Translator's note.* Vaneigem, *The Movement of the Free Spirit*, 147. An endnote following this passage (278 n. 128) refers the reader to Jan van Ruysbroeck, *The Spiritual Espousals*, trans. Eric College (London: Faber & Faber, 1952).

37. *Translator's note.* This sentence in ibid. 114 is followed by an endnote by the author: "Like most voluntary poverty movements, William's was opposed to the sale of indulgences. 'Before death', writes Colette Braeckman, 'man had four means of redeeming his soul from hell. Gratian's decree cites prayers for the dead, masses celebrated by priests, alms and legacies to ecclesiastical institutions. In the course of the thirteenth century there were great changes in the services surrounding the dead. Cumulative and anniversary masses were said for the soul of the dead person. They were no longer provided by the Church, but financed by a sum the dying man left for that purpose. This means of salvation was, from then on, for the rich only. In remission of his sins, the sick man would distribute alms. If he did not, the living would do so after his death, a practice that brought with it abuses that were condemned by the councils from the thirteenth century on. . . . At Lateran IV, Innocent III was worried by the extension of commercial activities,

and took measures to limit the duration of indulgences. . . . The Council of Béziers, in 1246, condemned money collectors who promised liberation from hell at bargain prices'" (270 n. 67). Vaneigem is quoting here from Colette Braeckman, "Guillaume Cornelisz", *Bulletin de la société d'histoire du protestantisme belge*, 9/4 (1982).

38. *Translator's note.* The textual interpolation here also appears in *The Movement of the Free Spirit*. This sentence is followed therein by an endnote by the author: "Almsgiving was criticized as being the least costly way of ensuring the rich a clear conscience. When it came from their surplus it did not reduce their wealth. Another proposition declared that 'no one who has two coats of the same sort can be saved'. The Church, of course, rebelled against a theory in which scorn for possessions was a guarantee of spiritual wealth, and the acquisition of possessions entailed the impoverishment of human status. 'At the University of Paris, in 1256, the regent defended the traditional theory of the secular Church against an adept of voluntary poverty, Master T. . . . With examples drawn from the lives of Saint Thomas and Saint Ambrose, he reminded his audience that the sharing of goods with the poor was an act of mercy rather than a total renunciation of worldly possessions'" (270–1 n. 68). Vaneigem is quoting here from Braeckman, "Guillaume Cornelisz".

39. *Translator's note.* This sentence is followed in *The Movement of the Free Spirit* by an endnote by the author: "Unlike the Church, which draws a distinction between the permitted possession of wealth and the mortal sin of avarice" (270 n. 69).

40. *Translator's note.* This sentence is followed in ibid. by an endnote by the author: "Stealing from the rich is not theft, as long as it provides the poor with subsistence they are otherwise denied. The same defense of theft turns up frequently among the Beguines and Beghards" (271 n. 70).

41. *Translator's note.* This sentence is followed in ibid. by an endnote by the author: "The idea of damnation seems to imply, as the Amaurians [*sic*] believed, that hell exists only here on earth. It is reserved for those who remain ignorant of the possibility of paradise, an ignorance which, according to [William] Cornelius, steams from private ownership" (271 n. 71).

42. *Translator's note.* This sentence is followed in ibid. 114–5 by an endnote by the author: "This proposition, like the ones that follow, bears the mark of the movement of the Free Spirit. The end of the world of possession implies the end of sin" (271 n. 72).

43. *Translator's note.* This sentence is followed in ibid. 115 by an endnote by the author: "It must be remembered that *fornication* is the clerical translation of 'the art of living', the refinement of which seems to have been a fundamental preoccupation of the

thirteenth century. The songs of the troubadours and trouvères [minstrels] were later eclipsed by the songs of death, which gradually proclaimed the triumph of Christianity on the eve of its desacrilization by the Renaissance" (271 n. 73).

44. *Translator's note.* This sentence is followed in ibid. 115 by an endnote by the author: "The critique of money is already beginning to give way to one of power, social representation and spectacle" (271 n. 74).

45. *Translator's note.* This sentence is followed in ibid. 115 by an endnote by the author: "The prohibition against making love to a pregnant wife, apart from offering women a reason for refusing, takes on a further meaning in relation to the proposition denying sins against nature, which, to the clerical mind of the thirteenth century signified not only homosexual or bestial relations, but any erotic relation not involved in procreation: mutual masturbation, *coitus interruptus* or *reservatus*, sodomy and so on. Here a politics of abortion is indirectly encouraged by William Cornelius, who must have been able to see the disastrous consequences of pregnancy for workers in the weaving trade and for the very poor" (271–2 n. 17).

46. *Translator's note.* This sentence is followed in ibid. 115 by an endnote by the author: "The freedom of nature practiced in the lower class not only implies equal rights between the sexes, it also requires—in Cornelius's conception—a real respect for women far removed from the misogyny of the bourgeoisie and the writers of fabliaux. It does not base itself on the worship of the object of seduction, but on a practical code of courtesy in which the woman—whether she comes from a poor background or whether she has embraced poverty voluntarily—has the right to give herself to, or refuse, whomever she likes. (There were many women workers exhausted by their jobs for whom the solicitations of exigent males were an additional burden.) Hence the restriction 'three times a week'" (272 n. 76).

47. *Translator's note.* Vaneigem, *The Movement of the Free Spirit*, 114–5, which refers the reader via an endnote (272 n. 77) to Frédéricq, *Corpus*, i. 119–20. Note that *The Movement of the Free Spirit* goes on to list one further allegation, one not included here: the belief that "If a woman is poor and indigent, she can give herself without sin".

BEGHARDS AND BEGUINES

1. Jundt, op. cit. 45 and 46.

2. *Translator's note.* German for "Bread for the sake of God".

3. Vaneigem, *Le Mouvement du libre-esprit*, op. cit. 149. [*Translator's note. The Movement of the Free Spirit*, 154–5, which refers the reader via an endnote (278 n. 134) to Giovanni Domenico Mansi, *Sacrorum conciliorum novas et amplissima collectio* (Florence:

NOTES

Expensis Antonii Zatta, 1759), xxiii. 997.]

4. *Translator's note.* Vaneigem notes in *The Movement of the Free Spirit* that "Beghards, Beguines, apostolic followers of Gerard Segarelli, partisans of voluntary poverty, Fraticelli and Joachites" were lumped together and condemned "in a single anathema" (155).

5. *Translator's note.* Ibid.

6. *Translator's note.* Ibid. 156, which refers the reader via an endnote (279 n. 146) to C. Baronius and O. Raynaldus, *Annales ecclesiastici una cum critica historico-chronologia* (Lucca, 1738–59).

7. *Translator's note.* Latin for *To Those of Us Who Longingly Wish* and *Concerning Certain Women.*

8. *Translator's note.* Latin for *Of the Nine Spiritual Rocks.*

9. *Translator's note.* Latin for 'Men of Intelligence'. Cf. Chapter 37 of the present work.

10. *Translator's note.* Cf. Vaneigem, *The Movement of the Free Spirit* (159–73).

11. *Translator's note. The Movement of the Free Spirit*, 177.

12. Guarnieri, op. cit. 459. [*Translator's note. The Movement of the Free Spirit*, 92.]

13. Ibid. 459.

14. *Translator's note.* Vaneigem, *The Movement of the Free Spirit* (180–7).

15. Vaneigem, *Le Mouvement du libre-esprit*, op. cit. 174. [*Translator's note. The Movement of the Free Spirit*, 182.]

16. J. L. von Mosheim, *De beghardis et beguinabus commentarius* (Leipzig: Weidmann, 1790).

17. Jundt, op. cit. 111.

18. *Translator's note.* A. Wautier D'Aygalliers, *Ruysbroeck the Admirable*, trans. Fred Rothwell (London: J. M. Dent & Sons Ltd., 1925), 43.

19. Herman Haupt, "Beiträge zur Geschichte der Sekte vom freien Geiste und des Beghartentums", *Zeitschrift für Kirchengeschichte*, 7 (1885), 503–76.

20. Karl Schmidt, *Nicolaus von Basel* (Vienna: W. Braumüller, 1866).

21. *Translator's note.* Original written in Middle English, *The Scale of Perfection* (circa 1380) was later translated into Latin.

22. Herbert B. Workman, *The Dawn of the Reformation* (London, 1901–2).

23. *Translator's note.* Latin for *Treatise Against Beghard, Lollard and Beguine Heretics.*

24. Jundt, op. cit. 108.

25. *Translator's note.* German for *The Book of Spiritual Poverty.*

26. *Translator's note.* Latin for 'uneducated layman'.

27. Jundt, op. cit. 108. [*Translator's note.* Translated from the French as quoted by Vaneigem.]

28. *Translator's note.* See Wilhelm Fraenger, *The Millennium of Hieronymus Bosch: Outlines of a New Interpretation* (Chicago: University of Chicago Press, 1951).

29. *Translator's note.* For Vaneigem's extended commentary on Bosch, see "A Thousand Erotic Games", *London Review of Books*, 38/17 (8 Sept. 2016).

THE MILLENARIANS

1. *Translator's note. The Movement of the Free Spirit*, 66. The author appends the following endnote to this sentence: "Whence the name chosen by Giles of Canter's group in Brussels: *Homines Intelligentiae* (the Men of Intelligence)" (260 n. 1).

2. *Translator's note.* Ibid. The author appends an endnote (260 n. 2) here citing Joachim of Fiore, *Concordia novi ac veteris testamenti* (1200), 2.5.21a and 3.7.28c.

3. *Translator's note.* Latin for 'the law of freedom'.

4. *Translator's note.* Latin for *Abbot Joachim of Florence Writing about the Prophet Isaiah*.

5. *Translator's note.* Latin for *Abbot Joachim's Excellent Interpretation of Jeremiah the Prophet*.

6. *Translator's note.* First published in French in 1854. Vaneigem wrote a preface titled "Terrorisme ou révolution" for a collection of Coeurderoy's writings titled *Pour la révolution* (Paris: Éditions champ libre, 1972).

7. *Translator's note.* Latin for *Introduction to the Eternal Gospel*.

8. Joachim of Fiore, *Concordia*, 3.7.28c.

9. Joachim of Fiore, *L'Évangile éternel*, trans. Emmanuel Aegerter (Paris: Rieder, 1928); Johann Chrysostomus Huck, *Joachim von Floris und die joachitische Literatur: Ein Beitrag zur Geistesgeschichte des hohenstaufischen Zeitalters* (Freiburg im Brisgau: Herder, 1938). [*Translator's note. The Chronicle of Salimbene de Adam*, trans. Joseph L. Baird, Giuseppe Baglivi, and John Robert Kane (Binghamton, NY: Medieval and Renaissance Texts and Studies, 1986), 253.]

10. *Translator's note.* Cf. Matthew 4: 17: "Repent, for the kingdom of heaven is at hand".

11. "Cronica fratris Salimbene de Adam Ordinis Minorum", in *Monumenta Germaniae historica: Scriptores*, ed. Oswald Holder-Egger (Hannover and Leipzig, 1905–13), 37.1.255 sq. [*Translator's note. The Chronicle of Salimbene de Adam*, 286, 249–50.]

12. Ibid. [*Translator's note. The Movement of the Free Spirit*, 81.]

13. Vaneigem, *Le Mouvement du libre-esprit*, 73. [*Translator's note*. See Vaneigem, *The Movement of the Free Spirit*, 80–1. In Italian, *leccatores* means 'lechers', *ghiottoni* means 'gluttons', and *scrocconi* means 'freeloaders'.]

14. *Translator's note*. Italian for 'humiliated person'.

15. *Translator's note*. Cf. Chapter 31 of the present work.

16. *Translator's note*. Italian for 'Bare Wall'.

17. *Translator's note*. Latin for *The Scale of Perfection*, the title of a work by Walter Hilton. Cf. Chapter 32 of the present work.

18. *Translator's note*. Rather than translating Ball back into English I have quoted from the original. 'Delved' means 'dug', as in digging the fields, and 'span' means 'spun', as in the spinning of fabric.

19. *Translator's note*. A leader of the peasants' revolt in England in the fourteenth century.

20. *Translator's note*. Here Vaneigem is supporting the central thesis of Norman Cohn, *The Pursuit of the Millennium: Revolutionary Millenarians and Mystical Anarchists of the Middle Ages* (rev. edn., New York: Oxford University Press, 1970).

21. Eugenio Anagnine, *Dolcino e il movimento ereticale all'inizio del trecento* (Florence: La nuova Italia, 1964).

THE FLAGELLANTS

1. Cohn, *Les Fanatiques de l'apocalpyse*, 134 and 135. [*Translator's note*. Vaneigem refers here to the French translation of Norman Cohn's *The Pursuit of the Millennium*, 128–9. Rather than translate Cohn back into English I have quoted directly from the original.]

2. Ibid. 147. [*Translator's note*. *The Pursuit of the Millennium*, 139.]

3. Cited in Jean Delumeau, *La Peur en occident: XIVe–XVIIIe siècles: Une cité assiégée* (Paris: Fayard, 1978), 313.

4. *Translator's note*. Known as 'the Angel of the Last Judgment', the ferociously anti-Semitic Ferrier was canonized by Pope Callixtus III in 1455.

5. Guarnieri, *Il movimento del libero spirito*, 427. [*Translator's note*. Vaneigem, *The Movement of the Free Spirit*, 88.]

THE FRATICELLES

1. Angelo Clareno, *Historia septem tribulationum ordinis minorum*, ed. Franz Ehrle, *Archiv für Literatur und Kirchengeschichte des Mittelalters*, ii (Berlin: Weidmannsche

Buchhandlung, 1886). [*Translator's note*. Translated from Vaneigem's French.]

2. Cited in Emile Gebhart, *L'Italie mystique: Histoire de la renaissance religieuse au Moyen Âge* (Paris: Hachette, 1908), 198. [*Translator's note*. Translated from the French as quoted by Vaneigem.]

3. *Translator's note*. Latin for 'The Poor Hermits of Lord Celestine'.

4. Henry-Charles Lea, *A History of the Inquisition of the Middle Ages* (New York: Harper & Brothers, 1887); translated by Salomon Reinach as *Histoire de l'inquisition au Moyen Âge* (Paris, 1900), i. 49.

5. *Translator's note*. Papal bulls issued by John XXII on 30 December 1317 and 23 January 1318 excommunicated both the Spirituals and the Fraticelles.

6. *Translator's note*. Cf. Vaneigem, *The Movement of the Free Spirit*, 124–8.

7. *Translation*: Latin for 'congregation of liberty'.

8. *Translator's note*. Latin for *The Tree of the Crucified Life of Jesus*.

9. *Translator's note*. Vaneigem, *The Movement of the Free-Spirit*, 128.

10. *Translator's note*. Vaneigem, *The Movement of the Free-Spirit*, 128, which appends an endnote to this paragraph: "Compare with Margaret Porete: 'The soul has no discomfort about its past sins, nor about the sufferings God suffered for it, nor for the sins and discomforts in which those close to them remain'" (277 n. 110).

11. Vaneigem, *Le Mouvement du libre-esprit*, op. cit. [*Translator's note*. Vaneigem, *The Movement of the Free-Spirit*, 128. An endnote added by the author (277 n. 111) refers the reader to Ubertino of Casale, *Arbor vitae crucifixae Jesu* (Venice, 1485).]

12. *Translation*: Latin for 'ecstatic love'.

13. *Translation*: Latin for 'Men of Intelligence'. See Chapter 37 of the present work.

14. Franz Ehrle, "Die Spiritualen, ihr Verhältnis zum Franziskanerorden und zu den Fraticellen", in *Archiv für Literatur und Kirchengeschichte des Mittelalters* (Berlin: Weidmannsche Buchhandlung, 1888), vol. iv. 78 *sq.*; Luigi Fumi, "Eretici e ribelli nell'Umbria dal 1320 al 1330", *Bolletino della regia deputazione di storia patria per l'Umbria*, 5 (1899), 349–82.

15. *Translator's note*. On 1 June 1428 Martin V ordered the Bishop of Ancona to strictly enforce his rulings against the Fraticelles in Maiolati, where all the suspects were tortured on the rack and where their village was destroyed.

16. *Translator's note*. Cf. Chapter 33 of the present work.

17. Pierre Bayle, "Fraticelli", in *Dictionnaire historique et critique* (Rotterdam: Chez Reinier Leers, 1697).

18. *Translator's note*. Italian for 'keg' or 'small barrel'.

19. Oliger, op. cit.; Guarnieri, 476; Ehrle, op. cit. 78 and sq.

20. Ehrle, op. cit. 127, 137, and 180.

THE EASTERN REFORMERS

1. *Translator's note.* Sometimes called John Huss, thus his followers were 'Hussites'.

2. Cohn, *Les Fanatiques*, op. cit. 226. [*Translator's note. The Pursuit of the Millennium*, 207.]

3. Cohn, *Les Fanatiques*, 232. [*Translator's note.* Cf. *The Pursuit of the Millennium*, 212: "This emerges quite clearly from an open letter distributed at that time: 'There are five of these cities, which will not enter into agreements with the Antichrist or surrender to him'".]

4. Cohn, *Les Fanatiques*, 232. [*Translator's note. The Pursuit of the Millennium*, 212. Cf. Jeremiah 48:10: "Cursed is he who does the work of the Lord with slackness, and cursed is he who keeps back his sword from bloodshed".]

5. Howard Kaminisky, "The Free Spirit in the Hussite Revolution", in *Millennial Dreams in Action: Essays in Comparative Study*, ed. Sylvia L. Thrupp (The Hague: Mouton, 1962), 47.

6. Ibid. 48.

7. *Translator's note.* After the siege and sacking of the self-governing community briefly established in Münster by radical Anabaptists in 1534 (see Chapter 42), Jan van Batenburg formed a new sect, one that was even more extreme than other Anabaptist movements.

THE MEN OF INTELLIGENCE AND THE PICARDS OF BOHEMIA

1. *Translator's note.* See Vaneigem, *The Movement of the Free Spirit*, 188–92.

2. Vaneigem, *Le Mouvement du libre-espirit*, op. cit. 180 and sq. [*Translator's note.* See Vaneigem, *The Movement of the Free Spirit*, 192–5. Note that at each point at which I have used an endnote to indicate overlaps between *The Movement of the Free Spirit* and the present work, I have retained the translation that is offered in the former.]

3. Lawrence of Brezová, "De gestis et variis accidentibus regni Boemiae", in *Fontes rerum bohemicarum*, ed. Jaroslav Goll (Prague, 1893), v. 431.

4. *Translator's note.* Vaneigem, *The Movement of the Free Spirit*, 288 n. 23. Vaneigem cites here Aeneas Silvius Bartholomeus (also known as Pope Pius II), "De hortu et historia Bohemorum", in *Omnia opera* (Basel, 1551).

5. *Translator's note. The Movement of the Free Spirit*, 193, which refers the reader via

an endnote (288 n. 235) to Karl Adolph Constantin Höfler, "Geschichtesschreiber der husitichen Bewegung in Boehmen", in *Fontes rerum austriacarum* (Vienna, 1856–66), section 1, vols. ii, v, and vii.

6. Lawrence of Brezová, *De gestis*, op. cit. 431. [*Translator's note. The Movement of the Free Spirit*, 193].

7. *Translator's note.* Author of *Histoire critique de Manichée et du manichéisme* (Amsterdam: J. Frederic Bernard, 1739).

8. Vaneigem, *Le Mouvement du libre-espirit*, op. cit. 186 and *sq*. [*Translator's note. The Movement of the Free Spirit*, 193–4, which refers the reader via a series of endnotes (288 n. 238–40) to Lawrence of Brezová's *De gestis*. The textual interpolations here also appear in *The Movement of the Free Spirit*.]

9. *Translator's note.* Thanks to the American television series *Star Trek: The Next Generation*, the word 'Picard' has stayed with us in the form of Jean-Luc Picard, the French captain (with an English accent) of the Starship Enterprise. In *The Drumhead*, the ninety-fifth episode of this series, which originally aired on 29 April 1991, Captain Picard says, "We think we've come so far. Torture of heretics, burning of witches, it's all ancient history. Then—before you can blink an eye—suddenly it threatens to start all over again".

THE VICTORY OF THE REFORMERS AND THE BIRTH OF THE PROTESTANT CHURCHES

1. Émile Gebhart, *L'Italie mystique: Histoire de la renaissance religieuse au Moyen Âge* (Paris: Librairie Hachette, 1890), 156. [*Translator's note.* Émile Gebhart, *Mystics and Heretics in Italy at the End of the Middle Ages*, trans. Edwin Maslin Hulme (London: George Allen & Unwin, 1922), 174.]

2. *Translator's note.* Cohn, *The Pursuit of the Millennium*, 226.

3. Cohn, *Les Fanatiques de l'apocalypse*, 247–54. [*Translator's note.* Cohn, *The Pursuit of the Millennium*, 228–9.]

4. *Translator's note.* Latin for 'extravagance' and 'greed', respectively.

5. *Translator's note.* According to Margaret L. King, *The Renaissance in Europe* (London: Laurence King Publishing, 2003), 190, Savonarola's followers were called *piagnoni* or 'Weepers', because they wept for their sins and the sins of the world.

6. *Translator's note.* Latin for 'Whose realm, their religion'—that is to say, the religion of the ruler becomes the religion of those who are ruled.

7. *Translator's note.* According to *The Catholic Encyclopedia: An International Work of Reference on the Constitution, Doctrine, Discipline, and History of the Catholic Church*, vol. ix, ed. Charles G. Herbermann, et al. (New York: The Encyclopedia Press,

Inc., 1913), "History presents few characters more unfortunate and pathetic than Tetzel. Among his contemporaries the victim of the most corrosive ridicule, every foul charge laid at his door, every blasphemous utterance placed in his mouth, a veritable literature of fiction and fable built about his personality, in modern history held up as the proverbial mountebank and oily harlequin, denied even the support and sympathy of his own allies—Tetzel had to await the light of modern critical scrutiny, not only for a moral rehabilitation, but also for vindication as a soundly trained theologian and a monk of irreproachable deportment" (entry on "Luther, Martin").

8. *Translator's note.* Translated from Vaneigem's French. Note that neither this insult (nor anything like it) appears on the rather extensive "List of Luther's Insults" that is hosted by <ergofabulous.org>.

9. *Translator's note.* English term 'marketing' used in the original text.

10. *Translator's note.* German for *Against the Bands of Looting Peasants and Assassins.*

11. *Translator's note.* Latin for 'Supreme Pontiff'.

THE DISSIDENTS FROM LUTHERANISM AND CALVINISM

1. *Translator's note.* Martin Luther, "That Jesus was Born a Jew", quoted by Hugh Schonfield, *The History of Jewish Christianity* (London: Duckworth, 1936).

2. *Translator's note.* Martin Luther, "That Jesus was Born a Jew", quoted by Armin Bachor, "The Secret of the Reformation", *Miskan: A Forum on the Gospel and the Jewish People,* 78 (2017), 37.

3. Delumeau, op. cit. 372 and 373. [*Translator's note.* The reader will surely notice that Delumeau presents his citations rather haphazardly, zig-zagging from one source to another and then back again.]

4. *Translator's note.* The World History/Archive Alamy includes a Nazi propaganda poster from 1933 that depicts Luther and a swastika, lists the dates 1483 (Luther's birth) and 1933, and, according to <facinghistory.org>, which reproduces this poster, proclaims "Hitler's fight and Luther's teaching are the best defense for the German people".

5. *Translator's note.* Martin Luther, "On the Jews and Their Lies", trans. Martin H. Bertram, *Luther's Works,* vol. xlvii (Philadelphia: Fortress Press, 1971).

6. *Translator's note.* Martin Luther, "On the Unknowable Name and the Generations of Christ", quoted by Gerhard Falk, *The Jew in Christian Theology: Martin Luther's Anti-Jewish* Vom Schem Hamphoras, *Previously Unpublished in English, and Other Milestones in Church Doctrine Concerning Judaism* (Jefferson, NC: McFarland & Company Inc., 1992).

7. *Translator's note.* Martin Luther, "On the Jews and Their Lies", trans. Martin H. Bertram, *Luther's Works*, op. cit.

8. *Translator's note.* Unknown source, translated from the French as quoted by Vaneigem.

9. *Translator's note.* Martin Luther, "On the Jews and Their Lies", trans. Martin H. Bertram *Luther's Works*, op. cit.

10. Delumeau, op. cit. 518. [*Translator's note.* Martin Luther, "That Jesus Was Born a Jew", translated from the French as quoted by Vaneigem.]

11. *Translator's note.* Translated from the French as quoted by Vaneigem. Luther did in fact write two letters to the Elector John of Saxony in 1526 (9 Feb. and 22 Nov.), but neither includes this sentence. In fact, none of the four hundred and ninety-seven letters reproduced by <lutherdansk.dk> include it or anything similar.

12. *Translator's note.* Caspar Schwenckfeld, quoted in Hartmann Grisar, *Luther*, ed. Luigi Cappadelta and trans. E. M. Lamond (London: Kegan Paul, Trench, Trübner & Company, Ltd. 1916), v. 155.

13. Delumeau, op. cit. 519.

14. Sébastien Castellion, *Traité des hérétiques: À savoir, si on les doit persécuter, et comment on se doit conduire avec eux, selon l'avis, opinion, et sentence de plusieurs auteurs, tant anciens, que modernes* (Geneva: Alexandre Jullien, 1913), 12.

15. Calvin, *Déclaration pour maintenir la vraie foy*, in *Opera omnia*. [*Translator's note.* Written and published in both Latin (*Defensio orthodoxae fidei de sacra trinitate*) and French (*Declaration pour maintenir la vraye foy que tiennent tous chrestiens de la Trinité des personnes en un seul Dieu*) in 1554, these texts are reprinted in *Ioannis Calvini opera quae supersunt omnia*, ed. Gulielmus Baum et al. (Brunswick, 1864–1900), vol. viii. I have translated the passage in question from the French as quoted by Vaneigem.]

16. Theodore Beza, quoted by Delumeau, op. cit. 520. [*Translator's note.* Translated from the French as quoted by Vaneigem.]

17. Ibid. 521. [*Translator's note.* Theodore Beza, *On the Right of Magistrates: Concerning the Rights of Rulers over Their Subjects and the Duty of Subjects towards Their Rulers. A Brief and Clear Treatise Particularly Indispensable to Either Class in These Troubled Times*, ed. Patrick S. Poole and trans. Henry-Louis Gonin <https://constitution.org/1-Constitution/cmt/beza/magistrates.htm>.]

18. *Translator's note.* Widely adopted by the anarchist movement in the nineteenth century.

19. Theodor Kolde, "Zum Process des Johann Denck und der drei gottlosen Maler

von Nürnberg", in *Kirchengeschichtliche Studien: Hermann Reuter zum 70. Geburtsag gewidmet*, ed. Theodor Brieger (Leipzig: J. C. Hinrichs, 1890).

20. "Johannes Denck", in *Dictionnaire d'histoire et de géographie écclesiastique*, ed. Alfred Baudrillart et al. (Paris: Librairie Letouzey et Ané, 1930).

21. *Translator's note*. German for *Those Who Truly Love the Truth*.

22. *Translator's note*. German for *On True Love*.

23. *Translator's note*. Written in the fourteenth century by an anonymous author (possibly John Tauler) and published by Martin Luther in 1516 and 1518, this mystical work was reprinted in 1528 by Ludwig Haetzer. It would appear that Denck was one of the many editors of this work. See George Huntston Williams, *The Radical Reformation* (3rd edn., University Park, Penn State University Press, 1995), who also notes that, "after a score of imprints there will appear in Worms in 1528 the first 'Anabaptist version', *Theologia Teütsch*, stylistically touched up by the Antitrinitarian Anabaptist Louis [sic] Haetzer and with an appendix, probably composed by the Anabaptist mystic John Denck, entitled *Etliche Hauptreden*, which in effect replaces Luther's foreword" (80).

24. *Translator's note*. Translated from Vaneigem's French.

25. "Johannes Denck", in *Dictionnaire d'histoire*, op. cit. [*Translator's note*. Translated from the French as quoted by Vaneigem.]

26. *Chroniques, annales et histoire de la Bible*. [*Translator's note*. Following Vaneigem, I offer a translation of the title, though the book itself has not to my knowledge been translated into either French or English: *Chronicles, Annals and History of the Bible*.]

27. Sebastian Franck, *Chronica, Zeitbuch, und Geschichtbibel* (Strasbourg, 1531).

28. *Translator's note*. Étienne de La Boétie, a contemporary of this period (1530–63), was the author of *Discours de la servitude volontaire* (*Discourse on Voluntary Servitude*).

29. Franck, *Chronica*, op. cit.

30. *Translator's note*. Latin for *On the Errors of the Trinity*.

31. *Translator's note*. Latin for *The Restoration of Christianity*.

32. Roland H. Bainton, *Hunted Heretic: The Life and Death of Michael Servetus, 1511–1553* (Boston: The Beacon Press, 1953); George Huntston Williams, *The Radical Reformation* (Philadelphia: The Westminster Press, 1962).

33. *Translator's note*. Translated from Vaneigem's French. See Stefan Zweig, *Castellio Against Calvin, or Conscience Against Violence*, trans. Robert Boettcher (independently published, 2021), which quotes Castellion's denunciation of Calvin's spiritual intolerance: "All the sects have founded their religions upon the word of God, and the members of each sect regard their own as being in exclusive possession of the truth. But, according

to Calvin, one sect alone is right, and the others must accommodate themselves to it. [...] Calvin [...] taking for granted his own infallibility, regards his views as right and the views of anyone who may differ from him as wrong" (128–9).

34. *Translator's note. De haereticis an sint persequendi* (Basle, 1554).

35. *Translator's note.* Sebastian Castellio, *Advice to a Desolate France*, ed. Marius F. Valkhoff and trans. Wouter Valkhoff (Shepherdstown, WV: Patmos Press, 1975), 17.

36. Ferdinand Buisson, *Sébastian Castellion: Sa vie et son oeuvre, 1515–1563: Étude sur les origines du protestantisme libéral français* (Paris: Hachette, 1892).

THE *ALUMBRADOS* OF SPAIN

1. *Translator's note.* The *Guerra de las Comunidades de Castilla* (The 'War of the Communities of Castile') was fought against Charles V between 1520 and 1521.

2. Marcel Bataillon, *Erasme et l'Espagne: Recherches sur l'histoire spirituelle du XVIᵉ siècle* (Paris: E. Droz, 1937), 73. [*Translator's note. The Movement of the Free Spirit*, 197. Note that *Alumbrados* can be translated as 'Illuminati'.]

3. *Translator's note.* Vaneigem, *The Movement of the Free Spirit* 198, appends an endnote here: "The phrasing is attributed to father Alcázar, a friend of Isabel" (290 n. 245).

4. *Translator's note.* Ibid. appends an endnote here: "Whence their rejection of sacraments, prayers and good works" (290 n. 246).

5. Marcelino Menéndez y Pelayo, *Historia de los heterodoxos españoles* (Madrid: V. Suárez, 1928), v. 526. [*Translator's note.* Vaneigem, *The Movement of the Free Spirit*, 198. The textual interpolation in the second sentence here also appears in that book.]

6. *Translator's note.* Spanish for 'beatified' or 'blessed'.

7. *Translator's note.* According to Katy Iverson, "Honor, Gender and the Law: Defense Strategies during the Spanish Inquisition, 1526–1532", MA diss. (College of William & Mary, 2010), "Hernández was one of the three female leaders of the *alumbrado* movement; she enjoyed a reputation as a spiritual healer and advisor. She was rumored not only to have the ability to heal, but also to interpret Sacred Scripture and rid priests of their sexual temptations" (34 n. 71).

8. Menéndez y Pelayo, *Historia de los heterodoxas españoles*, op. cit. 530. [*Translator's note.* Translated from Vaneigem's French.]

9. *Translator's note.* Vaneigem, *The Movement of the Free Spirit*, 199.

10. *Translator's note.* Quemadero De Tablada was a place for executions, built in Seville in 1481.

11. Vaneigem, op. cit. 193. [*Translator's note.* Vaneigem, *The Movement of the Free*

Spirit, 200, which refers the reader via an endnote (289 n. 250) to *Dictionnaire d'histoire et de géographie ecclésiastique* (Paris: Letouzey, 1930), vol. ii.]

12. Ibid. 194. [*Translator's note.* Vaneigem, *The Movement of the Free Spirit*, 201.]

13. *Translator's note.* Vaneigem appends an endnote to a similar passage in *The Movement of the Free Spirit* (202): "Connections have been made between the Alumbrados and the Guerinites, Illuminati, supports of Abbot Guérin, priest of Roye, who were subject to persecution in Picardy and Flanders in 1634" (289 n. 252).

THE SPIRITUAL LIBERTINES

1. *Translator's note.* Here I am matching the spelling adopted in *The Movement of the Free Spirit*. Other sources spell his first name Eligius and call his followers Loists.

2. *Translator's note.* See Vaneigem, *The Movement of the Free Spirit*, 200–13, 215–8 and 223–34.

3. *Translator's note.* Latin for 'illiterate and unskilled'. According to J. C. Margolin, "Libertins, libertinisme et 'libertinage' au XVIe siècle", published in *Aspects du libertinisme au XVIe siècle*, ed. Marcel Bataillon (Paris: Vrin, 1974), 1–33, this phrase was used by Calvin to describe Pruystinck.

4. *Translator's note.* An Anabaptist leader (1501–56) in the Netherlands.

5. Martin Luther, *Werke* (Weimar, 1883–1908), vol. xviii; French translation in Jundt, op. cit. 122–3. [*Translator's note.* Vaneigem, *The Movement of the Free Spirit*, 205–6.]

6. *Translator's note.* Vaneigem, *The Movement of the Free Spirit*, 207, which appends an endnote: "None of these has ever been found. It is probable that, like the spiritual treatises denounced by Calvin, their subversiveness was less in their literal than their cryptic meanings, which readers could discover at their will" (290–1 n. 268).

7. *Translator's note.* Vaneigem, *The Movement of the Free Spirit*, 207, appends an endnote to a similar sentence in that work: "Within the group, the rich found a kind of innocence of pleasure that all the gold in the world could not bring them while they remained under the control of the Church, paying for the redemption of their sins with remorse and expiatory masses" (290 n. 269).

8. Emanuel Van Meteren, *Historie der Neder-landscher ende haerder na-buren oorlogen ende geschiedenissen, tot den iare M.VIC.XII* (The Hague, 1623). [*Translator's note.* Vaneigem, *The Movement of the Free Spirit*, 207.]

9. Ibid. [*Translator's note.* Vaneigem, *The Movement of the Free Spirit*, 208.]

10. *Translator's note.* Vaneigem, *The Movement of the Free Spirit*, 208.

11. *Translator's note.* Ibid. 209–10.

12. French translation in Vaneigem, *Le Mouvement du Libre-Espirit*, 210. [*Translator's note.* See Vaneigem, *The Movement of the Free Spirit*, 218–23, which refers the reader via an endnote (292 n. 294) to Ignaz von Döllinger, *Beiträge zur Sektengeschicte des Mittelalters* (Munich: C. H. Beck, 1890), vol. ii, no. 62, 664–8, and, for the Latin text, to Jules Frederichs, *De Secte der Loisten of Antwerpsche Libertijnen (1525–1545): Eligius Pruystinck (Loy de Schaliedecker) en zijne Aanhangers* (Ghent: Vuylsteke, 1891).]

13. Georges Eekhoud, *Les libertins d'Anvers: Légende et histoire des loistes* (Paris: Mercure de France, 1912).

14. *Translator's note.* During the Dutch *Beeldenstorn*, known in English as the Great Iconoclasm or the Iconoclastic Fury, Catholic art and many forms of church fittings and decorations were destroyed by mobs of Calvinist Protestants.

15. *Translator's note.* Cf. Chapter 42 of the present work.

16. *Translator's note.* See James A. Wylie, *The History of Protestantism* (London: Cassell & Company, 1874), ii. 310: "'It is in this sense', she [Madame Ameaux] said[,] [...] 'we ought to take the communion of saints, spoken of in the Apostles' Creed; for this communion can never be perfect till all things are common among the faithful—goods, houses, and body'".

17. Jacob Spon, *Histoire de Genève: Rectifiée et considérablement augmentée par d'amples notes: avec les actes et autres pièces servant de preuves à cette histoire* (Geneva: Fabri & Barrillot, 1730), i. 399.

18. Jundt, op. cit. 127.

19. *Translator's note. Maraux* and *escervelés* are Middle French (Vaneigem calls it "the French of Rabelais") for 'scoundrel' and 'brainless idiot', respectively.

20. *Translator's note. Follastre* is Middle French for a 'truly crazy and stupid person'.

21. *Translator's note.* Middle French for 'very illustrious reader'.

22. François Berriot, "Un procès d'athéisme à Genève: L'affaire Gruet (1547–1550)", *Bulletin de la Société de l'histoire du protestantisme français*, 125 (Oct.–Dec. 1979), 577–92. [*Translator's note.* All Latin interpolations made by Berriot.]

23. Ibid. [*Translator's note.* Translated from the French as quoted by Vaneigem.]

24. John Calvin, *Contre la secte phantastique et furieuse des libertins, qui se nomment spirituels* (Geneva: Jean Girard, 1547).

25. *Translator's note.* See Vaneigem, *The Movement of the Free Spirit*, 224–32.

26. *Translator's note.* Literally 'Marguerite of the daisies' or perhaps the 'Daisy of the daisies'. An allusion to Marguerite de Navarre, the Queen of Navarre.

27. Jundt, *Histoire du panthéisme populaire*, op. cit. 128.

28. Ibid.

29. *Translator's note.* Vaneigem, *The Movement of the Free Spirit*, 292 n. 297. The full note runs as follows: "On September 13, 1542, at Valenciennes, 'Hughes Lescantelier, brewer, native of Maire les Tournai and Caso Hocq, native of this city', were sentenced to have 'their heads severed' for having supported a 'new sect called libertine', Hugues [*sic*] Lescantier in particular had affirmed that 'after men are washed . . . of their sins, they sin no more', while his companion had denied the Resurrection of Christ and declared 'that Jesus Christ was not hung on the cross, but the Devil in a fantastic body' (Bibliothèque municipale de Valenciennes, ms. 699, *Régistre des Choses communes*, folio 44)".

30. Calvin, *Contre la secte*, op. cit. 113. [*Translator's note.* Translated from the French as quoted by Vaneigem. On the Quintinists' use of dialect and jargon, see the quotation from Calvin's *Against the Fantastic and Furious Sect of the Libertines Who Call Themselves Spirituals* in Ferdinand Brunetière, "Calvin's Literary Work", *The Presbyterian and Reformed Review*, 47 (July 1901): "the loafers, as they are called, have a peculiar jargon which is understood only by their brotherhood, so that they deceive a man speaking in his presence without his knowing it, also the Quintinists have a barbarous language in which they chatter so that they are understood no better than are singing birds. Not that they do not use common words, as do others, but they so disguise their significance that one never knows what is the subject matter of which they speak, nor what it is they wish to affirm or deny" (399–400).]

31. *Translator's note.* Vaneigem, *The Movement of the Free Spirit*, 232, appends an endnote here: "This is the Calvinist translation of amorous passion, in which lovers, like children, dream of creating a world of innocence, without wrong or restraint" (293 n. 311).

32. Calvin, *Contre la secte*, op. cit. 113. [*Translator's note.* Vaneigem, *The Movement of the Free Spirit*, 232.]

33. Jundt, op. cit. 131. See also Vaneigem, op. cit. 215 and sq. [*Translator's note.* Vaneigem, *The Movement of the Free Spirit*, 224–32.]

THE ANABAPTISTS

1. *Translator's note.* Not discussed in the present work, the *Bagaudae* were insurgent peasants in the third century.

2. Cohn, *Les Fanatiques de l'apocalypse*, 255. [*Translator's note.* Cohn, *The Pursuit of the Millennium*, 119.]

3. *Translator's note.* German for 'tied-shoe alliance', the *Bundschuh* movement linked

together a series of peasant revolts in Germany between 1493 and 1517.

4. Maurice Pianzola, *Peintres et vilains: Les artistes de la Renaissance et la grande guerre des paysans en 1525* (Paris: Éditions cercle d'art, 1962). [*Translator's note*. Vaneigem adopted the name 'Ratgeb' in 1974 when he published *De la grève sauvage à l'autogestion généralisée* (Paris: Union générale d'éditions, 1974).]

5. Ibid.

6. Cohn, op. cit. 270. [*Translator's note*. Cohn, *The Pursuit of the Millennium*, 247.]

7. Ibid. 278. [*Translator's note*. Cohn, *The Pursuit of the Millennium*, 255.]

8. "Melchior Hoffmann", in *The Mennonite Encyclopedia: A Comprehensive Reference Work on the Anabaptist-Mennonite Movement*, ed. Harold S. Bender et al. (Scottsdale, PA: Mennonite Brethren Publishing House, 1956), vol. ii.

9. Cohn, op. cit. 279. [*Translator's note*. Cohn, *The Pursuit of the Millennium*, 255.]

10. Ibid. 280. [*Translator's note*. Cohn, *The Pursuit of the Millennium*, 255–6.]

11. Sebastian Franck, *Chronica, Zeitbuch und Geschictbibel* (Strasbourg, 1531). [*Translator's note*. Translated from Vaneigem's French.]

12. Pierre Barret and Jean-Noël Gurgand, *Le Roi des derniers jours: L'Exemplaire et très cruelle histoire des rebaptisés de Münster (1534–1535)* (Paris: Hachette, 1981).

13. Marcus van Vaernewyck, *Mémoires d'un patricien gantois du xvie siècle: Troubles religieux en Flandre et dans les Pays-Bas du xvie siècle*, trans. Hermann van Duyse (Ghent: Maison d'éditions d'art, 1905–6). [*Translator's note*. This book was published in Dutch under the title *Van die beroerlicke tijden in die Nederlanden en voornamelick in Ghendt, 1566–1568* (Ghent: C. Annoot-Braeckman, 1872–81).]

14. Karl Wilhelm Bouterwek, *Zur Literatur und Geschichte der Wiedertäufer: Besonders in den Rheinlanden* (Bonn: Marcus, 1884), 306.

THE INDIVIDUALIST MESSIAHS

1. Jundt, op. cit. 65. [*Translator's note*. Translated from the French as quoted by Vaneigem.]

2. Ibid. 166.

3. Gottfried Arnold, *Unparteiische Kirchen und Ketzerhistorie* (Frankfurt: 1699–1700). [*Translator's note*. German for *Impartial History of the Church and of Heresy*.]

4. *Translator's note*. Translation of this sentence taken from *The Movement of the Free Spirit*, 290 n. 258. The rest of the quotation is translated from the French as quoted by Vaneigem.

5. *Translator's note*. Wolfgang Fabricius Capito (1478–1541) was a German Protestant

reformer in the tradition of John Calvin who wrote an open letter "to the Reader" sometime after 22 May 1534, which was the day upon which Frey was drowned. Instead of using the German-to-French translation provided by Jundt and relayed by Vaneigem, I have called upon the more direct German-to-English translation of the "principal articles" against Frey that appears in *The Correspondence of Wolfgang Capito*, iii: *1532–1536*, trans. Erika Rummel (Toronto: University of Toronto Press, 2015), 231–2 (the textual emendation is Rummel's).

6. Jundt, op. cit. 178.

7. *Translator's note.* Friedrich Wilhelm Franz Nippold (1838–1918), a German Protestant theologian and the author of, among other works, *Handbuch der neuesten Kirchengeschichte* (Braunschweig: Schwetschke, 1880). The title in English would be *Textbook of Recent Church History*.

8. Jundt, op. cit. 201. [*Translator's note.* Translated from the French as quoted by Vaneigem.]

9. Christopher Hill, *Le monde à l'envers: Les Idées radicales au cours de la révolution anglaise*, trans. Simone Chambon and Rachel Ertel (Paris: Payot, 1977), 25. [*Translator's note.* Since this is a French translation of a work originally written in English (Christopher Hill, *The World Turned Upside Down: Radical Ideas during the English Revolution* (London: Temple Smith, 1972)), I have quoted directly from the original text (22–3). Note that, in the coming pages, Vaneigem will rely very heavily on Hill's work, both in his citations and his commentary.]

10. *Translator's note.* According to the Rosicrucian order AMORC, Torrentius was a member of the Brethren of the Rosy Cross.

11. *Translator's note.* At least one painting survived: *Still Life with Bridle* (1614), which is a part of the permanent collection at the Rijksmuseum in Amsterdam.

IRONISTS AND SKEPTICS

1. *Translator's note.* Written in 1548 by Étienne de La Boétie.

2. *Chroniken von Closener und Königshofen*, ed. Carl Hegel (Leipzig: Chroniken der deutschen Städte 8 and 9, 1870–1), extracts in *Livre secret du magistrat de Strasbourg* (Leipzig, 1871), ii. 1201; quoted in Jundt, *Histoire du panthéisme populaire*, op. cit. 106.

3. *Translator's note.* Latin for *A Little Book about the Happy Life That Is Not to Be Sought in Outside Trinkets, but Possessed in the Highest Good Within Ourselves*.

4. *Translator's note.* Dutch for *The Comedy of the Rich Man* and Latin for *The Consolation of Philosophy*, respectively.

5. *Translator's note.* Published in French in 1562.

6. Roland H. Bainton, *Bernardino Ochino: Esule e riformatore senese del cinquecento, 1487–1563*, trans. Elio Gianturco (Florence: Sansoni, 1940).

7. Rodolphe Peter, "Noel Journet, détracteur de l'écriture sainte (1582)", in *Croyants et sceptiques au XVIᵉ siècle: Le Dossier des 'Épicuriens'*, ed. Marc Lienhard (Strasbourg: Istra, 1981).

8. *Translator's note.* Quotations from Chassanion translated from the French as quoted by Vaneigem.

9. *Translator's note.* Latin for *The Art of Believing in Nothing*.

10. Frédéric Lachèvre, *Geoffroy Vallée (brûlé le 9 février 1574) et la "Béatitude des chrestiens": L'Ancêtre des libertins du XVIIᵉ siècle* (Paris: E. Champion, 1920).

11. *Translator's note.* See Geoffroy Vallée, *La Béatitude des chrétiens, ou Le Fléau de la foi*, ed. Alain Mothu (Paris: Les Éditions Demeter, 2005) and Geoffroy Vallée, *L'Art de ne croire en rien, suivi de Livre des trois imposteurs*, ed. Raoul Vaneigem (Paris: Éditions Payot & Rivages, 2002).

LEVELERS, DIGGERS, AND RANTERS

1. Hill, *Le Monde a l'envers*, 15. [*Translator's note.* Hill, *The World Turned Upside Down*, 12.]

2. *Translator's note.* The name 'the Diggers' was adopted in the 1960s by a group of radical community activists in the Haight-Ashbury neighborhood of San Francisco, California. Like their namesakes, they sought to create a new society outside of capitalism, money, and markets. Cf. Emmett Grogan, *Ringolevio: A Life Played for Keeps* (Boston: Little Brown, 1972).

3. Hill, *Le Monde a l'envers*, 88 and 89. [*Translator's note.* Hill, *The World Turned Upside Down*, 87–8.]

4. Ibid. 90. [*Translator's note.* Hill, *The World Turned Upside Down*, 88.]

5. Ibid. 207. [*Translator's note.* Hill, *The World Turned Upside Down*, 213.]

6. Ibid. 91. [*Translator's note.* Winstanley quoted in Hill, *The World Turned Upside Down*, 90.]

7. *Translator's note.* Hill, 95. Note that while Hill attributes the first quotation to Lilburne, *A Whip for the Present House of Lords* (Feb. 1647–8)—which is included in *The Leveler Tracts, 1647–1653*, ed. William Haller and Godfrey Davies (New York: Columbia University Press, 1944), 449—the second quotation is Hill's own summary.

8. Hill, *Le Monde a l'envers*, 105–7. [*Translator's note.* Hill, *The World Turned Upside*

Down, 106–7.]

9. Ibid. 112 and 113. [*Translator's note.* Hill, *The World Turned Upside Down*, 112–4.]

10. Note that the phrase "This is the flesh of Christ, take and eat" recalls Claushorn and his friends, who were banished from Strasbourg in 1359. Such was the typical treatment of God once language had been released from the bonds of religion by joy and drink.

11. Hill, *Le Monde a l'envers*, 159. [*Translator's note.* Hill, *The World Turned Upside Down*, 161.]

12. Ibid. [*Translator's note.* Hill, *The World Turned Upside Down*, 160.]

13. Ibid. [*Translator's note.* Hill, *The World Turned Upside Down*, 160.]

14. Jacob Bauthumley, *The Light and Dark Sides of God* (London: William Learner, 1650), 4. [*Translator's note.* Bauthumley quoted in Hill, *The World Turned Upside Down*, 165. Note that the third quotation is from Edward Hide's *A Wonder, Yet No Wonder* (1651), 35–41. Hide was in fact an opponent of the Ranters.]

15. *Translator's note.* Latin for 'Rejoice in the Lamb'; written between 1759 and 1763 while Christopher Smart (1722–71) was in a mental asylum.

16. Hill, 166–8. [*Translator's note.* Hill, *The World Turned Upside Down*, 168–70. See also Abiezer Coppe, *Selected Writings*, ed. Andrew Hopton (London: Aporia Press, 1987), 16, 20.]

17. *Translator's note.* Coppe quoted in Hill, *The World Turned Upside Down*, 169.

18. *Translator's note.* Hill, ibid.

19. *Translator's note.* Ibid. 169–70. See also Coppe, op. cit. 38.

20. *Translator's note.* Ibid. 169. See also Coppe, 24.

21. *Translator's note.* Ibid. 170, quoting the condemnation of Coppe. See also Coppe, 111.

22. *Translator's note.* Ibid. 170–1.

23. *Translator's note.* Ibid. 172.

24. *Translator's note.* Ibid. 172. These particular phrases are from Hill's summary of Clarkson's views.

25. *Translator's note.* Ibid. 172.

26. *Translator's note.* Ibid. 173.

27. *Translator's note.* Ibid. 173–4. The first of the quoted phrases here is Hill's; the subsequent two are Clarkson's.

28. *Translator's note.* Lodowicke Muggleton (1609–98).

29. *Translator's note. The World Turned Upside Down*, 178.

30. *Translator's note.* Cf. Christopher Hill, *Milton and the English Revolution*

(London: Faber and Faber, 1977).

31. *Translator's note. The World Turned Upside Down*, 176.

32. *Translator's note.* Ibid. 177.

33. *Translator's note.* All quotations attributed or referring to Thomas Webbe are from ibid. 182.

34. *Translator's note.* Note that the French translation of Hill used by Vaneigem renders this phrase as "une vraie Bible d'impiété et de communisme" ("a true Bible of impiety and communism").

35. *Translator's note.* Hill, *The World Turned Upside Down*, 177.

36. *Translator's note.* Ibid. 178.

37. *Translator's note.* Ibid. The first of these quotations is from Hill's historical summary; the second consists of Coppin's own words.

38. *Translator's note.* Ibid.

39. *Translator's note.* Ibid. 181–2.

THE JANSENISTS

1. *Translator's note.* Jean-Baptiste Lully (1632–87) was an Italian-born French composer who was attached to the court of Louis XIV. Jacques-Bénigne Bossuet (1627–1704) was a French bishop and theologian.

2. *Translator's note. Le Roi Soleil* (the Sun King) positioned himself at the center of the entire universe.

3. *Translator's note.* After the revocation of the Edict of Nantes by the Edict of Fontainebleau (1685), Protestants who publicly practiced their faith were subject to persecution and to prison terms aboard galleys as rowers.

4. *Translator's note. Le Tartuffe, ou l'imposteur*, a play by Jean-Baptiste Poquelin (1622–73)—better known as Molière—was banned by Louis XIV in 1664. Port-Royal-des-Champs was an abbey of Cistercian nuns known for their adherence to the ideas of Cornelius Jansenius.

5. Abbé Pluquet, *Mémoires pour servir à l'histoire des égarements de l'esprit humain par rapport à la religion chrétienne, ou Dictionnaire des hérésies, des erreurs et des schismes* (Besançon, 1817), ii. 213. [*Translator's note.* Most of the correspondence between Jansenius and Duvergier has been lost; what remains is collected in *Lettres de C. Jansénius á J. DuVerger de Hauranne*, ed. Gerberon (Cologne: 1703).]

6. Ibid.

7. *Translator's note.* Hyacinthe Robillard d'Avrigny, *Mémoires chronologiques et*

dogmatiques, pour servir à l'histoire ecclésiastique depuis 1600 jusqu'en 1716. Avec des réflexions & remarques critiques (Guerin, 1739).

8. "Arnauld", in *Dictionnaire d'histoire et de géographie ecclésiastique*.

9. Ibid.

10. *Translator's note. Julie's Garland* (1641) was a collectively written group of madrigals commissioned by Charles de Sainte-Maure for the purpose of wooing Julie d'Angennes.

11. *Translator's note.* Named for the first word in its opening phrase: "Unigenitus dei filius" ("The only begotten son of God").

PIETISTS, VISIONARIES, AND QUIETISTS

1. *Translator's note.* Latin for 'great mystery'.

2. *Translator's note.* Latin for *On the Principles of the Most Ancient and Most Recent Philosophy*.

3. Paul Vulliaud, "Fin du monde et prophètes modernes", *Les Cahiers d'Hermès*, 2 (1947), 112.

4. *Translator's note.* German for 'the Christian Education Society of Jesus'.

5. Serge Hutin, *Les Disciples anglais de Jacob Bœhme aux XVIIe et XVIIIe siècles* (Paris: Éditions Denoel, 1960), 16–9.

6. Ibid. 21.

7. *Translator's note.* The first two quotations from Gichtel here are taken from Johann Georg Gichtel, *Awakening to Divine Wisdom: Christian Initiation into Three Worlds*, ed. and trans. Arthur Versluis (St. Paul, MN: New Grail Publishing, 2004), 72, 89.

8. Serge Hutin, op. cit. [*Translator's note.* Unable to find it in Arthur Versluis' English translation of Gichtel, I have translated this passage from the French as quoted by Vaneigem.]

9. Louis-Claude de Saint-Martin, *Correspondance inédite avec Kirchberger, baron de Liebistorf 1792 à 1797* (Paris, 1862).

10. Sarane Alexandrian, *Histoire de la philosophie occulte* (Paris: Éditions Seghers, 1983), 366–7.

11. *Translator's note.* For the internal quotations here see *Theosophic Correspondence Between Louis Claude de Saint-Martin and Kirchberger, Baron de Liebistorf*, ed. and trans. Edward Burton Penny (Pasadena, CA: Theosophical University Press, 1982), 141–5, 150. All quotations come from Kirchberger's letter to Saint-Martin dated Morat, 25 Oct. 1794, except for the last one, which comes from Saint-Martin's letter to Kirchberger

dated 29 Brumaire, Year III.

12. *Translator's note.* Latin for 'With a grain of salt'.

13. *Translator's note.* Nicolas-Pierre-Henri, Abbé de Villars, *The Count of Gabalis, or, The Extravagant Mysteries of the Cabalists Exposed in Five Pleasant Discourses on the Secret Societies, Done into English by P. A. Gent., with Short Animadversions,* trans. Philip Ayres (London: BM, Printer to the Cabalistic Society of the Sages, 1680).

14. *Translator's note.* Greek for 'On the Energy of the Demons'.

15. *Translator's note.* German for the 'Enlightenment'.

16. *Translator's note.* Johann Christian Friedrich Hölderlin (1770–1843), a major lyric poet. Diotima appears in his 1799 novel *Hyperion*.

17. Leszek Kołakowski, quoted by Jean-Noël Vuarnet, *Extases féminines* (Paris: Hatier, 1991). [*Translator's note.* Kołakowski is the author of "Antoinette Bourignon. La mystique égocentrique", an essay included in his *Chrétiens sans église: La Conscience religieuse et le lien confessionnel au XVIIe siècle*, trans. Anne Posner (Paris: Gallimard, 1969).]

18. Quoted in Hutin, op. cit. 27 and 28.

19. Ibid. 28.

20. Vulliaud, op. cit. 114.

21. Hutin, op. cit. 25.

22. "It was at this time that two famous nuns from Montdidier were introduced at Maubuisson by one of the visitors, so that they could teach, he said, the secrets of the most sublime oration. The Mother of the Angels and the Angelic Mother did not act in accordance with the will of the Fathers, and they were often reproached for knowing no other perfection than that which was acquired by the mortification of the senses and by the practice of good works. The Mother of the Angels, who had learned at Port-Royal to distrust all novelty, observed these two young women closely. It transpired that, behind the jargon of pure love, annihilation, and perfect purity, they were concealing all of the illusions and horrors that the Church had condemned in Molinos. These women were indeed from the sect of the illuminati in Roye, who are known as the Guérinets, and for whom Cardinal Richelieu had made such a careful search. The Mother of the Angels notified the authorities of the peril that the convent was in, and these two nuns were confined very strictly by order of the court. The visitor who protected them had a great deal of difficulty extricating himself from the affair". Jean-Baptiste Racine, *Abrégé de l'histoire de Port-Royal* (Paris: Chez Lottin le jeune, 1767).

THE END OF THE DIVINE RIGHT

1. *Translator's note.* Antoine Louis Claude Destutt, Comte de Tracy (1754–1836) is generally credited with coining the term 'ideology'. Henri-Benjamin Constant de Rebecque (1767–1830) was a pioneering analyst thereof.

2. *Translator's note.* Briefly mentioned in Chapters 28, 44, and 45 of the present work, Jean Meslier (1664–1733) was an apparently unremarkable Catholic priest who turned out to have written a massive atheistic manuscript that its author called *Mémoires des pensées et sentiments de Jean Meslier*. It was only discovered after his death. Voltaire edited and published it under the title *Extraits des sentiments de Jean Meslier* in 1762.

3. *Translator's note.* Meslier's manuscript evokes a man who "wished that all the great men in the world and all the nobility could be hanged, and strangled with the guts of the priests". Thanks to Voltaire, Meslier has been credited with saying "Je voudrais, et ce sera le dernier et le plus ardent de mes souhaits, je voudrais que le dernier des rois fût etranglé avec les boyaux du dernier prêtre" ("I would like, and this would be the last and most ardent of my wishes, I would like it if the last king was strangled with the guts of the last priest"). Note that on 17 May 1968, during the occupation of the Sorbonne, members of the Situationist International sent out telegrams to various world leaders that included the following declaration: "HUMANITY WON'T BE HAPPY TILL THE LAST CAPITALIST IS HUNG WITH THE GUTS OF THE LAST BUREAUCRAT" or, depending on the intended recipient, "TILL THE LAST BUREAUCRAT IS HUNG WITH THE GUTS OF THE LAST CAPITALIST". See *Situationist International Anthology*, ed. and trans. Ken Knabb (Berkeley: Bureau of Public Secrets, 2006).

4. *Translator's note.* Rather than translate Woolston or, rather, 'his jailer' (who supposedly overheard his last words) back into English, I have quoted directly from the entry on Woolston in *The American Universal Cyclopedia: A Complete Library of Knowledge* (New York: S. W. Green's Son, 1882), xv. 547.

5. *Translator's note.* For the original English, see Woolston's *A Discourse on the Miracles of Our Saviour* (London, printed for the author, 1727), which includes a dedication "To the Right Reverend Father in God, Edmund, Lord Bishop of London". It concludes with the following words: "And what Pitty is it, that *Infidels* likewise are not to be quell'd with your Threats and Terrors! which (without the Weapons of sharp Reasonings and thumping Arguments, that others are for the Use of) would transmit your Fame to Posterity, for a notable Champion for Christianity, as certainly as, that your judicious Prosecution of the *Moderator* for Infidelity is here remember'd by, My Lord, The Admirer of Your Zeal, Wisdom and Conduct, Thomas Woolston" (iii and viii).

6. *Translator's note.* Woolston, *A Discourse on the Miracles of Our Saviour*, 34.

7. *Translator's note.* From the *Second Discourse on the Miracles of Our Saviour* (London: printed for the author, 1727), 34, 17.

8. *Translator's note.* Unable to locate the original, I have been forced to translate Woolston back into English.

9. *Translator's note.* From the *Fifth Discourse on the Miracles of Our Saviour* (London: printed for the author, 1729), 30.

10. *Translator's note.* Unable to locate the original, I have been forced to translate Woolston back into English.

11. *Translator's note.* Henri-Joseph Du Laurens, *Le compère Matthieu; ou Les Bigarrues de l'esprit humain* (London, 1777).

12. *Translator's note.* Latin for *The Three Impostors*. Cf. Chapter 28, n. 17, in the present work.

13. Gerhard Bartsch, preface to a reprinted edition of *De tribus impostoribus* (Berlin: Akademie-Verlag, 1960).

14. *Translator's note.* Translated from Vaneigem's French. Interpolations are mine. In the entry for "Qarmatians", Islam Wiki <mysobalanus.wordpress.com>, "conjuror" is replaced by "pickpocket".

15. Johann Lorenz von Mosheim, *Institutiones historiae ecclesiasticae novi testamenti* (Frankfurt and Leipzig: Meyer, 1726), translated as *Histoire ecclésiastique ancienne et moderne, depuis la naissance de Jésus-Christ jusques au XVIIIe siècle* (Maastricht: Chez Jean-Edme Dufour & Philippe Roux, 1776), 151; Prosper Marchand, *Dictionnaire historique, ou, Mémoires critiques et littéraires concernant la vie et les ouvrages de divers personnages distingués, particulièrement dans la république des lettres* (The Hague: De Hondt, 1758–9), vol. ii.

16. Johannes Nevisan, *Sylva nuptialis libri sex, in quibus materia matrimonii, dotium, filiationis, adulterii discutitur* (Lugduni, 1556). [*Translator's note.* Averroes quoted in the introductory "Disquisitions" in *The Three Impostors, Translated (With Notes and Illustrations,) from the French Edition of the Work, Published at Amsterdam, 1776* (New York: G. Vale, 1846), 8.]

17. Autbert Stroick, *Collectio de scandalis ecclesiae* (Florence: College of St Bonaventure, 1931).

18. Odorico Raynaldi, *Annales ecclesiastici* (Lucca: Mansi, 1752), vol. xiv. [*Translator's note.* According to "Sentiments Concerning the *Treatise of the Three Impostors*: Extract of a Letter or Dissertation of Mr. de La Monnoye on this Subject", in *The Treatise*

NOTES

of the Three Impostors and the Problem of Enlightenment: A New Translation of the Traité des trois Imposteurs *(1777 Edition)*, ed. and trans. Abraham Anderson (Lanham, MD: Rowman & Littlefield Publishers, Inc., 1997), Javinus de Solcia was "condemned [...] for having maintained this impiety that Moses, Jesus Christ & Mahomet had governed the world according to their fancy, *mundum pro suarem libito voluntatum rexisse*" (44).]

19. *Translator's note.* Latin for *Atheism Defeated.*

20. *Translator's note.* Latin for *Of the Tears of Christ.*

21. *Translator's note.* German for *A Conversation Between a Host and Three Guests of Different Religion* and Latin for *From a Friend to a Friend*, respectively. The latter text, also known as *Epistola amici ad amicum*, was published in Rome in 1674.

22. Matthias Knützen, *Ein deutscher Atheist und Revolutionär Demokrat des 17. Jahrhundert: Flugschriften und andere zeitgenössische sozialkritische Schriften*, ed. Werner Pfoh (Berlin: Akademie-Verlag, 1965). [*Translator's note.* Translated from Vaneigem's French.]

23. *Translator's note.* Pope Pius VI, "Charitas (On the Civil Oath in France)", 13 Apr. 1791 <ewtn.net>.

AUTHOR'S AFTERWORD

1. *Translator's note.* Hijabs have been burned during ongoing public protests against the arrest and beating of Mahsa Amini, a twenty-two-year-old Kurdish woman, by the Iranian 'morality police', which allegedly took place because she wasn't wearing her hijab properly. She died of her injuries in a hospital on 16 September 2022.

2. *Translator's note.* Charles-Henri Jean (Charles d'Avray) was a French anarchist poet, singer, and composer (1878–1960). These are the opening lines of his song "Le Triomphe de l'Anarchie" ("The Triumph of Anarchy"), written in 1901. The rest of this verse says: "From today on, let us live communism, | Let us group together only by affinities, | Our happiness will be born of altruism, | Let our desires become realities!" (Translation adapted from the one attributed to Naama21 on <lyricstranslate.com>.)

3. *Translator's note.* The name given to a relatively complete fossil of the prehistoric hominid *Australopithecus afarensis*, which was discovered in Ethiopia in 1974.

4. *Translator's note.* The location of famous prehistoric cave drawings discovered in 1940.

5. *Translator's note.* See Markos Moulitsas, *American Taliban: How War, Sex, Sin, and Power Bind Jihadists and the Radical Right* (Sausalito: PoliPoint Press, 2010).

6. *Translator's note.* See John Duffy, "Smallpox and the Indians in the American

Colonies", *Bulletin of the History of Medicine*, 25/4 (July–Aug. 1951), 324–41.

7. *Translator's note.* See Jeffrey M. Jones, "U.S. Church Membership Falls below Majority for First Time", Gallup News, Mar. 29, 2021 <https://news.gallup.com/poll/341963/church-membership-falls-below-majority-first-time.aspx>. Between 1998 and 2020, church membership among women declined from seventy-three percent to fifty-three percent.

8. *Translator's note.* Max Weber, *Die protestantische Ethik und der Geist des Kapitalismus* (1905), translated by Talcott Parsons as *The Protestant Ethic and the Spirit of Capitalism* (New York: Scribner, 1930).

9. *Translator's note.* A partial quotation of a famous remark by Karl Marx and Friedrich Engels: "[the bourgeoisie] has drowned the most heavenly ecstasies of religious fervor, of chivalrous enthusiasm, of philistine sentimentalism, in the icy water of egotistical calculation". *The Communist Manifesto*, trans. Samuel Moore (Chicago: Charles H. Kerr & Company, 1888), 38–9.

10. *Translator's note.* English in original.

11. *Translator's note.* English in original.

12. *Translator's note.* That is to say, the Roman Catholic Church.

13. *Translator's note.* The French word employed here, *écœurement* (italics in original), can also mean disillusionment.

14. *Translator's note.* A line from Karl Marx, *Critique of Hegel's 'Philosophy of Right'*, ed. Joseph O'Malley and trans. Annette Jolin and Joseph O'Malley (Cambridge: Cambridge University Press, 1972): "Religion is the sigh of the oppressed creature, the heart of a heartless world and the soul of soulless conditions" (131).

15. *Translator's note.* Louis Antoine de Saint-Just (1767–94), *Œuvres complètes de Saint-Just*, ed. Charles Vellay (Paris: Charpentier et Fasquelle, 1908), 414: "Those who make revolution half way only dig their own graves" (see use of this slogan in Guy Debord, Attila Kotányi and Raoul Vaneigem, "Theses on the Paris Commune", in *Situationist International Anthology*, ed. and trans. Ken Knabb (Berkeley: Bureau of Public Secrets, 1981), 316.

16. *Translator's note.* *L'Ère des créateurs* is the title of a book by Vaneigem that was published by Éditions Complexe (Brussels, 2002) and has not yet been translated into English.

Bibliography

'Abd al-Jabbār, *Critique of Christian Origins*, ed. and trans. Gabriel Said Reynolds and Samir Khalil Samir (Provo, UT: Brigham Young University Press, 2010).

"Acts of the Holy Apostle Thomas", trans. Alexander Walker, in *The Ante-Nicene Fathers: Translations of The Writings of the Fathers down to A.D. 325*, ed. Alexander Roberts, James Donaldson, and A. Cleveland Coxe (Buffalo, NY: Christian Literature Publishing Co., 1886), vol viii.

Aeneas Silvius, Piccolomini (Pius II). "De hortu et historia Bohemorum", in *Omnia opera* (Basel, 1551).

Aland, Kurt. "Augustin und der Montanismus", in *Kirchengeschichtliche Entwürfe: Alte Kirche, Reformation und Luthertum, Pietismus und Erweckungsbewegung* (Gütersloh: Gerd Mohn, 1960).

——. *Bibliographie zur Geschichte des Pietismus* (Berlin: De Gruyter, 1972).

Alexandrian, Sarane, *Histoire de la philosophie occulte* (Paris: Éditions Seghers, 1983).

Alfaric, Prosper, *Le problème de Jésus et les origines du christianisme* (Paris: Cercle Ernest-Renan, 1954).

Allier, Raoul, "Les Frères du libre-esprit", in Théodore Reinach et al., *Religions et sociétés* (Paris: F. Alcan, 1905).

Alphandery, Paul, *Les Idées morales chez les hétérodoxes latins au début du XIIIe siècle* (Paris: E. Leroux, 1903).

——. *De quelques faits de prophétisme dans les sectes latines antérieures au joachinisme*

(Paris: E. Leroux, 1905).

——. *Notes sur le messianisme médiéval latin (XIe-XIIe siècle)* (Paris: Imprimerie Nationale, 1912).

Altmeyer, J.-J., *Les Précurseurs de la réforme aux Pays-Bas* (Paris, 1886).

Alverny, Marie-Thérèse d', "Un fragment du procès des amauriciens", *Archives d'histoire doctrinale et littéraire du Moyen-Age*, 18 (1950–1).

Ambelain, Robert, *Jésus ou le mortel secret des templiers* (Paris: Robert Laffont, 1970).

Ammianus Marcellinus, *The Roman History of Ammianus Marcellinus during the Reigns of the Emperors Constantius, Julian, Jovianus, Valentinian, and Valens*, trans. C. D. Yonge (London: G. Bell and Sons, Ltd, 1911).

Anagnine, Eugenio, *Dolcino e il movimento ereticale all'inizio del trecento* (Florence: La nuova Italia, 1964).

Anderson, Abraham (ed. and trans.), *The Treatise of the Three Impostors and the Problem of Enlightenment: A New Translation of the* Traité des trois Inposteurs *(1777 Edition)* (Lanham, MD: Rowman & Littlefield Publishers, Inc., 1997).

Annequin, Jacques. *Recherches sur l'acte magique et ses représéntations (Ier et IIe siècles après J. C.)* (Paris: Les Belles Lettres, 1979).

Armand Hugon, Augusto and Gonnet, Giovanni, *Bibliografia valdese* (Torre Pelice, 1953).

Arnold, Gottfried, *Unparteiische Kirchen und Ketzerhistorie* (Frankfurt: 1699–1700).

Arnold, Klaus, *Niklashausen 1476: Quellen und Untersuchungen zur sozialreligiösen Bewegung des Hans Behem und zur Agrarstruktur einer spätmittelalterlichen Dorfes* (Baden-Baden: Verlag V. Koerner, 1980).

Arpe, P. F., *Apologia pro J. C. Vasnino* (Rotterdam, 1972).

Axters, Stephanus, *Geschiedenis van de vroomheid in de Nederlanden* (Antwerp: De Sikkel, 1953).

Babut, E.-Ch., *Priscillien et le priscillianisme* (Paris: Champion, 1909).

Bachmann, R. *Nicolas Storch* (Zwickhau, 1880).

Bachor, Armin. "The Secret of the Reformation", *Miskan: A Forum on the Gospel and the Jewish People*, 78 (2017).

Baerwald, Robert, *Die Schlacht bei Frankenhausen 1525* (Mülhausen: Urquell-Verl, 1925).

Bainton, Roland H., *David Joris: Wiedertaüfer und Kampfer für Toleranz in XVI. Jahrhundert* (Leipzig: M. Heinsius Nachfolger, 1937).

——. *Bernardino Ochino: Esule e riformatore senese del cinquecento, 1487–1563*, trans.

Elio Gianturco (Florence: Sansoni, 1940).

——. *Hunted Heretic: The Life and Death of Michael Servetus, 1511–1553* (Boston: The Beacon Press, 1953).

Baluze, E., *Miscellanea* (Paris, 1678–83).

Bar Konai, Theodore, *Livre des scolies* (Leuven: Peeters, 1980–2).

Barack, Karl August, "Hans Böhm und die Wallfahrt nach Niklashausen im Jahre 1476", *Archiv des historischen Vereines von Unterfranken und Asschaffenburg*, 14 (1856).

Barnabas, "The Epistle of Barnabas", trans. Alexander Roberts and James Donaldson, in *The Ante-Nicene Fathers: The Writings of the Fathers down to A.D. 325*, ed. Alexander Roberts, James Donaldson, and A. Cleveland Coxe (Buffalo, NY: Christian Literature Publishing Company, 1887), vol. i.

Baronius, C. and Raynaldus, O. *Annales ecclesiastici una cum critica historico-chronologia* (Lucca, 1738–59).

Barret, Pierre and Gurgand, Jean-Noël, *Le Roi des derniers jours: L'Exemplaire et très cruelle histoire des rebaptisés de Münster (1534-1535)* (Paris: Hachette, 1981).

Barthélemy, D. and J. T. Milik. *Discoveries in the Judean Desert, I Qumran Cave 1* (Oxford: Clarendon Press, 1955).

Bartsch, Gerhard. *De tribus impostoribus* (Berlin: Akademie-Verlag, 1960).

Bataillon, Marcel. *Erasme et l'Espagne: Recherches sur l'histoire spirituelle du XVIe siècle* (Paris: E. Droz, 1937).

——. (ed.), *Aspects du libertinisme au XVI siècle: Actes du colloque international de Sommières* (Paris: Vrin, 1974).

Baudrillart, Alfred et al. (eds.), *Dictionnaire d'histoire et de géographie ecclésiastiques* (Paris: Letouzey et Ané, 1912).

Bauthumley, Jacob, *The Light and Dark Sides of God* (London: William Learner, 1650).

Bayle, Pierre. "Fraticelli", in *Dictionnaire historique et critique* (Rotterdam: Chez Reinier Leers, 1697).

Beatrice of Nazareth, *Seven manieren van minnem* (Leuven: Vlaamsche boekenhalle, 1926).

Beausobre, Isaac de, "Dissertation sur les admaties de Bohême", in Jacques Lenfant, *Histoire de la guerre des hussities* (Amsterdam, 1731).

——. *Histoire critique de Manichée et du manichéisme* (Amsterdam: J. Frederic Bernard, 1739).

Bell, Harold Idris. *Juden und Griechen in römische Alexandria: Eine historische Skizze des alexandrinischen Antisemitismus* (Leipzig, 1926).

―. and Skeat, Theodore Cressy, *Fragments of an Unknown Gospel and Other Early Christian Papyri* (London: Trustees of the British Museum, 1935).

Belperron, Pierre, *La Croisade contre les Albigeois et l'union du Languedoc à la France* (Paris: Plon, 1948).

Bemmann, Rudolf, *Thomas Münzter, Mülhausen in Thuringen und der Bauernkrieg* (Leipzig, 1920).

Bender, Harold S. et al. (ed.) *The Mennonite Encyclopedia: A Comprehensive Reference Work on the Anabaptist-Mennonite Movement* (Scottsdale, PA: Mennonite Brethren Publishing House, 1955–9).

Berkhout, Carl T. and Russell, Jeffrey B., *Medieval Heresies: A Bibliography 1960–1979* (Toronto: Pontifical Institute of Mediaeval Studies, 1981).

Berriot, François, "Un procès d'athéisme à Genève: L'affaire Gruet (1547–1550)", *Bulletin de la Société de l'histoire du protestantisme français*, 125 (Oct.–Dec. 1979).

Beuzart, P. *Les Hérésies pendant le Moyen Âge et la Réforme jusqu'à la mort de Philippe II, 1598, dans la région de Douai, d'Arras et au pays de l'Alleu* (Le Puy: Peyriller, Rouchon et Gamon, 1912).

Beza, Theodore, *On the Right of Magistrates: Concerning the Rights of Rulers over Their Subjects and the Duty of Subjects towards Their Rulers. A Brief and Clear Treatise Particularly Indispensable to Either Class in These Troubled Times*, ed. Patrick S. Poole and trans. Henry-Louis Gonin <https://constitution.org/1-Constitution/cmt/beza/magistrates.htm>.

Bibliothèque municipale de Valenciennes, *Régistre des choses communes*, MS 699, fo. 44.

Bidez, Joseph *La Cité du monde et la cité du soleil chez les Stoiciens* (Paris: Les Belles Lettres, 1932).

Bignami-Odier, Jeanne, *Étude sur Jean de Roquetaillade* (Paris: Vrin, 1952).

Blond, G. "Les encratites et la vie mystique, Mystique et continence", in *Études carmélitaines* (Paris, 1957).

―. "Encratisme", in *Dictionnaire de spiritualité chrétienne* (1960).

Bloomfield, Morton W., "Joachim of Flora: A Critical Survey of his Canon, Teachings, Source, Biography, and Influence", *Traditio*, 13 (1957).

Bogaert, H. van den (Henricus Pomerius), "De origine monasterii Viridisvallis et de gestis patrum et fratum in primordiali fevore ibidem degenttium", *Annalecta Bollandiana*, 4 (1885).

Bolton, Brenda, "Innocent III's Treatment of the *Humiliati*", in *Popular Belief and Practice: Papers Read at the Ninth Summer Meeting and the Tenth Winter Meeting of the Ecclesiastical History Society*, ed. G. J. Cuming and Derek Baker (Cambridge: Cambridge University Press, 1972).

Bonner, Campbell. *Studies in Magical Amulets, Chiefly Graeco-Egyptian* (Ann Arbor: University of Michigan Press, 1950).

The Book of Common Prayer and Administration of the Sacraments and Other Rites and Ceremonies of the Church; Together with the Psalter or Psalms of David; According to the Use of The Episcopal Church (New York: Church Hymnal Corporation, 1979).

Bordenave, Jean and Vialelle, Michel, *Aux racines du mouvement cathare: La mentalité religieuse des paysans de l'Albigeois medieval* (Ouulouse: Privat, 1973).

Borst, Arno, *Les Cathares*, trans. Charles Roy (Paris: Payot, 1974),

Bouquet, Martin, *Recueil des historiens de la Gaule et de la France* (Paris, 1738–1876).

Bouterwek, Karl Wilhelm, *Zur Literatur und Geschichte der Wiedertäufer: Besonders in den Rheinlanden* (Bonn: Marcus, 1884).

Bovon, François, and Koester, Helmut (eds.), *Genèse de l'écriture chrétienne* (Turnhout: Brepols, 1991).

Braeckman, Colette. "Guillaume Cornelisz", *Bulletin de la société d'histoire du protestantisme belge*, 9/4 (1982).

Brandon, S. G. F. *Jesus and the Zealots: A Study of the Political Factor in Primitive Christianity* (Manchester: Manchester University Press, 1967).

Brandt, Otto H., *Thomas Müntzer: Sein Leben und seine Schriften* (Jena: E. Diederichs, 1933).

Brill, Jacques. *Lilith, ou, la mère obscure* (Paris: Payot, 1981).

Brownlee, William H., "Messianic Motifs of Qumran and the New Testament", *New Testament Studies*, 3/3 (May 1957).

Brox, Norbert, *Pseudepigraphie in der heidnischen und jüdisch-christlichen Antike* (Darmstadt: Wissenschaftliche Buchgesellschaft, 1977).

Brunetière, Ferdinand, "Calvin's Literary Work", *The Presbyterian and Reformed Review*, 47 (July 1901).

Buisson, Ferdinand, *Sébastian Castellion: Sa vie et son oeuvre, 1515–1563: Étude sur les origines du protestantisme libéral français* (Paris: Hachette, 1892).

——. *Le Rationalisme dans la littérature française de la Renaissance (1533–1601)* (Paris: Vrin, 1957).

Burton Penny, Edward (ed. and trans.), *Theosophic Correspondence Between Louis Claude de Saint-Martin and Kirchberger, Baron de Liebistorf* (Pasadena, CA: Theosophical University Press, 1982).

Büttner, Theodora and Werner, Ernst, *Circumcellionen und Adamiten* (Berlin: Akademie-Verlag, 1959).

Caldwell, Thomas, "Dositheos Samaritanus", *Kairos*, 4 (1962).

Callary, F. *L'Idéal franciscain au XIV*e *siècle: Étude sur Ubertin de Casale* (Leuven, 1911).

Calvin, John, *Contre la secte phantastique et furieuse des libertins, qui se nomment spirituels* (Geneva: Jean Girard, 1547).

——. *Ioannis Calvini opera quae supersunt omnia*, ed. Gulielmus Baum et al. (Brunswick, 1864–1900), vol. viii.

Cameron, Ron (ed.), *The Other Gospels: Non-Canonical Gospel Texts* (Philadelphia: The Westminster Press, 1982).

Capelle, Germaine Catherine, *Amaury de Bène: Étude sur son panthéisme formel* (Paris: Vrin, 1932).

Capito, Wolfgang, *The Correspondence of Wolfgang Capito*, iii: *1532–1536*, trans. Erika Rummel (Toronto: University of Toronto Press, 2015).

Carmignac, Jean. "Le Document de Qumran sur Melkisédeq", *Revue de Qumran*, 7/3 (Dec. 1970).

Castellio, Sebastian, *Advice to a Desolate France*, ed. Marius F. Valkhoff and trans. Wouter Valkhoff (Shepherdstown, WV: Patmos Press, 1975).

Castellion, Sébastien, *Traité des hérétiques: À savoir, si on les doit persécuter, et comment on se doit conduire avec eux, selon l'avis, opinion, et sentence de plusieurs auteurs, tant anciens, que modernes* (Geneva: Alexandre Jullien, 1913).

Cessario, Romanus, "Molina and Aquinas", in *A Companion to Luis de Molina*, ed. Matthias Kaufmann and Alexander Aichele (Leiden: Brill, 2014).

Chadwick, Henry, *Priscillian of Avila: The Occult and the Charismatic in the Early Church* (Oxford: Clarendon Press, 1976).

Chalus de la Motte, *Les Fourberies de l'église romaine* (Paris, 1706).

Chambrun-Ruspoli, Marthe de, *Le Retour du phénix* (Paris: Les Belles Lettres, 1982).

Charles, R. H., (trans.), *The Testaments of the Twelve Patriarchs* (London: Adam and Charles Black, 1908).

——. (trans.), *The Book of Enoch* (London: SPCK, 1917).

Châtellier, L., *L'Europe des dévots* (Paris: Flammarion, 1987).

Clareno, Angelo, *Historia septem tribulationum ordinis minorum*, ed. Franz Ehrle, *Archiv für Literatur und Kirchengeschichte des Mittelalters* (Berlin: Weidmannsche Buchhandlung, 1886), vol ii.

Clement of Alexandria, *Les Stromates* (Paris, 1951).

——. "The Stromata, or Miscellanies", trans. William Wilson, in *The Ante-Nicene Fathers: The Writings of the Fathers down to A.D. 325*, ed. Alexander Roberts, James Donaldson, and A. Cleveland Coxe (New York: Charles Scribner's Sons, 1913), vol. ii.

——. "On Marriage (*Stromateis*, III)", in *The Library of Christian Classics*, ii: *Alexandrian Christianity: Selected Translations of Clement and Origen*, ed. and trans. John Ernest Leonard Oulton and Henry Chadwick (Philadelphia: Westminster Press, 1954).

Clement of Rome, "The Clementine Homilies", trans. Thomas Smith, in *The Ante-Nicene Fathers: Translations of The Writings of the Fathers down to A.D. 325*, ed. Alexander Roberts, James Donaldson, and A. Cleveland Coxe, (Buffalo, NY: Christian Literature Publishing Co., 1886), vol. viii.

Coeurderoy, Ernest. *Pour la révolution* (Paris: Éditions champ libre, 1972).

Cohn, Norman, *The Pursuit of the Millennium: Revolutionary Millenarians and Mystical Anarchists of the Middle Ages* (rev. edn., New York: Oxford University Press, 1970); trans. Simone Clémendot, *Les Fanatiques de l'apocalypse: Millénaristes révolutionnaires et anarchistes mystiques au Moyen Age* (Paris: Payot, 1983).

Collins, Anthony, *Discourse sur la liberté de penser* (London, 1714).

Comestor, Petrus, *Scholastica historia magistri Petri Comestoris sacre scripture seriem breuem nimis et expositam exponentis* (Paris, 1513–9).

Comena, Anna, *The Alexiad of the Princess Anna Comnena*, ed. and trans. Elizabeth A. S. Dawes (London: Kegan Paul, Trench, Trubner and Company, Ltd., 1928).

Coornherdt, Dirck, *A l'aurore des libertés modernes. Synode sur la liberté de conscience de 1582* (Paris, 1992).

Corbin, Henry, "Nécessité de l'angélologie", in *L'Ange et l'homme* (Paris: A. Michel, 1978).

Cosmas, "The Discourse of the Priest Cosmas Against Bogomils (after 972)", in *Christian Dualist Heresies in the Byzantine World c. 650–c. 1450*, ed. and trans. Janet Hamilton, Bernard Hamilton, Yuri Stoyanov (Manchester: Manchester University Press, 1998).

Couchoud, P. L., *Le Dieu Jésus* (Paris, 1951).

Croze, M.-V., *Entretiens sur divers sujets d'histoire, de littérature, de religion et de critique* (Cologne, 1733).

Cueto Alas, Juan, *Los heterodoxos asturianos* (Barcelona, 1977).

Cullmann, Oscar, *Le Problème littéraire et historique du roman pseudo-Clémentin: Étude sur le rapport entre le gnosticisme et le judéo-christianisme* (Félix Alcan: Paris 1930).

Cuppé, Pierre, *Le Ciel ouvert à tous les hommes* (Amsterdam, 1767).

Cyprian of Carthage, "The Epistles of Cyprian", trans. Ernest Wallis, in *The Ante-Nicene Fathers: Translations of The Writings of the Fathers down to A.D. 325*, ed. Alexander Roberts, James Donaldson, and A. Cleveland Coxe (New York: Charles Scribner's Sons, 1888), vol. v.

Cyril of Alexandria, *Contra Julianum*, trans. Wilmer Cave Wright (1923) <https://www.tertullian.org/fathers/julian_apostate_galileans_1_text.htm>.

——. *Scholia on the Incarnation of the Only-Begotten*, trans. P. E. Pusey (1881) <https://www.tertullian.org/fathers/cyril_scholia_incarnation_01_text.htm>.

Czarnecki, Piotr, "If Not Bogomilism Than What? The Origins of Catharism in the Light of Sources", *Studia Ceranea*, 11 (2021).

Dando, Marcel, *Les Origines du catharisme* (Paris: Cercle Ernest-Renan, 1967).

Davies, Philip R., *The Damascus Covenant: An Interpretation of the "Damascus Document"* (Sheffield: Journal for the Study of the Old Testament, 1983).

De Smet, J. M., "De monnik Tanchelm en de Utrechtse Bisschopsozetel in 112–114", in *Scrinium Coraniense, Mélanges historiques Étienne von Cauwenbergh* (Leuven, 1961).

Decavele, Johan, *De dageraad van de Reformatie in Vlaanderen (1520–1565)* (Brussels: KAWLSK, 1975).

Delacroix, H., *Essai sur le mysticisme spéculatif en Allemagne au XIVe siècle* (Paris: Alcan, 1900).

Delatte, Armand, *Études sur la magie grecque* (Louvain: Fontemoing, 1914), vol. xviii.

Delumeau, Jean, *La Peur en occident: XIVe–XVIIIe siècles: Une cité assiégée* (Paris: Fayard, 1978).

Delvaux, Béatrice and Makereel, Catherine, "Les Racines élémentaires de Raoul Vaneigem: 'L'humanité meurt pour que survive une économie où l'argent fou tourne en rond'", *Le Soir*, 14 Nov. 2020.

Denifle, Heinrich and Chatelain, Emile, *Chartularium universitatis parisiensis* (Paris, 1889).

Denis, Albert-Marie, *Introduction aux pseudépigraphes grecs de l'Ancien Testament* (Leiden: Brill, 1970).

Deschner, Karlheinz, *Kriminalgeschicte des Christentums* (Hamburg: Rowohlt Verlag, 1986–2008), 9 vols.

Desroche, Henri, *Dieux d'hommes: Dictionnaire des messianismes et millénarismes de l'ère chrétienne* (Paris Editions Mouton, 1969).

Diesner, H. J., "Die Circumcelionem von Hippo Regius", *Theologische Literaturzeitung* (1960).

Dio, Lucius Cassius, *Roman History*, trans. Earnest Cary (London: William Heinemann, 1914), iii.

Dionysius the Areopagite, *The Works of Dionysius the Areopagite Part 1: Divine Names, Mystic Theology, Letters, Etc.*, trans. John Parker (London, James Parker and Co., 1897).

Döllinger, Ignaz von, *Beiträge zur Sektengeschicte des Mittelalters* (Munich: C. H. Beck, 1890), vol. ii.

——. *Prophecies and the Prophetic Spirit in the Christian Era*, trans. Alfred Plummer (London: Rivingtons, 1873).

Dondaine, Antoine, *Un traité néo-manichéen du XIIIe siècle. Le "Liber de duobus principiis", suivi d'un fragment de rituel cathare* (Rome: Istituto storico domenicano, 1939).

——. *La Hiérarchie cathare en Italie* (Rome: Istituto storico domenicano, 1949).

——. "L'Origine de l'hérésie médiévale", *Rivista di storia della chiesa in Italia*, 6 (1952).

Doresse, Jean, *Les livres secrets des gnostiques d'Egypte* (Paris: Plon, 1958–9).

——. *L'Evangile selon Thomas, ou les paroles secrètes de Jésus* (Paris: Librairie Plon, 1959).

Drijvers, H. J. W., (ed. and trans.), *The Book of the Laws of Countries: Dialogue on Fate of Bardaisan of Edessa* (Assen: Van Gorcum & Company, 1965).

——. *Cults and Beliefs at Edessa* (Leiden: Brill, 1980).

"The Drumhead", *Star Trek: The Next Generation*, Paramount Domestic Television, 29 Apr. 1991.

Dubourg, Bernard, *L'Invention de Jésus* (Paris: Gallimard, 1987).

Duhaime, Jean, "Étude comparative de *4QM^a FGG. 1–3* et *1QM*", *Revue de Qumrân*, 14/55 (Aug. 1990).

Dulière, Walter Louis, *De la dyade à l'unité par la triade: Préhistoire de la religion biblique, l'avenir du divin* (Paris: A. Maisonneuve, 1965).

Dunin-Borkowski, Stanislaus von, *Quellen zur Vorgeschicte der Unitarier des XVI. Jahrhundert in 75 Jahre Stella matutina* (1931).

Dupin, Louis Ellies, *Histoire des controverses et des matières ecclésiastiques traitées dans le XIIIe siècle* (Paris: Chez André Pralard, 1694; repr. 1842).

Duplessis D'Argentré, Charles, *Collectio judiciorum de novis erroribus* (Paris, 1755).

Dupont-Sommer, André, *La doctrine gnostique de la lettre 'wâw' d'après une lamelle araméene inédite* (Paris: Librairie Orientaliste Paul Geuther, 1946).

—. *Observations sur le Manuel de discipline decouvert près de la mer Morte* (Paris: Librairie Adrien-Maisonneuve, 1951).

—. *Les écrits esséniens découverts près de la mer Morte* (Paris: Payot, 1980).

Durand, David, *The Life of Lucilio (alias Julius Caesar) Vanini, Burnt for Atheism at Thoulouse. With an Abstract of His Writings. Being the Sum of the Atheistical Doctrine Taken from Plato, Aristotle, Averroes, Cardanus and Pomponatius's Philosophy. With a Confutation of the Same; and Mr. Bayle's Arguments in Behalf of Vanini Completely Answered* (London: W. Meadows, 1730).

Duvernoy, Jean (ed.), *Le Registre d'inquisition de Jacques Fournier, évêque de Parmiers (Benoit XII)* (Toulouse: Privat, 1965–6).

Eekhoud, Georges, *Les libertins d'Anvers: Légende et histoire des loïstes* (Paris: Mercure de France, 1912).

Ehlers, B., "Bardesan von Edesse. Ein syrische gnostiken", *Zeitschrift für Kirchengeschicte* (1970).

Ehrle, Franz, "Die Spiritualen, ihr Verhältnis zum Franziskanerorden und zu den Fraticellen", in *Archiv für Literatur und Kirchengeschichte des Mittelalters* (Berlin: Weidmannsche Buchhandlung, 1888), vol. iv.

Eisenberg, Josy, *Une histoire du peuple juif* (Paris: Fayard, 1974).

Eisenmann, Robert, *Maccabees, Zadokites, Christians and Qumran: A New Hypothesis of Qumran Origins* (Leiden: E. J. Brill, 1983).

Epiphanius of Salamis, *The Panarion of Epiphanius of Salamis: Book I (Sects 1–46)*, trans. Frank Williams (2nd edn., Leiden: Brill, 2009).

—. *The Panarion of Epiphanius of Salamis: Books II and III. De Fide*, trans. Frank Williams (2nd edn., Leiden: Brill, 2013).

Erbetta, Mario, *Gli apocrifi del Nuovo Testamento* (Turin: Marietti, 1966–81).

Erbstösser, Martin, *Les Hérétiques au Moyen Âge* (Leipzig: Edition Leipzig, 1984).

—. and Werner, Ernst, *Ideologische Probleme des mittelalterlichen Plebejertums: Die freigeistige Härerie und ihr sozialen Wurzeln* (Berlin: Akademie-Verlag, 1960).

Eusebius of Caesarea, "The Church History", trans. Arthur Cushman McGiffert, in *A Select Library of Nicene and Post-Nicene Fathers of the Christian Church: Second Series*, ed. Philip Schaff and Henry Wace (Buffalo, NY: Christian Literature Publishing Co., 1890), vol. i.

——. *Histoire ecclésiatique* (Paris: Cerf, 1952–60).

Falk, Gerhard, *The Jew in Christian Theology: Martin Luther's Anti-Jewish* Vom Schem Hamphoras, *Previously Unpublished in English, and Other Milestones in Church Doctrine Concerning Judaism* (Jefferson, NC: McFarland & Company Inc., 1992).

Fath, Abu'l, *The Kitāb Al-Tarīkh of Abū 'l-Fath*, ed. and trans. Paul Stenhouse (Sydney: Mandelbaum Trust, University of Sydney, 1985).

Fearns, James, "Peter von Bruis und die religiöse Bewegung des 12. Jahrhundert", *Archiv für Kulturgeschicte*, 48/3 (1966).

——. *Ketzer und Ketzerbekämpfung im Hochmittelalter* (Göttingen: Vandenhoeck & Ruprecht, 1968).

Ferguson, Everett (ed.), *Encyclopedia of Early Christianity* (2nd edn., New York: Taylor & Francis, 2013).

Fitzmayer, Joseph A., "The Contribution of Qumran Aramaic to the Study of the New Testament", *New Testament Studies*, 20/4 (July 1974).

——. "The Qumran Scrolls and the New Testament after Forty Years", *Revue de Qumrân*, 13/49–52 (Oct. 1988).

Ford, J. Massingberd, "Can We Exclude Samaritan Influence from Qumran?", *Revue de Qumrân*, 6/21 (Feb. 1967).

Fossum, Jarl E., "The Name of God and the Angel of the Lord: The Origins of the Idea of Intermediation in Gnosticism", Diss. (Utrecht University, 1982).

Franck, Sebastien, *Chronica, Zeitbuch, und Geschichtbibel* (Strasbourg, 1531).

Frederichs, Jules, *De Secte der Loisten of Antwerpsche Libertijnen (1525–1545): Eligius Pruystinck (Loy de Schaliedecker) en zijne Aanhangers* (Ghent: Vuylsteke, 1891).

——. *Robert le Bougre, premier inquisiteur général en France (première moitié du XIIIe siècle)* (Ghent: Clemm, 1892).

——. "Un luthérien français devenu libertin spirituel: Christophe Hérault et les loïstes d'anvers (1490–1544)", *Bulletin historique et littéraire (Société de l'histoire du protestantisme français)*, 41/5 (1892).

Frédéricq, Paul, *Corpus documentarum inquisitionis hereticae pravitatis neerlandicae* (Ghent, 1889–1900).

Frend, William Hugh C., *The Donatist Church: A Movement of Protest in Roman North*

Africa (Oxford: Clarendon Press, 1952).

——. *Martyrdom and Persecution in the Early Church: A Study of a Conflict from the Maccabees to Donatus* (Oxford: Basil Blackwell, 1965).

——. *The Rise of the Monophysite Movement: Chapters in the History of the Church in the Fifth and Sixth Centuries* (Cambridge: Cambridge University Press, 1972).

Freyburger-Galland, Marie-Laure, *Sectes religieuses en Grèce et à Rome dans l'antiquité païenne* (Paris: Les Belles Lettres, 1986).

Fumi, Luigi., "Eretici e ribelli nell'Umbria dal 1320 al 1330", *Bolletino della regia deputazione di storia patria per l'Umbria*, 5 (1899).

Gachard, Louis-Prosper, *Correspondance de Philippe II* (Brussels, 1848–1960).

Gaignebet, Claude and Jean-Dominique Lajoux, *Art profane et religion populaire au Moyen Âge* (Paris: Presses universitaires de France, 1985).

Garnier de Rochefort, "Contra Amaurianos", in *Beitrage zur Geschicte zur Philosophie und Theologie des Mittelalters*, ed. Clems Baeumker (Münster: Aschendorff, 1926), vol. xxiv.

Gaster, Moses, *Les Samaritains: Leur histoire, leurs doctrines, leur littérature* (Paris, 1984).

Gebhart, Émile. *L'Italie mystique: Histoire de la renaissance religieuse au Moyen Âge* (Paris: Hachette, 1908).

——. *Mystics and Heretics in Italy at the End of the Middle Ages*, trans. Edwin Maslin Hulme (London: George Allen & Unwin, 1922).

George, James Michael, "The Dualistic Gnostic Tradition in the Byzantine Commonwealth, with Special Reference to the Paulician and Bogomil Movements", Ph.D. diss. (Wayne State University, 1979).

Geremek, Bronisław, *Les Marginaux Parisiens aux XIV et XV siècles* (Paris: Flammarion, 1976).

Gerson, Jean Charlier de, *Opera Omnia* (Antwerp, 1706).

Gichtel, Johann Georg, *Awakening to Divine Wisdom: Christian Initiation into Three Worlds*, ed. and trans. Arthur Versluis (St. Paul, MN: New Grail Publishing, 2004).

Gilliam, Terry and Jones, Terry (dir.), *Monty Python and the Holy Grail* (Python (Monty) Films, 1975).

Giret, Stanislase, "Un courant judéo-chrétien à Rome au milieu du IIe siècle", in *Aspects du judéo-christianisme: Colloque de Strasbourg, 23–25 avril 1964*, ed. Marcel Simon (Paris: Presses universitaires de France, 1965).

Gonnet, Jean, "La figure et l'œuvre de Vaudès dans la tradition historique et selon les dernières recherches", in *Vaudois languedociens et pauvres catholiques* (Toulouse: Éditions Privat, 1967).

Goosen, A. J. M., "Achtergronden van Priscillianus' christelijike ascese", Diss. (Nijmegen, 1976).

Gouillard, Jean, *L'Hérésie dans l'Empire byzantin des origines au XIIe siècle* (Paris: Éditions de Boccard, 1965).

Goulder, Michael, "The Two Roots of the Christian Myth", in *The Myth of God Incarnate*, ed. John Hick (London: SCM Press, 1977).

Grant, Michael, *The Jews in the Roman World* (London: Weidenfeld and Nicholson), 1973.

Grant, Robert McQueen, *Gnosticism and Early Christianity* (New York: Columbia University Press, 1959); trans. Jeanne Henri Marrou. *La Gnose et les Orgines Chrétiennes* (Paris: Éditions du Seuil, 1964).

Graves, Robert, *The White Goddess* (London: Faber & Faber, 1948); *La Déesse blanche*, trans. Guy Trévoux (Paris: Editions Du Rocher, 1979).

Gregg, J. A. F. (ed.), *The Wisdom of Solomon in the Revised Version* (Cambridge: Cambridge University Press, 1909).

Grégoire, Henri, et al., *Les Persécutions dans l'empire romain* (Brussels: Palais des Académies, 1964).

Gregorovius, Ferdinand, *The Emperor Hadrian: A Picture of the Graeco-Roman World in His Time*, trans. Mary E. Robinson (London: Macmillan and Co., 1898).

Gregory of Tours. *Historia Francorum*, in *MGH scriptores rerum Mervoingicarum*, ed. Arndt and Krusch (Hannover, 1884).

——. *History of the Franks*, ed. and trans. Ernest Brehaut (New York: Columbia University Press, 1916).

Green, Charles M. (ed.), *The American Universal Cyclopedia: A Complete Library of Knowledge* (New York: S. W. Green's Son, 1882), vol. xv.

Grisar, Hartmann, *Luther*, ed. Luigi Cappadelta and trans. E. M. Lamond (London: Kegan Paul, Trench, Trübner & Company, Ltd. 1916), vol. v.

Grundmann, Herbert, *Studien über Joachim von Floris* (Leipzig: B. G. Teubner, 1927).

——. *Religiöse Bewegungen im Mittelalter* (Berlin: Ebering, 1935).

——. *Ketzergeschichte des Mittelalters* (Göttingen: Vandenhoeck & Ruprecht, 1963).

——. *Bibliographie zur Ketzergeschichte des Mittelalters, 1900–1966* (Rome: Storia e letteratura, 1967).

Guarnieri, Romana (ed.), *Il movimento del libero spirito: Testi e documenti* (Rome:

Edizioni di storia e letteratura, 1965).

Guibert, Joseph de, *Documenta ecclesiastica christianae perfectionis studium spectantia* (Rome: Pontifical Gregorian University, 1931).

Guillaume de Nangis, *Chronique latine de Guillaume de Nangis de 1113 à 1300, avec les continuations de cette chronique de 1300 à 1368*, ed. Hercule Géraud (Paris: J. Renouard, 1843).

Guillemin, Henri, *L'Affaire Jésus, L'Affaire Jésus* (Paris: Éditions du Seuil, 1982).

Hadewijch, *Visionen* (Leuven, 1926).

Hadot, Jean, *Histoire des religions* (Brussels: Presses universitaires de Bruxelles, 1980).

Haller, William and Davies, Godfrey (eds.), *The Leveler Tracts, 1647–1653* (New York: Columbia University Press, 1944).

Harnack, Adolf von, *Marcion. Das Evangelium vom fremden Gott: Eine Monographie zur Geschichte der Grundlegung der katholischen* (Leipzig: J. C. Hinrichs, 1921).

Harris, Maurice H. (ed. and trans.), *Hebraic Literature: Translations from the Talmud, Midrashim and Kabbala* (New York: Tudor Publishing, 1943).

Haupt, Herman, "Zur Biographie des Nicolaus von Basel", *Zeitschrift für Kirchengeschichte* (1825).

——. "Beiträge zur Geschichte der Sekte vom freien Geiste und des Beghartentums", *Zeitschrift für Kirchengeschichte*, 7 (1885).

——. "Husitische Propaganda in Deutschland", *Historisches Taschenbuch*, 6/7 (1888).

——. "Zur Geschichte der Geissler", *Zeitschrift für Kirchengeschichte* (1888).

——. "Zwei Trakate gegen Beginen und Begharden", *Zeitschrift für Kirchengeschichte* (1891).

Haureau, Jean-Barthélemy, *Histoire de la philosophie scolastique* (Paris, 1880).

Hausherr, P. I., "Le messalianisme", in *Atti del XIX Congresso internazionale degli orientalisti 23–29 settembre 1935* (Rome: Tipografia del Senato, 1938).

Heath, Richard, *Anabaptism from its Rise at Zwickau to its Fall at Münster, 1521–1536* (London: Alexander & Shepheard, 1895).

Hegel, Carl (ed.), *Chroniken von Closener und Königshofen* (Leipzig: Chroniken der deutschen Städte 8 and 9, 1870–1).

Heisterbach, Cesaire de, *Dialogus Miraculorum* (Cologne, 1851).

Herbermann, Charles G., et al., *The Catholic Encyclopedia: An International Work of Reference on the Constitution, Doctrine, Discipline, and History of the Catholic Church* (New York: The Encyclopedia Press, Inc., 1913).

Hermant, M., *Histoire des hérésies* (Paris, 1717).

Hermas, "The Pastor of Hermas", trans. F. Crombie, in *The Ante-Nicene Fathers: The Writings of the Fathers down to A.D. 325*, ed. Alexander Roberts, James Donaldson, and A. Cleveland Coxe (New York: Charles Scribner's Sons, 1913), vol. ii.

——. *Hermas. Le Pasteur*, trans. Robert Joly (Paris: Cerf, 1968).

Hermes Trismegistus, "<Discourse> of Hermes Trismegistus: Poimandres", in *Hermetica: The Greek Corpus Hermeticum and the Latin Asclepius in a New English Translation, with Notes and Introduction*, trans. Brian P. Copenhaver (Cambridge: Cambridge University Press, 1992).

Hill, Christopher, *The World Turned Upside Down: Radical Ideas during the English Revolution* (London: Temple Smith, 1972); trans. Simone Chambon and Rachel Ertel, *Le monde à l'envers: Les Idées radicales au cours de la révolution anglaise* (Paris: Payot, 1977),

Hillerbrand, Hans Joachim, *Bibliographie des Täufertums, 1520–1630* (Gütersloh: G. Mohn, 1962).

Hinrichs, Carl, *Luther und Müntzer: Ihre Auseinandersetzung über Obrigkeit und Widerstandsrecht* (Berlin: W. De Gruyter, 1952).

Hippolytus, *Philosophumena, ou, Réfutation de toutes les hérésies*, trans. A. Siouville (Paris: Rieder, 1928).

——. "Refutation of All Heresies", trans. J. H. MacMahon, in *The Ante-Nicene Fathers: Translations of The Writings of the Fathers down to A.D. 325*, ed. Alexander Roberts, James Donaldson, and A. Cleveland Coxe (New York: Charles Scribner's Sons, 1888), vol. v.

Hochhut, W. H. "Landgraf Philipp und die Wiedertäufer", in *Zeitschrift für die historische Theologie*, 29 (1859).

Hoffman, R. Joseph, *Marcion: On the Restitution of Christianity: An Essay on the Development of Radical Paulinist Theology in the Second Century* (Chico, CA: Scholars Press, 1984).

Höfler, Karl Adolph Constantin, "Geschichtesschreiber der husitichen Bewegung in Boehmen", in *Fontes rerum austriacarum* (Vienna, 1856–66).

Holl, Karl, "Luther und die Schwärmer", in *Gesammelt Aufsätze zur Kirchengeschicte* (Tübingen, 1923).

The Holy Bible: English Standard Version (London: HarperCollins, 2016).

Homer, *The Odyssey*, trans. Robert Fagles (New York, Penguin Books, 1996).

Horace Satires and Epistles; Perseus Satires, trans. Niall Rudd (London: Penguin, 2005).

Horsch, John, "The Rise and Fall of the Anabaptists of Münster", in *Mennonite Quarterly Review*, 9 (1935).

Huck, Albert, *Huck's Synopsis of the First Three Gospels*, ed. Ross L. Finney (Cincinnati: Jennings and Graham, 1907).

Huck, Johann Chrysostomus, *Joachim von Floris und die joachitische Literatur: Ein Beitrag zur Geistesgeschichte des hohenstaufischen Zeitalters* (Freiburg im Brisgau: Herder, 1938).

Hunt, A. S. and Edgar, G.C. (eds.), *Select Papyri* (Cambridge, MA: Harvard University Press, 1934), vol. ii.

Hutin, Serge, *Les Disciples anglais de Jacob Bœhme aux XVIIe et XVIIIe siècles* (Paris: Éditions Denoël, 1960).

—. *Les Gnostiques* (Paris: Presses universitaires de France, 1978).

Irenaeus, *Contre les heresies: Mise en lumière et réfutation de la prétendue 'Connaissance'*, trans. François Sagnard (Paris: Éditions du Cerf, 1979–82).

—. "Against Heresies", trans. Alexander Roberts and William Rambaut, in *The Ante-Nicene Fathers: The Writings of the Fathers down to A.D. 325*, ed. Alexander Roberts, James Donaldson, and A. Cleveland Coxe (Buffalo, NY: Christian Literature Publishing Company, 1887), vol. i.

Isser, Stanley, *The Dositheans: A Samaritan Sect in Late Antiquity* (Leiden: E. J. Brill, 1976).

Iverson, Katy. "Honor, Gender and the Law: Defense Strategies during the Spanish Inquisition, 1526–1532", MA diss. (College of William & Mary, 2010).

James, Montague Rhodes (trans.), *The Apocryphal New Testament: Being the Apocryphal Gospels, Acts, Epistles, and Apostles* (Oxford: Clarendon Press, 1924).

Jansenius, Cornelius, in *Lettres de C. Jansénius á J. DuVerger de Hauranne*, ed. Gerberon (Cologne: 1703).

Janssen, H. Q., "Tanchelijn", in *Annales de l'Académie Royale d'Archéologie de Belgique* (1867).

Jarry, Jacques, *Hérésies et factions dans l'empire byzantin du IVe au VIIe siècle* (Cairo: Institut français d'archéologie orientale, 1968).

Jaubert, Annie, *La Date de la Cène: Calendrier biblique et liturgie chrétienne* (Paris: Lecoffre, 1957).

—. *Origène: Homélies sur Josué* (Paris: Éditions du Cerf, 1960).

Jaujard, Georges, *Essai sur les libertins spirituels de Genéve d'apres de nouveaux documents* (Paris, 1890).

Jerome, *In Amos*, in *Patrologie latine*, ed. Jacques-Paul Migne (1844).

——. "Letter XII. To Eustochium", trans. W. H. Fremantle, G. Lewis and W. G. Martley, in *A Select Library of Nicene and Post-Nicene Fathers of the Christian Church: Second Series*, ed. Philip Schaff and Henry Wace (New York: Christian Literature Company, 1893), vol. vi.

Joachim of Fiore, *Concordia novi ac veteris testamenti* (1200).

——. *L'Évangile éternel*, trans. Emmanuel Aegerter (Paris: Rieder, 1928).

Josephus Flavius, "Against Apion", in *The Complete Works of Flavius Josephus*, trans. William Whiston (London: T. Nelson and Sons, 1854).

——. *Antiquitiés judaiques* (Paris, 1929).

——. "Antiquities of the Jews", in *The Complete Works of Flavius Josephus*.

——. *La Guerre des juifs*, trans. Pierre Savinel and Pierre Vidal-Naquet (Paris: Éditions de Minuit, 1977).

——. "The Wars of the Jews, or, the History of the Destruction of Jerusalem", in *The Complete Works of Flavius Josephus*.

Jundt, Auguste, *Histoire du panthéisme populaire au Moyen Âge et au seizième siècle* (Strasbourg: Fischbach, 1875).

Junod, Éric, *Histoire des Actes apocryphes des apôtres du III au IX siècle: Le Cas des Actes de Jean* (Geneva: Imprimerie La Concorde, 1982).

——. and Kaestli, Jean-Daniel, *L'histoire des Actes apocryphes des apôtres du IIIe au IXe siècle: Le cas des Actes de Jean* (Geneva, Lausanne and Neuchâtel: Cahiers de la Revue de théologie et de philosophie, 1982).

——. "Créations romanesques et traditions ecclésiatiques dans les Actes apocryphes des apôtres", in *Genèse de l'écriture chrétienne*, ed. François Bovon and Helmut Koester (Turnhout: Brepols, 1991).

Justin, *Die ältesten Apologeten*, ed. Edgar J. Goodspeed (Göttingen: Vandenhoeck & Ruprecht, 1914).

——. "The First Apology of Justin", trans. Marcus Dods and George Reith, in *The Ante-Nicene Fathers: The Writings of the Fathers down to A.D. 325*, ed. Alexander Roberts, James Donaldson, and A. Cleveland Coxe (Buffalo, NY: Christian Literature Publishing Co., 1885), vol. i.

——. *Dialog mit dem Juden Tryphon*, trans. Philipp Haeuser (Kempten: J. Kösel, 1917).

——. "Dialogue of Justin, Philosopher and Martyr, with Trypho, a Jew", trans. Marcus Dods and George Reith, in *The Ante-Nicene Fathers: The Writings of the Fathers down to A.D.*, ed. Alexander Roberts, James Donaldson, and A. Cleveland Coxe (Buffalo, NY: Christian Literature Publishing Co., 1885), vol. i.

——. *Les Oeuvres de St Justin, Philosophe et martyr, mises de grec en langage français par Jean de Maumont* (Paris, 1559).

Kaminsky, Howard, "Hussite Radicalism and the Origins of Tabor. 1415–1418", *Medievalia et humanistica*, 10 (1956).

——. "Chiliasm and the Hussite revolution", *Church History*, 26/1 (1957).

——. "The Free Spirit in the Hussite Revolution", in *Millennial Dreams in Action: Essays in Comparative Study*, ed. Sylvia L. Thrupp (The Hague: Mouton and Company, 1962).

King, Margaret L., *The Renaissance in Europe* (London: Laurence King Publishing, 2003).

Knabb, Ken (ed. and trans.), *Situationist International Anthology* (Berkeley: Bureau of Public Secrets, 1981).

Knibb, Michael A., *The Ethiopic Book of Enoch: A New Edition in the Light of the Aramaic Dead Sea Fragments*, 2 vols. (Oxford: Clarendon Press, 1978), 2 vols.

Knox, R. A., *Enthusiasm: A Chapter in the History of Religion* (Oxford: Clarendon Press, 1950).

Knützen, Matthias, *Ein deutscher Atheist und Revolutionär Demokrat des 17. Jahrhundert: Flugschriften und andere zeitgenössische sozialkritische Schriften*, ed. Werner Pfoh (Berlin: Akademie-Verlag, 1965).

Kołakowski, Leszek, "Antoinette Bourignon. La mystique égocentrique", in *Chrétiens sans église: La Conscience religieuse et le lien confessionnel au XVIIe siècle*, trans. Anne Posner (Paris: Gallimard, 1969).

Kolde, Theodor, "Zum Process des Johann Denck und der drei gottlosen Maler von Nürnberg", in *Kirchengeschichtliche Studien: Hermann Reuter zum 70. Geburtsag gewidmet*, ed. Theodor Brieger (Leipzig: J. C. Hinrichs, 1890).

Kolmar, Lothar, *Ad capiendas vulpes. Die Ketzerbekämpfung in Südfrankreich in der ersten Hälfte des 13. Jahrhunderts und die Ausbildung des Inquisitionsverfahrens* (Bonn: Röhrscheid, 1982).

Kryvelev, Iosif Aronovič, *Le Christ: Mythe ou réalité?* (Moscow: Social Sciences Today Editorial Board, 1987).

Kulcsár, Zsuzsanna, *Eretnekmozgalmak a XI–XIV szazadban* (Budapest: Tankönyvkiadó, 1964).

La Porta, Sergio (trans.), *Two Anonymous Sets of Scholia on Dionysius the Areopagite's Heavenly Hierarchy* (Louvain: Peeters, 2008).

BIBLIOGRAPHY

Labriolle, Pierre de, *La réaction païenne: Étude sur la polémique antichrétienne du 1er au IVe siècle* (Paris: L'Artisan du livre, 1934).

Lacarrière, Jacques, *Les Gnostiques* (Paris: Idées Gallimard, 1973); trans. Nina Rootes, *The Gnostics* (London: Peter Owen Ltd., 1977).

Lachèvre, Frédéric, *Geoffroy Vallée (brûlé le 9 février 1574) et la "Béatitude des chrestiens": L'Ancêtre des libertins du XVIIe siècle* (Paris: E. Champion, 1920).

Lacroze, Malthurin, *Entretiens sur diverse sujets d'histoire* (Cologne, 1711).

Langlois, Charles-Victor, "Instrumenta facta super examinacione M. Porete", in *Revue historique*, 54 (1894).

Laperrousaz, E. M., *Les manuscrits de la mer Morte* (Paris: Presses universitaires de France, 1961).

———. *L'Attente du messie en Palestine à la veille et au début de l'ère chrétienne* (Paris: A. et J. Picard, 1982).

Lawrence of Brezová, "De gestis et variis accidentibus regni Boemiae", in *Fontes rerum bohemicarum*, ed. Jaroslav Goll (Prague, 1893).

Lea, Henry-Charles. *A History of the Inquisition of the Middle Ages* (New York: Harper & Brothers, 1887); trans. Salomon Reinach, *Histoire de l'inquisition au Moyen Âge* (Paris, 1900).

Leff, Gordon, *Heresy in the Later Middle Ages: The Relation of Heterodoxy to Dissent, c. 1250–1450* (Manchester: Manchester University Press, 1967).

Lehrmann, Manfred R., "Ben Sira and the Qumran literature", in *Revue de Qumrân*, 3/1 (Feb. 1961).

Leisegang, Hans, *Die Gnosis* (Stuttgart: Kröner, 1941); trans. Jean Gouillard, *La Gnose* (Paris: Payot, 1951).

Leontius of Byzantium, *De sectis*, ed. Maryse Waegeman (Ghent, 1982).

Lerner, Robert E., *The History of the Free Spirit in the Later Middle Ages* (Berkeley: University of California Press).

Levy, Isidore, *Recherches esséniennes et pythagoriciennes* (Paris: Droz Minard, 1965).

———. *Corpus christianorum: Series apocryphorum* (Turnhout, 1983).

Lienhard, Marc (ed.), *Croyants et sceptiques au XVIe siècle: Le Dossier des 'Épicuriens'* (Strasbourg: Istra, 1981).

Lindsay, Philip, and Groves, Reginald, *The Peasants' Revolt of 1381* (London: Hutchinson, 1950).

Lucian of Samosata, "The Passing of Peregrinus", trans. A. M. Harmon, in *Lucian* (Cambridge, MA: Harvard University Press, 1936), vol. v.

Luther, Martin. "That Jesus Christ was Born a Jew", trans. Walter I. Brandt, in *Luther's Works* (Philadelphia: Fortress Press, 1971), vol. xlv.

——. "On the Jews and Their Lies", trans. Martin H. Bertram, in *Luther's Works*, vol. xlvii.

——. *Werke (Kritische Gesamtausgabe)* (Weimar, 1883–1908).

Luttikhuizen, Gerard P., *The Revelation of Elchasai: Investigations into the Evidence for a Mesopotamian Jewish Apocalypse of the Second Century and its Reception by Judeo-Christian Propagandists* (Tübingen: J. C. B. Mohr, 1985).

Maccoby, Hyam, *Revolution in Judaea: Jesus and the Jewish Resistance* (New York: Taplinger Publishing Company, 1981).

——. *The Mythmaker: Paul and the Invention of Christianity* (New York: Harper & Row, 1986); trans. Jean Gerber and Jean-Luc Allouche, *Paul et l'invention du christianisme* (Paris: Lieu commun, 1987).

Macek, Josef, *Le Mouvement hussite en Bohême* (Prague: Orbis, 1958).

Macewen, Alex R., *Antoinette Bourignon, Quietist* (London: Hodder and Stoughton 1910).

Mack, Rüdiger, "Libertinärer Pietismus", in *Pietismus und Frühaufkälrung an der Universität Giessen und in Hessen-Darmstadt* (Giessen: Justus-Liebig-Universität, 1972).

Magnien, Victor, *Les Mystères d'Éleusis* (Paris: Payot, 1938).

Maitland, S. R. (ed. and trans.), *Facts and Documents Illustrative of the History, Doctrine, and Rites of the Ancient Albigenses and Waldenses* (London: C. J. G. and F. Rivington, 1832).

Manselli, Raoul, *La lectura super Apocalipsim di Pietro di Giovanni Olivi* (Istituto Storico Italiano per il Medio Evo, Rome, 1955).

Mansi, Giovanni Domenico (ed.), *Sacrorum conciliorum nova et amplissima collection* (Florence and Venice, 1759).

Manteuffel, Tadeusz, *Naissance d'une hérésie: Les adeptes de la pauvreté volontaire au Moyen Âge* (Paris: Moulton, 1970).

Marchand, Prosper, *Dictionnaire historique, ou, Mémoires critiques et littéraires concernant la vie et les ouvrages de divers personnages distingués, particulièrement dans la république des lettres* (The Hague: De Hondt, 1758–9).

Marcus, Greil, *Lipstick Traces: A Secret History of the Twentieth Century* (Cambridge: Harvard University Press, 1989).

Margolin, J. C., "Libertins, libertinisme et 'libertinage' au XVIe siècle", in *Aspects du libertinisme au XVIe siècle*, ed. Marcel Bataillon (Paris: Vrin, 1974).

Marquès-Rivière, Jean, *Histoire des sects et des sociétés secrètes* (Paris, 1972).

Martène, Edmond, and Durand, Usin, *Veterum scriptorum et monumentorum dogmaticorum, moralium, amplissima collection* (Paris: Apud Montalant, 1724-33).

Martial, *Martial Epigrams*, trans. Walter C. A. Ker (London: William Heinemann, 1925), vol i.

Marx, Karl, *Critique of Hegel's 'Philosophy of Right'*, ed. Joseph O'Malley and trans. Annette Jolin and Joseph O'Malley (Cambridge: Cambridge University Press, 1972).

Matter, Jacques, *Histoire critique du gnosticisme: Et de son influence sur les sectes religieuses et philosophiques des six premiers siècles de l'ère chrétienne* (Paris: Levrault, 1828).

McDonnell, Ernest William, *The Beguines and Beghards in Medieval Culture* (New Brunswick, NJ: Rutgers University Press, 1954).

Mechtild of Magdeburg, *Offenbarungen der Schwester Mechtild von Magdeburg oder das fliessende Licht der Gottheit*, ed. Gall Morel (Regensburg: G. J. Manz, 1869).

Meeks, Wayne A., *The First Urban Christians: The Social World of the Apostle Paul* (New Haven: Yale University Press, 1983).

Meirinhos, J. F., "Was There a Portuguese Averroism in the 14th Century? Alphonsus Dionisii and Thomas Scotus", paper given at the 12th SIEPM Congress, Palermo, 17–22 September 2007 (published online: <http://ifilosofia.up.pt/inv/admins/meirinhos/docs/Meirinhos_averroism_14thCent_Portugal.pdf>).

Mellink, Albert F., *De Wederdopers in de Noordelijke Nederlanden (1531–1544)* (Groningen: J. B. Wolters, 1953).

——. "The Mutual Relations Between the Münster Anabaptists and the Netherlands", in *Archiv für Reformationgeschichte*, 50 (1959).

——. "Antwerpen als Anabaptismcentrum", *Nederlands Archief voor Kerkgeschiedenis*, 46 (1964).

Mellor, Ronald (ed.), *The Historians of Ancient Rome: An Anthology of the Major Writings* (2nd edn., New York: Routledge, 2004).

Ménard, Jacques (ed. and trans.), *L'Evangile selon Thomas* (Leiden: Brill, 1975).

——. (ed.), *Les Textes de Nag Hammadi: Colloque du Centre d'histoire des religions, Strasbourg, 23-25 octobre 1974* (Leiden: E. J. Brill, 1975).

Merx, Otto, *Thomas Müntzer und Heinrich Pfeiffer, 1523–1525: Ein Beitrag zur Geschicte des Bauernkrieges in Thüringen* (Göttingen: Vandenhoeck & Ruprecht, 1889).

Metzger, Bruce M., *The Early Versions of the New Testament: Their Origin, Transmission, and Limitations* (Oxford: Clarendon Press, 1977).

Meusel, Alfred, *Thomas Müntzer und seine Zeit* (Berlin: Aufbau-Verlag, 1952).

Meyer, Christian, "Der Wiedertäufer Nikolaus Storch und seine Anhänger in Hof", *Zeitschrift für Kirchengeschichte*, 16/1 (1896).

Middendorp, Theophil, *Die Stellung Jesu Ben Siras zwischen Judentum und Hellenismus* (Brill: Leiden, 1973).

Milano, Ilarino da, *L'eresia di Ugo Speroni nella confutazione del maestro Vacario* (Vatican City: Biblioteca apostolica Vaticana, 1945).

Mingana, Alphonse (ed. and trans.), *Woodbrooke Studies*, vi: *Commentary of Theodore of Mopuestia on the Lord's Prayer and on the Sacraments of Baptism and the Eucharist* (Cambridge: W. Heffer and Sons Ltd., 1933).

Mommsen, Theodor, *Römische Geschichte* (Leipzig: Reimer & Hirzel, 1854–6), 8 vols.; trans. C. A. Alexandre, *Histoire romaine* (Paris: Librairie A. Franck, 1863–72), 8 vols.

Monod, Bernard, *Le Moine Guibert et son temps (1053–1124)* (Paris: Hachette, 1905).

Montfaucon, Bernard de, *Lettres pour et contre, sur la fameuse question, si les solitaires, appelés Therapeutes, dont a parlé Philon le Juif, etaient chrétiens* (Paris, 1712).

Montgomery, James A., *Les Hommes du Garizim: Histoire, theologie, litterature des samaritains*, trans. Bernard Dubourg (Paris: OEIL, 1985).

Moreau, Gérard, *Histoire du Protestantisme à Tournai* (Brussels, 1962).

—. *Le Journal d'un Bourgeois de Tournai (Pasquier de La Barre)* (Brussels, 1975).

Mosheim, Johann Lorenz von, *Institutiones historiae ecclesiasticae novi testamenti* (Frankfurt and Leipzig: Meyer, 1726); trans. *Histoire ecclésiastique ancienne et moderne, depuis la naissance de Jésus-Christ jusques au XVIIIe siècle* (Maastricht: Chez Jean-Edme Dufour & Philippe Roux, 1776),

—. *De beghardis et beguinabus commentarius* (Leipzig: Weidmann, 1790).

Müller, Karl, "Calvin und die Libertiner", *Zeitschrift für Kirchengeschichte*, 48 (1922).

Müntzer, Thomas, *Thomas Müntzer Briefwechsel* (Leipzig: Teubner, 1931).

—. *Politische Schriften* (Halle, 1950).

Murphy-O'Connor, Jerome (ed.), *Paul and Qumran: Studies in New Testament Exegesis* (London: Priory Press, 1968).

Myers, James Edward, "Morality Among Cathar Perfects and Believers in France and Italy, 1100–1300", MA Thesis (Western Michigan University, 1976).

Naigeon, Jacques-André, *Encyclopédie méthodique: Philosophie ancienne et moderne*

(Paris, 1792).

Nauclerus, Johannes, *Chronica* (Cologne, 1544).

Nelli, René, *Dictionnaire des hérésies méridionales et des mouvements hétérodoxes ou indépendants apparus dans le Midi de la France depuis l'établissement du Christianisme* (Toulouse: Privat, 1968).

——. *Écritures cathares* (Paris: Editions Planète, 1968).

Nevisan, Jean, *Sylva nuptialis libri sex, in quibus materia matrimonii, dotium, filiationis, adulterii discutitur* (Lugduni, 1556).

Nider, Johannes, *Formicarius* (Strasbourg, 1517).

Nippold, Friedrich Wilhelm Franz, *Handbuch der neuesten Kirchengeschichte* (Braunschweig: Schwetschke, 1880).

Ogniben, Andrea, *I Guglielmiti del secolo XIII* (Perouse, 1867).

Oliger, Livarius, "De secta operitus libertatis, in Umbria seculo XIV. Disquistio et documenta", in *Storia e letteratura reccolta di studi et testi* (Rome: G. De Luca, 1943).

Optatus, *The Work of St. Optatus, Bishop of Milevis, Against the Donatists*, ed. trans. O. R. Vassall-Phillips (London: Longmans, Green, and Company 1917).

——. *Traité contre les donatistes*, ed. and trans. Mireille Labrousse (Paris: Éditions du Cerf, 1995).

Origen, *Contra Celsus*, trans. Frederick Crombie, in *The Ante-Nicene Fathers: Translations of The Writings of the Fathers down to A.D. 325*, ed. Alexander Roberts, James Donaldson, and A. Cleveland Coxe (New York: Charles Scribner's Sons, 1913), vol. iv.

——. *Origen: Homilies on Joshua*, ed. Cynthia White and trans. Barbara J. Bruce (Washington, DC: Catholic University of America Press, 2002).

——. *Opera omnia* (Leipzig: Hinrichs, 1899–1941).

Ory, Georges. *Le Christ et Jésus* (Brussels: Éditions du Pavillon, 1968).

Packull, Werner O., *Mysticism and the Early German-Austrian Anabaptist Movement, 1525–1531* (Scottdale, PA: 1977).

Pagels, Elaine H., *The Gnostic Gospels* (New York: Vintage Books, 1981).

Papebrochius, *Annales Antwerpienses* (Antwerp, 1845).

Parisot, Jean-Patrocle, *La Foi dévoilée par la raison* (Paris, 1681).

Patschovsky, Alexander, *Der Passauer Anonymous: Ein Sammelwerk über Ketzer, Juden, Antichrist aus der Mitte des 13. Jahrhunderts* (Stuttgart: Hiersemann, 1967).

Pelagius, Alvarus, *De planctu ecclesiae* (Ulm, 1474).

Pelayo, Marcelino Menéndez y, *Historia de los heterodoxos españoles* (Madrid: V. Suárez, 1928).

Pertz, Georg Heinrich (ed.), *Monumenta germaniae historica* (Berlin, 1826).

Pfeiffer, Franz, "Swester Katrei Meister Ekehartes Tohter von Strasburg", in *Deutsche Mystiker des vierzehnten Jahrhundert* (Leipzig: G. J. Göschen, 1857).

Philo, *The Works of Philo Judæus*, trans. Charles Duke Yonge (London: G. Bell, 1855).

Philonenko, Marc, *Les Interpolations chrétiennes des testaments des douze patriarches et les manuscrits de Quomrân* (Paris: Presses universitaires de France, 1960).

Philostorgius, *Annates* and *Epitomae Historiarum*, ed. Moritz Pinder and Theodor Büttner-Wobst (Bonn: Weber, 1841–97).

Philostorgue, *Epitome historiarum*, in *Patrologie grecque* (Paris: Imprimerie catholique, 1857–66).

Philostratus, *Life of Apollonius of Tyana*, ed. and trans. F. C. Conybeare (Cambridge, MA: Harvard University Press, 1912).

Photius: Bibliothèque, ed. René Henry (Paris: Société d'édition les belles lettres, 1960).

Pianzola, Maurice, *Peintres et vilains: Les artistes de la Renaissance et la grande guerre des paysans en 1525* (Paris: Éditions cercle d'art, 1962).

Picard, Jean-Claude, "Histoire des bienheureux du temps de Jérémie", in *Pseudépigraphes de l'Ancien Testament et manuscrits de la mer Morte*, ed. Marc Philonenko (Paris: Presses universitaries de France, 1967).

Picot, E., *Théâtre mystique de Pierre du Val et des libertins spirituels de Rouen au XVIe siècle* (Paris, 1882).

Plato, *Timaeus*, trans. Benjamin Jowett (Delhi: Lector House, 2019).

Plinval, Georges de, *Pélage: Ses écrits, sa vie, sa réforme* (Lausanne: Payot, 1943).

Pliny the Elder, *The Natural History of Pliny*, trans. John Bostock and Henry T. Riley (London: Henry G. Bohn, 1855).

Pluquet, François-André-Adrien, *Mémoires pour servir à l'histoire des égarements de l'esprit humain par rapport à la religion chrétienne, ou Dictionnaire des hérésies, des erreurs et des schismes* (Besançon: Petit, 1817).

Poquelin, Jean-Baptiste, *Le Tartuffe, ou l'imposteur* (Paris: Jean Ribou, 1669).

Porete, Marguerite, "Le miroir des simples âmes", in *Il movimento del libero spirito: Testi e documenti*, ed. Romana Guarnieri (Rome: Edizioni di storia e letteratura, 1965).

Porgès, Nathan, "Les relations hébraiques des persécutions des Juifs pendant la première croisade", *Revue des études juives* (1892).

Potthast, August, *Bibliotheca historica medii aevi* (Berlin, 1896).

Prateolus, Gabriel, *De Vitis, sectis et dogmatibus omnium haereticorum* (Cologne, 1659).

Preger, Wilhelm, *Geschicte der deutschen Mystik im Mittelalter* (Leipzig: Dörffling und Franke, 1874).

——. "Beiträge zur Geschicte der religiösen Bewegung in den Niederlanden in der zweiten Hälfte des vierzehnten Jahrhunderts", *Abhandlungen der Bayrischen Akademie der Wissenschaften*, 21 (1894).

Primov, Borislav, *Les Bougres: Histoire du pope Bogomile et de ses adeptes*, trans. Monette Ribeyrol (Paris: Payot, 1975).

Priscillian of Avila: The Complete Works, ed. and trans. Marco Conti (Oxford: Oxford University Press, 2010).

Pseudo-Dionysius the Areopagite, "Théologie mystique", in *Oeuvres complètes*, trans. Maurice de Gandillac (Paris: Aubier, 1943).

Pseudo-Tertullian. *Tertulliani Opera*, ed. V. Bulhart (Vienna: Tempsky, 1906).

Ptolemy, *Lettre à Flora*, ed. and trans. Gilles Quispel (Paris: Éditions du Cerf, 1949).

——. "Ptolemy's Epistle to Flora", in *The Gnostic Scriptures*, ed. and trans. Bentley Layton and David Brakke (2nd edn., New Haven: Yale University Press, 2021).

Puech, Émile, "(11QPsAp[a]): Un rituel d'exorcismes. Essai de reconstruction", *Revue de Qumran*, 14/55 (1990).

Puech, Henri-Charles, "Audianer", in *Reallexikon für Antike und Christentum: Sachwörterbuch zur Auseinandersetzung des Christentums mit der antiken Welt*, ed. Franz Joseph Dölger, Theodor Klauser, and Ernst Dassmann (Stuttgart: Hiersemann Verlag, 1950).

——. *Les Nouveaux écrits gnostiques découverts en Haute-Egypte (premier inventaire et essai d'identification)* (Boston: Byzantine Institute, 1950).

Pulver, Max "Jesus' Round Dance and Crucifixion, According to the Acts of Saint John", in *The Mysteries: Papers from the Erenos Yearbook*, ed. Joseph Campbell (New York: Pantheon Books, 1959).

Racine, Jean-Baptiste, *Abrégé de l'histoire de Port-Royal* (Paris: Chez Lottin le jeune, 1767).

Raschke, Hermann, *Die Werkstatt des Markusevangelisten: Eine neue Evangelientheorie* (Jena: E. Diedrichs, 1924).

Raynaldi, Odorico, *Annales ecclesiastici* (Lucca: Mansi, 1752), vol. xiv.

Rembert, Karl, *Die Wiedertäufer im Herzogtum Jülich* (Berlin: H. Heyfelder, 1899).

Reusch, Hinrich, *Die Indices librorum prohibitorum des XVI Jahrhundert* (Tübingen: Literarisches Verein, 1886).

Réville, Andrè, *Le soulèvement des travailleurs d'Angleterre en 1381* (Paris: A. Picard et fils, 1898).

Revillout, Carlos Eugenio (ed. and trans.), *Acta Pilatis* (Paris: 1913).

Robinson, J. Armitage, *Barnabas, Hermas and the Didache* (London: SPCK, 1920).

Robinson, James M. (ed.), *The Nag Hammadi Library* (rev. edn., San Francisco: Harper & Row, 1990).

Rochefort, Garnius von, "Contra Amaurianos", in *Beitrage zur Geschicte zur Philosophie und Theologie des Mittelalters*, ed. Clems Baeumker (Münster: Aschendorff, 1926).

Roersch, A. "La Correspondance de Pilse et de Torrentius", *Le Musée belge* (1926).

Roehrich, Gustave Guillaume, *Essai sur la vie, les écrits, et la doctrine de l'anabaptiste Jean Denck* (Strasbourg: Veuve Berger-Levrault, 1553).

Rokeah, David, *Jews, Pagans, and Christians in Conflict* (Jerusalem: The Magnus Press, 1982), 210.

Roquetaillade, Jean de (John of Rupescissa), "Vade mecum in tribulation", in Orthuinus Gratius, *Fasciculus rerum expetendarum et fugiendarum* (London, 1690).

Roscher, W., "The Status of the Jews in the Middle Ages Considered from the Standpoint of Commercial Policy", *Historia Judaica*, 6 (Apr. 1944).

Rosenstiehl, Jean-Marc, "Le Portrait de l'Antichrist", in *Pseudépigraphes de l'Ancien Testament et manuscrits de la mer Morte*, ed. Marc Philonenko (Paris: Presses universitaries de France, 1967), vol. i.

——. (ed.) *L'Apocalypse d'Élie* (Paris: Librairie Orientaliste, 1972).

Rougier, Louis, *Celse contre les chrétiens: La réaction païenne sous l'empire romain* (Paris: Copernic, 1977).

——. *Paganisme, Judaïsme, Christianisme: Influences et afforntements dans le monde antique* (Paris: De Boccard, 1978).

Rudolph, Kurt, *Gnosis: The Nature and History of Gnosticism* (San Francisco: Harper & Row, 1983).

Runciman, Steve, *The Medieval Manichee: A Study of the Christian Dualist Heresy* (Cambridge: Cambridge University Press, 1947); trans. Simone Pétrement and Jacques Marty, *Le manichéisme médiéval: L'Hérésie dualiste dans le christianisme* (Paris: Payot, 1972).

Russell, Jeffrey B., "Saint Boniface and the Eccentrics", *Church History*, 33/3 (September 1964).

Ruysbroeck, Jan van, *L'Ornement des noces spirituelles* (Brussels: Vromant, 1928).

——. *The Spiritual Espousals* (London: Faber & Faber, 1952).

Saint-Martin, Louis-Claude de, *Correspondance inédite avec Kirchberger, baron de Liebistorf 1792 à 1797* (Paris, 1862).

Salimbene of Parma, "Cronica fratris Salimbene de Adam Ordinis Minorum", in *Monumenta Germaniae historica: Scriptores*, ed. Oswald Holder-Egger (Hannover and Leipzig, 1905–13).

———. *The Chronicle of Salimbene de Adam*, trans. Joseph L. Baird, Giuseppe Baglivi, and John Robert Kane (Binghamton, NY: Medieval and Renaissance Texts and Studies, 1986).

Salles-Dabadie, Jean-Marie A., *Recherches sur Simon le Mage: L'Apophasis Megalè* (Paris: J. Gabalda et Cie, 1969).

Saulcy, Félicien de, *Dictionnaire des antiquités bibliques, traitant de l'archéologie sacrée, des monuments hébraïques de toutes les époques* (Paris: Migne, 1859).

Scheerder, Jozef, *De Inquisitie in de Nederlanden in XVIe eeuw* (Antwerp: Nederlandsche Boekhandel, 1944).

Schmidt, Karl, *Nicolaus von Basel* (Vienna: W. Braumüller, 1866).

Schmitt, Jean-Claude, *Mort d'une hérésie: L'Église et les clercs face aux béguines et aux beghards du Rhin supérieur du XIVe au XVe siècle* (Paris: Mouton, 1978).

Schonfield, Hugh, *The History of Jewish Christianity* (London: Duckworth, 1936).

Schroeder, H. J. (ed. and trans.), *Disciplinary Decrees of the General Councils: Text, Translation and Commentary* (St. Louis: B. Herder, 1937).

Sevrin, Jean-Marie, "Les noces spirituelles dans l'Evangile selon Philippe", *Museon*, 87/1–2 (1974).

Simon, Marcel, "La polémique anti-juive de S. Jean Chrysostome et le mouvement judaïsant d'Antioch", in Édouard Dumont et al., *Mélanges Franz Cumont* (Bruxelles: L'Institut de philologie et d'histoire orientales et slaves, 1936).

———. *Les Sectes juives au temps de Jésus* (Paris: Presses universitaires de France, 1960).

———. *Recherches d'histoire judéo-chrétienne* (Paris: Mouton & Co., 1962).

———. *Le Judaïsme et le Christianisme antique: D'Antiochus Epihane à Constantin* (Paris: 1968).

Simon, Otto, *Überlieferung und Handtschriftenverhältnis des Traktates "Schwester Katrei"* (Halle: Druck von E. Karras, 1906).

Skehan, Patrick W. (trans.), *The Wisdom of Ben Sira* (New York: Doubleday, 1987).

Smallwood, E. Mary, *The Jews under Roman Rule from Pompey to Diocletian: A Study in Political Relations* (2nd edn., Leiden: Brill, 1976).

Smith, Morton, *Clement of Alexandria and a Secret Gospel of Mark* (Cambridge, MA:

Harvard University Press, 1973).

Soden, Hans von, *Christentum und Kultur in der geschictlichen Entwicklung ihrer Beziehungen* (Tübingen: J. C. B. Mohr, 1933).

Spätling, Luchesius, *De Apostolicis pseudoapostolis apostolinis* (Munich, 1947).

Spizelius, Gottlieb, *Scrutinio Atheismi* (Krakow, 1585).

Spon, Jacob, *Histoire de Genève: Rectifiée et considérablement augmentée par d'amples notes: avec les actes et autres pièces servant de preuves à cette histoire* (Geneva: Fabri & Barrillot, 1730).

Starcky, J., "Un texte messianique araméen de la grotte 4 de Qumrân", in *Mémorial du cinquantenaire de L'École des Langues Orientales de l'Institut Catholique de Paris* (Paris: Bloud & Gay, 1964).

Stefano, Antonio De, *Riformatori ed eretici del Medioevo* (Palermo: F. Ciuni, 1938).

Stone, Jean Mary, *Reformation and Renaissance (circa 1377–1610)* (London: Duckworth, 1904).

Stork, Nancy P. (trans.), "Raymond de Sainte-Foy, Deacon of the Vaudois Sect: Confession 3" <https://www.sjsu.edu/people/nancy.stork/jacquesfournier/Raymond-de-Sainte-Foy-FINAL.pdf>.

Strobel, August, *Das Heilige Land der Montanisten: Eine Religionsgeographische Untersuchung* (Berlin: W. De Gruyter, 1980).

Stroick, Autbert (ed.), *Collectio de scandalis ecclesiae* (Florence: College of St Bonaventure, 1931).

Stroumsa, Gedaliahu G., "Aher: A Gnostic", in *Rediscovery of Gnosticism: Proceedings of the International Conference on Gnosticism at Yale, New Haven, Connecticut, March 28–31, 1978*, ed. Bentley Layton (Leiden: Brill, 1986), vol. ii.

Tacitus, *The Histories*, trans. W. Hamilton Fyfe (Oxford: Clarendon Press, 1912), vol. i.

Tardieu, Michel, "Le Titre du deuxième écrit du Codex VI", *Museon*, 87 (1974).

——. *Trois mythes gnostiques: Adam, Éros et les animaux d'Égypte dans un écrit de Nag Hammadi* (Paris: Études augustiniennes, 1974).

——. "Les livres mis sous le nom de Seth et les séthiens de l'hérésiologie", in *Gnosis and Gnosticism: Papers Read at the Seventh International Conference on Patristic Studies (Oxford, September 8th–13th 1975)*, ed. Martin Krause (Leiden: E. J. Brill, 1977).

——. *Le Manichéisme* (Paris: Presses universitaires de France, 1981).

Tatian, "Address of Tatian to the Greeks", trans. J. E. Ryland, in *The Ante-Nicene Fathers: The Writings of the Fathers down to A.D. 325*, ed. Alexander Roberts, James Donaldson, and A. Cleveland Coxe (New York: Charles Scribner's Sons, 1913), vol. ii.

——. "The Diatessaron of Tatian", trans. Hope W. Hogg in *The Ante-Nicene Fathers: Translations of The Writings of the Fathers down to A.D. 325*, ed. Allan Menzies (5th edn., New York: Charles Scribner's Sons, 1906), vol. ix.

——. *Oratio ad Graecos and Fragments*, ed. and trans. Molly Whittaker (Oxford: Clarendon Press, 1982).

Teicher, J. L., "The Teaching of the Pre-Pauline Church in the Dead Sea Scrolls", *Journal of Jewish Studies*, 3/3 (1952).

Tertullian, *Apologétique*, ed. and trans. Jean-Pierre Waltzing (2nd edn., Paris: Les Belles Lettres, 1961).

——. "Apology", trans. S. Thelwall, in *The Ante-Nicene Fathers: The Writings of the Fathers down to A.D. 325*, ed. Alexander Roberts, James Donaldson, and A. Cleveland Coxe (New York: Charles Scribner's Sons, 1918), vol iii.

——. *Ad Scapulam* (Vindobonae, 1957).

——. "The Soul's Testimony", trans. S. Thelwall, in *The Ante-Nicene Fathers*, vol. iii.

——. *De Anima*, ed. J. H. Waszink (Amsterdam: J. M. Meulenhoff, 1947).

——. "A Treatise on the Soul", trans. Peter Holmes, in *The Ante-Nicene Fathers*, vol. iii.

——. *Adversus Marcionem*, ed. and trans. Ernest Evans (Oxford: Clarendon Press, 1972).

——. "The Five Books Against Marcion", trans. Peter Holmes, in *The Ante-Nicene Fathers*, vol. iii.

——. *Contre les Valentiniens*, ed. and trans. Jean-Claude Fredouille (Paris: Éditions du Cerf, 1980–1).

——. "Against the Valentinians", trans. Alexander Roberts, in *The Ante-Nicene Fathers*, vol. iii.

——. "On the Resurrection of the Flesh", trans. Peter Holmes, in *The Ante-Nicene Fathers*, vol. iii.

——. *De paenitentia; De pudicita*, ed. Pierre de Labriolle (Paris: Picard, 1906).

——. "On Repentance", trans. S. Thelwall, in *The Ante-Nicene Fathers*, vol. iii.

——. "On Baptism", trans. S. Thelwall, in *The Ante-Nicene Fathers*, vol. iii.

——. *Adversos Judaeos*, in *Opera Omnia* (1528).

——. "On the Apparel of Women", trans. S. Thelwall, in *The Ante-Nicene Fathers: Translations of The Writings of the Fathers down to A.D. 325*, ed. Alexander Roberts, James Donaldson, and A. Cleveland Coxe (New York: Charles Scribner's Sons, 1913), vol. iv.

——. "On Exhortation to Chastity", trans. S. Thelwall, in *The Ante-Nicene Fathers*, vol. iv.

——. "On Modesty", trans. S. Thelwall, in *The Ante-Nicene Fathers*, vol. iv.

——. "De fuga in persecutione", trans. S. Thelwall, in *The Ante-Nicene Fathers*, vol. iv.

Theodore of Mopsuestia, *Une controverse avec les Macédoniens*, ed. and trans. François Nau (Paris: Firmin-Didot, 1913).

Théry, Gabriel, *Autour du décret de 1210*, i: *David de Dinant: Étude sur son panthéisme matérialiste* (Kain: Le Saulchoir, 1925).

Thiselton, Anthony C., *The First Epistle to the Corinthians: A Commentary on the Greek Text* (Grand Rapids, MI: William B. Eerdmans Publishing Company, 1997).

Thomas of Cantimpre, *Bonum universale de apibus* (Douai, 1627).

Thouzellier, Christine, *Une somme anticathare: Le Liber contra Manicheos de Durand de Huesca* (Leuven: Spicilegium sacrum Lovaniense, 1964).

——. *Catharisme et valdéisme en Languedoc à la fin du XIIe et au début du XIIIe siècle* (Paris: Presses universitaires de France, 1966).

The Three Impostors, Translated (With Notes and Illustrations) from the French Edition of the Work, Published at Amsterdam, 1776 (New York: G. Vale, 1846).

Tischendorf, Constantin von, *Apocalypses apocriphae* (Leipzig: Avenarius & Mendelssohn, 1966).

Tocci, Franco Michelini, *I manoscritti del mar Morto* (Bari: Laterza, 1967).

Torrey, Charles C., "Certainly Pseudo-Ezekiel", *Journal of Biblical Literature*, 53/4 (1934).

Tourniac, Jean, *Melkitsedeq ou La Tradition primordiale* (Paris: Albin Michel, 1983).

Tresmontant, Claude, *Le Christ hébreu: La Langue et l'âge des evangiles* (Paris: OEIL, 1983).

Trithemius, Johannes, *Annales hirsaugiensis* (St Gall, 1690).

Turmel, Joseph. *Histoire des dogmes* (Paris: Rieder, 1931–6).

Turner, John D., "Sethian Gnosticism: A Literary History", in *Nag Hammadi, Gnosticism, and Early Christianity*, ed. Charles W. Hedrick and Robert Hodgson, Jr. (Peabody, MA: Hendrickson Publishers, 1988).

Ubertino of Casale, *Arbor vitae crucifixae Jesu* (Venice, 1485).

Utenbogaerde, Hendrik, *De origine monasterii Viridisvallis una cum vitis B. Joannis Rusbrochii primi prioris hujus monasterii et aliquot coaetaneorum ejus* (1885).

Vaernewyck, Marc van, *Van die beroerlicke tijden in die Nederlanden en voornamelick in Ghendt, 1566–1568* (Ghent: C. Annoot-Braeckman, 1872–81).

——. *Mémoires d'un patricien gantois du xvie siècle: Troubles religieux en Flandre et dans les Pays-Bas du xvie siècle*, trans. Hermann van Duyse (Ghent: Maison d'éditions d'art, 1905–6).

Vaillant, André, *Le Traité contre les bogomiles de Cosmas le prêtre* (Paris: Imprimerie nationale, 1944).

——. *Les Livre des secrets d'Hénoch* (Paris: Institut d'études slaves, 1976).

Vallée, Geoffroy, *L'Art de ne croire en rien, suivi de Livre des trois imposteurs*, ed. Raoul Vaneigem (Paris: Éditions Payot & Rivages, 2002).

——. *La Béatitude des chrétiens, ou Le Fléau de la foi*, ed. Alain Mothu (Paris: Les Éditions Demeter, 2005).

Van Meteren, Emanuel, *Historie der Neder-landscher ende haerder na-buren oorlogen ende geschiedenissen, tot den iare M.VIC.XII* (The Hague, 1623).

Van Mierlo, "Hadewijch", in *Revue d'ascétique et de mystique*, 5 (1924).

——. "Bloermardinne", in *Dictionnaire d'histoire et de géographie ecclésiastiques* (Paris, 1926).

Vaneigem, Raoul, *Traité de savoir-vivre a l'usage des jeunes générations* (Paris: Gallimard, 1967); trans. *The Revolution of Everyday Life* by Donald Nicholson-Smith (Oakland: PM Press, 2012).

——. *De la grève sauvage à l'autogestion généralisée* (Paris: Union générale d'éditions, 1974).

——. *Le Livre des plaisirs* (Paris: Encre, 1979); trans. John Fullerton, *The Book of Pleasures* (London: Pending Press, 1983).

——. *Le Mouvement du libre-esprit: Généralites et témoignages sur les affleurements de la vie à la surface du Moyen-Age, de la Renaissance, et, incidemment, de notre époque* (Paris: Editions Ramsey, 1986); trans. Randall Cherry and Ian Patterson, *The Movement of the Free Spirit: General Considerations and Firsthand Testimony Concerning Some Brief Flowerings of Life in the Middle Ages, the Renaissance, and, Incidentally, Our Own Time* (New York: Zone Books, 1994).

——. *Adresse aux vivants sur la mort qui les gouverne* (Paris: Seghers, 1990).

——. "A Thousand Erotic Games", *London Review of Books*, 38/17 (8 September 2016).

Vermes, Geza (trans.), *The Dead Sea Scrolls in English* (3rd edn., Sheffield: JSOT Press, 1987).

Vernet, E., "Bogomiles" and "Les Frères du Libre-Esprit", in *Dictionnaire de théologie catholique* (Paris: Letouzey et Ane, 1920).

Villars (Abbé de), Nicolas-Pierre-Henri, *The Count of Gabalis, or, The Extravagant Mysteries of the Cabalists Exposed in Five Pleasant Discourses on the Secret Societies, Done into English by P. A. Gent., with Short Animadversions*, trans. Philip Ayres (London: BM, Printer to the Cabalistic Society of the Sages, 1680).

Vilmar, Eduard, *Abulfathi annales samaritani* (Gotha: Perthes, 1865).

Vogt, Hermann Josef, *Coetus Sanctorum: Der Kirchenbegriff des Novatian und die Geschicte seiner Sonderkirche* (Bonn: P. Hanstein, 1968).

Vos, K., "De doopgezinden te Antwerpen in de zestience eeuw", *Bulletin de la Commission Royale d'Histoire*, 84 (1919).

Vouaux, Léon, *Les Actes de Pierre* (Paris: Librairie Letouzey et Ané, 1922).

Vuarnet, Jean-Noël, *Extases féminines* (Paris: Hatier, 1991).

Vulliaud, Paul, "Fin du monde et prophètes modernes", *Les Cahiers d'Hermès*, 2 (1947).

Wattenbach, W., "Über die Sekte der Brüder vom Freien Geiste", *Sitzungsberichte der Königlichen Preussischen Akademie der Wissenschaft*, 29 (1887).

Werner, Martin, *Die Entstehung des christlichen Dogmas: Problemgeschichtlich dargestellt* (Bern: P. Haupt, 1953).

Whittaker, Molly, *Jews and Christians: Graeco-Roman Views* (Cambridge: Cambridge University Press, 1984).

Wilken Robert Louis, *The Myth of Christian Beginnings: History's Impact on Belief* (Garden City, NY: Doubleday, 1971); trans. J. Chambert, *Le Mythe des origines chrétiennes: Influence de l'histoire sur la foi* (Paris: Fayard, 1974).

William of Newburgh, *The History of William of Newburgh*, trans. Joseph Stevenson (London, 1856; repr. Felinfach: Llanerch Publishers, 1996).

William the Breton, "Gesta Philippi Augusti", in *Oeuvres de Rigord et de Guillaume le Breton*, ed. H. François Delaborde (Paris: Renouard, 1882–5), vol. i.

Williams, George Huntston, *The Radical Reformation* (3rd edn., University Park, PA: Penn State University Press, 1995).

Wilson, R. M., "Simon, Dositheus and the Dead Sea Scroll", *Zeitschrift für Religions- und Geistesgeschichte*, 9/1 (1957).

——. *Studies in the Gospel of Thomas* (London: Mowbray, 1960).

Winter, Jay (ed. and trans.), *The Complete Book of Enoch: Standard English Version* (Winter Publications, 2015).

Wippold, R., "Hendrik Niklaes", *Zeitschrift für Historische Theologie* (1862).

Woolston, Thomas, *A Discourse on the Miracles of Our Saviour* (London, printed for the author, 1727).

——. *Second Discourse on the Miracles of Our Saviour* (London: printed for the author, 1727).

——. *Fifth Discourse on the Miracles of Our Saviour* (London: printed for the author, 1729).

Workman, Herbert B., *The Dawn of the Reformation* (London, 1901–2).

Wünsch, Richard, *Sethianische Verfluchungstafeln aus Rom* (Leipzig: B. G. Teubner, 1898).

Wylie, James A., *The History of Protestantism* (London: Cassell & Company, 1874), vol. ii.

Yadin, Yigael, *The Ben Sira Scroll from Masada* (Jerusalem: The Israel Exploration Society and the Shrine of the Book, 1965).

Zweig, Stefan, *Castellio Against Calvin, or Conscience Against Violence*, trans. Robert Boettcher (independently published, 2021).

Name Index

Abrasax: 92, 119, 121, 228, 229, 230, 253, 345
Abu'l Fath: 97, 98, 99, 100
Adalbert: 361–2
Adamites of Bohemia (see Picards)
Albigensians: 393, 395
Alighieri, Dante: 417, 450
Alumbrados: 433, 468, 509–13, 607, 686 n.13
Amalric of Bena/Amalricians: 379, 381, 382, 383, 410–4, 440, 669 n. 1
Anabaptists: 351, 451, 479, 498, 500, 503, 517, 518, 529–45, 547, 548, 554, 558, 567, 680 n. 7, 684 n. 23
Antiochus IV Epiphanes: 45, 47, 61
Apollonius of Tyana: 111, 112, 168, 284
Apostolics: 173, 259, 342, 351, 444, 447, 448, 461, 467
Aquinas, Thomas: 339, 411, 523
Aristotle: 254, 381, 412, 462, 522, 524,
614
Arius/Arianists: 29, 90, 93, 156, 225, 232, 289, 295, 303, 307–14, 321, 327, 328, 335, 344, 505, 635–6 n. 42, 661 n. 6, 664 n. 4
Arnauld family: 587–91
Arnold of Brescia: 373–5
Asclepius: 112, 113, 184, 415
Audi: 295
Augustine of Hippo: 27, 57, 139, 238, 261–2, 265, 307, 318, 319, 321, 335–40, 383, 584, 585

Baius, Michel: 584–5
Ball, John: 434, 451, 530, 531, 569
Bar Kokhba: 50, 57, 70, 158, 172, 182, 193, 210, 267
Barbelo/Barbelites: 40, 82, 90, 92, 96, 106, 107, 111, 113, 115, 124, 125, 129, 132, 139–46, 149, 154, 163, 187, 206,

735

213, 221, 234, 279, 347, 364, 428, 469,
643 n. 78
Bardaisan of Edessa: 92, 130, 217, 291–5,
345, 347
Barnabas: 65, 79, 93, 94, 154, 157, 173,
177, 185, 194–7, 204, 271, 280, 285,
288–9
Basilides of Alexandria: 139, 162,
220–30, 231, 244
Bauthumley, Jacob: 576, 580–1
Beatrice of Nazareth: 263, 419, 672 n. 21
Beghards: 140, 173, 396, 403, 418,
425–36, 443, 447, 448, 449, 455, 461,
463, 467, 470, 674 n. 40, 676 n. 4
Beguines: 140, 403, 410, 417, 418,
425–36, 455, 461, 673 n. 34, 674 n. 40,
676 n. 4
Ben Sira: 44, 71
Bentivenga da Gubbio: 467–8
Bernard of Clairvaux: 363, 365, 366,
367, 374, 383, 667 n. 9, 670 n. 11
Bloemardinne, Heilwige: 420–2, 430, 477
Bodenstein, Andreas Rudolf (see Karl-
stadt)
Bogomils: 336, 351–8, 362, 363, 364,
365, 367, 385, 386–93, 396, 397, 418
Böhm, Hans: 485–8, 491
Böhme, Jakob: 501, 503, 575, 580, 593,
594, 595, 596, 598, 599, 600, 602, 605
Boneta, Prous: 465–6
Borborites: 326
Bosch, Hieronymus: 436, 677 n. 29
Bourignon, Antoinette: 420, 604–6
Bucer, Martin: 493, 501, 502, 525, 537,
538

CAINITES: 113, 123–6, 149, 268
Callixtus: 104, 275, 296, 304, 318
Calvin, John: 272, 354, 435, 483, 484,
490–4, 498, 500, 503, 505, 506, 507,
515, 517, 518, 520, 522, 525, 526, 527,
563–4, 565, 575, 584, 612, 623, 686 n. 3,
684–5 n. 33, 686 n. 6, 690 n. 5
Capito, Wolfgang Fabricius: 501, 538,
555, 689–90 n. 5
Carpocrates of Alexandria: 115, 219, 221,
230, 244, 251–4, 323
Cassius, Dio: 53
Castellion, Sebastian: 465, 498, 499,
503, 506–7, 553, 564, 684–5 n. 33
Cathars: 16, 336, 363, 364, 366, 371,
385–97, 399, 400, 401, 402, 411, 412,
418, 440, 454, 469, 668 n. 20, 671 n. 16
Celsus: 56, 61, 123, 268, 284, 285, 296
Cerinthians: 163
Christ (see Jesus Christ)
Christ of Bourges: 360–1
Circumcellions: 261, 278, 317, 321, 530
Clareno, Angelo: 461, 462, 463, 464, 468
Clarkson, Lawrence: 576, 579–80
Clement of Alexandria: 118, 144, 185,
194, 216, 221, 222–4, 232, 251–3, 278,
359, 377
Clement of Rome: 93, 634 n. 11
Coddians: 326
Cohn, Norman: 13–5, 370, 404–7, 485,
486–7, 628 n. 15
Comnena, Anna: 354–7
Constantine: 26, 28, 307–8, 309, 311,
313, 314, 315, 316
Coornhert, Dirck Volckertszoon: 503,

519, 563–5
Coppe, Abiezer: 577–9, 581
Coppin, Richard: 581–2
Cornelius, William: 373, 422–4, 674 n. 41, 675 n. 45, 675 n. 46
Cosmas: 351, 352–3, 354, 664 n. 5
Cyprian of Carthage: 44, 161, 304, 305, 341, 660 n. 5

DAVID: 34, 37, 66, 151, 196, 356
David of Dinat: 379, 382–3, 384, 412, 669 n. 2
Debord, Guy: 15–6, 699 n. 15
Délicieux, Bernard: 464–5
Denck, Hans: 499–501, 502, 504, 538, 557, 562, 564, 565, 593, 610, 684 n. 23
Diderot, Denis: 23, 429, 610
Diggers: 570–5, 691 n. 2
Diodorus of Tarsus: 329, 330, 331
Dolcino of Novara/Dolcinians: 445, 447–51, 457, 461, 463, 489, 492, 530
Donatus, Magnus/Donatists: 261, 278, 279, 286, 288, 289, 316–9, 321, 324, 341, 345, 359
Dositheos/Dunstan/Dusis: 52, 78, 92, 96, 97–101, 120, 124, 171, 187, 190
Duvergier de Hauranne, Jean-Ambroise: 585, 586, 587, 588, 693 n. 5
Dyophysites: 328, 330, 331

EBIONITES: 28, 42, 51, 71, 82, 87, 89, 100, 149, 162, 163, 165, 172–4, 180, 188, 193, 205
Eckhart, Meister: 419, 429, 430, 435
Elchasaites: 28, 65, 93, 97, 99, 154, 158,

174–5, 180, 187, 188, 190–1, 193, 200, 205, 211, 213, 219, 221, 232, 244, 254, 257, 268, 279, 285, 292, 297, 304, 307, 351, 385, 646 n. 2
Enoch: 47, 78, 80, 83, 84, 85, 87, 90, 92, 96, 99, 120, 155, 170, 174, 181, 184, 189, 465, 637 n. 9
Epiphanius of Salamis: 114, 115, 130, 132, 139-140, 141, 142, 143, 174, 193, 219, 231, 235, 251, 253–4, 261, 262, 265, 274, 296, 307, 314, 322, 328, 330, 347, 469, 646 n. 2
Eriugena, Johannes Scotus: 298, 378–81, 412
Essenes: 35, 42, 46, 48, 51, 58, 60, 62, 63, 64, 65, 68, 71, 72, 75–94, 96, 97, 131, 148, 149, 154, 155, 156, 160, 162, 168, 169, 173, 178, 180, 182, 187, 190, 194, 195, 210, 265, 270, 271, 284, 294, 297, 302, 310, 340, 395, 437, 636 n. 42
Euchites: 321–6
Eudo de Stella: 363–4
Eusebius of Caesarea: 26, 28, 159, 185, 187, 189, 203, 220, 260, 261, 274, 286, 292, 302, 303, 307, 308–10, 311, 314
Eve: 118, 120, 121, 127, 129, 134, 136, 139, 146, 149, 189, 338, 451, 478, 552, 643 n. 77

FAMILY OF LOVE/FAMILISTS (SEE HENRY NICLAES)
Flagellants: 16, 342, 442, 443, 453–9, 467, 487
Francis of Assisi/Franciscans: 342, 402, 406, 410, 439, 440, 441, 442, 448, 461,

737

463, 464, 465, 467, 510, 565, 671 n. 17
Franck, Sebastian: 502–3, 539, 563
Fraticelles: 27, 173, 403, 433, 442, 447, 448, 461–70, 475, 485, 489, 671 n. 17, 672 n. 21, 676 n. 4, 679 n. 5, 679 n. 15
Free Spirits: 16, 299, 378, 384, 396, 403, 409–24, 425, 427, 428, 429, 430, 431, 432, 433, 434, 435, 436, 441, 443, 449, 458, 463, 466, 467, 469, 470, 473, 477, 479, 492, 501, 502, 512, 520, 532, 547, 548, 567, 576, 671 n. 16, 672 n. 21, 674 n. 42
Frey, Nicolas: 554–6, 690 n. 5

GALAHAD: 662 n. 2
Gichtel, Johann Georg: 596–601, 602, 606
Gilles of Cantor: 477–8, 479
Gonnet, Jean: 400
Gregory of Tours: 359, 362
Groote, Gerhard: 418, 430, 432
Gruet, Jacques: 493–4, 506, 519–24, 526, 578, 612, 614
Guglielma/Guillelmites: 445–7
Gundulf: 362, 387, 396
Guyon, Madame: 420, 606–8
Guzmán, Dominic de: 27, 393, 510

HADEWIJCH OF ANTWERP: 263–4, 414, 417, 423–4, 446, 465
Hadrian: 268, 279
Hegesippus: 172, 174, 187
Henry of Lausanne: 364–7, 374, 375, 387, 389, 440
Herman of Rijswijk: 383–4

Hermas of Rome: 93, 162, 165, 200, 212, 230, 233, 259, 270–2, 273, 285, 287, 303, 322, 323
Hermes Trismegistus: 112, 131
Hernández, Francisca: 511–2, 685 n. 7
Herod: 63, 65, 66, 78, 81, 100, 123, 128, 137, 179, 465
Hildegard of Bingen: 298, 390, 596
Hildernissem, Willem van: 477, 478, 479
Hill, Christopher: 558, 577, 690 n. 9
Hippolytus of Rome: 104, 105, 216, 296, 304, 359
Hitler, Adolf: 495, 682 n. 4
Hoffmann, Melchior: 504, 518, 536–8, 539, 541
Homer: 637 n. 10, 640–1 n. 34
Horace: 56, 204
Hübmaier, Balthasar: 534–5, 536, 541
Hut, Hans/Huss/Hussites: 471, 473, 474, 479, 484, 534, 536, 680 n. 1
Hutter, John: 535–6

ICONOCLASTS: 349–50, 519, 536, 541, 542–5, 564, 687 n. 14
Irenaeus of Lyon: 27, 113, 114, 169, 185, 189, 190, 199, 201, 217, 220, 226, 228, 233, 243, 244, 254, 255, 259, 260, 264, 266, 272–4, 275, 277, 278, 437, 646 n. 44

JACOB/JAMES: 44, 60, 64, 68, 69, 71, 72, 77, 85, 87, 89, 98, 99, 100, 122, 128, 157, 160, 173, 174, 175, 182, 183, 184, 185–8, 189, 190, 192, 193, 194, 199, 202, 204, 211, 213, 248, 259, 279, 280, 285, 327, 337
James the Just: 71, 92, 110, 177, 178, 180,

185, 187, 203
Jansenius, Cornelius/Jansenists: 339, 583–7, 588, 590, 591, 693 n. 4
Jesus Christ: 132, 149, 220, 297, 298, 302, 308, 311, 455, 521, 572, 594, 596, 611, 612, 614, 637 n. 9, 647 n. 16, 658 n. 7, 664 n. 4, 688 n. 29, 698 n. 18
Joachim of Fiore/Joachimists: 15, 403, 412, 432, 433, 438–42, 445, 448, 450, 451, 453, 455, 462, 463, 465, 466, 478, 488, 492
Jochanaan (see John the Baptist)
John of Battenberg: 519, 541, 548
John of Lugio: 393, 395, 396
John the Baptist: 71, 92, 99, 159, 173, 174, 175, 177–82, 187, 193, 215
John the Essene: 87, 92, 173, 181
Joris, David: 516, 518, 541, 547–53, 558
Josephus, Flavius: 45, 52, 54, 56, 61, 63, 65, 68, 69, 70, 71, 75, 76, 80, 87, 92, 157, 160, 177, 181, 182, 188
Joshua: 27, 36, 38, 42, 68, 72, 85, 94, 95, 98, 100, 124, 149, 154, 157, 160, 161, 163, 164, 165, 180, 183, 248, 284, 286, 297, 659 n. 10
Joshua/Jesus: 27, 41, 42, 43, 52, 59, 72, 81, 84, 85, 86, 89, 92, 95, 104–105, 106, 111, 114, 115, 119, 126, 128, 143, 149, 150, 152, 153, 154, 155, 156–7, 161, 163, 164, 169, 172, 174, 175, 184, 185, 187, 191, 196, 205, 228, 232, 257, 280, 286, 287, 292, 296
Journet, Noël: 565–6, 578
Judah of Gamala: 45, 65, 66, 67, 68, 69, 71, 72, 157, 160, 182, 193

Judas: 71, 175, 183, 185, 204, 337, 496, 647 n. 16
Judeans: 35, 36, 72, 78, 92, 95, 114, 140, 166
Justin the Apologist: 110, 114, 150, 158, 164, 204, 214, 217, 266–9, 437
Justin the Gnostic: 132–9

KARLSTADT: 503–4, 537
Knutzen, Matthias: 615–6
Koukeens: 124

LA BOÉTIE, ÉTIENNE DE: 111, 503, 684 n. 28, 690 n. 1
La Motte, Jeanne-Marie Bouvier de (see Madame Guyon)
Lefebvre de la Barre, François-Jean: 628 n. 3
Leuthard of Vertus: 362, 386, 388
Levelers: 570–5, 577, 579
Lollards: 431, 434, 436, 451, 484
Luther, Martin: 154, 197, 435, 458, 483, 484, 490–3, 495, 496, 497, 502, 503, 504, 512, 515, 516, 531, 533, 536, 537, 562, 563, 565, 575, 682 n. 4, 683 n. 11, 684 n. 23

MACCABEES: 44, 47, 48, 52, 61, 62, 161
Mani/Manicheans: 139, 175, 214, 293, 302, 312, 336, 337, 342, 343, 348, 351, 352, 385, 389, 390, 394, 575, 667 n. 4
Marcion/Marcionites: 26, 28, 53, 57, 64, 75, 82, 84, 87, 89, 90, 91, 92, 96, 97, 98, 100, 111, 112, 126, 131, 132, 159, 167, 174, 175, 177, 184, 185, 190, 191, 193,

195, 199, 200, 201, 204, 205, 206, 207, 209–17, 222, 228, 230, 235, 238, 254, 258, 259, 261, 263, 264, 266, 267, 268, 270, 271, 272, 273, 275, 277, 289, 293, 302, 307, 312, 347, 349, 351, 385, 395, 396
Marcus: 28, 243–9, 272, 390
Marcus, Greil: 14, 18
Mariamne: 122, 123, 132, 155, 156, 167, 187
Martial: 57, 157
Mary of Magdalene: 45, 167, 168, 294
Marx, Karl: 451, 532, 602, 699 n. 9, 699 n. 14
Masoretes: 42, 43
Mechthild of Magdeburg: 263, 419, 465
Melchizedek: 60, 77, 80, 84, 92, 128, 154–6, 157, 163, 178, 191, 197, 598, 599, 644 n. 20
Men of Intelligence: 434, 477, 677 n. 1
Men of the Community (see Essenes)
Meslier, Jean: 383, 562, 581, 610, 666 n. 17, 696 n. 2, 696 n. 3
Messalians: 140, 173, 321, 322, 323, 324, 330, 336, 428, 429, 455
Miriam-Mary: 45, 123, 155, 156, 187
Mithras: 228–30, 257, 345
Monophysites: 324, 328, 331, 332, 333, 378
Montanus/Montanists: 28, 82, 90, 131, 174, 175, 191, 212, 231, 233, 234, 244, 258, 259, 261, 262–3, 264, 265, 267, 273, 275–6, 278, 279, 280, 284, 285, 286, 288, 289, 292, 296, 297, 299, 302, 303, 304, 305, 310, 318, 325, 337, 340, 341,

342, 344, 347, 351, 390, 655 n. 5, 657 n. 41
Moses: 34, 36, 38, 40, 41, 57, 76, 96, 97, 98, 99, 107, 118, 120, 127, 128, 132, 133, 134, 136, 160, 169, 189, 190, 194, 196, 203, 225, 235, 249, 253, 255, 283, 297, 298, 383, 384, 520, 522, 523, 556, 558, 566, 579, 613, 614, 637 n. 9, 659 n. 10, 698 n. 18
Münsterites: 518, 537, 538–41, 548
Müntzer, Thomas: 16, 492, 497, 499, 504, 532–3, 534, 536

Naas: 92, 122, 124, 133, 135, 136–7, 149
Naassenes: 28, 51, 53, 56, 82, 90, 100, 111, 113, 114, 115, 119–23, 124, 125, 126, 129, 131, 132, 149, 150, 152, 154, 155, 161, 181, 184, 187, 195, 196, 213, 221, 259, 279, 289, 347
Nazarenes: 28, 37, 42, 51, 52, 63, 65, 71, 76, 78, 79, 82, 83, 87, 89, 97, 98, 99, 100, 114, 119, 122, 149, 154, 157, 160, 162, 163, 168, 172–4, 180, 181, 183, 186, 188, 200, 205, 213, 219, 221, 268, 270, 297, 302, 307, 310, 337, 351
Nazis: 14, 15, 451, 682 n. 4
Nestorius: 323, 324, 328, 329, 330–1, 349
Niclaes, Henry: 519, 556–8, 563
Nicolaites: 124, 125, 206
Novatian: 28, 261, 279, 286, 288, 305, 310, 321, 341, 342, 344, 359, 660 n. 6

Ochino, Bernardino: 565, 614
Ophites: 119, 123, 130, 145

NAME INDEX

Optatus: 317, 318
Origen: 56, 59, 95, 104, 119, 123, 142, 157, 164, 185, 189, 202, 211, 251, 265, 273, 284, 286, 296–8, 302, 303, 305, 324, 328, 344, 359, 437, 610

PALUTIANS: 292, 295
Pastoureaux: 403–8, 442, 487
Patarins: 370–2, 373, 399, 400, 668 n. 2
Paul of Samosata: 298–9, 324, 333, 347, 348, 363, 660 n. 15
Paul of Tarsus (see Saul/Paul)
Paulicians: 299, 336, 347–50, 351, 352, 353, 385
Pelagius: 221, 335–40, 375, 466, 564
Perates: 124, 125, 126, 127, 129, 130
Peter (see Simon-Peter)
Peter of Bruys/Petrobrusians: 364–7, 374, 375, 387, 440, 665 n. 7
Pfeiffer, Heinrich: 533–4
Pharisees: 33–4, 38, 39, 42, 44, 46, 51, 52, 53, 60–5, 67, 68, 71, 73, 75, 77, 79, 81, 83, 88, 89, 90, 91, 92, 132, 147, 157, 169, 171, 172, 180, 195, 199, 201, 202, 211, 215, 257, 265, 271, 550
Phemionites: 326
Philo of Alexandria: 45, 55, 75, 82, 96, 157, 164, 171, 219, 294
Photios: 157
Picard, Jean-Luc: 681 n. 9
Picards/Pikarti: 434, 474, 478–81
Pietists: 263, 344, 504, 593–60
Pilate, Pontius: 27, 196, 258, 260, 282, 286, 328, 610
Plato: 46, 169, 232, 234, 254, 266, 267,
296, 377, 524, 653 n. 26
Pliny the Elder: 57, 82, 157, 172
Pliny the Younger: 65, 174, 188, 257
Pocquet, Anthony: 493, 525, 526
Polycarp: 201, 260
Pordage, John: 582
Porete, Marguerite: 16, 414, 417–20, 429, 433, 446, 448, 469, 510, 513, 525, 593, 679 n. 10
Priscillian of Avila: 130, 132, 143, 201, 313, 341, 342–4, 345, 510
Pruystinck, Eloi: 16, 515–19, 547, 553, 686 n. 3
Pseudo-Dionysius the Areopagite: 224, 298, 378, 379
Ptolemy: 40, 50, 164, 235–40, 646 n. 44

QUIETISTS: 420, 603–6, 607

RABELAIS, FRANÇOIS: 505, 565, 629 n. 11, 630 n. 19, 687 n. 19
Ranters: 434, 435, 519, 557, 575–7, 579, 580, 581, 582, 692 n. 14
Ratgeb, Jerg: 531, 689 n. 4
Rufinus, Tyrannius: 189, 261, 273, 296, 297
Ruysbroeck, Jan van: 418, 421, 422, 430, 477, 673 n. 33

SADDUCEES: 33, 39, 41, 42, 51, 59–62, 63, 64, 65, 72, 75, 77, 81, 83, 90, 169, 171, 172, 180, 257
Sadoq, the Sons of: 41, 59, 60, 62, 75
Salome: 141, 144
Samaritans: 33, 35–6, 40, 42, 59, 61, 72,

83, 90, 93, 95, 96, 97, 99, 106, 111, 114, 123, 169, 171, 175, 207, 230
Satan/Satanael: 83, 118, 131, 133, 165, 220, 267, 352, 353, 355, 356, 389, 390, 395, 396, 462, 474, 483, 497, 510, 580, 594, 599, 613, 660 n. 15
Satornilus: 114, 125, 163, 191, 212, 248
Saul/Paul: 26, 57, 72, 76, 77, 78, 80, 82, 83, 85, 86, 87, 89, 92, 97, 98, 100, 101, 105, 108, 110, 111, 125, 132, 148, 149, 154, 159, 166, 173, 174, 175, 186, 190, 191, 192, 194, 197–207, 211, 212, 213, 222, 223, 248, 254, 259, 265, 279, 285
Savonarola, Girolamo: 442, 469, 484, 488–90, 492, 509, 532, 681 n. 5
Schwenckfeld, Caspar: 497, 501, 502, 503, 504, 537, 553
Scoto, Thomas: 383–4, 499, 520, 612, 614
Segarelli, Gerard: 442–5, 448, 456, 462, 467, 676 n. 4
Seleucids: 44, 45, 50
Servetus, Michael: 494, 498, 502, 505–6, 507, 517, 553, 612, 614
Seth/Sethians: 28, 40, 51, 53, 56, 77, 80, 90, 92, 96, 124, 128, 148, 149–54, 155, 157, 163, 174, 181, 184, 187, 221, 253, 259, 268, 279, 289, 345, 347
Simon-Peter: 27, 28, 44, 64, 71, 72, 85, 87, 88, 89, 92, 98, 100, 108, 110, 172, 173, 174, 175, 177, 180, 183, 184, 185, 186, 188, 190, 192, 193, 194, 199, 202, 203, 204, 211, 212, 213, 216, 221, 248, 259, 262, 279, 280, 285, 288, 289, 298, 304, 305, 327, 328, 349, 411, 484, 526,

634 n. 11, 637 n. 9, 660 n. 5
Simon Cephas (see Simon-Peter)
Simon of Samaria: 16, 42, 52, 82, 98, 103–14, 121, 124, 127, 144, 150, 172, 203, 219, 251, 253, 254, 268, 272, 295, 325, 364, 409, 420, 513, 593
Simon the Essene: 71, 193
Simons, Menno/Mennonites: 535, 536, 541–2, 547, 548, 553, 563
Situationist International: 11, 14, 15, 18, 696 n. 3, 699 n. 15
Solomon: 34, 35, 45, 46, 60, 77, 287
Speroni, Hugo: 375
Spiritual Libertines: 435, 500, 515–27, 565
Spirituals: 321–6, 336, 403, 412, 441, 461, 462, 463, 464, 465, 466, 467, 488, 489, 492, 679 n. 5, 688 n. 30
Stalin, Joseph: 20, 26, 27, 28, 258, 303, 530
Storch, Nicholas: 504, 532–4
Stratiotics: 124, 326
Suetonius: 71, 158

TABORITES: 471, 473–5, 479, 480, 481, 484, 491, 531, 532
Tacitus: 57, 158
Tanchelm of Antwerp: 372–3, 405
Tany, Thomas: 582
Tatian: 26, 201, 213, 267, 274, 277–8, 284, 289
Templars: 408, 418, 444
Teresa of Ávila: 264, 344, 420, 465, 513
Tertullian of Carthage: 27, 154, 190, 191, 194, 197, 199, 201, 212, 217, 233, 258,

260, 261, 263, 264, 265, 266, 267, 268, 271, 273, 274–6, 277, 278, 280, 283, 284, 286, 288, 296, 303, 304, 305, 313, 318, 321, 327, 328, 337, 342, 344, 351, 359, 437, 662 n. 1

Tetzel, Johann: 491, 682 n. 7

Theodore of Mopsuestia: 299, 328, 329, 330, 331, 660 n. 15

Theodotus: 184, 216, 233, 293

Theophilus of Antioch: 261, 274

Therapeutes: 46, 75, 76, 80, 82

Theudas/Thomas: 68, 71, 72, 81, 87, 89, 92, 120, 141, 157, 162, 173, 175, 177, 182–5, 188, 199, 203, 205, 206, 211, 213, 248, 259, 279, 292

Thierry, Quintin: 493–4, 518, 524–7, 688 n. 30

Tiberius: 48, 51, 54, 55, 85, 196, 258, 283, 610

Torrentius, Jan: 558–9, 690 n. 10

Trajan: 65, 93, 158, 174, 188, 210, 254, 269, 279, 304

UBERTINO OF CASALE: 403, 461, 463, 467

VALENTINUS/VALENTINIANS: 185, 206, 220, 230–4

Vallée, Geoffroy: 384, 566–8, 667 n. 17

Vanini, Lucilio: 384, 568

Vaudoisians (see Waldo, Peter)

Virgin Mary: 156, 166, 372, 404, 405, 491, 521, 556, 671 n. 20

Voltaire: 198, 610, 612, 625, 696 n. 2, 696 n. 3

WALDO, PETER/WALDENSIANS: 140, 173, 342, 351, 365, 367, 375, 393, 394–5, 399–408, 411, 412, 414, 418, 423, 425, 439, 440, 442, 469, 473, 484, 507, 529, 534, 535, 668 n. 17, 668 n. 2

Webbe, Thomas: 581

Weigel, Valentin: 497, 503, 562–3, 595, 610

William of Newburgh: 363

William of Orange: 543, 544, 563, 564

Winstanley, Gerrard: 570, 572–5

Woolston, Thomas: 353, 610–2, 696 n. 5

Wycliffe, John: 433–4, 471, 484

YHWH: 31, 32, 33–4, 35, 36, 37, 38, 40, 41, 47, 52, 54, 60, 79, 84, 90, 91, 95, 96, 100, 114, 126, 139, 140, 155, 172, 182, 190, 200, 211

ZEALOTS: 34, 44, 45, 48, 51, 55, 56, 62, 63, 64, 65–73, 79, 85, 89, 98, 147, 158, 160, 161, 169, 171, 173, 188, 193, 257

Žižka, Jan: 474, 480, 481

Zoppo, Paolo: 468

Raoul Vaneigem is a historian and social theorist who was prominently associated with the Situationist International. He is the author of numerous books, including the highly influential *The Revolution of Everyday Life*. Among other of his works available in English are *The Movement of the Free Spirit* and *A Declaration of the Rights of Human Beings*.

Bill Brown has translated hundreds of letters, essays, and books, most of them by members of the Situationist International. He holds a doctorate in American and European literature from the University at Buffalo.